THE SAINTS

A Concise Biographical Dictionary

ANDREW: painting by Ferrari (*fl.* 1511 – 1535). (*National Gallery, London*)

PLATE 1

The Saints

A Concise Biographical Dictionary

EDITED BY JOHN COULSON

WITH AN INTRODUCTION BY

C. C. MARTINDALE, S.J.

NEW YORK

HAWTHORN BOOKS, INC.

Publishers

© 1958 by John Coulson. All rights reserved, including the right to reproduce this book or any portions thereof in any form except for the inclusion of a brief quotation in a review. All inquiries should be addressed to Hawthorn Books Inc., 70 Fifth Avenue, New York City 11. This book was designed and produced by Rainbird, McLean Ltd, London. The text and monochrome illustrations were printed in Holland by Drukkerij Holland N.V., Amsterdam. The monochrome plates were made by and the endpapers printed by Van Leer & Co. N.V., Amsterdam. The color plates were made by Austin Miles Ltd, London, and printed in England by Henry Stone & Son (Printers) Ltd, Banbury. The paper was supplied by Marshall & Co., London. The binding is by Van Rijmenam N.V., The Hague. *The Saints: A Concise Biographical Dictionary* was published simultaneously in Canada by McClelland & Stewart Ltd., 25 Hollinger Road, Toronto 16. Library of Congress Catalogue No. 58-5626.

SECOND PRINTING 1960

Nihil Obstat

DANIEL DUIVESTEIJN, S.T.D.

Censor Deputatus

Imprimatur

E. MORROGH BERNARD

Vicarius Generalis

Westmonasterii, die 18a Decembris 1957

CONTENTS

Introduction by C. C. MARTINDALE, S. J.   *Page*   8

Preface by JOHN COULSON   10

The Biographical Dictionary   13

The Calendar of Feast Days   471

For further reading   489

Acknowledgments   492

About the contributors   493

THE CONTRIBUTORS

Professor Hilary Armstrong

Deborah Armstrong

Rachel Attwater

The Rev. W. J. Battersby

Dame Anselma Brennell, O.S.B.

The Rev. Laurence Bright, O.P.

Maryvonne Butcher

The Rt Rev. B. C. Butler

Edward F. Caldin

The Rev. John Challenor

T. Charles-Edwards

John Coulson (Editor)

The Rev. Francis Courtney, S.J.

Alice Curtayne

The Rev. William Dalton

The Rev. Michael Day

Michael Derrick

Reginald James Dingle

The Very Rev. Illtud Evans, O.P.

H. O. Evennett

J. R. Foster

Adrian Green-Armytage

Dom Bede Griffiths, O.S.B.

Arnold L. Haskell

Renée Haynes

Christopher Hollis

The Rev. Bruno S. James

Julian Jebb

Eric John

The Rev. Alex Jones

The Rev. Professor David Knowles

Thomas Fanshawe Lindsay

Sir Arnold Lunn

Dr John Marshall

The Rev. Gervase Mathew, O.P.

The Rev. C. C. Martindale, S.J.

Dom Sebastian Moore, O.S.B.

Norman Painting

Alan Pryce-Jones

The Rev. Gabriel Reidy, O.F.M.

E. E. Reynolds

The Rev. H. J. Richards

The Rev. Etienne Robo

Dom Ralph Russell, O.S.B.

Joseph Rykwert

The Very Rev. Columba Ryan, O.P.

Professor Edward Sarmiento

George Irving Scott-Moncrieff

Roger Sharrock

Lancelot Sheppard

Walter Shewring

Dr Eric Strauss

Professor Jocelyn M. C. Toynbee

R. Trevett

Margaret Trouncer

Dom Aelred Watkin, O.S.B.

E. I. Watkin

Evelyn Waugh

Charles Wrong

THE COLOR PLATES

I ANDREW	*frontispiece*	9 JEROME	*facing p. 256*
2 ANTONY of PADUA	*facing p. 16*	10 JOACHIM (with Sabinus)	273
3 BENEDICT of NURSIA	64	II JOHN THE BAPTIST	304
4 BONAVENTURE	81	12 MARY THE BLESSED VIRGIN	321
5 DOMINIC	112	13 SEBASTIAN	352
6 FRANCIS	129	14 THOMAS AQUINAS	369
7 GREGORY THE GREAT	208	15 THOMAS THE APOSTLE	448
8 IGNATIUS of LOYOLA	225	16 VINCENT de PAUL	465

The end papers and jacket reproduce a detail from *The Last Supper* by
Leonardo da Vinci in the Convent of Santa Maria della Grazie, Milan

THE MONOCHROME PLATES

AGATHA	*page* 33	BERNARD of CLAIRVAUX	*page* 69	CLEMENT	*page* 122
AGNES	34	BERNARDINE of SIENA	70	COLUMBA *or* COLUMCILLE	123
ALBERT THE GREAT	35	BLAISE	71	COSMAS and DAMIAN	124
ALOYSIUS GONZAGA	36	BONIFACE	72	CUNEGUND	125
ALPHONSUS RODRIGUEZ	37	BORIS and GLEB	73	CUTHBERT	126
AMBROSE	38	BRIDGET of SWEDEN	74	CYPRIAN of CARTHAGE	127
ANGELO	39	BRIGID *or* BRIDE	75	DAVID *or* DEWI	127
ANNE (*with* JOACHIM)	40	BRUNO	76	DIONYSIUS *or* DENYS THE AREOPAGITE	128
ANSELM	41	CAJETAN	77	DOMINIC SAVIO	162
ANTONINUS of FLORENCE	42	CANDIDUS	78	DONATUS of AREZZO	163
ANTONY THE ABBOT	43	CANUTE *or* KNUT	123	DOROTHY	164
APOLLINARIS of RAVENNA	44	CASIMIR of POLAND	79	DUNSTAN	165
APOLLONIA	45	CATHERINE of ALEXANDRIA	80	EDMUND of ABINGDON	166
AUGUSTINE	46	CATHERINE of SIENA	113	EDMUND THE MARTYR	167
BARBARA	47	CECILIA *or* CECILY	114	EDWARD THE CONFESSOR	168
BARNABAS	48	CHARLEMAGNE	115	EDWARD THE MARTYR	168
BARTHOLOMEW	65	CHARLES BORROMEO	116	EGBERT	123
BASIL THE GREAT	47	CHRISTINA of BOLSENA	117	ELIGIUS *or* ELOI	169
BAVO *or* ALLOWIN	66	CHRISTOPHER	118	ELIZABETH and ZACHARY	170
BEDE (the Venerable Bede)	67	CHRYSOGONUS	119	ELIZABETH of HUNGARY	171
BERNADETTE SOUBIROUS	68	CLARE	120	ELIZABETH of PORTUGAL	172
		CLARE of MONTEFALCO	121	ERASMUS *or* ELMO	173

THE MONOCHROME PLATES continued

ETHELBERT *page* 123	JOSEPH *page* 268	PETER MARY CHANEL *page* 366
EUSTACE 174	JOSEPH BENEDICT LABRE 269	PETER of ALCÁNTARA 367
FABIAN 175	JOSEPH of ARIMATHEA 270	PHILIP BENIZI 368
FELIX I 176	JUDE 271	PHILIP NERI 401
FRANCES XAVIER CABRINI 209	KEVIN *or* COEGMEN 272	PHILIP THE APOSTLE 402
FRANCIS BORGIA 210	LAURENCE 305	PIUS V 403
FRANCIS of SALES 211	LEO I (THE GREAT) 306	PIUS X 404
FRANCIS XAVIER 212	LOUIS IX, KING of FRANCE 307	RAPHAEL THE ARCHANGEL 405
GABRIEL LALEMANT 161	LOUIS of ANJOU 308	RAYMUND NONNATUS 406
GALL 213	LUCY 309	RAYMUND of PENAFORT 407
GENEVIÈVE 214	MADELEINE SOPHIE BARAT 310	ROBERT BELLARMINE 408
GEORGE 215	MARGARET of CORTONA 311	ROSE of LIMA 409
GERMANUS *or* GERMAIN 216	MARGARET *or* MARINA 312	RUFINA 410
GERTRUDE THE GREAT 217	MARK THE EVANGELIST 313	SCHOLASTICA 411
GILES 218	MARTHA 314	SILVESTER I 412
GREGORY NAZIANZEN 219	MARTIN of TOURS 315	SIMEON 413
HELENA 220	MARTYRS of NORTH AMERICA 161	SIMEON STYLITES 414
HENRY THE EMPEROR 221	MARY MAGDALEN dei PAZZI 316	SIMON 415
HILARION 222	MARY MAGDALENE 317	SIMON STOCK 416
HUBERT 223	MATTHEW, APOSTLE and EVANGELIST 318	SIXTUS II 449
HUGH of LINCOLN 224	MATTHIAS 319	STANISLAUS of CRACOW 450
IGNATIUS of ANTIOCH 257	MENNAS 320	STEPHEN PROTOMARTYR 451
ISAAC JOGUES 161	MICHAEL 353	TERESA of AVILA 452
ISIDORE of SEVILLE 258	MONICA 354	TERESA of LISIEUX 453
JAMES THE GREATER 259	NICHOLAS of TOLENTINO 355	THOMAS MORE 454
JANUARIUS 260	NICHOLAS von (of) FLÜE 356	THOMAS of CANTERBURY 455
JOAN of ARC 261	NICODEMUS 357	URBAN I 456
JOHN BAPTIST de la SALLE 262	NORBERT 358	URSULA 457
JOHN BOSCO 263	OSWALD of WORCESTER 359	VALENTINE 458
JOHN CHRYSOSTOM 264	PANCRAS 360	VERONICA 459
JOHN de BRÉBEUF 161	PAUL 361	VINCENT FERRER 460
JOHN FISHER 265	PAUL THE FIRST HERMIT 362	WENCESLAUS of BOHEMIA 461
JOHN THE EVANGELIST 266	PERPETUA and FELICITY 363	WILFRID 462
JOHN VIANNEY (the 'Curé d'Ars') 267	PETER 364	WILLIAM of YORK 463
	PETER CANISIUS 365	ZENOBIUS 464

INTRODUCTION

The use of the words 'saint' and 'sanctity', 'holy' and 'holiness' is certainly much less frequent among us than it was. We respect a man who tells the truth, who is straight in money matters, who shows courage and good temper, who is faithful to his wife, and so forth. We may say a man is a very 'fine character', but are unlikely to call him 'holy', if only because we associate, however vaguely, the word 'holy' with 'religion', and a man such as I described might have no definite religion, or none at all, and never say any prayers. To come closer to 'saints', we hardly expect our contemporaries – at least in northern countries – to have 'patron saints', whom they expect to be interested in them and whom they invoke at a crisis and whose 'day' they celebrate in some particular way; they are unlikely to know anything about a St Charles or St Henry if they are called by those names.

I doubt if this is due chiefly to the fifteenth century revolt against the invocation or even the 'cult' of saints. It was said, then and since, that the saints 'took the place of God'. I do not believe this for a moment, though super-stitious homage may well have been paid to their relics. Then, as now, the central act of Christian worship was Holy Communion, and the central figures in Christian imagery were the Madonna with her Child, and the Crucifix. Nor, as is still sometimes happy-go-lucily said, did the saints merely 'replace' the heroes of paganism: the latter had nothing of 'holiness' about them: the saints always did. Nor again can we equate saints with fakirs or medicine-men, for though the latter were considered to possess magical powers and the former often lead a life of extreme asceticism, yet they are not necessarily associated with high virtue or with God. But the saint, as we understand him here, is essentially a man or woman of heroic virtue, due, we hold, to a most intimate union with God.

We think it quite possible that, in our age, the faculty of *admiration* has been weakened, if only because it contains an element of surprise, and life is making things seem common-place. Take a simple example – picture-postcards have made the world so familiar, that when I have seen something really out of the ordinary, like the Pyramids or the silhouette of Constantinople, I am inclined to feel: 'Yes, it's just like what one expected'. And we have got so accustomed to scientific 'advances' that we are not *astonished* to hear that after all a visit to Mars need not be brushed aside as absurd. This is really an impoverishment, if it means that we cannot see even the material world as marvellous.

But the disaster is still greater if we become unable to see human nature, or rather, this man or this woman, as someone extraordinary. And that, not only because of some remarkable thing they have done, but of something wonderful that they *are*. We even hear the 'cult of personality' condemned: we should all act collectively. This assumes that a man cannot be 'outstanding' without being conceited, as a minimum, and, at the maximum, a tyrant. But one fact you can assume about the saints is that they were supremely unselfish.

However, no one can be unselfish unless he cares for someone or something else; and complete unselfishness, going as far as self-forgetfulness, such that even self-*sacrifice* is at once accepted if it is so much as noticed, means that the 'something or someone' is *intensely* cared for. We know of some who, as they say, 'make money their god' and are ready to sacrifice no matter whom in order to get more of it. There are others who have 'lived for art', and have not only not cared for money, not even for wife nor children, if they can but follow their 'vision'. We do not associate sanctity with these, nor even, necessarily, with men or women who devote their lives to 'philanthropy', though we may doubt whether they can do that perseveringly without special help from God in whom they may actually profess to disbelieve. Our Lord's parable about those who fed the hungry, visited the sick or the prisoner, and were, said He, doing it to Himself though they did not know it, suggests that no good deed can be done alto-gether without His inspiration.

In fact it is part of Catholic doctrine that God is always He who takes the initiative, He who gives light to the mind and strength to the will, and that supernatural life which we call grace. In proportion as the soul advances to an ever fuller co-operation with grace, it advances towards sanctity.

Here I must interpolate two considerations. First, because there exists a 'calendar' or catalogue of persons to whose name the word 'saint' is prefixed, it does not follow that only *they* were saints. They are 'canonized' as saints: that is, the church has judged fit to 'placard' them, so to say, as saints. The first example of 'canonization' is found in 993 A.D., when Pope John XV officially recognized St Ulric as a saint. However, long before that, there were less authoritative ways of acclaiming saints, such as popular conviction. The few, then, who are canonized are, compared with the multitudes already thronging heaven, as those few stars that we see compared with those many myriads, afar in the universe, whose light has not yet reached us.

Secondly, we recall that, when reading the 'life' of a saint, we are not seeing forthwith an accomplished piece of perfection, but a *person* who is living and therefore growing. We are far from being bound to think that everything we read about a saint is, from the outset, perfectly wise or right, even when he was trying to fulfil the vocation that gradually dawned on him. Even the 'abnormal' experiences of the saint-to-be are not proofs of sanctity, though it may well be that they are a consequence of an invasion of grace (so to put it) into a soul not yet perfectly harmonized within itself. That is why St John of the Cross could compare an ecstasy (in which normal consciousness is *inhibited*) to a 'dislocation of the bones'. It is not, perhaps, hard to see that in a 'just man made perfect' (Hebrews 12:23), no one part of his total nature is perfected *at the expense* of any other. We can even see the rational foundation of that tremendous mystery – the resurrection of the flesh. We are not, in our *immortality*, to *get rid* of anything that has a share in making us men and women and we are never to be a kind of angel, so it does not follow that we should even *like* a saint till he has become exactly what God means him to be. If we would not like him even then, the defect may well be in ourselves, perhaps just because we cannot see everything all at once and from every aspect.

Yet those who grumble at anyone being better than anyone else on the human level, and quarrel with the idea of excellence, may object to the whole theory of a hierarchy of holiness – that some should be saints and others not. But all of the innumerable 'company of the saved' are saints! We have no space to discuss the doctrine of 'purgatory'; but those of us who are all too conscious of our faultiness, and nonetheless genuinely desirous of fulfilling God's plan for us, will all of us wear a halo. The dross will have been burned out of us, and the pure golden saint emerge. And since I in no way object to an infinite variety in human nature on the moral or social or intellectual level, and 'excellencies' of many sorts, so neither shall I rebel if star differs in loveliness from star (1 Corinthians 15:41) in the heavens of immortality.

We may trust that even this selection from the many thousands of 'saints' who have appeared in so many lands while nearly two thousand years have passed may, first, capture the interest of readers, and awaken in them an astonishment, and at last – when the motive of their lives has been recognized, that is, an *intense love of God* above and in all things – a dormant sense of awe: and thus the saints may become our own pathway back towards God and Christ without whom their existence would remain inexplicable.

C. C. MARTINDALE, S.J

PREFACE

This is as much a book to browse through as to consult. It is not a mere catalogue of dates and facts. Each main entry has been written by a leading authority, but in such a way as to be generally acceptable; since we believe that all our readers – Catholic and non-Catholic alike – will be more truly edified by an attempt to depict the true facts than by pious asides and the over-zealous acceptance of legends. Let the saints appear as they are, and the edification will look after itself. But this is, of course, a precept of perfection which we cannot claim to have consistently achieved, although, in order to do so, we have deliberately selected our contributors from as wide a field as possible; they range from some of the most distinguished theologians and biblical scholars to historians, psychiatrists, novelists and scientists, equally eminent.

In thus coming to see the saints from many different angles, the reader should be able to build up in his mind a rich and detailed picture of that complex and indefinable quality – sanctity. All that can be said without impertinence about this – the only quality common to all the saints – is that it exalts weakness into an irresistible strength, and causes its possessors, burning with the love of God, to behave in a way which is certainly unusual. It is therefore very easy for us who do not understand the sources of their power to consider some of the saints to have been abnormal almost to the point of insanity – especially when they have had visions, heard voices, received the stigmata or gone on hunger-strike. Because of the interest attached to these topics, they have been specifically treated within the context of the life of a particular saint. Levitation and other abnormalities are discussed in Joseph of Copertino, stigmata in Gemma Galgani, prolonged fasting in Lidwina of Schiedam, and the problems raised by the behavior of relics in Veronica, Pantaleon and Januarius.

Such discussions may also help to demonstrate the dangers of believing that sanctity can be measured by means of an external criterion, as though Simeon Stylites was a saint because he lived on top of a pillar. The saints have been called to behave in ways appropriate to particular occasions so that what may edify one generation revolts another, and it is sometimes wiser to know what sanctity is not than to seek for too rigorous a definition of what it is. Saints do not have to be committed to any particular political theories; some – William of York – were the dupes of political intrigue; others – Turibius of Lima – might be considered subversives. Some, like Francis, denounced social abuses, others, like Peter Claver, accepted them as providing the opportunity for their vocation. But what perhaps is hardest to accept is that sanctity is not quite the same as piety, and that although this quality may be as necessary to a saint as high speed is to an aeroplane – it cannot break the sound barrier without it – nevertheless sanctity is something beyond the barrier of mere piety, as a glance at the life of Teresa of Lisieux will soon show.

Many factors have had, therefore, to be taken into account in deciding how much space should be devoted to particular saints. Some have been included because they were politically important, others because interesting or even amusing things happened to them. No epic could be more exciting than that of the North American Martyrs, and no by-way more amusing than the 'cult' of 'St' Napoleon.

Certain saints have been treated as representatives of a class, so that although many of the early martyrs have been briefly noticed, an idea of their trials, tortures and executions may be gained in the longer accounts of Perpetua and Felicity, Maximilian of Theveste, Polycarp, Marcellus and Pothinus. In other cases a discussion of certain recurring theological references has been undertaken in the lives of particular saints – thus the primacy of the see of Peter and the place of his burial are dealt with by two of the leading experts on the subject in the life of Peter; the life of James the Less deals with the brethren of the Lord, Athanasius of Alexandria with the Arian heresy, and the status of Angels and Archangels is examined in the article of that name.

Legend is almost the major difficulty in hagiography, and where it is clearly evident that a saint did not exist we have said so, since nothing is to be gained by perpetuating mistakes and forgeries. But the relation of legend to reality is frequently more complex. To serve the ends of religious teaching, virtues have often received legendary embodiment in human form, or existing stories have been homiletically embellished. In many cases we are now quite unable to say what is fact and what is pious invention, and the symbolic blinding of Lucy, the derivation of Christopher's name, and the choice of a patron on the strength of a pun on his name (discussed under Expeditus) are but a few examples. Other facets of the infinitely various relationship of legend to facts have been treated in the articles on Agnes, Cecilia, Dionysius, Hippolytus and Joseph of Arimathea.

Illustrations

The illustrations to this book have usually but not always been chosen on their merits as works of art, and they add yet a further dimension to the subject by showing how infinitely complex is the relationship between hagiography and art. Sometimes, as in Jan Bruegel's 'St Eustace', the artist seems less interested in the saint than in the countryside and animals by which he is surrounded; and the greatest artists seem often to be attracted to those aspects of a saint's life which are least likely to have been true – at all events in a literal sense. Yet, as in Memlinc's 'Mystical Marriage of St Catherine', something is achieved which exists not merely in its own right as a work of art but as an effective aid to devotion.

Notes on the arrangement of the book

The saints are arranged in strict alphabetical order, for example John Baptist de la Salle will be found under *John B*, John the Good under *John T*, John of God under *John O*; similarly 'or' and 'and' have been included in the alphabetical arrangement. Christian names are anglicized throughout, so that Antony, Francis, Joan, John and Teresa appear in place of the sometimes more familiar Antonio, Francesco, Jeanne, Jean and Thérèse.

Where the dates of a saint's birth and death are known, they have been given. Otherwise the date of death, preceded by a "†" is stated, and in cases where this is not certain, the century is given instead. In cases of extreme uncertainty, no date is shown.

Since the entries in this dictionary are confined to saints, the prefix 'St' is frequently omitted in the text and consistently omitted from the titles to the entries. Cross-references are rarely specifically made to a saint unless an article is designed to be read in conjunction with another.

Each entry is followed by the date on which the saint is commemorated and at the end of the book there is included an up-to-date liturgical Calendar. This has been arranged so that there is a clear distinction between the main feast of the day according to the Roman Missal ('SMALL CAPITALS'), other feasts mentioned in the Roman Missal ('*Italics*'), and saints whose feasts are not mentioned in the Roman Missal but whose lives are included in this book ('ordinary type'). An asterisk '*' indicates those saints whose lives are of particular interest and are treated as main entries by our contributors. There is consequently a perfect cross-reference system between the Dictionary and the Calendar.

I am particularly grateful to the Abbot, Headmaster and Community of Downside Abbey for much advice and for permission to use the monastic library. I should especially like to thank Dom Ralph Russell, Dom Illtyd Trethowan and Dom Aelred Watkin. I am under a special debt of gratitude to Mr Lancelot Sheppard for his advice at all stages of the task and for the scholarly care with which he read the final manuscript, and to Mr E. I. Watkin, not only for the great thoroughness with which he read the proofs, but for his many valuable suggestions. No editor could have received greater assistance from his contributors than I, and I wish not only to acknowledge my gratitude, but to say how much this work owes to their advice so generously given.

JOHN COULSON

AARON, *see* Julius and Aaron.

ABACHUM, *see* Marius, Martha, Audifax and Abachum.

ABBO, *see* Goericus.

ABBO of FLEURY † 1004
After teaching at Ramsey, Huntingdonshire, he was recalled to France and made abbot of Fleury. He was stabbed while trying to pacify a monastic riot at La Réole in Gascony.
November 13th

ABDON and SENNEN † 303
Persians, they were brought to Rome and martyred during the persecution of Diocletian.
July 30th

ABERCIUS *Second Century*
In his seventy-second year, this bishop of Hieropolis made a pilgrimage to Rome which so impressed him that he caused a description of his journey to be carved upon his tomb.
October 22nd

ABIBUS, GURIAS and SAMONAS
Fourth Century
Martyred in Syria under the persecution of Diocletian, their bodies were contained in one of the principal shrines at Edessa in Syria.
November 15th

ABRAHAM † 422
Born in Cyrrhus, Syria, St Abraham was a solitary, and converted to Christianity pagans on Mount Lebanon and became bishop of Carrhae, Mesopotamia. He died in 422 in Constantinople, summoned there by Emperor Theodosius II, who greatly valued his advice.
February 14th

ABRAHAM KIDUNIA *Sixth Century*
Born in Edessa, Mesopotamia, he shunned marriage to become a hermit near Beth-Kaduna whose population of idolaters he evangelized after three hard years. A year later he returned to the desert, and died aged seventy. His biographer says of him that he was never seen to smile and that he lived every day as though it were his last.
March 16th

ABRAHAM of KRATIA 474–558
Born at Emesa in Syria, at twenty-six he was made abbot of Kratia in Bithynia. At thirty-nine he ran away to seek solitude, but was forced to return and to become bishop. Fifteen years later he again escaped, this time successfully, and passed the last twenty years of his life in a Palestinian monastery.
December 6th

ABRAHAM of ROSTOV *Twelfth Century*
Born at Galich, he was converted by being cured of a disease as a result of calling upon the Christian God. He became a monk and devoted his life to the conversion of Rostov, where he died in the monastery he had founded.
October 29th

ABRAHAM of SMOLENSK † 1221
A monk of the Bogoroditskaya monastery in Smolensk, he aroused opposition by his success as a preacher and spiritual director. He was tried on a number of trumped-up charges and apparently forbidden to say mass. His innocence was eventually proved and he died, beloved by all, as abbot of the Mother of God monastery at Smolensk.
August 21st

ABUNDIUS, ABUNDANTIUS and their Companions † c. 304?
Abundius was a priest, Abundantius a deacon. They are said to have been martyred, with the senator Marcian and his son John, by Diocletian.
September 16th

ACACIUS or ACHATIUS *Third Century*
Possibly bishop of Antioch, Pisidia, or of Melitene in Armenia. There is an extant report of his trial by Martian in which he argued so wittily against idolatry that the Emperor Decius pardoned him.
See also The Fourteen Holy Helpers.
March 31st

ACACIUS or AGATHUS † 303 or 305
A centurion in the Roman Army from Cappadocia, he is the only genuine, ancient martyr of Byzantium (excepting St Mucius). Constantine dedicated a church to him there, nicknamed the 'Walnut', because the tree upon which he was suspended for flagellation was incorporated into it.
May 8th

ACCA † 740

The protégé of St Bosa and then of St Wilfrid who made him abbot, he succeeded St Wilfrid in 709 as bishop of Hexham. The Venerable Bede praised him for his encouragement of learning.
October 20th

ACCURSIO, *see* Berard.

ACHARD, *see* Aichardus.

ACHATIUS, *see* Acacius.

ACHILLAS, *see under* Alexander of Alexandria.

ACHILLEUS, *see* Felix, Fortunatus and Achilleus.

ACHILLEUS, *see* Nereus, Achilleus and Domitilla.

ACISCLUS and VICTORIA   *Fourth Century?*

There is no agreement about the dates of these martyrs, although St Eulogius says that they came from Cordova and were brother and sister.
November 17th

ADALBALD of OSTREVANT   † 652

St Adalbald was the grandson of St Gertrude, the foundress of the Hamage monastery, and the son of Rigomer. As a courtier of King Dagobert I, he fought in Gascony, and there married St Rictrudis. His children became SS Mauront, Eusebia, Clotsindis and Adalsindis. The family devoted itself to pious works until Adalbald was murdered by his wife's kinsmen.
February 2nd

ADALBERT of EGMOND   † c.710?

A Northumbrian, he was one of those who converted Friesland. Egmond was the centre of his activities.
June 25th

ADALBERT of MAGDEBURG   † 981

A monk of Trier, Adalbert led an abortive missionary expedition to Russia in 961. In 962 he became the first archbishop of the city of Magdeburg which had been founded some years earlier by the Emperor Otto the Great to overawe the Slavs on the far side of the Elbe.
June 20th

ADALBERT of PRAGUE   † 956–997

Bohemian by birth, Adalbert was elected bishop of Prague when still a young man. He was twice forced to leave his bishopric for political reasons and eventually perished at the hands of the Prussians, whom he was trying to convert, possibly near Königsberg. A friend of the Emperor Otto III, he seems to have been an influential figure in the central Europe of his time.
April 23rd

ADALHARD or ADELARD   753–827

Son of Bernard, the son of Charles Martel, and first cousin to Charlemagne, he was abbot at Corbie, Picardy, until called to the Court. On Charlemagne's death, Louis the Debonair banished him to Heri (Noirmoutier), an island off Aquitaine. Recalled in 823, he returned to Corbie, and died there a great teacher.
January 2nd

ADAMNAN   c. 624–704

Born in Donegal, Adamnan was the ninth abbot of Iona and one of its most notable scholars. His best known work is his *Life of St Columba.*
September 23rd

ADAMNAN of COLDINGHAM   *Seventh Century*

He was an Irish monk of the monastery of Coldingham on the Berwick coast.
January 31st

ADAUCTUS, *see* Felix and Adauctus.

ADAUCUS   † 303

An Italian of high birth who suffered martyrdom while serving as *quaestor* (financial official) in a small town in Phrygia.
February 7th

ADDAI and MARI   *Second Century?*

Addai was possibly a missionary in Edessa, Mari may never have existed. They are venerated by the Chaldeans and Nestorians as the apostles of Mesopotamia.
August 5th.

ADELA, *see* Irmina and Adela.

ADELAIDE   931–999

Born in 931, St Adelaide was the daughter of Rudolph of Burgundy. Still a child she was betrothed for political reasons to Lothair of Provence, heir of King Hugh of Italy. Hugh married Adelaide's widowed mother. At the age of sixteen she married Lothair, now king of Italy, and a daughter, Emma, was born of the marriage. It was an unhappy union but a short one, for in 950 Lothair died. His successor, Berengar, imprisoned her when Adelaide refused to marry his son. After four months' confinement she escaped in August 951, and when that same year the German Emperor Otto appeared in Italy and proposed marriage, she accepted. Four children were born to them, the future Otto II and three daughters, two of whom became nuns. A revolt led by Ludolf, Otto's son by his first marriage, was crushed. It would appear to have been Adelaide's influence which encouraged, if it did not inspire, Otto's policy of close collaboration with the church. During a sojourn of six years in Italy Otto and Adelaide received the imperial crown from John XII.

When her husband was succeeded in 973 by their

son Otto II, Adelaide for some years exercised a powerful influence. Later, however, her daughter-in-law, the Byzantine princess Theophano, turned her husband against his mother, and she was driven from court. Finally a reconciliation was effected, and in 983 Otto appointed her his viceroy in Italy.

He died the same year, and the new emperor, Otto III, still a minor, was entrusted to the joint regency of his mother and grandmother. Theophano was able once again to oust Adelaide from power and the court. Her death in 991 restored the regency to Adelaide. She was assisted by St Willigis, bishop of Mainz. In 995 Otto came of age, and Adelaide was free to devote herself exclusively to pious works, notably the foundation or restoration of religious houses. She had long entertained close relations with Cluny, then the center of the movement for ecclesiastical reform and in particular with its abbots St Majolus and St Odilo (*see also* Cluny Saints). On her way to Burgundy to support her nephew Rudolph III against rebellion, she died at a monastery she had founded at Seltz. She had constantly devoted herself to the service of the church and peace, and to the empire as guardian of both; she also interested herself in the conversion of the Slavs. She was thus a principal agent – almost an embodiment – of the work of the Catholic church during the dark ages in the construction of the religion-culture of western Europe. Though she was never canonized, her feast is kept in many German dioceses.
December 16th

ADELAIDE of BELLICH † 1015
Daughter of Megengose, count of Guelder, she was abbess of Bellich, on the Rhine near Bonn, and of St Mary's, Cologne.
February 5th

ADELARD, *see* Adalhard.

ADELELMUS or ALEAUME † *c.* 1100
A French soldier, Adelelmus joined the Benedictine monastery of Chaise-Dieu, of which he became abbot. Constance of Burgundy invited him to Burgos, and he later fought against the Moors.
January 30th.

ADJUTUS, *see* Berard.

ADOLF † 1224
Related to the counts of Tecklenburg (Westphalia), Adolf became a canon of Cologne, but later entered the Cistercian monastery of Camp, and in 1216 replaced Gerard as bishop of Osnabrück. He died on June 30th, 1224, and has never been formally canonized.
February 14th

ADRIAN III † 885
Adrian III succeeded Macarius I as pope in 884.
July 8th

ADRIAN and EUBULUS † 309
Adrian and Eubulus came from Batanea, in eastern Palestine, in the seventh year of Diocletian's persecution to visit Christians at Caesarea. Stopped at the gates, they were tortured and killed for upholding their faith.
March 5th

ADRIAN and his Companions *Ninth Century*
Adrian and his companions were driven from their country by the Danes. We are not certain who Adrian was, whence he came, or how many companions he had. He has been identified with the Irish St Adrian, and with the Hungarian prince of that name who is said to have come to Scotland with 6605 companions and to have evangelized Fifeshire. Later they retired to a monastery on the Isle of May in the Firth of Forth, where they were massacred by invading Danes.
March 4th

ADRIAN and NATALIA † *c.* 304
Tradition makes Adrian an officer of the Roman court at Nicomedia who was converted by the sight of Christians being ill-treated and soon afterwards suffered martyrdom himself. Natalia was his wife.
September 8th

ADRIAN of CANTERBURY † 710
Adrian, a learned African, abbot of Nerida, near Naples, refused the archbishopric of Canterbury offered by Pope St Vitalian, but, as abbot of SS Peter and Paul, assisted St Theodore who had accepted the archbishopric. His instruction and example had a wide influence. He died on January 9th, 710.
January 9th

ADULF *Seventh Century*
A nobleman and brother of St Botulf, he was educated in Germany or Belgian Gaul. He became a monk and then a bishop, either at Utrecht or Maestricht.
June 17th

AEDH MAC BRICC *Sixth Century*
A disciple of St Illathan, he founded a monastery at Cill-air in Westmeath and became a bishop. He is alleged to have cured St Brigid of a headache by taking it upon himself.
November 10th

AELRED of RIEVAULX *c.* 1110–1167
St Aelred of Rievaulx was born at Hexham in Northumberland about the year 1110 and died in the year 1167 at the Cistercian monastery of Rievaulx of which he had been abbot for nearly twenty years. He was of pure

English stock and came on his father's side from a long line of hereditary priests. While still an impressionable youth, but not before he had received a sound grounding in letters and become thoroughly imbued with the new humanism of the time, he was sent to join the court of King David of Scotland. Here he won the confidence and friendship of the king, ultimately becoming High Steward of the royal household, and formed an intimate friendship with Earl Henry, the king's son. But, although things seemed to prosper for him, his soul was torn by an agonizing conflict from which, so he tells us, death seemed the only way of escape; for he felt himself called to seek God in the cloister and yet could not bring himself to break with his friend Henry. He was always a man with an enormous capacity for friendship, and in later life, when his affections had become transformed by charity, he composed a treatise on spiritual friendship after the pattern of Cicero's dialogue on the same subject that both for its theme and for the delicate beauty of its treatment is unique in Christian literature.

Release came to him and grace conquered in his soul when, returning from an interview with the archbishop of York, he visited the new Cistercian monastery at Rievaulx. From that visit he never went back to the court of Scotland. Walter Daniel, his disciple and biographer, tells us that Aelred had lived like a monk in the court of King David, but afterwards explains that he meant by this that he had led a humble life there, not that he had never 'deflowered his chastity'. After a stern struggle with himself his soul blossomed in the companionship of the cloister, and in the year 1143, after having occupied positions of responsibility in his own monastery, he was sent to become the first abbot of Revesby, a daughter house of Rievaulx, returning four years later to become abbot of Rievaulx in succession to Abbot Maurice.

As abbot of Rievaulx he very soon became known throughout the country for his holiness and prudence; he was admitted to the councils of the highest in the land and was constantly called upon to arbitrate in disputes. King Henry II of England was his friend, and, in 1160, during the papal schism of that time, he was able to influence him on behalf of Pope Alexander III. Attracted by his kindly and humane nature, men came from all over the country to seek admittance at Rievaulx, and he would turn no one away if he was satisfied he was in earnest, for he held that no monastery could call itself a house of God if it rejected the weak. But he would tolerate no soft living, and nowhere more than at Rievaulx was the Rule better observed.

He was the most delightful of companions, witty and of pleasant and easy speech, and he loved nothing better than to surround himself with his young and intelligent monks; yet he never allowed his natural inclinations to lead him into favoritism, and he could be firm to the point of obstinacy. His charming treatises on spiritual friendship, the boyhood of Jesus, the nature of the soul and other theological and historical subjects show a subtle and cultivated mind. They give the impression of having been written in some remote retreat by a scholar living far from the cares and troubles of life; but Aelred was a fine administrator and one of the busiest men of the day, and, during all the last years of his life, he was tortured by rheumatism and the stone. Broken by ill-health and over-work he died in the year 1167 at the comparatively early age of fifty-seven. He was canonized in 1191, and his feast day is kept on March 3rd, but on February 3rd by the Cistercians.
March 3rd/February 3rd

AEMILIUS and CASTUS   † 250
Two African Christians, they recanted after torture, but subsequently repented and were martyred during the persecution of Decius.
May 22nd

AENGUS, *see* Oengus.

AETERNUS, *see under* Aquilinus.

AFAN   *Sixth Century?*
All we know of this saint is that near Builth Wells, at Llanafan Fawr, which means Great Avanchurch, there is a thirteenth (?) century tombstone on which is inscribed 'Hic jacet Sanctus Avanus Episcopus' ('Here lies Saint Afan, bishop').
November 16th

AFRA   † 304
Afra was martyred, during Diocletian's persecution, at Augsburg, where she is still venerated.
August 5th

AGAPE
She is said to have been martyred at Terni in Umbria, but the evidence for her historical existence is very weak.
February 15th

AGAPE, CHIONIA and IRENE   † 304
Daughters of pagan Macedonian parents, they were tried before Dulcitius, the governor, for refusing to eat sacrificial meat, and for having in their possession copies of the Scriptures. Agape and Chionia were burned alive, and Irene sentenced to be kept in a brothel; but in the end she, too, was put to death.
April 3rd

AGAPITUS
All we know of this saint is that he was martyred and that a basilica was built to commemorate him at Praeneste (Palestrina) – the place of his birth and of his martyrdom.

Legend tells us that, at the age of fifteen, he was

ANTONY of PADUA: detail of painted
wooden polyptych by Schiavone
(1436-7 - 1504).(*National Gallery, London*)

PLATE 2

brought before the governor of Palestrina upon the order of the Emperor Aurelius, that he was condemned for being a Christian and tortured. He was flogged, put into a foul dungeon, had hot coals placed upon his head, boiling water poured over him and the bones of his jaw broken; but he remained firm. In despair, the governor had him thrown to the lions, but they refused to eat him, at which the governor had a seizure and died upon the spot. Agapitus was finally beheaded, but not before the example of his resolution and fortitude had converted the tribune Anastasius.

August 18th

AGAPITUS, *see* Sixtus II, Felicissimus, Agapitus and their Companions.

AGAPITUS I † 536
Agapitus succeeded John II as pope in 535. He died a few months later while on a visit to Constantinople.

April 22nd

AGAPIUS, *see* Timothy, Agapius and Thecla.

AGATHA *Third Century*
According to legend, she was born in Sicily of noble parents and martyred at Catania in 251. The governor of Sicily, Quintian, tried to force her to live with him, and, when she resisted his advances, had her arrested on suspicion of being a Christian. As all the efforts to talk Agatha round were useless, she was tortured; her flesh was ripped by iron hooks and her breasts were cut off, but she still resisted. She was then thrown upon burning coals, whereupon a violent earthquake shook the town of Catania, and Quintian, fearing that the people would rise up in protest, ordered Agatha to be taken back to prison. The tortures had been too great for her body, and she died soon afterwards.

Her martyrdom and early cultus are historically certain, and the church rejoices in Agatha's defence of her chastity in the introit to her mass: 'Let us all rejoice in the Lord, celebrating a festival in honor of Blessed Agatha, virgin and martyr; at whose passion the angels rejoice, and give praise to the Son of God.' The Epistle speaks of the way in which God has chosen the weak things of the world in order that he may confound the wise and strong. Agatha has also been made the patroness of nurses, and she is sometimes invoked against breast diseases and fire. ILLUSTRATION: page 33

February 5th

AGATHANGELUS and CLEMENT
Fourth Century
Clement, a teacher, bishop of Ancyra in Galatia, having miraculously survived torture was brought to Rome where he converted Agathangelus and ordained him deacon. Both were probably martyred at Ancyra.

January 23rd

AGATHO † 681
Agatho was a Sicilian Greek who became a monk at Palermo after being married and spending twenty years in secular activities. He succeeded Donus as pope in 678 and presided, through three legates, over the sixth general council at Constantinople in 680, confuting the Monothelite heresy in a letter.

January 10th

AGATHONICA, PAPYLUS and CARPUS
† 170 or 250
They were burned at Pergamos in Asia Minor for refusing to sacrifice to the gods. (*See* Carpus).

April 13th

AGATHOPUS and THEODULUS † 303
Deacon and lector respectively, they were drowned at Thessalonica for professing Christianity.

April 4th

AGATHUS, *see* Acacius.

AGERICUS or AIRY *c. 521–588*
He succeeded St Desiderius as bishop of Verdun and enjoyed the favor of King Sigebert I and of his son Childebert, whose counsellor he became.

December 1st

AGILBERT † 685
A Frenchman who had studied in Ireland, he was asked by Coenwalh, king of the West Saxons, to become bishop. He supported Rome at the synod of Whitby, and left England to become bishop of Paris when Coenwalh divided his see without consulting him.

October 11th

AGNES † *c. 304?*
A suitor, or suitors, chagrined by her refusal to wed, denounced Agnes to the prefect of Rome as a Christian. No threats could shake her determination to preserve her virginity as the bride of Christ and her faith. When she was taken by the order of the prefect to a brothel, divine power protected her purity; and a subsequent attempt to burn her failed, because the fire was miraculously extinguished. Her courage unshaken, she was beheaded.

Unfortunately the fifth century *Passion* is unreliable, although it has provided her office with beautiful antiphons and responsories. We are ignorant of the date of Agnes's death. Probably, as Père Jubaru has argued, she was stabbed in the throat. If, as is possibly the case, a skull preserved among the relics of the Sancta Sanctorum at Rome is in fact hers, she was a girl of about thirteen when she suffered.

The death of this brave child made a profound impression, and she became among the best known and most widely honored of the Roman martyrs. Her name is in the canon of the mass. Her body, headless, is enshrined in the basilica bearing her name, where on her feast day, are blessed the lambs whose wool is woven into the pallia sent by the Holy See to archbishops. St Ambrose's treatise *De Virginibus* (377) contains a panegyric of Agnes, who has always been regarded as the special patroness of bodily purity.

January 21st   ILLUSTRATION: page 34

AGNES of ASSISI   † 1253
Younger sister of St Clare, she too received the habit from St Francis. He made her first abbess of Monticelli in Florence, and she supervised the foundation of many other houses. The two sisters died within a few days of each other.

November 16th

AGNES of MONTEPULCIANO   *c.* 1268–1317
A nun at the age of nine, Agnes became head of a newly established convent at Procena when she was still in her 'teens. She subsequently founded a Dominican convent in her native town and was its prioress until her death. She led an extremely austere life and is reputed to have enjoyed many visions and raptures.

April 20th

AGRECIUS or AGRITIUS   † 329?
This bishop of Trier was succeeded by St Maximinus, and is known to have attended the council of Arles in 314. An unreliable account states that he received from St Helen several precious relics, including the 'Holy Coat of Trier' (our Lord's seamless coat), and the knife used at the Last Supper.

January 13th

AGRICOLA   † 580
Known as 'Arègle' in France, Agricola was bishop of Chalon-sur-Saône for forty-eight years. He was a friend of St Gregory of Tours, who tells us that Agricola led a very simple life, never breaking his fast until evening.

March 17th

AGRICOLA, see Vitalis and Agricola.

AGRICOLUS   *Seventh Century?*
Patron saint of Avignon since 1647, he is supposed to have been a seventh century bishop of that city. Because of his name, which means 'farmer', he is invoked to obtain fine weather or rain.

September 2nd

AGRIPPINA   *Third Century?*
Honored in Sicily and Greece, she may have suffered martyrdom in Rome in the time of Valerian or Diocletian.

June 23rd

AGRITIUS, see Agrecius.

AICHARDUS or ACHARD   † *c.* 687
Monk of the abbey of St Jouin in Picardy, abbot of Quinçay and later St Philibert's successor as abbot of Jumièges.

September 15th

AIDAN of LINDISFARNE   † 651
St Aidan was the leader of the Iona mission which was responsible for bringing Christianity to most of northern, midland and eastern England. At first it seemed that northern England would be converted by Roman missionaries from Canterbury, when King Edwin of Northumbria was baptized by Bishop Paulinus, who had come to him from Kent. But in 633 Edwin was killed in battle by the Welsh king Cadwallon. Paulinus accompanied Edwin's widow and his children south to Kent and only a single missionary, James the deacon, remained at work in the north. In 635 the Northumbrian prince Oswald defeated and killed Cadwallon and restored Northumbrian independence. Oswald had spent his exile at the Celtic monastery of Iona where he was baptized. He now asked his former hosts to send him a bishop for his people. They chose a monk of austere life who, expecting too much from the pagan Northumbrians, soon gave up in despair. On his return he was critized by a fellow monk called Aidan who thought he should have expected less and done more. Aidan was accordingly sent in his stead to see what he could do. He was consecrated bishop before his departure and on arrival in Northumbria he established his seat and a monastery on the tidal island of Lindisfarne, from where he undertook missionary journeys all over Northumbria, until his death in 651.

Aidan's religious allegiance created a problem for the new English church. Like the rest of the Iona community, Aidan held St Columba, the founder of Iona, in great veneration, and he celebrated Easter according to Columba's manner of calculating it. This had once been the practice of Rome and the west, but owing to the pagan Saxon invasions of England the Celtic Christians had been cut off from and had fallen out of step with their continental brethren. But now the conversion of England had been begun from Rome; and Wessex, Kent and East Anglia celebrated Easter in the Roman fashion while Northumbria, followed by Mercia and Essex, celebrated Easter in the Celtic fashion. Aidan himself refused to change and his prestige was sufficient to shelve the question for his lifetime. In spite of this difference Aidan was held in great respect by the 'Roman' bishops – as he was by all who knew him. He cared nothing for externals, he built only a thatched wooden church on Lindisfarne, he lived an austere life, he was never prevented by wordly rank from speaking his mind, and he was approachable by all. He was always more monk than bishop and Bede says of him that 'he was conspicuous for his discretion and adorned with other virtues too.'

August 31st

AIDAN or MAEDOC of FERNS   † 626
According to legend, he came from Connaught to study at St David's monastery. He returned home, built a monastery at Ferns, County Wexford, and became a bishop.

January 31st

AIGNAN of ORLEANS, *see* Anianus.

AIGULF   † c. 675
Appointed abbot of Lérins about 670, he aroused the opposition of some of his monks by his reforms. Two of them managed to secure his abduction by soldiers of the civil governor and he was subsequently killed, either by these soldiers or, more probably, by marauding Moors.

September 3rd

AIGULF or AYOUL   † 836
Aigulf was bishop of Bourges for twenty-four years.

May 22nd

AILBHE   † c. 526?
We know nothing reliable about this Irish saint who is supposed to have been the first bishop of Emly and to have preached in Ireland before St Patrick.

September 12th

AIRY, *see* Agericus.

ALBAN   *Fourth Century?*
The story of St Alban, the first British martyr, is told in Bede's *Ecclesiastical History*. During the persecutions of the Emperor Diocletian, Alban, a pagan, sheltered in his house a Christian priest. This priest by his virtuous example was the means of Alban's conversion, and when soldiers came to Alban's house to search out the Christian Alban put on the priest's cloak and was taken off in his stead. The judge, who was in the process of offering sacrifices to his gods, much enraged at Alban's temerity in taking the place of the wanted man, commanded Alban to be brought before the altar and demanded that he should offer sacrifice. But Alban confessed boldly that he was a Christian. 'These sacrifices . . . neither can help the worshippers nor satisfy the desires and prayers of the suppliants,' he said. The judge then ordered him to be beaten, but he bore this with such constancy and even joy that the judge commanded his execution.

They led him outside the city wall to the river, and there the people of the city who had flocked to see the spectacle ('almost all,' Bede says, 'so that the judge was left in the city without anyone to attend him') were crowded on to the bridge. But on Alban's prayer the river dried up to give him passage; seeing this the soldier appointed as executioner threw away his sword and prayed on his knees that he might have a part in Alban's fate, or even suffer for him. The procession continued its way up a beautiful hill with gentle slopes and covered in flowers; 'a place altogether worthy from of old, by reason of its native beauty, to be consecrated by the blood of a blessed martyr.' Here Alban prayed that God would give him water, and a spring appeared at his feet. And here a second executioner beheaded Alban. The first soldier also suffered with him, thus winning for himself the baptism of blood.

Bede says that Alban 'suffered death on the twenty-second day of June, near the city of Verulam.' Verulam, or Verulamium, was then a great Roman city, and the development of the present city of St Albans can be traced from that time. The tomb of St Alban was a place of pilgrimage in the fifth century; there was a church and shrine there in the early eighth century, and in 793 King Offa built a new church and founded a monastery. This was the beginning of the great Benedictine tradition of St Albans, and the abbey church is the cathedral today. Verulamium still exists as a park in which the Roman remains are protected and studied, and the landmarks of Bede's account of St Alban's death can be followed with ease. Doubts have been raised owing, among other things, to the fact that Diocletian's persecutions were not, at least officially, extended to Britain. But the solid weight of tradition goes clearly to support Bede's story, without of course necessarily establishing its every detail.

June 22nd

ALBAN or ALBINUS of MAINZ   *Fifth Century*
Alban is said to have been a Greek priest who came to Mainz, helped its bishop, St Aureus, in his struggle against the Arian heresy and was killed in a Vandal raid.

June 21st

ALBERIC   *Eleventh Century*
St Alberic was one of the hermits in the forest of Colon whom St Robert introduced, at their own request, to the Rule of St Benedict. After they had moved to Molesme in the year 1075 and had begun to increase in numbers and prosperity, their former fervor seemed to abate. They did not lead an evil life, but they took to the traditional modifications of St Benedict's Rule with rather too much alacrity to please either their abbot, St Robert, or his prior Alberic. Robert left the community in despair to live as a hermit somewhere in the neighborhood, and, not long after, Alberic accompanied by the Englishman, St Stephen Harding, a native of Dorset, also left Molesme.

They tried to live as hermits in the neighborhood of Langres, and, on the bishop of the diocese commanding them to return to their monastery, they seem to have moved further off and settled on a site called Cîteaux given to them by the Viscount of Beaune, where they were eventually joined by St Robert and about twenty monks from Molesme. Another account says that they returned to their monastery when told to do so by the bishop but left again a few years later with St Robert at their head to settle at Cîteaux. Certain it is that they were at Cîteaux with St Robert as their abbot in the year 1098, when the church there was consecrated. Their aim was not to start a new order but simply to live according to the letter of St Benedict's Rule.

After little less than a year St Robert returned to Molesme and Alberic became the abbot in his place. Under his rule the life began to take a definite shape and, according to tradition, the monks adopted for the first time the white Cistercian habit. It is said that this innovation was made at the command of our Lady to Alberic, but it could also have been for the purposes of economy, for the white of the habit was merely unbleached wool. After nine and a half years of rule Alberic, in the words of the Cistercian *Exordium Parvum*, 'departed to the Lord, a man glorious in faith and virtues'.
January 26th

ALBERT of CASHEL   *Seventh Century?*
Described by a twelfth century *Life*, in a near-pun dear to medieval writers, as 'by race an Angle, in speech an angel' (*natione Anglus, conversatione angelus*), he is supposed to have been archbishop of Cashel in Ireland; but it is unlikely that the see existed at the date usually assigned to him, and even his existence is doubtful.
January 19th

ALBERT of JERUSALEM   † 1214
Appointed Latin Patriarch of Jerusalem in 1205, St Albert, previously bishop of Vercelli and a diplomat of proved ability, worked tirelessly to keep the peace between Frank and Saracen. At the request of St Brocard, he gave the Carmelites a rule in sixteen chapters and must be regarded as the order's first legislator. He was murdered in the church of the Holy Cross at Akka.
September 25th

ALBERT of LOUVAIN   1166–1192
Son of the duke of Brabant, Albert was elected bishop of Liège in 1191. The election was disputed, and he travelled in disguise to Rome, where Pope Celestine III confirmed his election. He was murdered, however, on his return to France.
November 21st

ALBERT of MONTECORVINO   † 1127
Bishop of Montecorvino in Apulia (south-eastern Italy) and beloved by his flock, he is reputed to have once changed water into wine.
April 5th

ALBERT of TRAPAN   † *c.* 1307
A Sicilian Carmelite, he spent most of his life at the priory of Messina and his last years as a hermit near that city.
August 7th

ALBERT THE GREAT   *c.* 1206–1280
St Albert was one of the earliest generation of the Dominican order, founded in 1216; he took a large part in the momentous intellectual developments of the thirteenth century, and was declared patron of all those who devote themselves to the natural sciences, by Pope Pius XII in 1941. He is traditionally known as Albertus Magnus, Albert the Great. He was born in Swabia, within a few years of 1200 (the date is uncertain), the eldest son of a family belonging to the military nobility. He was educated at the University of Padua, already a scientific center, and joined the Dominicans as a young man. After completing his studies he taught theology; he went to Paris about 1240, and took the degree of master in sacred theology there in 1245 or 1246. For the next thirty years he led a very active life as teacher and administrator, including periods as provincial of his order in Germany and as bishop of Ratisbon, tramping the roads of Europe on long journeys. Yet his printed works, which were mostly composed in this period, fill thirty-eight quarto volumes and cover every field of learning. At Cologne and Paris he had St Thomas Aquinas as his pupil, and one of his last missions was to defend some of Thomas's writings against attacks at Paris in 1277. He died in 1280, after a pitiful period of dotage. He was canonized and declared a doctor of the church in 1931.

European Christendom in the thirteenth century was by no means the secure and static civilization it is often supposed to have been. Socially, materially and intellectually it was on the march. The church was changing with the times; the foundation of the mendicant orders, Dominican and Franciscan, opened up a new kind of priestly vocation, for the friars were bound neither to a parish like the secular clergy, nor to a monastery like the monks, so that they might be free to study and preach. The friars soon found themselves in key positions in the universities, still only a few decades old, which became the chief means by which the clergy were educated. The task before the universities was immense. Up to the twelfth century, the tradition of knowledge in the Latin-speaking western world had been based mainly on the Scriptures and the commentaries of the Fathers upon them, using a philosophy that may be loosely called Platonic. At the same time, the world of Islam had assimilated the logic and philosophy of Aristotle and much of Greek science and mathematics. In the twelfth century, these scientific and philosophical works became available in Latin translations. Thus the west was confronted with a new body of knowledge, obviously valuable but alien to the Christian tradition, and accompanied by Moslem commentaries which were very acute yet clearly heretical in part. This knowledge was the more suspect because it had been transmitted by the very enemies that most threatened Christianity.

St Albert's response to the difficulties of his time combined heroic sanctity with an astonishing universality of mind. That he should throw in his lot with the new mendicant order, despite the severe temptations of family pride, was already an indication of the humility and apostolic fire for which he was conspicuous throughout his long life. But great courage and intellectual honesty as well were needed to conceive and put into practice the policy of 'baptizing' the new learning. A lesser man might have either rejected it outright, or embraced it uncritically; St Albert proposed to understand it, to make it known, and to accept whatever parts of it might be found, after critical examination, to be true. This program was begun by him and completed by St Thomas. Neither of the two was a slavish follower of Aristotle; both differed from him on important points, and St Albert wrote, 'He who believes Aristotle to have been a god ought to suppose that he never made a mistake; but if he believes him to have been a man, doubtless he could make a mistake, just as we do'. But he accepted the main lines of Aristotle's realism, and showed that Christian doctrine could be expressed in terms of it.

Such a position implied a recognition of the autonomy of reason in its own sphere, in contrast with those who wished to make philosophy entirely subservient to theology; and of sense-experience as the origin of human knowledge, as against the Platonic view that it cannot give true knowledge. Both these conclusions are obviously important for natural science; indeed the changes in the intellectual climate brought about by the Aristotelean revival in the thirteenth century were probably a factor in the rapid development of science in the sixteenth. St Albert was himself a keen observer, with the interest of a true scientist in natural facts. He was not of course acquainted with scientific method and explanation as they are used today; but he had the scientific temper of mind, and in natural history he broke new ground, notably in the study of insects, as well as compiling critical encyclopedic works on the whole range of natural phenomena known to him, from astronomy and mineralogy to physiology.

St Albert is an especially apt patron for scientists because he made his love of truth about nature into an instrument of his love of Christ. Moreover, with all his scientific interest, he was no narrow specialist; he wrote also on logic, philosophy, theology and exegesis, with a universal and balanced outlook. Science itself is no danger to the Faith, but if a man becomes obsessed with the scientific mode of reasoning he may become blind to the truths of faith. St Albert's life shows how to meet this danger. If he appealed to observation in science, he knew that in theology he must take as his basis the doctrines of the church; if he was critical of the inaccurate observations of others, he was submissive to the teaching authority of Christ; if he was active in body and mind, he was eagerly passive to divine grace. Balance, universality and integrity might be his testament to scientists. Scholar and administrator; naturalist, philosopher and theologian; an innovator, yet a conserver of sacred doctrine; a man with an eye for detail, but always pursuing the integration of knowledge—St Albert is a mirror of the qualities that modern scientists need.
November 15th   ILLUSTRATION: page 35

ALBINUS of MAINZ, *see* Alban.

ALBINUS or AUBIN of ANGERS   † *c.* 550
A widely popular saint, of great charity and miraculous power, he was of English or Irish lineage and born at Vannes, Britanny. He was abbot of the Tincillac monastery and became bishop of Angers.
March 1st

ALCMUND   *Eighth Century*
Son or nephew of a Northumbrian king who lost his throne in 774, Alcmund may have perished helping his brother to win back the kingdom.
March 19th

ALCMUND and TILBERT   † 781 and 789
Seventh and eighth bishops of Hexham in Northumberland.
September 7th

ALDEGUNDIS   † 684
Born in Hainault about 635, daughter of SS Walbert and Bertilia, and sister of St Waldetrudis. She lived near Mons, and later in a hermitage which became the monastery of Maubeuge. She died of cancer.
January 30th

ALDEMAR   † *c.* 1080
Born in Capua, gifted with miracles, he became a deacon of the abbey of Monte Cassino, and director of Princess Aloara's convent in Capua. Because of hostility between the abbot and the princess, he built and directed the monastery of Bocchignano in the Abruzzi.
March 24th

ALDHELM   *c.* 640–709
Towards the middle of the seventh century an Irish hermit named Mailduib settled beneath the walls of a small stockade lying to the north fringe of the Selwood Forest at the place now called Malmesbury. In order to

live, Mailduib was forced to take pupils and at an unknown date a young man called Aldhelm joined the body, which from that moment grew in size and importance. Of Aldhelm's origin little can be said with certainty other than that he was born *c.* 640, was Saxon by birth and was related to the West-Saxon royal house.

According to a late tradition, Aldhelm received the tonsure in 661, and it is certain that in 671 he set out for Canterbury to study at the flourishing schools directed by Hadrian and Theodore. At Canterbury Aldhelm learned Roman law, astronomy, astrology, mathematics and some Greek and Hebrew and soon established for himself a reputation for unusual learning and brilliance. After only twelve months, ill-health forced him to return to Malmesbury, where for a time he seems to have been somewhat restless. Mailduib was, however, getting old and was depending more and more upon his pupil, while Aldhelm himself seems to have had some kind of experience which deepened his perception of spiritual truths, for, from that time onwards, he grew less inclined for secular learning and less ambitious to shine in the public eye as a brilliant scholar. His ordination to the priesthood seems to have marked the real turning-point in his career.

About the year 675 Mailduib died, and it was natural that Aldhelm should succeed him and should become the first abbot of Malmesbury. As abbot, he was an energetic and forceful superior; he introduced the Benedictine Rule, he acquired valuable estates for the monastery and used the proceeds to build three churches at Malmesbury itself. The number of monks greatly increased and Aldhelm was able to found two daughter houses, at Frome and at Bradford-on-Avon. He procured from the pope for these foundations and for Malmesbury itself a privilege which was later interpreted as placing them immediately under papal jurisdiction and exempting them from the control of the local bishop.

Aldhelm's merits as a scholar and administrator were early recognized. The Venerable Bede states that he was regarded as 'a wonder of erudition', and Pope Sergius I summoned him to Rome for consultation. An ecclesiastical synod meeting at Winchester deputed Aldhelm to remonstrate with the Celts of Devonshire and Cornwall on their differences from Roman practice with regard to the tonsure and the date of Easter.

As a writer Aldhelm was ingenious and learned, often to obscurity. He wrote in a tortuous and involved style – in which Irish influence is very marked – and perhaps his book of riddles is his happiest work, perverse as we may think its very conception. His Latin verses, in the writing of which he was almost a pioneer in England, are too mannered to be real poetry, and his largest work, the *Praise of Virginity*, contains little that is original save its style. Aldhelm also wrote poems in Anglo-Saxon to

which he set melodies of his own composition; though sung for generations after his death, they have now all perished. He was interested in music and mathematics.

The saint's character was praised by all who knew him, for he possessed a singular combination of qualities. His love of learning and practice of austerity never seem to have lessened his interest in everyday affairs nor stood in the way of what was almost a genius for friendship. His personality was an extremely powerful one, but he was never accused of being overbearing. As a practical administrator he was unwearied.

In the year 705 it was decided to subdivide the large diocese of Winchester and a bishopric was therefore established at Sherborne. King Ine of Wessex turned to Aldhelm when making the new appointment. For a long time the abbot demurred, pleading his advancing years and the loss of monastic peace; eventually, however, he agreed and was consecrated by the archbishop of Canterbury.

After a short, but extremely active, pontificate of under four years, Aldhelm was seized by his last illness while on visitation at Doulting in the Mendip Hills. He was carried into the little wooden church there and died on May 25th, 709. His body was taken to his own church at Malmesbury and buried. At Doulting a copious and perennial spring was for centuries a place of pilgrimage and today is still known as 'St Aldhelm's Well'.
May 25th

ALDRIC † 856
Born about 800, of noble family. After serving Louis the Pious at Charlemagne's court, he went to the bishop's school at Metz. He returned to the court as chaplain, and later became bishop of Le Mans.
January 7th

ALEAUME, *see* Adelelmus.

ALED or ALMEDHA or EILUNED *Sixth Century*
According to the legend, Aled was a Welsh maiden who dedicated herself to God. She fled from home to avoid a princely suitor but he followed her to her retreat, in the wood on Slwych Tump, lost his temper and cut off her head.
August 1st

ALEXANDER, *see* Epimachus, Alexander and their Companions.

ALEXANDER, *see* Epipodius and Alexander.

ALEXANDER, *see* Sisinnius, Martyrius and Alexander.

ALEXANDER AKIMETES † *c.* 430
Converted in Constantinople, he practiced asceticism in Syria for eleven years. Thereafter, he was a turbulent and restless missionary, founding monasteries by the

Euphrates, in Constantinople and at Gomon by the Bosphorus. He instituted an important form of perpetual choral service.

February 23rd

ALEXANDER, EVENTIUS and THEODULUS
Second Century

Three martyrs were buried in the Via Nomentana in Rome. All we know of them are their names.

May 3rd

ALEXANDER, JOHN III and PAUL IV
† 340, 577 and 784

All three were patriarchs of Constantinople. Tradition declares that Alexander obtained by his prayers the removal from the earthly scene of the heresiarch Arius. John was a lawyer who made the first systematic collection of canons of ecclesiastical law. Paul came from Salamis in Greece and instigated the council that, after his death, condemned iconoclasm in 787.

August 28th

ALEXANDER of ALEXANDRIA   † 328

He succeeded St Achillas as bishop of Alexandria, and was chiefly famous for his part in crushing the Arian heresy. At the first ecumenical council in Nicaea in 325 in which he took part, the heresy was condemned by Alexander's deacon and successor, St Athanasius.

February 26th

ALEXANDER of JERUSALEM   † 251

He studied with Origen in Alexandria's Christian school and was appointed bishop of his native Cappadocian city. During Severus's persecution he was imprisoned. When released, he visited Jerusalem and was made its coadjutor bishop. He died in Caesarea, imprisoned again for his faith.

March 18th

ALEXANDER SAULI   1534-1592

After joining the Barnabites at seventeen he became famous as a preacher, and was the friend of St Charles Borromeo, Gregory XIV and St Pius V. He was made bishop of Aleria in Corsica in 1570 and was known as 'the Apostle of Corsica'. In 1591 he became bishop of Pavia.

October 11th

ALEXANDER THE CHARCOAL-BURNER
Third Century

Dissatisfied with the nobly-born but unsuitable candidates for the vacant see of Comana in Pontus (northern Asia Minor), St Gregory the Wonder-worker turned to Alexander the Charcoal-Burner and, in spite of his rags and dirty face, chose him to be bishop. Alexander turned out to be a man of wisdom and is said to have eventually suffered martyrdom by fire.

August 11th

ALEXIS   *Fifth Century*

St Alexis is said to have been the son of two wealthy and powerful members of the Roman nobility. According to legend, on the night of his marriage, and with his wife's consent, he sailed to Syria and settled in the town of Edessa; there he lived for seventeen years as a beggar. At the end of this time a vision of the Virgin Mary appeared to the inhabitants of the town, saying, 'Seek the Man of God!' Alexis, realizing that he would be discovered, took ship for Tarsus but, because of bad weather, found himself back again in Italy. He returned to Rome and discovered that his parents were still living, so he presented himself at his father's house in the guise of a beggar, asking that he might be allowed to live under the staircase; this petition was granted, neither of his parents recognizing him for their son. Here he remained for a further seventeen years, living a life of great austerity, begging his bread and being ill-treated by his father's servants. His identity was discovered only at his death. Pope Innocent I, while celebrating mass before the emperor, heard a voice telling him to seek the Man of God in the house of Euphemian. The pope and emperor obeyed and, arriving at the house, discovered the body of Alexis beneath the staircase. A parchment was found on the body, giving details of the saint's name and history.

The epistle of his mass speaks of the evils which befall those who pursue material gain at all costs, 'for covetousness is the root of all evil.'

July 17th

ALEYDIS or ALICE   † 1250

Born at Schaerbeek, near Brussels, she entered a community of Cistercian nuns at the age of seven. After great suffering, she died of leprosy.

June 15th

ALFERIUS   *Eleventh Century*

Founder of the monastery of La Cava near Salerno, Alferius is said to have lived to the age of 120. Three of his successors as abbot of this famous monastery were also saints; many others are honored as blessed.

April 12th

ALFWOLD   *Eleventh Century*

A monk of Winchester, he succeeded his brother, Bertwin, as bishop of Sherborne and spread devotion to St Swithun in Dorsetshire.

March 25th

ALICE, *see* Aleydis.

ALIPIUS   *c. 360-c. 430*

The pupil and friend of St Augustine, he was baptized at the same time, became Augustine's principal assistant and, *c.* 393, bishop of Tagaste, his native town in Africa.

August 18th

ALLOWIN, *see* Bavo.

ALL SAINTS

On this day the church commemorates all those, known and unknown, who now enjoy the beatific vision of God in heaven. The origin of the feast (once called in England 'All Hallows') is obscure. We begin to find it mentioned early in the ninth century; for example, Alcuin kept it on November 1st. Its date suggests that it might be the Christianization of a Celtic festival marking the beginning of winter, but no evidence has been discovered to support this theory.
November 1st

ALL SOULS

Christians have prayed for the dead in Purgatory from very early times, believing that, in the words of Amalarius in the ninth century, 'many pass out of this world without at once being admitted into the company of the blessed'. For this reason, it came to be accepted that the commemoration of all the faithful departed should take place on the day following that of all the saints. The custom of devoting a special day to prayer for departed brothers and benefactors was widespread in monasteries of the western church by the seventh century; but it was St Odilo, abbot of Cluny, who decided, in about 998 that in Cluniac monasteries *all* the faithful departed should be commemorated on the day after the feast of All Saints. This Cluniac custom slowly spread and was general by the fourteenth century. All Souls' day has had its own office since 1913.
November 2nd

ALLUCIO   † 1134

Patron of Pescia in Tuscany, he devoted his life to the construction and care of almshouses and other hospices. He is also credited with making peace between Faenza and Ravenna.
October 23rd

ALMACHIUS or TELEMACHUS
Fourth Century

He was martyred by the angry crowd while attempting to end gladiatorial combats in Rome. According to Theodoret's *Ecclesiastical History*, the murder of Telemachus induced the Emperor Honorius to end these combats.
January 1st

ALMEDHA, see Aled.

ALNOTH   *Eighth Century*

A cowherd living near the monastery at Weedon, Northamptonshire, he became a hermit at Stowe, near Bugbrooke, where he was murdered by thieves.
February 27th

ALODIA, *see* Nunilo and Alodia.

ALOYSIUS GONZAGA   1568–1591

He was the eldest son of Ferrante, Marquis of Castiglione in Lombardy, who was offered the post of commander-in-chief to the cavalry of Henry VIII of England, but preferred the Spanish court. In Madrid Ferrante met Marta Tana who had come there with Isabel of Valois, Philip's third wife. He and Marta were married with incredible pomp in 1566, and Aloysius was born on March 9th 1568. The boy began soon to practise prayer and penance, and in 1585 renounced his birthright in favor of his brother Rodolfo and joined the Society of Jesus. In 1591 plague broke out in Rome: Aloysius caught it by carrying the sick to hospital on his back, and despite a brief recovery died on June 21st, a little over twenty-three years old.

It is impossible to estimate Aloysius's (Luigi's) career without some idea of his appalling heredity and environment. The Gonzaga tyrants rank with the Visconti, the Sforza, and the D'Este. They entered history about 1100; the first Gonzaga, lord of Mantua, was Luigi (1328), whose third marriage took place on the same day as his son's and grandson's: the three brides entered Mantua together in triumph. Already their cliff-like fortress was looming over the city. These despots displayed an amazing mixture of qualities. The Gonzaga clan survived one assassination after another and became allied to most of the reigning houses; but Luigi Gonzaga (1414) grimly surnamed 'The Turk', kept up three printing-presses and had for clients men like Platina, or Mantegna, who painted the scenery – now at Hampton Court – for the plays to which the Gonzaga were devoted. The French Parliament petitioned against the introduction of these plays into France – they were a 'high school of adultery' – and no one would now dare print the pictures with which some of the Gonzaga palaces were adorned. Yet these princes could care for agriculture, irrigation, checks on usury; and their insane debaucheries alternated with explosions of a genuine underlying faith. Their subjects, bled white by taxation, thrilled by their exotic pageantries, worshipped them till they broke into bloody but useless revolution.

Aloysius, convinced that such a society could not be reformed from within, and that he himself was 'a piece of twisted iron needing to be twisted straight', tore himself out of his setting and joined the new Company of Jesus, both because of its vow of poverty and because it vowed not to accept ecclesiastical dignities. These involved not only elaborate exterior homage but, usually, vast revenues: a kinsman of his had been appointed archbishop at the age of eight, and made a cardinal at fourteen. But apart from the violent shock to his family, Aloysius, being an imperial prince and allied to all the royal houses, became tied up in legal negotiations that seemed interminable. Even when he had done with courts, insane flatteries pursued him – doctors, feeling his pulse, would exclaim at the privilege of feeling Gonzaga blood throb beneath their fingers.

But in 1588 a quarrel broke out between Rodolfo and Vincent, duke of Mantua, head of the clan, over the fief of Solferino: not all the grandees, lay and ecclesiastical, with their army of lawyers, could settle the matter; the imperial authority was involved; even war seemed probable. Aloyisius had often helped his father, a reckless gambler, to settle his debts; and it was felt that only he, clear-headed, inflexible, unbribable, utterly unself-seeking, could be trusted to cope with the feud – although he was only just twenty-one. He went to Mantua and solved the business. There he was able to see his mother, whom he loved deeply, for his father by now had died. After his brother's death, Rodolfo ran riot: his exasperated vassals shot him, aged twenty-four, in 1593; his youngest brother Diego too was shot and ran to his mother's arms to die: she was stabbed and left for dead in the street but Aloysius, in a vision, cured her.

Aloysius himself had hoped for the missions overseas: others, that this youth of so mature a judgment would some day govern the Society of Jesus: but the plague cut short such hopes. Though the reek made him sick and faint, he served in hospitals heaped with dying men, obscene and blasphemous. If he had preserved his purity intact, his innocence was not ignorance; prudery in those days was impossible. He whose prayer was so deep never meant to be a recluse; if he could control quarrelling princes, so could he speak to the Roman rabble and lead them back to confession.

Such were the circumstances of Aloysius's life. They show the toughness of character that must have been his to have fought his way through such battalions of temptation, to victory. But human character alone would not have sufficed: it might have decided him to discard his coronet; but it would not have enabled his mother to see, before she died, his portrait above an altar and rays around his head. His life of prayer, and continuous war against that pride which he knew still remained deep in him, and his day-by-day response to grace, were what fitted him to become the patron of all young men, different though their circumstances are from those of the Gonzaga princes.

June 21st   ILLUSTRATION: page 36

ALPHAEUS and ZACHAEUS   † 303
Zachaeus was a deacon at Gadera beyond the Jordan and Alphaeus a lector. They were martyred together at Caesarea during the persecution of Diocletian.
November 17th

ALPHEGE   † 1012
Alphege became a monk at Deerhurst, then abbot of Bath. In 984 he succeeded St Ethelwold as bishop of Winchester, and he seems to have been especially concerned with the conversion of the Danelaw. He was translated to Canterbury in 1005. At this time England was continually under attack from pagan Vikings usually led by King Swein of Denmark. In 1012, after a particularly severe looting expedition, the Vikings were bought off by the English, but, in spite of this, they attacked Canterbury and seized Archbishop Alphege. The men of Kent had already been heavily taxed for the danegeld, and Alphege refused to allow them to ransom him. The Vikings were very angry and very drunk; they pelted him with meat bones left over from their banqueting until one of them, tiring of the sport, hit him with the iron head of an axe so that 'his holy blood fell upon the earth, and his holy soul was sent forth to God's kingdom'. The site of the martyrdom was traditionally the place on which Greenwich Church now stands.

After the Norman Conquest, Archbishop Lanfranc in an excess of reforming enthusiasm wished to strike his name from the calendar on the grounds that he had not been martyred for faith's sake. He was prevented by St Anselm who, instancing John the Baptist, claimed Alphege as a martyr for righteousness. St Thomas of Canterbury, in the hour of his martyrdom, invoked the aid of St Alphege.
April 19th

ALPHEGE of WINCHESTER   † 951
This bishop of Winchester is called the Elder, or the Bald, to distinguish him from St Alphege the Martyr. He helped indirectly to restore English monasticism by encouraging his kinsman, St Dunstan, to becom ea monk, and he was famous for his prophecies.
March 12th

ALPHIUS, CYRINUS and PHILADELPHUS   † 251
Their existence is doubtful. According to an unreliable story, they were natives of Vaste in the diocese of Atranto, and were martyred at Lentini in Sicily.
May 10th

ALPHONSUS LIGUORI   1696-1787
There is something paradoxical about this saint who lived in Naples almost through the whole of the eighteenth century. He said of himself, 'I have never preached a sermon which the poorest old woman in the congregation could not understand,' yet his *Moral Theology* is one of the subtlest books ever written, and most of us might be inclined to think of him as one who would be unintelligible to simple people.

He became a doctor of Civil Law at the age of seventeen and commenced to practise as a barrister immediately. His ability as an orator was such that a career of exceptional brilliance was expected; but it is possible that his youth led him to make the mistake which had such dramatic consequences for himself. In 1723 he was retained in a lawsuit involving hundreds of thousands of pounds and had made so masterly a speech that his case was thought to have been won; but the opposing counsel pointed out to him a small point that had escaped his notice: it destroyed his argument and, for a time, his reputation.

The shock prompted him to do what had probably always been in his mind. He dramatically renounced his career with the words, 'World, I know you now; courts you shall never see me more', and applied to join the Oratory. He was ordained in 1726.

His decision was not pleasing to his parents, although they were devout people. His father, who was captain of the royal galleys, had the cabin of his ship decorated with holy pictures, particularly those depicting the Passion. He made an annual retreat. Yet so horrified was he at the idea of his son's becoming a priest that he did his best to prevent it and tried to arrange an advantageous marriage. This opposition, however, was probably the result of the disrepute into which the Neapolitan clergy had fallen at the time.

There lay ahead of Alphonsus a long life, not merely of intellectual effort but of association with the common people. His delight was more in the confessional than in the study, and he soon made his mark as a mission priest. The upshot of his work was the formation of what we know today as the order of Redemptorists at Scala in November 1732. Although it was afflicted by dissension from the start – even the pioneers split up into two camps, and Alphonsus found himself beginning again with only two companions – the order nevertheless began to grow.

In 1748 he published his *Moral Theology*, which was approved by Pope Benedict XIV and became an immediate success. Alphonsus and his book achieved a certain fortuitous notoriety among Catholics and non-Catholics in the nineteenth century, for the part they were obliged to play in that great classic of spiritual autobiography: Newman's *Apologia pro Vita Sua*. Controversialists had seized upon some passages in the writings of Alphonsus in order to represent him as a teacher of laxity whose views had been endorsed by theological authority; and the Reformation Society in England published a book entirely composed of quotations from Alphonsus in order to prove 'that Romanism is immoral in its principles'.

Alphonsus said that, in certain special cases, equivocation – that is a play upon words which may have the effect of concealing the truth – is morally permissible. Newman's opponents used this as additional evidence for their charge that 'Father Newman informs us that truth for its own sake need not, and on the whole ought

not, to be a virtue with the Roman Clergy'. Newman's reply was trenchant: 'I shall give you my opinion on this point as plainly as any Protestant can wish . . . much as I admit the high points of the Italian character, I like the English character better.'

Two facts however, must be kept in mind in dealing with this aspect of Alphonsus's teaching: he was above all concerned with the welfare of souls, and in the times in which he lived the extreme doctrines of Jansenism were prevalent. Those who study the whole of his writings will find him protesting against the extremes both of rigorism and laxity. For controversial purposes it was only one side of his teaching that was selected. Nobody any longer sees any contrast between the subtle moral theologian, so easily misrepresented, and the founder of the intensely evangelical order which has been described as 'The Salvation Army of the Church'. He had a consuming love of souls: 'merciful towards others, he was severe only to himself and to those who by virtue of their sacred calling were obliged like him to achieve a life superior to that of the ordinary Christian'.

The truth of this statement was shown when he was made bishop of St Agatha in 1762. Priests who were in the habit of saying mass in fifteen minutes were suspended, and one 'star' preacher was rebuked in the following words: 'If you wanted to preach only yourself and not Jesus Christ, why come all the way to Ariola to do it?'

But Alphonsus continued to be concerned with the affairs of his order, and, in 1775, he persuaded Pope Pius VI to allow him to retire to his Redemptorist's cell at Nocera. Here he was to endure the bitterest sorrows of his life. To placate, as he thought, the hostility of the king towards his order, he was tricked into signing articles that split the Redemptorists into two factions which were reunited only after his death.

Worse was to come. His last years were clouded not only by papal displeasure but by acute illness; and for a year, at the age of seventy-eight he experienced 'a dark night of the soul'. But he passed through this into a tranquillity which lasted until his death in 1787.
August 2nd

ALPHONSUS RODRIGUEZ   *c.* 1533–1617
A wool merchant of Segovia who lost his wife and two children in quick succession, Alphonsus joined the Jesuits as a lay-brother in 1571 and spent the last forty-five years of his life as hall-porter at a Jesuit school in Majorca, well-known and beloved for his wisdom and sanctity.

St Peter Claver put himself under his direction and was encouraged to pursue his plans for working in America; while, at a later period, he aroused the admiration of that great Jesuit poet, Gerard Manley Hopkins, who must have felt that in this humble door-keeper

– 'much favoured by God with heavenly light and persecuted by evil spirits' – he had found someone who had undergone the same mental agonies as himself:

'..... while there went
Those years and years by of world without event,
That in Majorca Alfonso watched the door.'

October 30th   ILLUSTRATION: page 37

ALTMAN   † 1091
A native of Paderborn and bishop of Passau, Altman opposed the Emperor Henry IV over lay investiture, was driven from his see and spent the last years of his life in exile.

August 8th

ALTO   *Eighth Century*
An Irishman, he lived as a hermit near Augsburg, Germany. King Pepin gave him land at what is now Altomünster, Bavaria, and he founded a monastery which still exists as an abbey of Bridgettine nuns.

February 9th

AMADEUS   1110–1159
Born at Chatte, Dauphiné, son of Amadeus, lord of Hauterive, he was educated at Bonnevaux and Cluny. He served the Emperor Henry V, and subsequently became a Cistercian monk, abbot of Hautecombe, bishop of Lausanne, co-regent of Savoy and chancellor of Burgundy.

January 28th

AMADOUR
Popular tradition makes Amadour the first hermit in France and the founder of the shrine of our Lady at Rocamadour, but it is highly doubtful whether he ever existed.

August 20th

AMALBURGA   *Seventh Century*
The mother of SS Gudula and Reineldis and of Emebert, bishop of Cambrai, she spent the last part of her life as a Benedictine nun at Maubeuge.

July 10th

AMALBURGA   *Eighth Century*
Probably a nun at Munsterbilsen in Belgium, but nothing reliable is known about her.

July 10th

AMAND   c. 584–c. 679
A regionary bishop in Flanders and northern France during the Merovingian age, he founded a great many monasteries, including those of Tournai and Ghent.

February 6th

AMANDUS   † c. 431
The friend of St Paulinus of Nola, Amandus succeeded St Delphinus as bishop of Bordeaux in 400.

June 18th

AMATOR or AMATRE   † 418
Amator was bishop of Auxerre. The Latin *Life* of this saint by one Stephen is sheer fiction.

May 1st

AMATRE, *see* Amator.

AMATUS   † c. 630
Born at Grenoble, he became a monk at Luxeuil and converted a nobleman, afterwards St Romaric, who later founded the monastery of Remiremont (Romarici Mons). Amatus was its first abbot.

September 13th

AMATUS   † c. 690
This St Amatus was probably bishop of Sion, now capital of the Swiss canton of Valais.

September 13th

AMBROSE   c. 339–397
St Ambrose was born about the year 339 at Augusta Treverorum – the modern Trier. His father was Aurelius Ambrosius, prefect of the Gauls, and he belonged to the senatorial aristocracy. He was educated at Rome and entered the imperial service about 365. He was appointed governor of the provinces of Aemilia and Liguria about 371. His headquarters were at Mediolanum, the present Milan, and he was elected bishop there in the early winter of 373. As governor, he had gone to the assembly where the voting would take place to pacify a dispute between the candidates, and he was quite unprepared for the enthusiastic cry of 'Let Ambrose be bishop' which greeted his efforts at mediation. Though his family was Christian, he had not yet been baptized, but he was christened on November 24th, ordained priest and consecrated bishop on December 1st. He held the see of Milan till his death on April 4th, 397.

During most of his episcopate Milan was the capital of the western Empire, and he was the friend and counsellor of three very different emperors – Gratian, the boy Valentian and the great Theodosius, whom he once rebuked for presuming to enter the sanctuary during mass. 'The Emperor is in the church,' Theodosius was told, 'not over it.' Ambrose seems to have realized that the Roman world was plunging into darkness; within a few years of his death all the western provinces were over-run by the barbarians. More than any other man he handed on to the middle ages the legacy of Rome; the conception of objective justice and of law, the sense of the responsibility of office, pride in intergrity and in unbroken dignity. He christened Seneca and Cicero in his *De Officiis* and made their teaching part of the medieval heritage.

His life had as lasting an influence as his writings, and although he has been compared with St Augustine and St Jerome, his vocation was pastoral rather than literary.

He introduced the eastern custom of singing hymns into the western church, and he is perhaps better remembered for his hymns, such as *Aeterne Rerum Conditor* and *Veni Redemptor Omnium*, than for his more elaborate treatises on virginity (*De Virginibus*) and on faith (*De Fide*). And it is as a devoted pastor to his flock that he is seen by his greatest convert, Augustine, who sought baptism from him in 387. Consciously a Roman of senatorial rank, consciously the bishop of a great see, unconsciously a saint, Ambrose set an example that was never forgotten. He was a Father as well as a Shepherd, serenely and fearlessly independent of the state, the champion of the oppressed, a 'Christian Consul'.

December 7th　　　　　ILLUSTRATION: page 38

AMBROSE AUTPERT　　　　*Eighth Century*
An official at the court of Pepin the Short and at one time Charlemagne's tutor, he became a Benedictine monk and wrote a number of learned works highly thought of in medieval times.
July 19th

AMMON　　　　　†350
One of the first to establish a monastery in the Egyptian desert at Nitria.
October 4th

AMMON and his Companions　　　　†250
At one of the trials of Egyptian Christians during the persecution of Decius, several of the guards exhorted a prisoner to stand firm and not waver. By making their faith known, these guards – of whom Ammon was the chief – brought about their own deaths.
December 20th

AMICUS　　　　†c. 1045
A secular priest of Camerino, he became a hermit and, after an unsuccessful interval as a monk, settled in the Abruzzi to become a hermit once more.
November 3rd

AMPHILOCHIUS　　　　†c. 400
Born in Cappadocia, he was a close friend of his cousin St Gregory Nazianzen and of St Basil. He was made bishop of Iconium in 347 and prevailed upon Theodosius to forbid the Arians to hold any meetings, whether public or private.
November 23rd

ANACLETUS, *see* Cletus.

ANASTASIA, *see* Basilissa and Anastasia.

ANASTASIA and CYRIL
First venerated in the east, this patrician virgin and her attendant were martyred in Valerian's persecution.
October 28th

ANASTASIA of SIRMIUM　　　　†304?
Possibly martyred under Diocletian at Sirmium in Pannonia, she is commemorated at the second mass of Christmas.
December 25th

ANASTASIA PATRICIA
Her story is probably a pious fiction. The daughter of a patrician in Constantinople, she had to flee from the attentions of the Emperor Justinian. She reached the desert community of Abbot Daniel, told her story and was allowed a hermitage of her own. For twenty-eight years she lived in total solitude, wearing a monk's habit, and known as Anastasia the Eunuch.
March 10th

ANASTASIUS, *see* Astrik.

ANASTASIUS I　　　　†401
He succeeded St Siricius as pope in 399, and was the friend of SS Jerome, Augustine and Paulinus of Nola.
December 19th

ANASTASIUS I of ANTIOCH　　　　†599
Patriarch of Antioch, he was banished from his see for opposing erroneous doctrines supported by the Emperors Justinian I and Justin II, but later reinstated at the request of Pope Gregory I.
April 21st

ANASTASIUS II of ANTIOCH　　　　†609
He succeeded St Anastasius I as patriarch of Antioch in 599, and was murdered by a mob of Syrian Jews who were protesting against their forcible conversion to Christianity by the Emperor Phocas.
December 21st

ANASTASIUS of CLUNY　　　　†1085
Born in Venice, he was first a monk of Mont-Saint-Michel and then of Cluny. He was ordered to Spain but returned to Cluny for seven years, after which he settled in Aquitaine and lived as a hermit outside Toulouse.
October 16th

ANASTASIUS THE FULLER　　　　†304?
A fuller of Salona (Split) in Yugoslavia, he is said to have been thrown into the sea with a stone round his neck after painting a cross on his door during Diocletian's persecution. His original feast day was August 26th.
September 7th

ANASTASIUS THE PERSIAN　　　　†628
A soldier, converted after Chosroës had taken Christ's cross from Jerusalem to Persia, he was baptized and became a monk near Jerusalem. Anxious to suffer for Christ, he defied Persian beliefs in Caesarea, and was strangled, after terrible torture, in Bethsaloe, Assyria.
January 22nd

ANATOLIA, *see* Victoria and Anatolia

ANATOLIUS † *c.* 283
A learned Alexandrian who was bishop of Laodicea in Syria. Parts of his treatises on arithmetic are still extant.
July 3rd

ANATOLIUS of CONSTANTINOPLE † 458
He succeeded St Flavian as patriarch of Constantinople, and, although he protested his orthodoxy especially at the council of Chalcedon, he did not enjoy the complete confidence of the pope, St Leo, who accused him of being over-ambitious.
July 3rd

ANDREW *First Century*
The Gospels tell us that Andrew was the brother of Simon Peter, and that they were fishermen from Bethsaida; they also had a house at Capharnaum, as we hear that our Lord stayed there when he was preaching in the neighborhood. Andrew had been a disciple of St John the Baptist, and it was John who pointed out our Lord to him with the words, 'This is the Lamb of God'. Andrew and another of John's disciples immediately followed our Lord, and Andrew thus has the distinction of being known as the first of the disciples. He brought his brother Simon Peter to our Lord, and they became his disciples; but it was not until our Lord formally called them while they were casting their nets in the sea of Galilee that they 'dropped their nets immediately and followed him', leaving their families, their business and their possessions. It was at this time also that James and John were called, and Andrew appears with them and his brother at the head of the list of the twelve apostles. It was he who brought to our Lord the boy with the five barley loaves and two fishes at the feeding of the five thousand; and he and Philip told our Lord of the gentiles who had come asking if they might see him (John 12:20–22).

We have various accounts of the later life of St Andrew, but they are fragmentary and mainly not dependable. The Christian historian Eusebius tells us that he preached in Scythia. St Gregory Nazianzen says that he went to Epirus, St Jerome that he was in Achaia – and there seems a genuine tradition that he was indeed in Greece. The medieval tradition that he finally arrived at Constantinople and founded a church there is apparently unfounded; and the details of his martyrdom are equally uncertain. He is said to have incurred the enmity of the proconsul at Patras in Achaia, and to have been bound to a cross, where he remained two or three days preaching to the people who came to watch him, before he died.

Andrew is the patron of both Russia and Scotland. His connection with Russia is based on a tradition that in his missionary journeyings he preached in that country, reaching the city of Kiev in what is now the Ukraine, which was the center of the conversion of Russia in the eleventh century. Legend connects him with Scotland. It says that in the fourth century the guardian of the relics of Andrew at Patras was told in a dream to take part of them to a place that would be shown to him. He was led to what is now St Andrews in Scotland; he built there a church and preached to the heathen people. The St Andrew's cross – 'saltire' or X-shaped – of Scottish heraldry, often supposed to have been the form of cross on which Andrew was martyred, does not, in fact, seem to have been associated with the saint before the fourteenth century. ILLUSTRATION: frontispiece
November 30th

ANDREW AVELLINO 1520–1608
He was born in the Kingdom of Naples in 1520 and christened Lancelot. Before his ordination he had studied law and, when he became a priest, he became a pleader in the ecclesiastical courts. In the interests of one of his law-cases he was forced to tell a lie; but afterwards he was seized by such remorse that he gave up his legal career for ever, and devoted himself instead entirely to the conversion of souls.

At Naples, in 1556, he joined the Theatines, an order which had just been founded by St Cajetan. Because of his great love for the Cross, he asked to be given the name of Andrew. For ten years he was novice master, and he also founded houses in Piacenza and Milan. He was offered a bishopric by Gregory XIV but refused it and returned to Naples, where he became Superior of the Institute. Among his many friends were St Charles Borromeo and Scupoli, author of the *Spiritual Combat*. He was struck down by apoplexy in 1608 as he was reciting the first prayer of the mass, and for this reason he is often invoked against sudden death and apoplexy.

After his death his body lay in the church of St Paul so that it might be visited by the people of Naples; so great was their veneration for the dead man that they cut off locks of his hair for relics, grazing and piercing the skin of his face in doing so. Blood started to flow from these wounds and continued flowing for more than a day. It was preserved and is alleged to liquefy as does the blood of that other Neapolitan saint, Januarius, on the anniversary of Andrew Avellino's death. (*See* Januarius.)
November 10th

ANDREW BOBOLA 1591–1657
A Polish Jesuit who devoted most of his life to winning back members of the Orthodox church to Catholicism, he was martyred at Janow by Cossacks, who killed him slowly in the public slaughterhouse by the most barbarous methods.
May 21st

ANDREW CORSINI
1302–1373

He was born in Florence to Gemma Stracciabeni and Nicolas Corsini in 1302. The family was distinguished, and was to provide the church with a pope in a later century (Lorenzo Corsini, who reigned as Clement XII, 1730–40). Andrew's parents had long been childless and regarded his birth as an answer to their prayers; he was therefore regarded as devoted to God in a special manner from his birth. His temperament, however, was violent and undisciplined, and his pleasures were limited to hunting and the use of arms. But, at the age of fifteen, he underwent a sudden and violent conversion, the result – according to some – of his repentance after a brutal quarrel with his parents. A few days after this he took the Carmelite habit. He was professed in 1317. His manner now became extremely gentle and humble, and his mother told him that, before he was born, she had dreamed that she would give birth to a wolf, which, by entering a church, would be transformed into a lamb. These two animals are his usual emblems.

In 1328 he was ordained. He first preached in Florence, and then went to Paris for further study. After gaining his doctorate he went to Avignon, where the papal court resided, to study under his uncle, Cardinal Piero Corsini. He was elected bishop of Fiesole in 1360, but the election so distressed him that he hid in a Carthusian monastery, where he was found as the result of a child's dream. He was chiefly famous for his ability to settle quarrels and appease enemies, and was sent by Urban V to quell a rising in Bologna. This effort was so successful that the nobility and people remained at peace for the rest of his life. He fell ill during the midnight Mass of Christmas 372 and died on the Feast of the Epiphany 1373. He was canonized by Urban VIII in 1629 and his feast moved to February 4th, the anniversary of his consecration. His relics are venerated in the Carmelite church in Florence.
February 4th

ANDREW HUBERT FOURNET
1752–1834

Andrew Hubert Fournet de Thoiret, born in 1752, was thirty-seven when the French Revolution broke out. His early life had been somewhat undisciplined, and in one way and another he was a sore trial to his parents. He ran away from the school to which he had been sent. As a law student he played with the idea of becoming a soldier. Then he discovered a vocation to the priesthood and became, after ordination, parish priest of his native village. He still cultivated something of the grand manner (his parishioners referred to him as 'Seigneur de Thoiret'), and it needed a jolt to make him realize the full implications of his vocation. The reply of a beggar to whom he had refused alms brought full realization that his way of life was directly opposed to the spirit of the gospel.

He sold all his possessions and lived as poorly as his most needy parishioner.

Refusing to swear allegiance to the revolutionary constitution, he left for Spain, returning at the height of the Terror to minister secretly to the faithful. With the advent of more peaceful times he set about the restoration of his parish and then, in 1806, with the assistance of St Joan Elizabeth Bichier des Ages, he founded the Congregation of Daughters of the Cross for educational work and care of the sick poor; this was one of the influential factors in renewal of religion in France after the Revolution. Until his death in 1834 he continued to guide the institute with an unerring sense of the needs of souls.
May 16th

ANDREW of CRETE
† 740?

Archbishop of Gortyna in Crete, he was celebrated as a preacher and hymn-writer.
July 4th

ANDREW of CRETE
† 766

Sometimes called 'the Calybite' or 'in Krisi' to distinguish him from the earlier St Andrew of Crete, he was murdered by an iconoclastic mob because he defended the veneration of images from the attacks of Constantine IV.
October 20th

ANDREW of FIESOLE
Ninth Century?

Legend makes him an Irishman who was St Donatus's pupil, his companion on a pilgrimage to Rome and his archdeacon at Fiesole, but nothing certain is known about him.
August 22nd

ANDREW THE TRIBUNE
† c. 300

He may have been an officer in the Roman army who was discharged when he became a Christian. He and some companions took refuge in the Taurus mountains in Asia Minor, where they were tracked down and executed by the governor of Cilicia.
August 19th

ANDRONICUS and ATHANASIA
Fifth Century

According to an unreliable legend, this silversmith and his wife lived happily in Alexandria until the day when both their children died. St Julian appeared to Athanasia at the children's grave, and Athanasia became convinced that she and her husband must separate and live as hermits in the Egyptian desert.
October 9th

ANDRONICUS, TARACHUS and PROBUS
† 304

Their *passio* in the form of a dramatic dialogue is of doubtful authenticity. They may have been martyred in

Cicilia by gladiators during the persecution of Diocletian and Maximian, but it is even doubtful whether they existed.

October 11th

ANGADRISMA or ANGADRÊME   † 695

Educated by St Omer and St Lambert at Thérouanne, she was promised in marriage to St Ansbert; but, in answer to her prayers, she became a leper until the danger of marriage had past and she had been able to become a nun. She was later abbess of Oroër, near Beauvais.

October 14th

ANGEL, Guardian, *see* Guardian Angels *and* Angels and Archangels.

ANGELA MERICI   1474–1540

Angela Merici was born on March 21st, 1474, at Desenzano on Lake Garda; left an orphan at the age of ten she was brought up by her uncle and on his death went to live with her brothers. She was a devout girl and, having joined the Third Order of St Francis, devoted herself to teaching children. As her work became known she was asked to go to Brescia where a house was put at her disposal and a number of women came to join her; she was thus enabled to establish a religious association of women, under the patronage of St Ursula, who, remaining in the world, should devote themselves to every sort of corporal and spiritual work of mercy; but the particular emphasis was on education. Angela's methods were far removed from the modern idea of a convent school; she preferred to send her associates to teach girls in their own families, and one of her favorite sayings was, 'Disorder in society is the result of disorder in the family'. It was by educating children in the milieu in which they lived that she strove to effect an improvement in social conditions.

Angela Merici is known now as the foundress of the Ursuline *nuns* – and so she was, but despite her own inclinations. In reality she was in advance of her own times. Her plan of religious women without distinctive habit, without solemn vows and enclosure, was directly contrary to prevailing notions at her period, and under the influence of St Charles Borromeo at Milan and subsequent papal legislation (under St Pius V) the Ursulines were obliged to adopt the canonical safeguards then required of all nuns.

Angela Merici died in Brescia on January 27th, 1540.

June 1st

ANGELO   † 1220

The twin son of converted Jewish parents, he became a Carmelite and was stabbed to death while preaching at Leocata in Sicily by a certain Berengarius, who was infuriated by his denunciations of his sins. The story of his origin and life is, however, uncertain.

May 5th   ILLUSTRATION: page 39

ANGELS and ARCHANGELS

The teaching of the church about the world of spirits is constant and simple: there is such a world, it is important, it comprises good and evil beings, and it influences our world. For the first two of these statements consult almost any one of those compendia of Catholic faith that we call creeds, in which Creation is mentioned under two heads, 'visible and invisible'. For the third and fourth, consider the temptation of Eve and the annunciation to Mary. History, as portrayed in the Bible, has this invisible world for its background, whence mysterious beings suddenly come into our world to execute the divine will or to give God's word to men – the word 'angel' is Greek and means a messenger. In the Old Testament, good spirits are the more prominent, but in the New a more sombre note is struck, as the forces of evil rise to answer the challenge of the Son of Man.

The Bible mentions only three angels by name: Michael (Daniel 10:13, 21; Jude 9; Revelation 12:7) the champion against evil, Gabriel (Daniel 8:15; 9:27; Luke 1:19, 26) the angel of the Annunciation, and Raphael (Tobias 3:25 etc) the charming companion of Tobias, who shows him the secret of married life. There are also those mysterious generic names which St Gregory, collating various passages in Scripture in a way no modern Catholic scholar would accept, lists as the nine orders: Cherubim and Seraphim, Thrones, Dominations, Principalities, Powers, Virtues, Archangels, Angels.

The word 'angel' conjures up a certain image, suggested by pictures we have all seen. Can we get beyond images? Not only can we do so, but we do so every time we talk of images as 'only images'. We cannot but take the spiritual world seriously if we accept the devastatingly obvious fact that thought and talk about things is more than things, and that without this spiritual dimension, we contradict ourselves at every turn. But the practical recognition of this is difficult. The very fact that we *know* our thought to be impure suggests that we have, as it were, one foot in this greater world. This may help us to understand what the Bible is talking about when it describes angels bringing messages to men. They doubtless appear in human form, but this is only to give the eye something to rest on while the message is imparted to the mind. Significantly, they often come in sleep, when the mind is free. The most momentous communication ever made to the human race was made to St Mary at the Annunciation, as the collect says, 'through the message of an angel', and it involved an enlargement of the mind far beyond the horizons of a personal destiny.

In what relations do angels stand to God? Angels help to simplify our understanding of God's purpose, but, in so doing, they are doing nothing which is not happening to us in our everyday experience, because the more we know, the simpler our minds become. A genius like Einstein can understand the whole universe in the light of a single law of relativity. But to understand the very meaning of existence involves an incomparably greater simplicity of mind, and it should not surprise us to learn that there is a whole hierarchy of angels, each angel being placed in the hierarchy according to his degree of simplicity.

Returning now to the angelic Annunciation, we can show its other, deeper dimension. The angel enlarges the mind, in so far as the finite mind can be enlarged, to embrace the design of God: thus simplified, Mary surrenders, falls far beyond anything the angel can show her, into the embrace of God, whose own son enters her heart, enters, on this supreme and unique occasion of surrender, so perfectly as to take flesh in her womb.

The most exciting book on the angels is *The Celestial Hierarchy* by Dionysius, a sixth century writer; it was he who brought out the intellectual or mystical implications in the angelic hierarchy revealed to us in scripture. Each angel, according to its degree, understands and manifests (for an angel, the two are synonymous; it can't keep anything to itself) a more or less exalted idea which it has from God. The Cherubim ('they who shine') and Seraphim ('they who burn') are the highest, for they reflect respectively the divine knowledge, in which the Word or Son is eternally born, and the divine love in which the Spirit is eternally breathed forth. But even their 'ideas' are infinitely short of God, of whom there can be no created comprehensive idea. This gap is bridged only by God himself, and grace is as necessary for the Cherubim as it is for us. Dionysius, who has extolled more than any other writer the glories of the celestial host, is of all writers the most austerely negative about God himself. He takes you in, through ever greater splendors, to the great negation, the 'not this, not that' which is the unanimous cry of all mystics, Christian and non-Christian alike. The angels show us the first step towards God, but the second step, the real step, is taken by God himself.

Spirituality means control of material forces as well as detachment from them, and the spirit world influences our world, as well as our thoughts, for good and evil. The fallen angels – those who preferred their spiritual power to grace – have staked out a claim in this world: hence exorcisms of salt and water, and, for that matter, of the infant about to be baptized. The Guardian Angels represent this angelic power working for our good. Here again, the thought of angels should enlarge our thought of God. It is natural for man, harried by the shocks and ironies of temporal existence, to think of God primarily as protector. This tendency is corrected

by locating this office in the world of spirits, and God is left free to be simply God, our final vision and delight, the rest of our infinitely restless spirit.

(*See also* Gabriel, Guardian Angels, Michael *and* Raphael).

ANGILBERT † 814

A pupil of Alcuin, raised in Charlemagne's court, he became a monk. He was a particular favorite of Charlemagne and held important court positions as well as the abbacy of Centula, near Amiens.

February 18th

ANIANUS *First Century*

He was said to have been consecrated bishop that he might govern in the absence of St Mark, whom he later succeeded as bishop of Alexandria.

April 25th

ANIANUS or AIGNAN of ORLEANS † 453

Bishop of Orleans in succession to St Evurtius.

November 17th

ANICETUS † c. 165

A Syrian, he became pope towards the end of the reign of the Emperor Antonius Pius. He endeavoured to settle the controversy over the date of Easter, and St Polycarp visited him in Rome to discuss the matter, but the conference was unsuccessful.

April 17th

ANNE

About the mother of our Lady nothing is known for certain. All information concerning her that we possess comes to us from the apocryphal writings, which are notorious for their legendary character. When scripture or tradition failed to give the details demanded by popular curiosity, pious imagination filled the breach. The Protogospel of James in particular, the second century source of most of the information concerning our Lady's parentage and early life, is so closely parallel to the story of the childhood of Samuel in 1 Samuel 1–2 (the mother's childlessness, the reproach of her neighbors, the heavenly answer to her prayer, the promise to dedicate the child from birth, the child's upbringing in the sanctuary) that scholars have judged it to be nothing more than an imitation. The very name of Anne remains uncertain, because of its identity with the name of Samuel's mother. (It seems likely that the figure of Joachim was based, at least partially, on the husband of Susannah in Daniel 13.) When St Luke used the same chapters of 1 Samuel as a ground sketch for his account of the birth and infancy of John the Baptist, he took care to allow historical fact to control the parallelism.

For all that, there is great beauty in the story, and it has, like most legends, its symbolic value. If Anne is called upon to bear insults and sufferings, it is because

AGATHA: detail from painting by Bernardino Luini (*c*.1480 – 1531-2). *(Galleria Borghese, Rome.)*

AGNES: seventh century mosaic. *(Ch. di Sta Agnese, Rome.)*

ALBERT THE GREAT: painting by Justus van Ghent
(*fl.* 1446 – 1480-5). *(Ducal Palace, Urbino.)*

ALOISIVS GONZAGA MARCHI
EILIVS FERDINANDI

ALOYSIUS GONZAGA: portrait by an unknown artist. *(Kunsthistorisches Museum, Vienna.)*

ALPHONSUS RODRIGUEZ: painting by Murillo (1617–1682).
Although Alphonsus Rodriguez was neither a priest nor a martyr, Murillo has
chosen to depict him as both. *(Gemäldgalerie, Dresden.)*

Photo: Mella

AMBROSE: fifth century mosaic.
(Basilico di S. Ambrosio, Milan.)

ANGELO: painting by Ludovico Carracci (1555 – 1619). The Carmelite legend says that Angelo was stabbed, but Carracci has shown him hanging upon a tree and shot by an arrow.*(Pinacoteca, Bologna.)*

ANNE (with JOACHIM): fresco by Giotto *c.*1266 – 1337). *(Cappella degli Scrovegni all'Arena, Padua.)*

ANSELM: terracotta altarpiece by Luca della Robbia, (1400 - 1482). *(Galleria della Collegiata, Empoli.)*

ANTONINUS of FLORENCE: tomb effigy by Portigiani (1536–1601). (Ch. di S. Marco, Florence.)

ANTONY THE ABBOT: painting by Pisanello (*c.*1395–1455).
(*National Gallery, London.*)

APOLLINARIS of RAVENNA: seventh century mosaic. *(S. Apollinare in Classe, Ravenna.)*

APOLLONIA: early fifteenth century rood screen, showing her with pincers. *(Ashton, Devon.)*

AUGUSTINE: detail of a tempera painting by Simone Martini (1283 – 1344).
(*Fitzwilliam Museum, Cambridge.*)

(A) BASIL THE GREAT: mosaic (1148).
(Duomo, Cefalu, Sicily.)

(B) BARBARA: detail from a painting
by Botticelli (1444 – 1510).
(Pinacoteca, Lucca.)

BARNABAS: (figure on right) detail from a painting by Botticelli (1444 – 1510). (*Uffizi, Florence.*)

all cooperation in the work of redemption involves sharing the cross of Christ. At an even deeper level, Anne's childlessness evokes a theme which is dear to the Old Testament, where children are the gift of God. This is especially emphasized in the traditions of the great patriarchs Isaac, Jacob and Joseph (as well as of Samson, the last of the Judges, and Samuel, the first of the Prophets), each of whom is presented as the son of a mother who had no hope of bearing children. The destiny of God's people rests not in human likelihood and planning, but in the hands of God alone. The true Israelite must learn to see that he is not self-sufficient, and that what is required of him is utter abandonment to a God on whose initiative alone his salvation depends. Our legend places Anne's child, Mary, in this line of thought, in much the same way as the New Testament sees the theme come to its climax in the son of this virgin Mary, for whom childbirth is not merely humanly unlikely, but humanly impossible. It is in the nothingness of his own creatures that God is born into the world.

The cult of St Anne can be traced back to the sixth century in the east, and to the early eighth century in Rome. By the late middle ages it had spread throughout Europe, as is attested by the numerous churches built in her honor and the popularity of the paintings against which Luther inveighed. It seems that it was at the instance of England, in 1382, that her feast was first given an annual celebration, although it was not inserted in the general calendar of the Roman rite until two centuries later. ILLUSTRATION: page 40

July 26th

ANNE or SUSANNA   *c. 840–c. 918*

Born in Constantinople of well-to-do parents, at the age of twenty-eight Anne fled, so the story goes, to Epirus in the north-west of Greece, where she spent the rest of her life as a hermit.

July 23rd

ANNEMUND   †658

Bishop of Lyons and the friend of St Wilfrid of York.

September 28th

ANNO   1010–1075

The political turmoil that was his public life began with his unpopular appointment as archbishop of Cologne in 1056. He was regent for Henry IV, but was dismissed when Henry came of age, and it is rather for his blameless private life that he is remembered than for his political skill, although he was a successful reformer and founder of monasteries.

December 4th

ANSANUS   †304

The first apostle of Siena, where his memory is still perpetuated, he was martyred during the persecution of Diocletian.

December 1st

ANSBERT   *Seventh Century*

Chancellor to King Clotaire III, he later became a monk and abbot at Fontenelle. Appointed bishop of Rouen in 684, he was banished upon false accusations to the Hautmont monastery in Hainault.

February 9th

ANSEGISUS   *c. 770–833*

A monk of Fontenelle, he became one of Charlemagne's advisers, reorganized several monasteries and returning to Fontenelle as abbot made a celebrated collection of the capitularies or edicts of the Frankish kings.

July 20th

ANSELM   1033–1109

St Anselm was born in Aosta in 1033. He may have shown signs of his mature vocation in childhood and he certainly passed through a period of instability in his adolescence, but at the age of 27 he found his place in the world of the flesh and the spirit; he became a monk of Bec in Normandy. Normandy, rather later than the rest of France, was undergoing a monastic revival, and Bec, under the Italian monk and teacher Lanfranc, was the center of Norman monasticism and perhaps the most famous school in Europe. Anselm was happy and successful at Bec. He succeeded Lanfranc both as prior and abbot and his fame as teacher soon eclipsed that of Lanfranc. In 1066 the duke of Normandy conquered England and in 1072, with papal aid, William I reorganized the English church and normanized the English episcopate. Lanfranc became archbishop of Canterbury, and from then on Norman monks were frequently appointed to English sees. Anselm remained a close friend of Archbishop Lanfranc and was also held in respect by William the Conqueror, but there was never any suggestion of electing him to either a Norman or an English see. It is plain that Anselm had no talent for politics either secular or ecclesiastical, and under normal circumstances he would no doubt have remained happily at Bec for the rest of his life. But circumstances were not normal.

In 1087 William I died, and in 1089 he was followed by Lanfranc. The new king, William Rufus, was not without many of the qualities which made for a good king by contemporary standards, but he was homosexual and his morals must have roused as much horror as his power as ruler created fear of expressing it. After Lanfranc's death, Canterbury was left vacant for four years. The papacy was in schism, and Rufus, by refusing to recognize either of the papal claimants, effectively prevented anyone from exercizing moral supervision over England or its king. But in 1093, while Anselm was visiting England, Rufus was struck with a mysterious illness, probably more psychical than physical, and in terror that he would go to Hell if he died with Canterbury vacant, he begged Anselm to accept the primatial see. Anselm refused, whereupon he was seized by the bishops and forcibly invested with the archiepiscopal insignia. The pope later ordered Anselm to accept this 'election'. By this time it was holiness and moral reputation, rather than sagacity, which churchmen wanted in their archbishop. But the king recovered and repented of his repentance. Forced by Anselm to recognize Urban II as pope, he tried to make a disgraceful bargain with the pope for Anselm's deposition. The pope refused, and Anselm then tried to hold a synod of the English church to condemn sodomy; the king refused his permission, and, by adroit use of his undoubted legal rights over the material possessions of Canterbury, he persuaded the English bishops to renounce their obedience to their archbishop, although most of them had helped to force Anselm to accept the see only two years before. The lay magnates, however, warned Rufus that they would not tolerate Anselm's deposition but in 1097 after a constant and fruitless quarrel with the king, Anselm gave up and voluntarily went into exile. In 1100 Rufus was killed in what was probably a hunting accident, in spite of sinister rumors to the contrary, and he was succeeded by his normal, profligate, pious and very able brother, Henry. Anselm was recalled from exile, but, during his stay in Rome, he had heard the pope condemn the ceremonies by which lay rulers were wont to confer the material possessions of their sees on new bishops. Anselm accordingly refused to do homage to the new king, and precipitated a crisis, which under a ruler less tolerant than Henry I, would have meant a serious conflict between church and state. The pope was really concerned with the freeing of episcopal appointments from lay control, but Anselm never saw this, and, over a point of ceremony only, he was prepared to excommunicate half the English episcopate. In the end Anselm spent another term of exile abroad, and the king and the pope negotiated a compromise behind his back which Anselm only accepted with the greatest reluctance. Peace was restored in 1106 and Anselm returned to rule the English church uneventfully until his death in 1109.

Anselm was no politician, because he was without any sense of compromise or proportion in worldly matters; he had a wholly intransigent conscience, but he had also a sweetness of disposition, a humility and a control of his temper that disarmed even the hardest headed men of affairs. He had a moral greatness which was also an intellectual and a spiritual greatness. He is the first doctor of the church after the dark ages who is still a living force in philosophy and theology. His argument for the existence of God, sometimes known as the ontological proof, asserts that because our idea of God is what it is – 'than which no greater can be thought' – we are already, thereby, committed to a belief in God's existence. The apparent simplicity of this demonstration hides a subtlety of analysis which has appealed very strongly to some contemporary thinkers in England and France. Anselm's theology was part of a new spirituality based on a gentle compassion for the sufferings of Christ, which, taken up by the Cistercians, swept through the church. We owe to this movement the familiar representation of the suffering Christ on the cross which replaced that of a crucified but glorified Christ.

As archbishop of Canterbury, Anselm was not at his greatest, but he did one thing of lasting value: he put an end to the denigration of the 'rustic' English saints by the new Norman churchmen. Lanfranc had even struck St Dunstan out of the calendar, Anselm put him and many others back. He encouraged devotion to the traditional English saints, and he undoubtedly helped to promote that affection for all things English which is found even among churchmen of Norman ancestry after his day. He thus helped to heal that emotional schism which the Norman Conquest had opened in English life.   ILLUSTRATION: page 41
April 21st

ANSELM of LUCCA   1036–1086
Born in Mantua, of which he is the patron, he was the nephew of Pope Alexander II. His discipline and dislike of secular authority in ecclesiastical matters forced his retirement from the bishopric of Lucca. He became papal legate in Lombardy.
March 18th

ANSELM of NONANTOLA   † 803
Duke of Friuli and brother-in-law of King Aistulf. When a soldier, he founded monasteries at Fanano, and nearby at Nonantola where he was later abbot. Banished by Desiderius, he was restored by Charlemagne.
March 3rd

ANSFRID   † 1010
Count of Brabant, and a noted soldier, he succeeded Bishop Baldwin of Utrecht at the suggestion of the Emperor. He founded a convent at Thorn, near Roermond, and the abbey of Heiligenberg, where he retired when he lost his sight.
May 11th

ANSKAR   † 865
Born near Amiens of noble family, he became a monk of Old Corbie, Picardy. He undertook successful missions to Sweden and Denmark, became abbot of New Corbie, Westphalia, papal legate to the northern peoples and first archbishop of Hamburg, later united with Bremen.
February 3rd

ANSOVINUS † 840

Born at Camerino, Umbria, he became a priest at Castel-Raimondo, near Torcello. Later he was confessor to Louis the Pious and bishop of Camerino. Greatly revered for wisdom and charity, he died of fever.

March 13th

ANSTRUDIS or ANSTRUDE † 700

The daughter of St Salaberga, whom she succeeded as abbess of Laon, St Anstrudis defended her life and the income of her convent with such intrepidity that Bd Pepin of Landen became her protector.

October 17th

ANTHELM 1107–1178

Two years after joining the Carthusians in 1137, he was elected seventh prior of the Grande Chartreuse and restored the avalanche-damaged buildings. He summoned the first general chapter, and became virtually the first minister-general of the order. After helping to secure the papal throne for Alexander III against the imperial nominee, he was made – much against his will – bishop of Belley.

June 26th

ANTHERUS † 236

He is believed to have been elected pope in 235 to succeed St Pontian, but he died after reigning only 43 days. According to the *Liber Pontificalis*, he was killed for trying to preserve the official documents of the proceedings against martyrs.

January 3rd

ANTHIMUS † 303

Bishop of Nicodemia, he was one of the many martyrs who suffered there during the persecution under Diocletian and Maximian.

April 27th

ANTONINA † 304?

She may have been martyred under Diocletian, either at Nicaea or Nicomedia, but there are no fewer than three different references to her in the Roman martyrology.

June 12th

ANTONINUS of APAMEA *Fourth Century*

A stonemason of Aribazus in Syria, he overturned the statues in a pagan temple near Apamea. The villagers took their vengeance by attacking and killing him one night in Apamea. He was only twenty when he died.

September 2nd

ANTONINUS of FLORENCE *c.* 1390–1459

He was born in Florence on March 1st 1390 (or 1389) to Tommasa di Cenni and Niccolo di Pierozzo, an affluent and well-connected notary. He was christened Antonio, but the diminutive – Antonino – soon became attached to him, possibly because of his frailty. Even as a child he liked listening to sermons, and he came under the influence of Bd Giovanni Dominici, who had just established a Dominican priory of the strict observance outside Florence, and was a noted preacher. In 1404 St Antoninus asked to join the order but was refused on account of his youth and bad health, until he had learned the whole of the decretals of Gratian, a huge tome of canon law, by heart. He did this in a year, and entered the novitiate. During the following year he was joined by El Giovanni da Fiesole, the great painter known as Fra Angelico, who was to remain one of his closest friends. For the next few years the life of the community was affected by the schism between the various claimants to the papacy: it was moved to Cortona where Antoninus was elected prior in 1417. In 1430 he was the prior of the main Dominican house in Rome and was also, as a leading canonist, auditor of the Rota; some years later he became vicar-general of his whole congregation.

Late in the '30s he moved back to Florence and had a leading part in the taking over of the monastery of St Marco by the Dominicans, under Medici patronage, and he became its first prior in 1439. This foundation was to become one of the greatest centers of humanist learning in Italy. It housed the first important public classical library, bequeathed by the great bibliophile Nicolo Nicoli, and was decorated by a series of frescoes by Fra Angelico. There was a cell set aside for Cosimo dei Medici, to which he would retire frequently, and the priory became the home of a brilliant circle of artists and scholars.

In 1445, Pope Eugenius IV, who had met Antoninus during the council of Florence, decided after long hesitation to appoint him archbishop of Florence. His first reaction was to run away to Sardinia to avoid the appointment. He was persuaded by friends to return to Florence, where he petitioned the city government to have the appointment cancelled; but it was extremely popular, both because of the saint's personal position, and because he promised to be the first non-absentee bishop of Florence for some time. In fact, when he did finally take possession of his cathedral, he started on a series of reforms. The bishop's entourage was reduced, the daily offices were regularly to be performed in the cathedral, even if by the bishop alone. The charitable organization of the see was extended, going beyond the provision of food and shelter to help in business and the provision of dowries for impecunious families. As a canonist, Antoninus became one of the leading arbiters both of litigation and of cases of conscience in Italy, while the reputation of his ecclesiastical court was so high that the pope would not allow appeals from it to Rome. As might be expected of an archbishop of the most flourishing commercial center in Europe in the fifteenth century, he was much concerned with the moral implications of economic activity. Familiar as he was with the economic practices of his time, he was realistic and sober in his judgments. He sanctioned, within very close limits, a form of capitalism, although he condemned the rigging of prices by cartels; but he was convinced of the duty of the state to limit commercial abuses and to provide the essentials of social security, such as a health and hospital service, for all citizens. Preaching also concerned him greatly: he went round to every church in Florence preaching regularly, until he had shamed the parish clergy into imitating his example; and it was of his preaching and its effect that Pope Nicolas V was thinking when he said that Antoninus living was as good a saint as Bernardino dead. He was also a skilled Latin orator, and this endeared him – his latinity was very elegant – to the intellectual élite of his time, to whom oratory was the most prized accomplishment. He represented the Florentine republic as chief spokesman and orator on several occasions – notably at the coronation of Pope Pius II in 1458.

St Antoninus died on May 2nd 1459. His funeral, with the pope as mourner and the patriarch of Venice as celebrant, seemed already like a canonization procession. He had been a saint very much in the public eye, an affable and civilized person, a perfect modern bishop, circumspect but fearless in his dealings with civil authority, completely familiar with the concerns and interests of his people – both intellectual and economic – and sensible as well as strict in his directives. His sanctity was never in doubt, and he was canonized in 1522 by Adrian VI. In 1589 his body, incorrupt, was moved into a new shrine in San Marco, where it has remained.

May 10th   ILLUSTRATION: page 42

ANTONINUS of SORRENTO   † 830
Born at Picenum, Southern Italy, this solitary became abbot of St Agrippinus, Sorrento. He was made the town's principal patron, and his intercessions became its chief protection against the Saracens.
February 14th

ANTONY (983–1073) and THEODOSIUS of PECHERSK   † 1074
They are the fathers of Russian monasticism. Antony was the founder of the famous monastery of the Caves of Kiev, which flourished until the Bolshevik Revolution, and Theodosius its first real organizer. A man of great humility and charity, he was not afraid of emerging from his monastery to help those outside, and his influence was felt far and wide in Russia.
July 10th

ANTONY CLARET   1807–1870
Sallent, in the north of Spain, was the birthplace in 1807

of this saint whose influence was by no means confined to his own country. He came of poor parents and, since his father was a weaver, was put to the loom at an early age, learning Latin and mastering the elements of printing when he had time. He went to the seminary at Vich in 1829 and was ordained priest six years later. Unable for reasons of health to follow his wish to become a Carthusian, and after an abortive attempt to enter the Jesuits, he settled down to an energetic career preaching popular missions in his native land; to ensure the greater extension of this work he managed to establish a religious congregation – the Missionary Sons of the Immaculate Heart of Mary (the 'Claretians') – and then, such was now his fame, he found himself appointed archbishop of Santiago in Cuba.

Here was full scope for his activities; to re-christianize his diocese he was obliged to begin practically everything anew: the clergy needed considerable reformation and to be imbued afresh with a sense of their vocation, the laity required to be recalled to the fundamental notions of Christianity. All this was not achieved without opposition from political, clerical and other vested interests: fifteen attempts were made on his life, one of which nearly succeeded. In eight years Antony Claret was able to effect a very great change in Cuba.

He returned to Spain to act as confessor to Queen Isabella II, and managed to combine the not too onerous duties of this post with much work for the popular apostolate, particularly by means of the printing press. The revolution of 1868 banished both the Queen and her confessor from the country, and Antony Claret, after a short sojourn in Rome, died in France in 1870. He was essentially a man of prayer, and this deep spiritual life was the mainspring of all his activity.
October 24th

ANTONY DANIEL, see Martyrs of North America.

ANTONY DEYNAN, see Martyrs of Japan.

ANTONY, EUSTAGE and JOHN   † 1342
These household officers of the duke of Olgierd, ruler of Lithuania, were converted to Christianity, and executed for their faith at Vilna.
April 14th

ANTONY GIANELLI   1789–1846
Born at Cerreto in 1789, and ordained in Genoa at twenty-three, he organized two religious congregations, the Missioners of St Alphonsus Liguori, and the Sisters of Santa Maria dell' Orto. He was appointed bishop of Bobbio in 1838.
June 7th

ANTONY KAULEAS   † 901
Abbot of a monastery near Constantinople, his birth-

place. When Stephen, brother to Leo VI, died, Antony was chosen patriarch of Constantinople. He was a prudent administrator and possessed 'the discretion of a pure mind that keeps its balance and is not deceived'.
February 12th

ANTONY MARY ZACCARIA   1502–1539
A doctor of medicine as well as a priest, Antony was the founder of the Clerks Regular of St Paul, often known as the Barnabites after their headquarters, the church of St Barnabas in Milan.
July 5th

ANTONY of LÉRINS   † 520
Born at Valeria in Lower Pannonia, he spent his life in search of solitude and, for a time, lived in a cave on the shores of Lake Como; but, fearing that his fame would make him vain, he became a monk of Lérins in France.
December 28th

ANTONY of PADUA   1195–1231
The universality and vigor of the cult of St Antony of Padua are mysterious in view of the facts of his life. He was born in 1195, probably near Lisbon, receiving the name of Ferdinand. His father was a revenue officer and knight at the court of Alfonso II, king of Portugal. Ferdinand was sent to the cathedral school in Lisbon, but, at the age of fifteen, he joined the Canons Regular of St Augustine.

At the end of two years in this house, he asked to be transferred to Coimbra, a day's journey to the north of the city, because he was finding visits from relatives too disturbing in Lisbon. The Coimbra monastery had a renowned school of biblical studies, which Ferdinand found a most congenial environment. He studied with intense application for eight years and became a profound theological and scriptural scholar.

One day, in his capacity as guest-master, he had to look after five Franciscan friars, who were on their way to Morocco. Later it became known that they had no sooner arrived at the mission when they were savagely butchered. Their remains were brought back to Coimbra where they were given a state funeral. Ferdinand was completely unsettled by his fleeting acquaintance with the martyrs. His studies became meaningless. He longed to give his life on some distant mission field.

Fired with this new ambition, he took the painful and unusual step of leaving the Canons Regular of St Augustine in order to join the Franciscans. These soon conceded him permission to go to Morocco. But the longed-for martyrdom was not for him. Illness supervened at once and he was ordered home. On the return journey, his ship was driven out of its course by a storm, and he had to land at Messina in Sicily. He then joined his Franciscan brethren in Italy. He was probably present at the famous Chapter of Mats in Assisi in 1221, where he could have met St Francis. Shortly afterwards he was sent to a little hospice near Forlì, in Emilia, where he was given duties that were chiefly menial.

Within a year, however, his brilliant gifts were discovered quite by accident. At an ordination ceremony at Forlì, the special preacher engaged for the occasion failed to appear. None of the others present would agree to fill the gap and oblige with an extempore sermon. To get out of his predicament, the Father Provincial briefly ordered Antony to preach. His performance astonished the audience, who saw at once that Antony had all the gifts of a first-rate speaker: poise, delivery, conviction, personal charm, amazing memory, mastery of theology and scripture. The immediate sequel was his appointment as preacher to the whole of Italy. It was a period when the church never had greater need of preachers to combat the prevailing heresies and, as it happened, few of the first Franciscans were effective controversialists.

From that hour, the Forlì hospice saw no more of Antony. He was always on the road, travelling ceaselessly from the south of Italy to the north of France, devoting all his time, talents and energy to the work of preaching. The people's response was his greatest stimulus. The churches could not hold the crowds who came to hear him. A platform had to be set up for him out of doors. Soon the streets and squares could not accommodate the people and the platform had to be carried outside the town, or city, to a plain, or a hillside, where twenty, thirty, forty thousand would gather to hear him. At the rumor of his coming, shops were shuttered up, markets suspended and the law courts closed. During the night before the sermon, the whole countryside became alive with flitting lights as people began to converge from all sides to the venue. It seemed that to those who had once come within the sphere of Antony's influence, nothing whatsoever could rival the interest of his sermons.

His favorite line was a virulent attack on the weakness of the secular clergy and on the prevalent sins of contemporary society: their greed, their luxurious living, their tyranny. A typical anecdote was of the famous occasion when he was invited to preach at a synod at Bourges, presided over by the Archbishop Simon de Sully. With the words *Tibi loquor cornute* ('as for you, there, with the mitre on your head'), Antony launched into a denunciation of the prelate who had invited him, which petrified his audience.

The last Lent he preached happened to be in Padua. It was long remembered for the furore it caused in the city. The Paduans could find neither food nor accommodation for the crowds who invaded them. After Easter, Antony and his two companions went to a friend's country estate outside the city for a rest. Walking through the woods, they were whimsically delighted with a giant walnut tree which had six branches growing upwards from the crown. They bound the branches together with woven willows and roofed them with rushes to make a cool, airy cell for the tired preacher.

He was far from well. Ten years' preaching had taken all his physical reserves. He had developed dropsy, which made breathing difficult. He was finding it increasingly difficult to get about because his swollen body refused to respond. He had worn it out at the age of thirty-six.

In this characteristic Franciscan retreat, he had an intimation of death on June 13th 1231. He told his companions to take him back to St Mary's in Padua, because he did not want to be a trouble to their kind host. They placed him on a peasant's cart, therefore, drawn by an ox, and began the doleful journey back to the city through the summer dust and heat. Soon he was beyond speech, so they halted at the convent of the Poor Ladies at Arcella. Here they placed him sitting upright again to help him to breathe. He began to chant a Lauds hymn and, so singing, he died.

Shortly after his death, his fame shifted focus. His posthumous glory has concentrated almost solely on his miracles. But when the prodigies recorded for his canonisation are sifted, out of the fifty-six then accepted it is worth noting that only one occurred during his lifetime. His fame in life was not due to the working of prodigies. He mostly earned his success in the human way that is open to everyone. He was canonised in less than a year after his death.

Such, then, is the paradox of his life. The well-known representations of him suggest the cloistered contemplative, but the world was his cloister and the two notes of his life work were militant activity and ceaseless travel. He has become so monopolised by the Italians, and particularly by Padua, that it is generally forgotten that he was a Portuguese. An aristocrat by birth, he has become the special advocate of the poor and the downtrodden. A scholar who had no living rival as a biblical expert, called by his contemporaries 'Hammer of the Heretics' and 'Living Ark of the Covenant', he has become the patron of the illiterate, the finder of lost trifles, the saint of the trivial appeals. One of the most effective preachers the world has ever known is now mostly invoked against the most petty, almost the comical, little ills of life.

Following the artists, his devotees complacently think of him as sweet and meek, but a truthful biographer would have difficulty in maintaining such a viewpoint. Sweetness of disposition was not his most notable trait; he had a tongue that could blister; he was bold rather than meek. However he may have since endeared himself to the world as the steadfast friend of the scatter-brained, he is surely a far more imposing figure in the larger context of reality.

June 13th ILLUSTRATION: facing page 16

ANTONY THE ABBOT *Fourth Century*

Known also as St Antony of the Desert, this saint was born in 250 near Hieracleus in Upper Egypt. Upon the death of his parents, he sold everything – staying only to see that his sister's education was completed – and retired into the desert. He began to live a life of great austerity, eating only bread and water, and that only once a day, after sunset. The devil attempted to frighten him from his retreat by assuming many terrible shapes, but St Antony stuck fast.

His admirers became so many and so insistent that he was eventually persuaded to found two monasteries for them and to give them a rule of life. These were the first monasteries ever to be founded, and St Antony is, therefore, the father of cenobites or monks. In 311 he went to Alexandria to take part in the Arian controversy (*see also* St Athanasius) and to comfort those who were being persecuted by Maximinus. This visit lasted for a few days only, after which he retired into a solitude even more remote so that he might cut himself off completely from his admirers. When he was over ninety, he was commanded by God in a vision to search the desert for St Paul the Hermit, and he is said to have survived until the age of a hundred and five, when he died peacefully in a cave on Mount Kolzim near the Red Sea.

St Antony was so greatly venerated that the Emperor Constantine himself wrote and asked to be remembered in his prayers, while St Athanasius paid him many visits and wrote an account of his life. To those who implored him to lengthen his stay in Alexandria, he replied, 'As fish die if they are taken from the waters, so does a monk wither away if he forsake his solitude.' The gospel of his mass reminds us, 'Blessed are those servants whom the Lord, when he cometh, shall find watching'.

January 17th ILLUSTRATION: page 43

ANYSIA † 304?

She was martyred at Thessalonica during the persecution of the governor Dulcitius.

December 30th

ANYSIUS † c. 407

He was appointed bishop of Thessalonica in 383 and became a firm supporter of St John Chrysostom. St Damasus made him patriarchal vicar in Illyricum, a territory whose jurisdiction was disputed by Rome and Constantinople.

December 30th

APHRAATES † c. 345

Of Persian family, he was converted to Christianity and

lived as a hermit at Edessa in Mesopotamia, and then at Antioch, where he emerged from seclusion to aid the Christian community in the Arian persecutions.
April 7th

APOLLINARIS of HIERAPOLIS *Second Century*
A famous Christian teacher and bishop in Hierapolis, he was called 'the Apologist' from his celebrated apology for Christianity which he addressed to Marcus Aurelius.

The Emperor had nearly gained a victory over the German tribe of the Quadi as a result, it was alleged, of the prayers of the Christians in his army.

St Apollinaris may have written his apology to remind the Emperor of this victory and of his promise to protect Christians.
January 8th

APOLLINARIS of RAVENNA *First Century?*
By tradition he was the first bishop of Ravenna.
July 23rd   ILLUSTRATION: page 44

APOLLINARIS of VALENCE *c. 453–c. 520*
Son of St Hesychius and brother of St Avitus, Apollinaris was bishop of Valence, where he is known as 'Aplonay'.
October 5th

APOLLINARIS SYNCLETICA
The little that is known of her belongs entirely to legend. She was an emperor's daughter who ran away from home disguised as a man in order to live as a hermit.
January 5th

APOLLO   † *c. 395*
After many years as a hermit, at the age of eighty Apollo founded a community of monks near Hermopolis in Egypt. He emphasized the importance of cheerfulness and was noted for his joyful expression. He is said to have kept his monks alive for four months during a famine by miraculously multiplying bread.
January 25th

APOLLONIA   † 249
She was a deaconess well advanced in years who was martyred at Alexandria during an outbreak of popular violence towards the end of the reign of the Emperor Philip. When the mob seized her, her teeth were knocked out and she was threatened with burning, but so anxious was she to achieve martyrdom that she flung herself into the flames before her persecutors were ready.

She is shown in pictures with a golden tooth suspended on her necklace and holding a tooth in a pair of pincers, and she is invoked against toothache.
February 9th   ILLUSTRATION: page 45

APOLLONIUS, *see* Philemon and Apollonius.

APOLLONIUS THE APOLOGIST   † *c. 185*
A Roman senator, Apollonius was denounced as a Christian by one of his slaves in the reign of Commodus. He was allowed to defend his Christianity before the Senate (a substantially reliable account of the debate is extant), but was condemned to death.
April 18th

APPHIA, *see* Philemon and Apphia.

APPHIAN and THEODOSIA   † 306
Apphian was nineteen when he was sentenced to be drowned at Caesarea for protesting against the Governor's order that all should attend public sacrifice.

Theodosia was found speaking to some condemned prisoners; for this her breasts were torn off with iron claws, and she was thrown into the sea. She was eighteen years old.
April 2nd

APULEIUS, *see* Marcellus and Apuleius.

AQUILA and PRISCA   *First Century*
Disciples and assistants of St Paul, this Jewish tent-maker and his wife are mentioned in the Acts of the Apostles (18:1–3, 26) and in St Paul's Epistles (I Corinthians 16: 19; Romans 16:3; 2 Timothy 4:19). They probably died in Asia Minor but may have been martyred in Rome.
July 8th

AQUILINA   *Third Century?*
Her parents were Phoenician Christians. She was only twelve years old when she was arrested, and after a whipping had failed to shake her faith, she was beheaded.
June 13th

AQUILINUS   *c. 620–c. 695*
After forty years as a soldier, he forsook the world and, with his wife, looked after the poor at Evreux. Aquilinus succeeded St Aeternus as bishop, but continued to spend long hours in his hermit's cell.
October 19th

ARAGHT, *see* Attracta

ARBOGAST   *Sixth Century*
Arbogast, who seems to have been a native of Aquitania, was bishop of Strasbourg.
July 21st

ARCADIUS   *Third Century*
Martyred in North Africa under Valerian or Diocletian. Legend has it that he died by progressive mutilation, losing all his limbs, joint by joint, until only the trunk remained.
January 12th

ARCADIUS and his Companions   † 437
They were martyred during the Vandal persecution in Africa for refusing to subscribe to the Arian heresy.
November 13th

ARCHELAUS

This bishop of Kashkar in Mesopotamia was celebrated for a book of disputations between himself and the Manichee Manes. His authorship is now discredited.
December 26th

ARCHINIMUS, *see* Armogastes, Archinimus and Saturus.

ARDALION   † *c.* 300

His is the legend of an actor who, while impersonating a Christian martyr on the stage, was himself converted and burned alive for his declaration of faith.
April 14th

ARDO   † 843

Born at Languedoc, he is chiefly remembered for a biography of his superior, St Benedict of Aniane. He was raised in the monastery and eventually became headmaster of its famous school.
March 7th

ARETAS and the Martyrs of Najran, and St Elesbaan
Sixth Century

In the sixth century, the Jews of Yemen rose in revolt against the Aksumite Ethiopians and after a long siege massacred the inhabitants of the Christian city of Najran, whose defendants were led by St Aretas.

The Aksumite king, Elesbaan, launched a punitive expedition against the Yemen Jews. He was hardly less cruel than they had been, but in later life he resigned his throne and became an exemplary anchorite.
October 24th

ARMEL   *Sixth Century*

A Welshman who crossed over to Brittany he founded two monasteries and gave his name to Ploërmel.
August 16th

ARMOGASTES, ARCHINIMUS and SATURUS   *Fifth Century*

Martyred when the Vandal king, Genseric, renounced the orthodox faith and ordered persecution of Catholics. Armogastes was banished from the king's household with terrible degradation; Archinimus of Mascula was tortured; Saturus, master of Huneric's household, was reduced to beggary.
March 29th

ARNOUL of METZ, *see* Arnulf.

ARNOUL of SOISSONS, *see* Arnulf.

ARNULF or ARNOUL of METZ   † *c.* 643

A statesman and soldier of the court of Theodebert II of Austrasia and an ancestor of the Carolingian kings of France, Arnulf later became bishop of Metz. He con-tinued to take part in public affairs, but eventually withdrew to a hermitage in the Vosges, where he died.
July 18th

ARNULF or ARNOUL of SOISSONS
c. 1040–1087

A soldier in his youth, Arnulf became a monk at Soissons and, in 1081, bishop of that see.
August 15th

ARSACIUS   † 358

According to the historian Sozomen, Arsacius lived alone in a tower at Nicomedia. When the city was destroyed by an earthquake the tower was one of the few buildings that remained upright. Arsacius was found kneeling in it, dead.
August 16th

ARSENIUS   † *c.* 450

A Roman of senatorial family, he may have been tutor to the emperors, Arcadius and Honorius, but this is no longer certain. After ten years at the court of Constantinople, Arsenius sailed to join the monks of the Egyptian desert, where he lived a notably humble and ascetic life until he died, aged ninety-five, at the rock of Troë, near Memphis.
July 19th

ARTALDUS or ARTHAUD   † 1206

A Carthusian, he founded the community at Arvières and gained so great a reputation that at the age of eighty-seven he was obliged to become bishop of Belley. He resigned two years later and returned to Arvières where he died aged 105.
October 7th

ARTEMAS

Mentioned in the *Hieronymianum* as a saint martyred at Pazznoli near Capua. At San Prisco, also near Capua, he was named and depicted in mosaics which no longer exist.
January 25th

ARTEMIUS   † 363

Prefect of Egypt under Constantine the Great and be-headed by Julian the apostate, he was an Arian and a persecutor of catholics. It is not certain that this is the Artemius whose shrine at Constantinople was famous for its cures.
October 20th

ARTHAUD, *see* Artaldus.

ARTHELAIS   *Sixth Century*

Daughter of Lucius, proconsul of Constantinople, such was her beauty that the Emperor Justinian asked for her to be delivered to him. She fled to Benevento where she devoted herself to ceaseless prayer and fasting, and died at the age of sixteen.
March 3rd

ASAPH
Seventh Century

He is said to have been left in charge of the monastery of Llanelwy in Denbighshire after the departure of St Kentigern. When the Normans developed an episcopal see there, it was named after him.

May 11th

ASCLAS
Third Century

According to legend, he was born in the Thebaid and was tried for his religion. During his trial, he miraculously stranded the governor, Arrian, in the Nile, until he would profess Christian belief. Arrian did so, returned to land and had Asclas drowned.

January 23rd

ASICUS or TASSACH
† 470

He is regarded as the first bishop of Elphin in County Rosscommon, having been appointed by St Patrick. He failed as a ruler and fled, but was found by his monks after seven years, dying on the journey home at Raith Cungi, or Racoon.

April 27th

ASTERIUS, *see* Claudius, Asterius, Neon, Domnina and Theonilla.

ASTERIUS
† 410

This bishop of Amasea was an able preacher, and he encouraged the invocation of saints and the belief in their intercession.

October 30th

ASTRIK or ANASTASIUS
† *c.* 1040

There are many people with whom Astrik, the first archbishop of Hungary, may be identified. He was probably Astrik Radla who undertook the evangelization of the Magyars in the reign of St Stephen I.

November 12th

ASTYRIUS, *see* Marinus and Astyrius.

ATHANASIA, *see* Andronicus and Athanasia.

ATHANASIA
Ninth Century

A Greek of Aegina, when her second husband decided to become a monk she made her house into a convent, with herself as abbess. She may have spent some time at Constantinople as the Empress Theodora's adviser but the details of her life are unreliable.

August 14th

ATHANASIUS of ALEXANDRIA
c. 295–373

St Athanasius was born some time about the year 295 and most probably at Alexandria. His family was apparently of some wealth – years later he was to hide among their sepulchres. It is certain that he received a fairly elaborate and conventional classical education; he quotes Euripides, Pindar and Homer, and refers to 'great Plato'. Perhaps later he studied at a Christian catechetical school, possibly of Caesarea, for all his thought is impregnated not only by a knowledge of all the Scriptures but of commentaries on Scripture and a sense of the tradition of the Fathers. It is known that as a young man he taught as Lector, or Didaskalos, in the catechetical school of Alexandria. Some time during the first crucial twenty-five years he had been in the desert and known St Anttony the Abbot. Most probably he had tried to live as a hermit, for all his life he would seem to have been a contemplative. Perhaps that is the key to much in the character of his sanctity and in his personality. Few saints seem to have changed so little as Athanasius. He was fully formed when he first took part in history about 320; everything that mattered most to him seems to have happened before he was thirty.

About the year 320 St Athanasius was deacon to Alexander, bishop of Alexandria. Arius, who was to give his name to Arianism, was then parish priest of Boucalis in the same city, a popular preacher, an admired ascetic and a director of consecrated virgins. He was already teaching that the Son of God had come 'into being out of non-existence' and that 'once he was not'. For Arius, the Son was a divine being and our Saviour, but he was the link between man and God, and pure eternal Godhead was the prerogative of the Father only. Arianism was to take many forms, sometimes more extreme, often more moderate than that which Arius had preached. Athanasius was to fight them all for more than fifty years. It is likely from the style and content that he was the true author of the encyclical against the new teaching which Bishop Alexander published in 322. It is certain that he attended the council of Nicaea three years later as Alexander's councillor and had at least some share in the final formulation of the definition there, that the Son was of the same substance as the Father. He came back to Egypt with his bishop and, in the summer of 328, succeeded him in the see of Alexandria.

During the first seven years of his episcopate, St Athanasius created for himself a position in Egypt which was to prove ultimately impregnable. He visited, taught and administered southward down the Nile valley. He sent the first mission into inner Africa, and under the leadership of St Frumentius it converted the kingdom of Axum in Ethiopia. Everywhere he established close relations with the monks and hermits who were to revere him as a wonder-worker and to name him 'Truth-teaching Father' and 'Christ-Bearer'. No previous bishop of Alexandria had ever had such power. It was perhaps political as much as theological intrigue which led the Emperor Constantine to summon him to Byzantium and then to exile him to Trier on the German border in 335.

He did not return to Egypt till two years later, when he found that the Arian factions were beginning to gain a rather hesitant patronage from the new Emperor in the east, Constantine's son Constantius. From 337 to 366 his life became primarily a struggle, at times almost single-handed, against all those tendencies which would have led to the undoing of the work of Nicaea. It is fairer to describe his opponents as anti-Nicene rather than as Arians. They included bishops who were addicted to some variant of Arian teaching, others of personal if lax orthodoxy who were ready to compromise for the sake of peace, and others who were rigorously orthodox and old fashioned, who abhorred the Nicene definition as a novelty and feared that it might cloak the revival of the heretical tendencies that had minimized the distinction between the Father and the Son. Behind them all was the power of the Emperor and of the great civil servants, probably quite uninterested in doctrine but intent on enforcing unity in what was rapidly becoming the state religion. It was the policy of Constantius to replace the definition of Nicaea by a compromise formula which could be accepted by all and dictated by the State. St Athanasius was to be the champion, not only of the single substance of the Trinity, but of the autonomy of the church.

Three other times he was arrested and sent into exile – each time he returned. From 356 to 361 he was in hiding in Egypt, sometimes in desert hermitages, sometimes in cisterns and in tombs. There were short lulls, and, for the last few years of his life, he was left undisturbed in Alexandria. But he was never secure and when he died a little before dawn on the May 2nd 373 the struggle seemed still undecided; Valens, then emperor in the east, was anti-Nicene and many of the bishops supported the imperial policies. Five years later Valens was dead and the Nicene cause had triumphed.

St Athanasius had written the greatest of his works during the thirty years of turmoil; his *De Incarnatione Verbi* seems to have been completed in 337. His *De Virginitate* and his *Orationes* may date from about 357. The *Contra Arianos* may be later than 362. He had written so much, but again and again all his thought, like his life, centers in a double conception; the Son the manifestation of the Father, the church the manifestation of the Son. Perhaps no saint has been more like St John; all later theology has been affected by him either directly or through St Ambrose and Damascene. In the west he was remembered as the doctor of the Trinity, so that long afterwards the Latin, and probably African, 'Quicumque Vult' came to be called the Athanasian Creed. But primarily he was the doctor of the Incarnation and of grace. As he contemplated Christ, 'The invisible Godhead made visible', he saw each member of His Body as a vine branch of the Vine: 'I say ye are

gods and all sons of the Highest'; 'We are sons and gods by reason of the Word within us'; 'the Word became man so that we should be deified'. To St Athanasius the Church was not only a visible society linked by a single Faith, 'One House', 'One Tunic', 'One Sheepfold'. It was also 'the Sanctuary in which is shed the Blood of Christ'. Christ's presence rendered it unchangeable and indestructible. For St Athanasius there was one retort to heresy: 'This is not the faith of the Catholic church, this is not the faith of the Fathers'. For him the Faith of the Catholic church was Christ as Light.
May 2nd

ATHANASIUS of NAPLES † 872
Bishop of Naples before he was twenty, Athanasius did much for his native city until his efforts were thwarted by his nephew, the tyrannical duke, Sergius II, who put him in prison at Sorrento and eventually forced him into exile, where he died.
July 15th

ATHANASIUS THE ATHONITE *c.* 920–*c.* 1000
Born at Trebizond, he became a professor at Constantinople, and then the founder or at least the first real organizer of the celebrated monasteries on Mount Athos which to this day still house monastic communities.
July 5th

ATHENOGENES † *c.* 305
A bishop and theologian who suffered martyrdom under Diocletian, apparently somewhere in Asia Minor.
July 16th

ATTALAS † 627
A native of Burgundy, he entered St Columban's monastery at Luxeuil and when the community was exiled to Bobbio, Lombardy, he succeeded Columban as abbot.
March 10th

ATTILANUS, *see* Froilan and Attilanus.

ATTRACTA or ARAGHT *Fifth or Sixth Century*
Attracta is said to have founded a hospice for travellers on the shores of Lough Gara in Ireland and also to have performed a number of somewhat unlikely miracles.
August 11th

AUBERT † *c.* 725
Founder of the church of Mont-Saint-Michel, which was dedicated in 709.
September 10th

AUBERT of CAMBRAI † *c.* 669
The bishop of Cambrai and Arras took part in the translation of St Fursey's relics to Péronne and signed grants of privilege to several monasteries.
December 13th

AUBIN, *see* Albinus of Angers.

AUDIFAX, *see* Marius, Martha, Audifax and Abachum.

AUDOENUS or **OUEN** *c.* 600–684
Audoenus was chancellor of King Dagobert I. He founded a monastery in the forest of Brie, and was eventually elected bishop of Rouen.
August 24th

AUDOMARUS or **OMER** † *c.* 670
Audomarus was a monk of Luxeuil who became bishop of Thérouanne in north-eastern France and left his diocese in an extremely flourishing condition.
September 9th

AUDREY, *see* Etheldreda.

AUGUSTINE 354–430
St Augustine was born on November 13th 354 at Thagaste in Numidia (now Souk-Ahras in Algeria). His parents were probably both native Numidians, i.e. Berbers. His father Patricius, a small landowner and town councillor, was a pagan (though he became a Christian at the end of his life). His mother, St Monica, was a Christian; and it was she who by her prayers and her unwearying patience and affection was responsible, more than any other human being, for her son's conversion. As was common at that time, he was entered in infancy among the candidates for baptism, but the actual baptism was indefinitely postponed, to avoid the risk of post-baptismal sin. He was in fact baptized, by St Ambrose, only after his conversion, when he was thirty-two. He went through the usual course of literary studies of his time (he loved Virgil and hated Greek, which he probably never perfectly mastered) at Thagaste and Madaura, and eventually trained and began to practise as a rhetorician at Carthage. His morals during this period were probably no worse, perhaps rather better, than those of his contemporaries, and we should not take his fierce condemnations of his own behavior in the *Confessions* too literally. He certainly took a concubine; but he was faithful to her till he sent her away at Milan in 385, and had a dearly loved son, Adeodatus, by her. At this period he became a Manichee, attracted by the intellectual pretensions of Manichaeism and the slick and easy solutions it offered to problems about the nature of God (corporeal, a sort of glorified gas), the scriptures (rejected or allegorized) and the origin of evil (due to an independent uncreated principle).

In 383 he went to Rome as a teacher of rhetoric, and in 384 obtained a post at Milan. He had already begun to see through Manichaeism, and was in a painful state of scepticism and uncertainty. At Milan he came into contact with the city's great bishop, St Ambrose, whose sermons showed him for the first time how he could believe the scriptures interpreted according to the teaching of the Church without sacrificing his intelligence: and he also read the books of the Neoplatonists, Plotinus and Porphyry, which cured him of Manichaean materialism and gave him a spiritual philosophy which he found in harmony with the Christian revelation. He became intellectually convinced of the truth of Christianity, but held back from any decisive step till in September 386 he underwent the great experience of conversion, instantaneous though long prepared, and complete, which he describes unsurpassably in the eighth book of his *Confessions*. It was a conversion both to Christianity and to the pursuit of Christian perfection by an ascetic life. After it he gave up his profession of rhetorician and retired to Cassiciacum, in the country near Milan, with his mother St Monica, his son Adeodatus, and several friends. Here he began to write, and produced a group of philosophical dialogues, the earliest of his works that we have.

He was baptized by St Ambrose at Easter 387, and started back with his mother and friends to Africa. St Monica died on the way at Ostia. In Africa he was persuaded by Bishop Valerius of Hippo to become a priest, and was ordained in 391. In 395 he was consecrated bishop as coadjutor to Valerius, and succeeded him as bishop of Hippo on his death soon after. He spent the remaining thirty-five years of his life as a hard-working diocesan bishop, somehow finding time to produce, besides his best known and loved works, the *Confessions* and the *City of God*, that vast series of theological writings which have made his thought a living force throughout Western Christianity from his own day to ours, and which are read and studied now perhaps more than ever before.

He lived a monastic common life with his clergy and did all he could to encourage the formation of religious communities. Two sermons on ascetic communal life and a long letter on its principles which he wrote to a community of women he had founded, with his sister as its first head, form the so-called 'Rule of St Augustine', which is the basis of the rules of a great many communities of canons regular, friars and nuns. The account of his life as a bishop by his friend St Possidius is a most attractive one, and shows St Augustine as a very human, kindly and charitable person, devoted to the service of the community, living very simply himself and with a real love of poverty, though not ostentatiously ascetic, but practising a very liberal hospitality. He always had wine at the common meals, as a sign of respect for the good gifts of God (perhaps he remembered the perverted puritanism of his Manichaean days). The one thing he would not tolerate at his table was malicious gossip and scandal, even when it came from fellow-bishops. He was continually engaged in the defence of the Catholic faith against schismatics, heretics and pagans; he had to deal in turn with his old friends the Manichees, with the wild Berber schism of the Donatists, and with the formidable Briton, Breton, or Irishman Pelagius and his followers, who denied original sin and did not believe that God's grace was needed for salvation. This last controversy produced St Augustine's writings on grace, which have had so great an influence on later Christian thought (though his influence extends far wider than this one field). But, though he opposed heresy with vigor, he was on the whole, for his period, courteous and charitable in dealing with individual heretics and pagans.

St Augustine lived to see the savage Vandal invasion of Africa which began in 429, and died on August 28th 430 at the age of seventy-six, while the Vandals were besieging his episcopal city of Hippo, in a spirit of the greatest courage, humility and penitence. He made no will, for he had no possessions to leave: but, from the time of his death to our own day, his legacy of thought has been recognized by most western Christians as the richest left by any Christian teacher after St Paul.

August 28th   ILLUSTRATION: page 46

AUGUSTINE of CANTERBURY   † c. 605
St Augustine was the agent of a greater man than himself, Pope St Gregory the Great. In Gregory's time, except for the Irish monks, missionary activity was unknown in the western Church, and it is Gregory's glory to have revived it. He decided to begin with a mission to the pagan English, for they had cut off the Christian Celts from the rest of Christendom. The time was favorable for a mission since the ruler of the whole of southern England, Ethelbert of Kent, had married a Christian wife and had received a Gaulish bishop at his court. Gregory himself wished to come to Britain, but his election as pope put an end to any such idea, and in 596 he decided to send an Italian monk following the comparatively new Rule of St Benedict. Augustine set out with some companions, but when they reached southern Gaul a crisis occurred and Augustine was sent back to the pope to beg them off. In reply the pope made Augustine their abbot and subjected the rest of the party to him in all things, and with this authority Augustine successfully reached England in 597, landing in Kent on the Isle of Thanet. Ethelbert and the men of Kent refused to accept Christianity at first, although an ancient British church dedicated to St Martin was restored for Augustine's use; but very shortly afterwards Ethelbert was baptized and the pope having been consulted, a plan was prepared for the removal of the chief see from Canterbury to London and the establishment of another province at York. Events prevented either of these

projects from being fulfilled, but the progress of the mission was continuous until Augustine's death, somewhere between 604 and 609.

The only defeat Augustine met with after he came to England was in his attempt to reconcile the Welsh Christians, to persuade them to adopt the Roman custom of reckoning the date of Easter, to correct certain minor irregularities of rite and to submit to his authority. Augustine met the leaders of the Welsh church in conference but he unfavorably impressed them by remaining seated when they came into his presence – it is likely that in this he unfavorably impressed St Bede too. Augustine was neither the most heroic of missionaries, nor the most tactful, but he did a great work, and he was one of the very few men in Gaul or Italy who, at that time, was prepared to give up everything to preach the gospel in a far country.

May 28th

AUNACHARIUS or AUNAIRE   † 605
Bishop of Auxerre from 561 until his death.

September 25th

AUREA   *Eleventh Century*
Daughter of Nunnio and Amunia, villagers in Villavelayo, Calahorra, during the Moorish occupation of Spain, she entered the nearby convent of San Millán where she was famous for her visions and miracles.

March 11th

AURELIAN   † 551
Bishop of Arles from 564 to 551.

June 16th

AURELIUS   † 429
A friend of St Augustine and bishop of Carthage for thirty-seven years, he had to devote much of his time to combating the Donatist and Pelagian heresies.

July 20th

AURELIUS, NATALIA, FELIX
and their Companions   † c. 852
They were martyred at Cordova during the Mahommedan domination of Spain.

July 27th

AUREUS, *see* Alban.

AUSTREBERTA   † 704
Born near Thérouanne, Artois, the daughter of Count Palatine Badefrid and St Framechildis, she became abbess of the Port nunnery on the Somme, which she left in order to reform a newly and laxly established convent at Pavilly.

February 10th

AUSTREGISILUS or OUTRIL † 624

He retired from the court of King Guntramnus at Chalon-sur-Saône and was ordained, and later nominated abbot of Saint-Nizier at Lyons, by St Aetherius. In 612 he was elected bishop of Bourges, his native city, where he remained until his death.

May 20th

AUSTREMONIUS or STREMOINE
Fourth Century

A missionary in Auvergne, he is the apostle and first bishop of Clermont.

November 1st

AUXENTIUS † 473

Son of Addas and one of the horse-guards of Theodosius the Younger, he became a hermit on Mount Oxia, Bithynia. He was unsuccessfully accused of the Eutychian heresy and went with many disciples to Mount Skopa. His women disciples were known as 'Trichinaraeae' – 'the nuns dressed in haircloth'.

February 14th

AVERTINUS † 1180?

A Gilbertine canon, he was supposed to have attended St Thomas of Canterbury in exile and after the death of the archbishop to have settled in Touraine, where he devoted himself to the poor. He is invoked against dizziness and headache. All we really know is that there may have been a hermit of this name who certainly had no connection with St Thomas.

May 5th

AVITUS *Sixth Century*

An abbot in the province of Perche, he was buried near Orleans.

June 17th

AVITUS of VIENNE *Sixth Century*

Born in Auvergne, he was the son of Isychius, bishop of Vienne, whom he succeeded in 490. He caused Sigismund of Burgundy to repent the murder of his son, Sigfric.

February 5th

AYBERT 1060–1140

Born in 1060 at Espin in Tournai, he lived as a hermit near the abbey of Crespin. For twenty-five years he was procurator and cellarer, but later he retired to his hermitage where he was ordained. His habit of repeating the Hail Mary fifty times successively and of dividing the psalter into fifty parts may have had something to do with the origin of the Rosary.

April 7th

AYOUL, *see* Aigulf.

BABYLAS *Third Century*

Although he was the most famous of former bishops of Antioch, few facts remain of his life. He was either beheaded or died in prison during the persecution of Decius.

January 24th

BACCHUS, *see* Sergius.

BADEMUS † 376

He was imprisoned during the persecution under King Sapor II of Persia. Nersan, another Christian prisoner, was promised pardon if he would kill Bademus, which he did.

April 10th

BAGNUS or BAIN † c. 710

A monk of Fontenelle, and a disciple of St Wandregisilus, in 689 he was appointed to the see of Thérouanne, the region around Calais, of which town he is the patron. After twelve years he retired to Fontenelle, where he was obliged to become abbot. The village of Bainghien is named after him.

June 20th

BAIN, *see* Bagnus.

BALBINA

She was invested by Ado, an unscrupulous martyrologist, to account for the name of that cemetery in Rome which is between the Via Appia and the Via Ardeatina, and is known as the cemetery of Balbina.

March 31st

BALDOMERUS or GALMIER *Seventh Century*

A pious locksmith of Lyons, he is sometimes regarded as patron of that trade. According to an unreliable story, he entered the monastery of St Justus, and was later ordained subdeacon by Bishop Gundry.

February 27th

BALRED and BILFRED *Eighth Century*

A priest, Balred lived as a solitary at Tyningham, and later on the Bass Rock. He died at Aldham, but his relics were buried at Durham with those of St Bilfred, a goldsmith and hermit, who had decorated the binding of St Cuthbert's book of the Gospels, now in the British Museum.

March 6th

BARACHISIUS and JONAS † 327

Monks of Beth-Iasa, they went to encourage Christians at Hubaham during persecution by Shapur, the Persian king. For this they were tried, but willingly accepted terrible deaths rather than renounce God.

March 29th

BARADATES *Fifth Century*

An anchoret of Cyrrhus, he is referred to as 'the admirable Baradates' in Theodoret's *Philotheus*. Although a learned

theologian, he was more celebrated for the ingenuity of his mortifications. He encased himself entirely in leather, leaving only his mouth and nose free, and lived in a trelliswork hut in which he could not stand upright.
February 22nd

BARBARA

Barbara was an extremely popular saint in the Middle Ages, but it is doubtful whether she ever existed. According to legend, she was shut up in a tower by her father because of her great beauty. During her father's absence on a journey, she became a Christian, received baptism and caused some workmen who were building two windows into her tower to add a third in honor of the Trinity. When her father returned and she told him what she had done, he tried to kill her, but she was miraculously transported to a mountain. Her father, however, found her place of refuge and took her before the magistrates, where she was condemned for being a Christian, the father himself asking to be allowed to carry out the sentence of execution.
See also The Fourteen Holy Helpers.
December 4th ILLUSTRATION: page 47 (B)

BARBASYMAS and his Companions † 346

He succeeded his brother, St Sadoth, as bishop of Seleucia and Ctesiphon. He and sixteen priests were arrested by King Sapor II, tortured for their Christian faith and martyred at Ledan in Huzistan.
January 14th

BARBATUS † 682

A priest of Benevento, which had relapsed into paganism, he restored Christianity by prophesying the unsuccessful siege of the town by Constans II. He succeeded Hildebrand as bishop of Benevento. His *Life*, however, is late and unreliable.
February 19th

BARDO c. 980–1053

Born about 980 at Oppershofen, and educated at the abbey of Fulda, he became abbot of Kaiserswerth, superior of Hersfeld, and finally archbishop of Mainz, where he took part in two synods under Leo IX, who appointed him his legate for Germany.
June 15th

BARHADBESABA † 355

Deacon of Arbela, he was martyred during the persecution of the church in Persia that began in 340.
July 15th

BARLAAM Fourth Century?

Although St John Chrysostom wrote a panegyric of this saint, scarcely anything certain is known of him other than that he was tortured at Antioch.
November 19th

BARLAAM and JOSAPHAT

In order to prevent his son, Josaphat, from becoming a Christian, the king, his father, had him confined; but an ascetic, Barlaam, disguised himself as a merchant and converted the boy.

This story is now known to be a Christian version of the legend of Siddartha Buddha.
November 27th

BARLAAM of KHUTYN † 1193

This saint, who is remembered in the Russian form of the Byzantine mass, came from a wealthy Novgorod family. He gave his property to the poor and became a hermit at Khutyn on the Volga. His numerous disciples had eventually to be formed into a monastic community of which he became abbot.
November 6th

BARNABAS First Century

St Barnabas plays a prominent part in the early chapters of the Acts of the Apostles, less for his own sake than for the purpose of introducing the hero of the book, St Paul. A Cypriot Jew and a member of the first Christian church at Jerusalem, it is through his services that, about the year 39, the neo-convert Saul is welcomed into the apostolic community (Acts 9:27). Four years later he enlists the aid of Saul for the task of guiding and directing the newly established Christian community at Antioch (Acts 11:19–26), a town which then ranks in importance second only to Rome, and which is to become the center of Gentile Christianity and the powerhouse of the evangelization of east and west. It is again with Saul that he is entrusted with the relief fund sent to Jerusalem (Acts 11:27–30), where the two are joined by John Mark, a relative of Barnabas (Colossians 4:10), who will form the third member of the missionary journey they undertake about the year 45 (Acts 13 and 14). From here Barnabas gradually fades into insignificance. Although it is his native Cyprus that is first evangelized, it is Saul under his new name of Paul who takes the lead, 'Paul and his company' who make their way to the mainland of Asia Minor, Paul who does the talking (the semi-comic incident at Lystra, [Acts 14:8–18], where Barnabas is mistaken for the stately Zeus and Paul for the mercurial Hermes, is eloquent testimony to the mutual rôles they played) and Paul finally who on their return three years later receives the approbation of the council of Jerusalem for the policy that has been followed in the journey (Acts 15:1–35). When in the following year a projected second missionary journey involves a dispute over the inclusion of John Mark (Acts 15:36–41), Paul chooses other companions and Barnabas returns to Cyprus. His task of introducing St Paul is fulfilled, and his name is not mentioned again in the Acts. A passing reference in Paul's correspondence with the church at Corinth tells us that he is still alive about the year 56 (1 Corinthians 9 : 5); Paul's request six years later that his companion Mark should join him in Rome (2 Timothy 4 : 11) allows us to infer that by then Barnabas was dead.

A later tradition speaks of Barnabas's journey to Alexandria, Rome and Milan, of which town he became the first bishop. A possibly more reliable tradition describes his death by stoning at Salamis in his native country. Fragments exist of an apocryphal *Gospel of Barnabas* and of a fifth century work known as the *Acts of Barnabas*, but these offer no information that is not already known from the Acts of the Apostles. The so-called *Epistle of Barnabas*, which many of the Fathers included in their canon of scripture, is now acknowledged to be the second century work of a Jewish Christian of Alexandria.

The very first mention of Barnabas in the Acts (4 : 36) has singled him out as a supreme example of the charity which was to characterize those on whom the Holy Spirit had descended, and through which the precious unity of the Church was to be preserved. It is here that this man, whose proper name was Joseph, is given the new name by which he will be known ever after – Bar-Nahba, the 'man of encouragement'. It is Barnabas whose selflessness forms a vivid contrast with the hypocrisy of Ananias, whose real charity befriends Paul when the rest of his fellow 'cradle-Catholics' can see nothing but ground for suspicion, whose thoughtfulness rescues Paul out of oblivion to launch him on his life's work, whose guidance directs the new Antioch community to the charity which is so practically expressed in the relief sent to Jerusalem and in the missionaries sent to the pagan world. He is willing to adapt himself to the Jewish-Christian way of life at Antioch rather than offend their susceptibilities (Galatians 2 : 13), yet he shares with Paul the hardships of a 1500 mile journey to take the good news to the Gentiles. At the end he steps back into second place and even fades out of the picture altogether rather than curb the genius that was Paul's. If it needed the intense fire of a Paul to set the mediterranean world alight, it needed the quiet encouragement of a Barnabas to make of that fire the light that would enlighten the world.

June 11th   ILLUSTRATION: page 48

BARNARD, *see* Bernard.

BARONTIUS   *Seventh Century*
He withdrew from the world to the abbey of Lonray in Berry but secretly retained some possessions. St Peter having reproved him in a vision, he reformed and retired to Pistoia with another hermit, Desiderius.
March 25th

BARSABAS   † c. 342
An abbot, martyred with ten monks at Ishtar in about 342.
December 11th

BARSANUPHIUS   *Sixth Century*
An Egyptian, he lived alone in a cell adjoining a monastery at Gaza in Palestine, where he was renowned for his austerity, keeping in touch with the outer world by means of written messages only.
April 11th

BARSIMAEUS   *Third Century?*
He is usually taken to have been the third bishop of Edessa, but he may have been Barsamja, successor to Palut. Various dates make it evident that he could not have been martyred under Trajan, as the Roman Martyrology states.
January 30th

BARTHOLOMEA CAPITANIO   1807–1833
Born at Lovere in northern Italy, she early made a vow of perpetual chastity and, obtaining a teacher's diploma, devoted herself to the apostolate of the young, with outstanding results. Eventually she and Catherine Gerosa (St Vincentia Gerosa) founded the *Suore della Carità* (Sisters of Charity of Lovere), a congregation which has its headquarters in Milan. She died at twenty-six from consumption aggravated by her ceaseless exertions, leaving behind her two volumes of 'Spiritual Writings' and many letters.
July 26th

BARTHOLOMEW   *First Century*
The Synoptic Gospels and the Acts of the Apostles mention Bartholomew as one of the Twelve, but offer no further information about him except to link his name with that of Philip. The Fourth Gospel, which has no explicit list of the Apostles although it names most of them and speaks frequently of 'the Twelve', makes no reference to Bartholomew, but mentions an otherwise unknown Nathanael, linked with Philip in his call (John 1 : 43–51) and closely associated with the other Apostles after the Resurrection (John 21 : 1–14). Since the sixteenth century many scholars have identified Nathanael with Bartholomew, and have seen in the latter name merely the patronymic or 'surname' by which Nathanael is specified as the son (*bar*) of Tolmai (or possibly Ptolemy) in the same way as Simon Peter is specified as the son of Jona.

If the identification is accepted, we have more detail about the vocation of our saint than about that of any other Apostle (Luke 5 : 4–10 seems to be a doublet of John 21 : 4ff). The scene is not without humor. In his very first words in reply to Philip's invitation to come and recognise the awaited Messiah in the preacher from Nazareth – 'What can you expect from Nazareth?' – Nathanael has expressed the universal rivalry between neighboring villages (he is from Cana, John 21 : 2) and has set the tone for what is to follow. For there is a smile behind Christ's own words as he greets this 'sincere son of Jacob' who has none of that 'double-dealing' which tradition had connected with the name; and there is guarded caution behind Nathanael's inquiry about the extent of Christ's knowledge of him. When he sees his deepest thoughts being read in Christ's second playful allusion to his kinship with Jacob the dreamer, he is sufficiently overcome to recognize Christ as the Messiah. But the last word goes to Christ as he smilingly promises that this Jacob will see in reality what the other only dreamed of – the coming of heaven to earth. Paradoxically, the messianic 'son of God' whom Nathanael is willing to recognize in this thought-reader is something less than the heavenly 'son of Man' whom Christ will reveal to him.

If the identification with Nathanael is rejected (and indeed many of the Fathers rejected it explicitly), Bartholomew remains a featureless figure. Later tradition has made the usual attempt to provide the missing details, and from the fourth century on there are conflicting accounts of his missionary activity in Asia Minor, Armenia, Mesopotamia, Persia, India and Egypt. Of these Armenia has the strongest support, and although its earliest writers make no mention of our saint he is honored as the Apostle of that country. A tradition that he was flayed alive lies behind the knife and the skin which have been adopted as his symbols. His body is reputed to have been later taken to Benevento. It remains disputed whether it was these alleged relics or others which were transported to Rome in the tenth century by the Emperor Otto III and which now lie in the church of 'St Bartholomew-on-Tiber'. These surface features can offer us no precision, but behind them stands the figure of one who was an intimate friend of Christ, whose weakness was turned into strength by that close union, and who, like his Master, offered his life for love of the church. It is this aspect alone that the liturgy has chosen to underline, to remind us that it is upon such foundation stones that we are built.

August 24th   ILLUSTRATION: page 65

BARTHOLEMEW of FARNE   † 1193

Born in Whitby, he was ordained in Norway, and became a monk of Durham. He later retired to the desolate island of Farne, where he lived forty-two years.

June 24th

BARTHOLOMEW of GROTTAFERRATA
† *c.* 1050

The third abbot, he completed the monastery of Grottaferrata, founded by St Nilus, and made it a center of learning. By tradition it is here that Pope Benedict IX retired after his scandalous reign, and was brought to true repentance by the saint.

November 11th

BASIL of ANCYRA,   † 362

A priest who opposed Arianism and the semi-Arianism of Bishop Basil in Ancora, he was martyred under Julian the Apostate for condemning idolatry.

March 22nd

BASIL THE GREAT   329–379

St Basil was one of the group of great oriental theologians to whom, under God, we owe our right belief in the Trinity and the Incarnation, and also the chief organizer of ascetic community life in the East. He was born in 329 at Caesarea, the capital of Cappadocia, far up in the interior of Asia Minor. A surprizing number of his family are honored as saints; his grandmother St Macrina the Elder, his father and mother, St Basil the Elder and St Emmelia, his brothers St Gregory of Nyssa and St Peter of Sebaste, and his sister St Macrina the Younger. He studied at Constantinople and went on from there to Athens, which was still the great university city of the Greek-speaking world. Here his fellow-student and close friend was another young Cappadocian, St Gregory Nazianzen, who with the two brothers Basil and Gregory of Nyssa, makes up the trio of Cappadocian doctors of the church.

When Basil returned to Caesarea he taught rhetoric for some years in the city. Then he retired from the world, inspired by the example of his elder sister Macrina, who with her widowed mother, had already founded her own community of nuns on one of the family estates at Annesi on the river Iris. He travelled through all the monastic centers of the east, Egypt, Syria, Palestine and Mesopotamia, to study the monastic life wherever it was flourishing. Then he returned and founded his own community not far from that of his sister; and the way of life which he worked out for it, on the basis of what he had seen on his travels, is still that which is followed by all the monks of the eastern Orthodox churches and by some Catholic monks of the Byzantine rite. Furthermore it deeply influenced St Benedict, who knew St Basil's ascetic writings in a Latin translation by Rufinus, and through him the whole of western monasticism. It was a way of life better balanced and more humane than the most important earlier form of ascetic common life, the Egyptian monasticism of St Pachomius. There was more loving obedience and less harsh discipline; a moderate communal asceticism (extreme enough, certainly, by modern standards) instead of individual competition in austerities; and an emphasis on work, intellectual (the prayerful study of the Scriptures) and manual (useful labor for the benefit of the monastic community). St Basil only lived for five years as a monk in his monastery. But what he did and wrote then was the most immediately and lastingly successful part of his life's work.

BENEDICT of NURSIA : detail of predella panel by Lorenzo di Monaco (c.1372 - c.1422) (National Gallery, London)

PLATE 3

BARTHOLOMEW: statue by Marco Agrati (1500 – 1571). *(Duomo, Milan.)*

BAVO or ALLOWIN: detail from the right outer shutter of 'The Last Judgment' by
Hieronymus Bosch (*c.* 1460 – 1518). (*Acad. Fine Arts, Vienna.*)

BEDE: (The Venerable Bede): illumination from Bede's MS 'Life of Saint Cuthbert' (Late twelfth century). *(British Museum.)*

BERNADETTE SOUBIROUS: photograph taken *c.* 1866.

BERNARD of CLAIRVAUX: detail from a painting of St Bernard's 'Vision of the Virgin' by Filippo Lippi (1406 – 1469). *(National Gallery, London.)*

BERNARDINE of SIENA: painting from the school of Squarcione (1397 – 1468).
(Academia Carrara, Bergamo.)

BLAISE: detail from triptych painted on wood by Hans Memlinc (1430–35 – 1494). *(Dom, Lübeck.)*

BONIFACE: detail of a silver statue by an eighteenth century silversmith.
(Fuldaer Domschatz, Augsburgh.)

BORIS and GLEB: fourteenth century icon, tempera painted on wood, of Suzdal
School. *(Russian Museum, Leningrad.)*

St. BRIGITTE
Canonisée au Concile

BRIDGET of SWEDEN: engraving.

BRIGID or BRIDE: painting by Gabrielle Hayes (*b.* 1909.)

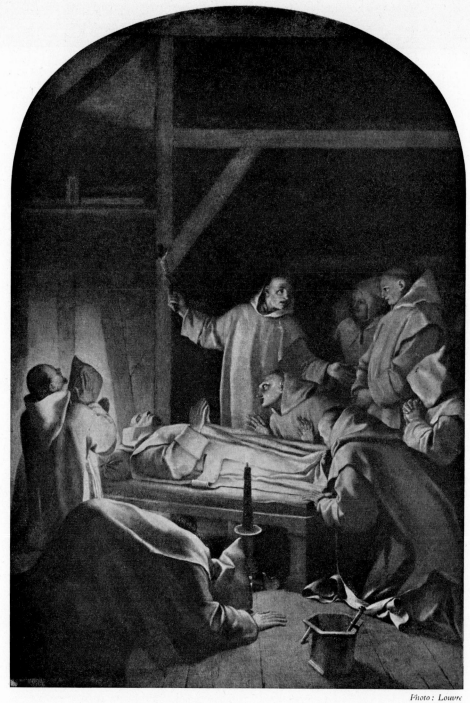

BRUNO: painting by Le Sueur (1617 – 1655). (*Louvre, Paris.*)

CAJETAN: sculpture by Bernini (1598 – 1680). *(Bas. Sta Maria Maggiore, Rome.)*

CANDIDUS: reliquary (thirteenth century).
(St Maurice d'Agaune treasury.)

CASIMIR of POLAND: painting by Bartholomaeus Zeitblom (1455-60 – 1518-22).
(Alte Pinakothek, Munich.)

CATHERINE of ALEXANDRIA: 'The Mystical Marriage of St Catherine 'by Hans Memlinc
(1430–35 – 1494). *(Hôpital S. Jean, Bruges.)*

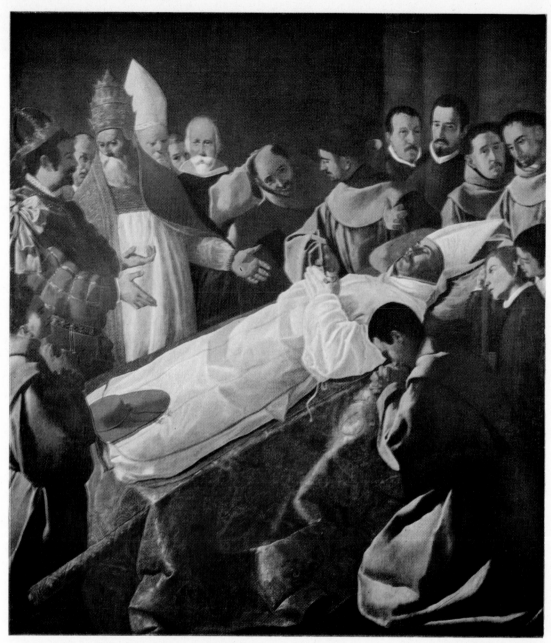

BONAVENTURE: painting by Zurbaran (1598 - 1663). (*Louvre, Paris*)

PLATE 4

In 370 he became archbishop of Caesarea. At that time the Arian heresy, which denied that Christ was God, in the sense of his being of the same substance with the Father was at the height of its influence. The Emperor Valens was an Arian, and was vigorously persecuting the Catholics. St Basil's primary task as archbishop was the defence of the Catholic faith, which he carried out for the rest of his life with unflinching courage, great intellectual power, and a charity and desire for agreement with his opponents (though not at the price of orthodoxy) unusual among theological controversialists. He so overawed the Prefect of the east, Modestus, and the Emperor Valens himself, that he and his diocese were left alone, though there was persecution everywhere else. His answer to the Prefect, recorded (perhaps with some embellishments) by St Gregory Nazianzen, may explain why, and gives an excellent idea of the quality of the man. Modestus had threatened him with confiscation, exile, torture and death. St Basil said, 'Well, in truth, confiscation means nothing to a man who has nothing, unless you covet these wretched rags and a few books; that is all I possess. As to exile, that means nothing to me, for I am attached to no particular place. That wherein I live is not mine, and I shall feel at home in any place to which I am sent. Or rather, I regard the whole earth as belonging to God, and I consider myself as a stranger wherever I may be. As for torture, how will you apply it? I have not a body capable of bearing it, unless you are thinking of the first blow you give me, for that will be the only one in your power. As for death, this will be a benefit to me, for it will take me the sooner to the God for whom I live . . .' The Prefect said that nobody had ever spoken to him like that. St Basil replied, 'Perhaps that is because you have never had to deal with a bishop.'

Besides defending the Catholic faith against heresies, St Basil was a model diocesan bishop. He visited every part of his diocese continually, he organized a great hospital for the sick poor, and like all ancient bishops he preached very frequently; some of his courses of sermons, which are major theological works, have been preserved. Heresy was by no means his only trouble. There was every sort of division among the Catholics of the east and very considerable misunderstandings between east and west. St Basil's life as a bishop, in fact, was lived in the midst of the sort of miserable muddles so common in the history of the church, when everybody is more or less in the wrong, no one trusts anybody else, and Christian charity is very little in evidence. His own charity never failed, and he worked unceasingly for peace and unity. But he was misunderstood and misrepresented; all his efforts to unite the Catholics seemed to go wrong. He did just live to see the death of Valens, which meant the end of the Arian persecution: but he

died very soon after, worn out, at the age of only forty-nine, on January 1st (the date on which the eastern churches keep his chief feast) 379.

June 14th　　　　　ILLUSTRATION: page 47 (A)

BASIL THE YOUNGER　　　† 952
Legends color the history of this monk, who lived at Constantinople when Leo VI and Alexander reigned. He was accused as a spy but was miraculously saved from all the torture inflicted upon him.
March 26th

BASILIDES, QUIRINUS or CYRINUS, NABOR and NAZARIUS
These martyrs are often incorrectly referred to as a group and given their own feast on June 12th. See the separate entries under Quirinus, Nabor and Nazarius.
June 12th

BASILISSA, *see* Julian and Basilissa.

BASILISSA and ANASTASIA　　*First Century?*
Legend says that these were two noble Roman ladies who arranged for the burial of SS Peter and Paul and were condemned to death for their pains, but the evidence for their existence is slender and unreliable.
April 15th

BASILLA or BASILISSA　　　† 304
A maiden of the Imperial family, who vowed chastity when converted to Christianity, she was given the choice between fulfilling her marriage contract and death; she chose the latter. So runs the legend. All we know for certain is the fact of her martyrdom.
May 20th

BASLE, *see* Basolus.

BASOLUS or BASLE　　　† c. 620
Born at Limoges, he was a soldier before becoming a monk. Zealous for solitude, he was allowed to live as a hermit for the rest of his life, and St Sindulf became one of his disciples.
November 26th

BATHILDIS　　　† 680
She was an English girl who was sold as a slave into the household of the mayor of the palace at Paris. King Clovis II married her, and when he died she became regent. She founded the abbey of Corbie and the nunnery of Chelles to which she retired in 665.
January 30th

BAUDELIUS　　　*Fourth Century*
His cultus is old, but his story is unreliable. He may have arrived at Nîmes as a missionary during a feast of Jupiter, and been beheaded when he criticized the populace for their paganism.
May 20th

BAVO or ALLOWIN † *c.* 655
A dissolute nobleman and a widower, he was converted by St Amand, gave away his money, and lived as a hermit. He is the patron of the dioceses of Ghent and of Haarlem. ILLUSTRATION: page 66
October 1st

BEAN *Eleventh Century*
Founder of the bishopric of Banff in Mortlach, which later became that of Aberdeen.
October 26th

BEATRICE, *see* Simplicius.

BEATUS of LIEBANA *Eighth Century*
A monk of Liebana in the Asturian mountains, he led a successful campaign, much of it in writing, against Elipandus, archbishop of Toledo, and his Nestorian heresy that Christ was only God's adopted son.
February 19th

BEATUS † 112?
He was, according to legend, a hermit who lived on the slopes of St Beatenberg (which is named after him) above the lake of Thun. He should not be confused with St Beatus of Vendôme, who preached at Vendôme and Nantes, and died near Laon at the end of the third century.
May 9th

BEDE (The Venerable Bede) *c.* 673–735
Bede tells us practically all we know of his early life in a few brief sentences appended to his *Ecclesiastical History*. He was born in 673 or 674 on land to the south of the Tyne which afterwards became the property of the twin monasteries of Wearmouth and Jarrow where his whole life was spent. At the age of seven he was given to the care of Abbot Benet Biscop to be educated. Ordained a deacon at the age of eighteen, he became a priest in 702 or 703 when he was twenty-nine.

His monastic life was an uneventful one and we can sum it up in his own words: 'I have spent the whole of my life ... devoting all my pains to the study of the Scriptures, and, amid the observance of monastic discipline and the daily task of singing in the church, it has ever been my delight to learn or teach or write.' This summary is in very truth the whole of Bede's life. He seldom left the monastery, and we hear of two journeys only. Once he visited York to see Archbishop Egbert and to inspect the flourishing schools there, and on an earlier occasion, to gain material for his life of St Cuthbert, he stayed at Lindisfarne and from there visited Farne Island to examine the remains of the saint's cell.

It was as a teacher that Bede was supreme. He had no interest in speculation and no desire to be original; his genius was that of one who, with infinite pains, educates himself and transmits not only what he has learned but a deep sense of the value of such knowledge. Of his oral teaching – to which he attached great importance – of course we cannot speak, but his books became standard works of reference in his own lifetime. His carefulness and sobriety of approach, his pains to be accurate, his obvious orthodoxy, gave to them a unique authority. Bede's works fall into three well-defined classes. His theological writings consist mainly of a teacher's commentaries on the Bible, based very largely on the western Fathers and written for the most part in the allegorical manner of Christian tradition. Bede used his knowledge of Greek and displayed what we may think was an innocent vanity in making the most of such Hebrew as he had learned. Yet, despite the lack of originality in his approach, the commentaries of Bede remain even today one of the best means to arrive at the thought of the early Fathers.

His scientific writings consist partly of traditional explanations of natural phenomena, in which the poetic approach of St Ambrose is sometimes reflected, and partly of treatises on the calendar and the calculation of Easter – a matter of moment, as the Paschal controversy between Saxons and Celts had by no means entirely died down. It was Bede's popularization of the method of calculating calendar years from the supposed date of our Lord's birth which more than anything else ensured its universal acceptance in western Christendom.

The saint's historical writings are perhaps best remembered today. The chief of these was *The Ecclesiastical History of the English People*, one of the most important pieces of historical writing of the early middle ages. It is the sole source of much of our information about early Saxon history, and (apart from occasional bias against the Celtic church) it is written with sober objectivity and balance of judgment, dependent upon documentary sources and trustworthy witnesses. Bede also wrote a short history of the abbots of Wearmouth and prose and verse lives of St Cuthbert.

Bede, then, remained from 679 onwards in the monasteries of Wearmouth and Jarrow, carrying out meticulously the duties of his monastic life and engaged unceasingly in writing and teaching. Of his holiness, none of his contemporaries had any doubts, and it is refreshing to see that it was accompanied by none of the phenomena dear to the conventional hagiographer, for he worked no miracles, saw no visions and taught no new path to God.

His death was as sober and undeterred as was his life. In the early summer of 735, when he was sixty-three, his health began to fail, and he suffered much from asthma. He was, however, at work until the very end. On the Tuesday before Ascension Day he summoned the priests of the monastery, made them little gifts of pepper and incense and begged their prayers. At intervals during the next forty-eight hours, propped up in bed, he dictated to the very last sentence an English rendering of the Gospel of St John upon which he was engaged at the onset of his illness. Finally, asking to be laid on the floor, he sang the anthem 'O King of Glory' from the Office of Ascension Day and so died. It was May 27th, 735.

He is still usually referred to by that title given him in his lifetime – 'the Venerable Bede' – but since his recognition in 1899 as a saint and doctor of the church, he is sometimes known as St Bede the Venerable.

May 27th   ILLUSTRATION: page 67

BEE, *see* Bega.

BEGA or BEE   *Seventh Century*

A Northumbrian recluse, she lived on the headland called after her, St Bee's Head. Whether she was the St Heiu referred to by Bede as the first woman to take the veil in Northumbria, or the daughter of an Irish king who travelled miraculously to England to avoid marriage is uncertain.

September 6th

BEGGA   † 693

The elder daughter of Bd Pepin of Landen and of Bd Itta, and sister of St Gertrude of Nivelles. She married Ansegisilus, son of St Arnulf of Metz, and gave birth to Pepin of Herstal, founder of the Carlovingian dynasty. As a widow she established the convent of Andenne, of which she became abbess.

December 17th

BENEDICT II   † 685

By birth a Roman, he was elected pope in 683. He persuaded the Emperor Constantine IV to abolish the imperial sanction for papal elections, but, notwithstanding, some later elections to the papacy were still subject to the emperor's confirmation.

May 8th

BENEDICT CRISPUS   † 725

Archbishop of Milan, he is known to have lost an important lawsuit in Rome, and to have written the epitaph for Caedwalla, the Anglo-Saxon prince buried in St Peter's.

March 11th

BENEDICT JOSEPH LABRE, *see* Joseph Benedict Labre.

BENEDICT of ANIANE   † 821

Son of Aigulf of Maguelone. From a hermit by the brook Aniane in Languedoc with Widman and others, he rose to become the chief reformer of all monasteries in the Empire and one of the greatest influences on western monasticism. *Concordia Regularum* (A Harmony of Rules) is his most important work. It aims to show the common properties possessed by all the important codes of monastic observance.

February 11th

BENEDICT of BENEVENTO and his Companions
† 1003

He was sent by Otto III from his monastery near Ravenna to evangelize the Slavs of Pomerania, but he and his companions were murdered by thieves in Poland.

November 12th

BENEDICT of NURSIA   *c. 480–c. 547*

St Benedict, patriarch of western monasticism, was born about the year 480, and died about the year 547. These dates are quite uncertain, but they are accurate enough for practical purposes. It was a turbulent period. The Goths, who were Arian heretics, had established a kingdom in Italy, and were striving to defend it against the Emperor Justinian's great general Belisarius. In 546 the Gothic king, Totila, who figures in St Benedict's story, captured the city of Rome, and left it in ruins and deserted for forty days. Justinian's armies won a final victory so costly that the historian Gibbon wrote: 'The deliverance of Rome was the last calamity of the Roman people.' Such was the setting within which St Benedict established the monastic system which was to preserve religion, art, science and agriculture for Europe throughout the dark ages.

There are two main sources for St Benedict's life, the second *Dialogue* of St Gregory the Great and the saint's own *Rule*. The *Dialogue* is a collection of miracles attributed to St Benedict, the value of which may be admitted or discarded according to individual taste and critical fashion, but it contains much valuable factual information. Benedict was born in a country town of the Sabine hills called Nursia. His parents were probably what we should now describe as country gentry in a small way. Tradition connects him with the princely Roman clan of the Anicii, but this is most unlikely. Having been brought up at home, at about the age of fourteen he was sent to Rome to complete his education. Modern readers will be surprised to find that he was accompanied by his nurse Cyrilla.

But the decadence of Rome horrified the young countryman. Still followed by his nurse, he fled from the city two or three years later, knowing only that God was calling him to the life of a monk or a hermit. After a brief stay with some holy men at Enfide, thirty-five miles distant from Rome, he set off once more, this time quite alone, to adopt the solitary life of an anchorite. Having received the monastic habit, which in those days was nothing but a sheepskin, from a monk called Romanus, he buried himself in a cave at Subiaco, on the steep face of Monte Calvo, and there endured a three-year probation of silence, penance and prayer.

This was the type of monasticism which had arisen in the east in the third century. The accent was heavily laid on penance, which often reached exaggerated and unbalanced extremes. It was St Benedict's achievement to modify this system, and to evolve a form suitable to the west. Before long he was joined at Subiaco by postulants, some of them Goths, some of them nobles, who wished to share his way of life, and he built twelve little monasteries for them. St Gregory tells us that St Benedict left Subiaco owing to the persecution of an envious priest. Mark, a poet of the Carolingian period, says that he received a divine call to migrate to Cassinum. Be that as it may, at some date between 520 and 530 St Benedict set out from Subiaco with a few companions, reached Cassinum, climbed the mountain, destroyed the pagan temples he found on the summit, and established the world-famous abbey of Monte Cassino.

Here he settled down for the remainder of his life and wrote the *Rule,* the code which was to dominate western religious life for 600 years. It is a remarkable document, Roman in its strength and balance and in its sound practical detail; exquisitely charitable; fervent in faith. St Benedict laid his emphasis upon community life. He divided the monk's day between prayer, study and manual labour. He mitigated the austerities of the Egyptian desert, urging the abbot, whose rule was to be paternal and monarchic, 'so to temper all things that the strong may still have something to long after, and the weak may not draw back in alarm'. If no detail was too trivial to interest him – from the clothes and shoes of the brethren to their portions of food and drink – he could point the way to great spiritual heights, as in his *Prologue* and in his famous 72nd chapter *On Good Zeal.* The virtues he specially enjoined were those of obedience and humility, and he would not tolerate 'murmurers'.

St Benedict's own character stands revealed in every page of the *Rule.* Here is a man of natural Roman virtue, elevated and inspired by supernatural Christian faith. He knows how to govern; if necessary, how to punish. But his heart is filled with paternal love and compassions; love is the principle of the community life, and its purpose is 'that in all things God shall be glorified'. For St Benedict, God is to be found everywhere and in all things – in the abbot and brethren, in the guests and pilgrims, in the divine office which is the monk's principal duty, even in the spades and hoes which he uses for his field work. The *Rule* shows St Benedict's familiarity with Scripture and with the Fathers. There is a quotation or two from the Latin classics, but these may well have passed into proverbs in his day, their origin lost. He writes with touches of irony and kindly humor. If his feet are firmly planted on the way of the practical and the possible, his hand and his eye are raised constantly to the heights. He is above all, as St Gregory loves to call him, 'the man of God'.

Among the many miracles of which we read in the *Dialogue* is St Benedict's recognition of the disguised king Totila, and his prediction of the latter's subsequent career and of the date of his death. He prophesied too that Monte Cassino would be destroyed, but that his monks would escape alive. This prophecy came true about the year 590, when the monastery was sacked by the Lombards; again in 883, when it fell a prey to the Saracens; and a third time in 1943, when it was utterly destroyed by Allied bombs. The great Benedictine Order, too, has had its periods of decline and of revival, but it still stands throughout the world as the type of western monachism, justifying the claim asserted in the proper preface for its founder's mass that he is 'the guide and master of an innumerable multitude of sons'.

St Benedict was buried at Monte Cassino, in the same grave as his sister, St Scholastica. There is considerable controversy about his relics, which are said to have been removed to the abbey of Fleury-sur-Loire about the year 673, while Monte Cassino was still lying an empty ruin after its first destruction. The Monte Cassino tradition claims that the removal never took place, or that the relics were returned in the eighth century. St Benedict's feast occurs in the general calendar of the church on March 21st, but the Benedictine Order adds a second celebration on July 11th. This second feast was originally established to commemorate the translation of the saint's relics to France, but it is now only described liturgically as the Translation by the French Congregation. The rest of the Order knows it as the Solemnity. *March 21st*   ILLUSTRATION: facing page 64

BENEDICT or BENET BISCOP   † 690

St Benedict Biscop was a Northumbrian of good family who was born about the year 628. He therefore grew up amongst the first generation of Northumbrian Christians. He himself was a *gesith*, or warrior-companion of King Oswy of Northumbria, but, in 633, he abandoned his military career and set out for Rome on pilgrimage. He met and joined St Wilfrid at Canterbury, and they travelled to Lyons together. Benedict went on to Rome, and he returned to Northumbria a convinced supporter of the Roman obedience. After the Roman triumph at Whitby in 664, when the Northumbrian church conformed to Roman custom and law, Benedict made a second visit to Rome. He then became a monk at Lérins for some months, visited Rome again and escorted the new archbishop of Canterbury, Theodore of Tarsus, to England in 669. After a short spell as abbot of St Peter's, Canterbury, and another visit to Rome, Benedict returned to Northumbria, where he founded the great monasteries of Jarrow and Wearmouth. After further visits to Rome, Benedict amassed a remarkable collection of books for his monasteries, and the library he created at Wearmouth was to make Bede's great historical work possible. He built his abbey, moreover, in the Roman style then new to England, and he imported a Roman monk to take charge of the chant and ceremonial in his new monastery. Apart from his undoubted spirituality, he earned an eternal debt of gratitude by linking English art and culture with the mediterranean tradition.

January 12th

BENEDICT THE BLACK † 1589
The son of an African slave in Sicily, he was freed by his master and became a hermit. Later he joined the Observant branch of the Fransiscans, first serving as a cook, then as superior of the house of St Mary near Palermo. On his retirement he returned to the kitchen, saying that the greatest mortification was not to fast altogether but to eat a little and then stop.

He is the patron of the negroes of North America.

April 4th

BENEDICT THE HERMIT † 550
A hermit in the Campagna, mentioned by St Gregory the Great, he was shut into an oven when the Goths under Totila ravaged Italy, but miraculously survived.

March 23rd

BENEN, *see* Benignus.

BENET BISCOP, *see* Benedict Biscop.

BÉNEZET † 1184
During an eclipse, he heard a voice bidding him to build a bridge over the Rhône at Avignon. He convinced the bishop of Avignon, and work was begun in 1177. He was buried on the bridge itself, and his body – which remained incorrupt for several hundred years – was afterwards transferred to a specially constructed chapel on the bridge. He is the patron of Avignon.

April 14th

BENIGNUS of DIJON *Third Century?*
He is venerated at Dijon, although nothing was known about him until the discovery of his spurious *passio*, which has been shown to be one of a set of romances produced to account for the origins of the churches of Autun, Besançon, Langres and Valence.

November 1st

BENIGNUS or BENEN † 467
The son of an Irish chieftain and disciple of St Patrick, he became his successor as chief bishop of Ireland. He is given the credit for the evangelization of Clare and Kerry. One tradition asserts that he joined St Patrick in retirement at Glastonbury, but this is wholly unreliable.

November 9th

BENJAMIN *Fifth Century*
A deacon, he was martyred in fearful manner when Abdas, an unwise bishop, burnt a Persian temple and

caused King Yezdigerd to recommence the persecution of Christians.

March 31st

BENNO † 1106
He was deposed from the bishopric of Meissen by prelates subservient to the Emperor Henry IV, because he supported Pope Gregory VII. He regained his see three years later by submission to the anti-pope, but changed his allegiance to Urban II in 1097.

June 16th

BENVENUTO † 1282
Born at Ancona, he was appointed by Pope Alexander IV archdeacon of Ancona, a city which had supported Frederick II against the pope until Benvenuto reconciled it. Later he became bishop of Osimo, and governor of the Ancona Marches.

March 22nd

BERARD and his Companions † 1202
Five friars, SS Berard, Peter, Odo, Accursio and Adjutus, were sent by St Francis to the Mohammedans of the west. From Seville they went to Morocco, where the sultan, annoyed by their preaching, cut off their heads with his scimitar.

January 16th

BERCHARIUS † 696?
St Nivard recommended him for the priesthood and made him the first abbot of Hautvillers. St Bercharius himself established Montier-en-Der. He was murdered by a monk whom he had reproved and whom he freely forgave before dying.

October 16th

BERHTWALD † 1045
A monk of Glastonbury, this St Berthwald was the last bishop of Ramsbury in Wiltshire, the see being removed after his death to Old Sarum. Known in his lifetime for his visions and prophecies, he was buried in his own abbey of Glastonbury.

January 22nd

BERHTWALD of CANTERBURY † 731
Abbot of Reculver, archbishop of Canterbury for thirty-seven years (692–731) and a friend of St Aldhelm and St Boniface. A letter to Berhtwald from the bishop of London is the oldest letter extant from one Englishman to another.

January 9th

BERNADETTE SOUBIROUS 1844–1879
Bernadette Soubirous, the eldest of a large family, the poorest in Lourdes, was born on January 7th, 1844.

On February 11th, 1858 she set off with her sister Marie and a friend, Jeanne Abadie, to gather firewood from the common land by the banks of the river Gave. A delicate girl, she lagged several paces behind her companions, who had already waded across the cold waters of a shallow mill stream that separated them from the grotto of Massabielle. She was removing her shoes and stockings when she suddenly heard the roar of a great wind and felt it on her cheeks. Seeing the motionless poplars, she thought that she must be mistaken, and went on with her preparations to cross the stream. Once again she heard the rushing wind, and looking up she saw bathed in a bright light in a niche in the grotto, a girl no larger than herself. The girl was dressed in a pure white robe with a sky blue girdle knotted in the middle and reaching down to her feet, which were unshod, and which rested on golden roses. Over her head, and reaching to her shoulders, she wore a white veil. In her hands she clasped a rosary of white beads threaded on a golden chain.

Bernadette stuck to this description, but she was to disapprove of its sentimental rendering as a statue, which she called a caricature.

Bernadette went down on her knees, clutching her rosary. She tried to make a sign of the cross but trembled too much to raise her hand. Then, as the lady smiled and beckoned, Bernadette lost her fear, and recited the rosary as the lady let the beads run through her fingers. The rosary ended, she disappeared.

To Bernadette's astonishment the others had seen nothing, but her story carried conviction. She asked them to keep it a secret, but Marie told her mother, who scolded them both and forbade Bernadette the cave. After many entreaties, however, she relented, and two days later, after Sunday mass, they set out again; the first Lourdes pilgrims, four or five children armed with a bottle of holy water. The lady appeared, and the same thing happened. The following Thursday the children were accompanied by two adults. This time the Lady gave Bernadette a message; she wished her to be gracious enough to visit the grotto for fifteen days. She promised Bernadette that she would make her happy, but not in this world.

At the sixth appearance, on February 21st, Bernadette convinced the sceptic, Dr Dozous, the most prominent physician in Lourdes, who had come to investigate, that she was both sane and sincere. Dr Dozous became her champion, and later was the first doctor to look after the sick at Lourdes.

The matter had now spread far and wide and was causing grave concern to the town officials. Bernadette was bullied, cajoled and cross-examined, but stuck to her story.

It was at the ninth visitation that the spring appeared and with it the first of the miraculous cures.

The Church had been cautious from the start, resisting strong pressure from believers and anti-clericals. The Abbé Peyramale – 'a gruff bear of a man' – had for-

bidden his clergy to have anything to do with the grotto. When Bernadette brought him a message from the Lady asking for processions, he said bluntly that first he must know with whom he was dealing.

It was on March 25th at the sixteenth appearance – there were to be two more – that the Lady told Bernadette in the local patois, 'I am the Immaculate Conception.'

This message, not understood by Bernadette herself, and only recently proclaimed as a dogma, carried conviction. A commission was appointed by the bishop of Tarbes to examine the phenomena, and after four years of patient investigation, its finding was that 'the apparition which called herself the Immaculate Conception which Bernadette both saw and heard is none other than the most Holy Virgin.'

Bernadette was now so famous, that privacy became impossible. After an interval of two years spent in dealing with a daily stream of visitors, many of whom were merely curious, some even hostile, she went as a boarder to the Convent of the Sisters of Nevers. She remained there for eight years and finally entered the mother house where, on July 29th, 1866, she took the habit as Marie Bernard.

Lourdes and its continuing miracles have in a sense obscured the life of a remarkable saint. Her life was a hard one; in her own words, 'she was ground like a grain of corn'. The Reverend Mother and the Mistress of the Novices were strict to the point of harshness and took every opportunity to humiliate her. She suffered too from constant ill health, realizing that the healing spring was not for her. But she accepted everything, expressing her position with the homely phrase, 'The Virgin used me as a broom, to remove dust. When the work is done the broom is put behind the door and left'. After eight years, seven of which were spent as an assistant nurse in the infirmary, and the last of which was a true martyrdom –'the more pain I suffer, the more I shall unite myself with his heart' – she died on the Wednesday of Easter Week 1879 at the age of thirty-six. Her last words were, 'Holy Mary, Mother of God, pray for me a poor sinner.'

She was buried in the convent chapel at Nevers, where her body is exposed to full view. She was beatified in 1925, and canonized on December 8th, 1933.

April 16th   ILLUSTRATION: page 68

BERNARD of ABBEVILLE, *see* Bernard of Tiron.

BERNARD of CAPUA   † 1109
Chaplain to Duke Richard II, son of the prince of Capua, he was appointed bishop of Foro-Claudio. He moved the bishop's residence to Caleno where he built a new cathedral, transferring to it the relics of St Marcius, a local hermit.
March 12th

BERNARD of CLAIRVAUX 1090–1153

St Bernard of Clairvaux was born in the year 1090 at Fontaines-lès-Dijon, and he died sixty-three years later in his monastery at Clairvaux.

It is not very hard to find the lineaments of the grown man in the childhood of Bernard. Like many gifted and highly strung characters he suffered all his life from megrim, and one of the first things we know about him is that, when he was only a child, he drove from the room a local 'wise-woman' who had been called in to charm away his headache. He seems to have been a youth of uncommon good looks and intelligence; yet, if we may judge the child from what we know of the man, there could have been little of the prig about him. Nevertheless, when he was twenty-two years old, he chose to become a monk. This would have been nothing out of the ordinary in those days if he had elected to join one of the rich and powerful monasteries of Benedictine monks, where his gifts and the influence of his family would have assured for him a distinguished career; but he did nothing of the sort, instead he chose to enter an obscure house a few miles to the south of his home, that was known locally as the New Monastery or, for some reason that is not perfectly clear, Cîteaux.

This monastery had been founded some years previously by a group of enthusiasts who wanted to live quite simply according to the letter of St Benedict's Rule; but the place had not prospered, the life was austere, and the whole project was crumbling for lack of recruits. Naturally enough Bernard's family were horrified at his choice, they thought it madness for a delicate young man like Bernard to attempt such a life; but he ended by taking his uncle, all his brothers, and most of his friends with him. Altogether he led no less than about thirty young men to Cîteaux – all the gilded youth of his neighborhood. In his *Apologia* Bernard gives us the reason for this surprising choice of his when he implies that, much as he admired the usual Benedictine way of life, his own nature was so passionate that it needed stronger medicine, and nothing that we know of him contradicts this view that he had of himself.

This influx of new blood very soon infused Cîteaux with life; the fashion started by Bernard and his companions was presently followed by an ever-increasing number of young men. The Englishman St Stephen Harding was abbot at the time, and fortunately he was an administrator of genius as well as a saint and a scholar. Very soon he was sending out small groups of monks to found other monasteries on the same pattern as the mother house, and, within three years of his arrival, Bernard's turn came. He set out at the head of twelve other monks and chose, as the site for his new monastery, a valley not far from Bar-sur-Aube and adjoining the territory of his kinsmen. It was known as the Valley of Wormwood; soon it became even better known as the Valley of Light, or Clairvaux.

The first years of the new foundation were not easy, the community suffered every sort of privation, the monks went short of even the bare necessities, and Bernard himself fell ill. Clearly he had been driving both himself and his monks too hard; when he recovered sufficiently to take his place again as abbot, he had learned how to be gentle and tolerant with others if not with himself. By this time his fame had spread, men came from great distances to seek his help, and he was repeatedly being called in to arbitrate in disputes. This did not please everyone, for Bernard was no respecter of persons: he held strong views and did not fear to express them, his wit could be devastating, and he had little understanding of lesser men than himself or patience with their pettiness. Very soon he got a curt letter from Rome telling him to stay in his monastery and not meddle with what did not concern him. Nothing would have pleased him better than to stay in his monastery, but he felt the good of the church did concern him, and he was not afraid to write back a very spirited reply.

He was an ardent advocate of the Hildebrand reforms, but he thought the centralization of the church had gone far enough and, while staunchly upholding the prerogatives of the Holy See, he did not believe it necessary to flatter the Pope. But when the schism in the papacy threatened to shipwreck the church, and he was called out of his monastery again, he went forth with reluctance; but it was due to him that the anti-pope was defeated and the church was able to right herself. By this time he was known all over Europe, and the whole world seemed to turn to him for advice and help. When men could not visit him in person they wrote to him, and Bernard made a point of answering all his letters, even those from the most humble people. Only a part of his huge correspondence survives, but it is one of our chief sources for the history of the time, and, better still, it gives us a vivid impression of the writer, no etherial spirit but a man of flesh and blood like ourselves.

As the protagonist of the Cistercian reform he came into controversy with the Benedictine monks of the great congregation of Cluny (*see also* the Cluny Saints). He respected their way of life but could not condone the abuses prevalent in some houses of the order. Yet the abbot of Cluny, Peter the Venerable, remained one of his most loyal friends. Bernard's fierce opposition to Peter Abelard is well known. He objected to the novel theories of Abelard, but he objected even more strongly to the way he discussed sacred matters in the market place and to his bumptious behavior. The first thought of Bernard was always for the faith of simple people and in every controversy he was on the side of conservatism against novelties; but he was a friend of learning and a patron of scholars, notably of our own Robert Pullen and John of Salisbury.

During all this time Clairvaux had been growing and founding daughter houses all over Europe, so that it seemed that, under Bernard's influence, all the world was becoming Cisterian. Although one of the most busy men of his times, he did not neglect his monks; he remained all his life a monk and a mystic before all else and always found time to instruct his monks, as well as to compose his superb commentaries on the mystical meaning of the Song of Songs, besides several other theological and mystical treatises. But his declining years were saddened by the failure of the second Crusade. The pope imposed upon him the duty of preaching it and, at his words, all Europe sprang to arms; but it was always his weakness that he could not understand the base motives of lesser men than himself. As soon as they were away from his influence the Crusaders forgot the high ideals with which he had inspired them and ruined the expedition by fighting among themselves and by deeds unworthy of Christian men. Nevertheless this did not prevent them from blaming Bernard for the catastrophe they had brought upon themselves, so that, like many other saints and like Christ himself, he died, on August 20th in the year 1153, under the cloud of apparent failure.

After his death men realised that a prophet had passed from their midst, and all Europe mourned. Twenty-one years later Pope Alexander III canonized him, and his feast day is kept on the anniversary of his death. In the year 1830 he was formally accorded the title of 'doctor of the church'. He lived before the birth of Scholasticism, and, because his teaching is still in the main stream of the patristic tradition, he is often known as the last of the Fathers.   ILLUSTRATION: page 69
August 20th

BERNARD of MENTHON or MONTJOUX
Eleventh Century

An aura of enchanting legend surrounds the name of St Bernard of Menthon, but little is known about him. He lived in the eleventh century at Annecy and may have been the son of the count of Menthon, hence his traditional surname; but this view is questioned and he is now more frequently called St Bernard of Montjoux after a hospice established on Mons Jovis. According to his legend, he completed his education in Paris and returned home to find that his parents had arranged a suitable marriage for him; but this did not please him at all because he had set his heart on becoming a priest. He therefore fled from home, some say on the eve of his marriage, and took refuge with Peter, archdeacon of Aosta. Some time after his ordination he was appointed vicar general of the diocese by the bishop of Aosta and

devoted his life to visiting the remote Alpine valleys of the diocese – no small undertaking in those days – founding schools, and restoring clerical discipline. But he is best known for his love and care of pilgrims and travellers, and for the hospices he founded for them on the summits of the Great and Little St Bernard passes high up in the Alps. A charming story is told of how Bernard's parents discovered their long lost son when they took refuge in one of his hospices on their way to seek him in Italy. He entrusted the care of his two foundations to the Canons Regular of St Augustine, and the same order is there to this day.

Everyone has heard of the Great St Bernard dogs. These fine creatures were introduced by the canons long after the time of Bernard to assist in finding travellers who had lost themselves in the snow and ice on their way over the mountains. In the past the canons and their dogs have saved many lives, and they are deservedly renowned for their work of mercy, but nowadays, people do not attempt to cross these mountain passes during the winter: it is safer, more simple, and probably cheaper, to make the short journey by train. The dogs are still kept on, but they are no longer used to save lives. About eight canons live in their vast and austere hospice eight thousand feet up on the Great St Bernard pass. In winter they are completely snowbound, but when the passes are open, that is to say from June until October, they are much visited by tourists. Lately they have tried to open another hospice in the Himalayas for the benefit of travellers into Tibet. The date of Bernard's death is not certain, but is thought to have been in the year 1081. He was made the patron of all mountain climbers by Pius XI in 1923.
May 28th

BERNARD of PARMA   1055–1133

Renouncing the advantages of his noble Florentine birth to become a Vallombrosan monk, he was also remarkable for his refusal to insist upon the temporal claims of his see when he became bishop of Parma. He supported the reforms of Gregory VII, was exiled by one of the anti-popes which his diocese housed, and was made a cardinal whilst he was still abbot-general of his order.
December 4th

BERNARD of TIRON   † 1117

Sometimes known as St Bernard of Abbeville, he was recalled from his hermitage to become abbot of St Cyprian's, near Poitiers. He resigned after a quarrel with Cluny, and built a Benedictine monastery in the forest of Tiron.
April 14th

BERNARD or BARNARD   † 842

Born about 778 of distinguished family, he served under

Charlemagne, married, and founded the Ambronay monastery of which he later became abbot. In 810 he became archbishop of Vienne.

January 23rd

BERNARDINE of SIENA 1380-1444

This 'star of Tuscany' came of the noble Sienese family of the Albizeschi. Born at Massa Marittima, where his father was governor, on September 8th 1380, and left an orphan at six, he was brought up by his aunts. At school in Siena he was remarkable for intelligence and a general popularity in no way lessened by outstanding goodness and purity. When he was seventeen, he joined a Marian confraternity at the La Scala hospital and began a secluded spiritual life. Yet in 1400, he willingly emerged to become the successful organizer of the hospital services during a severe outbreak of the plague. Although he escaped infection, he fell ill through exhaustion and never entirely recovered.

In 1402 he joined the Franciscans, throwing in his lot with the 'Observant' reform-party. Their spectacular growth in the ensuing period owes much to his influence; for twelve years (1430–1442) he was to be their vicar general. His ordination in 1404 was followed by a dozen years hidden life, but the rest of his career is a record of indefatigable preaching journeys, usually afoot, all over Italy. He was the greatest popular preacher of his time, a worthy successor to St Vincent Ferrer, a true 'apostle of Italy'.

His habitual topics were the need of penance and denunciation of prevalent vices, especially civil and political strife, usury, gambling and 'vanity' in dress and social behaviour. He treated these worn themes in a fresh manner, using pregnant anecdotes and illustrations, holding vast crowds for hours and bringing about impressive conversions.

He will be remembered for his promotion of the cult of the Holy Name of Jesus, of Mary as dispenser of the graces merited by her divine Son, and of St Joseph. He was accustomed to preach holding a board on which were the first three letters of the Saviour's name in its Greek form – 'IHS' – surrounded by rays, and he persuaded people to copy these plaques and erect them over their dwellings and public buildings. His last sermons – on *Inspirations* – show him to have been a profound psychologist of the mystical way and a liberal-minded teacher of the theory of contemplative prayer.

He died, worn out with missionary labours, on May 20th, 1444, at Aquila in the Abruzzi, and was buried there. The miracles at his tomb induced Nicholas V to canonize him only six years later. In the Roman rite both mass and office on his feast day are taken from the Common of Confessors, but the Franciscans have a proper mass and office, including the hymn *Sidus Etruscis*

and a homily on apostolic poverty from one of his own sermons.

The preaching of St Bernardine, especially the *verbatim* versions of his popular sermons in Italian, still deserves attention in an age no longer much addicted to pulpit oratory. Modern readers will at least admire the rugged forthrightness, often earthiness, of his style. They will applaud his social awareness and the eminently practical methods he adopted to drive his lessons home and make them permanent. ILLUSTRATION: page 70

May 20th

BERNARDINO REALINO 1530-1616

Born in 1530 at Carpi, he was a lawyer before he became a Jesuit in Naples. He was later appointed rector of the college at Lecce in Apulia. Much interest was aroused after his death when it was found that blood drawn from his body continued to remain in a liquid state.

For a discussion of similar manifestations, see the articles on SS Januarius and Pantaleon.

July 3rd

BERNO of CLUNY † 927

See the Cluny Saints.

January 13th

BERNWARD † 1022

Ordained priest by St Willigis, he became chaplain and tutor to Otto III and then bishop of Hildesheim. He is known as a patron of the arts, and was possibly himself a craftsman in metals. His last years were troubled by a dispute with St Willigis over episcopal rights which was settled in Bernward's favor by the pope.

November 20th

BERTHA † c. 725

She is supposed to have been the widow of a nobleman, and to have retired to the convent she had founded at Blangy in Artois. Once the house was set in order she left her daughter Deotila in charge and lived as a solitary.

July 4th

BERTHA and RUPERT Ninth Century

Bertha's pagan husband was killed in battle when her son Rupert was an infant. She devoted herself to his education and, as he grew older, they provided for the poor and retired to hilly country later called Rupertsberg near Bingen in Germany, where Bertha outlived her son by twenty-five years.

May 15th

BERTHOLD Twelfth Century

According to legend he reformed crusaders in Antioch; but what is more certain is that he formed a community of hermits on Mount Carmel, and became the founder of the Carmelites.

March 29th

BERTILIA of MAREUIL *Eighth Century*
Born of noble family, on her husband's death she became a solitary at Mareuil in Arras, where she built a church.
January 3rd

BERTILLA † *c. 705*
Strictly trained at Jouarre, she was sent to establish the abbey at Chelles, endowed by St Bathildis, wife of Clovis II. Her rule gave the house such a reputation that Hereswitha, widow of the king of the East Angles, and St Bathildis herself both joined the community.
November 5th

BERTINUS *Seventh Century*
When St Omer became bishop of Thérouanne, SS Bertinus and Bertrand were sent from Luxeuil to help him. As a center for their missionary work, they built a monastery at Sithiu, of which Mommolinus and then Bertinus were abbots.
September 5th

BERTOUL or BERTULF *Eighth Century*
Born in Germany of pagan parents, he migrated to Flanders, became a Christian, and was made steward and heir to Count Wambert. On the Count's estates at Renty, he built a monastery to which he retired.
February 5th

BERTRAND of COMMINGES † 1123
He became bishop of Comminges in about 1075 and ruled his see, now a part of the Toulouse diocese, for fifty years with a zeal and strictness which sometimes made him unpopular.
October 16th

BERTRAND of LE MANS † 623
Ordained by St Germanus at Paris, he became bishop of Le Mans in 587. He was often in exile through political troubles, but was reinstated by King Clotaire in 605.
June 30th

BERTULF, *see* Bertoul.

BERTULF † 640
Converted to Christianity by his kinsman St Arnoul of Metz, he entered the monastery of Luxeuil but moved with St Attalas to Bobbio, where he succeeded him as abbot. He was the first abbot to have immunity from episcopal control confirmed by the pope.
August 19th

BESAS, CRONION and JULIAN, † 250
Under the persecution of Decius in Alexandria, Julian, a man disabled by gout, and his bearer Cronion, confessed their Christianity and were publicly burned. For protesting against this, Besas, a soldier, was beheaded.
February 27th

BESSARION *Fourth Century*
A wanderer in the Egyptian wilderness, he may have been the disciple of St Antony and St Macarius.
June 17th

BETTELIN *Eighth Century*
According to an unreliable historian, he lived with St Guthlac at Croyland, and was so envious of his master's reputation that once when he was shaving him he was tempted to cut his throat. Overcoming the temptation, he later became St Guthlac's favorite disciple. He must not be confused with Bettelin, the legendary patron of Stafford.
September 9th

BEUNO † *c. 642*
One of the greatest of the saints of Wales, St Beuno probably died in 642 on April 21st, which became his feast day. Wonder-worker and aristocrat, monk and master of monks, patriot, challenger of tyrants: that was the medieval picture of the man which is reflected in his Life, and which survives, carved in stone on the fourteenth-century pulpit of the Black Monks of Shrewsbury. He looks out a trifle sternly across what used to be the refectory and is now a goods-yard.

Round such a man legend necessarily gathered. It was his custom, we are told, to preach each Sunday at Llanddwyn, walking over the water as if on dry land from his monastery at Clynnog, with his staff and his book of sermons. One Sunday, however, he dropped his book, which was swept away by the waves. The saint reached the shore in as much of a bad temper as is possible for a saint, only to find the precious volume, safe and sound, on a large stone with its rescuer, the pious curlew, standing guard. The saint blessed the creature; and that is why it is so peculiarly difficult to find the curlew's nest.

To what extent is it possible for the historian to penetrate behind the medieval reflection to the seventh-century saint, behind the fourteenth-century monk, carved on the pulpit, to the primitive six-foot monolith, Maen Beuno, his preaching-stone, which still stands by the Severn at Aber-rhiw? Dr Nash-Williams has established that there were considerable Gallo-Roman Christian settlements in North Wales. Later, it appears, these became active centers of Welsh monastic Catholicism. The monastic foundations of north Wales differed from those of the south in that they had no scholastic tradition, and their founders were not indigenous saints as were Dyfrig and Illtud. The single exception would appear to be St Beuno; and he, according to tradition, had to go to south-east Wales for his monastic formation. As Professor Bowen suggests in his book *The Settlements of the Celtic Saints in Wales* (University of Wales Press, 1954), the conclusion would appear to be that St Beuno was the leader of a mission from Powys by way of north-east into north-west Wales; that he played the same part there as did St David in the south; and that, at a time when the first wave of barbarian invasion was sweeping up to the eastern borderlands, he established Catholicism in a framework of monastic settlements. In so doing, he systematically made choice of places which in the past had been centers of Gallo-Roman settlement, and which were linked together by Roman roads. The distribution of church dedications to those saints whom tradition represents as his disciples follows the same pattern and reinforces the same conclusion. The tradition of his high lineage fits exactly into this picture. In the circumstances of Welsh society in the seventh century only a man of princely family could have made the number of foundations which bear his name.

As late as the early nineteenth century, sick men were still being brought from great distances across the mountains to be laid, in hope of a cure, on the tomb of this founding-father of his nation.

As he lay dying, tradition says that he saw heaven opened and the Trinity in Unity. 'And I see seven angels standing before the throne of the most high Father, and all the fathers of heaven singing their songs, and saying: "Blessed is he whom Thou hast chosen, and taken, and who does for ever dwell with Thee".'
April 21st

BEUZEC, *see* Budoc.

BIBIANA or VIVIANA
According to the untrustworthy source of her notice in the Roman Martyrology, she suffered under Julian the Apostate.
December 2nd

BILFRED, *see* Balred and Bilfred.

BIRINUS † *c.* 650
A Roman missionary, he arrived in England in 634, intending to evangelise the Midlands, but he found that the West Saxons had relapsed, and, assisted by St Oswald, king of Northumbria, he baptised Cynegils, king of the West Saxons. He was given Dorchester (Oxfordshire) for his see.
December 5th

BLAISE † 316?
One of the Fourteen Holy Helpers, St Blaise is held in great honor in France and Germany. He was said to be bishop of Sebaste and to have been martyred in the persecution of Licinius. His legend tells us that his powers of healing extended to animals, that hunters who had come out into the mountains to seek wild beasts for the amphitheater were amazed to see them clustered around the saint, and that on another occasion he cured a boy who was suffocating because a fish-bone had stuck in his throat.

St Blaise is the patron of wild animals and wool-combers and of sufferers from afflictions of the throat. *See also* The Fourteen Holy Helpers.
February 3rd ILLUSTRATION: page 71

BLANDINA † 177
St Blandina was one of the martyrs who suffered with St Pothinus and many others at Lyons during the persecutions there in 177. According to the account written from the churches of Lyons and Vienne to the churches of Asia and Phrygia, Blandina, a slave, was first tortured until her persecutors pronounced themselves weary, and then taken into the amphiteater with her companions, Maturus, Sanctus and Attalus to be attacked by wild beasts and in other ways tormented. She was hung up on a kind of cross to be the prey for the animals, but as none of them would touch her she was for a time returned to prison. She and Ponticus, a boy of fifteen, were taken daily to the arena to see the sufferings of their fellows, but nothing could move them; and at last the boy was put to death, having been supported always by the encouragement of Blandina. On the same day Blandina herself was tied up in a net and thrown to a bull: 'She was herself offered up, the very heathen confessing that they had never known a woman endure so many and so great sufferings'.
June 2nd

BLANE † *c.* 590
According to his untrustworthy legend, he returned to his birthplace in Bute after having studied for seven years in Ireland under SS Comgall and Canice. He was ordained by St Cathan, his uncle, became a bishop and died at Kingarth in Bute. Dunblane Cathedral was built on the site of his monastery.
August 11th

BLESILLA † 383
Daughter of St Paula. When her husband died, she devoted the rest of her twenty years to austere piety. At her request, St Jerome began to translate the book of Ecclesiastes.
January 22nd

BODO, *see* Salaberga and Bodo.

BOETHIUS, *see* Severinus Boethius.

BOGUMILUS † 1182
One of twin sons of noble parents, he was educated at Paris and became priest of the church he himself built at Dobrow. In 1167, he succeeded his uncle as archbishop of Gniezo, but failed as a ruler and became a hermit.
June 10th

BOISIL or BOSWELL † 664

He succeeded St Eata as abbot of Melrose on the Tweed. His famous prophecies included one of his own death during the great plague of 664. St Cuthbert was trained by him.

February 23rd

BONAVENTURE 1221–1274

The baptismal name of St Bonaventure, the 'Seraphic Doctor', was Giovanni. He was the son of Giovanni di Fidanza and Ritella, born at Bagnorea near Viterbo in 1221. As a young man he joined the Roman Province of the Franciscans and was sent to complete his education at Paris University. Here he studied under Alexander of Hales, the English scholar who joined the friars and laid the foundations of the Franciscan school of philosophy and theology. Both as student and later as teacher in Paris, Bonaventure had St Thomas Aquinas as his colleague and friend. They were associated in a defence of their respective Orders and the whole Mendicant version of the religious life against the attacks of the secular master William of St Amour.

In 1257, despite his youth, Bonaventure was elected as minister general of the whole Franciscan Order, an exacting position which he filled for sixteen years almost till his death. The situation he had to face was delicate; the Order was internally divided between the *Spirituales* or zealots for the literal observance of the Rule, and the *Relaxati* who desired mitigations. It is a tribute to his holiness as well as his abilities that he solved this problem so well as to merit the title of 'Second Founder' of the Friars Minor. At the general chapter at Narbonne in 1260 he gave the Order its first constitutions, and he was untiring in his visitation of the different provinces to see that this legislation was being put into practice. It was he also who organised the studies of clerics in the Order and so made possible the wide apostolate of both learned and popular preaching which we have come to associate with the best of the medieval friars. He himself was a much sought-after preacher to clerical and lay congregations, to regulars and seculars, to the learned and to the simple. Nonetheless he managed all the time to pour forth a series of writings bearing on Franciscan history and spirituality, as well as more general treatises on philosophy, theology and scripture which were the outcome of his Paris professorship. Amongst them we may signalize his Commentary on the Franciscan Rule, his biography of St Francis (a peace-making rather than a critical essay) and the celebrated *Itinerarium mentis in Deum* (*Journey of the Soul to God*) written in 1259 at La Verna, where St Francis had been stigmatized just thirty-five years previously.

The early controversy with William of St Amour was only the first phase in a long struggle to get the Franciscan

ideal accepted in all contemporary circles. We find St Bonaventure upholding the same cause later on against Gerard of Abbeville, and in the council of Lyons. He had also to curb the excesses of those of his brethren who followed the prophetic notions of the Calabrian Cistercian, Joachim of Flora, and looked for the establishment of an apocalyptic 'eternal gospel' of which the 'Spiritual' Franciscans would be the natural heralds. Again, on a wider plane, we see him helping to resist the rise of 'Latin Averroism' (*see* St Thomas Aquinas) in the philosophical arena at Paris.

It is, however, as a saint and as one of the greatest of mystical theologians, that he was prized by contemporaries and is still studied by the enlightened. Everyone was impressed by his authentically Franciscan devotion towards the Passion of our Saviour; amongst his works is to be found an office of the Passion which he composed for the personal use of the saintly King Louis IX. Bonaventure was the first to give the mystical movement inaugurated by St Francis of Assisi a solid theological and psychological basis. His spiritual teaching, like his whole system of thought, centers about Christ. In him the tender affective love of Francis for the humanity of Christ is united with the traditional Augustinian theology (rather than the newer Dominican Aristotelianism), and there is, in consequence, a stress on love and the part played by will rather than on knowledge and the part played by intellect. He did not hesitate to teach that an idiot might love God as well as the most learned divine. For him the Incarnation and Redemption are the crowning glory of God's work for man, the supreme purpose of all creation and therefore, necessarily, the focus of all spiritual life. The practical goal of spiritual endeavour for all, according to Bonaventurian teaching, is a lofty contemplative prayer, union with the divine wisdom. This attitude is to be discovered in all that he wrote, but as an example of its explicit statement we may point to the much commented *De triplici via* (*The Threefold Way*), a miniature but nevertheless complete *summa* of medieval mystical doctrine.

His solid, even obstinate, humility enabled him to evade, in 1265, the burdens of the archbishopric of York to which he was appointed by Pope Clement IV, but it proved unavailing eight years later when Pope Gregory X compelled him to accept the see of Albano and made him a Cardinal. It is related that when the legates arrived with the red hat they found that the saint was doing the washing-up. He asked them to hang the hat on the branch of a tree until he had finished. The last months of his life were passed in close association with the Pontiff in preparing for a forthcoming. Ecumenical council by means of which it was hoped to re-unite Greeks and Latins. When the council met at Lyons St Bonaventure was its moving spirit until his premature death on July 14th, 1274.

Although he had been an almost universal object of veneration during life, for his saintliness and for his repute as miracle-worker, the process of his canonization was, owing to the unfortunate dissensions within his own Order, unduly deferred. The great popular esteem in which he was held may be gauged with fair accuracy from the prominent part assigned to him by Dante in *Paradiso*, XII, 127ff, where his disinterested spiritual outlook, even when holding high ecclesiastical office, fits him both to relate the story of St Dominic and to criticize some of his relaxed followers. The popular cult of St Bonaventure was greatly enhanced in 1434 when his remains were translated and his head found incorrupt. But it was still not until 1482 that he was canonized by pope Sixtus IV. His tomb was plundered by the Huguenots, but the head was safely hidden, only to disappear finally in the troubles of the French Revolution. In 1588 pope Sixtus V pronounced him a doctor of the universal church.   ILLUSTRATION: facing page 81

July 14th

BONET or BONITUS   † 706

Chancellor to St Sigebert III of Austrasia, and governor of Marseilles, he succeeded his brother St Avitus II as bishop of Clermont, but doubting the legitimacy of his election, retired to the abbey of Manglieu.

January 15th

BONIFACE   675–754

St Boniface was originally called Wynfrid. He was a West Saxon, born near Exeter, traditionally at Crediton, in 675. He was brought up from childhood in the Benedictine monasteries of Exeter and Nursling, where he was subjected to the influence of the West Saxon monastic culture stemming from St Aldhelm. By 717 Wynfrid was an outstanding West Saxon cleric, and he was asked to accept election as abbot of Nursling, but he had already decided to join the Anglo-Saxon mission; and, in 718, he left for Frisia. He retained the greatest interest in English affairs for the rest of his life, he had many English correspondents, but he never visited England again. Naturally Wynfrid went first to Willibrord in Frisia, and, not surprisingly, he began his missionary career as Willibrord had begun his, with a visit to Rome for a papal commission. This he got, together with his new name, Boniface – after the Roman martyr whose feast fell on the eve of the day on which the commission was granted. In 722, after another visit to Rome, Boniface was consecrated bishop, and for the first time a bishop from a distant see followed local Italian practice and made a personal profession of obedience to the pope.

Boniface would not stay in Frisia and work under Willibrord, he preferred to open up new territory in western Germany. He began at Hesse in Thuringia, where he felled the sacred oak of Donar. His courage in doing this has often been justly commended, but it is unlikely that Boniface had much to fear from incensed pagans, since Carolingian arms were near at hand. Preaching and baptism were not the whole of the missionaries' task. It was also necessary to provide for the recruitment and education of a native clergy. Under contemporary conditions this meant the planting of monasteries and the mingling within the new communities of newly converted monks and monks from older established monasteries elsewhere.

Willibrord had already founded Echternach in Luxembourg, and Boniface founded many more, of which Fulda is the best known. Through these foundations, not only was the Rule of St Benedict established in some very dark places, but the remarkable tradition of thought and letters summed up in the work of Bede was also taken to circles far wider than those for which it was originally intended. We can trace a direct connection through these new monasteries between the culture of Bede and Aldhelm and that of the Carolingian renaissance: in many ways the Anglo-Saxon missionaries were the Carolingian renaissance.

Boniface was responsible for organizing the West German church, and he was the first occupant of two new sees, Cologne and Mainz. He was also given the task of reforming the Frankish church, and one consequence of his reforms was the arrangement of the Frankish sees into provinces whose metropolitan archbishops were for the first time placed in direct and necessary contact with the Roman see. In 751 the Pope authorized and encouraged Pepin to depose the last Merovingian puppet king of the Franks, and Boniface himself anointed Pepin as king: a ceremony from which all later royal coronations take their origin. But in spite of the political importance of his work and its ecclesiastical consequences, Boniface was no politician. He never showed much political understanding or tact, and he roused a good deal of perfectly well-intentioned opposition. He was always the missionary, the reformer, the enthusiast, and it was a fitting climax to his life that, in 754, he should lose it – an old man murdered by pagans when he was about to administer the sacrament of confirmation to his last converts.

June 5th   ILLUSTRATION: page 72

BONIFACE, *see* Bruno.

BONIFACE I   † 422

An old man when elected to the papacy, he had to overcome the supporters of the anti-pope Eulalius before he could take office. He supported St Augustine in the struggle against Pelagianism.

September 4th

BONIFACE IV † 615

As pope, he converted the Pantheon into a Christian church now known as Santa Maria Rotonda. He was the recipient of the famous letter from St Columbanus criticising the doctrinal attitude of the papacy.

May 8th

BONIFACE of LAUSANNE † 1260

Born in Brussels, he was a famous Paris lecturer who, two years after disputes had driven him to Cologne, became bishop of Lausanne. Zealous but disastrously tactless, after eight years he retired to the La Cambre nunnery in Brussels.

February 19th

BONIFACE of TARSUS † 306?

Boniface is said to have been the steward of a beautiful young Roman lady called Aglaë, who sent him to the East to fetch some relics of martyrs. Suddenly converted from an immoral life by his mission, he himself courted martyrdom and perished at Tarsus in Cilicia.

May 14th

BONITUS, *see* Bonet.

BONOSUS and MAXIMIAN † 363

Two army officers stationed at Antioch, they were executed for refusing to revert to pagan practices under an edict of Julian the Apostate. The story is, however, doubtful.

August 21st

BORIS and GLEB † 1015

Sons of St Vladimir of Kiev, they were deprived of their patrimony by their elder brother, Svyatopolk. Though both had the ability and the forces to resist, they forebore to do so on conscientious grounds, and were killed by their brother's hirelings.   ILLUSTRATION: page 73

July 24th

BOSA † 705

A monk of Whitby, he was appointed bishop of Deira after St Wilfrid had been banished by King Egfrid and the York diocese divided. St Acca was among his pupils.

March 9th

BOSWELL, *see* Boisil.

BOTULF or BOTOLPH *Seventh Century*

He returned to England after being educated abroad with his brother Adulf and built a monastery at Boston (i.e. 'Botulf's stone'). Seventy English churches are named after him.

June 17th

BOTVID † 1100

Of Swedish birth, he was converted in England and returned to Sweden as a missionary. He was murdered by a Finnish slave whom he had baptized and freed.

July 28th

BRAULIO † 651

A most celebrated saint, patron of Aragon. After studying at Seville under St Isidore, he succeeded his brother John as bishop of Saragossa, and was renowned as pastor, scholar and writer.

March 26th

BRENDAN *c. 484–c. 577*

Although little of St Brendan's history can be affirmed with certainty, his name is possibly the most widely known of all the Irish saints. Centuries after the golden age of missionary expansion had become only a memory, it was chiefly through him that Ireland was known to the world. He was born near Tralee, in Kerry, probably in the year 484. According to the ancient Irish custom of fosterage, he was placed as an infant in the care of St Ita, who reared him until he was six. Later he was sent to St Jarlath's monastic school in Tuam, and he was finally ordained priest by Bishop Erc.

Like his master, Jarlath, he became a founder of monasteries. When he had established a number of settlements in Kerry, he sailed up the Shannon to found a monastery at Clonfert in Galway. This became a great founthead of missionary enterprise for hundreds of years. St Senan, from his point of vantage on Scattery Island at the mouth of the river, counted in one day seven ships, all crowded with overseas students, sailing up the Shannon for Clonfert. This once populous venue is today a bosky solitude, loud with bird-song, hidden in a maze of leafy side roads. All that now remains of its former splendor is a superb twelfth-century Hiberno-Romanesque doorway.

The most spectacular event in Brendan's life was his expedition with sixty chosen companions to discover the legendary Island of the Blessed. They sailed the Atlantic ocean in two hide-covered coracles, taking with them sufficient provisions for a month's journey. All the rules of the monastic life were strictly observed on board. There may even have been two such voyages. The monks came back with tales of incredible adventures and their odyssey became one of the most popular Christian sagas first in Ireland and, later, all over Europe.

While on a visit to a convent at Annaghdown where his sister, Briga, was abbess, the great navigator-saint became ill. It was about the year 577, and he was over ninety. The last conversation between brother and sister strikes a very human chord. Knowing that it was the end, he asked her to help him with her prayers. She not unreasonably said:

'What have *you* to fear?'

'I am afraid of the loneliness,' he told her, 'on this dark journey to the unknown land. I fear the presence of the King and the sentence of the Judge.'

St Brendan's feast day is on May 16th. He is then

particularly invoked by the people of his homeland who live in the numerous places commemorating his name, such as Brandon Well, Brandon Point, Brandon Bay and Brandon Headland. But his traditional 'pattern day' is June 29th, when a romantic pilgrimage takes place in his honor to the summit of Mount Brandon, 3,127 feet high. Prayers are said on the climb at cairns marking the ancient route. The habitual silence of the heights is broken that day by the crowds assisting at Mass in the ruined primitive oratory where Brendan is said to have planned his voyages. Very fittingly it is, while standing in awe before the tremendous vista of sky and ocean which so powerfully allured him, that his twentieth-century devotees salute his memory.

The oldest version now extant of the *Navigatio Brendani* is said to have been written in the early part of the tenth century, but scholars are agreed that it is a ninth century composition, written in Ireland by an Irishman. All the great medieval libraries of Europe vied in their possession of manuscript versions of the heroic tale, in prose and verse, in Latin, Irish, French, Saxon, English, Flemish, Welsh and Breton. Although so largely embellished by fancy, by common assent it was rated excellent entertainment. It gave a new impulse to the literature of allegory. Even Dante is reputed to have drawn from this source for some of the episodes in his *Commedia*. The unknown author of the *Navigatio* was certainly a genius, because in the guise of a heroic saga of the sea, he succeeded in painting a most careful and accurate picture of the ideal monastic life.

Incredible as it sounds today, geographers accepted without question the reality of Brendan's island. Century after century it continued to be marked on ancient maps in varying positions to the west of Ireland. It was a particularly fixed idea of the Spanish and Portuguese cartographers, who caused several official expeditions to be fitted out for its rediscovery. Only about the middle of the eighteenth century was belief in its existence finally abandoned.

May 16th

BRICE or BRITIUS † 444

Formerly a monk of St Martin's monastery, Brice preferred the life of a worldly secular priest, immaculately dressed, the owner of many slaves and a stable of horses. He became leader of the opposition to Martin. He insulted him in public, jeering at his 'empty superstitions, imagined visions and ridiculous ravings'. If he begged his bishop's pardon, he did it with little sincerity, for he continued his opposition. When a sick man, hoping for a cure, asked for Martin, Brice replied: 'If you are in search of that maniac, look over there. As usual he's gazing up at the sky like a lunatic'. Martin bore with him patiently. 'Since Christ,' he said, 'put up

with Judas, why should I not put up with Brice?' He is even said to have foretold that Brice would be his successor, although this may not perhaps have been prophecy but a shrewd estimate of the state of opinion among the future electors.

Brice did in fact succeed Martin in 397. According to St Gregory of Tours he vindicated himself from a charge of fathering his washerwoman's child by walking unscathed over burning coals; but his flock, it is certain, were unconvinced of his innocence, and they deposed and expelled him. He went to Rome, where Pope Zozimus pronounced him innocent. The Pope, however, conducted no local inquiry; he was no doubt prejudiced against rebellious diocesans, and took no steps to deprive Brice's successor of his see. Our verdict surely must be not proven rather than not guilty.

After seven years' exile and the death of two bishops, Brice returned to Tours and his episcopal office. His latter years at any rate must have been edifying, for he was awarded the honors of sanctity, and, in medieval western calendars, his feast followed two days after Martin's. The Dominicans still give him a memorial on November 14th.

November 13th

BRIDGET of SWEDEN 1303–1373

St Bridget (sometimes called Birgitta) was born about the year 1305 (by tradition on June 14th) in Upland, the chief province of Sweden, where her father, Birger, was governor. Her mother, Lady Ingeborg of Finsta, was a daughter of the governor of East Gothland. When only seven Bridget had a vision in which our Lady placed a crown on her head, and when ten, after a sermon on the Passion, she saw in a dream Christ wounded and bleeding. These two experiences seem to have been the formative ones of her life.

Her mother died in 1314, and she lived with an aunt until, in 1316, obediently but against her inclination, she married Ulf Gudmarsson. They had four boys and four girls. Two of the boys died young; Karl, the eldest, was worldly but devoted to our Lady; Birger, the second, though married, later became his mother's companion and brought her body home to Sweden from Rome to be buried. Three of the girls married: Merita and Cecilia staying in Swedish society, while Catherine lost her husband and lived with her mother; the fourth, Ingebord, became a Cistercian.

Twenty-eight years after their marriage, Ulf died and Bridget went to live the penitential life she longed for near the Cistercian monastery at Alvastra. While there, she planned the Rule and Office of the order she was called to found but which she never saw in existence. After two years, in 1344, she went to Rome, where she died on July 23rd, 1373. Her canonization took place only eighteen years later, on October 7th, 1391.

St Bridget had the gift of prophecy and worked many marvellous cures. Once widowed, she lived an ascetic life, eating very little, sleeping short hours, and praying continually. She followed a strict rule and practiced every possible kind of charitable work, even reducing herself to begging. She received constant inspirations which were either taken down by her chaplain and put into Latin, thus becoming known as her 'Revelations', or took the form of letters to the succeeding popes, cardinals, and secular rulers of the day, telling them of their wickedness and how to reform their lives. Both in Sweden and in Rome she was either hated violently or loved as a saint. 'Strong and full of courage,' she was 'homely and kind and had a laughing face.'

The Bridgettine order of nuns no longer has monks attached to it. There are twelve convents at the present time, Syon Abbey in Devonshire being the only religious house in England to have unbroken organic continuity since before the Reformation. All Bridgettines pray for the restoration of the mother house at Vadstena in Sweden, which really started after St Bridget's death but with her daughter, St Catherine of Sweden, as first abbess. It was under the patronage of the bishop who had once been tutor to her sons, a circumstance she foretold years before. The Bridgettines cultivate a special devotion to our Lady and to the Passion of Christ, thus stemming naturally from the childhood visions and the whole life of their foundress.   ILLUSTRATION: page 74
October 8th

BRIEUC, *see* Brioc.

BRIGID, *see* Maura and Brigid.

BRIGID or BRIDE   *Fifth Century*
St Brigid flourished in the second half of the fifth century, and was probably born near Faughart, two miles from Dundalk in the county Louth. The accepted traditional account is that she was the daughter of a pagan chieftain named Dubthach and that her mother, Brocessa, was a Christian bondwoman in his household. St Patrick in his brief *Confession* makes a troubled mention of Christian slave women. Their plight was on his mind. If, as in Brocessa's case, their master happened to be a pagan, they were denied Christian rights and the practice of their religion became – as he says – extremely difficult.

Nevertheless Brigid was brought up a Christian and became a nun as soon as she was allowed to determine her future. She was not among the first to take this step. Again in his *Confession*, St Patrick says that the number who did so surprised him. They remained in their own homes, helping the church and striving as best they could to live a dedicated life, often even in pagan house-holds. They were not organized in any way. Brigid was the pioneer of Irish feminine monasticism in that she was the innovator of community life for women. She rallied together both bondwomen and free in adequately protected communities up and down the land. Of all her settlements, the greatest, the best known and the most enduring in fame was Kildare, a double monastery for monks and nuns under the joint rule of an abbot-bishop and an abbess.

It is the fashion to decry the Brigidine legends for their naïve credulity, contradictions and *lacunae*. Nevertheless, however disappointing in factual detail, they are to be prized for their delineation of a strongly defined character, familiarly Irish. They are consistent in depicting Brigid as generous and gay, vehement and energetic.

Her compassion for the poor was the cause of trouble at home while she was still a child. She would hand out to them valuable articles of attire, or perhaps a flitch of bacon, or a sheep from the flock, or even her father's valuable sword. In later life her friends were to protest about the same trait. One of them once brought her a basket of choice apples, and then had to stand by and watch her distribute them amongst the crowd of sick poor who seem to hover in the background of every legend:

'They were for you, not for them,' said her friend.

'What is mine is theirs.'

Even her community complained about her habit of converting every little treasure given to the convent into food, or comforts, for the poor. But she loved gaiety and music too, and delighted in showing hospitality to friends who were not in need. Her warmth of heart expressed itself in prodigality.

She was not hesitant to 'use anger', which is not the same as losing one's temper. Once she took two of her sisters on a long journey to a friendly monastery where she meant to beg for a loan of corn to tide her community over a famine period. On arrival, they were regaled with a meal of bread and bacon, even though it was Lent, when normally all the religious of the Celtic Church abstained from meat. Under the special circumstances, Brigid began to eat the bacon, but her companions refrained. When she noticed this, she sprang up, seized them by the shoulders and put them out of the room.

She was immensely energetic. Her work as foundress carried her over large areas of Ireland; and she usually travelled in the heavily built chariots of the time, on roads that were mere tracks. Numerous legends deal with her adventures on such journeys. Once she was thrown from the car and cut her head on a stone. Once the horse bolted and came to a halt only at the edge of a precipice.

She belonged to a race whose way of life was agricultural, and she is always shown busy at rural pursuits. When St Brendan went to visit her 'she came from her sheep' to welcome him; she took her place with the reapers in the cornfields; she was a butter-maker; she was renowned for her home-brewed ale. She had the same love of nature and power over the animal kingdom displayed by all the Celtic saints: the wild duck came to her at her call; she tamed a young fox and a wild boar.

She is supposed to have lived to about the age of seventy and to have been buried in Downpatrick in the same grave as Patrick and Columcille. Her head is said to have been taken to Portugal late in the thirteenth century by three Irish knights who were going to join a crusade to the Holy Land. But they left their treasure in the parish church of Lumiar, three miles outside Lisbon. A tablet set into the wall of the church records the event. It is a twelfth century church and contains a chapel dedicated to St Brigid, containing a statue of her, dressed in white. Portions of this relic were brought back from Lumiar in 1929 for veneration in a new church of St Brigid in Dublin.

Her feast is celebrated on February 1st and, in addition to Ireland, it is observed in northern Italy where her cult is surprisingly strong; in parts of France, particularly Brittany; in Portugal; as also in Wales, Australia and New Zealand.

Her cultus appears to have taken over certain features of the pagan worship of a namesake Brigid, the goddess of fire, notably the perpetual fire kept alight for many centuries at her abbey of Kildare.

February 1st   ILLUSTRATION: page 75

BRIOC or BRIEUC   *Sixth Century*

St Brioc is most famous in Brittany. He is said to have built a monastery near Tréguier and another one at the present Saint-Brieuc; in this latter place, having reached the age of one hundred, he died. His relics were preserved there until the middle of the ninth century, but the attacks of the Normans caused them to be sent for safety's sake inland to Angers. However, in 1210 a portion of these relics was returned amid great rejoicing, and these are still in the cathedral of Saint-Brieuc. The bishopric of Saint-Brieuc was not founded directly by the saint, but it was his monastery which became the seat of that see. His name is found in other places in Brittany, and also in Cornwall and in Wales, and it seems probable that he was one of the many Celtic travelling missionary bishops.

The medieval *Life* of Brioc tells us that he was born of pagan parents in a neighborhood identified as Cardiganshire, and was sent to France to be educated, where he became a Christian and was ordained. He returned to his home and converted his parents, but went back to Brittany with many companions and founded his first monastery. Later he paid another visit to his home, when he came to the aid of his country people in a time of pestilence. But he returned once again to Brittany, where he settled for the rest of his life, in his second monastery, at what is now Saint-Brieuc. *May 1st*

BRITIUS, *see* Brice.

BROCARD   † *c.* 1231

He succeeded St Berthold as head of the Frankish hermits on Mount Carmel, and he obtained from the papal legate, St Albert of Jerusalem, the first body of rules for the Carmelite Order. *September 2nd*

BRUNO   *c.* 1035–1101

Bruno the Carthusian was born about the year 1035 at Cologne in Germany, and he died in Calabria, in the south of Italy, in the year 1101. Very little is known of Bruno's early life, but it is plausibly conjectured that he came of the noble der Hautenfaust family and was educated at the school of St Cunibert in the town of his birth. He then seems to have left Cologne to study humanities at Rheims, and he may have gone on from there to study philosophy at Tours. We next hear of him as head of the schools of Rheims, chancellor of the diocese, and canon of the metropolitan see. He was undoubtedly one of the most learned men of his day, and young men of parts came to Rheims in order to sit under him, amongst whom were Odo of Châtillon, who afterwards became Pope Urban II, and several others who were to make their mark in the world. His commentaries on the psalms, and the epistles of St Paul, which are the only writings of his that have come down to us, are perhaps more notable for solid scholarship than for any great depth or originality of thought, but it is clear from them that he had some knowledge of Greek and Hebrew – a rather rare accomplishment in those days.

Troubles began for him with the death of Archbishop Gervase in 1068 and the appointment of Manasses. Manasses was a gentleman of rather unsavoury and violent habits, who had obtained the see of Rheims by simony. Bruno, at the head of a few other canons, opposed him and appealed to Rome; Manasses retaliated by confiscating their property and forcing them to fly the city. Bruno took refuge at a place called Le Rocher, in the house of a friend called Adam. One day while he was walking in the garden of Adam's house with two friends, Ralph and Fulcius, the conversation turned on the deceitful nature of the world's pleasures and the joys of contemplation. Carried away by their topic they felt their hearts burn within them and thereupon decided that at the first opportunity they would leave the world and devote themselves to a life of prayer. But nothing could be done at the moment, for Fulcius had to go to Rome in order to put before the pope the case against the archbishop, and Bruno felt he could not leave Rheims while the archbishop was still in possession. In the meantime the fervor of his friends grew cold, so that when at last Manasses was deposed, in the year 1080, only Bruno remained faithful to his resolution.

After the deposition of Manasses, the papal legate, Hugh de Die, seems to have mentioned Bruno as a suitable successor, but by that time he had fled from Rheims, and with a few companions settled as a hermit at a place called Sèche-Fontaine. His hermitage was near to the abbey of Molesme, where St Robert was abbot, and it is possible that he became a monk there for a short time. He did not stay long at Sèche-Fontaine; finding his solitude there apt to be troubled by visitors, he set off in the year 1084 to seek a more remote site in the mountains of Savoy, accompanied by six companions. On his way he stopped at Grenoble to consult the saintly bishop, a former pupil, Hugh de Châteauneuf. It so happened that the night before St Hugh had seen in a dream seven stars settle on a remote site in the Chartreuse mountains and, recognising in Bruno and his six companions the seven stars of his dream, he lost no time in taking them to the place that had been indicated to him. Here was a site sufficiently solitary to satisfy even Bruno, and he immediately settled down with his companions to build a small chapel with seven wooden hermitages round it. Such were the modest beginnings of the great monastery that stands there to this day, the mother house of the Order that bears its name. High up amongst the mountains and forests of Savoy, few monasteries can have a more spectacular situation or one more in keeping with the spirit of prayer. But Bruno was too well known to be left in peace for long.

In the year 1090, Odo of Châtillon, his former pupil, who had become Pope Urban II, bethought himself of his old master and summoned him to his assistance in Rome. It was a command from the highest authority, and Bruno could not but obey. However, it was not long before Pope Urban saw that the court was no place for Bruno, and before the year was out gave him permission to leave Rome, providing he remained at hand in Italy. During the short time that he had been at the papal court, Bruno had met Count Roger of Sicily, the brother of Robert Guiscard, and when he left Rome he settled on property the count had given him at La Torre in Calabria, founding there his second monastery, on the same pattern as the Grande Chartreuse. Here he died on October 6th in the year 1101, without ever having lived to visit again his first monastery.

From the little that we know of him, Bruno seems to have been a lovable personality, with an intense affection for his friends, and, what is rare in men of those times, a deep appreciation of the natural beauty of his surroundings. In a charming letter to his old friend Ralph, one of only two that have survived, he describes with great sensitivity the beauty of the country round his hermitage in Calabria. He died without leaving any written rule behind him, but the way of life which his ideals of prayer, solitude and simplicity inspired, has lived down the centuries to our own day. The Carthusians, as his monks are called from the site of their mother house in the Chartreuse mountains, live a modified solitary life in small three-roomed cells opening on to a common cloister. They meet together for the main canonical offices which are always sung, and once a week for a long walk. On great feasts they eat in common, but at other times in their cells. They have retained the medieval externals of their life more rigidly than other monks, and it is their proud boast that their way of life is deemed the most perfect in the church and that they have never been reformed, because they have never stood in need of it. Nevertheless their life has undergone profound modifications since the days of their founder, some of which, such as the prolonged vocal prayers and multiplicity of devotions, might make it harder than it was in Bruno's day, for the man who seeks nothing else than to be left alone, to live to God alone in utter simplicity. Since the time of Bruno the offices of Matins and Lauds have been placed in the middle of the night so that sleep is broken, and the Little Office of our Lady, the Office of the Dead, and various other prayers are said in addition to the canonical office.

October 6th　　　　　ILLUSTRATION: page 76

BRUNO of SEGNI　　　　　† 1123

He was chosen as bishop of Segni by Pope Gregory VII after his defence of Catholic doctrine at the council of 1079 in Rome. After a long fight for church reform, he retired to Monte Cassino of which he became abbot in 1107. He was forced to resign his abbacy and return to his see, however, when he criticized some concessions made by Pope Paschal II.

July 18th

BRUNO of WÜRZBURG　　　　　† 1045

Great-nephew of St Boniface of Querfurt, he became bishop of Würzburg. When at dinner with Emperor Henry III at Bosenberg on the Danube, he was killed by the collapse of a balcony.

May 17th

BRUNO or BONIFACE of QUERFURT
974–1009

As chaplain to Otto III, he visited Italy, became a monk

in Rome and joined St Romuald. He set out to evangelize Eastern Europe and was made a missionary bishop. He was killed at a place which was later called Braunsberg in his memory.
June 19th

BRUNO THE GREAT of COLOGNE 925–965
Not to be confused with the founder of the Carthusians, this saint was the son of the Emperor Henry the Fowler, and chancellor to his brother, Otto I. He became archbishop of Cologne in 953 and proved to be not only a good man but a successful statesman.
October 11th

BUDOC or BEUZEC   *Sixth Century?*
It is hard to know if there was one Budoc or several, and the stories which surround the name belong more to magic than to religion. St Budoc has been venerated in Brittany and Pembrokeshire, and there is a place called Budock in Cornwall.
December 9th

BURCHARD   † 754
He went from Wessex to help St Boniface in the evangelization of Germany, and became bishop of Würzburg. He supported the claims of Pepin the Short to the Frankish throne.
October 14th

BURGUNDOFARA or FARE   † 657
Her father, Count Agneric, at first opposed her wish to become a nun. He relented and built a convent for her, later named Faremoutiers, of which she was abbess for thirty-seven years.
April 3rd

CADFAN   *Sixth Century*
He founded the monastery at Towny, Merioneth, which became a famous seminary, and the communities at Bardsey and Llangadfan.
November 1st

CADOC   † *c.* 575
The earliest biography extant of this well-known Welsh saint was written some six hundred years after his death. He seems to have visited Brittany, Cornwall and Scotland and to have founded more than one monastery. He is known as one of the builders of Christian Wales.
September 25th

CADROE or CADROEL   † 976
Son of a Scottish thane, he was educated in Armagh, Ireland. After training Scottish priests, he went to England, where he miraculously saved London from

fire, and went to France, where he became abbot of Waulsort on the Meuse and of St Clement at Metz.
March 6th

CADWALLADER   † 664
'Not for Cadwallader and all his goats,' shouted Pistol as Fluellen presented him with the famous leek. How came a seventh-century Welsh saint into a comic brawl on the Elizabethan stage? And not only on the stage in London. In Rome, too, his name was a battle-cry. For in the dispute over Maurice Clynnog's management of the English College, the Welsh students maintained that the college was of Cadwallader's foundation, and that the English students were, at best, tolerated guests.

The son of the redoubtable Cadwallon, he was a child at his father's death, and he did not become king until 654. He died in the Great Plague of 664. He must have spent his last years as a monk, for there are seven foundations of which he is the founder and patron saint. Three churchs are dedicated to him, in one of which (Llangadwaladr in Anglesey) his grandfather is commemorated by a seventh century inscription; and his feast is included in no fewer than fourteen western calendars of the fifteenth and sixteenth centuries.

His cult is of great interest to the historian. With the rise to supremacy of the house of Aberffraw, the cult provided its princes with that memory of a sainted ancestor which was so eagerly desired by all medieval rulers. Geoffrey of Monmouth, by confusing him with Caedwalla, had given him a striking legend in which he died a pilgrim at Rome, assured by an angel that his seed should recover the crown of Britain. The heralds ascribed a coat of arms to him, azure a cross paty fitchy or; and the already traditional Red Dragon was declared to be his particular emblem. In 1485 Henry VII, claiming direct descent from the saint, marched to Bosworth under the saint's banner.

Today, in the twentieth century, when the Welsh XV takes the field at Cardiff, the Red Dragon flags and the famous red shirts derive ultimately from the invocation of a seventh century saint who left a crown to become a monk, and became the patron saint of Welsh royalty.
November 12th

CAEDMON   *Seventh Century*
Caedmon is the first English poet we know by name; his work is unfortunately lost. A herdsman attached to the monastery of Streoneshalch (Whitby), he was visited in his sleep, so Bede tells us, by one who bade him sing of the creation. When the abbess of the monastery, St Hilda, discovered his poetic gift she invited him to join the community which was a double one. This he did, submitting willingly to monastic discipline until his exceptionally happy and peaceful death.
February 11th

CAEDWALLA
† 689

A king of Wessex who died on a pilgrimage to Rome immediately after he had been baptized; his epitaph has been preserved in the Crypt of St Peter's from the original stone in the old church.

April 20th

CAESARIA
Sixth Century

First abbess of a large nunnery founded by her brother, St Caesarius, bishop of Arles, she ruled with a remarkably generous spirit for which she was praised by Gregory of Tours amongst others. It is believed that this was the first properly organized community for women in the west.

January 12th

CAESARIUS and JULIAN

They were martyred – according to their legend – at Terracina in Italy for protesting against the custom of making human sacrifice to Apollo.

November 1st

CAESARIUS NAZIANZEN
† 368

Brother of St Gregory Nazianzen and son of the bishop of Nazianzus he became a famous physician in Constantinople. He defended his faith against the disapproval of Julian the Apostate, and died a recluse.

February 25th

CAESARIUS of ARLES
470–543

A monk at Lérins and brother of St Caesaria, he was forced by ill-health to go to Arles, where the bishop was so impressed with him that he obtained his release from Lérins. In 503 he succeeded to the bishopric, and was famous for the simplicity of his preaching. He protected his flock in war and against heresy.

August 27th

CAGNOALD, *see* Chainoaldus.

CAIUS, *see* Soter and Caius.

CAIUS FRANCIS, *see* Martyrs of Japan.

CAJETAN
1480–1547

St Cajetan (Gaetano da Thiene) was an important figure among those who laid the foundations of the sixteenth century Catholic reform in Italy. Born in 1480 at Vicenza, in the dominions of Venice, of a well-to-do and respected family, he obtained his doctorate in civil and canon law at Padua in 1504, and in 1508 embarked on an administrative ecclesiastical career in Rome, where he bought, as was then common, a secretarial office in the papal chancery. He appears to have enjoyed the favour of Julius II and may have been employed by that pontiff in his dealings with Venice at the time of the League of Cambray and the subsequent wars, 1509–1516, which brought so much suffering and desolation, and which seriously impaired the prosperity of Cajetan's family.

It seems probable that these circumstances first stirred in Cajetan something of a real religious conversion. In 1516 he joined the Roman Oratory of Divine Love, a confraternity, of Genoese inspiration, pledged to the cultivation of the spiritual life of its members by prayer, frequentation of the Sacraments, and the performance of charitable works in hospitals, orphanages, penitentiaries and so forth. He was ordained priest on September 30th, 1516 and, after his first mass some months later, began to celebrate daily, an unusual practice at that time. Through the instrumentality of a friend from Brescia, Bartolomeo Stella, he came under the influence of an Augustinian nun of that city, Laura Mignani, with whom he entered into regular correspondence, but whom he probably never saw. On returning to Vicenza in 1517 for his mother's last illness, he took as his confessor the well-known Dominican Fra Battista Carioni da Crema, under whose influence he now decided to devote his life wholeheartedly to the service of God. Having regulated the affairs of his relations and given up his ecclesiastical preferment, he spent the next six years working in the spiritual and charitable confraternities in Vicenza, Verona and Venice which were the counterparts in those cities of the Roman Oratory of Divine Love. Here he preached frequent communion, eucharistic devotion, prayer and mortification, and worked at the meanest tasks in hospitals for syphilitics and homes for reformed prostitutes. He became the leading spirit, and his example helped to fire St Jerome Emiliani to his new religious foundation of the Somaschi.

It was not, however, until his return to Rome, under the guidance of Fra Battista, in 1523, that Cajetan met the companions with whom he made his own new foundation in 1524. Chief among these was Gian Pietro Carafa, later Pope Paul IV. In natural temperament wholly dissimilar, these two men found themselves united in a burning zeal for the reform of the church, especially in Rome which Cajetan had likened to a new Babylon. Their society of Clerks Regular, who came to be called Theatines – Carafa was known as 'Theatinus' from the Latin version of his bishopric of Chieti – set up a new model of clerical life and deportment marked by an extreme austerity and a complete devotion to pastoral work. Though secular priests, living in community and engaged in pastoral work, the Theatines took the monastic vows of poverty, chastity and obedience. Divesting themselves of all ownership of property, both as individuals and communities, and abstaining even from mendicancy, they relied entirely on the charity of others for their material support. It was a heroic venture in which they assaulted the clerical abuses of the day and sought to restore the spiritual prestige of the priesthood. Their community in Rome – small, select, even aristocratic in composition – soon became a center of spirituality, charity and liturgical study. But it was driven from Rome when that city was sacked in 1527 and took refuge in Venice. Its members suffered cruelly, not least Cajetan himself who was brutally tortured by Spanish soldiers who believed him possessed of hidden wealth. The Theatines did not return to Rome until 1555 when Carafa was pope and Cajetan dead.

Cajetan's spirituality took final expression and was embodied in the mixture of the pastoral and the contemplative that constituted the life of the Theatines and set the model for other subsequent foundations of Clerks Regular. But while Carafa became more and more active in public affairs, especially after his elevation to the Cardinalate in 1536, Cajetan retired increasingly into a hidden life in the Theatine houses of Venice and Naples. Influential as the Theatines became in the reform of the church in Italy, they shunned all publicity and self-advertisement. Gaetano's extreme humility became legendary. He left comparatively few letters and no literary works. Yet it is evident that he reached the extremes of sanctity and was venerated as a saint before his death. His tirelessness in prayer and preaching, his eucharistic devotion, his ascetic life, his ceaseless charity and apostolate, display all the hall-marks of counter-reformation spirituality. He had, however, a strong liturgical sense. He was punctilious in the extreme in attendance in choir, for the Theatines recited their office in common, and liturgical study was a speciality of the order. Stories of miracles multiplied during his own life-time. He himself related in a letter to Laura Mignani an early mystical experience in which our Lady entrusted to him the care of the Divine Infant. On his death-bed he is said to have undergone, as the climax of his spiritual evolution, all the pains of the crucifixion. He died at Naples in 1547. He was beatified in 1629, and in 1691 Innocent XII published the Bull of his canonization which had been drawn up twenty years previously.

August 7th   ILLUSTRATION: page 77

CALAIS, *see* Carilefus.

CALEPODIUS   † 222
We know only that a catacomb bore his name. His legend says that he suffered as a martyr during the reign of Alexander Severus, in an attack by the populace on the Christians.
May 10th

CALLISTUS or CALIXTUS   *Third Century*
For our knowledge of St Callistus we depend mainly on St Hippolytus's account of him (*Philosphoumena,*

Book IX). It is unfortunate, for it is the account of an unscrupulous enemy. Nevertheless making the qualifications suggested by common sense – nor could Hippolytus have falsified public facts – we can learn from it more of Callistus's life than is known of any other primitive pope. He was the slave of a Christian, Carpophorus, who, in consideration no doubt of his talent for finance and organisation, placed him in charge of a bank. The venture was unsuccessful, though Callistus, we may be sure, was innocent of the misappropriation of funds with which Hippolytus charges him. To recover debts owed by Jews he forced his way into a synagogue. The Jews charged him with the crime of Christianity. The perfect of Rome had him scourged and sent him to forced labor in the Sardinian mines. When Marcia, mistress of the Emperor Commodus, obtained the release of these captives, Callistus returned. Pope Victor sent him to Antium, the Roman Brighton or Coney Island, to recover his health, and settled a pension upon him. This disproves Hippolytus's allegation that Victor had excluded him from the list of confessors sent to Marcia. Victor's successor, St Zephyrinus, appointed Callistus his archdeacon and placed him in charge of the cemeteries. He opened the catacomb on the Via Appia which bears his name. It was the property and gift of his friend, the heiress Cecilia. He proved himself so capable an administrator that in 217 he was chosen to succeed Zephyrinus as pope.

It was probably Callistus who organized the titles of Rome, parish churches in houses belonging to the donors who gave the title its name. He condemned the monarchist Unitarian Sabellius whom he had formerly patronized. He introduced wise and charitable disciplinary relaxations. In the Trastevere the Cecilii possessed at least one 'insula', a block of tenements. Cecilia gave the property to Callistus, who established there the title, church and offices, which long bore his name, now Santa Maria in Trastevere. In 222 he met a violent death, traditionally and most probably thrown down a well in Trastevere by an angry mob. The supposition presents itself that his death was due to the hostility aroused by his evacuation of the pagan tenement dwellers. From first to last he was a strong minded and high handed man. He was buried, not in the catacomb bearing his name, but in a cemetery near at hand on the Via Aurelia.
October 14th

CALOCERUS and PARTHENIUS   † 304
Brothers who were said to have been eunuchs in the household of the wife of the Emperor Decius, they were burned alive for their faith.
May 19th

CAMERINUS, *see* Luxorius, Cisellus and Camerinus.

CAMILLUS de LELLIS 1550–1614

Born in 1550 at Bocchiancio in the Abruzzi, he was the son of a soldier and grew to be a hot-tempered giant – he once threatened to throw a blasphemer out of a coach in which they were travelling – over six foot six inches tall and broad in proportion, with piercing black eyes. At the age of seventeen he enlisted, together with his father now aged seventy-six, in the Venetian army; but it was not long before his father died, and Camillus was reduced to destitution by his persistent craze for gambling. Although some Capuchins at Mangredonia took pity on him, he did not see his life for what it was until 1575, when he decided to enter the hospital of San Giacomo in Rome.

Henceforth he devoted the rest of his life to the care of the sick in conditions which it is almost impossible to imagine: patients were left to rot in their own filth, they were hurried off to the mortuary before they were dead and were even beaten by their attendants. Camillus was determined to found an order, whose members would bind themselves to help the sick, the plague-ridden and the dying; so he became a priest and, after his ordination, founded the ministers of the sick, or Camillans. For most of his life he was crippled by a diseased leg which required constant dressing, by a rupture, and by feet so calloused that he had to walk with a stick; yet he continued the full duties of a priest with the regular visiting and care of the sick, even to the extent of denying himself more than three or four hours sleep nightly.

By the time he retired from the generalship of his Order in 1607, there were three hundred members, fifteen houses and eight hospitals. At least 170 members had died in the exercise of their vocation, and the first 'field ambulances' to serve troops in the field had also been established. Camillus has sometimes been called the Red Cross saint, because his order wear a black habit with a red cross on the right of the breast, and he is the patron of the sick and of all nurses.

July 18th

CANDIDUS, *see* Maurice, Candidus and their
Companions. ILLUSTRATION: page 78

CANICE or KENNETH Sixth Century

St Canice was a native of Derry who lived in the second half of the sixth century. Many of the Celtic saints were of royal blood, or the sons of chiefs, but Canice was the son of a bard, one of those poets who entertained the chiefs with their verses. He was a poet himself. The friend and colleague of Columba, he spent some time with him in Iona and also helped him in the evangelization of western Scotland, where his name is rendered as Kenneth, or Kenny. He was with Columba when he made his first visit to the Pictish King, Brude, at Inverness. Thereafter, Canice worked in many parts of Scotland, probably founding a monastery at St Andrews, leaving his name as a mark of his activities in both highlands and lowlands: notably at the great abbey of Cambuskenneth. Unlike Columba, however, Canice returned to Ireland in middle life and was responsible for a notable foundation at Aghaboe in Ossory. He probably also established a monastery in Kilkenny, as the ancient cathedral there is dedicated to him, and he is patron of the diocese.

A story from his school-days provided the Celtic church with a moral tale. One day, when he was practising writing as a boy of thirteen, he was suddenly called away to work with his companions in the fields. He dropped his pen in the middle of forming the letter O. Later on, when his master saw the copy, he reproved him for the unfinished letter, saying sarcastically that the boy must have been glad of the call, when he could not even wait to finish his letter. Canice answered soberly that he did not like working in the fields, but that he was trying to learn obedience which was harder than writing. This story went the round of all the monastic schools, and Canice's O became proverbial among them as the symbol of perfect obedience.

The lovely little Hebridean island of Inchkenneth has the remains of a chapel and monastery founded by the saint. When Boswell and Dr Johnson visited the island in 1773 they were much moved by its beauty and associations. Boswell records that he knelt before the cross there, and 'prayed with strong devotion, while I had before me the image of that on which my Saviour died for the sins of the world. The sanctity of venerable Columba filled my imagination. I considered that to ask the intercession of a departed saint was at least innocent and might be of service'.

October 11th

CANTIUS, *see* John of Kanti.

CANTIUS, CANTIANIUS and
CANTIANELLA Fourth Century

It seems that these two brothers and sister were left orphans and brought up by a Christian guardian. All four were beheaded in the persecutions under Diocletian.

May 31st

CANUTE or KNUT Eleventh Century

Canute, who became king of Denmark in 1080, was the nephew of the celebrated King Canute of England. He was an able ruler who favored the church. A generous patron of individual churches such as that of Lund, he helped to establish the tithe in his dominions; but, in spite of this, he was not remarkable for holiness of life. In 1085 he planned a great invasion of England, but the taxation which he imposed in Denmark to pay for this expedition provoked a revolt. Canute was defeated by the rebels and took sanctuary in the church of St Alban at Odense, where he was killed as he knelt before the altar. The monks of Odense accepted him as a saint, buried him under their altar and promoted his cult.

In some ways St Canute seems to be the Danish answer to Norway's St Olaf, but it should be remembered that the monks of Odense who first promoted his cult were English, and Canute's murder alone prevented him from leading a great invasion of England. It may be that St Canute had a genuine claim to sanctity: there is, however, little evidence of it in his biographies.
January 19th   ILLUSTRATION: page 123 (A)

CANUTE LAVARD   † 1131
He was second son of Eric the Good of Denmark. As duke of southern Jutland and then king of the Wends, he supported the missionary St Vicelin. He was killed by a jealous uncle.
January 7th

CAPRAIS, *see* Caprasius.

CAPRASIUS   *Third Century*
St Caprasius was long supposed to have been executed by the Roman Prefect in France for refusing to sacrifice to Diana. This story is now discredited, but the church at Agen is dedicated to him, and he certainly did exist.
October 20th

CAPRASIUS or CAPRAIS   † 430
Spiritual director of St Honoratus of Lérins, he accompanied him to the east, and returned with him to Gaul where he assisted St Honoratus in founding the monastery of Lérins.
June 1st

CARADOC   † 1124
After a false accusation was brought against him at the court of a Welsh prince where he was harper, he became a monk and a recluse. His shrine is in the cathedral church of St David.
April 14th

CARANTOC or CARANNOG   *Sixth Century*
He founded the church of Llangrannog in Cardiganshire and a community in Somerset or Cornwall called Cernach; he also seems to have spent some time in Brittany.
May 16th

CARILEFUS or CALAIS   † *c*. 540?
According to unreliable sources, he was educated at the monastery of Menat near Riom, and was a friend of St Avitus with whom he was ordained at the abbey of Micy near Orleans. Later he lived as a hermit in Maine,

where his disciples formed a community which became known as Anisole.
July 1st

CARPUS   † *c*. 165
During the persecution under Emperor Marcus Aurelius, bishop Carpus and the deacon Papylus were brought before the Roman governor at Pergamos in Asia Minor. The governor interrogated them both publicly, using all his powers to persuade them to offer sacrifice to the gods. But Carpus said, 'I am a Christian. I worship Christ, the Son of God, who came in these latter times for our salvation and delivered us from the snares of the devil. I will not sacrifice to such idols.' And, as he remained unmoved, he was taken to the torture. Papylus also refused, with the words, 'I have served God from my youth up and I have never sacrificed to idols. I am a Christian . . .' He too was taken away to be tortured. But as they were both steadfast the governor ordered them to be burned at the stake in the amphitheater, Papylus suffering first and then Carpus. The last words of Carpus were: 'Blessed art thou, Lord Jesus Christ, Son of God, because thou didst judge me, a sinner, worthy to have this part in thee!' There was a woman in the crowd, named Agathonica, and she, seeing the death of Carpus and Papylus, knew that she also was called to share with them in their martyrdom. She too was condemned: and when she was touched by the flames she cried out three times, 'Lord, Lord, Lord help me, for I fly unto thee.' And their fellow Christians came and took away their remains and cherished them.
April 13th

CARTHAGE, CARTHACH or MOCHUDA   † 637
Originally a swineherd in Kerry, he came under the care of St Carthach the Elder who ordained him and whose name he adopted. He established a monastery at Rahan which became famous after it was forced to move to Lismore. The rule established by him still exists, and he is regarded as first bishop of Lismore.
May 14th

CASIMIR of POLAND   † 1484
Son of King Casimir IV of Poland, he never occupied the throne himself and died at the age of twenty-three from a lung disease aggravated by his ascetic mode of life.
March 4th   ILLUSTRATION: page 79

CASPAR del BUFALO   1786–1837
Son of a chef, he became a priest and was exiled when Napoleon took Rome. He founded the Congregation of the Precious Blood, setting up missionary houses in the most vice-ridden quarters of Italy. He was canonized in 1954.
January 2nd

CASSIAN, *see* Marcellus and Cassian.

CASSIAN of IMOLA
A Christian schoolmaster, he was probably the first, but certainly not the last member of that profession to be martyred by his pupils.
August 13th

CASSIUS † 538
This bishop of Narni was told that he would die in Rome on the feast of St Peter and St Paul. On the eve of the feast he made one of his annual visits to Rome, and in the seventh year the prophecy was fulfilled.
June 29th

CASTOR † c. 425
He and his wife both retired from the world. He became abbot of his own foundation of Mananque in Provence, and later bishop of Apt.
September 2nd

CASTULUS † 286
According to legend, he was Diocletian's chamberlain. He was betrayed by an apostate, martyred by the prefect Fabian and buried in the catacomb called by his name.
March 26th

CASTUS, *see* Aemilius.

CATALD and CONLETH
Seventh and Sixth Centuries
St Catald was a monk and teacher at Lismore who, on return from pilgrimage to Jerusalem, was chosen bishop of Taranto. St Conleth is known to have been a skilled metalworker. Through his friendship with St Brigid, he became bishop of Kildare.
May 10th

CATHERINE dei RICCI 1522–1590
Of a distinguished Florentine family, she became prioress of St Vincent's convent at Prato, and outstanding among mystics for the intensity of her ecstasies. These began in 1542, and occurred continuously every week for twelve years, beginning regularly at midday each Thursday and ending at four o'clock on Friday, twenty-eight hours afterwards.

In addition to receiving the stigmata, St Catherine is said to have been given a ring by Christ to mark her spiritual espousal. Evidence is conflicting. Three nuns of her community were convinced that they had seen such a ring – of gold set with a pointed diamond – on the index finger of her left hand. What cannot be disputed is that at certain times a red circle and lozenge appeared in such a way on her finger that they were plainly and unmistakably visible.
February 13th

CATHERINE LABOURÉ 1806–1876
Save for the events of 1830, the life of this peasant woman, who became a Sister of Charity at the age of twenty-four, contains little or no biographical incident worthy of chronicling. She was born in 1806, the daughter of a smallholder and entered the Sisters of Charity in 1830 at Châtillon-sur-Seine; after a few months she was sent to the motherhouse in the rue du Bac in Paris. It was there that she underwent the great experience of her life – a series of visions in which our Lady is said to have shown her the form of a medal which should be struck in honor of the Immaculate Conception. Catherine told no one save her confessor and, convinced of her sincerity, he obtained the archbishop's sanction for the striking of the medal. This has come to be called the 'Miraculous Medal' and is known throughout the Catholic world; 'miraculous', say some, owing to the circumstances of its origin; 'miraculous', say others, owing to the extraordinary graces obtained through invoking our Lady in the terms of its inscription revealed to Catherine Labouré: 'O Mary conceived without sin, pray for us who have recourse to you!'

For upwards of forty years Catherine spoke to no one save her confessor of her experience: she enjoined silence on him, and, when the medal was world famous, her part in the whole affair remained unknown until shortly before her death. She was sent from the rue du Bac after a year there to the convent at Enghien-Reuilly on the outskirts of Paris where she looked after the poultry and acted as doorkeeper. There she died in 1876. She was canonized in 1947.

This appearance of our Lady to a Sister of Charity at the beginning of the nineteenth century is notable on two counts: it was the first in a series that occurred in France during the nineteenth century – La Salette, Lourdes, Pontmain are the most famous – and it is particularly remarkable for the conduct of the person concerned. Her self-effacement and humility, her seeking of holiness in a very ordinary humdrum life, all show her to have been a woman whose character and virtues were of an outstandingly high order.
November 28th

CATHERINE of ALEXANDRIA
The heroine of a pious fiction, we know little of her before the ninth century. By tradition she was a beautiful and a learned young woman of Alexandria who, at her conversion, underwent a 'mystical marriage' with the infant Jesus, our Lady herself placing the gold ring on Catherine's finger. Catherine was brought before the Emperor Maxentius to be tried. Fifty philosophers were opposed to her in argument, but she vanquished them all, and they were burned by the Emperor for their failure. She was condemned to be killed on a spiked wheel (hence 'catherine-wheel'). The wheel broke, and she was

beheaded. Once extremely popular (her voice was heard by St Joan of Arc), she is the patron of Christian philosophers, and is venerated as one of the Fourteen Holy Helpers. ILLUSTRATION: page 80
November 25th

CATHERINE of BOLOGNA † 1463

Daughter of John de' Vigri, she was a Franciscan tertiary under Lucy Mascaroni, and became superior of the Corpus Christi convent at Bologna. She is famous for her artistic talent, her piety and her visions. Her body was buried without a coffin, remaining in the ground for nearly three weeks, and when it was exhumed it was found to be incorrupt. It may still be seen in the convent church at Bologna.
March 9th

CATHERINE of GENOA 1447–1510

In the year 1463, the Adorni and Fieschi, Montagues and Capulets of the Genoese nobility, sought to exchange hostility for an alliance by marrying Giuliano Adorno to Caterinetta Fiesca, a girl of sixteen. Unfortunately this Romeo was not in love with this Juliet, and this Juliet was, moreover, temperamentally unsuited to marriage. In consequence while Giuliano sought consolation elsewhere, his young wife moped for some years in their palace, then attempted to fill her life with a round of amusements.

Suddenly in March 1474 the inner void was filled by a whole-hearted conversion to God. As Catherine knelt in a convent chapel she was overwhelmed by the love of God. She kept crying out to herself: 'No more world, no more sins.' Soon afterwards she made a general confession.

Henceforward she never turned back. She was soon a daily communicant, a practice then extraordinarily rare, though for many years, not finding a congenial director and not being obliged by mortal sin, she did not confess. She passed twenty-three Lents and twenty-two Advents fasting from solid food. During these fasts, which lasted for as long as thirty days in Advent and forty in Lent, she was as active as when she was eating normally. (The problem of prolonged fasting is more fully discussed in the account of St Lidwina of Schiedam). She reformed her husband, and together they undertook the care of the sick in the hospital of Pammatone. In 1479 they moved into the hospital of which in 1490 she was appointed matron. During the plague of 1493 she was unsparing in her service of the sick and the organization of relief, though she was brought to death's door when she contracted the infection by impulsively kissing a dying man. In 1497 Giuliano died.

Catherine's external activities stemmed from a life of prayer in which love of God cleansed her from every taint of self-seeking. It was a vehement love which carried her into prolonged ecstasies, from which, however, she would emerge at the call of duty. When a friar suggested that, as a religious, he could love God better than a laywoman, she repelled the suggestion indignantly, face aflame, hair falling about her shoulders: 'If I thought your habit would enable me to love God better I would tear it from your back'. Returned home, she exclaimed: 'O Love, who shall hinder me from loving thee? Though I were ... in a camp of soldiers I could not be hindered from loving thee.'

She was the center of a group of friends and disciples, who remembered and recorded the profound sayings which make her a teacher of mystical theology. Prominent among them was Ettore Vernazza, an organizer of charitable works whose daughter, a nun, was herself a mystic, her directors Don Carenzio and Don Marabotto and her maid Argentina. She also undertook the care of her husband's illegitimate daughter, Thobia.

Catherine's later years were years of weakness and painful illness, compelling her to resign her post as matron. Even the surface, so to speak, of her interior life suffered. She was indeed being consumed in a purgatorial fire of divine love, at once agonizingly painful and blissful. Physicians were baffled by a disease even more psychological than physical. Finally on September 15th 1510 she passed from her earthly purgatory to heaven.

Disciples, probably Vernazza and Marabotto, gradually put together a life and collection of sayings, Catherine's *Vita è Dottrina*. It included a particular collection of sayings, an Explanation of Purgatory, which in process of time was detached and came to be regarded as a composition of the saint. A dialogue between Body and Soul, early attached to the *Vita*, was also considered to be her composition. It was in fact composed by Vernazza's daughter. The treatise on Purgatory which understands and explains Purgatory in the light of its earthly counterpart – the purgatory of consuming love – is one of the two most illuminating views of Purgatory given to the Church; the other is the *Divine Crucible of Purgatory* by Mother St Austin.

Catherine is the subject, victim and teacher of a love no less powerfully experienced for the lack of those human images in which it most commonly finds expression. She was canonized in 1737, and her feast is observed at Genoa on March 22nd.
September 15th

CATHERINE of PALMA † 1574

Catherine Tomas spent her whole life in Majorca, where, after a hard childhood, she was accepted by the convent of St Mary Magdalen. She was subject to trances sometimes lasting for a fortnight, to visions and to assaults from invisible sources.
April 1st

Catherine Benincasa was born in Siena in 1347, the youngest of a very large family. Her father, Giacomo, was a prosperous wool-dyer, the comfort of whose home may be gauged even today by visiting the large house in which he brought up his family, still preserved though considerably altered, through the intervening centuries. His wife, Monna Lapa, was the capable and energetic ruler of this lively family.

Catherine spent a normal, contented infancy during which only excessive gaiety singled her out from among her brothers and sisters. But in adolescence she became attracted to prayer and solitude. Lapa vigorously disapproved and for a period considered Catherine a difficult daughter, in fact a problem teenager, who rebelled against her mother's direction in such matters as dress and amusements, resisted any suggestion of marriage and refused just as positively to become a nun.

There was a truce to their disagreement when Catherine, at the age of sixteen, gained admittance to the Third Order of St Dominic, then flourishing in Siena. The rules of this group allowed her to dress in the black and white habit of a Dominican nun while remaining in her own home. Thenceforward for three years she never left her room, except to go to mass and confession, and spoke to no one except her confessor. This good priest said afterwards that he always felt incompetent to guide her. During this period Catherine trained herself to live on a spoonful of herbs a day and to make a couple of hours' sleep every night suffice. Though apparently so uneventful, those years were of major importance to her, for it was on them she built her life's achievement.

Having been told by God to resume family life, she then began to do her share of the work of the house, to nurse the sick and to help the poor. Almost at once it became known that she had discernment of souls and people began to flock to her from all sides. A motley band of men and women of all ages and ranks gathered around her, forming the singular 'club' of Fontebranda, the name of the district where she lived. They included scions of the principal Sienese families, men of fashion, priests and religious, soldiers and artists, merchants, lawyers, politicians.

The plain people of Siena did not care for the novelty. Here, said her neighbors in effect, is a young woman, a kind of nun, said to be holy; yet she goes about freely with numbers of young men, who are in and out of her house at all hours of the day. Who ever heard of such a thing? They nicknamed her derisively the 'Queen of Fontebranda', and they called her friends, who they said must be bewitched, the 'caterinati'. But the unique club, or the 'bella brigata', as they called themselves, was not to be dispersed by jeers. The disapproval did not even cloud their happiness. They persevered. Ecclesiastical history has since given them the noble title 'School of Mystics'. They were attracted to Catherine by her gaiety as well as by her asceticism; by her practical common sense as well as by her spiritual insight; by her serenity and personal charm.

There was at this time a severe crisis in the church, owing to the papacy's desertion of Rome for Avignon. This had particularly bad effects on the Italian Communes who were always at strife with the French papal legates. When Florence declared war on the papal states in protest against the legates' rule, eighty towns joined them in ten days. While Catherine was in Pisa, working in the cause of peace, she received the stigmata on the fourth Sunday of Lent, 1375, although the marks remained invisible until after her death. At a certain stage in this war, Florence asked Catherine to go to Avignon and there intercede with Pope Gregory XI on behalf of their embassy. She at once agreed and reached Avignon in the third week of May, 1376, accompanied by twenty-three members of the 'bella brigata', including four priests.

The ensuing three months were among the most fateful in the whole history of the church. Catherine had to endure every kind of rebuff in Avignon: the society ladies who had great power in the papal court openly made fun of her; inquisition-minded prelates subjected her to a merciless examination in doctrine; when the Florentine envoys arrived, they rudely refused to accept her mediation: Florence had merely used her as a pawn in order to gain time. But the pope favored her, and now she fully understood his irresolution of character and his difficulties. She succeeded in convincing him that peace could be won only by restoring the papacy to Rome.

The might of France, the Sacred College and the pope's own family immediately closed in around him to prevent him from taking this step. It was a terrifying struggle of wills in which the victory went to Catherine. Pope Gregory XI left Avignon for ever on September 13th 1376.

The change of climate and the difficulties with which he had to cope took a heavy toll of Gregory's frail physique. He died within a year. The new pope, Urban VI, was a Neapolitan who began his pontificate with a zeal for reform which immediately alienated the French cardinals. They withdrew to Anagni, where they issued a statement that the occupier of the Holy See was in reality an intruder, whom they had only pretended to elect in fear of the Roman mob who had dominated the election with their clamor for an Italian pope. Shortly afterwards the French cardinals elected a rival pope, who went to live in Avignon. Thus began the great western Schism which lasted for seventy years and proved to be the most terrible ordeal which the church has ever had to suffer.

Catherine went to Rome at the request of Urban VI to organize spiritual help towards ending the schism. Before leaving Siena for the last time, she dictated a book called *The Dialogue of St Catherine*, which together with her four hundred *Letters*, comprise a great treasury of spiritual writing.

Once again in Rome she pitted herself against the powers of evil that threatened to engulf the church. For a whole year she lived corporally on the Blessed Sacrament and took less than an hour's sleep every night while she sent her zealous letters all over Europe, beseeching help for the restoration of unity and for peace, as daily she offered her life for this cause. One evening in January 1380, while dictating a letter to Urban, she had a stroke. Partially recovering, she lived in a mystical agony, convinced that she was wrestling physically with demons. She had a second stroke while at prayer in St Peter's and died three weeks later on April 29th, 1380, aged thirty-three. She was buried under the high altar in the Dominican church of Santa Maria sopra Minerva, but her head was afterwards removed and taken to Siena, where it is enshrined in the Dominican church. She was canonized eighty-one years after her death. Her feast is celebrated in Siena on the April 29th, but elsewhere in the church on the next day.

April 30th   ILLUSTRATION: page 113

CATHERINE of VADSTENA   † 1371
A daughter of St Bridget of Sweden, she spent most of her life with her mother in Rome. After St Bridget's death she retired to the convent of Vadstena in Sweden.
March 24th

CEALLACH, *see* Celsus.

CECILIA or CECILY
A Roman maiden of noble family, devoted to prayer, she was given in marriage against her will to a pagan youth named Valerian. On the wedding day 'while the pipes (organs) were playing' for the festivities, 'she sang in her heart' to Christ, praying that her virginity might be preserved intact. A misunderstanding of these words as meaning that she sang to the accompaniment of an organ has made Cecilia the patroness of music. Alone with her husband in the bridechamber she informed him that an angel was keeping guard over her, and, if he attempted to consummate the marriage, he would experience God's punishment. If he respected her maidenhood he would be rewarded by divine grace. Valerian asked to see the angel which alone would convince him. He could see the angel, she told him, only if he were instructed and baptized, for which she sent him to Pope Urban. On his return he saw the angel offering Cecilia and himself floral crowns. They converted her brother-in-law Tiburtius who was also baptized by Urban. The

brothers were condemned to death for their faith by the prefect Almachius. They converted the soldier on guard, his family and the executioner, who were all baptized by night by priests brought by Cecilia. Next day all were beheaded. Almachius proceeded to arrest Cecilia, whose eloquence converted more than four hundred. He ordered her to be taken back to her house in the Trastevere, now St Cecilia's Church, and burned in her bath room. When the attempt failed he sent a soldier to behead her. After three blows he failed to decapitate her, but left her mortally wounded. At her prayer, death was delayed three days to give her time to have her house consecrated as a church.

This in outline is the story told by the 'Passion' which has found its way into the Breviary. Composed in Rome shortly before 500, it is a fabrication devoid of historical truth. Valerian and Tiburtius are indeed authentic martyrs but have no connection with Cecilia; and the story of her virginal marriage has been plagiarized from a genuine episode in Victor of Vitis's History of the Vandal Persecution. The romance, however, endowed with a martyr's cultus as St Cecilia a lady who had been hitherto but the owner and donor of the property bearing her name in the Trastevere. The heiress, a virgin probably, though possibly a childless widow, came of a noble family, the Cecilii, and she endowed the church of Rome with the cemetery opened by Callistus where her tomb, long since empty, is the central feature of a crypt adjoining the papal crypt. Inscriptions discovered have proved it to be the family vault of the Ceciliani, an allied family succeeding the Cecilii, presumably, at Cecilia's death. This lady bountiful also gave Pope Callistus at least one tenement house in the Trastevere, where he founded the church bearing his name and another bearing hers. The adjoining bathroom, according to the Passion the scene of her imaginary martyrdom, was in fact the bathroom attached to the tenements. The date of her death is unknown. It may have been under Callistus's successor, Pope Urban, with whom the Passion associates her, during the years when the tolerant syncretists, Alexander Severus, gave the church peace and protection. Her body is alleged to have been concealed from the Lombard invader Aistulf in 756, discovered in consequence of a dream by Pope Paschal I, 817–824, who enshrined it where it is now venerated, in her titular church. The latter statements rest on contemporary evidence. But the story is puzzling. How came it that when the body was concealed, the pope was not informed of the fact and place?

November 22nd   ILLUSTRATION: page 114

CECILIUS   *Third Century*
This Carthaginian priest converted St Cyprian. His name was probably Cecilianus, but he is often confused with a

Cecilius Natalis who was the chief magistrate of Cirta in Africa in 210.
June 3rd

CECILY, *see* Cecilia.

CEDD, *see* Chad or Ceadda and Cedd.

CELESTINE I † 432
Born in Campania, he was conspicuous in Rome as deacon before his election to the papacy in 422, where he acted vigorously in counteracting Pelagianism and in opposing Nestorius, as well as in promoting missionary work in Ireland.
April 6th

CELESTINE V (Peter Morone) *c.* 1210–1296
Born about 1210 in the Abruzzi of peasant stock, Peter di Morone betook himself as a youth to the mountain solitudes to live a hermit's life. Willynilly his life of prayer and extreme austerity – he fasted every weekday and kept three Lents a year on bread and water – attracted disciples, whom he formed into a new order of monks, 'The hermits of St Damian', later called 'Celestines'. In 1274 their rule was approved by Gregory X. Peter became the superior of thirty-six communities. Resigning his office, he retired to a solitary hermitage on Mount Morone near Sulmona.

After the death of Nicholas IV on April 4th 1292, irreconcilable feuds kept the Holy See vacant for more than two years. A letter addressed by Peter to one of the cardinals denounced the scandal and threatened God's wrath. The eleven cardinals unanimously elected the writer pope on July 5th 1294.

Reluctantly Peter bowed to what seemed the will of God. His short pontificate, as Celestine V, was a disaster. His knowledge of men was confined to unworldly monks. He could neither understand nor oppose those who sought to exploit his simplicity for political or pecuniary advantage. Moreover, he devised the impracticable project of retiring at intervals from his government of the church to enjoy a hermit's contemplation. He therefore became the tool of King Charles of Naples and lavished benefices and privileges on unworthy suitors. By Advent he was convinced of his incapacity and, encouraged by his successor the future Boniface VIII, resigned the papacy – not an unprecedented step. In vain he attempted to resume his hermit's life in the mountains. Boniface arrested him and kept him in confinement till death. His guards insulted and ill-used him, but he bore his sufferings with patience, even joy. It was not long before death released him, May 19th, 1296. Clement V at the request of Boniface's enemy, Philip of France, canonized him in 1313.
May 19th

CELSUS, *see* Nazarius.

CELSUS or CEALLACH † 1129
The see of Armagh was hereditary in the family of Ceallach mac Aedha for several generations. He was a layman when he succeeded to it in 1105, but he broke the family tradition by nominating St Malachy, his archdeacon, as his successor.
April 7th

CEOLFRID 642–716
After some time at the monasteries of Gilling and Ripon, he went, at St Benedict Biscop's request, to Wearmouth where he became prior. He was made abbot of a new foundation at Jarrow and, in 690, succeeded Benedict Biscop, ruling both Wearmouth and Jarrow. He resigned his office in order to make a pilgrimage to Rome, but died on the way at Langres.
September 25th

CEOWULF *Eighth Century*
A Northumbrian king and a celebrated contemporary of Bede, who dedicated the *Ecclesiatical History* to him, he died as a monk of Lindisfarne.
January 15th

CERATIUS or CÉRASE *Fifth Century*
He was bishop of Grenoble and was present at the council of Orange in 441.
June 6th

CERBONIUS † *c.* 575
Driven out of Africa with St Regulus by the Vandals, St Cerbonius came to Populonia in Tuscany and became its bishop. Another St Cerbonius, bishop at Verona, of whom nothing is known, is probably the same person.
October 10th

CERNEUF of BILLOM, *see* Serenus the Gardener.

CHAD or CEADDA and CEDD *Seventh Century*
SS Chad and Cedd were two brothers who were amongst the earliest native bishops of the English church. They were both monks of the Celtic type, probably disciples of St Aidan. Cedd converted the East Saxons – the men of London were notoriously and obstinately pagan even in Anglo-Saxon times – and became their bishop. He died in 664. His brother Chad was one of the most prominent of the party in favor of maintaining Celtic customs and rejecting Roman ones at the synod of Whitby in 664. But after the synod had decided in favour of Rome, Chad acquiesced. His episcopal career began under a cloud. The triumphant 'Roman' leader, Wilfrid had been elected bishop of the Northumbrians, but, during his long absence in Gaul, Chad seems to have been intruded into the see and to have been uncanonically consecrated. When St Theodore of Tarsus came to England in 669, one of the first things he did

was to depose Chad and restore Wilfrid. Being convinced of Chad's holiness and eligibility, he remedied the defect in his orders and later in the same year sent him to Mercia as Bishop. Chad settled the Mercian see at Lichfield and rapidly acquired a reputation for sanctity. Although he died in 672 his reputation had already spread to Ireland, and he remained throughout the middle ages one of the most popular English saints. His relics are enshrined in the Catholic Cathedral at Birmingham.

March 2nd (St Chad), October 26th (St Cedd)

CHAEREMON, ISCHYION and other martyrs
† 250
St Dionysius of Alexandria, speaking of the Egyptian Christians who were driven into the desert to starve, mentions especially St Chaeremon, bishop of Nilopolis. He also mentions St Ischyion who was martyred for refusing to sacrifice to the gods.

December 22nd

CHAINOALDUS or CAGNOALD   † c. 633
He joined St Columbanus at Luxeuil and followed him into exile. He was later elected bishop of Laon.

September 6th

CHARITY, *see* Faith, Hope, Charity and Wisdom.

CHARLEMAGNE   742–814
This famous king of the Franks and founder of the Holy Roman Empire has never been formally canonized. Devotion was paid to him in the twelfth century, and St Joan of Arc associated him with St Louis of France in her prayers. In 1475 a feast in his honor was instituted in France, and this is still celebrated in Aachen.

The reasons leading to this 'canonization' of a powerful emperor were probably political, because he owed his success very largely to his championship of the rights of the church (*see also* St Leo III). An instructive modern example will be found in the life of 'St' Napoleon, although the two cases are, of course, not parallel.

(In Aachen) January 28th   ILLUSTRATION: page 115

CHARLES BORROMEO   1538–1584
St Charles Borromeo may be said to have incarnated the spirit and ideals of the Counter-Reformation. Sprung from a noble Lombard family he was born at Arona on October 2nd, 1538, and as a second son was early destined for the church, to which also his youthful piety inclined him. He took a doctorate in Canon Law at Pavia in 1559, but in the following January was summoned to Rome by his maternal uncle who had just become pope as Pius IV. There he was forthwith created a cardinal, heaped with valuable ecclesiastical preferment including the archbishopric of Milan, and despite his youth entrusted with the responsible post of Papal Secretary of State. In this capacity he controlled all the official papal correspondence, including the difficult negotiations concerned with the completion of the council of Trent between 1560 and 1564. St Charles' ability amply justified his uncle's trust; but he was content with a subordinate role and except perhaps on a few special occasions probably did not exercise any decisive influence on Pius IV's policy. The council ended, St Charles remained in Rome occupied with the heavy business left over, and was not allowed by the pope to take up residence in his diocese until September 1565. But hardly had he made his triumphal entry into Milan than he was summoned back to attend his uncle on his deathbed and take part in the election of his successor, St Pius V. He returned to Milan in April 1566.

From that time up to his death on November 3rd, 1584, St Charles's life was devoted entirely to his duties as archbishop. The much needed restoration of the pastoral episcopate was central in the scheme of reform of the council of Trent and St Charles set out to become the 'new-model' Tridentine bishop. So fully did he succeed that his example became a pattern and an inspiration for the whole church, and he probably did more than any other single man to get the decrees of the council into action throughout the Catholic world. In both the diocese and the province of Milan he effected a renewal and a reorganization of clerical and spiritual life, signalized by the great mass of detailed legislation promulgated in six provincial and eleven diocesan synods.

Constantly travelling on visitation throughout his vast diocese, preaching and administering the sacraments, he exercised a direct personal ministry even in the remotest villages and Alpine valleys. The revival of Catholicism in Switzerland, parts of which lay within his jurisdiction, was decisively influenced by him. He founded a number of colleges and seminaries. He was a friend to the Jesuits, the Barnabites and other new pastoral orders of the age, and he founded a company of special helpers of his own, the Oblates of St Ambrose (now of St Charles). He was also actively concerned with the reform of the older orders. It was a group of discontented members of the order of the *Umiliati*, which he tried to reform, and which was soon afterwards suppressed, that made the dramatic attempt at his assassination during evening prayers in his Palace in 1569. He encouraged all sorts of pious associations, re-organizing the valuable Company of the Christian Schools to which he attributed the greatest importance. He preserved for Milan the Ambrosian Rite when this was threatened, and in all ways sought to model himself on St Ambrose. But the firmness and uncompromising logic with which St Charles sought to vindicate to the uttermost what he conceived to be the duties and rights of his office, and the severity of his moral principles, inevitably provoked opposition. This came not only from some clerical quarters but also from the lay power represented by the Spanish governors of Milan and by the city's Senate. A running conflict concerning the archbishop's rights of coercive jurisdiction over the laity and the validity of his decrees against dancing, the theatre, tournaments, and public spectacles of all kinds, as well as other controverted matters, marked the course of his episcopate, during which accusations of clerical tyranny on the one hand were met by excommunications and threats of excommunications on the other.

A saint, however, as well as a reformer, St Charles asked nothing of others that he did not perform himself. His private charity was immense and he stripped himself and his household for the needy. He attained to sainthood only gradually, and by the exercise of sheer will-power and progress in prayer. In 1562 the death of his elder brother, so far from causing him to resign his Cardinalate and take up the headship of his family, as was generally expected, only moved him to seek immediate ordination, and to adopt an ascetic mode of life unusual at that time in Rome. In Milan his life of prayer and self-denial was intensified side by side with his pastoral labours. His heroic behaviour during the great plague of 1576-8 was another turning point, leading him to the extremes of detachment and mortification which marked his later years. Though he ate practically nothing at all and slept only for a very few hours on the hardest pallet, his energy seemed boundless. Endless visitations, audiences and pilgrimages, a vast correspondence, regular reading, careful preparation for constant preaching – an art that did not come naturally to him, but for which he schooled himself relentlessly – all still left him time to pass many hours wrapped in continuous prayer. He literally wore himself away; yet he outlived his four sisters whose affairs he attended to with such careful prudence. He left no revelations of his own spiritual life nor, apparently, was he a contemplative in the exact theological sense, yet he cultivated the spirit of Camaldoli and other remote places of recollection. He also greatly valued the *Spiritual Exercises* of St Ignatius and took a Jesuit for his confessor. He had a special devotion to the Holy Shroud of Turin, to Loretto, and to the early saints of the Milanese church, whose relics he delighted to honor and translate.

In St Charles Borromeo, with his well-known ascetic but deeply reflective features, the energy and efficiency of the true Lombard were turned with overwhelming – indeed frightening – will-power to the service of God, and to the interests of the people of Milan, of the papacy and of the full canonical rights of the church. Yet this selfless life of devotion was not achieved without effort, nor without the sacrifice of personal interests which he had cultivated in earlier life, when he had hunted freely, played the 'cello, and taken part in philosophic discussions in Rome. He remained a man of culture and taste. His requirements in church architecture and music were always exact, and the contents of his private library impressive. He was canonized by Paul V on November 1st, 1610. ILLUSTRATION: page 116
November 4th

CHARLES GARNIER, *see* Martyrs of North America.

CHEF, *see* Theuderius.

CHELIDONIUS and EMETERIUS   † 304
Patrons of Santander, they were soldiers, sons of St Marcellus, martyred under Diocletian at Calahorra.
March 3rd

CHIONIA, *see* Agape, Chionia and Irene.

CHRISTINA of BOLSENA and CHRISTINA of TYRE
Thrown into the lake of Bolsena by her father for destroying his household gods, Christina survived only to be subjected to elaborate tortures; these, too, she survived. The story of Christina of Tyre is substantially the same. Although both saints are probably legendary, there is some evidence for the existence of Christina of Bolsena.   ILLUSTRATION: page 117
July 24th

CHARLES of SEZZE   1613-1670
One of the first acts of Pope John XXIII was the canonization on 12 April 1959 of Joachima de Vedruna (q.v.) and Charles of Sezze, an Italian peasant who became a Franciscan lay-brother.
January 6th

CHRISTINA THE ASTONISHING   1150-1224
An orphan born at Brusthem in 1150, she is said to have returned from death to try to liberate some of the souls she had seen in Purgatory. She could no longer tolerate the smell of human-beings, and earned her nick-name by the ways she adopted to escape human contact: climbing trees, hiding in ovens and, on one occasion, flying like a bird into the rafters of a church.
July 24th

CHRISTOPHER   *Third Century*
The patron of travellers, Christopher died a martyr, probably in Lycia, during the persecution of the Emperor Decius in 250. He had no official biographer; but stories about him containing elements of folk-tale, allegory and word-play upon his name have persisted. His legend appears to have been formulated first in the east in the sixth century and to have reached the west some three centuries later. In succeeding years, pious story-tellers have added to the story, or altered its setting. To some, Christopher was a peasant (one tradition says that before his conversion he had the head

of a dog); whilst to others he was a prince who, through the intercession of our Lady, was born to a heathen king. Some have set the scene in Syria, some in Canaan and some in Arabia. His name, before his conversion, is given as Offerus, Offro, Adokimus, Reprobus or Reprebus.

The essence of his legend, though, has the beauty of simplicity: Christopher, a man of great strength but of a sensitive nature, vows to serve the greatest king in the world. Thus begin the travels of this gentle giant in search of truth which are commemorated in many a journey today.

First, Christopher serves the greatest king of the region, but he soon finds that there is one whom he fears: the Devil. So Christopher seeks out Satan, and serves him, until he finds that there is one of whom even Satan stands in awe: Jesus Christ. Christopher's search for Christ is long and hard; eventually he encounters a hermit – some say it was St Babylas of Antioch – who converts him, and tells him that he can serve Christ best by doing well the earthly task for which he is best fitted. So Christopher becomes a ferryman, carrying on his broad shoulders any traveller who wished to cross a nearby river.

One night of storm and driving rain, Christopher carries over the river a small child who insists on making the journey at that moment. With each step he takes, Christopher's burden becomes heavier; half-way over he feels certain that his strength will fail, and that he and his passenger will sink to the depths of the river. When at last he reaches the opposite bank, the child tells him that he has carried on his shoulders all the sins of the world, and asks him to plant his great walking-staff in the ground. At once a wonderful tree springs up miraculously. Then Christopher recognises the Christ-Child, and sees face to face the King whom he has vowed to serve.

Some legends say that, having borne Christ, he should now bear his name, and so henceforth Offero becomes Christ-Offero. As the Golden Legend puts it: 'And afterwards he was named Christopher, which is as much as to say bearing Christ'.

After such an experience it is not surprising that, in spite of all dangers, Christopher should preach Christ to all who came his way, with such conviction and zeal that the earthly agonies of martyrdom were as nothing to him. It is not surprising either that, despite lack of hard facts, such an inspiring story should remain and grow in the minds of men; that in the middle ages his picture was to be found at the entrance of churches or at the gates of cities, prompted by the belief that those who gazed upon his image should not that day be a prey to sudden death: and that today, no matter where men may travel, St Christopher should go with them.

See also The Fourteen Holy Helpers.

July 25th   ILLUSTRATION: page 118

CHRODEGANG   † 766

Born near Liège, he became bishop of Metz while still a layman. His greatest achievement was instituting the practice by which all clergy lived together under the same regulations either conventually or in clergy-houses. His church at Metz was one of the first to adopt the pure Roman liturgy and to use Gregorian chant; and its high traditions endured for many years.

March 6th

CHROMATIUS   † c. 407

Bishop of Aquileia and the friend of St Jerome, whose translation of the Bible he helped to finance.

December 2nd

CHRYSANTHUS and DARIA

Authentic Roman martyrs about whom we unfortunately know nothing for certain. They may have been husband and wife, and have been stoned in a sand pit on the Via Salaria Nova.

October 25th

CHRYSOGONUS   † 304?

Although he is mentioned in the canon of the mass, nothing is known of him except that he was probably a Roman official who was martyred in Aquileia. At Rome he was identified with his namesake after whom the church of Chrysogonus was named.

November 24th   ILLUSTRATION: page 119

CIARAN or KIERAN   c. 511-544

On a broad loop of the river Shannon in the middle of Ireland, halfway between Banagher and Athlone, lie the ruins of the most remarkable of all Irish monastic foundations, Clonmacnoise. A city of the dead, it comprises the shell of a cathedral, the ruins of seven other churches, three high crosses, two stumps of round towers, and hundreds of tombs and headstones. Fifty kings are said to be buried here among the graves of the abbots and monks, including the last High King of Ireland, Roderick O'Conor: 'Battle-banners of the Gael, that in Ciaran's plain of crosses their final hosting keep.'

Clonmacnoise differed from – and surpassed – all the other monastic schools in that it was immediately recognised as the principal school of Ireland, rather than of a province, or of a tribe. As such it was endowed by the High Kings, and its abbots were elected in turn from every part of Ireland. Students flocked to it from all over Ireland as well as from England and France. Its famous alumni number great names like Alcuin, Charlemagne's educational adviser; Tigernach, the chronicler; and Dicuil, the geographer. It had passed its thousand years when Henry VIII suppressed it. Oxford will not be as old as Clonmacnoise for another hundred years.

This was and is St Ciaran's enduring monument. Born in Connacht about the year 511, he was trained by

Finnian at Clonard, and later by Enda at Aran. He died prematurely of plague at the age of thirty-three, only seven months after the foundation of Clonmacnoise. He is said to have prophesied the Viking destruction of the school. His monks asked him what they should do in the face of such an assault; run before the storm, or cling to the place sanctified by his relics. His counsel was: 'Hasten to other quiet places and leave my remains just like the dry bones of a stag on a mountain, for it is better to be with my spirit in heaven than to remain dishonored beside my bones on earth.' His words were often recalled during the penal night of the seventeenth century when a similar choice confronted so many religious. The Gael's independence of shrines was a factor in the Irish recovery.

Ciaran's death-scene lives on in the racial memory. He asked to be taken outside and laid on the ground. Then he looked up at the heavens and murmured something about the way being steep and difficult. His companions encouraged him, and he answered that even David and Paul the Apostle feared death. They tried to take away a stone from under him for his comfort, but he prevented them, saying that he wanted to preserve some conformity with Christ until the end.

St Ciaran's feast-day is kept on September 9th, the traditional pattern day at Clonmacnoise, which never fell wholly into desuetude. Mass is again being celebrated in the ruins, which come to life on that day, when thousands converge on the site. The reappearance of pleasure launches on the Shannon in the last few years has once again made the place easily accessible by water, and this too has brought about a renewal of interest in Clonmacnoise.

September 9th

CIARAN or KIERAN of SAIGHIR
Sixth Century

The Irish claim him as the first-born of their saints, but we know little of him except from marvellous but mutually inconsistent legends. He probably assisted St Patrick in evangelizing Ireland, built the monastery of Saighir, and became first bishop of Ossory.

March 5th

CISELLUS, *see* Luxorius, Cisellus and Camberinus.

CLARE
c. 1193–1253

St Clare (Clara) was born of patrician parents at Assisi in Umbria in 1193/4. After hearing a sermon by St Francis and taking counsel with him she and a companion left her father's house secretly by the door reserved for the passage of a corpse on the evening of Palm Sunday, March 18th, 1212, to meet Francis at the Porziuncola. It is perhaps the most astonishing as well as the most beautiful of all the episodes of the early years

of the brotherhood; the courage and faith and simplicity of the principal actors – the eighteen-year-old girl, leaving all that was familiar and secure, for the unknown; the thirty-year-old and penniless Francis, accepting her as a spiritual and material responsibility; the spring night in the wooded valley, the torches of the brethren, the girl's hair hanging loose at the altar to be cut by Francis. Acting entirely unconventionally and without canonical authority, he accepted her bill of divorce from the world and lodged her in a Benedictine nunnery nearby. There she was joined by her sister Agnes, and others, and the group was settled by Francis at San Damiano, where ultimately Clare's mother, Ortolana, and younger sister joined her. For some time the community was as independent as the early friars; Francis gave Clare a short rule of life, and strict rules of diet, and there are indications that Clare, in the matter of physical austerity, went even further than Francis would have wished. In 1215 he appointed her abbess, and probably gave her the Rule of St Benedict, but an eye-witness speaks of the informality as well as the fervor of the sisterhood, which rapidly multiplied.

In Francis's later years relations with San Damiano were interrupted and the beautiful story of his midnight supper with Clare is almost certainly unauthentic; but in his last illness he was sheltered by her in a hut of branches in the garden of San Damiano, and there composed the *Canticle of Brother Sun*. He gave her his final blessing, departing to die at the Porziuncola, and commanded the brethren to carry his dead body to Assisi by way of the convent, where Clare and her sisters received it and gazed on the wounds in hands and feet.

Clare, truly interpreting the ideals of Francis, obtained from Innocent III a privilege, written in part by the Pope himself, guaranteeing absolute poverty, but Gregory IX, who as Cardinal Ugolino had taken a hand in regulating the friars, insisted on endowing the nuns with land and buildings. Clare resisted, and in a celebrated interview in 1228 withstood the Pope and obtained the desired privilege. When Gregory offered to absolve her from the vow of absolute poverty Clare replied, 'Holy Father, absolve me from my sins, but not from the obligation of following our Lord,' and the Pope yielded.

In the years that followed, Innocent IV in 1247 once more sanctioned the holding of property, but Clare replied by herself composing a rule based on that of Francis, enjoining absolute poverty, and this was approved in haste by Innocent IV two days before her death. The original bull was discovered in the saint's tomb in 1893.

The surviving letters of Clare are not revealing; they are formal in style and abound in flowers of speech, but the recently discovered process of canonization,

DOMINIC: painting by Giovanni Bellini (c.1426 – 1516). (National Gallery, London)

PLATE 5

CATHERINE of SIENA: fresco by Andrea Vanni (*c.*1332 – *c.*1414).
(*Ch. di S Domenico, Siena.*)

Photo: Villani

CECILIA or CECILY: painting by Raphael (1483 – 1520). *(Pinacoteca, Bologna.)*

CHARLEMAGNE: sculpture by Agostino Cornacchini (1685 – 1740). *(Ch. di S. Pietro, Rome.)*

CHARLES BORROMEO: portrait by Guiseppe Maria Crespi (1664 – 1747). *(Ambrosiana, Milan.)*

CHRISTINA of BOLSENA: painting by the Master of the Boissière
Bartholomew (1490 – 1530). (Alte Pinakothek, Munich.)

CHRISTOPHER: silverpoint drawing by Jan van Eyck (1380-90 – 1441). *(Louvre, Paris.)*

CHRYSOGONUS: painting attributed to Jacopo Bellini (*c.*1400 – *c.*1470).
(*Ch. dei SS Gervasio e Protasio, Venice.*)

Photo: Alinari

CLARE: fresco by Cimabue (d. *c.*1302). *(Ch. di S. Francesco, (upper), Assisi.)*

CLARE of MONTEFALCO: detail of painting by Francesco Melanzio (1487 – 1524).
(Ch. di S. Francesco, Montefalco.)

CLEMENT: mural by Ghirlandaio (1449 – 1494). *(Cappella Sistina, Vatican.)*

(A) CANUTE or KNUT: silver penny
(struck at Slagelse, *c.* 1085). (*British
Museum.*)

(B) EGBERT: silver sceatta (struck *c.* 750)
found in the sixteenth century.
(*British Museum.*)

(C) ETHELBERT: silver penny (struck
in East Anglia, *c.* 790). Similar to a piece
found near Rome. Part of the legend is in
Runic. (*British Museum.*)

(D) COLUMBA or COLUMCILLE:
ceramic relief by Brigid ni Rinne (b. 1936.)

COSMAS and DAMIAN: painting by Emmanual (seventeenth century). *(National Gallery, London.)*

CUNEGUND: limewood figure, waxed white and gilded, by Ignaz
Günther (1725 – 1775). *(Rottam Inn, Bavaria.)*

CUTHBERT: MS illumination from Bede's 'Life of Saint Cuthbert' (late twelfth century).
(British Museum.)

(A) CYPRIAN of CARTHAGE: painting
by Bartholomeus Zeitblom
(1455-60 – 1518-22).
(Alte Pinakothek, Munich.)

(B) DAVID or DEWI: chestnutwood figure,
by the studio of Prinknash Abbey, 1948.
*(Church of God of the Holy Ghost, Newtown,
Montgomeryshire.)*

DIONYSIUS or DENYS THE AREOPAGITE: detail from painting by J. de Malouel (d. 1419), and H. de Bellechose (*c.* 1400 – 1419). *(Louvre, Paris.)*

Photo: Mella

FRANCIS: fresco by Cimabue (1240 - *c*.1302). (*Ch. di San Francesco, Assisi*)

PLATE 6

conducted less than two years after her death, gives many vivid touches and the picture of a strong and lofty sanctity, with extreme austerity of life and an illness of thirty years' duration. On a celebrated occasion in 1241 she repelled the looting soldiers of Frederick II, and protected the city of Assisi with her prayers. Other more gentle facets of her character appear; her love of flowers, her custom of passing through the dormitory and pulling the blanket over a sleeping nun, and the well authenticated incident of the bedridden abbess ordering the cat to bring a towel across the room and 'not to drag it on the floor like that'. The witnesses – her own sisters, her nuns and citizens of Assisi – all show us the ardent, determined girl grown into a commanding yet exquisitely gracious figure. She died on August 11th, 1253, and on the morrow Pope Alexander offered the white mass of virgins in her honor. She was canonized in 1255.

St Clare is justly accounted the Foundress of the Second Order of St Francis, that of the Poor Ladies (Minoresses, Poor Clares or Clarisses). Like their brethren they have experienced many divisions and reforms, but they have as their patroness and model a saint given by God to share the ideals and sufferings of Francis; one who by her sanctity and personality could win and in a sense subdue three of the greatest popes of the century in her fidelity to the call of poverty.

August 12th   ILLUSTRATION: page 120

CLARE of MONTEFALCO   † 1308
She became a member of a group of young women – Franciscan tertiaries – led by her sister. When they decided to adopt a more formal conventual life, the bishop of Spoleto recommended them to live according to the Rule of St Augustine. On her sister's death, St Clare became abbess, and so great was her devotion to the Cross that it was alleged that, when her heart was examined after her death, an image of the Cross was imprinted upon it. Her body was certainly still incorrupt in 1881, the year of her canonization, and an eye-witness testified to the 'exquisitely beautiful outline of her face'.

August 17th   ILLUSTRATION: page 121

CLARUS   *Seventh Century*
So named for the brightness of his spiritual perception. He probably entered the abbey of St Ferréol, became director of the convent of St Blandina, and abbot of the St Marcellus monastery at Vienne in Dauphiné.

January 1st

CLARUS   *Eighth Century?*
A popular saint in France in the ninth century, he is one of the English saints represented in the murals of the chapel of the English College in Rome.

November 4th

CLAUD   *Seventh Century*
A priest in Besançon, he retired to the monastery of Condate or Saint-Claude in the Jura, where he became abbot. He was elected bishop of Besançon in 685, but retired again to Condate after ruling for five years.

It is possible, however, that the bishop and the abbot were different people who possessed the same name.

June 6th

CLAUDIA   *First Century*
She is mentioned by St Paul (2 Timothy 4:21), and she may have been a Briton, the wife of St Pudens and mother of Linus who succeeded St Peter.

August 7th

CLAUDIUS, ASTERIUS, NEON, DOMNINA and THEONILLA   † 303?
According to a not wholly reliable legend they were put to death by the proconsul of Cilicia under Diocletian.

August 23rd

CLAUDIUS, HILARIA and his Companions
Claudius was a Roman tribune who suffered with Hilaria, his wife, and others under Numerian, after being converted by the constancy of the martyrs SS Chrysanthus and Daria.

December 3rd

CLEMENT   *First Century*
Around the year 100, a faction of Corinthian Christians revolted against the rulers of their church. Third in succession to St Peter, Clement wrote a letter in the name of the church of Rome to the church of Corinth exhorting, indeed commanding, a return to obedience. He takes for granted the primacy of the Roman church and her right to intervene with authority in the affairs of other churches. He insists upon the necessity of discipline and order as witnessed everywhere, from the divine government of the world to the Roman army. The letter breathes the spirit of imperial Rome baptized as the *ethos* of the church of Rome: authority, but also peace and charity. We are surely entitled to identify Clement with the Clement mentioned in the *Shepherd of Hermas* 'whose duty it is to write to cities abroad'. He may also be, as the Roman missal supposes, the Clement mentioned by St Paul in his epistle to the Philippians. But we cannot be certain. He was not Domitian's cousin, Flavius Clemens, probably a Christian martyr, but he may have been his freedman. Nor was he himself a martyr; nothing is heard of his alleged martyrdom till the closing decades of the fourth century. And Irenaeus, when in his list of the early popes he mentions that Telesphorus was a martyr, implies that the others were not. We do not know the exact date of Clement's death.

Clement was later made the hero of utterly unhistoric

romances composed in Syria, the Clementine *Homelies*, *Recognitions* and *Epitome*.

About the middle of the third century a house in the valley between the Caelian and Esquiline hills was adapted to serve as a Christian church with the title of Clement. This Clement, the donor, and legal owner of the property, cannot have been the first century saint; but by the time of Pope Siricius (384–399) he had been identified with him. For the title of Clement had become attached to the church where Pope Clement was venerated and, moreover, as a martyr. The church, which has been excavated, was enlarged and richly decorated. Above it is the present basilica of San Clemente built about 1100.

Towards the close of the fifth century a Roman writer composed the 'Passion' of St Clement enshrined in the Roman breviary. St Clement banished by Nerva and Trajan to the quarries of the Chersonese, not yet in fact imperial territory, miraculously produced a spring of water for the benefit of his fellow convicts and converted multitudes of pagans. At the command of Trajan's representative 'Duke' Aufidianus, an anchor was tied to his neck and he was drowned. The sea receded three miles and showed his body buried by angels in a marble mausoleum. The story is obvious fiction, but the spring and the anchor occur in a mosaic substantially reproduced in the present San Clemente. St Clement is mentioned in the canon of the Roman Mass.

November 23rd   ILLUSTRATION: page 122

CLEMENT, *see* Agathangelus and Clement.

CLEMENT MARY HOFBAUER   1751–1820
One of the most remarkable of the many figures behind the scenes at the Congress of Vienna (1814–15) was Father Hofbauer, a Redemptorist, who had introduced that Congregation to the countries north of the Alps from its native Italy, despite the opposition of the Austrian Emperor whose policy of state control of the church and its affairs was inimical to all religious orders.

Clement Mary Hofbauer was born in 1751 of a Czech father and a German mother. After working as a baker, he was enabled to study for the priesthood through the generosity of two benefactors encountered in Rome while he was on pilgrimage there. There, too, he fell in with the Redemptorists and entered among them. His first mission was to Warsaw, where he was in charge of the German church, and he soon enjoyed a certain repute as a confessor and the instigator of good works to remedy the social evils of the day. Thus he founded an orphanage, a poor school and a secondary school. In 1808 the invading French cast him into prison, whence, after four weeks, he was able to go to Vienna. Here he became the inspiration and religious leader of a group of German romantics – von Müller, Schlegel, Werner and others – and exerted tremendous influence not only among the poor but also, and despite his rather scanty education, with officials, statesmen and scholars. In this way he was able to defeat the project for a German national church at the Congress of Vienna, and eventually succeeded in arranging for the legal establishment of the Redemptorists north of the Alps, though he did not live to see this occur, since he died in 1820. As a consequence he is regarded by the Redemptorists as their second founder (*see* St Alphonsus Liguori). He was a man of great energy and drive, seeing clearly the end in view and always indefatigable in his work for souls, in the confessional especially, and among the poor.

March 15th

CLEMENT of OKHRIDA and his Companions, the Seven Apostles of Bulgaria   *Ninth - Tenth Century*
These were SS Methodius, Cyril, Gorazd, Clement, Nahum, Sabas and Angelarius. Cyril and Methodius are noticed separately, and of the others, Clement was probably the chief. He was the first Slav to be made a bishop, and founded a monastery at Okhrida.

July 17th

CLEOPATRA and VARUS   *Fourth Century?*
St Varus was a soldier who took pity on some condemned monks and shared their death. Cleopatra, a Christian woman, retrieved his body and built a shrine to him at Dera'a, east of Lake Tiberias. Their story is, however, a fiction and there is little reason to believe in their existence.

October 19th

CLETUS and MARCELLINUS   † 91 and 304
In the present canon of the mass, Cletus is referred to as the third pope, but we are not sure whether he was the third or fourth. He died in 91.

Marcellinus reigned eight years in succession to Pope St Caius and died in 304.

April 26th

CLODOALD, *see* Cloud.

CLODULF or CLOUD   *Seventh Century*
St Clodulf and Ansegis were sons of St Arnoul, bishop of Metz. Ansegis married and was an ancestor of the Carlovingian kings. Clodulf, however, became bishop of Metz in 656, and ruled for about forty years.

Iune 8th

CLOTILDA   † 545
She converted her husband Clovis, king of the Salian Franks, to Christianity. After her husband's death she was troubled by the quarrels of her sons, and retired to do charitable work in Tours.

June 3rd

CLOTSINDIS, *see* Adalbald of Ostrevant.

Brought up by St Clotilda, his grandmother, he and his brothers were the heirs to the Frankish throne. The brothers were murdered by their uncles Childebert and Clotaire; but St Cloud escaped and lived as a solitary. Because of a pun on *clou* (nail), he is regarded as the patron of French nail-makers.

September 7th

CLOUD, *see* Clodulf.

THE CLUNY SAINTS: Berno, Odo, Mayeul, Odilo, Hugh, Bd Aymard and Peter the Venerable

910–1157

It is natural to take these seven saintly men together, because they found their vocations in the same nursery of saints, the abbey of Cluny. Cluny restored the true monastic ideal, it created the first religious order, it was one of the sources of the ideals and practices of the reforming papacy, it gave bishops to the church of a standard of life and breadth of vision hardly known since the days of the early church. It taught by its example a mingling of authority with humility, command more than tempered with love. Not unnaturally the seven saintly men who between them ruled the abbey of Cluny for more than two centuries, bear witness to the quality of the religious life in that abbey: they show the impress of a peculiarly Cluniac sanctity, and their lives impinge upon one another until one seems to see a holy tradition rather than a series of individual exploits. The story of the Cluny saints is the story of Cluny itself.

St Berno was abbot of the remote abbey of Baume in the early years of the tenth century. He was a Burgundian of the highest birth; a man fitted by nature to command and supplied with connections which insured he would have every opportunity. Berno chose to rule a monastery, however, and he made it one of the few genuine centers of Benedictine life in Europe. In 910 the duke of Aquitaine wished to found a monastery as penance for the sins of his youth and insurance against the life to come. He wanted Berno to rule his monastery and together they chose the magnificent site of Cluny. From the first the new monastery differed from almost all its contemporaries. Most monasteries were to a greater or lesser degree subject to 'secular tyranny', to the rights and demands of local great persons, for whom monastic offices and monastic lands provided a convenient means of settling younger sons in life, with or without a monastic vocation. This was made impossible at Cluny by freeing the new abbey from all subjection to any man whatsoever, except the pope. Berno ruled both Cluny and Baume and, to ensure continued independence, he disposed of the abbacy of Cluny in his own lifetime and secured the election of St Odo as second abbot.

St Odo was also of noble birth, with Angevin con-

nections which had secured him a valuable prebend from the canons of Tours. But he had an authentic monastic vocation, and he joined Berno at Baume the year before the foundation of Cluny. As abbot of Cluny he set the characteristic 'tone' of the Cluniacs: aristocratic but genuinely humble, politic but utterly devout, with a pervasive, sophisticated simplicity. He had an extraordinary spiritual gaiety – he sometimes made his monks laugh till they cried and could as easily move them to tears of compassion. He once allowed a beggar to ride on his horse and himself carried the beggar's wallet containing stale and evil-smelling bread and garlic. One of his monks could hardly bear the smell and moved away; Odo turned to him and said, 'It is the smell of poverty which you cannot endure'. Odo, like Berno, was a reformer of monasteries, and he was responsible for reviving the strict Benedictine Rule in a number of French and Italian monasteries. It is not too much to say that when Odo died in 944 monasticism had been transformed.

Bd Aymard, his successor, was not such an able statesman and, unlike Odo, could not enter into easy relationships with princes; but he had all Odo's simplicity and holiness. By now Cluny had such a hold on the respect of men of the time that statesmanship was hardly needed, and the abbey grew easily under Aymard's rule. In old age he went blind and resigned Cluny to another saint, Mayeul.

St Mayeul was a man of striking appearance and again of remarkable humility. A Benedictine biographer remarked of his election: 'Invited, he resisted; beseeched, he refused; rebuked, he trembled; commanded, he submitted'. He resumed the tradition of piety and politics which had marked St Odo's abbacy, he revived many abbeys, and he advised emperors; but when Otto II offered him the papacy he refused. In 994 he was succeeded by St Odilo, one of his closest disciples.

St Odilo was a little man, of insignificant appearance and immense force of character; under him Cluny was at its greatest. Already in the days of St Berno, Cluny had been something more than the normal self-governing institution envisaged in the Rule of St Benedict. It had been linked with the abbey of Baume by St Berno, who intended the union to continue. The idea was that each should help the other to maintain proper Benedictine practice. At the same time, the early abbots of Cluny were constantly called to reform other monasteries which, however, preserved their independence once the reform was complete. In many cases nothing further was needed – the English monastic reform undertaken by SS Dunstan, Ethelwold and Oswald under Cluniac influence is a conspicuous instance of Cluny's success by example – but many reformed communities soon slipped back into their old ways. St Odilo sought to prevent this by extending the original connection between Baume and Cluny very much further. He no longer merely reformed monasteries but subjected them permanently to Cluny; he appointed every prior of every Cluniac house, and the profession of every monk in the remotest monastery was made in his name and subject to his sanction. He periodically visited the monasteries subject to Cluny and saw to it that discipline was strict. Consequently monasticism was given a greater stability, and there was never again any danger, as there had been since the days of Cassian and St Benedict, of monasticism dying from internal corruption. What is more, Odilo had given the church its first religious order, properly so-called. Odilo left another legacy of a different kind. He started the practice of commemorating the dead of his order on the day after All Saints, so that it is from him that the celebration of All Souls' day has come down to us. He died in 1049 and was succeeded by St Hugh, the sixth successive saintly abbot of Cluny.

St Hugh maintained the abbey of Cluny as well as the Cluniac order, which he planted in Italy, England and Spain. It is certainly under Hugh that Cluny reached the height of its worldly reputation and power although spiritually there was some decline from the great days of St Odilo. When Hugh died, a very old man, in 1109, Cluny's best days passed with him. The next abbot, Pons, was a secular-minded, contentious yet pious nobleman, who was made a cardinal, but nearly destroyed Cluny. He created so many factions that his resignation was accepted by the pope in 1122. A few months later Cluny elected its last great abbot, Peter the Venerable.

Bd Peter was faced with the fruits of Abbot Pons's factious abbacy from the first, but much worse followed in 1125, when Pons, repenting of his resignation, returned to Cluny, which he seized by force and misused terribly. The pope succeeded in ejecting Pons, however, who died in prison in 1126. By this time the order was on the verge of collapse, and the finances of Cluny itself in chaos. It was Peter's achievement to restore the order, to return Cluny to an economically sound basis, and, above all, to repair the abbey's shattered reputation; all of which he did with conspicuous success. In addition he played a part in the church life of his time second only to that of his contemporary St Bernard of Clairvaux, a man whose virtues are easier to admire than they can have been to live with. Bernard was the spokesman of the new Cistercian order, and he occasionally transgressed the limits of justice in dealing with what he could not help considering the rival order of Cluny. Immensely provoked, Abbot Peter never lost his temper with the great Cistercian, nor ever regarded the Cistercians as anything but fellow-Christians and fellow-monks. His moderating rôle in the dispute between Bernard and Abelard shows him as orthodox as Bernard and a good deal more

charitable; his letter to Héloise announcing Abelard's death clearly reveals his saintly character. He would take no part in preaching the second Crusade, and Cluny was the home of the first doubts as to the efficacy of Christianity imposed by the sword.

The great days of Cluny, however, were over. Its reputation under Peter the Venerable was not equal to that of its abbot, and it is natural to compare it unfavourably with Cîteaux. But if Cîteaux was magnificent under SS Stephen Harding and Bernard, it declined into respectability soon after their deaths; whereas the grandeur of Cluny had lasted for at least two centuries – centuries, moreover, which began in the dark ages when monasticism was virtually extinct, and ended in the twelfth century renaissance, with the Rule of St Benedict triumphant. At the beginning the church had been almost indistinguishable from the feudal society in which it lived, but it became a great spiritual corporation firmly led by the pope; and because of its contribution to this renaissance, Cluny must stand with the Society of Jesus as one of the most influential religious orders the church has so far seen.

April 29th

CODRATUS and his Companions   *Third Century*
He came of a Greek Christian family in Corinth, and is said to have lived in the wilderness before studying medicine. With five of his disciples, Cyprian, Dionysius, Anectus, Paul and Crescens, he was tried by Jason, prefect of Greece under Decius and Valerian, and beheaded.

March 10th

COEGMEN, *see* Kevin.

COLETTE   † 1447
Born in Picardy of humble parents, St Colette reformed the Poor Clares; one branch of the order is still known as the Colettines. She travelled all over France and Flanders founding or reforming convents, and is said to have met St Joan of Arc at Moulins in 1429.

March 6th

COLMAN of CLOYNE   *Sixth Century*
There are no fewer than 226 saints bearing the name of Colman. This one was known as the 'sun-bright bard', and was the royal poet at Cashel. While still a pagan, he assisted St Brendan in the discovery of the relics of St Ailbhe. He later became the first bishop of Cloyne.

November 24th

COLMAN of DROMORE   *Sixth Century*
He was the first bishop of Dromore, in county Down, and founded a monastery there.

June 7th

COLMAN of KILMACDUAGH   † c. 632
It is said that because he was made a bishop against his

will, he hid himself in the mountains of County Clare and became a hermit. He later founded a monastery at a place called after him Kilmacduagh.

October 29th

COLMAN of LANN ELO   *c.* 555-611

After visiting his uncle St Columba at Iona, he returned to Ireland and founded the monastery of Lann Elo (Lynally) in Offaly.

September 26th

COLMAN of LINDISFARNE   † 676

Lindisfarne, known in a later day as Holy Island, and still later, as St Cuthbert's Island, is situated in the North Sea two miles from the coast of Northumberland. Its monastic ruins had a revival of tourist popularity in the nineteenth century on account of Sir Walter Scott's description of them in his poem *Marmion*:

> A solemn, huge, and dark-red pile,
> Placed on the margin of the isle,
> Yet still entire the Abbey stood,
> Like veteran, worn but unsubdued.

Oswald, king of Northumbria made an appeal to the monastery of Iona in the year 635 to send him missionaries who would complete the evangelization of his realm. One of the Iona community, an Irish monk named Aidan, was thereupon made bishop of Northumbria and put in charge of the work. In imitation of his great master, St Columba, Aidan settled a little community on the island of Lindisfarne, which he modelled on Iona and used as a base of operations for their missionary work. Lindisfarne thus became the residence of the first sixteen bishops of Northumbria, and it flourished for centuries as the religious capital of the north of England and the south of Scotland. The see was afterwards transferred to Durham.

Colman was the third occupant of the see in succession to Aidan. He, too, was an Irishman trained in Iona and sent from there to take charge of Northumbria. Colman was not long in office when his diocese was disturbed by controversy over the date of celebrating Easter. After several changes, Rome had evolved a fixed method of computing this date. But Celtic usage had never altered the method taught by St Patrick. The Celtic monks and especially the Iona community were tenacious in preserving their traditions. It seemed to them like a betrayal of their founder, Columba, to deviate from his original discipline. Even when the parent body in Ireland showed a growing inclination to observe Roman customs, Iona still held out.

The most influential supporter of Roman practice in Northumbria was St Wilfrid, abbot of Ripon. He had been educated in Lindisfarne but had later studied in Rome, and he returned an enthusiast for bringing England into line with Rome. Soon the whole kingdom of Northumbria was divided on this question, a discussion of which will be found in the article on St Wilfrid.

A settlement became so imperative that in 664 the king summoned a synod to meet at Whitby, in Yorkshire, to discuss the matter and come to an agreement. After a full discussion, during which feeling ran high, the assembly voted in favour of making the Roman practice universal in the diocese. But disagreement persisted among the Celtic monks, who influenced the many Celtic peoples in Northumbria. In the interests of peace and order, Colman gave up the bishopric after only three years in office and returned to Iona with his band of Celtic monks.

After a short stay in Iona, he led his followers to Ireland to make a new foundation. Always devoted like Columba, Enda and Senan to an island habitation for its natural seclusion, he chose the hitherto uninhabited island of Inishbofin off the coast of Mayo, where he created a new outpost of monastic life that resembled Iona and Lindisfarne.

The historian St Bede, while disagreeing with Colman on the point at issue, paid a glowing tribute to the fame of the Celtic monks in Northumbria. They were not attracted by pomp, and insisted on such simple buildings as were absolutely necessary. When kings and nobles visited Lindisfarne, they were regaled with the same fare as the monks, who refused grants of lands and kept only the cattle essential for their needs. In a place and period when a good horse was a coveted possession, they still travelled everywhere on foot, including the bishop. When nobles showered gifts on them, these were passed on to the poor. The Celtic monks' indifference to worldly possessions was the secret of their influence in Northumbria.

Some years later, Colman established another foundation on the mainland of Mayo for the Anglo-Saxon brethren who had refused to be parted from him. This became known as the Abbey of the English Saints and flourished up to the eighth century, always inhabited by English monks. It became a bishop's see which was later merged with that of Tuam. Colman died at Inishbofin in the year 676, nine years after he had left Lindisfarne.

February 18th

COLOMAN   † 1012

On his way as a pilgrim to Jerusalem he was arrested in Vienna as a spy and hanged. He came to be venerated as one of the patrons of Austria.

October 13th

COLUMBA   † 853

A nun, she was martyred at Cordova during the moorish persecution.

September 17th

COLUMBA of SENS

Her story – that she was a Spaniard who came into Gaul and settled at Sens – is probably a deliberate fiction. All that is certain is that she was martyred at Sens.

December 31st

COLUMBA or COLUMCILLE 521–597

St Columba is a saint who still, after fourteen hundred years, exerts an appeal upon our imaginations. Born in Ireland, in Donegal in the year 521, he was of the blood royal, and might indeed have become High King of Ireland had he not chosen to be a priest. His vital, vigorous personality has given rise to many legends, and it is a little hard to sift fact from what is more probably fiction. We do know that he was a man of tremendous energy, probably somewhat headstrong in his youth, but with his tendency to violence curbed by a gentle magnanimity.

It seems certain that he left Ireland as an act of penance, although it is less certain how far this was connected with his quarrelling over a copy of the Gospels he had made, a dispute that led to a bloody battle. He came from Ireland to Scotland, to the colony of Dalriada founded on the west coast by his fellow Irish Scots who were at that time somewhat oppressed by the dominant Picts. With twelve companions he founded his monastery on Iona in the year 563. These Celtic monks lived in communities of separate cells, but Columba and his companions combined their contemplative life with extraordinary missionary activity. Amongst his many accomplishments, Columba was a splendid sailor. He sailed far amongst the islands and travelled deep inland, making converts and founding little churches. In Ireland he had already, it is said, founded a hundred churches.

Of all the Celtic saints in Scotland, Columba's life is much the best documented, because manuscripts of his *Life*, written by St Adamnan, one of his early successors as abbot of Iona, have survived. Iona itself remains a place of the greatest beauty, a serene island set in seas that take on brilliant colors in the sunshine, recalling the life and background of this remarkable man whose mission led to the conversion of Scotland and of the north of England, and indeed carried its influence far further afield. It later became the site of a Benedictine Abbey and of a little cathedral. These were dismantled by the Scottish reformers in 1561, and part of Columba's prophecy was fulfilled:

> In Iona of my heart, Iona of my love,
> Instead of monks' voices shall be lowing of cattle,
> But ere the world come to an end
> Iona shall be as it was.

When Dr Samuel Johnson visited the island in 1773 he observed, 'That man is little to be envied, whose patriotism would not gain force upon the plain of Marathon, or whose piety would not grow warmer among the ruins of Iona!'

Columba was a poet as well as a man of action. Some of his poems in both Latin and Gaelic have come down to us, and they reveal him as a man very sensitive to the beauty of his surroundings, as well as always, in St Adamnan's phrase, 'gladdened in his inmost heart by the joy of the Holy Spirit'. He died in the year 597.

June 9th ILLUSTRATION: page 123 (D)

COLUMBANUS † 615

St Columbanus was born in either Kildare, or Carlow, about the middle of the sixth century, a period when the fame of the Irish monastic schools had begun to resound throughout the Christian world.

He was educated first at a school on Cleenish Island, Lough Erne, and afterwards at Bangor, which was at that time the foremost school in Ireland. Here he remained until he was almost forty. He then left Ireland for Gaul with twelve chosen companions, 'in order to preach the gospel to pagans and to lead a solitary life'. This group were the pioneers of a movement which developed into an apostolic crusade during the Celtic golden age.

The king of Austrasia, the most easterly of the three Frankish kingdoms, received the missionaries kindly and gave them a ruined Roman fort called Annegray on the border of his kingdom, where it touched Burgundy. Annegray is now a village in the commune of Faucogney, Haute-Saône. Here the Irish monks set to work with a will, clearing and cultivating the land and building wooden huts for their needs. Presently they became a center of interest to the two kingdoms. Both nobles and serfs were strongly attracted to their way of life and flocked to join them. Annegray was soon too small for the numbers, and Columbanus was given another site at Luxeuil, seven miles away. In a short time a third foundation became necessary and this was established at Fontaine, four miles west of Annegray. In ten years, all three monasteries were humming with life.

But neither the Frankish bishops nor the two courts between whose kingdoms Columbanus was poised, viewed with unanimous enthusiasm this spectacular increase in strength and influence. The Irish monks continued to celebrate Easter according to Celtic, instead of Roman, usage, and the bishops made this a pretext to summon Columbanus to appear before a synod. He excused himself from personal attendance in an eloquent letter in which he appeals to them to allow him 'to live in silence in the depth of these forests, near the bones of our seventeen brethren who have died here'. But he suggests that more urgent matters than a liturgical difference of opinion claimed the bishops' attention. The king of Burgundy had four illegitimate children and was not married. The fact that the bishops frequented his court and never adverted to the scandal shows to what a low state Christianity had fallen. However, there could be only one end to such a quarrel: Columbanus and all his brethren of Irish blood were expelled from Luxeuil. The monastery was allowed to carry on its work, but he and they were to go back 'whence they came'. They were escorted out of the kingdom and conveyed to Nantes. Here, before he embarked, Columbanus wrote a touching letter of farewell to the brethren at Luxeuil: charged with emotion, it reveals not only the writer's nobility of character, but also the training he had had in the Irish schools. Part of the letter is addressed particularly to the monk he had nominated to succeed him, to whom he says: 'As for me, my soul is rent asunder. I have desired to serve everybody, I have trusted everybody, and it has made me almost mad. Be thou wiser than I: I would not see thee taking up the burden under which I sweated . . . While I write, they come to tell me that the ship is ready – the ship which is to carry me back against my will to my country . . . The end of my parchment obliges me to finish my letter. Love is not orderly: it is this which has made it confused.'

But the ship was driven back by a storm and ran aground again on the coast of Gaul. Since their military escort had meanwhile returned home, the Irish group were free again. Traversing Gaul once more, they preached the gospel to the pagan peoples on the banks of the Rhine. They then sailed up that river and its tributaries to the Lake of Zürich and finally settled for a period at Bregenz on the Lake of Constance. The hostility of the pagan tribes in this region eventually forced the monks to leave. Columbanus and one companion travelled south, crossed the Alps and entered the kingdom of Lombardy where he was well received. He was then in the seventies, and both legend and record combine in presenting a remarkable picture of the indomitable missionary, with the bow-shaped frontal tonsure of Celtic usage, in a white habit and cowl, his pastoral staff in his hand, his only possession a codex of the Gospels in a leather satchel suspended from his neck.

The king of Lombardy gave him the site of a ruined oratory in the Apennines. Here once again the two monks began the work of clearing, cultivating, building. There is mention of the aged Columbanus carrying great logs on his shoulder to hasten on the work. This was the origin of the Bobbio monastery. Columbanus thought that he had found another Luxeuil where he could contemplate in solitude the death which he knew was approaching. But he had little leisure. The Arian heresy was rife in Lombardy; the king himself was an Arian, yet he asked Columbanus to write to the pope, appealing for an end to the schism caused by this heresy.

This drew from Columbanus the famous statement of the Irish position in the seventh century which is so often quoted by apologists:

'We, Irish, living at the furthest extremity of the world, are the disciples of St Peter and St Paul, and of the other apostles who have written under the dictation of the Holy Spirit. We receive nothing more than the apostolic and evangelical doctrine. In Ireland there have never been either heretics, Jews, or schismatics . . . The native liberty of my race gives me boldness. With us it is not the person, but the right which counts . . . We are bound to the chair of St Peter; for however great and glorious Rome may be, it is this chair which makes her great and glorious in our eyes . . .'

Some distance from Bobbio, Columbanus had discovered a cave in the side of a huge rock. This he transformed into a chapel dedicated to our Lady, and here he lived, returning to the monastery only for Sundays. But he died within a year of Bobbio's foundation, on November 23rd, the day on which his feast is now celebrated, in the year 615.

Although to the dissolute Merovingian courts and their subservient bishops, Columbanus may well have been a disturbing figure, vehement and gaunt like an Old Testament prophet; in the imitacy of community life he was kindly and affectionate, with the same gift of poetry and power over the animal kingdom as St Francis of Assisi displayed in a later century. The squirrels used to come down from the trees to nestle in the folds of his cowl. He tamed wolves in the forest and subdued a bear and her cub.

His work prospered exceedingly after his death. Luxeuil became the foremost monastic school in seventh-century Gaul and survived up to the time of the French Revolution. Bobbio became the Monte Cassino of Northern Italy and earned for Columbanus the fame of 'Saint Benedict's rival'. His cult is still fervent today in northern Italy, where thirty-four parishes are dedicated to him.

But it is not the Columban foundations alone which make his name so significant in the history of Europe. Many of his Irish companions became in their turn great founders, and between them they formed a solid bulwark against the onrush of paganism in the dark ages. It was their combined work that eventually saved the faith in Europe.

November 23rd

COLUMCILLE, *see* Columba.

COMGALL   † 603
Born in Ulster and ordained by Bishop Lugid, he founded the great abbey of Bennchor, or Bangor. Three thousand monks are said to have lived under his rule, including St Columbanus.

May 11th

COMGAN
Eighth Century

A prince of Leinster, he fled to Scotland after a defeat in battle and founded a community in Lochalsh, opposite Skye. He is buried at Iona.
October 13th

CONAN
Seventh Century?

He was probably a missionary in Ireland or in the Isle of Man and the Hebrides. Place names seem to prove his existence, but dates disprove his title, 'bishop of Sodor'.
January 26th

CONCORDIUS
Second Century

A subdeacon living in the desert during the reign of Marcus Aurelius. Tried at Spoleto by Torquatus, governor of Umbria, he joyfully endured torture rather than worship idols, and was beheaded.
January 1st

CONDEDUS
† c. 685

An English wanderer in France, he became a monk of Fontenelle, but reverted to the solitary life on an island in the Seine called Belcinac.
October 21st

CONLETH, *see* Catald and Conleth.

CONRAD of CONSTANCE
† 975

A member of the Guelf family, he was made bishop of Constance in 934 and settled his estates upon the church. He is usually represented with a chalice and a spider because once when he was celebrating mass, a spider dropped into the chalice, and although all spiders were then thought to be deadly poisonous, Conrad swallowed it out of respect to the Eucharist.
November 26th

CONRAD of PARZHAM
† 1894

Of humble Bavarian parentage, he became a Capuchin lay-brother and was sent to Altötting, where as porter he ministered to the needs of pilgrims for forty years.
April 21st

CONRAD of PIACENZA
† 1351

A nobleman of Piacenza, he accidentally set fire to a large stretch of countryside. His delay in owning up nearly caused the death of an innocent man who was wrongly accused; and this, together with the heavy fine he had to pay, turned Conrad's thoughts to religion. He became a friar and a hermit celebrated for piety and miraculous cures at Noto in Sicily.
February 19th

CONRAN

A legendary bishop of Orkney. No evidence whatsoever supports his existence.
February 14th

CONSTANTINE, *see* Theodore, David and Constantine.

CONSTANTINE
Sixth Century

King of Cornwall, he became a menial at St Mochuda monastery in Rahan, Ireland, and later helped SS Columba and Kentigern in Scotland. Murdered by pirates in Kintyre, he is regarded as Scotland's first martyr.
March 11th

CONTARDO
† 1249

While on pilgrimage to Compostella, he climbed a hill which afterwards bore his name, overlooking Broni, and prayed that if he had to die away from home, it should be there. Almost immediately he was taken ill and died in a wretched hut.
April 16th

CONVOYON
† 868

He was the founder and abbot of the monastery of St Saviour at Redon in Brittany, where he is greatly revered. During his last days he was exiled from Redon by Norse invasions.
January 5th

CORBINIAN
† 725

After fourteen years in a hermitage near Melun in France, he went to Rome, and was sent by Pope St Gregory II as a missionary bishop to Bavaria.
September 8th

CORENTIN or CURY
Sixth Century?

During the seventeenth century St Corentin's *cultus* became widespread because of the preaching of Bd Julian Maunoir. He was probably the first bishop of Cornouaille in Brittany.
December 12th

CORNELIUS
† 253

Fifteen months after Fabian's martyrdom in the persecution of Decius, the Roman church was able to elect Pope Cornelius. He was faced with the schism of Novatian, a rigorist, who would refuse absolution even on their deathbed to all who denied their faith, leaving them to the divine mercy. As soon as he was assured of Cornelius's canonical election St Cyprian acknowledged and supported him, and his intervention brought back to Catholic unity several confessors (men who had suffered short of death) who had supported Novatian. Despite some misunderstandings, Cornelius and Cyprian were allies, indeed close friends, and decrees of a Carthaginian council condemning Novatus and Novatian were ratified by a Roman council. In a letter to Bishop Fabius of Antioch, Cornelius informs him that the church of Rome possessed forty-six priests, seven deacons, seven sub-deacons, forty-two acolytes, fifty-two exorcists, lectors and doorkeepers, and supported 1500 widows and poor people.

When Gallus renewed the persecution, Cornelius was arrested. He was banished to Centumcellae, the modern Cività Vecchia. In a letter of congratulation Cyprian wrote: 'Let us pray each for the other in these days of persecution, support each other by a mutual charity and, if God does one of us the favor to die shortly and before the other's death, may our friendship continue in the Lord's presence and our prayer for our brethren and sisters continue to solicit the Father's mercy'. Cornelius in fact did not live long. He died in exile in June 253 and was buried at Centumcellae; but his body was later transferred to a crypt adjoining the catacomb of Callistus. The friendship of these two saints, Cornelius and Cyprian, survives to this day and throughout a world beyond their imagining in a common festival on September 16th and in the canon of the Roman mass, where Cyprian, the sole non-Roman bishop mentioned, is coupled with his friend.
September 16th

COSMAS and DAMIAN

Legend relates that they were two brothers, doctors who took no fees from their patients, and that they were martyred for their faith amid the conventional extravaganza of tortures and marvels. Their early *cultus* at Cyr, a city in Southern Syria, attests their existence and martyrdom. But this is all that is known about them.

Their fame, based on miraculous cures of those who invoked their aid, spread throughout the church, and the Emperor Justinian I, grateful for a cure, did much to foster the devotion. A sanctuary at Aegae in Cilicia led to the localization of their martyrdom in that city. At Rome Pope Symmachus (498–514) built an oratory in their honor, Felix IV (526–530) a basilica. Their Roman festival, September 27th, was probably the date of a dedication. Its mass was used by Gregory II (eighth century) for the station mass of the fourth Thursday in Lent, the September festival receiving a new mass composed of liturgical bits and pieces. The pagan practice of sleeping in the precincts of a temple of Aesculapius that the god might indicate a cure in a dream was transferred, so Gregory of Tours informs us, to sanctuaries of Cosmas and Damian. With St Luke, Cosmas and Damian are the patrons of surgeons and physicians.
September 27th   ILLUSTRATION: page 124

CRESCENTIA, see Vitus, Modestus and Crescentia.

CRISPIN and CRISPINIAN

The patrons of shoemakers, they are said to have preached the Gospel in France and to have mended shoes for their bread. A tradition connects them with Faversham in Kent, and they are referred to by Shakespeare in Henry V's speech before the battle of Agincourt.
October 25th

CRISPINA   † 304

St Augustine refers quite frequently to this saint, and a written summary of the evidence at her trial has come down to us which is reasonably authentic. She was martyred at Theveste in Africa for refusing to sacrifice to the gods.
December 5th

CRONAN of ROSCREA   *Seventh Century*

He built his first settlement at Puayd, but he is said to have built fifty houses which he relinquished in turn to needy anchorites, including Lusmag in Offaly and Monahincha near Roscrea.
April 28th

CRONION, see Besas, Cronion and Julian.

CUBY, see Cybi.

CUMIAN   *c. 590–c. 665*

He probably founded a community at Kilcummin in Offaly and introduced the Roman method of fixing the date of Easter – a practice which gained him a rebuke from the abbot of Iona.
November 12th

CUNEGUND   † 1033

Daughter of Siegfried of Luxemburg and Hedwig, she married Henry, duke of Bavaria, later king of the Romans. The royal couple founded the cathedral and monastery of Bamberg, and after Henry's death Cunegund entered the convent she had founded at Kaufungen in Hesse.   ILLUSTRATION: page 125
March 3rd

CUNGAR   *Sixth Century*

St Cungar is an example of a saint about whom it is difficult to know much in the sense of dependable written records, yet who has survived in human memory through his close association with a neighborhood. As a Celtic saint his name is known by the dedication of churches and in place-names in Wales, Cornwall and Brittany. And there are legends about him which suggest that he was one of the great monks who journeyed in the Celtic countries preaching and converting and, above all, establishing monasteries.

He is remembered, however, most clearly in Somerset. Somerset in Cungar's time was suffering from the Saxon invasions but was not yet engulfed; yet his fame survived the heathen influx. Congresbury near Yatton is named after him, and a church nearby is dedicated in his honor. There is a ninth century mention of a monastery, and many medieval references exist to his body being preserved at Congresbury; and it was in Somerset in the early middle ages that a *Life* of Cungar was produced. As a *Life* it is not perhaps very satisfactory, since it appears to have been written for admonitory rather than historical purposes, but it has chapter

headings calculated to engage the reader's attention: 'How King Poulentus was blinded', 'How Prince Pebiau was liquefied'. This saint, whose memory has survived heathen invasion and the kind of hagiography which tends to cast doubts on his very existence, still has his feast observed in the diocese of Clifton today.
November 27th

CUNIBERT *Seventh Century*
He became bishop of Cologne in 625 and founded the church of St Cunibert in that city.
November 12th

CURY, *see* Corentin.

CUTHBERT *c. 634–687*
There has been much dispute about the ancestry and race of St Cuthbert, but it is fairly certain that the saint was born within a year or two of 634 and that he started life as a shepherd on the Lammermuir Hills to the south of Edinburgh. Inspired by some kind of spiritual experience, in 651 Cuthbert joined the monastery of Old Melrose in the valley of the Tweed about two miles from the present Melrose. Of his early life in the monastery we know nothing of significance; it was when he had been at Melrose for ten years that he was appointed prior of Lindisfarne or Holy Island – both monasteries being under the jurisdiction of Abbot St Eata at the time.

It was as prior of Lindisfarne that the two most prominent sides of St Cuthbert's character began to make themselves apparent. First, there was the extraordinary influence exercised by his personality, an influence which can be explained by the way in which he made the interests of other persons his own. He really seems to have been able to enter into the feelings of others, especially of penitent sinners, and he threw himself wholeheartedly into the task of reconciling a community much divided both ideologically and racially. The other prominent characteristic of the saint was his vivid interest in archaeology and in the beauties of nature. He was the protector of the sea-birds, he used to wander round the isle of Lindisfarne during the long summer nights 'inspecting and examining everything' as the Venerable Bede describes it. It was characteristic that, in later years, it was while he was gazing with great interest at a Roman fountain on the walls of Carlisle that he had his sudden and vivid intuition of the disastrous defeat of Nechtansmere, which was then taking place across the fells.

Nevertheless, despite this interest in persons and things, Cuthbert was possessed by a strong desire to lead a life of complete solitude. At first he went to live at 'St Cuthbert's Isle', which lies a short distance from the coast of Holy Island and is joined to it by a stretch of sand at the ebb. From this isle, away to the south, the tall black cliffs of the Inner Farne are clearly to be seen, and it must have been the daily sight of this more remote retreat which drew Cuthbert thither.

It was in 676 that Cuthbert retired to the Inner Farne. He made himself a cell from which the mainland could not be seen, and he constructed a small guest-house a few yards away for the housing of visitors from Lindisfarne. For nearly nine years the saint remained in this strikingly beautiful spot, until, in 684, at the request of a synod held at Twyford, he reluctantly undertook to become bishop of Hexham, a see which he soon changed for that of Lindisfarne. His life as a bishop differed little from that which he had led as prior of Lindisfarne, save for the long journeys through the hills of the border country which he carried out with tireless energy, and about which many miraculous doings of his were afterwards related. It seems that the energy he displayed undermined his health, for, though still only in his early fifties, he became convinced that he had not much longer to live and thereupon returned to his hermitage at Farne to prepare himself for death.

It was immediately after Christmas in the year 686 that Cuthbert left Holy Island for the Inner Farne. At first he was active enough to meet the brethren from Lindisfarne when they came over to see him, but gradually his strength began to fail and he was unable to walk down to the landing-stage. On February 27th his last illness came upon him and from that time he was hardly able to move. After receiving the sacraments he died in the early morning of Wednesday March 20th, 687.

He was buried at Lindisfarne; later, moved to Chester-le-Street during the Danish raids, his body eventually rested at Durham.

The bare record of St Cuthbert's life does not perhaps enable us fully to express the fascination exercised by the saint, not only upon contemporaries but also upon those who came afterwards such as the Venerable Bede, King Alfred and St Aelred of Rievaulx. Indeed his memory is reverenced by northerners to the present day. He has given his name in popular parlance to the eider duck, 'cuddy's ducks', to a local variety of sea-weed, 'St Cuthbert's Beads', and to many spots on the coastline of Lindisfarne and of Farne. According to the early *Lives* of him, St Cuthbert tamed the eider ducks of Farne; in the breeding-season they are tame to this day.

St Cuthbert's body was moved from Lindisfarne to a shrine in Durham Cathedral, and, at the Reformation, it was again moved to avoid desecration. The English Benedictines claim that, by means of a secret known only to three monks at any one time, they alone can say where St Cuthbert's body now is; but there is some evidence for supposing that bones and relics discovered in 1827 are, in fact, those of the saint.
March 20th ILLUSTRATION: page 126

CUTHBURGA † c. 725

The sister of King Ine of Wessex, her husband, King Aldfrid of Northumbria, allowed her to enter the convent of Barking. With her sister St Quenburga, she founded the abbey of Wimborne in Dorset, of which she was head.

September 3rd

CUTHMAN Tenth Century

Of simple but cheerful piety, he obeyed his parents unconditionally. He went from place to place seeking work and wheeling his widowed mother in a cart. With his own hands he built a church at Steyning in Sussex.

February 8th

CYBARD, see Eparchius.

CYBI or CUBY Sixth Century

Although an important Celtic saint, very little is reliably known of his life. He was almost certainly in Angelsey, the stronghold of his cult, and the monastery of which he was abbot was built on the site of what is now Holyhead, which is in Welsh *Caer Gybi* (Cybi's Fort).

November 8th

CYNEBURGA, CYNESWIDE and TIBBA
Seventh Century

Cyneburga, daughter of the Mercian king, Penda, married Alcfrid, son of Oswy of Northumbria. She founded and entered a convent at Castor, where she was succeeded as abbess by her sister, Cyneswide, married to Offa, son of the East Saxon king. Tibba, their kinswoman, probably inhabited a cell nearby.

March 6th

CYPRIAN, see Felix and Cyprian.

CYPRIAN of ANTIOCH and JUSTINA

The story of Cyprian of Antioch and the lady Justina is a pious fiction which, as far as we can tell, has no foundation in fact whatever. It was already in circulation in the fourth century and was believed to be true by such eminent but uncritical Christian writers as St Gregory Nazianzen and the poet Prudentius, who already confuse the fabulous converted magician, Cyprian of Antioch, with the great and undoubtedly genuine bishop and martyr Cyprian of Carthage. But all modern Catholic scholars agree that the legend is entirely fictitious. It runs, briefly, as follows.

Cyprian the magician was a native of Antioch and an adept in every branch of the black art, which he studied in all the schools of magic in the East. (Professional magicians, whose intentions were often as evil, even if their results were not as remarkable, as anything in the stories, were a genuine enough feature of the life of the Roman Empire.) In the course of his nefarious career he met and fell in love with a Christian girl called Justina. She overcame, by the power of prayer and the sign of the cross, all his attempts to win her with the help of the demons. The result was that Cyprian was converted to Christianity; he burned his magical books in the presence of the bishop, and behaved with such edifying piety and humility that he was ordained priest and eventually became bishop of Antioch. Finally he and Justina were martyred together in the persecution of Diocletian. After the miraculously unsuccessful attempt to give them a sensationally horrid death (in this case by boiling in pitch) which is common form in fictitious acts of martyrs, they were beheaded by order of the Emperor himself.

The story remained very popular in east and west throughout the middle ages, and long after, and is the theme of a play by Caldéron entitled *El Mágicò Prodigioso* (*The Wonder-Working Magician*).

September 26th

CYPRIAN of CARTHAGE † 258

Caecilius Cyprianus Thascius Cyprian, among the most outstanding figures of the primitive church, was an African. In early life a pagan of brilliant endowments and considerable learning, teacher of rhetoric and advocate, he indulged all the pleasures of the young people of his time. Converted to the Christian faith, through the instrumentality of a priest Cecilianus, who on his death bed entrusted his widow and children to Cyprian's care, he devoted himself wholeheartedly to the service of Christ. He pledged himself to celibacy, sold his possessions and home, giving all the proceeds to the poor, renounced heathen literature for the Bible and Tertullian, never again quoting a pagan author. A number of treatises and a collection of letters are his contribution to Christian literature. Though devoid of speculative ability he handled vigorously the rhetorical style of his period.

It is not surprising that soon after his conversion he was ordained priest and, in 249, was elected bishop of Carthage by an overwhelming majority of the clergy and laity. An attempt to escape the dignity by flight was frustrated. He displayed all the gifts and virtues a bishop should possess, and he did his utmost to raise the moral and spiritual standards of his flock, relaxed by many years of freedom from persecution. In particular he wrote a tract against the worldliness, not vice, of the consecrated virgins, the earliest type of nuns. They must not use make up or tint their hair. The year following Cyprian's election, 250, the Emperor Decius launched a dangerous, because systematically organized, persecution: all must sacrifice to his genius. Many Christians obeyed. Others compromised by purchasing from venal officials certificates, *libelli*, that they had complied with the law; Cyprian went into hiding. The church, he considered, should not be deprived during the storm, of a bishop, and his presence at Carthage would provoke the enemy; so he kept in touch with his flock by letter. Nevertheless he found himself obliged to defend his conduct.

When persecution ceased with Decius's death the lapsed Christians sought to return to the church. Cyprian presided over a council of bishops and priests which decided that those who had sacrificed might be absolved only in danger of death, those who had obtained *libelli* after a period of penance. A priest, Novatus, and a deacon, Felicissimus, had created a schism in favor of laxity, indiscriminate and immediate reconciliation. Cyprian supported Pope Cornelius against the schism of Novatian and his adherents, and, together with several letters, sent the Roman Christians a treatise on the unity of the church, *De Unitate Ecclesiae*, in which he insists on the supremacy of St Peter's successor as the cornerstone of Catholic unity.

In 253 a plague raged throughout the Empire. The Christians of Carthage spent themselves generously in the service of the victims, pagans as well as Christians. Nevertheless superstition ascribed the plague to divine anger against the Christians, and the Emperor Gallus renewed persecution. Under these circumstances another council decided to absolve all penitents prepared to stand firm for their faith. The persecution, however, may not have been severe at Carthage, for Cyprian was not disturbed.

Unhappily a serious conflict broke out between Cyprian and Cornelius's successor, Pope Stephen. Cyprian continued and defended the established African custom of rebaptizing heretics reconciled to the church. Stephen championed the Roman usage, later accepted by the entire church, of recognizing heretical baptism as valid. Somewhat highhandedly he attempted to impose his view on the Africans, but a council of eighty-seven African bishops supported Cyprian. It was at this time that Cyprian produced a revised version of his treatise on unity. He omitted the affirmations of papal supremacy and, in veiled language, charged the Pope and his supporters with destroying Catholic unity. Schism seemed inevitable, but Stephen died, and his successor, Sixtus II, a man of peace, let the matter drop. Local churches would be free to follow their own practice.

In 257 persecution was revived by the Emperor Valerian. Cyprian was among its victims. Our accounts of his appearances before the proconsuls and his martyrdom are based on official documents and the report of an eye-witness. Summoned before the proconsul Paternus, he confessed his faith and refused to betray the names of his priests. He was banished to Curubis, a town on the coast, lonely but healthy, where he was able to correspond with his flock and compose his last treatise, an exhortation to martyrdom. On the eve of his departure a symbolic dream had assured him that he would be beheaded in a year's time. In fact a year later, autumn 258, since an imperial decree had sentenced members of the clergy to death, he was recalled and brought before another proconsul, Galerius Maximus. Remanded for one night, which he spent with members of his flock, on the morning of September 14th he stood once more before his judge: 'You are Thascius the Pope of these sacrilegious people'. 'Yes.' 'Our most holy Emperors command you to sacrifice.' 'I will not do it.' 'Think it over.' 'Follow your instructions. When the right course is so plain there is no room for reflection.' Reluctantly Galerius pronounced sentence of decapitation, and Cyprian was led off to execution. He prayed, took off his cloak and tunic, and stood up in his linen undergarment. He ordered twenty-five pieces of gold to be given to the executioner. The Christians spread out cloths to receive his blood as a relic. A priest and archdeacon tied his hands. He was beheaded.

The following night the Christians bore his body to burial triumphantly in a torchlight procession to the graveyard of Macrobius Condidianus, the procurator, 'on the road to Mappala near the reservoirs.' A few days later the proconsul followed him to the tomb. We possess Cyprian's biography written by his deacon Pontius.   ILLUSTRATION: page 127 (A)

September 16th

CYRAN, *see* Sigiramnus.

CYRIACUS, LARGUS and SMARAGDUS
Fourth Century

We know that there was a St Cyriacus, because he is buried at Rome on the Ostian way at a place called Cyriacus, but whether he is the saint of the celebrated legend is most uncertain.

According to that legend Maximianus, in order to please his father-in-law Diocletian, started to build a great palace with magnificent thermal baths. Many Christians were forced by Maximianus to labor at the construction of these baths, and SS Cyriacus, Largus and Smaragdus went among their fellow Christians helping and consoling them. Pope St Marcellus was so impressed by their devotion that he had them ordained deacons, but they were discovered and arrested. Cyriacus was, however, able to cure the Emperor's daughter, Artemia, of a severe illness; and to show his gratitude, Diocletian gave him a house which he promptly turned into that church which now bears his name.

The king of Persia, hearing of Cyriacus's reputation as a healer, sent to Diocletian to know if he would allow him, to go to Persia where the king's daughter was 'possessed of a demon'. Diocletian gave permission, and

Cyriacus went to Persia, cured the king's daughter, converted her, her father and many Persians to Christianity, and then returned to Rome. He and his companions were left in peace, until one day, during Diocletian's absence from Rome, Maximianus arrested Cyriacus, Largus and Smaragdus, put them to the torture and had them executed outside the walls of the city.

The Gospel of their Mass reminds us 'In my name shall they cast out devils ... they shall lay their hands upon the sick, and they shall recover'.

August 8th

CYRIACUS or JUDAS QUIRICUS
Second Century

The principle patron of Ancona, where local legend says that he was a Jew who revealed the hiding place of the Cross to the Empress Helen, he became bishop of Jerusalem and suffered martyrdom under Julian the Apostate.

See also The Fourteen Holy Helpers.

May 4th

CYRICUS and JULITTA *Third Century?*

The story of the widow Julitta is probably a fabrication. To escape the enforcement of the edicts of Diocletian against Christians, she fled to Tarsus with her three-year old son Cyricus. There she was recognized and arrested. In his rage the governor killed her son, while Julitta was first tortured and then executed.

June 16th

CYRIL, *see* Anastasia and Cyril.

CYRIL and METHODIUS † 869 and 884

Natives of Thessalonica, these two brothers preached the Gospel (in Slavonic) in Moravia. Cyril died in Rome, probably before he could be consecrated bishop Methodius became archbishop of Sirmium and persuaded the pope to allow a vernacular liturgy in Slavonic. These brothers are regarded as the apostles of the southern Slavs and the patrons of the unity of the Eastern and western churches.

July 7th

CYRIL of ALEXANDRIA † 444

In the year 412 St Cyril succeeded his uncle, Theophilus, as bishop of Alexandria. He was perhaps already middle-aged, but nothing is known of his earlier life except that he had been present at the condemnation of St John Chrysostom in 408, that he had apparently at one time been a monk in the desert and that clearly he had received an elaborate education in the Greek classics.

By the fifth century the patriarchs of Alexandria had become the wealthiest and most politically powerful bishops in the empire. Now that Egypt was Christian they had come to represent all that was left of Egyptian national sentiment. They styled themselves the sucessors of St Mark, but they were also the successors of the High Priests of Amen Ra and in some fashion of the Pharaohs. There was always to be something of the Pharaoh in Cyril even though before the end he was a saint.

During the first fifteen years of his episcopate he broke the power of two successive governors and of the Jewish bankers in Alexandria. The philosopher Hypatia and the prefect Callistus were both murdered by Cyril's supporters, not by Cyril, but it is true there is no evidence that he condemned them. His practical charity towards the poor and sick and his deep compassion towards all penitent sinners were combined with a certain quality of ruthlessness. He does not seem to have doubted that his enemies were the enemies of God. Passionate in his zeal for souls, passionate in his defence of Catholic truth, he was ready to use any weapon that came to hand: his wealth, the mobs that his eloquence could rouse so easily, his steady body-guard of monks with their long staves and heavy leather boots. This may help to explain why the Christological controversy in which he played so great a part kept for so long a semi-political character.

The monk Nestorius had become patriarch of Constantinople in 428. He does not seem to have merited the sympathy so warmly accorded to him by nineteenth-century historians. He seems to have been a court prelate, vehemently ambitious, subservient to the emperor and the civil service, convinced of the outstanding efficacy of his personal prayer and intent on the persecution of all heretics. On the other hand there is no convincing evidence that he himself was ever intentionally heretical. All early fifth century theologians accepted the teaching of the church that Christ was both divine and human. No definition had yet solved the problem of the inter-relation of his Godhead and his Manhood. St Cyril held that the two were united so closely that the Mother of the child Christ could be termed the God-Bearer, Nestorius that they remained so separate and distinct that the Mother of the child Christ should be termed Christ-Bearer only. Each accused the other of heresy.

St Cyril rallied the majority of the Eastern monks to his support, he gained the support of Rome and was authorized to act as its representative in the east. Strengthened by this mandate he condemned and anathematized Nestorius at a synod at Alexandria in 430, and then, in the summer of 431, opened and presided at a general council at Ephesus, where Nestorius was not only condemned but deposed, and where the Virgin was acclaimed as Mother of God.

The council of Ephesus was recognised and confirmed by Rome, but the imperial government refused any recognition on the ground that St Cyril had refused to wait for the arrival of forty-three bishops who were sympathizers with Nestorius. St Cyril was arrested in

Asia Minor and imprisoned for two months. The patriarch of Antioch and all his suffragans declared they were no longer in communion with him. He escaped to Egypt. He achieved reunion with Antioch in 433, and forced the emperor to recognize the decrees of Ephesus. But the imperial government remained suspicious and Antioch radically hostile. St Cyril was still engaged in Christological controversy when he died in 444.

There was no greater Greek theologian than St Cyril. He possessed a power of synthesis and of vision which can be compared with that of St Augustine. He held that our self-chosen darkness had been broken by the coming of the Son and Paraclete, the wisdom and the love of God, and that the Catholic church was the perpetuation of that coming. For St Cyril the church is personalized, she is both Virgin and Mother, unsoiled, untainted, the channel of all grace. Mary, the sinless, the Godbearer, is both her symbol and her prototype. In the church God's compassion abides for ever. 'We also have the power to remit sins.' 'There is no sin that cannot be remitted.' 'He wills Iscariot to be saved as well as Peter.' Christ, being love, is also mercy. He came to us to heal, and because it is his touch that heals he assumes human nature utterly. This is the key to St Cyril's Christology and to his theology of the Eucharist, at once a sacrifice and a banquet at which Christ's body and blood become 'the leaven of our dough'.

No saint has been critized so bitterly as St Cyril, and few saints have shown themselves so vehement. None even of those who hated him could query his greatness, and behind all the vehemence lay the strength of his personal love for Christ and the strength of his personal trust in Christ's compassion. In the eastern phrases he is 'The Seal of all the Fathers', he is 'Great Cyril'.

February 9th

CYRIL of CAESAREA   *Third Century*

A Cappadocian he was cast out by his pagan father when he was converted to Christianity. The governor sought to frighten him by condemning him to be burned, but was so infuriated when Cyril complained at being led away from the pyre, that he had him killed.

May 29th

CYRIL of CONSTANTINOPLE   † c. 1235

He is often confused with the more famous SS Cyril of Alexandria and Cyril of Jerusalem, and a great deal of fictitious history has been invented about him. All we know for certain is that in 1232 he became prior general of the Carmelites in Palestine, an office he held for three years.

March 6th

CYRIL of HELIOPOLIS and MARK
Fourth Century

When Julian the Apostate succeeded the Christian emperor Constantius, Cyril, a deacon of Heliopolis, was martyred. Mark, bishop of Arethusa, was horribly tortured; he was beaten, thrown into the sewers, given up to schoolboys to the tormented, and eventually smeared with honey and plagued by gnats. Yet he was pardoned, since Julian feared the strength martyrs gave to Christianity.

March 29th

CYRIL of JERUSALEM   † c. 387

We first hear of Cyril as a priest in the church of Jerusalem under its bishop St Maximus. It was his duty to instruct the catechumens, and a series of his conferences delivered in the Lent and Easter of 348 have come down to us. He succeeded Maximus as bishop and, it has been suggested, employed his authority to organize liturgical commemorations of the events of Holy Week and Easter at their local sites. He would seem to have elaborated the ceremonial of the mass and introduced the eastern theory that the consecration is effected by an invocation (*epiclesis*) of the Holy Spirit.

Though his conciliatory temper made him averse from enforcing the Nicene term 'Homoousios', 'consubstantial', he was no Arian, and suffered accordingly at the hands of the Arian bishop of Caesarea and the Arian Emperor Constantius. Towards the close of his life, when orthodoxy had become the imperial creed, he took part in the council of Constantinople, which re-imposed the 'Homoousios' and defined clearly the godhead of the Holy Spirit, which he had himself emphasised in his Catecheses.

Cyril witnessed and reported the appearance of a luminous cross seen by the entire city of Jerusalem, and saw the failure of Julian's attempt to rebuild the Jewish temple. The probable date of his death is 387. He is a doctor of the church.

March 18th

CYRIL of TUROV   † 1182

A monk and a recluse, he left his cell to become bishop of Turov. He was one of the best early Russian biblical scholars, and was renowned for his preaching.

April 28th

CYRINUS, *see* Alphius, Cyrinus and Philadelphus.

CYRINUS, *see* Basilides, Quirinus or Cyrinus, Nabor and Nazarius.

CYRUS and JOHN   *Fourth Century*

Especially praised in eastern literature, Cyrus, an Alexandrian physician, went with John to help Athanasia and her three daughters, Christians persecuted in Canopus. They were all tortured and beheaded.

January 31st

DAGOBERT II of AUSTRASIA † 679

The son of the saintly king Sigebert III, he was exiled to Ireland. He was befriended by St Wilfred of York, who brought about his restoration to the throne of Austrasia in 675.

December 23rd

DAMASUS I † 384

He succeeded Liberius as pope in 366 amid much and long continuing opposition. He is especially remembered for the encouragement he gave to St Jerome whom he made his secretary. It was Damasus who began the draining and enlarging of the Catacombs, placing on the tombs of the martyrs inscriptions and verse epigrams, which must be regarded rather as aids to devotion than as guides to accurate archaeological reconstruction. One of his most celebrated epigrams is that on himself, which he placed in the cemetery of St Callistus: 'Here I, Damasus, would like to have been buried, but I feared to profane the ashes of the saints'. He was, therefore, buried in a church on the Via Ardeatina.

December 11th

DANIEL and his Companions † 1227

St Daniel, minister provincial of Calabria, with six other Franciscans, was put to death for preaching to the Mohammedans in Morocco.

October 10th

DANIEL THE STYLITE † 493

He became a disciple of St Simeon the Stylite and after his master's death determined to follow his example. He had a pillar constructed near Constantinople, and proceeded to make his residence there for the rest of his life, undeterred by the frosts and high winds to which that country is liable. He showed marked prophetic gifts, and the Emperor Leo and his successor Zeno frequently consulted him.

December 11th

DARIA, see Chrysanthus and Daria.

DASIUS † c. 303

As a soldier in the Roman army, Dasius was elected 'Lord of Misrule' for the Saturnalia, but, as he was a Christian, he refused to take part, and was executed. His relics are supposed to rest at Ancona. He certainly existed but his story is a pious romance.

November 20th

DATIUS † 552

A bishop during troubled times, he was driven out of Milan by the Goths and went to Constantinople, where he supported Pope Vigilius in his controversy with Justinian.

January 14th

DATIVUS, see Saturninus, Dativus and their Companions.

DAVID, see Theodore, David and Constantine.

DAVID I, KING of SCOTLAND † 1153

In 1113 he married Matilda, widow of the earl of Northampton and became earl of Huntingdon, succeeding to the Scottish throne in 1124. He was a close friend of St Aelred of Rievaulx and established the bishoprics of Brechin, Dunblane, Caithness, Ross and Aberdeen, as well as many monasteries, including Holyrood.

May 24th

DAVID of MUNKTORP † c. 1080

An English monk who went as a missionary to Sweden, he became the first bishop of Västeras.

July 15th

DAVID or DEWI c. 460–c. 500

David (Welsh, *Dewi*), patron saint of Wales, may have lived from c. 460–500. (?520–?589, the dates usually given are even less certain). His father was Sant, a king of South Wales, and his mother, Non, to whom a number of ancient Welsh churches are dedicated. His fame is largely due to the *Life* written six centuries after his death by Rhigyfarch, whose concern was to exalt the claims of the see of St David's against the primacy of Canterbury, and who, for that reason, endowed David with a national importance and with powers of jurisdiction which he certainly never possessed. David was primarily a monk, and it was at Mynyw (Latin, *Menevia*, the medieval name for the diocese of St David's and now the title of the Catholic see), on the North Pembrokeshire coast, that he established his first monastery. He founded many other houses, and like all the Celtic saints he seems to have travelled much, though the tradition that he went to Jerusalem (there to be consecrated 'archbishop') is unlikely to be true. He was present at a synod at Brefi in Cardiganshire, and its decrees for the regulation of religious life in South Wales seem to owe much to his influence. At Brefi, while he was speaking, the field where he stood is said to have been raised up into a hill and a white dove appeared on his shoulder, and so David is usually represented in art standing on a mound. David died on March 1st, and more than fifty ancient churches in South Wales are dedicated to him.

It is necessary to distinguish David, the 'archbishop' of medieval chroniclers, from the monk (also a bishop) whose greatness lies in the influence he had on the growth of Welsh monasticism in the fifth and sixth centuries. The severity of Welsh monastic life is reminiscent of the traditions of the Thebaïd and was probably inspired by them. Hard manual labor was the rule; absolute silence and a rigorous fast were imposed, and abstinence from any drink but water earned for David the name of 'Waterman' – a quality that later commended him to nonconformist taste, which in other respects could scarcely find him a congenial patron. The example of a disciplined and sacrificial life was David's legacy to his people, and his dying words are its summary: 'Be cheerful: keep the faith: observe exactly all the little things that you have learned of me'. The attempt to make of David a symbol of religious independence of Canterbury (and, for that matter, of Rome itself) has grossly distorted the achievement of a saint who exemplifies the contemplative life and the apostolic zeal which is fostered by prayer.

St David's cult was approved in 1120 by Pope Callixtus II, who is said to have granted an indulgence to those who visited his shrine in the cathedral that bears his name. His feast was kept in Wales and in the province of Canterbury throughout the middle ages, and medieval ingenuity was quick to play on the name he shares with the king of Judah. A sequence in his honor (from a manuscript in the Cathedral Library at Hereford) ends thus: 'O David, our leader and strong champion, do thou overcome by thy prayers Goliath, the enemy of our earthly course.' ILLUSTRATION: page 127 (B)
March 1st

DAVNET, *see* Dympna and Gerebernus.

DECLAN *Sixth Century?*
A native of county Waterford and a bishop, his episcopal church was at Ardmore.
July 24th

DEICOLUS or DESLE *Seventh Century*
A monk who went from Ireland to Luxeuil with St Columbanus, he later founded the abbey of Lure in Besançon, where he lived and died a hermit. Columbanus once asked him why he was smiling. Deicolus replied: 'Because no-one can take my God from me'.
January 18th

DEINIOL † *c.* 584?
Known as 'Daniel of the Bangors' from his foundation of Bangor Fawr on the Menai Straits, and Bangor Iscoed on the Dee, he was made a bishop and was also notable for his opposition to a revival of Pelagianism.
September 11th

DELPHINUS † 403
The second bishop of Bordeaux, he was a friend of St Ambrose and of St Paulinus of Nola, whom he converted.
December 24th

DEMETRIAN † *c.* 912
One of the greatest saints of Cyprus, he lost his wife three months after marriage and became a monk of

St Antony's monastery of which he later became abbot. After forty years of monastic life he unwillingly consented to become bishop of Khytri, governing his diocese for twenty-five years.
November 6th

DEMETRIUS
Probably a deacon martyred at Sirmium, he was transformed by popular imagination into a warrior saint, second only to St George in popularity. His cult developed in Salonika, where he was known as 'The Great Martyr'.
October 8th

DEMETRIUS of ALEXANDRIA † 231
The eleventh bishop of Alexandria in succession to St Mark, he appointed Origen head of the catechetical school at Alexandria, but was obliged later on to call together the synod that forbade Origen to preach. He died at the age of a hundred and five.
October 9th

DENIS, *see* Dionysius of Paris.

DENYS, *see* Dionysius the Areopagite.

DEODATUS or DIÉ *Seventh Century*
Bishop of Nevers in 655, he retired, according to a late and unreliable *Life*, first to the Vosges and then to an island near Strasburg. Returning to the Vosges he founded the monastery of Jointures which followed the Rule of St Columban.
June 19th

DEOGRATIAS † 457
Consecrated bishop of Carthage fourteen years after the Vandals had expelled Bishop Quodvultdeus, he restored the church's spirit and among other excellent works, redeemed slaves brought from Rome by Genseric.
March 22nd

DERFEL GADARN *Sixth Century?*
He may have been a Welsh warrior who died a monk of Bardsey. Before the Reformation, his statue was in the church of Llandderfel in Merioneth, but because of the superstitions which abounded concerning it, it was ordered to be destroyed, and was used in the burning of Bd John Forest at Smithfield in 1538.
April 5th

DESIDERATUS *Sixth Century*
One of three brothers born in Soissons and locally venerated as saints (Desiderius and Deodatus were the other two), this secretary of state to King Clotaire became bishop of Bourges.
May 8th

DESIDERIUS or DIDIER † 655
An official of the court of King Clotaire II of Neustria,

he there met St Arnulf of Metz and St Eligius. He was, in 630, elected bishop of Cahors while still a layman.
November 15th

DESIDERIUS or DIDIER   † 607
Bishop of Vienne, he denounced Queen Brunhildis and many attempts were made to discredit him. He was eventually killed by hired assassins.
May 23rd

DESLE, *see* Deicolus.

DEUSDEDIT   † 618
Known also as Adeodatus I, he was pope for three years, and is said to have begun the use of the leaden *bullae* (seals) from which papal 'bulls' take their name.
November 8th

DEUSDEDIT   † 664
A South Saxon named Frithona, he took the name 'Deusdedit' when in 653 he succeeded St Honorius, becoming the first Englishman to hold the see of Canterbury.
July 14th

DEWI, *see* David.

DIDACUS or DIEGO   † 1463
Born of poor parents at San Nicolas del Puerto in the diocese of Seville, he spent some time as a hermit before becoming a lay-brother of the observant Friars Minor at Arrizafa. He became a missionary in the Canary Islands, and in 1445 was made head of the chief convent there. He was recalled to Spain after four years, and spent the rest of his life in that country.
November 13th

DIDIER, *see* Desiderius.

DIDYMUS, *see* Theodora and Didymus.

DIÉ, *see* Deodatus.

DIEGO, *see* Didacus.

DIONYSIA, MAJORICUS and their Companions.
                † 484
A mother and son, they were among those martyred with great savagery by the vandal king Huneric in Africa.
December 6th

DIONYSIUS   † 269
Though many of the early popes were not in fact martyrs, their deaths occurred during times of persecution, and they are therefore remembered liturgically as martyrs. Dionysius, who succeeded St Sixtus II as pope, was the first to live in times of toleration, and he is thus the first pope from whom the title 'martyr' was withheld.
December 26th

DIONYSIUS of ALEXANDRIA   † 265
At first a pupil of Origen, and then his successor at the catechetical school at Alexandria, he became bishop of Alexandria in 247. He ruled for seventeen years during a time of plagues and persecutions, being himself twice exiled.
November 17th

DIONYSIUS of CORINTH   *Second Century*
As bishop of Corinth, he was one of the leaders of the church in the second century in combating heresy, both in his diocese, and by a wide correspondence. Although he died peacefully, he is venerated as a martyr by the Greeks because of his sufferings for the faith.
April 8th

DIONYSIUS of MILAN   *Fourth Century*
Dionysius was banished from his see of Milan for supporting St Athanasius at the synod convened by the Emperor Constantius to condemn him.
May 25th

DIONYSIUS or DENYS THE AREOPAGITE and DIONYSIUS or DENIS of PARIS
Among the handful of converts made by St Paul at Athens (Acts 17) was a member of the Athenian Council of the Areopagus, Dionysius the Areopagite. Nothing more is certainly known of him. A tradition, however, going back to Dionysius of Corinth, about 170, affirms that he became bishop of Athens.

About the year 500 a Syrian monk, whose identity is unknown, composed a number of treatises, of which four are extant, possibly all actually written. They are concerned with the ranks and the functions of the angels, a symbolic interpretation of the church's liturgy and hierarchy, the names given to God, in what sense they are applicable to him and 'mystical theology', the absolute transcendence of the Godhead. Our truest knowledge of God is therefore ignorance, an experience which, because it exceeds image and concept, must be expressed in negative terms. This writer makes considerable use of the Neoplatonist philosopher, Proclus (died 485). To give his writings authority, he represents himself as St Paul's convert, the Areopagite, supporting the identification by fictitious letters. The device was successful and Denys became the accepted teacher of angelology and mystical theology. Disproof of his pseudonym detracts nothing from the great intrinsic value of his treatises.

About the middle of the third century, a bishop named Dionysius preached at Lutetia Parisiorum, the future Paris, and organized a church. Whether he was the first missionary is unknown. He was probably assisted by a priest named Eleutherius and a deacon, Rusticus. He (and they?) suffered martyrdom at a place named Vicus

Catulliacus, the present St Denis, in the persecution of Decius (250) or Valerian (258). On the site of his death rose the abbey of Saint-Denis, the burial place of the French kings.

In the early years of the ninth century, an anonymous writer, possibly for the first time, identified the martyr, bishop of Paris, with Dionysius the Areopagite, and therefore with the pseudo-Denys whose writings had already reached France. He also relates that after decapitation the martyr carried his head two miles from Montmartre to Saint-Denis. A little later, Abbot Hilduin, who translated and used the works of the 'Areopagite', put the finishing touches to this preposterous legend.

October 9th   ILLUSTRATION: page 128

DIOSCORUS, *see* Nemesius, Dioscorus and their Companions.

DISIBOD   † *c.* 674
Said to have been an Irish bishop, he went to Germany where he founded the monastery known as Disibodenberg.

September 8th

DISMAS   *First Century*
It was not much later than midday when the procession halted outside the walls at the northern end of Jerusalem on April 7th in the year 30 A.D. There was a small rocky mound there just above the city gates. Planted on the mound were several upright stakes about twelve feet high, like a cluster of dead trees. There seemed to be more priests in the crowd than usual, otherwise it was the scene of just another crucifixion.

Dismas watched as the two men who were to die with him were stripped of their clothes and made to lie on their backs on the ground. He watched as their wrists were nailed to the beams they had carried through the crowded streets from the Antonia.

A woman offered him a flask of wine mixed with myrrh to deaden his senses, and he drank gratefully.

Then his turn came.

At length, a rope, rough with dried blood, was under his arms and around his chest, and he was hoisted up, his legs dangling free until the beam was fixed to the upright stake; then his feet were nailed to the wood.

Soon he felt his body sink under its weight; the nails through the nerve centers in his wrists sent waves of pain through his body, and the terrible cramp began and the thirst. The man next to him had refused the opiate.

His life ebbed away with his blood, dripping from hands and feet; above his head vultures circled. He looked down and saw a group of women; among them was one of great beauty, gazing at him with compassion and through the mists of pain he heard the words: 'Behold thy mother'.

He heard, too, the priests in the crowd acknowledge that the man next to him had worked miracles. He had heard much talk about him as the Christ, had heard him preach about a kingdom he was to establish. He was a good man and now they were mocking him. His other companion began to shout: 'Save thyself and us too, if thou art the Christ'.

To speak was an agony, for to draw breath he must lift himself up on the cross, but he made the effort and turning his head, he rebuked him.

'What! Hast thou no fear of God, when thou art undergoing the same sentence? And we justly enough; we receive no more than the due reward of our deeds; but this man has done nothing amiss.' Then he said to the man next to him: 'Lord, remember me when thou comest into thy kingdom'.

And the reply came: 'I promise thee, this day thou shalt be with me in Paradise'. (Luke 23:39-43).

Whatever his crimes he had passed judgment on himself, had acknowledged his guilt in accepting his punishment as just, and on account of this one act of repentance (Summa: III Q5: art. 2) he had been forgiven, and his gaze had been directed beyond death, for what kingdom could the Christ enter now except one beyond the grave?

For three hours he hung there, while thick darkness spread over the land, until the Christ cried out with a loud voice: 'Father, into thy hands I commend my spirit,' and he was left with only one companion.

Then soldiers came with clubs and broke his thighs to hasten his death, for the Jews had asked Pilate that the bodies might be buried before nightfall, when the Sabbath began, and this was a special Sabbath. Cramp twisted his body; he could no longer press down upon his feet to relieve it and so he died, conformed to the image of Christ crucified.

A portion of the cross on which Dismas died is alleged to be preserved at Santa Croce in Rome, and he is the patron of those condemned to death.

March 25th

DOGMAEL   *Sixth Century*
Four churches were dedicated to him in Pembrokeshire; this Welsh saint had a considerable cult in Brittany as Dogméel, or Toël.

June 14th

DOMETIUS THE PERSIAN   † *c.* 362
This Persian convert entered a monastery at Nisibis and after his ordination as a deacon retired to a cave. By the order of Julian the Apostate, whom he had criticized, he was stoned to death.

August 7th

DOMINIC   1170-1221
St Dominic Guzman, founder of the Dominicans or Order of Friars Preachers, was born at Calaruega in

Castile in 1170. Until he was thirty-five he led a life cloistered and studious. He studied first under his uncle, archpriest of Gumiel, then for ten years at the University of Palencia. When he was twenty-four he was invited by Diego, bishop of Osma, to join his reformed canons regular, of which in due course he became subprior, then prior. Blessed Jordan of Saxony, his first biographer, hints at the apostolic zeal burning within him at this period: 'God had given him a special grace of prayer for sinners, for the poor, for those in suffering; he bore their affliction in the close sanctuary of his compassion, and his tears ... betrayed the ardor of the feeling within him.'

Then in 1205 Dominic accompanied Diego on an official mission for Ferdinand of Castile across Europe. On their way back the two men visited Rome and petitioned Pope Innocent III to release them from their duties at Osma for work in the foreign mission field around the Dnieper.

Innocent III had long been looking for men to carry out the work of preaching in the south of France, to counteract the influence there of the Albigensian heretics who taught that everything material was evil and of the devil. Perfection consisted in an inhuman self-denial and austerity; short of this, it became a matter of indifference whether, for example, one married or committed fornication, as both belonged to the material order and were, therefore, evil. Marriage was, if anything, the worse evil for being set up as good and virtuous. Such doctrines utterly undermined the social institutions of property and the family, and the heretics did not scruple to work secretly, setting children against parents, wives against husbands. They had their own rites and hierarchy, and were divided into the *perfecti*, the extremely austere leaders, and the mass of their followers, who found in the new doctrines a convenient excuse for unbridled moral freedom.

The heresy sprang from the unrest of a period of transition, and the accompanying ferment of new and challenging ideas. Catholics, and in particular the clergy, were not only living in the past, but had little or no grasp of Christian doctrine. Innocent III had appealed two years earlier to the Cistercian Order. They had responded generously; and two of them had gone as Papal Legates to Languedoc, where they had become absorbed in political and administrative schemes for the reform of the clergy and the expulsion of heretics. What was needed was an evangelical example as inspiring as that of the heretics' own leaders. In Innocent's words, 'A famine has come into the land, the little ones cry out for bread, and there is found none to break it to them'.

Instead of allowing Diego and Dominic to go to the foreign missions, Innocent sent them to the south of France. The two newcomers rallied the dispirited legates,

Cistercian reinforcements arrived, and by April 1207, within a year of the new start, there were forty missionaries in the field. Initial successes came, but they did not last. It was not easy, after all, to change the heretics. The end of the year brought disaster: the Cistercian monks, deeply discouraged, went home; Diego, returning to Spain to fetch auxiliaries, died there; one of the legates also died; and, worst of all, Peter of Castelnau, the other legate, was assassinated by the heretics. It was a fate largely the result of his own froward disposition which had, all along, been no help to the preachers, but it was the signal for war. The Catholic lords launched a civil war of religion against the Albigensians, and Dominic was left preaching where he could, matching the austere example of the *perfecti* by his own exacting mortifications. 'A man who governs his passions is master of the world,' he said. 'He must either rule them or be ruled by them. It is better to be the hammer than the anvil.'

For six years Dominic weathered the storm. He had founded earlier at Prouille a religious community of women, converts from heresy; they were now almost his only support. At last in 1215 peace came, and in the reorganization that followed the bishop of Toulouse turned to him to re-establish Innocent's 'preaching' in his diocese; but there had matured in Dominic's mind wider designs. He had only six companions, yet he proposed to Innocent, in that same year, that they should form not a diocesan body but a world-wide Order of Preachers. This enlargement of Innocent's original conception had no precedent in Christian history, but Dominic's quality had been proved, and Innocent consented. Dominic was told to draw up a constitution, and, a year later, the new Pope, Honorius III, approved the Order of Friars Preachers.

St Dominic immediately dispersed his followers, by now sixteen in number, throughout Europe; and he, himself, travelled the whole of Europe on foot, organizing the Order. In 1220 he convened the first Chapter at Bologna, where the final constitutions of the Order were determined. These, based upon the experience gained and St Dominic's outstanding gifts of clarity and flexibility, are one of the most remarkable legislative achievements of western Christendom, and to them must be attributed the continuing vigor and unity of the Dominican Order.

Dominic had but one more year to live. Before his death Dominicans were sent to Oxford, to Hungary, Denmark and Greece. Everywhere the Order gathered to itself the flower of university life, though remaining at the same time broadly popular in appeal. St Dominic died at Bologna, surrounded by his brethren, on August 6th, 1221. He was canonized in 1234.

St Dominic's character was one of extraordinary

integrity and completeness. To an exquisitely sensitive nature, reflected even in his bodily beauty, he united a rare discipline of mind and soul; and he was the perfect instrument to combat the gloomy heresy of Albigensianism. His order has ever since stood for the value of all things creaturely as well as divine; and it has always welcomed new ideas while holding fast to well-understood principles from the past.

August 4th   ILLUSTRATION: facing page 112

DOMINIC LORICATUS   † 1060
When he discovered that his parents had bribed the bishop to make him a priest, he refused ever again to say mass, and became an anchorite. His title, 'Loricatus', refers to the mailed shirt he wore next to his skin. St Peter Damian made him prior of a hermitage near San Severino.

October 14th

DOMINIC of SILOS   † 1037
For refusing to give up monastic property, this prior of San Millán de la Cogolla was exiled by Garcia III, king of Navarre. Welcomed by Ferdinand I of old Castile, St Dominic was given the decayed monastery of St Sebastian of Silos and turned it into one of the greatest in Spain.

December 20th

DOMINIC of SORA   † 1031
A monk famous in his birthplace Foligno, Etruria, for his power over thunderstorms. He devoted his life to founding Benedictine monasteries and churches throughout Italy, and died at Sora in Campania.

January 22nd

DOMINIC of the CAUSEWAY *Eleventh Century?*
After trying unsuccessfully to become a Benedictine, he lived as a solitary. His name derives from the road he made for pilgrims bound for Compostella.

May 12th

DOMINIC SAVIO   1842–1857
A peasant's son from Riva, Piedmont, he was only fifteen when he died. He was educated by St John Bosco at the Turin Oratory, and organized the Company of the Immaculate Conception among the boys to help St John in running the school. Dominic was continually having to be restrained from violent mortifications by St John Bosco, who used to say: 'The penance God wants is obedience . . . Religion must be around us like the air we breathe; boys must not be wearied by too many devotions and observances'.

March 9th   ILLUSTRATION: page 162

DOMINICA, *see* Indractus and Dominica.

DOMINICA   † *c.* 303?
Her legend, of doubtful authenticity, states that she was born in Campania and suffered martyrdom on the banks of the Euphrates.

July 6th

DOMITIAN   *Sixth Century*
Bishop of Tongres, he was active in evangelizing the Meuse valley. At the synod of Orleans in 549, he distinguished himself by his refutation of heresies.

May 7th

DOMITILLA, *see* Nereus, Achilleus and Domitilla.

DOMNINA, *see* Claudius, Asterius, Neon, Domnina and Theonilla.

DOMNOLUS   *Sixth Century*
He seems to have been abbot of a monastery in Paris before his election to the see of Le Mans in 560, where he ruled for twenty-one years.

May 16th

DONALD   *Eighth Century*
He lived at Ogilvy in Forfarshire. After his wife's death, his nine daughters formed themselves into a religious community which he supervised.

July 15th

DONATIAN and ROGATION   *Third Century*
Donatian, a native of Nantes, converted his brother Rogatian to Christianity. Under the decree of Emperor Maximian, both were imprisoned, and after being tortured on the rack, beheaded.

May 24th

DONATIAN, LAETUS and their Companions
† *c.* 484

St Donatian and four other bishops all died in the desert after being banished by the Arian king Huneric. St Laetus of Leptis Minor was singled out for special attention and burned to death.

September 6th

DONATUS of AREZZO   † 362
The second bishop of Arezzo, he is venerated as a martyr.

August 7th   ILLUSTRATION: page 163

DONATUS of BESANÇON   *Seventh Century*
Born of noble parents, St Donatus became bishop of Besançon. In that city he founded the monastery of St Paul, and his mother founded St Mary's Abbey for nuns. Donatus drew up a rule for the nuns of this foundation, basing it so closely on the Rule of St Benedict that some paragraphs were copied down word for word; but he permitted himself a few innovations which can hardly be regarded as within the Benedictine tradition. The nuns were encouraged to make frequent

confessions to the mother superior, they were forbidden to provide meals for visiting bishops, abbots, monks or priests, and corporal punishment was to be administered for the following offences: eating and drinking without saying grace, talking at meals, and claiming that something was one's own property. The punishment in each of these cases was six strokes of the cane.

St Donatus took part in the councils of Clichy (627) and Chalon-sur-Saône (650).

August 7th

DONATUS of FIESOLE   † 876
An Irish pilgrim on his way back from Rome, he arrived at Fiesole as the people were about to elect a new bishop. When he entered the cathedral the bells rang out, and the congregation took this to be a sign that Donatus must be their next bishop.

October 22nd

DONNAN and his Companions   † 617
Very little is known of St Donnan except that he must have been one of the most active of those early Scottish saints who converted the country to Christianity. Like many of them, he was a native of Ireland. He must have associated himself rather with the Pictish Church of St Ninian than with the newer missionary activities of St Columba, of whom he was a contemporary. We know of Donnan's activities through the trail of place-names, usually *Kildonan*, signifying the site of a church originally founded by the saint, which stretch from Ninian's countryside in Galloway, up to Perth and on to Aberdeenshire. The very routes taken by him are revealed to us by the disposition of his churches. He went north to Sutherland, and to several islands on the west coast. And it is here, on one of these islands, that St Donnan and fifty-two companions were martyred in the year 617. The story has it that the woman ruler of the island of Eigg was concerned with the martyrdom, carried out by pirates (who were probably those Viking raiders who so constantly harassed the Celtic Christian communities), after St Donnan and his companions had celebrated Easter mass.

April 17th

DOROTHEUS, *see* Peter, Gorgoneus and Dorotheus.

DOROTHEUS of TYRE   *Fourth Century*
A priest, or possibly bishop, of Tyre, he was exiled in the reign of Diocletian, and again under Julian the Apostate. At Odyssopolis in Thrace (now Varna in Bulgaria) he was arrested and beaten to death, it is said at the age of 107.

June 5th

DOROTHEUS THE YOUNGER
Eleventh Century
A patrician's son from Trebizond on the Black Sea, he

shunned marriage and entered the Genna monastery at Amisos under Abbot John. Through his prophetic and miraculous gifts he founded a great monastery, Khiliokomos, and became its abbot.

January 5th

DOROTHY   *Fourth Century*
She was tortured by Fabricius, governor of Caesarea, Cappadocia, for refusing to marry and to worship idols. As she was on her way to execution, Theophilus, a young lawyer, asked her with a sneer to send him some of the apples and roses from the garden to which she was going. She agreed, and an angel appeared with a basket in which were three apples and three roses. Theophilus was converted and died a martyr.

February 6th   ILLUSTRATION: page 164

DOSITHEUS   *Sixth Century*
A monk of the monastery of Gaza, he was physically frail and died young, probably from tuberculosis of the lungs.

February 23rd

DRAUSIUS or DRAUSIN   *Seventh Century*
Educated by St Anseric, and appointed archdeacon by Bettolin, bishop of Soissons, whom he succeeded, he founded a monastery at Rethondes, a nunnery, a church and religious houses at Soissons.

March 7th

DRITHELM   † c. 700
A graphic account of his death, vision and return to life is given by Bede in his *Ecclesiastical History*. Drithelm was a Northumbrian who returned to life on the morning after his death, sitting up suddenly 'to the great consternation of those weeping round the body, who ran away; only his wife, who loved him more dearly, remained with him'. He told her that he must now live a different life, and, dividing his property among his family, he became a monk of Melrose.

In the interval between his death and his coming back to life, he had received a vision in which he had been taken by a handsome man in a shining robe 'in what appeared to be an easterly direction' to a valley, on one side of which were great fires and on the other icy blizzards. This he had thought to be Hell, but he was told that it was 'the place where souls are tried and punished who had recourse to repentance at the hour of death'. At the end of the valley, it began to grow dim and darkness concealed everything; 'masses of black flame suddenly appeared rising and falling as from a great pit'. This was Hell. 'When my guide had brought me to this place, he suddenly disappeared and left me alone'. This, Drithelm was afterwards told, was in order that he might discover what his future should be. His guide rejoined him and led him to a broad and pleasant meadow enclosed by a high wall and filled with the scent of spring flowers. Here there were many parties of happy people. Drithelm assumed that this was Heaven, but his guide replied, 'No, this is not the Kingdom of Heaven as you imagine'. It was instead the place where those who had done good but were not yet perfect waited for entry into the Kingdom of Heaven.

At this point Drithelm was restored to life. To protests that, as a monk, he exposed himself unnecessarily to intense cold or to a dicipline that was more severe than was needful, he replied, 'I have known it colder . . . I have seen greater austerity'.

September 1st

DROCTOVEUS or DROTTÉ   *Sixth Century*
Born at Auxerre, he entered the abbey of Saint-Symphorien at Autun under St Germanus. He became abbot of a new monastery on the site of what is now Saint-Germain-des-Prés, when Germanus was appointed bishop of Paris.

March 10th

DROGO or DRUON   † 1189
Orphan of a noble family, he lived piously as a pilgrim and then as a shepherd, of which calling he is the patron. After suffering a disfiguring hernia, he retired to a solitary existence at Sebourg.

April 16th

DROSTAN   † *c.* 610
Of royal Irish descent, he was a disciple of St Columba and became the first abbot of a community at Deer in Aberdeenshire.

July 11th

DROTTÉ, *see* Droctoveus.

DRUON, *see* Drogo.

DUNSTAN   *c.* 909–988
St Dunstan was born *c.* 909 at Baltonsborough near Glastonbury in Somerset. His parents were of high rank; an uncle, Athelm, was bishop of Wells and later archbishop of Canterbury, two other kinsmen were bishops and he was related to the Lady Ethelfreda, niece of King Athelstan. He was brought up in the semi-monastic community of Glastonbury, a shrine where old traditions of learning were irrigated by the fresh streams brought by pilgrims, Irish and English. He was tonsured, but took neither vows nor orders for a time, and spent some years living now at Glastonbury and now at King Athelstan's court in Wessex. He had rivals and enemies, and was undecided whether to marry or to take religious vows, which at that time in England did not necessarily imply entering a monastery, for there was no fully organized abbey in being. A severe illness decided him, and he received the monk's habit from

his uncle, Archbishop Alphege, *c.* 934, and was ordained priest *c.* 939. When Edmund succeeded King Athelstan, Dunstan joined the royal household, but once more there were rivalries, and Dunstan was disgraced. It was then that the king, in danger of death when hunting near Cheddar, vowed to restore him, and in consequence duly appointed him head of the community at Glastonbury with the title of 'abbot'. From that moment, probably in 940, may be dated the rebirth of medieval English monasticism which was to last undisturbed till the Reformation.

Dunstan reorganized Glastonbury as a monastery following the Rule of St Benedict, and soon attracted disciples, of whom the most celebrated was Ethelwold, and when King Edmund was murdered in 946 Dunstan became chief adviser to his successor, King Edred. During his reign the first of the new monastic foundations was made at Abingdon by St Ethelwold, but Edred's successor exiled Dunstan, who took refuge in the newly reformed abbey of St Peter at Ghent where he imbibed the spirit of the most observant continental monasteries. Thence he was recalled to be bishop first of Worcester, then of London and finally in 960 of Canterbury. The last appointment was due to King Edgar (959–75), the young and enthusiastic patron of Dunstan and of the monastic revival. During his reign and thenceforth with few intermissions almost till his own death, Dunstan was the king's chief adviser in church and state; he has indeed been called the first 'Prime Minister' of England. Besides guiding the rapid spread of monasticism, which was given unity and a common observance by a common code, the *Regularis Concordia* (974), Dunstan reorganized the church by promoting monastic bishops, and took a large part in the creation of a united England. He lived to see the end of the great age of revival, and the beginning of sorrows and Danish invasions in the reign of Ethelred 'the Unready'. He died, an old man, in 988, and was immediately venerated as a saint all over England.

No letters or books written by Dunstan have survived, and we have no means of knowing the precise part he took in the events of his day. We can, however, gain some idea of his personality from an early *Life*, and from scattered notices by contemporaries. He was unusually handsome, with fair hair that became white and earned him the adjective 'angelic'. Though his contemporaries remarked upon his energy as a young man and his unshakable strength in later life, they are also unanimous in making of him a creative artist both in painting and metal work and music; it is highly probable that a well-known drawing still in existence of the monk Dunstan adoring Christ is a self-portrait, and it is equally probable that he was the composer of the beautiful plain chant *Kyrie Rex Splendens*. As the sole unchanging figure in high office in England during an epoch of rapid change which, while disorderly, was yet one of great national and intellectual revival, he may fairly be given credit for much of the permanent good that resulted: the establishment of many of the great abbeys, such as Glastonbury, Westminster, and Ramsey, the replacement of the unsatisfactory clergy at many of the cathedrals by monks, the educational and artistic achievements of the time, and the diffusion of the monastic culture throughout the land by means of the monk-bishops. He may certainly stand, with Theodore of Tarsus and Lanfranc, as one of the greatest of the medieval archbishops of Canterbury.

There is plenty of evidence that he was beloved not only by his disciples and colleagues, but by a succession of kings on the one hand, and by the common people on the other. The episodes of conspiracy and opposition in his early life probably do no more than reflect the feuds and ambitions of the court, while at the same time they show that Dunstan was always one to be reckoned with as a strong and resolute personality. Above all, there is testimony to his reputation for holiness, and for holiness of character and personality rather than of reputed signs and wonders. He died, immediately after receiving Viaticum at a mass celebrated by his deathbed; his last words, clearly referring to the sacrament he had just received, were those of the Psalmist: 'The merciful and gracious Lord hath made a remembrance of his marvellous works; he hath given food to them that fear him.'   ILLUSTRATION: page 165
May 19th

DUTHAC   *Eleventh Century*
A Scotsman educated in Ireland, he returned to Scotland and was appointed bishop of Ross. He was famous for predictions and miracles, and Tayne, his burial ground, became a place of pilgrimage.
March 8th

DYFRIG   *Fifth Century*
St Dyfrig (in Latin, Dubritius) is the principal saint of south-east Wales, and in particular of the two districts of Ergyng and Ewias. He flourished in the fifth century, and he was thus an earlier contemporary of SS Illtud and Samson. He is described as the son of Efrddil, daughter of the Romano-British king of Ergyng, herself a saint and a founder of churches. Her grandfather, Constantine, a son of Magnus Maximus, had come under the influence of St Martin of Tours, and he is the founder and patron saint of Welsh Bicknor. Here in the penal times, after the Reformation, stood Courtfield, the home of the Vaughans and a main center of Welsh Catholicism. Dyfrig was born near Madley, probably at Chilstone. He grew up a notable scholar. His first foundation was at Hentland, and thence he moved to

Moccas. At Ynys Bŷr (Caldey) he was wont to spend Lent; and on the death of St Pŷr he appointed St Samson abbot, and later consecrated him bishop. In extreme old age, he retired to live as a hermit on Ynys Enlli (Bardsey) where he died and was buried.

St Dyfrig stands out in two respects. First, linked by ancestry with the work of St Martin, he was, like St Martin, both abbot and bishop; and he played the part of St Martin, not only, if principally, in Ergyng, but further afield in all the territories of the Britons. Secondly, he represented and carried forward the tradition of Romano-British Catholicism into the next age, initiating the great movement of missionary monasticism. A great man, he stands at the origin of a great epoch.
November 14th

DYMPNA and GEREBERNUS   *Seventh Century*
St Dympna was one of those fascinating hidden saints whose 'delayed action' in the thirteenth century is very like the mysterious reappearance of St Philomena in the nineteenth. The relics of two saints, Dympna and Gerebernus, were discovered in the town of Gheel, Belgium, in the thirteenth century. Little attention was paid to the matter until it was found that invocation to St Dympna was extraordinarily efficacious in the case of epileptics, lunatics and the mentally deranged, who began to throng in great numbers to her shrine. Almost as miraculous was the attitude of the people of Gheel, who welcomed these afflicted people and treated them with great kindness. Dympna quickly became the patroness of the insane, and Gheel became renowned for the help the inhabitants gave to those so afflicted. Before the close of the thirteenth century a hospital was built there for mental patients. Today, Gheel has an excellent state hospital and numerous private homes for the same purpose, where several thousand patients receive treatment and after-care. The excellence of the Gheel system, never rivalled elsewhere, is that as soon as patients can dispense with institutional care they are taken into private homes in the district where they can resume family life and help with domestic and agricultural work. A whole colony of defectives is thus cared for by the people. When a relapse occurs, the patient is taken back to the hospital. This is commonly agreed to be the most humane treatment ever devised for the insane, and it gives results second to none. But a whole district has to collaborate in such a scheme and only at Gheel, under the patronage of St Dympna, has this been found possible.

The dossier of the saint has been lost and the legend attached to her is so remote from the control of history that it is hardly worth repeating. She is supposed to belong to the mid-seventh century and to have been the daughter of an Irish pagan king and a Christian mother, who died when Dympna was still a child.

When she grew to girlhood, she resembled her dead mother so much that her father wanted to marry her; and she fled from her home in the care of a couple of servants and the priest, Gerebernus. The group took ship to Antwerp and finally settled at a place now occupied by the town of Gheel. The enraged father followed them and had Gerebernus put to death by his attendants. When Dympna still refused to return home with her father, he killed her. Afterwards the local people buried the two and venerated them as martyrs.

Dympna's identification with the Irish saint Davnet has also been suggested, but not proved.
May 15th

EANSWIDA † *c.* 640
The granddaughter of St Ethelbert of Kent, she refused to marry a pagan prince and founded a convent near Folkestone.
September 12th

EATA † 686
Selected for the priesthood by St Aidan of Lindisfarne, he became abbot of Melrose, and then took charge of Lindisfarne after the synod of Whitby. He changed dioceses with St Cuthbert and became bishop of Hexham.
October 26th

EBBA THE ELDER † 683
One of the supporters of St Wilfrid, she was given some land by her brother Oswy of Northumbria, and founded the abbey of Ebbchester upon it. She later established a double monastery at Coldingham, on a promontory still known as St Abb's Head.
August 25th

EBBA THE YOUNGER † *c.* 870
Abbess of Coldingham, she disfigured herself and her nuns to preserve their chastity from the Danish invaders, who burned them with their convent in 870.
April 2nd

EBERHARD † 1164
Born in Nüremburg of noble family, he was educated by the Benedictines at Paris University. In 1146, he became archbishop of Salzburg, where he was famous as a reformer and peacemaker.
June 22nd

EBREGISLUS or EVERGISLUS *Fifth Century*
He was educated by St Severus whom he succeeded as bishop of Cologne. He is said to have been murdered by robbers while at prayer.
October 24th

EBRULF or EVROULT † 596
A member of the court of Childebert I, he parted from his wife by mutual consent to become a monk of Bayeux. Later he and three companions retired to the forest of Ouche in Normandy and lived as anchorites. The community multiplied, and St Ebrulf founded several monasteries.
December 29th

EDBERT † 698
He succeeded St Cuthbert as bishop of Lindisfarne, where he was renowned for his charity and biblical scholarship.
May 6th

EDBURGA † 751
A disciple of the abbess St Mildred whom she succeeded at Minster-in-Thanet, she is chiefly remembered as a friend of St Boniface who valued her friendship and her talent as a calligrapher.
December 12th

EDBURGA of WINCHESTER † 960
Her parents, King Edward the Elder and his third wife, Edgiva, intending that she should become a nun, placed her in the abbey of Winchester, of which she later became abbess.
June 15th

EDITH of POLESWORTH *Tenth Century*
The sister of King Athelstan and wife of the Viking Sihtric, she was buried at Tamworth, near Polesworth. There are, however, other accounts of her, and her identity is uncertain.
July 15th

EDITH of WILTON 962–984
This daughter of King Edgar and St Wilfrida lived most of her life in Wilton Abbey, of which her mother was abbess, and in which Edith was placed at a very early age; so that it was said of her that she had not so much forsaken the world as never known it.
September 16th

EDMUND of ABINGDON † 1240
St Edmund was born at the end of the twelfth century at Abingdon. His mother was devout but entertained an excessive belief in hairshirts and short-commons; and her husband eventually retired into a monastery of less strict obedience than his family circle, where he combined a life of contemplation with an ampler diet. Edmund was brought up to sanctity and in adolescence was something of a prig. He underwent a symbolic engagement to our Lady, and when later a young woman made an assignation with him, he kept it accompanied by his university teachers; and they, together, beat the 'offending Eve out of her' – as the young woman

afterwards recalled. Edmund was educated at Paris but returned to England to become an early luminary of the University of Oxford. He was a member of Stephen Langton's circle, and treasurer of Salisbury – the most distinguished chapter in England at that time.

In 1233, his reputation for learning and sanctity was such that he was elected archbishop of Canterbury. He was a compromise candidate and his pontificate saw an unseemly brawl between king and pope, from which neither emerges with much credit. In 1240 he set out on a journey to Rome, but when he reached Pontigny his health gave way; he decided to return to England but died soon after setting out. His remains are still venerated at Pontigny. It is commonly said that he went to Pontigny as a voluntary exile, but this is mere hagiographical rumor.

It cannot be said that St Edmund was a great archbishop, but his position between papal and royal policies, neither of which he could quite approve, was difficult. His personal charm, learning and virtue, however, are beyond question. ILLUSTRATION: page 166
November 16th

EDMUND THE MARTYR 841–870
St Edmund was born in 841. Nothing seems to be known of his very early years. In 855, on Christmas Day, when only fourteen, he was made king of Norfolk, in Attleborough. It was a time of danger to the people who suffered much from the invasions of the still heathen Danes; the king was chosen by the clergy and nobles as their leader in battle and defender of the faith. There is a tradition that shortly before his early death, King Edmund defeated part of the Danish army which had been setting fire to Thetford; reinforcements arrived for the enemy, who then offered him peace, but at the expense of the Christian religion and the welfare of his people. These terms he refused and fled towards Framlingham Castle. He was pursued and captured. A second time he refused offers of peace, and in consequence he was put to death. These details are not historically substantiated: the only certain fact about his death is that he was killed by the Danes in the winter of 870.

The other certain fact about him is that he was a very holy king. He learned the Psalms by heart, partly at least in honor of King David upon whom he modelled himself. David also had been a king whose life had involved him in battle against the heathens. There are legends about St Edmund's miracles, and it is certain from the large number of churches dedicated to him that he was widely loved and revered. This is the more remarkable because he had died defeated in battle; but his defeat was recognized as a martyrdom.

His body was first buried at Hoxne where he died; in 903 it was translated to Bury St Edmunds (Beodrics-

worth), where it became the principal relic in the church of the Benedictine Abbey of St Edmundsbury. In 1010 the relics were taken for safety to London and returned after two years. There has recently been a revival of devotion to him in Bury St Edmunds, which bears witness once more to the holiness of his life, his greatness as a ruler and the inspiration of his example.
November 20th ILLUSTRATION: page 167

EDWARD THE CONFESSOR † 1066
Son of Ethelred the Unready and of his Norman wife Emma, Edward was sent for safety to Normandy with his brother Alfred, when Sweyn conquered England. He was ten years old. In Normandy he grew up, and he remained in Normandy even when his mother married the Danish King Canute. During the reign of Harold Harefoot, his brother, Alfred, visiting England, was arrested by Earl Godwin, and, whether or not with his complicity, was blinded and put to death. In his heart Edward never forgave Godwin. On his accession Harthacanute sent for his half brother, showed him favor and apparently recognized his right of succession. Shortly afterwards, in 1042, Harthacanute died and Edward became king. He was obliged to come to terms with Godwin and married his daughter Edith. The marriage however was not consummated: William of Malmesbury is uncertain of Edward's motive. Since the succession was doubtful and, as the event proved, would be contested, it is difficult to approve his decision. Once during his reign Edward shook off Godwin's tutelage. He turned to the Normans: Duke William was invited to England and promised the succession. Even the Queen was banished to a nunnery. The following year however Godwin returned to England and power, to which on his death his son Harold succeeded. Edith returned to court.

Edward showed mildness and courtesy to all, led a life of devotion, austerity and generous alsmgiving. His sole earthly pleasure was the hunt, but he never allowed it to interfere with daily attendance at mass. Since the unsettled condition of his kingdom made it inadvisable to fulfil a vow of pilgrimage to Rome, it was commuted by the Pope, and as part of the terms Edward restored and endowed Westminster Abbey. He was the first English monarch to touch victims of scrofula, otherwise known as the King's evil, because of the traditional belief that the king had power to heal this disease. Nevertheless he was, it would seem, a better man than monarch, and the favor he showed the Normans paved the way for the Norman Conquest. When his abbey was consecrated, December 28th, 1065, Edward was absent. He had contracted a mortal illness from which, on January 5th of the new year, he died, obliged at last to recognize Harold as his successor. His body, alone of

English saints of known identity, still rests in its shrine at Westminster.

Gracious legends attached themselves to Edward's memory. At the Consecration he saw our Lord blessing him from the altar. He dispatched an embassy to the cave of the Seven Sleepers at Ephesus. It was reported that they had turned over, a sign of future calamity. A ring given to an aged beggar was returned to the king by St John the Evangelist with a warning of speedy death and the promise of Paradise. When Edward woke to see a thief helping himself to his treasure, he warned him to make off with his plunder before his chamberlain caught him.

Edward was canonized in 1161. October 13th is the date of the translation of his relics.

October 13th   ILLUSTRATION: page 168 (A)

EDWARD THE MARTYR   † 979
The son of King Edgar, Edward ruled England for three years and was then murdered outside Corfe Castle, probably by retainers of his young step-brother Ethelred.

March 18th   ILLUSTRATION: page 168 (B)

EDWIN   † 633
King of Northumbria, he married Ethelburga, a Christian, but it was many years before he himself could decide to become one: he would sit alone for hours, silently deliberating which religion he should follow. At last in 627 he and his counsellors were baptised by St Paulinus of York, and for seventeen years the kingdom was so peacefully administered that it was said that a woman could carry her new-born child across the island from sea to sea without suffering any harm.

St Edwin was killed in 633 while resisting a Welsh invasion.

October 12th

EGBERT   † 729
An English monk of Lindisfarne, he was anxious to go on the mission to Germany. His destiny, however, was less heroic but quite important. Settling on Iona, he succeeded in persuading the monks to adopt the Roman usage over the celebration of Easter – a task which took thirteen years of gentle persuasion.

April 24th   ILLUSTRATION: page 123 (B)

EGWIN   † 717
Said to have been descended from the Mercian kings, he became bishop of Worcester in 692 and founded the abbey of Evesham, which later became one of the great Benedictine houses of England.

December 30th

EILUNED, see Aled.

ELESBAAN, see Aretas and the Martyrs of Najran.

ELEUSIPPUS, *see* Speusippus, Eleusippus and Meleusippus.

ELEUTHERIUS
This martyr, a Roman soldier, was among those falsely accused of burning down the palace of Diocletian at Nicodemia.

October 2nd

ELEUTHERIUS   † c. 189
Little is known of this pope who is supposed to have corresponded with St Lucius, the British king, about the conversion of his kingdom – a story which is no longer accepted.

May 30th

ELEUTHERIUS   *Sixth Century*
Abbot of St Mark's monastery near Spoleto, he was the friend of St Gregory who mentions him several times in his *Dialogues*.

September 6th

ELEUTHERIUS and RUSTICUS   † 258
They were the companions in martyrdom of St Denis, and the abbey of St Denis near Paris is reputed to have been built over their tombs. (*See* St Dionysius).

October 9th

ELEUTHERIUS of TOURNAI   † 532
The relics and records of this bishop of Tournai perished in the fire which destroyed Tournai Cathedral in 1092. He is said to have been a great preacher, and to have been killed by heretics as he was leaving his church.

February 20th

ELFLEDA   † 714
Daughter of Oswy, king of Northumbria, she was placed by him in the Hartlepool convent. She accompanied the abbess, St Hilda, to Whitby, and later governed as joint abbess with her mother, Eanfleda. She was instrumental in helping to reconcile St Theodore of Tarsus and St Wilfrid.

February 8th

ELIAS, see Flavian and Elias.

ELIAS, JEREMY and their Companions   † 309
During persecution by Maximian and Maximus, Elias and four companions were arrested at Caesarea, Palestine, after visiting fellow-Christians in Cilicia. Since torture failed to shake their faith, the governor, Firmilian, had them executed together with two Christian bystanders.

February 16th

ELIGIUS or ELOI   c. 588–660
The son of a working man, he was born at Chaptelat near Limoges and became famous as a goldsmith. Clotaire II made him master of the mint and was so

impressed by his honesty and holiness that he gave him land on which to build the first of his several monastic foundations. Court life did not spoil him, and it was said that a stranger might always recognise his house from the crowd of poor people who were received at its doors.

In 641 he became bishop of Noyon. He is the patron of all smiths and workers in metal.

December 1st   ILLUSTRATION: page 169

ELIZABETH and ZACHARY

In the year 7 B.C., in a time of peace, under the Emperor Augustus, an aged priest named Zachary, from a small town four miles south-west of Jerusalem, made his way to the Temple to fulfil the duties assigned to him by lot. His life was overshadowed by a circumstance tragic to a Jew: he and his wife were childless. For many years they had prayed that this 'reproach among men' (Luke 1:25) might be taken away.

The priests who served the Temple were divided into twenty-four groups, and their term of office, which came round twice a year, lasted for one week. Zachary belonged to the eighth group under the headship of the priest Abia, and on this occasion he had been assigned the privilege of offering incense in the Holy Place, the ante-room to the Holy of Holies, an offering which was made twice a day, at the morning and evening sacrifice.

While Zachary was performing his duties in the Holy Place the faithful remained standing outside, praying and watching the ceremony from a distance. Suddenly, unseen by the people, an angel appeared to him, to the right of the altar of incense, and he was overcome by fear. But the angel said, 'Zachary, do not be afraid; thy prayer has been heard, and thy wife Elizabeth is to bear thee a son, to whom thou shalt give the name of John.' (Luke 1:13). This name was an omen, for 'Jehohanan' meant 'Yahweh has shown mercy'. The angel told Zachary that his son would be filled with the Holy Spirit in his mother's womb, would bring many Israelites back to God, and, with the spirit and power of an Elias, prepare the way for the Messiah.

Zachary asked, 'By what sign am I to be assured of this? I am an old man now, and my wife is far advanced in age.' (Luke 1:18). The Angel answered, 'I am Gabriel, and my place is in God's presence ... thou shalt be dumb ... until the day when this is accomplished; and that because thou hast not believed my promise'. (Luke 1:19-21.)

Zachary had asked for a sign and had been given one; a sign which served also to purify his faith.

When Zachary at length came out from the Holy Place he was unable to satisfy the curiosity of the faithful, who wondered what had delayed him for so long; from his behavior they guessed that he had seen some vision in the sanctuary, but his muteness prevented them from learning its exact nature.

When his term of office was at an end, he returned home, and writing, probably, on a small wax tablet, he made known to his wife the circumstances and nature of Gabriel's promise.

Soon after Zachary's return Elizabeth did in fact conceive a child, but she and her husband kept this mysterious and wonderful news to themselves for five months. In the sixth month of her pregnancy Elizabeth was visited by her cousin Mary, to whom Gabriel had revealed the secret at the time of the Annunciation.

'No sooner had Elizabeth heard Mary's greeting than the child leaped in her womb, and Elizabeth herself was filled with the Holy Ghost' (Luke 1:41), so that she recognized in her cousin the mother of the Lord.

Three months passed and Elizabeth gave birth to her son. Her relatives and neighbors flocked to the house on hearing this extraordinary news and congratulated her. They returned on the eighth day for the prescribed ceremony of circumcision, when the child was to be named. Normally the child would have been given his grandfather's name, to avoid confusion between father and son, but as Zachary was old enough to be a grandfather the fond relatives suggested that the child should bear his name. Elizabeth, however, said, 'No, he is to be called John'. (Luke 1:61). Her relatives were puzzled by this choice, because it was not a family name, and they made signs to Zachary appealing to him to settle the dispute. Zachary understood their signs and answered in the only way he could. He wrote upon his wax tablet: 'His name is John'. (Luke, 1:63.)

At once Zachary recovered his speech and broke the long silence of nine months with a canticle of praise, the 'Benedictus', used ever since in the Christian liturgy. He rejoiced in the fulfilment of God's promises to Israel, and made known the destiny of his son as the precursor of the Lord and the prophet of God's merciful salvation.

Mary returned to Nazareth, and Elizabeth and Zachary were left to watch over their child as he grew, 'and his spirit achieved strength.' (Luke 1:80.)

November 5th   ILLUSTRATION: page 170

ELIZABETH of HUNGARY   1207-1231

St Elizabeth is traditionally represented as dressed in rich clothes, bearing in her top skirt–which is gathered up at the front to form an apron–a profusion of red roses, while behind her back she holds a loaf of bread; these are the symbols of her life, her inherited position as Queen of Hungary, and the life she elected for herself of penance and asceticism.

The contrast between the two callings is everywhere apparent in the twenty-four years which made up her life. Even before her wedding at the age of thirteen to the saintly Louis of Thuringia, she was marked out for suffering. Her mother-in-law tried to prevent the wedding out of jealousy and constantly mocked Elizabeth for her charity and humility. She said that she behaved 'like a tired old mule', when she prostrated herself before the crucifix, and that she was totally unfitted to be Queen.

Her mortifications took the form of wearing the simplest clothes woven of coarse untreated wool and of eating as little as possible; she refused to wear her jewelled crown, when our Lord wore one of thorns. However, more important than these mortifications was her constant and remarkable charity, which was expressed in every detail of her life, inward and outward. When she was not actively engaged in the business of government she spent all her time either in prayer or visiting the poor and the sick, with the result that, after her husband's death in 1227, his family accused her of squandering the royal purse on the vagrants of the land.

Her husband's family gained control of the government and ousted her from the palace with her four children, and Louis's brother declared himself regent. He forbade any citizen to take her in, and such was his reputation for savagery that she was reduced to spending the first days of her banishment in a pigsty. She refused the asylum offered by her father, but finally accepted the hospitality of her own uncle, the bishop of Bamberg.

Since 1226 her confessor had been Master Conrad of Hamburg, a severe and unpopular inquisitor of heretics. St Elizabeth now placed herself unreservedly under his direction, which was so severe as to seem sadistic: he banished all her followers, substituting two ugly and disagreeable waiting women; and for infringements of his discipline he would administer a beating, sometimes for merely missing a sermon.

Eventually her husband's comrades returned from the Crusades, entrusted with the duty of protecting Elizabeth. This they were preparing to do when the usurper changed his attitude to her; she was recalled and the rights of her son recognized.

She had few more years of life to run, but she spent them in constant prayer and practical charity, and became universally loved and revered. She died on November 19th, 1231, and was canonized four years later by Pope Gregory IX. ILLUSTRATION: page 171
November 19th

ELIZABETH of PORTUGAL 1271–1336

Daughter of Peter II of Aragon and of Constance, grand-daughter of Frederick II, she was given the name of her great aunt, St Elizabeth of Hungary. Her birth began the work of peacemaker which distinguishes her, for it reconciled her father and grandfather. At the age of twelve she was married to King Denis of Portugal, though one is glad to know that she was almost nineteen before she gave birth to the elder of her two children.

As a queen she led a life of prayer, austerity and charitable works. Every day she recited not only the Divine Office but the Offices of our Lady, and the Dead. With her maids of honor she devoted much time to working for the poor or the sick and visiting hospitals. Though a capable ruler, Denis was an unfaithful husband. In fairness, however, we should remember that his marriage was a political arrangement and that, among kings, chastity has been the exception, not the rule. Elizabeth not only bore with his infidelities with patience and gentleness but gave his illegitimate children a mother's care. Denis's son Alfonso was less tolerant of his affection for them, and twice rebelled against his father. On both occasions she reconciled father and son, riding between the combatants. She was banished for a time on the slanderous suggestion that she was encouraging her son's revolt; but the truth soon came to light, and Denis showed his confidence in her by trusting her with the government of Torres Vedras. She also stopped two other wars. In 1325 Denis died a penitent and holy death, devotedly nursed by his wife through a long and painful illness.

Divesting herself of every ornament or token of rank, Elizabeth became a Francisan tertiary, wearing the habit and living in a house adjoining the convent of Poor Clares she had founded at Coimbra. Her life was a model to the nuns.

In 1336 her son, King Alfonso, began a campaign against the king of Castile, who had ill-treated his wife, Alfonso's daughter. Despite failing health, through days of burning heat, Elizabeth followed the army. She caught up with it at Estremoz and was successful in making permanent peace between the hostile kings. But the effort proved mortal. Her last illness, attended by her son and daughter-in-law, was brightened by divine consolations, and a vision of our Lady greeted her last breath. Her birth had been peace, her work had been peace, and for peace she gave her life. She died on July 4th. She was canonized by Urban VIII, who furnished her office with special hymns. When mankind is faced with the alternative of peace or suicide, the intercession of this saint of peace is more than ever valuable. ILLUSTRATION: page 172
July 8th

ELIZABETH of SCHÖNAU †1164

She entered the Benedictine house of Schönau at the age of twelve, and ten years later had the first of a number of visions which were to continue for the rest of her life.
June 18th

ELMO, *see* Erasmus.

ELOI, *see* Eligius.

ELZEAR   1285–1323
Educated at the monastery of St Victor at Marseille, where his uncle was abbot, he married Delphina of Glendèves who was herself beatified. When he entered into his inheritance, he pacified his turbulent vassals without using force and acted as justiciar to King Robert of Naples.
September 27th

EMERENTIANA   † 304
An authentic Roman martyr, her tomb was close to St Agnes's basilica. Legend connected her, therefore, with Agnes, and it was said that Emerentiana was her foster-sister and that she was stoned to death when praying by her sister's grave.
January 23rd

EMETERIUS, *see* Chelidonius and Emeterius.

EMILIAN CUCULLATUS   † 574
A patron of Spain, he was a shepherd who lived as a hermit for forty years near Burgos. The bishop of Tarazona made him receive ordination and become a parish priest, but he gave so much of his church's wealth away that he was deprived of his parish and returned to his mountain hermitage.
November 12th

EMILIANA, *see* Tharsilla and Emiliana.

EMILY de RODAT   1787–1852
For a long while she was unable to find a community which satisfied her, although most of her time was spent at the Maison Saint-Cyr at Villefranche. This she was able to turn into a school for the poor, which was to grow into the Congregation of the Holy Family of Villefranche. In daughter houses, nursing and social work were added to teaching, and there were thirty-eight such establishments when she died.
September 19th

EMILY de VIALAR   1797–1856
Born at Gaillac in Languedoc, she was the granddaughter of Baron de Portal, physician to Louis XVIII and Charles X. When her grandfather died she used her legacy to found a community for the education of children and the care of the sick at Gaillac. It became the Sisters of St Joseph of the Apparition; and forty houses throughout the world were established in her lifetime.
June 17th

EMMA   *Eleventh Century*
After the death of her husband and son, she devoted herself to religious work, founding several monasteries, including that of Gurk in Corinthia.
June 29th

EMMELIUS, *see under* Basil the Great.

EMMERAMUS   *Seventh Century*
Reputed to have been bishop of Poitiers, this missionary later turned his attention to Germany. He died from injuries he received when he was attacked by the agents of Duke Theodo.
September 22nd

EMYGDIUS   † 304
He was entirely unknown before the discovery of a body claimed to be his towards the end of the tenth century. His legend says that he was a German who went to Rome, and was beheaded in the persecution under Diocletian. He is invoked against earthquakes.
August 9th

ENCRATIS, *see* Optatus and his Companions and Encratis.

ENDA and FANCHEA   *Sixth Century*
A warrior, he was persuaded to live peaceably by his sister, Fanchea, a nun; Enda was ordained in Rome, built churches at Drogheda, and established the famous monastery at Killeany on Aran which really started organized monasticism in Ireland.

He seems to have retained something of his war-like spirit as abbot of Killeany, for, to test his monks, he used to set them afloat on the open sea in a coracle. If the coracle sank, the monk was a sinner. All the community were exposed to this test, and the only one to fail was the cook who was promptly banished.
March 21st St Enda; January 1st St Fanchea

ENECO or IÑIGO   † 1057
King Sancho the Great was determined to restore discipline to his father-in-law's monastery at Ona and called upon Eneco, a hermit, to govern it in the spirit of the Cluniac reform; this he did with great success.
June 1st

ENGELBERT   † 1225
The son of the count of Berg, he held important ecclesiastical preferment while still a boy, and by skilful manoeuvring became archbishop of Cologne at the age of thirty. Although his personal life was blameless, he defied the pope several times, took the field as a soldier and was murdered while defending the rights of an oppressed convent.
November 7th

ENGELMUND   *Eighth Century*
An English monk, he assisted St Willibrord in his missionary work in the Netherlands.
June 21st

ENNODIUS † 521

Brought up in Milan, he married a wealthy woman but afterwards decided to become a deacon. His wife became a nun, and he began to make a reputation as a teacher and writer. An unsympathetic comment on his writings was that he shrank from making himself intelligible in case he should be thought commonplace. He was made bishop of Pavia, and went twice to Constantinople on papal missions.

July 17th

EOGHAN, *see* Eugene.

EPARCHIUS or CYBARD † 581

He lived as a hermit near Angoulême, and after ordination, accepted disciples.

July 1st

EPHRAEM SYRUS THE DEACON † c. 373

The details of Ephraem's life are uncertain. For most of them there is at best but probability. Born at Nisibis in Mesopotamia about the beginning of the fourth century, on his conversion to Christianity he was expelled from home by heathen parents. He was befriended by the bishop of Nisibis and his successors and, at a date unknown raised to the diaconate, though, it would seem, declining priesthood from humility. When Nisibis was surrendered to the Persians by the Emperor Jovian, he withdrew into solitude, finally to a cave overlooking the city.

His prolific pen poured out devotional, theological and controversial writings, mostly in verse, in particular commentaries on the Scriptures and his hymns inaugurated the use of hymnody into the liturgical offices. He anticipated later developments by his devotion to the humanity of Jesus and to our Lady, whom he declared free from any taint of sin. He appears to have visited St Basil the Great in Cappadocia. On the occasion of a famine he overtaxed his strength, organizing and administering relief and caring for the sick, for he died only a month after his return to his cave, probably June 373. In his testament he asks that incense be used only in worship, not for his funeral, and that masses be said for his soul. Benedict XV declared him a doctor of the church and placed his feast in the Roman Calendar.

June 18th

EPIMACHUS, ALEXANDER and their
Companions † 250

Dionysius, bishop of Alexandria, witnessed their martyrdom at Alexandria during the persecution of Decius. (*See* Gordian and Epimachus).

December 12th

EPIPHANIUS of PAVIA † 496

This bishop of Pavia devoted his life to acts of charity and goodwill, and his popular titles, 'glory of Italy' and 'light of bishops' show how greatly Italy loved him.

January 21st

EPIPHANIUS of SALAMIS c. 310–403

After a visit to Egypt, he became abbot of a monastery he built at Eleutheropolis, and in 367 was chosen bishop of Salamis in Cyprus. He had a hasty temper and seems to have taken sides rather too easily, so that his later years were marred by some regrettable incidents. St Jerome referred to him as 'a last relic of ancient piety'.

May 12th

EPIPODIUS and ALEXANDER † 178

Childhood friends, they escaped from the massacre of Lyons in 177, but were soon discovered and executed.

April 22nd

EPISTEME, *see* Galation and Episteme.

EQUITIUS † c. 560

Founder of many monasteries, including that at Terni, his simplicity and the fact that he was not ordained aroused the hostility of the Roman clergy.

August 11th

ERASMUS or ELMO † 303?

A bishop of Formiae in the Campagne and a martyr, sometimes known as St Elmo, he is one of the Fourteen Holy Helpers and was once widely honored as the patron saint of sailors. Just before or after a storm at sea, electrical discharges on the masthead give off a bluish light which used to be known as St Elmo's light, because it was thought to be a sign that the particular ship had been taken under his protection. ILLUSTRATION: page 173

June 2nd

ERCONGOTA, *see* Ethelburga, Ercongota and
Sethrida.

ERCONWALD Seventh Century

Little is known of St Erconwald. A member of the East Anglian royal family, he was consecrated bishop of London in about 675 by Archbishop Theodore of Canterbury (St Theodore of Tarsus). He was probably the first to attempt to organize regular diocesan life in London, now that the 'mission' period was over, and he founded two famous medieval abbeys, Chertsey, and Barking nunnery.

This saint was the subject of a remarkable legend. While repairs were being made to St Paul's Cathedral, the body of a pagan but righteous nobleman was found, incorrupt. Erconwald, stirred by the thought of such righteousness in Hell, was moved to prayers and tears. His prayers united the dead man's soul to his body long enough for the tears to baptize him. The story is a variation on the more famous legend of St Gregory the

Great and the Emperor Trajan, which was circulating in England before 700. Behind these legends lies a genuine concern for the salvation of those who had led a good life but were unbaptized. It is pleasant to find such a concern in England at so early a date, and it is to St Erconwald's credit that he should be the subject of such a legend.
May 13th

 EREMBERT   *Seventh Century*
A Benedictine monk of Fontenelle Abbey under St Wandregisilus, he retired there when ill-health forced him to resign from his bishopric of Toulouse in 668.
May 14th

ERENTRUDE   *Eighth Century*
She assisted St Rupert, her kinsman, in organizing the religious life for women in the new city of Salzburg. She became abbess of a convent in that city.
June 30th

ERHARD   † 686
Probably bishop of Ratisbon, where local place names make it likely that his cultus dates back to the eighth century. Some relics remain, but no biographical facts.
January 8th

ERIC of SWEDEN   † 1161
As king of Sweden, he had the constitutions of his kingdom codified, and the book was known as *King Eric's Law*. Once Christianity was established in Sweden, he evangelized Finland which he had conquered. A conspiracy between Prince Magnus of Denmark and Swedish rebels brought about his death.
May 18th

ERMENGILD or ERMENILDA   † 703
Daughter of St Sexburga and Ercombert of Kent, she was wife of Wulfhere the Mercian king, and mother of St Werburga. In succession, Sexburga and Ermengild became abbesses of Ely after St Etheldreda, Sexburga's sister.
February 13th

ERMINOLD   † 1121
He resigned the abbacy of Lorsch after disputes, and was appointed abbot of the new monastery at Prüfening. Though a charitable man, he was strict; he died from a blow struck by a turbulent monk.
January 6th

ESKIL   *Eleventh Century*
This Englishman set out to reconvert Sweden where the work of St Anskar was being undone. He became regionary bishop of Strängnäs and was stoned to death by a heathen mob for protesting at a pagan festival.
June 12th

ESTERWINE   † 686
A popular courtier who became a monk at Wearmouth, an abbey recently founded by his relative St Benedict Biscop. After Benedict's retirement Esterwine ruled until his death four years later.
March 7th

ETHBIN   *Sixth Century*
After his father's death he was cared for by St Samson, and later became a monk in Brittany under St Winwaloe. When his monastery fell to the Franks, he fled to Ireland.
October 19th

ETHELBERT   † 794
The son and successor of Ethelred, king of the East Angles, he was murdered at the court of King Offa of Mercia, and his remains were later buried at Hereford.
May 20th   ILLUSTRATION: page 123 (c)

ETHELBERT of KENT   † 616
He is honored for his noble reception of the missionaries under St Augustine, for although he was still a heathen he assisted them; and when he was converted, he aided Christianity without ever enforcing it. He married Bertha, the Christian daughter of the king of Paris.
February 25th

ETHELBURGA, ERCONGOTA and
  SETHRIDA   *Seventh Century*
Ethelburga, her niece Ercongota and her half-sister Sethrida were members of the royal family of the East Angles. In order to live the religious life they travelled to Gaul and entered the abbey of Faremoutier in the forest of Brie. Sethrida later became abbess, and she was succeeded by Ethelburga.
July 7th

ETHELBURGA of BARKING   † c. 678
She was the sister of St Erconwald who founded the monastery at Barking of which she became abbess.
October 12th

ETHELBURGA of LYMINGE   *Seventh Century*
Daughter of King Ethelbert of Kent, she married Edwin, the pagan king of Northumbria, St Paulinus accompanying her as chaplain. She eventually converted her husband, but after his death was obliged to return to Kent where she founded and ruled the abbey of Lyminge.
April 5th

ETHELDREDA or AUDREY   † 679
A widow, she married the boy Egfrid, son of the king of Northumbria; when he grew up, she refused to consummate the marriage, and was supported by St Wilfrid. She retired to Ely where she founded a double monastery. The unfortunate Egfrid married again.
June 23rd

ETHELNOTH † 1038

Appointed archbishop of Canterbury in 1020, he encouraged King Canute to build a shrine to St Alphege at Canterbury and to support the rebuilding of Chartres.
October 30th

ETHELWALD *Eighth Century*

After assisting St Cuthbert, he became prior then abbot of Old Melrose in Scotland, and later succeeded Eadfrith as bishop of Lindisfarne. His relics are in Durham Cathedral.
February 12th

ETHELWALD or OIDILWALD THE HERMIT
† 699

A monk from Ripon, noted for his wisdom and miracles, he occupied, for twelve years, the cell on Farne Island formerly used by St Cuthbert. His relics are at Durham.
March 23rd

ETHELWOLD † 984

Born in Winchester, he became a monk of Glastonbury under St Dunstan and, in 954, abbot of Abingdon. Nine years later he became bishop of Winchester, replacing the lax cathedral canons with his own monks. A keen reformer of monastic usage, he repaired and revived many ancient foundations which had suffered during the Danish raids.
August 1st

EUBULUS, *see* Adrian and Eubulus.

EUCHERIUS of LYONS † 449

Both his sons became monks of Lérins and then bishops. Eucherius himself retired to Lérins, but was appointed bishop of Lyons in 434.
November 16th

EUCHERIUS of ORLEANS † 743

A monk at Jumiège who became bishop of Orleans, his birthplace; he was exiled to Liège by Charles Martel for opposing the confiscation of church revenues. He was allowed to retire to Saint-Trond near Maestricht.
February 20th

EUGENDUS or OYEND *Sixth Century*

Coadjutor to Minausius whom he succeeded as abbot of Condat. He prayed and fasted continually, promoted learning and founded a church, but never consented to become a priest.
January 1st

EUGENE or EOGHAN *Sixth Century*

With two other boys, Tigernach and Coirpre, he was supposed – according to legend – to have been sold into slavery in Brittany. Returning to Ireland, he settled at Ardstraw in Tyrone and was consecrated bishop. From this bishopric grew the see of Derry.
August 23rd

EUGENIA

According to legend she was the daughter of the duke of Alexandria. She disguised herself as a man, became a monk and then an abbot. To answer a charge of adultery she was obliged to reveal her sex in order to prove her innocence.
December 25th

EUGENIUS I † 657

His predecessor – St Martin I – was still alive in exile when St Eugenius was appointed pope, probably at the instigation of the Emperor Constans II. Eugenius refused to enter into communion with the Byzantine patriarch, Peter.
June 2nd

EUGENIUS of CARTHAGE † 505

Because of the persecution of the Vandals, the see of Carthage had long been vacant. In 481 King Huneric gave the Catholics permission to elect a bishop and Eugenius was their choice. He was so successful that the Vandals were forbidden to enter his churches. After an abortive conference with the Arians in 484, he was banished and except for a few years, passed the rest of his life in exile.
July 13th

EUGENIUS of TOLEDO † 657

Archbishop of Toledo, he was a musician and poet, and tried to improve the standard of church singing.
November 13th

EUGRAPHUS, *see* Mennas, Hermogenes and Eugraphus.

EULALIA of MERIDA † 304

This girl of twelve, the most famous virgin martyr of Spain, died during the persecution of Diocletian. She is the subject of a hymn by Prudentius.
December 10th

EULAMPIUS and EULAMPIA † 310?

They are said to have been a brother and his sister who were martyred at Nicomedia under Galerius; but there is no reliable evidence that they even existed.
October 10th

EULOGIUS of ALEXANDRIA † c. 607

In 579, this abbot of a monastery at Antioch became the patriarch of Alexandria. There he fought against Monophysites, and was a close friend of St Gregory the Great.
September 13th

EULOGIUS of CORDOVA † 859

A priest known from his friend and biographer, Alvarez, with whom he studied under Sperandeo. Under Moorish persecution in Cordova, he fearlessly encouraged the

A

B

Photos: Universal Lens Craft

C

(A) JOHN de BRÉBEUF.
(B) GABRIEL LALEMANT.
(C) ISAAC JOGUES.

Three of the Martyrs of North America.

Engravings by N. G. Huret.

DOMINIC SAVIO: photograph from a likeness made after his death.

DONATUS of AREZZO: detail from painting 'Canon with patron saints' by Gerard David (1450 – 1523). *(National Gallery, London.)*

DOROTHY: with the Infant Christ by Francesco di Giorgio (1439 – 1501).
(National Gallery, London.)

DUNSTAN: alleged self-portrait of Dunstan, at the foot of Christ (second half of tenth century).
(Glastonbury MS, Bodleian Library, Oxford.)

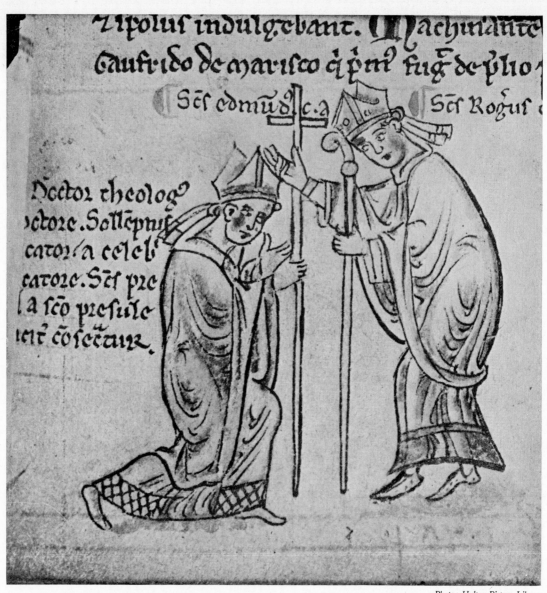

EDMUND of ABINGDON: MS drawing by Matthew Paris (d. 1259) of 'The Consecration of St Edmund', from the *Historia Anglorum. (British Museum.)*

EDMUND THE MARTYR: (with arrow), Edward the Confessor, John the Baptist and King Richard II (kneeling): Panel from the Wilton Diptych. (French school, fourteenth century). *(National Gallery, London.)*

Photo: British Museum

(A) EDWARD THE CONFESSOR: silver penny
(struck at Winchester *c.* 1066). One of six discovered in
the armpit of an executed felon on Stockbridge Down.
(British Museum.)

Photo: British Museum

(B) EDWARD THE MARTYR: silver penny (struck
at London). The coin is from a hoard found at Chester in
1941, concealed (*c.* 980) when a Viking fleet was ravaging
the Wirral. *(British Museum.)*

168

ELIGIUS or ELOI: painting by Petrus Christus (*fl.* 1444 – 1472-3). (*Lehman Collection, New York.*)

ELIZABETH and ZACHARY: detail of painting by Ghirlandaio (1449 – 1494). *(Louvre, Paris.)*

ELIZABETH of HUNGARY: detail of painting 'The Virgin and Child with saints' by Jan van Eyck (1380-90 – 1441). *(Frick Collection, New York.)*

ELIZABETH of PORTUGAL: painting thought to be by a Portuguese pupil of Quentin
Matsys (c. 1466–1530), probably Eduardo Portugues.

ERASMUS or ELMO: painting by Matthias Grunewald (1470-80–1528-30). *(Alte Pinakothek, Munich.)*

EUSTACE: painting by Jan Bruegel (1568 – 1625). (*Prado, Madrid.*)

174

FABIAN: detail of restored painting attributed to Diamante (*c.* 1430 – 1498). *(Cappella Sistina, Vatican.)*

FELIX I: sixth century mosaic. *(Ch. dei SS Cosmas e Damian, Rome.)*

faithful, urging many to the martyrdom he eventually suffered himself.
March 11th

EUPHEMIA † 303
Martyred at Chalcedon, she was once widely venerated. The fourth general council, which condemned the heresy of Monophysism in 451 was held in the church built in her honor at Chalcedon.
September 16th

EUPHRASIA or EUPRAXIA *Fifth Century*
Related to Theodosius who protected her when her father Antigonus died, at seven years old she entered an Egyptian convent. Here her lifelong asceticism and humility inspired great devotion: she would often pass a week without eating, and once remained standing in the same place for thirty days until she collapsed.
March 13th

EUPHROSYNE *Fifth Century?*
No evidence supports the existence of this saint, though she is much honored in Greece. Her legendary history which echoes that of St Pelagia the Penitent asserts that, in order to avoid detection, St Euphrosyne presented herself at a local monastery disguised as a boy, and that she passed the rest of her life as a monk there.
January 1st

EUPHROSYNE of POLOTSK † 1173
The only virgin canonized by the Russian church, she was the daughter of Prince Svyatoslav of Polotsk, and lived as a solitary nun, earning money for charity by copying books.
May 23rd

EUPLUS † 304
He was brought before the governor, Calvisian, at Catania in Sicily during the persecution of Diocletian, and was beheaded.
August 12th

EUROSIA *Eighth Century?*
The story that she was killed by the Saracens when she refused to marry a Moorish chieftain is probably a myth. She had a great vogue among Spanish soldiers in the sixteenth century, and is invoked against bad weather.
June 25th

EUSEBIA *Seventh Century*
Daughter of St Adalbald of Ostrevant and St Rictrudis, she was the great grand-daughter of St Gertrude whom she succeeded as abbess of Hamage when only twelve. Though summoned by Rictrudis to Marchiennes, she secretly returned to Hamage and ruled with remarkable wisdom.
March 16th

EUSEBIUS † 310
He succeeded St Marcellus as pope and was faced with the problem of what to do with those who had lapsed during Dioletian's persecution. Led by Heraclius, they sought readmission so furiously that the emperor banished the pope and Heraclius from Rome to Sicily where Eusebius died.
August 17th

EUSEBIUS † 884
After leaving Ireland, he entered the Saint-Gall abbey in Switzerland and became a hermit on Mount St Victor in the Vorarlberg. A peasant, whose heathen ways he was denouncing, struck him with a scythe and killed him.
January 31st

EUSEBIUS, NESTABUS, ZENO and NESTOR † c. 362
Eusebius, Nestabus and Zeno were three brothers who together with Nestor were lynched by a mob in Gaza on the charge of taking part in the destruction of a temple.
September 8th

EUSEBIUS of CREMONA *Fifth Century*
A lifelong friend of St Jerome whom he accompanied to the Holy Land. At Rome, where he returned to collect funds, he influenced Pope St Anastasius I to condemn Origen's writings. He died in Italy.
March 5th

EUSEBIUS of ROME *Fourth Century*
It is certain that he lived in Rome, but our information is otherwise highly unreliable.
August 14th

EUSEBIUS of SAMOSATA *Fourth Century*
A bishop of Samosata, he distinguished himself in opposing the Arians, especially in the choice of bishops for neighboring sees. Exiled during the persecution under Valens, he returned in 378, and was murdered by an Arian woman.
June 21st

EUSEBIUS of VERCELLI † 371
A Sardinian, he was bishop of Vercelli in Piedmont. At the council of Milan in 355 he opposed the Arians and was banished by the Emperor Constantius to Palestine. He returned to his diocese after Constantius's death in 361. The cathedral at Vercelli possesses a manuscript of the Gospels which may be in his hand.
December 16th

EUSTACE, *see* Antony, Eustace and John.

EUSTACE and his Companions
Little is known of this patron of huntsmen, who is also one of the Fourteen Holy Helpers. Legend has it that he was a Roman general who was converted while

hunting, and suffered martyrdom with his family by being roasted in a bronze bull.
September 20th   ILLUSTRATION: page 174

EUSTATHIUS, *see* Eutychius.

EUSTATHIUS of ANTIOCH   † *c.* 340
He was translated from the see of Beroea in Syria to that of Antioch, and took an active part in opposing Arianism, especially at the council of Nicaea. This led to his banishment to Thrace in 330.
July 16th

EUSTOCHIUM   † *c.* 419
Like her mother St Paula, she was strongly influenced by St Jerome, and took a vow of chastity. When her mother went to Palestine, she accompanied her, and stayed at Bethlehem. Both tended St Jerome when his sight failed, and Eustochium succeeded her mother as superior of the three communities she had helped to found.
September 28th

EUSTORGIUS of MILAN   † 518
Bishop of Milan from 512 until his death in 518.
June 6th

EUSTRATIUS and his Companions
All these martyrs suffered under Diocletian in Armenia, and their bodies were afterwards taken to Rome, being entombed in St Apollinaris.
December 13th

EUTHYMIUS THE GREAT   † 473
A priest of Melitene in Armenia he spent his long life in austere solitude near Jericho, instructing his community of monks, advising and curing all in distress, and ruling as bishop over the many Arabs he had converted. So great was his love of solitude that he delegated the duty of ruling his community to vicars, to whom each Sunday he gave his instructions.
January 20th

EUTHYMIUS THE ILLUMINATOR   † 1028
Son of St John the Iberian, he helped his father to found the monastery of Iviron on Mount Athos, and succeeded him as abbot. He retired after fourteen years in order to concentrate on his task of translating sacred commentaries and other biblical works into Iberian.
May 13th

EUTHYMIUS THE YOUNGER   † 898
Born at Opso, near Ancyra, he left his wife and child to become a monk on Mount Olympus in Bithynia. He then moved to Mount Athos and after many years founded a monastery at Peristera. He passed some time on a pillar.
October 15th

EUTROPIUS, *see* Tigrius and Eutropius.

EUTROPIUS of ORANGE   *Fifth Century*
He was ordained after the death of his wife and, as bishop of Orange, set about repairing the damage done by the Visigoths.
May 27th

EUTROPIUS of SAINTES   *Third Century*
He was sent from Rome to evangelize the south-west of France, and became the first bishop of Saintes. He was executed for converting Eustella, the daughter of the Roman governor. His story is unreliable but the tradition of his cultus is ancient.
April 30th

EUTYCHIAN   † 283
This pope is buried in the catacomb of Callistus and is called a martyr; but it is unlikely that he was martyred, because he did not live in a time of persecution.
December 7th

EUTYCHIUS   † 582
He was a monk of Amasea in Pontus who became patriarch of Constantinople in 553, but was banished after a dispute with the Emperor Justinian. He was restored to his see after a twelve years' exile.
April 6th

EUTYCHIUS or EUSTATHIUS   † 741
A patrician, he lived during a time of double persecution, for the Emperor Leo the Isaurian persecuted Christians, who venerated images, while invading Arabs killed them for defending their faith. Eutychius was captured by the Arabs and martyred at Carrhae in Mesopotamia.
March 14th

EVARISTUS   † *c.* 107
Fourth in succession to St Peter, he succeeded St Clement as pope and reigned for eight years.
October 26th

EVENTIUS, *see* Alexander, Eventius and Theodulus.

EVERGISLUS, *see* Ebregislus.

EVERILD   *Seventh Century*
Of noble birth, she left her family to found a community of women near York with the help of St Wilfrid.
July 9th

EVERMOD   † 1178
Inspired by St Norbert, he left Cambrai, joined the Premonastratensian canons and eventually succeeded Norbert as superior of the Gottesgnaden monastery. The first bishop of Ratzeburg near Schleswig-Holstein, he is known as the apostle to the Wends.
February 17th

EVODIUS   *First Century*
He was consecrated as bishop of Antioch by the Apostles themselves, and is supposed to have coined the word 'Christian'.
May 6th

EVROULT, *see* Ebrulf.

THE TWO EWALDS   † 695
These two Northumbrian brothers, known as 'Ewald the Dark' and 'Ewald the Fair' were murdered by suspicious tribesmen soon after leaving St Willibrord, whose mission they had just joined.
October 3rd

EXPEDITUS
There is a delightful but apocryphal story to account for the origins of this saint who never existed, but is sometimes regarded as the patron saint of 'hustle' and invoked against procrastination.

Some Parisian nuns, we are told, received a box of relics from Rome for a newly-commissioned chapel. No clue to the identity of these relics could be found except for a label on the outside of the box, which had the words 'è spedito' followed by the date. As they were innocent of Italian the nuns did not know that 'è spedito' meant 'sent off', but assumed instead that it was the name of the saint whose relics they had received. Their chapel was dedicated accordingly, and the cult of St Expeditus had begun.

The nature of the invocation made – that causes committed to the saint's care are expedited *(sic)* – gives us a clue to the real origin of the cult: a play upon words. There are many such associations which can be ascribed to the same kind of source, and the choice of a patron saint seems frequently to have been made on the strength of a pun. In France, St Clare is considered to help us to see more *clearly*, St Ouen restores *hearing* and St Cloud cures boils *(clous)*, while in Germany diseases of the eye *(auge)* are referred to St Augustine.
April 19th

EXSUPERANTIUS   † 418
Successor to St Ursus as bishop of Ravenna, he persuaded Stilicho, who was besieging the city, to leave the cathedral unharmed.
May 30th

EXSUPERIUS   † *c.* 412
He succeeded St Silvius as bishop of Toulouse and completed the church of St Sernin. He was famous for his boundless charity.
September 28th

EXSUPERIUS or HESPERUS and ZOË
      Second Century
A family of Christian slaves, it was the sons, Cyriacus and Theodulus, who encouraged their parents, Exsuperius and Zoë, in their religion. All four were roasted to death when they professed their faith.
May 2nd

EYSTEIN   † 1188
Eystein (*i.e.* Augustine) Erlandsson was the second archbishop of Nidaros (Trondheim). He spent most of his life securing the church in Norway from interference by powerful laymen; hence probably his devotion to St Thomas of Canterbury, whom he may have met in Paris, and whose shrine he may well have visited when he was forced to take refuge in England in 1181.
January 26th

FABIAN   † 250
He succeeded St Antherus as pope in about 236 and reigned for about fourteen years. He was martyred in the persecution of Decius.   ILLUSTRATION: page 175
January 20th

FABIOLA   † 399
A Roman lady of great wealth and position, she divorced her dissolute husband and married again. On the death of her second husband she did public penance in the basilica of St John Lateran and was restored to communion by pope St Siricius. She used her wealth to found the first Christian public hospital in Europe, working there until 394 when she went to visit St Jerome at Bethlehem. He must have liked this passionate and determined woman, for he wrote a charming description of her after her death. As his pupil she flung herself into a study of the scriptures with an enthusiasm that nothing could satisfy, subjecting the saint to a strict and detailed cross-examination upon the minutiae of Old Testament exegesis, which provoked him to write a short treatise in his own defence – especially for Fabiola.

She returned to Rome when the community at Bethlehem had to withdraw temporarily before a threatened invasion, but she could not rest; thinking only of the desert, she still lived on there in spirit. She burned to be free of Rome, and started to make plans to leave, but amidst the feverish preparations for her departure she died.
December 27th

FACHANAN   *Sixth Century*
Traditionally the founder of the great school of Ross, of whose diocese he is patron and the first bishop, this disciple of St Ita also founded the monastery of Molana.
August 14th

FAITH   *Third Century*
This young girl is said to have been martyred at Agen,
and there are still chapels dedicated to her in St Paul's
Cathedral and Westminster Abbey in London.
October 6th

FAITH, HOPE and CHARITY and their mother
  WISDOM
Misplaced piety rather than fact is probably responsible
for the legend that Faith, Hope and Charity were the
children of Wisdom, and that all four were martyred at
the same time during the persecution of Hadrian.
August 1st

FANCHEA, *see* Enda and Fanchea.

FANTINUS   *Tenth Century*
He was abbot of the Greek community of St Mercury
in Calabria before he began his wanderings. These led
him eventually to Salonika, where he died. It is possible,
however, that the Calabrian Fantius has been wrongly
identified with a Fantinus of Salonika.
August 30th

FARE, *see* Burgundofara.

FARO   † *c. 672*
The most illustrious bishop of Meaux, he was made
chancellor to Dagobert I. We have little reliable knowledge of his life and works.
October 28th

FAUSTINUS, *see* Simplicius, Faustinus and Beatrice.

FAUSTINUS and JOVITA
These brothers were of noble birth and belonged to the
city of Brescia which honors them as its chief patrons,
claiming to possess their relics; but there is little reliable
evidence even of their existence, let alone of their
martyrdom.
February 15th

FAUSTUS, JANUARIUS and MARTIAL
                                        † 304?
They were known as the 'Three Crowns of Cordova',
because they were martyred in that city.
October 13th

FAUSTUS of RIEZ   *Fifth Century*
A monk of Lérins, he succeeded St Maximus as abbot
and then as bishop of Riez. Although he was to a certain
extent guilty of semi-Pelagian errors, he was a staunch
opponent of Arianism and was for a time banished from
his see.
September 28th

FEARGAL, *see* Virgil.

FEBRONIA   *Fourth Century*
The story of this beautiful nun who was supposed to
have been tortured and martyred at Nisbis in Mesopotamia is probably fictitious.
June 25th

FECHIN   † 665
Once widely honored, this Irish monk was the founder
and ruler of a monastic community at Fobhar in
Westmeath. He died in the Irish plague of 665.
January 20th

FELICIAN, *see* Primus and Felician.

FELICIAN and MESSALINA   *Third Century*
When Felician, bishop and missionary, was imprisoned
during persecutions by Decius, a maid, Messalina, tended
him so devotedly that she also was arrested. Both refused
to worship idols, and died after torture. The measure of
truth there may be in this story can be determined.
January 24th

FELICISSIMUS, *see* Sixtus II, Felicissimus and
  Agapitus.

FELICITY, *see* Perpetua and Felicity.

FELICITY and
  THE SEVEN HOLY BROTHERS
On July 10th the *Depositio Martyrum* records seven
martyrs; Felix and Philip buried in the catacomb of
Priscilla, Martial, Vitalis and Alexander in the catacomb
of the Jordani, Silanus in the catacomb of Maximus,
Januarius in the catacomb of Praetextatus.
    They were certainly seven authentic martyrs, but
nothing suggests relationship between them. Indeed the
fact of burial in four different cemeteries suggests that
their martyrdoms were independent. It happened that
the body of a martyr Felicity was buried near the body
of Silanus in the catacomb of Maximus. Since her feast
day is November 23rd, her martyrdom is unlikely to
have been in any way connected with his, not to speak
of the six other martyrs of July 10th. Unfortunately, a
hagiographer, wishing to present his devout public with
a Christian version of the passion of the seven Maccabees
in their mother's presence, composed a *Passio* which
made these seven martyrs Felicity's sons, tortured and
put to death in her presence and encouraged by her
exhortations. The *Passio*, only too successful, must have
been written before the middle of the fifth century, for
St Peter Chrysologus was acquainted with it. To
account for burial in four distinct catacombs the writer
despatches his seven martyrs to four different judges.
November 23rd Felicity; *July 10th* The Seven Brothers

FELICULA   *First Century*
Her legend states that after the martyrdom of her foster-

sister Petronilla, Count Flaccus, a rejected suitor, handed her over to the Roman magistrates. She was tortured and eventually suffocated in a sewer.
June 13th

FELIM, *see* Nathy and Felim.

FELIX, *see* Aurelia, Natalia, Felix and their Companions.

FELIX, *see* Nabor and Felix.

FELIX I   † 274
He succeeded St Dionysius as pope and is frequently confused with another Felix who is buried on the Via Aurelia. St Felix died on December 30th, 274, and is buried in the cemetery of Callistus.
May 30th   ILLUSTRATION: page 176

FELIX 'II'   † 365
This anti-pope was neither saint nor martyr, but a Roman deacon who, after the expulsion of Pope Liberius, was consecrated by three Arian bishops, and fled when Liberius returned.
July 29th

FELIX II (III)   † 492
This pope, St Felix, is referred to as the Third to distinguish him from the mis-titled anti-pope, Felix II. He is chiefly known for his work in restoring the African church, and for excommunicating the patriarch Acacius, who ignored the decisions of the council of Chalcedon when dealing with the Monophysites.
March 1st

FELIX III (IV)   † 530
He was nominated to the papacy by King Theodoric, in succession to St John I. During his rule the tenets of the Semi-Pelagians were condemned at the synod of Orange in 529, clerical immunity from lay jurisdiction was strengthened, and the basilica of SS Cosmas and Damian was built.
September 22nd

FELIX and ADAUCTUS   † *c.* 304
When St Felix was being taken to execution, he was met by a stranger who was so impressed by his bearing that he made an immediate profession of faith, asking that he might join St Felix in martyrdom. For this reason the unknown stranger was called 'Adauctus' (the one added).
August 30th

FELIX and CYPRIAN and their Companions † *c.* 484
These two bishops were among the 4966 Christians who were driven into the African desert by the Vandal king Huneric. Felix, an old man, had been bishop for forty-four years.
October 12th

FELIX and FORTUNATUS   *Third Century*
Although natives of Vicenza, these two brothers suffered martyrdom at Aquileia, in the persecution under Diocletian and Maximian.
June 11th

FELIX, FORTUNATUS and ACHILLEUS † 212
They were sent by St Irenaeus, bishop of Lyons, to evangelize the people of Valence, where they became martyrs.
April 23rd

FELIX of BOURGES   *Sixth Century*
He was bishop of Bourges and took part in the council of Paris in 573. The dust from his tombstone was said to have worked many amazing cures.
January 1st

FELIX of CANTALICE   *c.* 1515–1587
He joined the Capuchin monastery of Città Ducale, and later spent forty years in Rome as questor to the community, begging alms. There he became friendly with SS Philip Neri and Charles Borromeo. He walked bare-foot and wore, not a hair shirt, but one of mail studded with spikes.
May 18th

FELIX of DUNWICH   † 648
A French bishop, he took over the see of Dunwich in Suffolk. Helped by Sigebert, the newly converted king of East Anglia, he evangelized a large area and founded a school.
March 8th

FELIX of NANTES   † 582
His wife became a nun in 549, when, at the age of thirty-six, he was made bishop of Nantes. He completed the cathedral and improved the navigation of the Loire.
July 7th

FELIX of NOLA   † *c.* 260
We know of St Felix chiefly through the enthusiasm of St Paulinus of Nola, who, coming to that place rather more than a hundred years after the death of Felix, found his tomb cherished by the faithful. Paulinus, too, became devoted to the memory of the saint; he claimed to have received many favors through his intercession, and he gathered the traditions of the neighborhood into the story of his life.

According to this, Felix was the elder son of a prosperous farmer; he became a priest, and was the great aid and comfort of St Maximus, bishop of Nola, during the persecutions under the Emperor Decius. Felix himself was imprisoned, but was miraculously set free by an angel that he might go to the help of his bishop who was suffering alone in his retreat in the desert. At the death of Maximus, when the persecution had come to an end, there was a movement to make Felix bishop, but he insisted on standing down in favor of a man senior to him in the priesthood. He refused to make a claim for his possessions among those which had been confiscated during the persecutions and which the authorities were restoring to their owners, but lived on his own scrap of land, cultivating it himself, and giving all that he received to the poor. He died at an advanced age on the date of his feast.

The tomb of St Felix speedily became a center of devotion, as St Paulinus relates; and we hear from no less a person than St Augustine of the miracles performed there.
January 14th

FELIX of THIBIUCA   † 303
One of the first victims of the persecution of Diocletian, this bishop of Thibiuca was beheaded in Carthage for refusing to surrender his sacred books to be burned.
October 24th

FELIX of TRIER   *Fourth Century*
A most devout and charitable bishop of Trier, who, as his electors were not acceptable to Pope St Siricius, retired to the monastery he had founded.
March 26th

FELIX of VALOIS   † 1212?
This saint never existed save in the imagination of Trinitarian authors at a loss for some means of enhancing the glory of their order. He is supposed to have been a member of the royal family living as a hermit at Cerfroid in the province of Valois, who was encouraged by his disciple St John of Matha to found a society for the redemption of captives, otherwise known as the order of the most Holy Trinity. It is also claimed that he was in charge of the French Province and of the mother-house at Cerfroid.
November 20th

FERDINAND III of CASTILE   † 1252
He became king of Castile at the age of eighteen, and of Leon thirteen years later in 1230. Besides founding the University of Salamanca, he fought continually and successfully against the Moors, building churches in the conquered territory.
May 30th

FERGAL, *see* Virgil.

FERGUS   *Eighth Century?*
An Irishman, he came as a missionary to Scotland, where he founded many churches, Glamis among them. He may have been Fergustus, bishop of the Scots, who attended a synod in Rome in 721.
November 27th

FERREOLUS   *Third Century?*
He was a tribune of Vienne and was arrested for his failure to persecute Christians. It was then discovered that he was himself a Christian and he was beheaded.
September 18th

FERREOLUS and FERRUTIO   *Third Century*
They were sent by the bishop of Lyons, St Irenaeus, as missionaries to the district of Besançon. Their work ended in their martyrdom in the reign of Caracalla.
June 16th

FERREOLUS of LIMOGES   *Sixth Century*
He was bishop of Limoges and died sometime after 591.
September 18th

FIACRE   *Sixth Century*
St Fiacre lived approximately between the years 600 and 670. He was one of the numerous band of Irish missionaries who travelled to Europe in the wake of St Columbanus. The bishop of Meaux, who had known Columbanus, gave a kindly welcome to Fiacre and enabled him to set up his hermitage at a spot later known as La Brie, seven miles from Meaux on the banks of the Marne in Normandy, now one of the most fertile districts of France.

Here Fiacre settled down to live the religious life as he had lived it in Ireland – a patch of the Celtic church translated to Gaul. Soon the natives of the district began to seek him out in his forest solitude to learn the Christian faith. The hardships these pilgrims suffered, far from their homes without shelter or food, troubled Fiacre. The friendly bishop of Meaux gave him additional land and Fiacre felled trees to build a hospice for them near his oratory; he cleared the soil in order to grow corn and vegetables to feed them. His life of self-sacrifice won to the faith all the surrounding district and he was particularly honored for his work with the spade. The patron saint of gardeners, he is indeed the saint of the spade, which is also his symbol in art.

The cult of St Fiacre grew steadily in France and reached an extraordinary peak of fervor in the seventeenth century, a thousand years after his death, when his shrine was famous for miraculous cures. His name became attached to the four-wheeled cab because, when this vehicle first came into use in Paris in 1640, it was chiefly hired at the Hotel St Fiacre to take pilgrims on the first stage of their journey to his shrine at La Brie. The name was later transferred from the hotel to the vehicle.

He was the favored saint both of the common people and of royalty. The personal histories of Louis XIII, his wife Anne of Austria, and their son, the Grand Monarch, abound in anecdotes describing the saint's answers to prayers.
September 1st

FIDELIS of COMO † 303?

The *cultus* of this saint at Como is very old, but we know nothing for certain about him. He may have been an army officer who ministered to Christians captured by Maximian until he was himself caught and beheaded.
October 28th

FIDELIS of SIGMARINGEN † 1622

A Swabian from Hohenzollern and protomartyr of the Congregation *de Propaganda Fide*, Mark Rey started his career as a lawyer. Disgusted with the tricks of the legal profession, he joined the Capuchins, taking the name of Fidelis. Appointed leader of the first attempt since the Reformation to re-convert the Zwinglians of the Grisons, after considerable success he was murdered by a gang of armed men on the road from Sewis to Grüsch.
April 24th

FILLAN or FOELAN Eighth Century
and KENTIGERNA † 734

The son of St Kentigerna and Feriach, Fillan became an abbot near St Andrews, but retired and built a church at Glendochart in Perthshire. Kentigerna, a prince's daughter, became a nun.
January 19th Fillan; *January 7th* Kentigerna

FINA or SERAPHINA † 1253

Of wonderful patience and faith, her brief life was mainly spent on a board, paralyzed and terribly neglected, at St Geminiano in Tuscany. When she died, white violets were found to be growing on the board on which she had lain. To this day the peasants of her village call the violets which bloom at the time of her feast Santa Fina's flowers.
March 12th

FINAN † 661

An Irish monk of Iona, he became second bishop of Lindisfarne in succession to St Aidan. During his peaceful rule, he baptized Penda, prince of the Middle English, and Sigebert, king of the East Saxons; he consecrated St Cedd, upheld the Celtic use as against the Roman, and built a cathedral on Holy Island. It was of wood thatched with sea-grass.
February 17th

FINBAR † c. 633

Said to have voyaged to Rome several times, often by miraculous means, he founded a monastery at the mouth of the river Lee; around it grew the city of Cork, of which he was the first bishop. The island of Barra takes its name from him.
September 25th

FINNIAN LOBHAR Sixth Century?

Born in Leinster, he was a descendant of the royal family of Munster and named 'the Leper' from a skin disease

he suffered, which appeared to be like leprosy. He was abbot either of Clonmore or of Swords abbey.
March 16th

FINNIAN of CLONARD † c. 549

Known as the 'teacher of the saints of Ireland', he founded many churches, schools and monasteries of which the most famous was at Clonard on the Boyne, near Meath. This was the religious center of the diocese of which he may have been bishop.
December 12th

FINNIAN of MOVILLE † c. 579

No certainty attaches to the details of his life. He is believed to have been an Ulsterman educated under St Colman, who went to Rome and was ordained, after scandal had made it desirable for him to leave Strathclyde. His foundations at Moville, in county Down, and Dromin, in Louth, both became famous centers of learning.
September 10th

FINTAN of CLONEENAGH † 603

Described as the Irish counterpart of St Benedict of Nursia, he founded and ruled the celebrated Cloneenagh monastery in Leix. Although surpassingly austere himself – he is said to have existed on barley bread and muddy water –, he was gentle and tolerant towards others. His personal appearance must have been striking, as he was described by St Columba as having a ruddy face, gleaming eyes and hair flecked with white.
February 17th

FINTAN of RHEINAU Ninth Century

An Irishman carried off by Norsemen as a slave to the Orkneys, he escaped to Scotland. On his way back from a pilgrimage to Rome he met some hermits at Rheinau in the Black Forest and stayed with them until his death.
November 15th

FINTAN or MUNNU of TAGHMON † c. 635

He wished to become a monk of Iona but was sent back because the abbot had been told in a vision that St Fintan was destined to found an Irish monastery. He did so at Taghmon in County Wexford.
October 21st

FIRMINUS Fourth Century?

He is said to have been a bishop of Toulouse who undertook missionary work in Northern France and suffered martyrdom at Amiens. But the sources are late and unreliable. All we can really accept is that this bishop and martyr was venerated at Amiens during the ninth century.
September 25th

FLANNAN Seventh Century

First bishop of Killaloe, he was the son of the chieftain

Turlough who became a Christian as a very old man, inspired by his son's life and teaching.
December 18th

FLAVIAN † 449
He became patriarch of Constantinople in 447 under Pope Leo I. As a result of the unending contrivances of the chamberlain to Theodosius II, Chrysaphius, he was so brutally beaten up for condemning Eutyches – the Monophysite heretic – at the 'Robber Synod' that he died from his injuries.
February 18th

FLAVIAN and ELIAS *Fifth Century*
When in 457 St Elias was banished from Egypt, he went to Palestine, where he was elected patriarch of Jerusalem. Both he and St Flavian, the patriarch of Antioch, were exiled for their opposition to Monophysism.
July 20th

FLORA and MARY † 851
These two girls were martyred in Cordova by Abdur Rahman II. They promised to intercede in heaven for the release of St Eulogius, also imprisoned in Cordova, and he and his companions were in fact released a week later.
November 24th

FLORA of BEAULIEU † 1347
Scruples drove this young nun into such a state of depression that her companions made fun of her. Later, she underwent a series of mystical experiences.
October 5th

FLORENTIUS of STRASBOURG
Seventh Century
An Irishman, he settled as a hermit in Alsace, gaining the patronage of King Dagobert, and founding a monastery at Haslach. He became seventh bishop of Strasbourg *c.* 678.
November 7th

FLORIAN † 304
He was a high-ranking officer in the Roman Army who gave himself up to the governor of his province and was thrown into the River Enns. He is regarded as the patron saint of Poland, Linz and Upper Austria, and is invoked against dangers from water and fire.
May 4th

FLORIBERT † 746
He was the son of St Hubert, and succeeded his father as bishop of Liège.
April 27th

FLORUS and LAURUS
These two brothers were stone-masons who were martyred in Illyria. They were converted after they had built a heathen temple. It is probable that this story fictious, and they may even be doublets of the Four Crowned ones.
August 18th

FOELAN, *see* Fillan and **Kentigerna**.

FOILLAN † c. 655
Brother of SS Fursey and Ultan, he worked as a missionary in England before going to Gaul where he established a monastery at Fosses near Nivelles. He was murdered by robbers near his church.
October 31st

FORANNAN † 982
He gave up the Irish bishopric of Domhnach–Mor and, travelling with twelve companions, recognized Waulsort on the Meuse as the valley which was shown to him in a dream as his future home. He became first a monk and then, in 962, abbot of the monastery at Waulsort.
April 30th

FORTUNATUS, *see* Felix and Fortunatus.

FORTUNATUS, *see* Felix, Fortunatus and Achilleus.

FORTUNATUS, *see* Hermagoras and Fortunatus.

THE FOUR CROWNED ONES † 306?
Although there are confusing traditions about the identity of these martyrs, it is likely that their names were Claudius, Nicostratus, Simpronian, Castorius and Simplicius and that there were five, not four, martyrs. They worked for Diocletian in the stone quarries at Sirmium. The emperor tolerated their Christian beliefs because of their great skill as carvers but was eventually persuaded to order their execution for refusing to sacrifice to the gods. They were placed alive in leaden coffins, and thrown into the river. Their relics were later taken to Rome, where the confusion over their identity arose.

A basilica was built and dedicated to them on the Coelian hill, and they are the patrons of sculptors and stonemasons.
November 8th

THE FOURTEEN HOLY HELPERS
In the middle ages it was sometimes more customary to honor saints for their supposed ability to do things than for their piety, and it is to this period that the cult of the Fourteen Holy Helpers belongs. It was particularly strong in Germany, whence it spread into France, Italy and other countries. It seems never to have made much mark in England, but in other parts of the world many churches, institutes and shrines were named after the Holy Helpers, and, in some dioceses, the feast was permitted on August 8th. A church is called after them in Baltimore, Maryland. Further information about the individual saints forming the group of the Holy Helpers

will be found under the appropriate entries. The Fourteen Holy Helpers are invoked as follows:

1. Achatius, against headaches.
2. Barbara, against lightning, fire, explosion and sudden death.
3. Blaise, against diseases of the throat.
4. Catherine, by philosophers, students and lawyers.
5. Christopher, by travellers.
6. Cyriacus, against maladies of the eye.
7. Denis, against headaches and rabies.
8. Erasmus, against cramp and diseases of the intestines.
9. Eustace, by hunters and sometimes to save us from fire of all kinds, including eternal fire.
10. George, by soldiers and sometimes against skin diseases.
11. Giles, against epilepsy, insanity, sterility and cases of demonic possession.
12. Margaret, by pregnant women and during childbirth.
13. Pantaleon, against phthisis and other wasting diseases.
14. Vitus (or Guy), against epilepsy and against the 'dance' bearing his name.

In France it was customary to include our Lady, thus bringing the number of Helpers to fifteen. Local variations occurred elsewhere, and, at one time or another, the following saints were included: Dorothy, Leonard of Noblac, Magnus of Füssen, Magnus of Altino, Oswald, and Nicholas of Myra (Santa Claus).

August 8th

FRANCA of PIACENZA † 1218

When Franca Visalta became abbess of the Benedictine convent of St Syrus in Piacenza, her reforming zeal proved too much for the inmates, she was deposed, and later transferred to the new Cistercian foundation at Montelana.

April 26th

FRANCES of ROME 1384–1440

Married at thirteen, this noble Roman lady devoted much time to works of piety and charity, while remaining a model housewife. She founded the Oblates of Tor de' Specchi, and is said to have been guided for the last twenty-three years of her life by an archangel visible only to herself.

March 9th

FRANCES XAVIER CABRINI 1850–1917

St Frances-Xavier (Maria Francesca) Cabrini was born on 15th July, 1850, in the old Lombard town of Santangelo.

She was the youngest of an exemplary Catholic family, although her father's cousin, Agostino Depretis, was an enthusiast for Mazzini, a prominent anti-clerical, and subsequently prime minister of the new Italian government.

Although a delicate, shy child, she was very intelligent, hard-working, obedient, yet with an iron will and precociously devout, given to prayer, and from very early years an enthusiast for the foreign missions, above all those in China. This inclination needs stressing in view of her later career, for until ordered by Leo XIII to labor elsewhere her life's resolve and ideal was to enter some religious institute with convents in the far east. She was educated by the Daughters of the Sacred Heart and, being destined for the teaching profession, obtained the certificates required by the government; but her earlier life seemed a series of frustrations.

Soon after qualifying, she lost both parents within a year. At the request of the priest of a neighboring town, she taught successfully in the local school, besides doing fine apostolic work, but, feeling that as regards her vocation she was wasting time, she applied for admission first to the convent above mentioned and then to the Sisters of Cannossa, whose work was devoted to oriental missions. To her dismay, both superiors rejected her on the grounds of insufficient health.

Very unwillingly, but obeying her Ordinary, the bishop of Lodi, she accepted the position of superior of a small orphanage known as the House of Providence at Codogno, badly mismanaged by three women who professed to wish to make religious vows. Six miserable years followed until, in 1880, realising the hopelessness of the task, the bishop closed down the orphanage, and thus addressed Sister Cabrini: 'You want to be a missionary. I know no institute of missionary sisters, so found one yourself'.

Frances quietly consented and, with some half-dozen girls from the former orphanage, founded the Missionary Sisters of the Sacred Heart. They began in a small former Franciscan friary, and, as was the case with most of their convents, almost without means. However, heroic trust in God was Mother Cabrini's great characteristic, and to the end she lived up to the motto chosen for her congregation: 'I can do all things in Him who strengtheneth me' (Philippians 4:13). The episcopal approval was received on December 29th, 1880, and it was said that the institute 'never knew an infancy'.

Foundations followed quickly in Milan and elsewhere in northern Italy and finally a house in Rome, although opposition and disapproval from the Cardinal Vicar and others had to be overcome first. That foundation led to the complete re-orientating of Frances's career and to the sacrifice of her life's longing. In 1888 she secured the decree of papal approbation of the congregation.

At that period, the pope, most of the clergy, and, it might be added, very many serious-minded Italians, were deeply concerned over the mass emigration to the Americas of millions of their poor, illiterate countrymen, the results of which threatened to be socially and religiously catastrophic. Ignorant of the real conditions overseas, unable to speak a word of any language but their own, the emigrants were in the hands of agencies whose sole object was to exploit them. The repayment of the passage money advanced by these agencies meant a crippling burden for years, even after the debtors had found work. The Italian government made no attempt to help them on their arrival, to see that they settled down satisfactorily, or to care for them in any way. Disliked by most Americans, not excepting many of their fellow Catholics, they lived crowded into the 'Little Italies' of the great cities under lamentable moral and material conditions. The death rate was high, while, to crown all, the notorious Cahensly agitation began in 1886, causing suspicions that foreign intrigue lay behind this dumping of poverty-stricken aliens on American soil.

The bishop of Piacenza, Monsignor Scalabrini, aided by other zealous clergy, determined to devote himself to solving the problem, and they founded in New York the Society of Saint Charles to care for the emigrants, but Italian Sisters were desperately needed. In 1887, being in Rome, the bishop proposed that Mother Cabrini should undertake the work.

At first she firmly refused, but a curious series of happenings finally compelled her to face the question, and she laid the whole situation before Leo XIII. His decision was thus expressed: 'Not to the east, but to the west,' adding, 'You will find a vast field for labor in the United States'. Peter had spoken. At once, Frances Cabrini relinquished her plans and threw herself into the new enterprise, which, although she had pronounced it 'too easy', she soon found was to provide her with crosses innumerable for the rest of her life.

After having twice invited her and informing her that an orphanage, school, and convent were being prepared, the archbishop, a well-meaning but change-able man, told her when she arrived in New York, in March 1889, that the plans had fallen through, and advised her and her companions to return to Italy. He had disagreed with the temporal foundress and with-drawn his permission. However, Mother Cabrini recon-ciled the parties and the foundation was made, to be followed by a chain of others, spanning the continent from New York to California.

Besides schools of all grades and charitable institutions of all kinds, she founded four great hospitals, with nurses' homes attached; one each in New York and Seattle, and two in Chicago. To these homes, as to her schools, she readily admitted non-Catholics who were willing to keep the rules. Houses were opened also in Central America, the Argentine, Brazil, France, Spain and England, besides several more in Italy. Leo XIII supported the foundress unfailingly, as did his successors. Not that all went smoothly always, by any means. She had to face opposition from clergy and laity. Parties

formed against her; two revolutions destroyed her Central American convents; two lawsuits imperilled her work in Italy. Yet she persevered undismayed. Money came in as she needed it; Catholics and non-Catholics were generous. When all failed, God seemingly worked miracles.

Side by side with business capacities which called forth unstinting admiration, a practical knowledge of building and of hospital and school organisation which amazed experts, she could show the simplicity of a Friar Juniper. When negotiating for the purchase of a large property in Chicago, she suspected she was being defrauded, so sent two Sisters to measure the whole with ordinary tape-measures, to the decided suspicion of the police. Having set her heart upon acquiring a fine college, which was not for sale, in order to turn it into an orphanage, she persuaded the owner to sell it to her, we know not how. When seeking to buy a derelict hotel in Seattle for a hospital, and finding it belonged to someone named Clark, she simply ordered the Superior of New York to ring up every person of that name – there were over a hundred – in the telephone directory until she found him.

Spiritually, her life is an interesting study in develop-ment. She is an encouraging saint. Certain natural characteristics might have made her an unlovable woman. Very able – there was 'no fooling Mother Cabrini', said one who tried – a strict disciplinarian, she could have been an autocrat. Owing to want of experience, she was at first narrow in some respects. She had never received a normal noviciate training and had to learn by ex-perience. She knew nothing of conditions in foreign, especially non-Catholic, countries and she could be tactless.

But grace perfected nature. She had faith, she was a woman of prayer, and she was humble. She was ready to learn, to recognize her faults and to work at them. She became noted for gentleness, loved and revered. Her character mellowed, and her great gifts had full play. Her wide-mindedness was remarkable as time went on. She was ready to minister to the criminals in Sing Sing prison; and she would work among the most abandoned souls. She became a saint. In 1909 she set the seal, as it were, upon her utter giving of herself to the vocation, which had been God's choice and not her own, by becoming an American citizen at Seattle.

She died at Chicago on December 22nd, 1917, which is kept as her feast day. On August 6th, 1938 she was beatified by Pius XI, and on July 7th, 1946, canonized by Pius XII. On September 8th, 1950, the latter declared 'Heavenly Patroness of all Emigrants' (to whom in these days is often added 'and of Displaced Persons') her whom he described as 'an extraordinary woman . . . whose courage and ability were like a shining light'.

December 22nd   ILLUSTRATION: page 209

He was born at Assisi in Umbria in 1181/2. His father, Piero Bernardone, a prosperous merchant, was in France at the time, and named him after that country; but a greater influence in his childhood and boyhood came from his devout and loving mother. He was gay, adventurous, generous and popular, and though prepared to follow his father's trade he dreamt also of a knight's career. In 1201 he took part in an attack on Perugia, was taken prisoner and remained a hostage there for a year. This experience, and a severe illness, began the process of his conversion, but c. 1205 he enlisted in another military expedition to Apulia. Halted by a dream, in which Christ called him to his service, he returned and gave himself to the care of the sick. On April 16th, 1206 he again heard the voice of Christ calling him to rebuild his church of San Damiano. Always impetuous and whole-hearted, he renounced his old life, and adopted that of a hermit; and when his father first imprisoned him and then brought him before the bishop as disobedient, he abandoned all his rights and possessions, even to his clothes. Two years later, possibly February 24th, 1209, he heard in the Gospel at mass (Matthew 10:9) the call to the preaching of penance (i.e. the turning from the world to Christ); it was the decisive moment; he abandoned the hermit's dress, took a rough tunic and cord and began to preach Christ; he was soon joined by two companions to whom he gave as a Rule three Gospel texts (Matthew 20:21; 10:9; Luke 9:23). When his companions numbered eleven, he wrote for them a short Rule (the lost *Primitiva*), and in 1209 led them to Rome to seek approval from the Pope.

Innocent III, after a short hesitation, had the insight to see in this single-minded, ardent layman a true apostle, and gave a verbal approbation (June 1210). The brotherhood returned to Assisi where they settled in huts at Rivotorto near the Porziuncola and preached penance throughout central Italy. It was the golden dawn of simplicity; the friars turned their hands to every kind of work or lived on gifts of food; they had as example and guide the spiritual wisdom and angelic simplicity of Francis, their brother and 'mother'. There was no organization and no friary: the brethren with Francis's leave went where they would, as the Poor Brothers of Penance of Assisi. In 1212 Francis encouraged Clare, a girl of noble birth and family in the city, to found a sisterhood of poverty and prayer at San Damiano; they became the Poor Ladies, now called the Poor Clares. Neither at this nor any other time did Francis wish to found an 'order', indeed he consciously turned away from the cloistered, formalized, secure life of the monasteries he knew and from the new technical learning of the schools: he wished only to follow literally and perfectly the Christ of the Gospels. The brotherhood, however, inevitably took something of the form of a monastic body; they said the divine office, and slept and ate in common like monks. When they grew in numbers with phenomenal rapidity, Francis had to delegate his authority to leaders or, as he called them, 'mothers' or 'servants' *(ministri)*, of groups; and all the brethren met each year in a great 'chapter' at the Porziuncola.

In 1216 Francis assisted the dying Innocent III, and obtained from his successor, Honorius III, the great indulgence for the Porziuncola church; in the following year he won the friendship of Cardinal Ugolino, who remained ever after his staunch ally and protector. In 1219 the brotherhood, fast growing unwieldy, was divided into provinces, and the first great 'missions' were sent across the Alps. Francis himself, with a complete disregard of all prudential considerations, left Italy to join the crusaders and win his way into the presence of the Sultan. In his absence the brotherhood, which now contained many recruits of education and clerical standing, drifted without a pilot into a crisis which was only resolved by the recall of Francis, the diplomacy of Ugolino, and the adoption of the normal canonical framework of the religious life.

In response to persistent pressure Francis now wrote a more detailed Rule (the *Regula Prima*), but even this was too simple and spiritually exigent for the new leaders of the body, and it was only a revised and somewhat conventionalized version (the *Regula Secunda* or *Bullata*, still in use) that ultimately received papal approval from Honorius III in 1223. Meanwhile Francis, broken in health and anxious in spirit, made over the rule of the brotherhood to a vicar who became in fact minister-general; the post from 1221 was filled by the enigmatic Brother Elias. Francis himself retired into the mountains, and on September 14th, 1224, at the end of a period of seclusion, experienced the mysterious visitation, that left on his body the marks of the Sacred Wounds (or Stigmata) of Christ, which remained with him as an acute physical suffering for the rest of his life. Henceforward his maladies increased, and he became almost wholly blind; he was borne from place to place by the faithful 'four companions' who were to be the apostles of his purest teaching. In 1224 (probably) he wrote the *Canticle of the Sun*, the earliest masterpiece of the young Italian language, and in 1226 in his short *Testament* he repeated with solemn emphasis and foreboding his teaching on absolute poverty, literal obedience to the Rule, and the refusal of all privileges. After a last visit to Clare and her sisters, and a last blessing to the city of Assisi and his brethren, he died at the Porziuncola on the evening of October 3rd, 1226. He was canonized two years later by his friend Ugolino (then Gregory IX) and in 1228 his body was translated to the crypt of the great basilica, the work of Brother Elias, where it still rests.

Francis, long venerated by Catholics as the founder of a great order and a seraphic lover of the infant Jesus and the crucified Savior, has in recent years attracted multitudes outside the church. He has been hailed as 'the most lovable of the saints', the 'only true Christian in history', and even as the first socialist and the first of the reformers. Others have seen in him a lover of flowers and animals, a poet, a romantic, and a humanitarian. In so doing many fail to understand him. He lived always on the spiritual level and spoke the language of the soul not of the mind, and those who do not know that language are misled or repelled by his words. Francis was a man of extreme simplicity. He had only one aim, to love Christ and to imitate him and his life perfectly, even literally, and he followed this aim ever more completely from his conversion to his death. He was by nature impulsive and sensitive, with an immense capacity for self-sacrifice; he had found Christ without book-learning; the words of Christ had been enough for him and he could not understand those who wished for more or who gave less than all. Above all, he was a son of the church to the marrow of his bones; her sacraments, her teaching and her priesthood were all manifestations of Christ, and his simple faith ultimately became a mystical contemplation of the incarnate word, the crucified Jesus. He gave to the church at a critical epoch a new form of the religious life, and he gave to all Christians, more simply and fully than any other saint of the middle ages, the vision of a life lived wholly in the power and spirit of the cross of Christ.

October 4th   ILLUSTRATION: facing page 129

FRANCIS BLANCO, *see* Martyrs of Japan.

FRANCIS BORGIA   1510–1572
He was born in Gandia in Spain in 1510, the first of fourteen children of Juan Borgia, duke of Gandia (the grandson of Pope Alexander VI), and Frances de Castro. Two of his brothers were appointed cardinals, one an abbot, one an archbishop, and two of the sisters abbesses. Francis was first sent as a page to the court of the Infanta Catalina, who was engaged to the king of Portugal; after the marriage he was sent to study rhetoric and philosophy under his step uncle, archbishop John of Aragon. At seventeen the saint was already well known for his remarkable appearance as well as for his courtly accomplishments, and he entered the entourage of his distant cousin, the Emperor Charles V. Two years later, on his marriage to Leonora of Portugal, he was created Marquis of Lombay by the Emperor, and of this marriage – which appears to have been very happy – eight children were born. In 1536 the saint took part in the emperor's ill-advised campaign in Provence; and in 1539, when the Empress Isabella died, he and his wife were instructed to accompany the funeral procession from Toledo to the imperial tombs at Elvira. The coffin was opened for recognition on arrival at the tombs, and at the sight of the decayed body of the Empress – the face was by then unrecognizable – Francis suffered a violent conversion. The same year the Emperor named him Viceroy of Catalonia, and he took effective measures to reform the hidebound judicial and administrative system of the province. This period of office led to more fervent prayer and to more frequent communion, whilst the first contacts with itinerant Jesuit preachers were also made at that time. On the death of his father, in 1543, Francis succeeded to the dukedom of Gandia and returned to court, becoming master of the household to Princess Mary of Portugal, who was engaged to the future Philip II, the emperor's son; she died before the marriage could take place and the saint retired to his duchy where he was now planning to build a Jesuit college, and his wife a Dominican nunnery.

The Duchess died in 1546, and, as he was praying for her recovery during her last illness, Francis was addressed by the crucifix before which he knelt. It told him that his wife's life would be spared if he so decided, whereupon he surrendered himself entirely to God's will. After his wife's death he was introduced to the *Spiritual Exercises* of St Ignatius, and at his special request the Pope issued a bull approving them. Soon he was in correspondence with Ignatius, asking to be admitted into the Society of Jesus. As preliminaries to entering that body, Ignatius counselled secrecy, the study of theology and the arranging of suitable matches for his children. When his duties to his family were fulfilled, Francis set out for Rome, and at once wrote to the Emperor asking to renounce all his titles and properties in favor of his son; meanwhile Ignatius insisted that he must keep to the station to which he was called. He was highly esteemed at the papal court, and the threat of a cardinal's hat made him turn back to Spain. In February 1551, having received the emperor's dispensation, he at once joined the Jesuits and was ordained six months later. The grandee, who had renounced the world, had of course also attracted much notoriety. 'The Holy Duke', as he was now known, celebrated his second mass in public, and the pope granted a special indulgence to all who made their communion at it (there were so many that the mass, which began at 9 a.m., did not finish till 3 p.m.). Ignatius sent him to preach in Portugal, where he was very successful, and a new offer of the cardinalate was made and refused. He was soon appointed Provincial of the Society for Spain and the Indies, establishing several new houses and the first Jesuit novitiates in Spain.

The Emperor Charles V sent for Francis on his deathbed – he arrived to find the Emperor dead, and himself named executor in the Emperor's will. This was in 1558. In 1561, while the general of the Jesuits was at the council

in Trent, Francis went to Rome to act as vicar general, and four years later, was unanimously elected third superior of the society. The intransigent Pope Pius V, no respecter of titles, stopped his coronation procession by the Jesuit college to pay his respects to the saintly general. When the Pope decided to launch his crusade against the Turks he sent his nephew, Cardinal Bonelli, and Francis on an embassy to engage the help of Christian princes. Though it had several important by-products, this mission failed in its principal aim: discouraged and weakened, Francis returned to Rome and died two days later. There is something paradoxical about this saint because, although he achieved undeniable heroic sanctity and the heights of asceticism, he was never able to leave the stage of counter-reformation dynastic politics. Francis was beatified by Pope Gregory XV in 1623 and canonized by Clement XI in 1671. His relics – except an arm, which remained in the Gesu in Rome – are on the high altar of the church dedicated to him in Madrid. ILLUSTRATION: page 210
October 10th

FRANCIS CARACCIOLO 1563-1608
A letter delivered in error to Ascanio Caracciolo decided his vocation, for he read in it the description of an intended religious Congregation which seemed exactly to fit in with his needs. He was at that time a secular priest, having taken orders in gratitude for the cure of a skin disease which seemed likely to kill him.

The religious Congregation described in the letter was that known later as the Minor Clerks Regular; Caracciolo joined it taking the name of Francis instead of his baptismal name, and to all intents and purposes became the co-founder. There is little incident to record in the rest of his life. The Clerks Regular led penitential lives and busied themselves giving missions all over Italy, together with visiting hospitals and the spiritual and bodily care of the sick. Francis, who became superior-general and saw the institute increase throughout the length and breadth of Italy, died at Agone in a house that had just come into his possession as a gift from St Philip Neri, who desired it to be used as a noviciate for the Minor Clerks Regular. Francis was forty-four.
June 4th

FRANCIS de SALES, *see* Francis of Sales.

FRANCIS di GIROLAMO 1642-1716
Born near Taranto, he became a Jesuit at Naples, where his preaching was famous. Among his penitents was Mary Alvira Cassier who had murdered her father and, disguised as a man, had served in the Spanish Army.
May 11th

FRANCIS of MIAKO, *see* Martyrs of Japan.

FRANCIS of PAOLA 1416-1507
An unlettered Italian from Paola in Calabria, Francis

began to live as a hermit at the age of fifteen. Joined by disciples, he founded the Minim Friars (i.e. *minimi*, least in God's household). He spent the last part of his life in France, whither he had been summoned by the dying Louis XI, who had heard of his miraculous powers.
April 2nd

FRANCIS-OF-ST-MICHAEL, *see* Martyrs of Japan

FRANCIS of SALES 1567-1622
Francis Bonaventure was born on August 21st 1567, at the castle of Sales in Savoy; his father was lord of Nouvelles and (by his marriage) of Boisy; as the eldest son of a prominent nobleman, he was destined, by a father proud of his nobility, for a career in the world and a seat in the senate of Savoy. He received his school education at Annecy which, in its beautiful setting by the lake, was to be the scene of his life-work. His outward charm of manner could not conceal from his fellows the depth of his religious life; but it masked a firmness of purpose leading him gradually towards the priesthood, in spite of all the contrary pressures of his feudal background. When sent to Paris to complete his education in 1582 he refused to attend the College of Navarre, his father's choice, because he feared its temptations, and chose instead the Jesuit College of Clermont. Here he came in contact with the riches of post-Tridentine humanism, enlisting the classical learning of the Renaissance in the service of the Christian mind and spirit; Francis wore the garb of that humanism more easily and naturally than any: as he said, those who would be religious should avoid ostentation but wear clothes that fitted them.

He struggled with doubts about his hope of salvation; one day in the church of St Etienne des Grès he prayed fervently in his trouble before a statue of our Lady, taking at the same time a vow of chastity; the temptation fell away from him 'like the scales of leprosy'. From 1586 to 1591 he attended the University of Padua to study law and left after taking the Doctor's degree. But his vocation was now clear, though only to himself; he surmounted with quiet, firm dignity the inevitable clash with his father; he was ordained priest on May 13th, 1593, becoming a senior canon of the chapter of Geneva.

His fervor soon brought him to the notice of Claude Granier, bishop of Geneva, and he was allowed to offer himself for what seemed the well-nigh impossible task of winning back from Calvinism the people of the Chablais district. To an age torn by the folly and scandal of religious wars Francis brought a spirit of mission which was charitable and persuasive; but his early efforts in the Chablais were bitterly disappointing, and he underwent a hard discipline of insult and of disillusion with the promises of princes.

Sent to Paris in 1602 to negotiate about the condition of Catholics in the reconverted territories, he came in contact with the great figures of the religious and mystical revival taking place behind the worldly façade of the court of Henri IV: Henri de Joyeuse, Berulle, and Mme Acarie (Bd Mary of the Incarnation). In July on the death of Granier he became bishop of Geneva and returned to Annecy. Constantly journeying and preaching, without pomp or fuss he gradually drew the entire diocese into the intimate habitude of his own holiness. He exerted himself particularly in the sacrament of penance, carrying his knowledge of the soul to both prince and peasant. One of the most celebrated of his penitents was St Joan Frances de Chantal, whom he entrusted with his scheme for the foundation of a new order, the Visitation, 'an order where the charity and gentleness of Jesus Christ shall rule, where the weak and infirm can be admitted, which shall be able to give attendance to the sick and to visit the poor.'

In the midst of his constant pastoral work he found time to write the book which has made him best known to succeeding ages, the *Introduction to the Devout Life* (1609), a work which sprang immediately from his care for souls, and which was based particularly on his counsel to another penitent, Mme de Charmoisy, on the problem of how to live a Christian life in the world.

When he visited Paris again in 1618 it was as a famous preacher and an acknowledged spiritual force. He preached often twice a day with the unpretentious simplicity and directness of a great, highly disciplined intellect. In his last years he was dying slowly from overwork, moving humbly among all ranks, ever mindful of the necessary detail; a saint who provides a pattern for the responsible administrator in an age busier and more hurried than his own. He died on December 28th, 1622, at Lyons, with the word 'Jesus' on his lips. He was canonized by Alexander VII in 1665.

Francis's great work was to show how ordinary life can be sanctified – every type of ordinary life, but especially that of busy, well-to-do people. No problem is too small for him, dress, entertainments, flirtations, the daily interchange of husband and wife, but he deals with them all so as to guide his reader to the final end: the love of God and the imitation of Christ. In his teaching there is no perpetual struggle between nature and grace, flesh and spirit, no violent tension wresting the human life that would be Christian out of and away from its ordinary sphere of social duties. But neither is there any descent into softness or sentimentality; with all his grace and poise and gentleness he demands an approach to perfection and a total harmony of the personality in the framework of the Christian virtues. He learned from the Renaissance the easy grace of style which is also a graciousness of mind; he added, however,

the traditional rural wisdom of Savoy, that sense of the Catholic verities which he had always taken for granted and which for that very reason he could make more lucidly explicit to the outsider or to those in trouble. Sweetness and graciousness are his key-words (they come in the collect of his Mass); they represent a reconciliation of the outward beauty and the tough inner core of the Christian life. In the age after Calvin and before Jansenism he had much to teach the world, and has, too, in our own, when a preference for the extraordinary and melodramatic solution in every province from theology to fiction may make us overlook someone who tells us that saintliness is both desirable and possible.

January 29th   ILLUSTRATION: page 211

FRANCIS SOLANO   1549–1610
A Spanish Franciscan, he spent the last twenty years of his life as a missionary in South America, where his untiring efforts made numerous converts. He was known as 'The Wonder-worker of the New World'.

July 13th

FRANCIS XAVIER   1506–1552
Francis Xavier was born on April 7th, 1506 in the Spanish kingdom of Navarre; and his native language, like that of Ignatius Loyola, whose devoted disciple he was to become, was Basque. He inherited the proud and passionate temperament of his race and could show himself both fiery and autocratic even to the end of his life. As a boy he was ambitious and fond of sport, but he had a largeness of heart and generosity of nature which made him capable, once he had been converted, of heroic love and endurance.

His first encounter with Ignatius took place at the University of Paris, where Francis went at the age of nineteen. Ignatius was much the elder man, and it took him some time to win Francis from his worldly ambitions. But eventually Francis capitulated and gave himself with his whole soul to the new life which the *Exercises* of Ignatius opened up to him. He became one of the first members of the Society of Jesus and made his vows with Ignatius and five others on August 15th, 1534, and was finally ordained priest on June 24th, 1537.

The first object of Ignatius and his companions had been to make a pilgrimage to Jerusalem, but events turned out otherwise. Ignatius was asked by King John of Portugal to send priests to the new missions in India, and his choice fell eventually on Francis. Francis, it must be said, had no particular qualifications for this task. Though he took his degree at the University, he was possessed of no great learning, and the only books he took with him on all his missionary journeys were his breviary and a book of meditations. His ignorance of the religion of the people to whom he went to preach the gospel was complete. He regarded all 'moors' and 'pagans' as enemies of God and slaves of the devil, to be rescued at all costs from his power. His attitude never changed, and the devout Muslim, the learned Brahmin and the Buddhist monk made equally little impression on him.

In this respect his mind remained essentially medieval. He saw a vast new world opening before him and his one desire was to win it to Christ. He brought with him nothing but his consuming love for God and for the souls of his fellow men. It is noticeable that he never criticized the social, political or ecclesiastical institutions of his time. He accepted the slave trade and the Inquisition alike apparently without question and, although he complained bitterly of the abuse of power, he never questioned the right of the Portuguese power in India and was prepared at all times to make use of it in the interests of the gospel.

Yet though he might accept the external circumstances of life as he knew it, he preserved an absolute detachment of heart. He deliberately chose to live in the most complete poverty and refused to accept any of the material conveniences which were offered to him. His food was reduced to so small a quantity that it was a miracle that he kept alive. The only concession he would make in clothing for his long missionary journeys under a tropical sun was a pair of boots. He could put up with the most appalling conditions on his long sea voyages and endure the most agonizing extremes of heat and cold. Wherever he went he would seek out the poor and the sick and spend his time in ministering to their needs. Yet while he was occupied all day with these incessant labours, he would spend the greater part of the night in prayer. And all this was done with a gaiety and lightness of heart, which remind one of the other Francis – of Assisi.

The story of his journeys is an epic of adventure. He arrived in Goa in May 1542 and went on from there to Cape Comorin in the south of India. Here he spent three years working among the pearl-fishers, or Paravas, of the Fishery Coast. From there he went on to the East Indies, to Malacca and the Moluccas, and, finally, in 1549 he set out for Japan. He died on December 3rd 1552 on a lonely island, vainly seeking to obtain entrance into China. Thus in ten years he traversed the greater part of the Far East. When one considers the conditions of travel, the means of transport, the delays and difficulties which beset him at every stage, it is, even physically, an astounding achievement. It is even more remarkable when one considers that he left behind him a flourishing church wherever he went and that the effects of his labours remain to the present day.

Many miracles have been attributed to St Francis. He was said to have possessed the gift of tongues, to have healed the sick and even to have raised the dead; but for the last, at least, there is no real evidence. That he possessed the gift of prophecy seems to be certain, but he can hardly have possessed the gift of tongues. The evidence is, on the contrary, that he had to rely throughout on interpreters to translate his message into the different languages he required, and was often sadly misled. The real miracle of his life, as has been said, was the miracle of his personality, by which he was able to convert thousands to the faith wherever he went and to win their passionate devotion.

He died abandoned with but one companion, without the sacraments or Christian burial. But within a few weeks his body was recovered and found to be perfectly incorrupt. It was brought to Goa and received there with a devotion and an enthusiasm which showed that the people had already recognized him as a saint. He was beatified by Pope Paul V in 1619 and canonized together with St Ignatius by Pope Gregory XV, on March 12th, 1622. He is now the patron of all the missions of the catholic Church.

December 3rd   ILLUSTRATION: page 212

FRANCIS XAVIER BIANCHI   1743–1815
He was born in Arpino, became a Barnabite, a priest, and later superior of two colleges in Naples. Notwithstanding severe physical suffering and some persecution, he continued his great work as a confessor. He was canonized in 1951.
January 31st

FREDERICK of UTRECHT   † 838
He was elected bishop of Utrecht, and expanded the missionary activities of the see. He is said to have made himself unpopular with the Empress Judith and others by his outspoken denunciation of immorality, and may have been murdered at Walcheren.
July 18th

FREDIANO, *see* Frigidiano.

FRIDESWIDE   † 735?
The earliest account of the legend of this saint is probably that of William of Malmesbury and belongs to the first part of the twelfth century.

Because of her beauty Frideswide was pursued for many years by a royal suitor. Eventually he tried to carry her off, but when she invoked the help of SS Catherine and Cecilia, he lost his sight.

Frideswide established herself in a cell near Binsey, and is the patron saint of Oxford, where she founded a monastery on the site of which Christ Church now stands.
October 19th

FRIDOLIN   *Sixth Century?*
According to unreliable legend this itinerant Irish

missionary, sometimes known as 'Fridolin the Traveller', made foundations generally dedicated to St Hilary, at Poitiers – where he was an abbot –, on the Moselle, in the Vosges mountains, at Coire in Switzerland and at Säckingen on the Rhine.
March 6th

FRIGIDIAN or FREDIANO   *Sixth Century*
A monk, possibly a prince of Ulster, he became an anchorite in Lucca, and later bishop. Though banished by invaders, he returned, formed a clerical community, which did not merge into any other order until 1507, and was much honored for his holiness and miracles.
March 18th

FROILAN and ATTILANUS   *Tenth Century*
St Attilanus was a disciple of St Froilan, and together they did much to restore monasticism in Spain. Attilanus became bishop of Leon, and Troilan bishop of Zamora.
October 3rd

FRONTO and GEORGE
St Fronto, a Jew, was alleged to have been a follower of St Peter. He and St George travelled to France, where St Fronto became bishop of Périgueux and St George, bishop of Le Puy.
October 25th

FRUCTUOSUS of BRAGA   † 665
His large inheritance as son of a Spanish general was devoted to charity and to the foundation of monasteries. These proved embarrassingly popular, particularly those which he formed at the request of whole families who wanted to live the religious life. For them he adapted the Rule of St Benedict, insisting that the fathers and sons should live in a separate part of the monastic building from that occupied by the mothers and daughters.

Although he wanted to become a hermit, he was elected bishop of Dumium and later archbishop of Braga.
April 16th

FRUCTUOSUS of TARRAGONA   † 259
Under the persecution of Valerian and Gallienus, the governor Emilian arrested this much beloved bishop of Tarragona and the deacons Augurius and Eulogius. They remained faithful to God, and were burned alive. The detailed *Acta* are unquestionably authentic.
January 21st

FRUMENTIUS   *Fourth Century*
One of the first to preach the gospel in Ethiopia (Abyssinia), he was appointed bishop of Aksum in that country by St Athanasius of Alexandria.
October 27th

FULBERT   † 1029
It was he who, as chancellor of Chartres, developed the cathedral schools into one of the best institutions in Europe, and he was referred to as a reincarnation of Plato and Socrates – such was his learning. Later he became bishop of the diocese, describing himself as 'the very little bishop of a very great church'. To him, we owe the beautiful Easter hymn, 'Ye choirs of New Jerusalem'.
April 10th

FULGENTIUS   468–533
Scion of a senatorial family of Carthage, he was pro-curator of Byzacena until he withdrew from the world to become a monk. Scourged by order of an Arian priest in 499, he later composed a confutation of Arianism, '*Three Books to King Thrasimund*'. Consecrated bishop of Ruspe (now Kudiat Rosfa, in Tunisia) in 508, he was forced to retire to Sardinia by Arian opponents, but returned to Ruspe to die a peaceful death.
January 1st

FULRAD   † 784
After founding three monasteries in his native Alsace – Lièvre, Saint-Hippolyte and Salone – he became abbot of Saint-Denis, near Paris. As such, he was a close adviser of the Carlovingians and often their intermediary with Rome.
July 16th

FURSEY   *c. 567–c. 649*
It is impossible to be precise about any of St Fursey's dates until considerably more research is done on the sources for his life. On the other hand we know with certainty that he was a real person, whose lifework illuminated the Christian history of Ireland, England and France in the first half of the seventh century.

He was born in Munster about the year 567 and was taught in his early boyhood by none other than the great St Brendan. Later on he attended the School of Clonfert and after ordination he established a number of monastic settlements all over Ireland. The wide sphere of his influence is indicated by the fact that at least three place names still perpetuate his memory in districts far distant one from the other: one in county Galway, one near Dundalk and one in county Cork.

Although when Brendan died Fursey cannot have been more than ten or twelve, the young man showed how he had been influenced by that pioneering spirit. Fursey, too, was daring and adventurous; he suffered from the same restless longing which finally drove him into exile to find new lands to win to the Faith.

After twelve years' work in Ireland, he crossed over to England and founded a monastery in East Anglia, probably near Yarmouth in the former Roman fort, Caistor Castle, some time after the year 640. Some few years later, he extended his travels to France, where he set up a monastery at Lagny on the Marne a few miles from Paris. He was about to return to England when he died, probably in the year 649. He was buried, therefore, at Péronne, of which he is the patron saint. Many miracles took place around his tomb, which became the mecca of Irish pilgrims for many generations. This was the origin of a close and fruitful association between northern France and Ireland.

It is for his visions of the spirit world and the after-life that Fursey is really famous. While thus rapt, he used to fall into a trance-like state so like death that on several occasions his brethren had begun to prepare him for burial. He afterwards described the struggle between the angels and the powers of evil for possession of the soul when it leaves the body, saying that he had been permitted to witness that struggle. He also tasted the joys of Heaven, saw the fires of Hell, and was conducted through the regions of the damned. He used to show the mark of a burn on his neck and explain that it happened when the demons hurled against him a lost soul whom he had known in life.

The *Vision* of Fursey was afterwards committed to writing. It had a great influence on medieval literature, as it was the starting-point of all the subsequent *Vision* accounts which were to beguile the Christian mind of Europe for many generations. Dante in his *Divine Comedy* repeated several of Fursey's episodes and both writings have many other points of similarity, especially in the changing atmosphere from the confusion of Hell to the peace of Paradise.

We owe it to the Venerable Bede's enthusiasm that Fursey's name was saved from oblivion. A *Life* was written shortly after his death by a contemporary. Fortunately it came into Bede's hands, and he made great use of it in his *Ecclesiastical History*, which was completed in 731. The success of this work made Fursey the best known of the Irish saints in England and France.
January 16th

FUSCIAN, VICTORICUS and GENTIAN
Their legend is that they were Roman missionaries in Gaul who visited St Quentin and, shortly after his martyrdom, were themselves put to death by Rictiovarus.
December 11th

GABRIEL LALEMANT, *see* Martyrs of North America.   ILLUSTRATION: page 161 (C)

GABRIEL POSSENTI (Gabriel of our Lady of Sorrows)   1838–1862
The son of a lawyer, he was educated in Spoleto. Four years before his death he entered the Passionist Order at Morrovalle.
February 27th

GABRIEL THE ARCHANGEL
Gabriel was sent to Mary at Nazareth to tell her of her destiny (Luke 1:26). He also came to Zachary to tell him of the birth of John the Baptist (Luke 1:11, 19), and he prophesied the coming of the Messiah to the prophet Daniel (Daniel 9:21).

He is the patron of postal and telephone workers.
See Angels and Archangels.
March 24th

GAIANA, *see* Rhipsime.

GALATION and EPISTEME
Cardinal Baronius added their names to the Roman Martyrology, but it is certain that they are merely characters in a pious legend in which Galation, a Christian youth, marries a beautiful pagan girl, Episteme ('knowledge'), converts her and ensures their joint martyrdom.
November 5th

GALDINUS   † 1176
As archdeacon to Hubert, archbishop of Milan, whose successor he became, he was forced into exile when Frederick Barbarossa besieged Milan. Later, in co-operation with the Lombard League, he did much to repair the damage done during the war.
April 18th

GALL   † 646
Nothing is known about St Gall's birth, or childhood, in Ireland. He was a fellow-student of St Columbanus at the great school of Bangor and was one of the twelve who accompanied him into exile to preach the gospel to pagan peoples. He assisted him in founding the monasteries of Annegray, Luxeuil and Fountains in Gaul and was one of the band eventually driven out of Burgundy with Columbanus. He was at his master's side in all their subsequent travels up to their stay in Bregenz in Austria. Gall was a clever linguist and quickly mastered the local dialects, knowledge that was most useful to him in his missionary work.

Gall should be the patron saint of fishermen, because all the legendary stories are about fishing, which to him was both a duty and a sport. During his time in Luxeuil, Columbanus sent him one day to fish in a certain river so as to provide food for the community. Gall was delighted with the order, but displeased with the suggested venue. He went to what he considered a much better place in a different river. Here he let down his net in a pool, but although he could see the fish, they turned back when they came to the net and he caught nothing. Downcast, he returned empty-handed to the monastery, where Columbanus reproved him for his disobedience and sent him back to the river first suggested where he made a wonderful catch. When the Irish monks established themselves near the Lake of Constance, Gall was once again knotting his nets and fishing the lake. There was also a good fishing-pool on the river Steinach on the shores of which he made his final settlement.

When two of the monks were killed by the pagans near Bregenz, many of whom were very hostile, Columbanus decided to travel south into Italy. Gall was not well at the time and, on the day fixed for departure, he was too ill to travel. He asked Columbanus's permission to remain behind. The abbot was grieved at the separation. One of the legendary accounts says that he did not believe Gall was too ill to travel and that, as a penance for breaking away on his own, he forbade him to say mass again during the lifetime of Columbanus.

However that may be, Gall immediately began a work which was in every way worthy of his great master. As soon as he recovered, he set out to find a site for a hermitage, with the help of a local guide. As they went along together, Gall tripped and fell. Immediately he fashioned a rude wooden cross, set it upright in the ground and hung on it some relics of saints that he always carried with him. He believed that Providence had shown him the exact spot and he began his thanksgiving. It was a desolate place in the valley of the river Steinach, which flowed into the Lake of Constance.

On their first night here, as Gall was again praying before the cross and the guide was trying to sleep, the latter saw a bear shuffle into the circle of the camp fire. He thought they were both doomed, but before he could cry out, Gall had looked up and calmly told the bear to put a log of wood on the fire. The bear obeyed. Gall then threw it some bread, commanding it to keep to its forest home and not molest them in any way. The bear shuffled away. The guide then jumped up, threw himself at Gall's feet, saying that he was indeed a man of God. Next day they constructed a hermitage beside the cross. In the course of time so many disciples were drawn to this place, that Gall became known as the Apostle of Switzerland. This was the origin of the famous abbey of St Gall and the reason why the modern town of the same name and other towns in eastern Switzerland have for emblem a bear holding a log of wood.

Gall knew by a vision, or a dream, when Columbanus died, and he sent one of his brethren to Bobbio for confirmation. The messenger returned with news of the day and hour of Columbanus's death, which confirmed Gall's vision. He also brought back Columbanus's pastoral staff, which he had left to Gall in token of forgiveness. Two fragments of this staff, encased in silver croziers, are still preserved in Bavaria, one at Kempten and the other at Füssen.

Gall died in 646, on October 16th, on which day his feast is kept. The famous abbey of St Gall arose on the site of his hermitage and within a hundred years of his death it had acquired European fame. It maintained a close relationship for hundreds of years with the Bobbio monastery founded by Columbanus. During the middle ages, St Gall became the leading west European center of literature and the arts, particularly music. Its famous library still survives in large part, adjoining the cathedral of the diocese dedicated to St Gall.   ILLUSTRATION: page 213
October 16th

GALL of CLERMONT   486–551
A young nobleman, he entered the monastery of Couron, and became bishop of Clermont in 526. He educated his nephew, St Gregory of Tours.
July 1st

GALLA   † *c.* 550
Although her doctor warned her that unless she married again she would grow a beard, this young patrician widow persevered in her resolve to become a nun. St Gregory tells her story in his *Dialogues*.
October 5th

GALLICANUS   *Fourth Century*
A Roman patrician and consul in 300, he was a generous benefactor of the church.
June 25th

GALMIER, *see* Baldomerus.

GATIAN   *Third Century*
Venerated as the first bishop of Tours, he came from Rome to Gaul at the same time as St Denis of Paris.
December 18th

GAUCHERIUS   † 1140
Born at Meulan-sur-Seine, he took up a solitary life when he was eighteen. The community which grew under him at Aureil adopted the Rule of the canons of St Augustine.
April 9th

GAUDENTIUS   † *c.* 410
A pupil of St Philastrius, he succeeded him as bishop of Brescia *c.* 387. He was one of those deputed to defend St John Chrysostom.
October 25th

GAUGERICUS or GÉRY   † *c.* 625
Born at Yvoi in the Ardennes, he became bishop of Cambrai, and founded the abbey of St Médard. He is also supposed to have made the original settlement on an island in the Senne, from which Brussels developed.
August 11th

GELASIUS I   † 496
He succeeded St Felix II as pope in 492. His insistence

on the supremacy of the Holy See at a time of possible distintegration contributed much to the unity of the early church.

November 21st

GEMMA GALGANI 1878–1903

There is little to be said about her life. Born at Camigliano in Tuscany, she suffered from 'tuberculosis of the spine with aggravated curvature', and, though she considered herself cured by a vision of the young Saint Gabriel Possenti, she could not obtain a certificate of health enabling her to enter a convent, as she wished. She had many 'abnormal' experiences from June 1899 onwards, including the 'stigmata' in hands and feet, carefully examined by her confessor and biographer, the Passionist Fr Germano. These began to appear about 8 p.m. on a Thursday and lasted till 3 p.m. on the Friday. No pain preceded their apparition, but only a deep recollection. There was seen first a discoloration on the back and palm of each hand; then a 'rent in the flesh' under the skin which then split, and a deep laceration was observed, at least usually: the holes above and below corresponded and the perforations seemed complete, but it was hard to judge of this because they kept filling up with blood, partly flowing, partly congealing. Fr Germano measured the diameters and shapes of the wounds carefully, and noted that 'a few times' a sort of fleshy swelling, like a nail-head, about an inch across, covered the wounds in the hands (though not those in the feet): 'The deep wounds were the more usual state of Gemma's stigmata – I say, the more usual state'. He also says that directly the Friday ecstasy was over, 'the flow of blood from all *five* wounds ceased immediately; the raw flesh healed; the lacerated tissues healed too': at least by Sunday not a vestige remained of the deep 'cavities'; the new skin was smooth, though 'whitish marks' remained on it. Much more could be said about this saint, but this account suffices as occasion for explaining the principles governing the Church's approach to these and allied phenomena.

First, the Congregation of Rites, declaring that Gemma practiced the Christian virtues to a heroic degree, explicitly refrained from passing judgment on the preternatural character of the recorded phenomena; a matter (it adds) 'upon which no decision is ever made' (see *Acta Apostolicae Sedis* vol. xxiv [1932], p. 57, and Thurston: *Physical Phenomena of Mysticism*, ed. J. H. Crehan, chapter II, especially pp. 52–54).

We must first register the alleged *facts* presented to us for observation, and then consider the evidence. Only then may we tentatively embark on *interpretation*. So we notice that before the time of St Francis of Assisi there can be quoted only two or three instances of stigmatization of doubtful character: but since St Francis, instances become almost innumerable up to the present day. We start by excluding those where self-inflicted wounds can even be suspected; for there have been instances of downright imposture, of misguided asceticism – conscious or possibly unconscious. This cannot apply to Gemma Galgani, since the gradual appearance and disappearance of her wounds was scrupulously *watched*. Again, all instances of complete stigmatization (save probably two) are found in women, and usually (though by no means always) in women who lead an enclosed and constantly meditative life; this suggests that the mind can influence the body – as it obviously can: a *thought* can make one blush, or turn pale. Further, an ecstatica's stigmata (or visions) not seldom correspond with some picture or effigy that she habitually sees: the marks of the scourging on Gemma are said to reproduce those on a crucifix she contemplated; Catherine Emmerich and others 'see' our Lord on a Y-shaped cross like one they were accustomed to; some will see Him crucified with three, others with four, nails; the wound of the lance may be on the right, or again on the left. We may therefore grant that *even if* a supernatural grace be granted to the soul, the mind, helped by the imagination, may proceed to interpret it to itself by means of such ideas or images as it possesses or prefers. But how far can the 'mind' influence the body? 'Dermatography' – marks on the skin, usually disappearing soon – can undoubtedly be induced by suggestion, whether it be self-suggestion or administered by another; but can suggestion cause lesions of the tissues, persisting and not becoming gangrenous? The word 'hysteria' should now be left aside – the ugly word 'pithiatism' may be replacing it – it merely means 'suggestibility'. Now there is no fault in being 'suggestible'; one person may lie abnormally open to the stimulus of anger, fear, sex or pity. If then we seek the nature of the stimulus lying behind the bodily manifestations observed in one who, on other grounds, is judged to be of exceptional holiness, we can prudently suppose that it is love for God, for Christ incarnate, or crucified, which so moves the entire 'subject' – body-mind – as to produce the exterior phenomena. The miracle would then lie in the intensity of the love for God granted to a human soul; the physical consequences of so super-human a love might be quite incalculable, by no means necessarily the stigmata, though possibly including them: indeed, disconcerting symptoms might well co-exist with those that might be expected, and should by no means be at once ascribed to diabolic influences. The description of all abnormal symptoms of the sort under discussion should be purely clinical, not rhetorical or pietistic.

For a discussion of further aspects of this problem, see the article on St Joseph of Copertino.

St Gemma Galgani was beatified in 1933, and canonized in 1940.
April 11th

GENESIUS of ARLES † 303?
A clerk to the court before which Christians were tried, he refused to go on with his note-taking. He was martyred on the banks of the Rhône. Venerated at Rome, he came to be regarded as a Roman martyr and to be transformed by legend into the fictitious St Genesius the Comedian.
August 25th

GENESIUS of CLERMONT *Seventh Century*
Of a senatorial family, he became bishop of Clermont, his birthplace.
June 3rd

GENESIUS THE COMEDIAN
A Roman actor, he was suddenly converted while impersonating a Christian and receiving a mock baptism on the stage. After making a public profession before the emperor who was in the audience, he was beheaded. It is, however, unlikely that this saint ever existed, other than as a doublet or legendary offshoot of St Genesius of Arles.
August 25th

GENEVIÈVE *Fifth Century*
For our knowledge of St Geneviève we depend upon a *Life* which purports to have been written by a contemporary shortly after her death. Its authenticity, denied by some authorities, is defended by others. The layman may accept it at least provisionally. She certainly lived in Paris during the latter part of the fifth century, when the city was conquered by the Franks; and by her holiness, austerity, constant prayer, and miracles, as well as by the beneficent influence she exercized over the Frankish rulers, won the veneration of the Parisians, becoming after her death the patroness of their city.

Born at Nanterre, a village close to Paris, she was dedicated to God at the early age of seven by St Germanus of Auxerre. At the age of fifteen she received the 'virgin's veil' from the bishop of Paris. She soon became a center of controversy because of the miracles and predictions attributed to her, but the friendship and esteem shown her by St Germanus put an end to a campaign of calumny. When Paris was blockaded by Childeric, she led a convoy of boats provisioning the city. Her exhortations, supported by a miraculous supply of wine to the workmen, secured the erection of a basilica over the tomb of St Denis; and her prayers saved Paris from Attila's hordes. She died about 500, in favor with Clovis, the first Christian king of the Franks. A magnificent basilica rose over her shrine. Her

life and character remind us in many respects of St Joan a thousand years later. ILLUSTRATION: page 214
January 3rd

GENGULF or GENGOUL † 760
A Burgundian knight and friend of Pepin the Short, when his wife proved unfaithful to him, he retired to Avallon and lived as a recluse, but was murdered by one of her lovers. The story of his life and murder is, however, as unreliable as it is grotesque.
May 11th

GENNADIUS † c. 936
Abbot of the monastery of San Pedro de Montes in Cantabria and later bishop of Astorga, he is regarded by Spaniards as a protector against fever.
May 25th

GENOU, *see* Genulf.

GENTIAN, *see* Fuscian, Victoricus and Gentian.

GENULF or GENOU *Third Century?*
He was traditionally the first bishop of Cahors in Gaul where his feast is still kept, but this seems extremely improbable.
January 17th

GEORGE, *see* Fronto and George.

GEORGE † 303?
St George was martyred at Lydda in Palestina, probably before the time of Constantine. This is all that can be ascertained about this famous saint. There are many and various, but unfortunately not very dependable, *Lives* of St George, telling of the wonders of his martyrdom: how he encouraged his fellow Christians by public avowal of his faith, how he was arrested and how he was executed after many sufferings, not indeed only on his part, for his persecutors received their punishment. But the story of the slaying of the dragon, the story which is vividly associated with him and which has acquired such symbolical power, not to speak of its literary uses from Spenser's *Faerie Queene* to children's tales of the Seven Champions of Christendom, does not make its first definite appearance until the twelfth century. It is then that we find a story of his martyrdom to which has been added an account of St George as knight and dragon slayer. George, it says, a Christian knight, came to the city of Sylene in Lybia, which was being persecuted by a terrible dragon; and the people had been reduced to supplying it with prey from among their own company. On this occasion the king's daughter herself had to go forth, but George attacked and subdued the monster, and the princess led it back to the city with her own girdle round its neck. Here St George slew the dragon on the condition that

the people should be baptized. With some words of admonishment on being good Christians he then goes on to his martyrdom; the complete transformation of the saint into a knight of chivalry in which he marries the princess is a still later development.

In spite of the lack of detailed information, George was, and is, a great figure in the east. It is remarkable also that his fame spread so far and so comparatively fast. He was known in England by the eighth century, his *Life* was translated into Anglo Saxon, and English churches were dedicated to him. The middle ages saw a steady development of his identification with England. In an age of elaborate chivalric ideals and ritual, when saints were given the attributes of knighthood and Langland in *Piers Plowman* could speak of our Lord riding to Jerusalem to joust for our salvation, George became patron of knighthood and arms, and finally patron of England. The famous flag appears in 1284, and in the fourteenth century the red cross on the white ground was worn by both soldiers and sailors. This of course survives in the white ensign of the British Navy, in the flag flown on high days by English parish churches, and it is incorporated in the Union Jack. The Order of the Garter, the premier order of knighthood in England, was established by Edward III about 1347 and placed under the principal patronage of St George – as it still is; St George's Chapel, Windsor, was built as the chapel of the order. The saint's feast became of increasing importance during the middle ages, and remained a holiday of obligation for English Catholics until 1778.   ILLUSTRATION: page 215
April 23rd

GEORGE MTASMINDELI of the BLACK MOUNTAINS   1014–1066
For some time abbot of Iviron on Mount Athos, he was famous for his treatises and translations into Iberian.
June 27th

GEORGE of AMASTRIS   *Ninth Century*
A hermit on Mount Sirik, he entered the Bonyssa monastery when his companion anchorite died. Appointed bishop of Amastris, his birthplace, he organized a successful defence against the Saracens.
February 21st

GEORGE THE YOUNGER   *Ninth Century*
A native of the island of Lesbos, he was one of three Saints George who were bishops of Mitylene. St George the Younger was exiled when he opposed the iconoclasm of Leo the Armenian.
April 7th

GERALD of AURILLAC   855–909
The biography of this nobleman was written by St Odo of Cluny. He remained a layman, but founded a monastery at Aurillac and lived a life of great austerity rising at two each day to say the office and serve mass.
October 13th

GERALD of MAYO   † 732
He accompanied St Colman to Ireland after the Celtic way of observing Easter was forbidden in Northumbria. He became abbot of the English monastery at Mayo, while Colman ruled the Irish one.
March 13th

GERALD of SAUVE-MAJEURE   † 1095
A monk of Corbie in Picardy, he visited Rome and Jerusalem and became abbot of St Vincent at Laon. He resigned, however, through the lack of discipline there, and with some companions founded the abbey of Sauve-Majeure (Silva Major).
April 5th

GERARD MAJELLA   1726–1755
The son of a tailor, he was born at Muro, south of Naples and became a Redemptorist lay-brother at the age of twenty-three. He died when he was twenty-nine, and even in his lifetime was famous throughout Europe for his miracles. He was alleged to be able to make himself invisible and to be in two places at once, but his claim to sanctity rests on a firmer foundation – that of his love of God and a deep humility, which he carried to such lengths that when he was falsely accused of a serious offence against a young girl, he remained silent. Some months later he was exonerated and asked why he had not protested his innocence. He replied that it was against the rule of the order to produce excuses.
October 16th

GERARD of BROGNE   † 959
Although he wanted to be a recluse, he was persuaded by the count of Flanders to devote the last twenty years of his life to the inspection and reformation of all monasteries in Flanders.
October 3rd

GERARD of CSANAD   † 1046
A monk of San Giorgio Maggiore in his native Venice, he passed through Hungary on pilgrimage to Jerusalem and decided to remain there. The king, St Stephen, nominated him the first bishop of Csanad; but the king died in 1038, and Gerard was martyred during the ensuing revolt against Christianity.
September 24th

GERARD of GALLINARO and his Companions
The legend is that Gerard, Arduin, Bernard and Fulk were Englishmen who died in Italy while on pilgrimage.
August 11th

GERARD of TOUL   † 994
He was chosen bishop of Toul in 963, after serving as a

cathedral canon in his native city, Cologne. Famous for his preaching and charity, he made Toul a center of learning by encouraging Greek and Irish monks to settle there.
April 23rd

GERASIMUS   † 475
A monk from Lycia in Asia Minor, he was saved from the Eutychian heresy by St Euthymius, and condemned himself to a life of perpetual penance for his lapse. Many great men were trained in his famous community on the Jordan near Jericho, which survived for a hundred years after his death. A lion attached itself to Gerasimus, in gratitude for his having healed its paw, and stood guard over the monastic donkey. It is possible that, in art, St Jerome (Geronimus) has annexed the lion of Gerasimus, owing to a similarity in the latin form of their names.
March 5th

GEREBERNUS, *see* Dympna and Gerebernus.

GEREMARUS or GERMER   † *c.* 658
He retired from the court of Clovis II, to the monastery of Pentale, near Brionne, of which he became abbot; but his strictness made him unpopular, and he resigned in order to live as a recluse. Towards the end of his life he founded a community at Flay.
September 24th

GEREON and his Companions
The Roman Martyrology asserts that St Gereon and 318 companions suffered under Maximian at Cologne.
October 10th

GERLAC   *Twelfth Century*
After his wife's death, this soldier became a devout hermit at Valkenburg in Holland, living in the hollow of a tree. Because he entered no religious order, the neighboring monks refused him the last sacraments, but they were administered to him by a mysterious stranger.
January 5th

GERLAND   † 1100
Born at Besançon, he may have been related to the Norman conquerors of Sicily who made him bishop of Girgenti.
February 25th

GERMAIN, *see* Germanus.

GERMAINE of PIBRAC   *c.* 1579–1601
The daughter – ugly and deformed – of a farm laborer, Germaine was thoroughly disliked by her stepmother, who treated her like Cinderella. She spent her short life as a shepherdess, never failing to get to mass whatever the weather and sharing her meager rations with beggars. Her relics still lie in the church at Pibrac, near Toulouse.
June 15th

GERMANICUS   *Second Century*
A letter from the Christians at Smyrna told how Germanicus, during a persecution, encouraged a wild beast to consume him, the sooner to escape the company of the wicked men, among whom he lived.
January 19th

GERMANUS of AUXERRE   *c.* 389–448
Germanus's life is related in a biography written by a priest named Constantius about thirty years after his death. Born at Auxerre about 389, he studied rhetoric and law at Rome, where he practised as a barrister and married. The Emperor Honorius sent him back to Gaul as provincial governor ('*dux*'). His headquarters were his native town. He had always been a Christian, but his religion was conventional rather than fervent. In 418, however, much against his will, he was made bishop of Auxerre in succession to St Amator. Henceforward he was a changed man, his life a life of prayer and rigid austerity. He gave away his possessions to relieve the poor and endow his cathedral. He lived in continence with only coarse barley bread to eat, and not before evening, often fasting for several days. He wore a monk's garb and slept on a bed of ashes. He built a monastery, which he frequented.

Miracles attested the sanctity of this second Martin, in particular the exorcism of demoniacs; and such was his repute that in 429 Pope Celestine I despatched him in company with St Lupus, bishop of Troyes, to Britain to combat the Pelagian heresy. He calmed a storm at sea by his rebuke and by oil literally poured on the troubled waters. At a public disputation with the Pelagian leaders held at Verulamium (St Albans) the latter were silenced. Some years later he returned to Britain to extirpate the persistent remnants of the heresy. The small body of vocal Pelagians was banished.

On one of these two visits the Britons, threatened by a joint attack of Saxons and Picts, turned to the former general for help, and Germanus took command of their army. He lured the enemy into a defile, and at his instructions the Britons posted on either slope raised the cry of Alleluia. Their enemies, believing themselves faced with a large army, fled panic-stricken. When a savage and redoubtable force of barbarians, who had been commissioned by the Roman general Aetius, was advancing against Armorica (Brittany), Germanus met their chief, intrepidly seized the bridle of his horse and turned him back overawed. It remained to obtain an imperial pardon for the Armorican rebels. To that end Germanus travelled to Ravenna, where he was welcomed and received with honor by the bishop, St Peter Chrysologus, the Emperor Valentian III and his mother Galla Placidia. There he died July 31st, 448. His body was taken back in a triumphant procession to Auxerre,

198

where it was buried. His relics were scattered by the Huguenots.

July 31st

GERMANUS of CAPUA † *c. 540*

This bishop of Capua was a close friend of St Benedict and was sent by Pope St Hormisdas as one of the delegation to persuade the Emperor Justin to end the Acacian schism.

October 30th

GERMANUS of CONSTANTINOPLE † 732

The son of a senator, he was brought up in the church and appointed successively bishop of Cyzicus and then patriarch of Constantinople. Within a year of this appointment, he called a synod which refuted the Monothelite heresy.

May 12th

GERMANUS of GRANFEL *Seventh Century*

Brought up by Modoard, bishop of Trier, he entered St Arnulf's monastery at Romberg and later became abbot of Duke Gondo's monastery, Granfel. He was killed while remonstrating with the soldiers of Gondo's cruel successor.

February 21st

GERMANUS of VALAAM, *see* Sergius and Germanus of Valaam.

GERMANUS or GERMAIN † 576

Abbot of St Symphorian in his native Autun, he was chosen bishop of Paris by King Childebert I who founded, and was buried in, a church now known as St Germain-des-Prés. Germanus tried unsuccesfully to pacify and correct the warring descendants of Childebert.

May 28th ILLUSTRATION: page 216

GERMER, *see* Geremarus.

GERMERIUS *Sixth Century*

Said to have been chosen bishop of Toulouse at the age of thirty, he occupied the see for fifty years. At Dux, he built a church and a monastery in which he was buried.

May 16th

GEROLDUS † 978

In middle-age he became a recluse, and after his death, his sons Cuno and Ulric occupied his cell, watching over his tomb.

April 19th

GERONTIUS † 501

Bishop of Cervia (Ficocle), he was murdered at Cagli, near Ancona, when he was returning from a synod in Rome.

May 9th

GERTRUDE of NIVELLES † 659

Patroness of travellers, and invoked against mice and rats, she was born at Landen, daughter of Bd Pepin and of Bd Itta who founded the Nivelles monastery. As its superior Gertrude ruled wisely, but died young worn out by her austerities.

March 17th

GERTRUDE THE GREAT † *c. 1301*
and MECHTILDE † *c. 1298*

Of noble birth, Mechtilde of Hackeborn, at the age of seven, was placed as an oblate with the nuns of Russdorf, where shortly afterwards her sister, Gertrude, was elected abbess. In 1258 the nuns moved to Helfta.

St Gertrude the Great was born on the Epiphany 1256, of unknown parentage, and before the age of five, she was made an oblate of Helfta. Unfortunately she has been confused with her namesake the abbess. Helfta was, it seems, a Benedictine House, which adopted certain Cistercian usages. Mechtilde had been given charge of studies, and Gertrude was therefore her pupil. Though content with her life, Gertrude was for many years far from fervent, and more interested in the humanities than theology or devotion.

At the approach of her twenty-fifth birthday, a vision of Jesus converted her to the ardent and sacrificial love of God which made her a saint. She was favored by mystical graces of a markedly liturgical flavor. Her heart symbolically united in a vision to the heart of Jesus, she was a precursor of the later devotion to the Sacred Heart foretold to her by St John the Evangelist. She also advocated frequent communion and devotion to St Joseph. Five books of her visions and spiritual instructions were compiled, *The Messenger of God's Loving-kindness*, but only the second is certainly and completely her composition. Whereas her genuine work combines profound spirituality with prose poetry of high quality, much attributed to her is sugary sentiment. From her pen are also seven meditations, *exercitia* on decisive moments and themes of the Christian and monastic life, liturgical in spirit and arrangement. 'All the great themes of human poetry', it has been remarked, 'are treated by Gertrude – nature, love, and death, but as seen by the Christian faith, experienced by Christian love'. Gertrude was subprecentor under Mechtilde. She died on October 17th 1301 or 1302.

The Book of Extraordinary Grace, a record of mystic graces bestowed on Mechtilde, was compiled by Gertrude, revised and approved by herself. Mechtilde died on November 19th, 1298 or 1299. She must not be confused with another mystic, also a nun at Helfta, Mechtilde of Magdeburg.

Neither saint has been officially canonized, but Gertrude's feast is in the general Calendar of the Roman

rite, and Mechtilde's is kept by some Benedictine convents.   ILLUSTRATION: page 217
November 16th

GERVASE and PROTASE
Their remains were discovered by St Ambrose during excavations at Milan, and since then they have been accounted the first martyrs of that city.
June 19th

GERVINUS   † 1075
A canon of Rheims, his birthplace, he entered the abbey of St Vanne at Verdun and became abbot of Saint-Riquier. Towards the end of his life, he suffered from leprosy.
March 3rd

GÉRY, *see* Gaugericus.

GETULIUS and his Companions   *Second Century*
The husband of St Symphorosa, he was an officer in the Roman Army until his conversion to Christianity. Cerealis, a court official, was also converted when he came to arrest him, and finally both they and the small community adhering to Getulius were executed. The story is, however, most probably a fiction.
June 10th

GHISLAIN, *see* Gislenus.

GIBRIAN   *Sixth Century*
According to an unreliable legend he was the eldest of seven brothers – the others were SS Helan, Tressan, German, Veran, Abran and Petran – and three sisters who all migrated to Brittany. He lived as a recluse at the confluence of the rivers Coole and Marne.
May 8th

GILBERT of CAITHNESS   † 1245
Bishop of Caithness, he was elected in 1223. According to a most unlikely legend, he led the Scottish bishops at the council of Northampton in 1176 in refusing to recognize the jurisdiction of York over them.
April 1st

GILBERT of SEMPRINGHAM   † 1189
St Gilbert was born in the late eleventh century, the son of a Norman knight and an English mother. His family had estates and influence in Lincolnshire. As a boy Gilbert was useless at knightly pursuits and was, therefore, considered a weakling; yet when he died, worn out by austerities, he was just over 100 years of age. He was pushed into the church and the family living at Sempringham, but became a man of learning and a teacher of repute.

He wished to start a religious order for women, but later changed his mind and substituted double monasteries for men and women. He established his first house at Sempringham, and the idea caught the imagination of his contemporaries, including King Henry II. But royal benefactions did not prevent St Gilbert from openly favoring St Thomas of Canterbury during his quarrel with the King.

The papacy was not at first enthusiastic about the new order, but Gilbert secured the ear of St Bernard of Clairvaux and through him the support of the Cistercian pope, Bd Eugenius III. On Gilbert's death in 1189, there were thirteen Gilbertine houses, with altogether 700 men and 1500 women. This was the only medieval religious order founded in England; but it also had some success in France.

The discipline of the order was severe, and St Gilbert was noted for his austerities. At meal-times he caused a plate to be put beside him which he called 'the plate of the Lord Jesus', and into it he put all the best parts of the dishes served to him in order that they might be given to the poor. He was canonized in 1202.
February 16th

GILDAS THE WISE   *Sixth Century*
A most celebrated teacher, born about 500 in the valley of the Clyde, he is known chiefly for his much-condemned exposition of British vice, *De excidio Brittaniae*. Among his travels he visited Ireland and did much for monasticism. He died in Brittany *c.* 570, surrounded by disciples.
January 29th

GILES
Possibly a hermit near the mouth of the Rhône in the sixth or eighth century, he was a popular saint in the Middle Ages, the patron of cripples, beggars and black-smiths, and was commemorated as one of the Fourteen Holy Helpers. His emblems in art are a hind and an arrow, because his hand was pierced by an arrow when he was protecting a hind against a hunting-party led by King Flavius. The king apologised and, later on, was persuaded by Giles to found, at what is now Saint-Gilles in Province, a monastery of which Giles was the first abbot.   ILLUSTRATION: page 218
September 1st

GISLENUS or GHISLAIN   † *c.* 680
A hermit, he later founded the monastery of St Ghislain, near Mons; and it is said that it was he who persuaded SS Waldetrudis and Aldegundis to found their convents.
October 9th

GLADYS, *see* Gundleus and Gwladys.

GLEB, *see* Boris and Gleb.

GLYCERIS   *Second Century*
A Christian girl martyred at Heraclea in the Propontis, she was supposed to have been the daughter of a Roman

official. She refused to sacrifice, smashed an image of Jupiter and unaffected by torture died peacefully.
May 13th

GOAR   † *c.* 575
He left his parish in Aquitaine to live as a hermit on the Rhine; but his popularity soon led to false accusations, and he was brought before Rusticus, bishop of Trier. The trial raised such a storm of protest that Rusticus was deposed by King Sigebert I. Goar was invited to take his place but died before he could do so.
July 6th

GOBAN or GOBAIN   *Seventh Century*
This Irishman went with St Fursey to East Anglia, and then with St Ultan to Gaul. Near La Fère, he built a cell and a church later named Saint-Gobain. He was killed by German raiders.
June 20th

GODEBERTA   *Eighth Century*
She was taken to court by her parents to arrange a suitable marriage, but met St Eligius, bishop of Noyon, who became her spiritual director. King Clotaire III gave her his palace at Noyon, where she set up a convent.
April 11th

GODEHARD or GOTHARD   † 1038
When the Bavarian monastery of Nieder-Altaich was restored to Benedictine rule, St Godehard took the habit there and later became abbot. In 1022, however, he was nominated to the see of Hildesheim, and although over sixty, his energy and efficiency were outstanding.

The St Gothard pass takes its name from a chapel built on its summit and dedicated to this saint.
May 4th

GODELVA   † 1070?
When she married Bertulf of Ghistelles, a Flemish nobleman, she fell foul of her mother-in-law, and ran away as a protest against her cruelty. After a reconciliation she returned, only to be murdered by her husband's servants.
July 6th

GODFREY of AMIENS   1065–1115
He so efficiently transformed the abbey of Nogent that, in 1104, he was made bishop of Amiens. His discipline was so severe and he became so unpopular that in 1114 he retired to the Carthusians until recalled by his archbishop.
November 8th

GODRIC   † 1170
Norfolk-born, Godric started as a peddlar, then became a seafaring merchant (if not pirate). After a pilgrimage to Jerusalem and a short spell as steward to a Norfolk landowner he finally settled down as a hermit in a

forest at Finchale, near Durham. There he lived for nearly sixty years, the trusted friend of bird and beast and famous for his piety and gift of prophecy – he foretold the martyrdom of St Thomas of Canterbury. We have a biography by a contemporary, the monk Reginald of Durham; it includes the words and tunes of four holy songs taken down from Godric's lips.
May 21st

GOERICUS or ABBO   † 647
Goericus became a priest and succeeded St Arnulf as bishop of Metz.
September 19th

GOHARD and his Companions   † 843
This bishop of Nantes, together with the priests assisting him, was slain while singing mass at his own altar by raiding Norsemen who had sailed up the Loire.
June 25th

GOMMAIRE, *see* Gummarus.

GONSALO GARCIA, *see* Martyrs of Japan.

GORDIAN and EPIMACHUS   *Third Century*
Gordian was a boy martyr, and there is little else we know about him which is reliable. He may have been buried in the same tomb as that of the translated relics of St Epimachus, who was martyred at Alexandria in 250, and whose feast is kept on December 12th. Gordian and Epimachus are, however, commemorated jointly on May 10th.
May 10th

GORGONIA   † *c.* 372
What we know of this saint is taken from the panegyric preached by her brother St Gregory Nazianzen. She was the daughter of St Gregory Nazianzen the Elder and St Nonna, and sister to St Caesarius.
December 9th

GORGONIUS
A Roman saint of this name was buried on the Via Lavicana, and he is sometimes confused with St Gorgonius of Nicomedia.
September 9th

GORGONIUS of NICODEMIA, *see* Peter, Gorgonius and Dorotheus.

GOTHARD, *see* Godehard.

GOTTSCHALK   † 1066
A Wendish prince, he gave up Christianity after his father's murder by a Christian Saxon, but returned to the faith on his marriage. He recovered his lands, but was killed in an anti-Christian revolt raised by his brother-in-law.
June 7th

GREGORY
† c. 603

Born in Sicily and educated by St Potamion, he travelled widely. He was made bishop of Girgenti and wrote a Greek commentary on *Ecclesiastes*.

November 23rd

GREGORY II
† 731

Born in Rome, he succeeded Constantine as pope in 715. He was celebrated for his buildings (he re-erected the walls of Rome and re-established Monte Cassino) and his apostolic zeal. During Leo III's persecution, St Gregory showed noteworthy tact in his dealings with both emperor and Christians.

February 11th

GREGORY III
† 741

At the funeral of St Gregory II in 731, the crowd carried off this Syrian priest who was renowned for his holiness, and made him pope by popular acclamation. He dealt firmly with the iconoclastic emperor Leo III; and towards the end of his life was troubled by the Lombard invasions.

December 10th

GREGORY VII
c. 1023–1085

Gregory VII, or Hildebrand, to give him his baptismal name, was born about 1023. His family were not noble and may have been of Jewish origin. Hildebrand became a Benedictine monk in Rome, but his peculiar ability soon drew him from the cloister into the service of the papacy. He was exiled from Rome with Gregory VI but returned with the first reforming pope, Leo IX. Pope Leo was the first of the popes of the so-called Gregorian reformation, which is named, somewhat unfairly, after its most spectacular representative, but Leo was its progenitor. From then onwards Hildebrand was influential in the counsels of a series of popes. He played a decisive part in the controversy over the theology of the Eucharist between Lanfranc and Berengar of Tours which led eventually to the definition of the doctrine of Transubstantiation. Hildebrand supported Lanfranc's orthodoxy but moderated the vigor of his opposition; in this, the most serious doctrinal controversy since the days of the Fathers, it is Hildebrand who comes out best, orthodox in conviction but moderate and gentle in exposition. But theology was to occupy little of Hildebrand's official life.

Guided by Hildebrand the papacy was becoming more and more anti-German and anti-imperial. An alliance was formed with the Norman rulers of Southern Italy against the Hohenstaufen emperors; the papacy supported the popular anti-imperial movement in Milan, but the kernel of the new papal policy was expressed in the new papal election arrangements which vested the right of election of a pope in a college of cardinals. In other words, imperial influence was to be greatly reduced if not quite eliminated. It is not surprising that Hildebrand should have been so strong for the election decree, since he had seen the Emperor dispose of the see of Peter at will and had twice taken part in humiliating negotiations for the imperial acceptance of a new pope. In 1073 Hildebrand, at the height of his influence, was elected pope, as Gregory VII.

The Emperor, Henry IV, although aware that he had a dangerous enemy in the new Pope, acquiesced in his election. But, by 1075, Henry felt strong enough to open a counter-offensive against papal pretensions, and, in consequence, the German bishops renounced their allegiance to Gregory and supported the emperor in his call for a new papal election. Gregory replied by excommunicating and deposing Henry, and he won a remarkable victory. The German princes followed the pope and renounced their allegiance to the emperor, and Henry himself only saved his throne by going to the pope at Canossa and doing penance for his faults. Thus Gregory had won one of the most spectacular victories for the spiritual power in history. Unfortunately the German princes were not moved by spiritual intentions alone, and they continued their opposition to Henry for selfish political ends. The pope at first remained neutral, but when the princes seemed to have complete victory within their grasp, Gregory was unable to resist the temptation to join the winning side and to excommunicate and depose the emperor once again. This time the result was very different: Henry gained a great deal of sympathy and the pope lost almost everything except his title. Henry went from triumph to triumph; when he entered Italy, thirteen cardinals went over to his side, Rome welcomed him and Gregory was forced to take refuge with his Norman allies, among whom he died a bitter exile. 'I have loved justice,' he said, 'and I have hated iniquity, therefore I die in exile.'

Gregory's ideal was a noble one. He saw the clergy as a body of men set apart from other men by their ordination, organized in a supernatural community defined by its sacramental powers and ruled by the successor of Peter, the pope. He was equally concerned that men in orders should live lives which showed the fruits of their supernatural office, and he was a zealous supporter of clerical celibacy and a bitter opponent of any form of simony – at a time when the higher clergy commonly paid money for their offices to layman and thought nothing of it. Equally Gregory was eager to eliminate all lay interference from episcopal elections, but especially imperial interference from papal elections. Neither he, nor later popes, altogether succeeded, but they undoubtedly transformed men's attitude to the Church and her priests. Unfortunately, from his very position, Gregory had to mix reform with politics, and

it cannot be said that he was sensitive about using dubious political allies for what were undoubtedly good intentions. He did not fail to recognize in theory that lay rulers had their rights and their powers, but he thought that the pope, as representing the spiritual power, could interfere at any time and in any place. Had it been made clear that this interference was to be reserved for great moral issues it might have been made acceptable, but Gregory sought to persuade the kings of England and Denmark to accept him as feudal overlord, to hold their kingdoms as papal fiefs. He thus seemed to want to absorb the secular into the spiritual power and to rule laymen as he claimed to rule churchmen. Even devout reformers thought he went too far – St Peter Damian called him a 'holy Satan'. But whatever his faults his tragic last years surely expiated them, and, after his death, the ideal of church reform was clearer, sharper and a little nearer realization. He was canonized after the counter-reformation and has never been the object of a popular cult.
May 25th

GREGORY MAKAR *Eleventh Century*
He was so greatly praised as bishop of Nicopolis in Little Armenia, that to prevent himself from becoming conceited he left the city and travelled through Italy and France. Finally he became a hermit, austere and still famous, at Pithiviers in Orleans.
March 16th

GREGORY NAZIANZEN *c. 329–390*
St Gregory Nazianzen was by nature a gentle man and by genius and training a scholar, but throughout his life he was involved in controversies, disputes and misunderstanding in which his sensitive and essentially reasonable temperament suffered much, and not only from his ostensible 'enemies'. Nevertheless he has been declared a doctor of the church, and he won for himself the title 'the Theologian'; he is an outstanding example of those saints whose lives, as far as immediate results go, seem a series of disappointments and ill-success, yet who with the passage of times are seen increasingly to be great both in themselves and in their work.

Gregory was born at Arianzus in Cappadocia into a family of saints; his father was bishop of Nazianzus – in that place and time a married clergy was the normal rule. He was educated in Cappadocia, in Palestine, at Alexandria, and then went on to spend some ten years studying in Athens. It was during this time that he became a close friend of St Basil. When he was thirty Gregory left Athens and joined St Basil in a life of retreat, prayer and study which foreshadowed the pattern of monastic life both in the east and in the west. Gregory then went home to help his ageing father, who in a manner not uncommon at the time almost forcibly

ordained him. Shocked deeply at the task that had been forced on his own profound sense of unworthiness, Gregory fled to Basil, but soon returned, and wrote a treatise, an apology for his flight. Gregory was one of those who could touch nothing without leaving on it the seal of a mind of exceptional power and fineness: this treatise is a study of the priesthood which has been a source of inspiration to such as St Gregory the Great, and is still to all who deeply consider the subject today.

After a period of troubled work at Nazianzus, during which his friendship with St Basil was marred by his own inability to be belligerent where the things of the church were concerned, he spent five peaceful years in retirement from the affairs of church government. He was then invited to go to Constantinople, where most of the churches were given over to the Arian heresy. Here the popular method of solving religious disputes was by fighting in the streets or by what was even more distasteful to such a person – intrigue. Gregory went, with many misgivings. His lack of pomp made him personally unpopular, the Arian rabble set out to annoy him, and friends whom he trusted betrayed him. Yet his famous sermons on the Trinity won him and the church increasing respect and renown, and even St Jerome came in from his desert to hear him. He was made bishop of Constantinople, but the opposition was so noisy that Gregory insisted on resigning. As soon as he could he went into retirement, spending his last years contentedly in study, writing and mortification.
May 9th ILLUSTRATION: page 219

GREGORY of LANGRES † 539
A stern but just governor of Autun and great-grandfather of St Gregory of Tours. When his wife Armentaria died, he was appointed bishop of Langres, and ruled with all charity and virtue.
January 4th

GREGORY of NYSSA *c. 330–395*
St Gregory of Nyssa was a member of that remarkable Cappadocian family of saints which included the two St Macrinas and St Basil the Great; he was the younger brother of St Basil and St Macrina the Younger. St Basil intended him for the church, but he had ideas of his own about his career, married, and became a professional rhetorician. However, he was eventually persuaded by St Basil and his friend St Gregory Nazianzen to become a priest (continuing to live as a married man with his wife, as was then the general custom). St Basil managed to get him chosen as bishop of Nyssa, near the borders of Lower Armenia, in 372, so that he could help in the great struggle against Arianism.

During St Basil's lifetime St Gregory was rather overshadowed by his elder brother, and his well-meaning attempts to give the help required of him were not very effective. It was only after St Basil's death on January 1st, 379, that he really came into his own as the inheritor and finisher of his brother's work. He soon came to be recognized as the leading Catholic theologian of the east and was greatly esteemed by the Catholic Emperor Theodosius. He played a dominant part at the General Council of Constantinople in 381, which marked the triumph of his and St Basil's ideas. From then till his death (the date of which is not precisely known) he carried on an intense and successful activity as ecclesiastical statesman, theologian, preacher and writer. A large quantity of his writings has been preserved, and they are more and more in our own time attracting the attention of scholars and theologians.

St Gregory of Nyssa, like St Augustine, is both a theologian and a philosopher. His works contain an original and most influential form of Christian Platonism, and a magnificent theology of the Trinity and the Incarnation which develops the ideas of St Basil. He is also deeply influenced, both as a theologian and a commentator on the Scriptures, by Origen. But it is perhaps as one of the earliest and greatest of eastern Christian writers on the spiritual life that he attains his highest eminence. Of course his theology and philosophy are not separated from his spiritual teaching, any more than they are in any of the great early doctors. All his thought is integrated and directed to show the way by which the mind can ascend to God. And the path of individual spiritual progress is not shown in isolation from the sacramental life of the church, but rather as one and the same with it. It is this integration of thought, prayer, and sacrament which makes St Gregory so acceptable a spiritual master to many people in our own time.
March 9th

GREGORY of SPOLETO   *Fourth Century?*
Supposed to have been martyred at Spoleto, there is much doubt whether this saint ever existed.
December 24th

GREGORY of TOURS   538–594
Born at Clermont-Ferrand he is the most famous bishop of Tours after St Martin, succeeding St Euphronius in 573. In spite of the forthrightness of his criticisms he remained on good terms with the Merovingian kings, and his diocese flourished. Besides writing his celebrated *History of the Franks*, he was a renowned collector of religious legends.
November 17th

GREGORY of UTRECHT   *c.* 707–*c.* 775
He was a disciple of St Boniface, who made him abbot of the monastery of St Martin at Utrecht. For twenty years after the death of St Eoban, he successfully administered the see of Utrecht, in addition to being abbot of a leading missionary center; but he never received episcopal consecration.
August 25th

GREGORY THE GREAT   *c.* 540–604
Few of the famous men in history to whom the title of 'Great' has been accorded have earned it so thoroughly as St Gregory, pope and doctor of the church. He was born in Rome about the year 540, the son of a noble and wealthy patrician, the senator Gordianus. Nothing is known of his childhood, but he must have experienced at least the effects of the savage wars between the Gothic kings and the generals of the Emperor Justinian, during which Rome herself was sacked. Gregory adopted a legal and political career, and in 573 became city prefect, a post of great distinction although of diminished power. But he had always had thoughts of the religious life – it was one of the reasons why he never married – and in the following year, 574, he resigned from public life and took the monastic habit.

Gordianus was dead, and Gregory had succeeded to his vast estates. This enabled him to found six monasteries in Sicily, and to turn the family mansion on the Coelian hill into a seventh, dedicated to St Andrew, where he himself lived as a simple monk. It is likely that the Rule which he established there was that of St Benedict, which is so highly praised in his later writings. These were the happiest years of his life, and he never ceased to be homesick for his monastery. They did not last long. In 578 the Pope ordained him, and made him deacon of one of the seven ecclesiastical regions of Rome. In 579 he was despatched to Constantinople as papal ambassador. He took some of his monks with him, and found leisure enough to preach to them the sermons on the book of Job now known as the *Morals*. Here, too, he managed to convert Eutychius, the patriarch of Constantinople, to a belief in the resurrection of the body.

His embassy lasted for about seven years, and in 586 he returned to Rome, where for a time he re-entered St Andrew's Abbey, this time as its abbot. In 590 the Pope, Pelagius II, died, and Gregory was elected to succeed him. Rome was being devastated by the plague, and the pope-elect organized pilgrimages throughout the city, during which a vision of St Michael was seen above the spot now known as Castel Sant Angelo, waving a drawn sword. The plague suddenly abated, and Rome hailed the new pope as a worker of miracles.

St Gregory's pontificate lasted fourteen years, and called for all his strength of spirit and will, all his experience in administration and diplomacy. The Roman Empire was falling apart. The emperor in Constantinople was represented in Italy only by an exarch with a court at Ravenna, who possessed very little moral or material power. Lombard armies were harrying the peninsula, and Rome was besieged in 593. Gregory found that he had to organize the military defence of the city, and to make such terms as he could with the invaders. Food supplies had to be procured if the citizens were not to starve. The functions of nearly every department of the decadent civil state were thrust upon the Pope.

Meanwhile Gregory was reorganizing the church. Dioceses had to be amalgamated, or their boundaries re-defined. The scattered papal estates had to be efficiently administered. The pope's own household needed reform. Nothing was more remarkable, in all St Gregory's dealings with the churches both of the west and of the east, than his insistence on the supremacy of the Roman See. With great deference for the rights of bishops in their own dioceses, he asserted the principle of the primacy of St Peter unswervingly. 'Who can doubt,' he wrote in one of his letters, 'that the church of Constantinople is subject to the Apostolic See?' So also in his relations with the Emperor, St Gregory combined great deference for the undoubted rights of the civil power with vigilance to defend his own rights and those of the ecclesiastical and monastic orders.

Many liturgical reforms are attributed to St Gregory. It is at least certain that he instituted the 'Stations', decreeing that during the season of Lent the pope, his clergy and people should meet every day and go in procession to one or other of the Roman churches, and there celebrate mass with special solemnity. He added the phrase beginning *diesque nostros* to the *Hanc igitur* in the canon of the Mass, and made certain other structural alterations. But the extent to which he influenced church music – in spite of the fact that it now bears his name, 'Gregorian' – is much disputed. So too is the attribution of the 'Gregorian' sacramentary and the 'Gregorian' antiphonary. He was a prolific writer and an effective preacher. Apart from the *Morals*, the authentic works of St Gregory still extant include two series of sermons, one on the book of Ezechiel and the other on Gospels of the day; four books of the *Dialogues*, a collection of miracles attributed to Italian saints; the *Book of Pastoral Care*, a moving exposition of what the life of a bishop or priest should be; and an important collection of his *Letters*.

St Gregory is known as the Apostle of England. He had himself hoped to undertake a mission to convert the pagan Saxons, who had destroyed or driven out what remained of the former Christian culture of Britain. The story that he exclaimed, 'Not Angles, but angels.' when he saw a group of Saxons in Rome is probably true, but the Saxons in question were probably tourists, not slaves. Unable to carry out the mission himself, he entrusted it in 596 to a group of monks from St Andrew's,

headed by the man who later became St Augustine of Canterbury.

St Gregory died on March 12th, 604. He was buried in the basilica of St Peter's, and his first tomb – the second was constructed by order of Pope Gregory IV – bore a Latin inscription of inferior merit, which yet sums up the great Pope's life in one magnificent phrase. He is called 'God's consul'. The consuls of republican Rome had gone. Imperial Rome herself was in her death-agony. But St Gregory stands as a link between the age of the patricians and that of the pontiffs, between the glory of the historical city of Rome and the glory of the City of God.   ILLUSTRATION: facing page 208 *March 12th*

GREGORY THE ILLUMINATOR   † *c.* 330
Although his origin is unknown, his life's work was in Armenia, where, by converting King Tiridates, he secured the recognition of Christianity as the official religion. When he became a bishop, he may have established his see at Ashtishat. He was the first supreme Bishop Catholicus of Armenia, and the position was hereditary in his family for a century.
September 30th

GREGORY THE WONDERWORKER   † 268
Born at Neocaesarea in Pontus, he was converted to Christianity in his youth and became not only a disciple of Origen, but an influential teacher of his philosophical theology. On his return home in 238 he became bishop of the seventeen Christians in Neocaesarea; but at his death only seventeen pagans remained.

According to St Gregory of Nyssa, he was favored with the first recorded apparition of our Lady; and he also acquired the reputation of being an extraordinary miracle-worker, being credited with the changing of the course of a river, and even with the moving of a mountain.
November 17th

GRIMBALD   † 903
Born at St Omer, he was brought to England by Alfred the Great and became superior of the secular canons at Winchester.
July 8th

GRIMONIA
On becoming a Christian, this Irish girl took a vow of chastity and fled to France where she lived as a recluse. When her father's messengers found her, she refused to return and was killed.
September 7th

GUALFARDUS or WOLFHARD   † 1127
A saddler from Augsburg who settled in Verona, his piety attracted so much attention that he retired to a

solitary life. The Veronese persuaded him to return, and he became a hermit-monk of the Camaldolese priory of the Holy Redeemer.
April 30th

GUARDIAN ANGELS
A reference to angels as individual guardians is made indirectly in the oldest extant Roman sacramentary, and votive masses are mentioned by Alcuin in the eighth century. The feast was inserted in the calendar of the Roman rite in 1670. *See* Angels and Archangels.
October 2nd

GUARINUS † 1159
He left Bologna to join the Augustinian canons at Montaria. For his humility and holiness Pope Lucius II appointed him cardinal-bishop of Palestrina, where he was greatly venerated.
February 6th

GUARINUS or GUÉRIN † 1150
A monk of Molesmes, he was appointed abbot of St John of Aulps near Geneva. A letter from St Bernard of Clairvaux establishes that he became bishop of Sion in the Valois.
January 6th

GUDULA † 712?
Daughter of St Amalberga and god-daughter of St Gertrude of Nivelles, by whom she was educated, she led a life of fasting and prayer. She used to walk two miles to mass every morning. Legend has it that once her wax taper went out and was miraculously relit as she prayed. Her remains lie in the Brussels church named after her.
January 8th

GUDWAL or GURVAL Sixth Century?
One of the earliest missionaries to Brittany, he established several monasteries, notably the one at Locoal.
June 6th

GUÉNOLÉ, *see* Winwaloe.

GUIBERT † 962
After he had founded the Benedictine monastery of Gembloux in Brabant on his own land, this Lotharingian nobleman retired to the monastery of Gorze; but he had to defend his foundation against the claims of the emperor and the count of Namur.
May 23rd

GUMMARUS or GOMMAIRE † c. 774
One of Pepin's courtiers, he married a woman so unreasonable and oppressive that his attempts to rescue his marriage elevated him to heroic sanctity. After many unsuccessful years he gave up his efforts to achieve matrimonial peace and became a recluse.
October 11th

GUNDLEUS and GWLADYS or GLADYS Sixth Century
A chieftain of south-east Wales, Gundleus stole his wife, Gwladys, from Brychan of Brecknock in a raid. Reformed from violence by their son St Cadoc, husband and wife lived separately and devoutly at Newport in Monmouthshire.
March 29th

GUNTRAMNUS † 592
Although his private life cannot be admired, he was a just ruler of Burgundy and an enthusiastic promoter of religious work.
March 28th

GURIAS, *see* Abibus, Gurias and Samonas.

GURVAL, *see* Gudwal.

GUTHLAC c. 673–714
For our knowledge of Guthlac we are indebted to a trustworthy *Life* written in the century of his death. Born about 673, he was related to the royal house of Mercia. In his youth he took an active part in dynastic warfare. He commanded a band of armed men who attacked townships, slaughtered foes, and looted indiscriminately. Soldier or Freebooter? In the circumstances there was no practical distinction. Even so he restored to his victims a third of the plunder: an avenue opened to future grace. About the age of twenty-four he was converted and entered the double monastery of Repton, then ruled by the Abbess Elfrida. Unpopular at first for his extreme austerities, in particular his refusal of alcoholic drinks, his holiness was soon appreciated. His vocation, however, was to a hermit's life, and, with the abbess's permission, he settled with two companions in a swampy island in the fens, the future site of Crowland Abbey. Here his meal was barley bread and muddy water not tasted before sundown. Subject to the temptations and torments which beset the fathers of the desert, he endured horrific visions of Hell, assaults by fiends of hideous aspect, assuming at times the form of wild beasts and serpents: phantasies no doubt, whether of subconscious or diabolic origin, but, in his belief, objective realities. Moreover he was beaten up by beings whom his biographer, perhaps himself, regarded as devils, who spoke Welsh. These no doubt were Britons who resented the invasion of their refuge by one of the conquering race. There is other evidence, place names in particular, of the survival in eastern England of Welsh communities. St Bartholomew, to whom Guthlac had a special devotion, often came to his relief on these

occasions. Under diabolic inspiration a disciple plotted to kill him and make his profit from pilgrims to his tomb; but Guthlac was aware of his design, rebuked him and brought him to repentance.

The creatures of the wild loved him. Fish swam to his call, birds frequented his cell and rested in the places he chose for them. When crows pilfered his scanty possessions, he bore it patiently. While he conversed with a visitor two swallows perched upon him, twittering. As time passed a group of disciples occupied neighboring cells. Though his sister, St Pega, was an anchoress close by at Peakirk (Pega's Kirk) he refused to see her, but when the approach of death was made known to him, invited her to his funeral. The abbess of Repton sent a coffin. He died April 11th, 714. Before and after his death his cell was fragrant with the scent of roses and balm, and it was brilliantly illuminated. Ethelbald, now king of Mercia, built a monastery on the island. Though sacked by the Danes it was restored, and Crowland Abbey continued until the dissolution. Its church is partly a ruin, partly a parish church.
April 11th

GUY of ANDERLECHT
c. 1012

Born near Brussels, he became a sacristan. In order to have more to give to the poor, he engaged in a commercial undertaking which proved unsuccessful, and as a penance for having undertaken it, he went on pilgrimage for seven years.
September 12th

GUY of POMPOSA
† 1046

Born near Ravenna, he received the tonsure in Rome and went to live with a hermit, Martin, on the River Po. Later he became abbot of St Severus and of the Pomposa monastery near Ferrara, living in great austerity.
March 31st

GWLADYS, *see* Gundleus and Gwladys.

HALLVARD
† 1043

Patron of Oslo, he was supposed to have been a trader who was killed when trying to protect a woman accused of theft.
May 15th

HARVEY, *see* Hervé.

HEDDA
† 705

A monk of Whitby, he became a bishop of the West Saxons in 676 and later moved his see from Dorchester to Winchester. As bishop he was a close adviser of King Ine, helping to draw up his code of law.
July 7th

HEDWIG
c. 1174–1243

Hedwig and her husband, Henry I of Silesia, did much to promote religion in Silesia, founding many monasteries, including the great Cistercian nunnery at Trebnitz (near Breslau) whither Hedwig retired for the last thirty years of her life.
October 16th

HEGESIPPUS
Second Century

Although he was a Jew who was born and died in Jerusalem, he spent much of his life in Rome and is reputed to have been the first church historian.
April 7th

HEIMRAD
† 1019

It has never been officially decided whether Heimrad was a saint or merely an eccentric. The son of a serf in Swabia, he was appointed chaplain to the lady who owned the estate; but he was too restless to stay, and spent his whole life in wandering.
June 28th

HEIU, *see* Bega or Bee.

HELDRAD
Ninth Century

A nobleman, born at Lambesc near Aix, his inclinations led him to Novalese, a monastery in the Alps devoted to the care of travellers over the Mount Cenis pass. He became its abbot, built another hospice on the Lautaret Pass, and in some ways anticipated the work of the canons of Great St Bernard (*see* Bernard of Menthon).
March 13th

HELEN of SKÖVDE
c. 1160

A member of the Swedish nobility and a widow, she devoted herself to the care of the poor; she was executed on the false charge of having caused the murder of her son-in-law.
July 31st

HELENA
c. 247–c. 330

There are saints who are remembered for a single act and to this class Helena eminently belongs. She was, at one time, the most important woman in the world, yet we know next to nothing about her. Two places claim to be her birth-place: Colchester in England and Drepanum, a seaside resort, now quite vanished, in Turkey. The evidence for neither is so strong that Englishman or Turk need abandon his pretension. The Emperor Constantius married her early in his rise to power and abandoned her later for a royal match. She may have been brought up at one of the post-stables on an Imperial trunk road and have there attracted Constantius's attention on one of his official journeys. Or she may, conceivably, have been what legend makes her, the daughter of a British chief. She bore one son, Constantine the Great, probably at Nish in Serbia. After her divorce she settled at Trier (Trèves) where the Cathedral probably stands on the foundations of her palace. Almost certainly it was there that she became Christian. At the very end of her life she suddenly emerged for her great adventure: the finding of the true Cross. She died at Constantinople and her body was thereupon or later moved to Rome.

But for her final, triumphant journey she would have no fame. We should think of her, if at all, as we think of Constantine: someone who neatly made the best of both worlds. The strong purpose of her pilgrimage sheds a new and happier light on the long years of uneventful retirement showing us that it was by an act of will, grounded in patience and humility, that she accepted her position. In a court full of intrigue and murder she formed no party, took no steps against her rival when her husband tired of her, but quietly accepted her disgrace; her son Constantine rose to power, proclaimed her empress, struck coins in her honor, opened the whole imperial treasury for her use. And she accepted that too. Only in her religious practices did she maintain her private station, slipping in to mass at Rome among the crowd, helping with the housework at the convent on Mount Sion. She accepted the fact that God had his own use for her. Others faced the lions in the circus; others lived in caves in the desert. She was to be St Helena Empress, not St Helena Martyr or St Helena Anchorite. She accepted a state of life full of dangers to the soul in which many foundered, and she remained fixed in her purpose until at last it seemed God had no other need of her except to continue to the end, a kind old lady. Then came her call to a singular peculiar act of service, something unattempted before and unrepeatable—the finding of the true Cross.

She had gone out to Jerusalem to superintend the construction of Constantine's Basilica on Mount Calvary, and it is possible that during the excavation of the site, the Cross was found. The old sneer, that there was enough 'wood of the Cross' to build a ship, though still repeated, has long been nullified. All the splinters and shavings venerated everywhere have been patiently measured and found to comprise a volume far short of a cross. We know that most of these fragments have a plain pedigree back to the early fourth century. But there is no guarantee, which would satisfy an antiquary, of the authenticity of Helena's discovery. There are certain elements about the surviving relics which are so odd that they seem to preclude the possibilities of imposture. The 'Label' for example – the inscription *Jesus of Nazareth, King of the Jews* – now preserved in Santa Croce seems the most unlikely product of a forger's art. But it *is* nevertheless possible that Helena

was tricked, or that she and her companions mistook casual baulks of timber, builders' waste long buried, for the wood they sought; that the Label somehow got added to her treasure later.

Even so her enterprise was something life-bringing, for she was not merely adding one more stupendous trophy to the hoard of relics which were everywhere being unearthed and enshrined. She was asserting in a sensational form a dogma that was in danger of neglect. Power was shifting. In the academies of the eastern and south-eastern Mediterranean sharp, sly minds were everywhere looking for phrases and analogies to reconcile the new, blunt creed for which men had died, with the ancient speculations which had beguiled their minds, and with the occult rites which had for generations spiced their logic. Everything about the new religion was capable of interpretation, could be refined and diminished; everything except the unreasonable assertion that God became man and died on the Cross; not a myth or an allegory; true God, truly incarnate, tortured to death at a particular geographical place, as a matter of plain historical fact. This was the stumbling block in Carthage, Alexandria, Ephesus and Athens, and at this all the talents of the time went to work, to reduce, hide and eliminate.

Constantine was no match for them. Schooled on battle fields and in diplomatic conferences, where retreat was often the highest strategy, where truth was a compromise between irreconcilable opposites; busy with all the affairs of state; unused to the technical terms of philosophy; Constantine not yet baptized, still fuddled perhaps by dreams of Alexander, not quite sure that he was not himself divine, not himself the incarnation of the Supreme Being of whom Jove and Jehovah were alike imperfect emanations; Constantine was quite out of his depth. The situation of the church was more perilous, though few saw it, than in the days of persecution. And at that crisis suddenly emerged God-sent from luxurious retirement in the far north, a lonely, resolute old woman with a single concrete, practical task clear before her; to turn the eyes of the world back to the planks of wood on which their salvation hung.

August 18th ILLUSTRATION: page 220

Other feasts connected with the Cross:
May 3rd Finding of the Cross; *September 14th* Exaltation of the Cross

HELIER *Sixth Century*
A native of Tongres in Belgium, he was converted to Christianity when he was a boy and had to flee from the wrath of his father. He eventually established himself as a hermit in a cave on the island of Jersey, where the town of St Helier is named after him.
July 16th

GREGORY THE GREAT: painted panel of polyptych by Antonello da Messina (*fl.* 1446 - 1479).
(*Galleria Nazionale, Palermo*)

PLATE 7

Photo : courtesy of the Mother Cabrini High School, New York

FRANCES XAVIER CABRINI: photograph.

FRANCIS BORGIA: painting by an unknown artist. (English College, Valladolid, Spain.)

Photo : Mella

FRANCIS of SALES: painting by an unknown artist. *(Monastero della Visitazione, Turin.)*

FRANCIS XAVIER: painting by Carlo Maratta (1625 – 1713).
(Ch. del Gèsu, Rome.)

GALL: painting by W. Dürr (1815 – 1890). (*Museum, Carlsruhe.*)

GENEVIÈVE: painting by Puvis de Chavannes (1824 – 1898).
(Panthéon, Paris.)

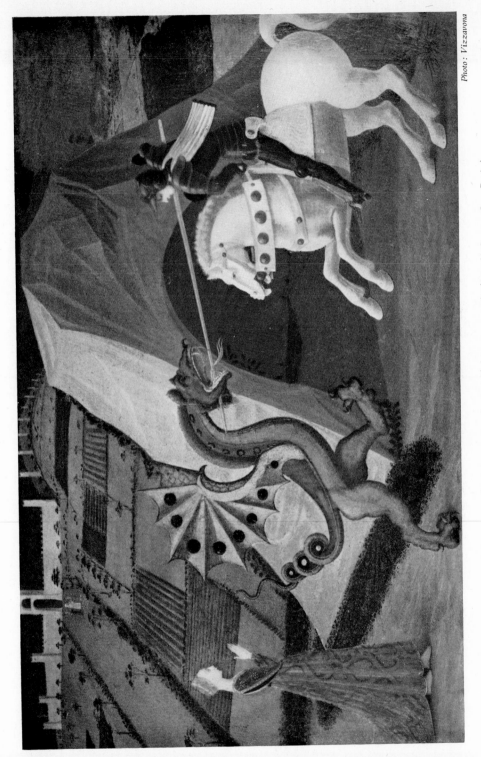

GEORGE: painting by Vittore Carpaccio (died 1523 – 1526). (*Musée Cognac-Jay, Paris.*)

Photo: Vizzavona

GERMANUS or GERMAIN: French enamel, (*c.* 1400). (*British Museum.*)

GERTRUDE THE GREAT: engraving.

GILES: detail painting by the Master of St Giles (*fl. c. 1500*). (*National Gallery, London.*)

GREGORY NAZIANZEN: mosaic (1148).
(Duomo, Cefalu, Sicily.)

HELENA: detail of painting by Piero della Francesca (*c.1420 – c.1492*). (*Ch. di S. Francesco, Arezzo.*)

HENRY THE EMPEROR: sculpture on Adams porte (1240). *(Dom, Bamberg.)*

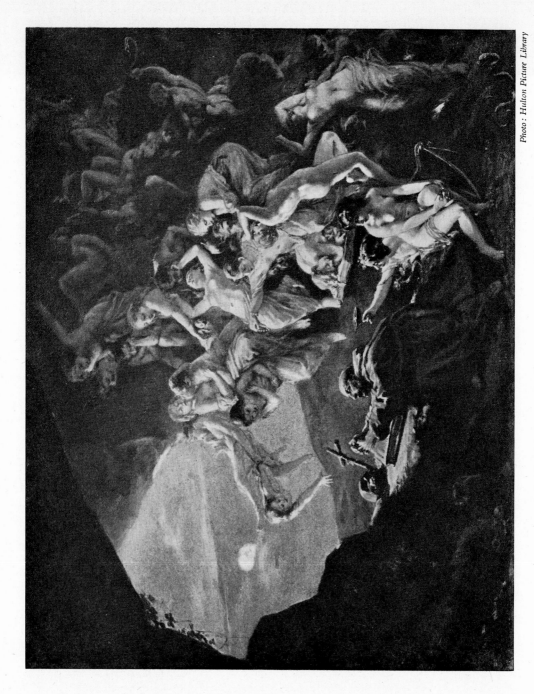

HILARION: painting by N. F. O. Tassaert (1800 – 1874). (Exhibited at the Paris Salon 1857.)

HUBERT: painting by the Master of Werden (late fifteenth century). *(National Gallery, London.)*

HUGH of LINCOLN: sculpture.

IGNATIUS of LOYOLA: painting by Rubens (1577 - 1640). (*Kunsthistorisches Museum, Vienna*)

PLATE 8

HELIODORUS † c. 400

An ex-soldier, he became a disciple of St Jerome, and lived with him in the Holy Land. Much to St Jerome's disappointment, he returned to Italy and became bishop of Altino. This account, however, is based upon a late and unreliable *Life*.

July 3rd

HELLADIUS † 633

As an eminent official of the Visigoth court, he frequently visited the Agali monastery near the river Tagus. Eventually he entered it, became abbot and was later archbishop of Toledo.

February 18th

HENRY of COCKET † 1127

A Dane, he crossed to Northumberland when the English missionaries were exercising great influence in Denmark. He became a hermit on Cocket, an island of the River Cocket belonging to the Tynemouth monastery, and died there.

January 16th

HENRY of UPPSALA Twelfth Century

An Englishman resident in Rome, he accompanied Cardinal Breakspear (afterwards Pope Adrian IV) to Scandinavia and was consecrated bishop of Uppsala in 1152. He accompanied St Eric of Sweden in an expedition against the pagans in Finland, and remained there on missionary work until an unruly Finnish convert killed him.

January 19th

HENRY THE EMPEROR 972–1024

Born in 972, he was educated by St Wolfgang of Ratisbon, succeeded Otto III as emperor in 1002 and was crowned by Pope Benedict VIII at Rome in 1014. He is not entirely free from the charge that he used ecclesiastical power to reinforce secular power, and his purpose in creating the see of Bamberg in 1006 was as much to keep the Wends in order, as to save their souls.

He was a supporter of the Cluniac reforms (*see* The Cluny Saints); and the story is told that he once presented himself to the abbot of Saint-Vanne at Verdun with the request that he should accept his obedience and make him a monk. The abbot accepted the emperor's obedience but, in return, commanded him to go on ruling the Empire.

Henry died at the castle of Grina on July 15th, 1024.

July 15th ILLUSTRATION: page 221

HERBERT † 687

In answer to his prayers, this anchorite of Lake Derwentwater died at the same time as his lifelong friend, St Cuthbert of Lindisfarne. St Herbert's island is still honored by pilgrims, the present Catholic church in Windermere is dedicated to him, and Wordsworth wrote a poem on his hermitage.

March 20th

HERCULANUS † c. 547

This bishop of Perugia was put to death by King Totila after the Goths had captured Perugia. He can probably be identified with the other St Herculanus who is also venerated in Perugia.

November 7th

HERIBALD Ninth Century

Abbot of St Germanus, he became bishop of Auxerre.

April 25th

HERIBERT † 1021

Born at Worms and appointed archbishop of Cologne while chancellor to Otto III, he did outstandingly good work for the church and among the poor, besides obtaining great miracles through prayer. He is still invoked for rain.

March 16th

HERMAGORAS and FORTUNATUS
First Century?

St Hermagoras was supposed to have been installed as the first bishop of Aquileia by St Peter, with St Fortunatus as deacon, and to have been executed at the order of Nero.

July 12th

HERMENEGILD † 585

His father was Leovigild, king of Spain, who brought him up in the Arian heresy from which he was converted by his wife and St Leander. This caused war with his father, and though there was for some time a reconciliation, his continuing opposition to Arianism so annoyed his father that he ordered his execution. Whether Hermenegild's death in those circumstances can be regarded as a martyrdom has been much disputed.

April 13th

HERMENLAND Eighth Century

A courtier of Clotaire III, born at Noyon, he entered Fontenelle Abbey in Normandy and was chosen to lead a party of monks sent as missioners to Nantes. Their monastery in the Loire estuary became famous for its education and Hermenland for his miracles.

March 25th

HERMES Second Century?

A martyr, he was buried on the old Salarian Way in the cemetery of Basilla.

August 28th

HERMOGENES, *see* Mennas, Hermogenes and Eugraphus.

HERVÉ or HARVEY Sixth Century

One of the most popular saints in Brittany, he was

supposed to have been the blind son of a Briton who settled in Brittany. Head of the community of Plouvien, he transferred it to Lanhouarneau.

June 17th

HESPERUS, *see* Esuperius and Zoë.

HESYCHIUS   *Third Century*
He was martyred at Durostorum (now Silistria) soon after the martyrdom of St Julius, his friend.

June 15th

HESYCHIUS   *Fourth Century*
A disciple of St Hilarion whom he followed from Palestine to Sicily, he remained with him until his death and brought his body back to Palestine for burial in the monastery at Majuma.

October 3rd

HIDULF   † *c.* 707
He was probably an auxiliary bishop of Trier, but he had a great desire for a monastic life and founded the abbey of Moyenmoutier to which he retired.

July 11th

HILARIA, *see* Claudius, Hilaria and their Companions.

HILARION   *Fourth Century*
A life of St Hilarion was written by no less a person than St Jerome. He did not know Hilarion himself, but received an account of him from St Epiphanius of Salamis, who visited St Hilarion just before he died. Hilarion was born at Tabatha, a village near Gaza. He was sent to that great center of culture, Alexandria, for his education, and at the age of fifteen became a Christian. This was the time of the beginnings of eremitical life in the desert, and Hilarion made one of those who flocked out to St Antony where he was attempting to live in solitude. However, Hilarion had a deep desire for such a life himself, whereas those who came to St Antony were seeking miracles and cures, and finding this altogether too populous Hilarion sought out the desert for himself. First of all he returned home, and, his parents having died, gave away his possessions to his relations and to the poor. Then he found himself a place between the sea shore and a swamp, where he could live in true isolation. His austerities were severe. His clothes were of the simplest, the most notable garment being a hair shirt; he lived on fifteen figs a day until the moral duty of supporting his own life made him take a few vegetables, bread and oil. His cell was of the size to enable him to sleep protected from the weather and no more. He went up to Jerusalem only once in all the long years he spent near Majuma in Palestine, and the reason he gave was that he would not even seem to make little of what the church honored, but neither would he keep on going there as if there were only certain places where God could be found and worshipped.

The life of the hermit is for a few, but the judgment of the saint would seem to have universal application. After twenty years in this way of life miracles were brought about by Hilarion's intercession, and as he grew older his precious solitude was increasingly sapped away both by the crowds who came to him for help and by the disciples who had attached themselves to him; for the sake of these brethren, he lamented, he even had to own a farm. He decided to leave his no longer desert place, and thus began the struggle which took up the rest of his life between his search for solitude and his personal fame. He tried living in the Egyptian desert but found it impossible to remain unnoticed. An attempt to hide himself in Sicily was equally unsuccessful. The only thing to do, he thought, was to go to a land where he could not speak the language, and he journeyed to Dalmatia. But people's need still evoked his help, and miracles demand no language to be understood. He finally found refuge in Cyprus, and there, having reached the age of eighty, in a remote and peaceful spot he died.   ILLUSTRATION: page 222

October 21st

HILARUS   † 468
Papal legate at the infamous 'Robber Council' where St Flavian of Constantinople was killed, he succeeded Leo the Great in 461 as pope. He built the chapel of St John the Apostle in the baptistry of St John Lateran in Rome.

February 28th

HILARY of ARLES   † 449
As a youth he joined his kinsman St Honoratus at Lérins, and succeeded him as bishop of Arles. Although efficient, his zeal was sometimes excessive: he deposed Bishop Chelodius, who appealed successfully to Rome, and, in another diocese, appointed a successor to an old and infirm bishop before the latter's death. The sick man recovered, and the diocese had two bishops. The pope however decided in favor of the original bishop.

May 5th

HILARY of GALEATA   † 558
His hermitage near the river Ronco attracted many disciples for whom he built a monastery which he called Galeata, although it was later known as Sant' Ilaro.

May 15th

HILARY of POITIERS   *c.* 320–*c.* 368
St Hilary of Poitiers was one of the greatest champions of the Catholic faith against Arianism in the west. Not much is known about his life. He was an adult convert from paganism, and became bishop of Poitiers about 350. Because of his vigorous opposition to the attempts of the Emperor Constantius II to impose Arianism on the western church he was exiled to Phrygia in 356.

But he showed himself so effective a defender and propagator of Catholic belief in the east that the emperor decided he would be less trouble if he was allowed to return to his diocese, and sent him back to Gaul in 360. He continued to fight Arianism in the west till his death about 368.

St Hilary learnt much from his contacts with the Catholic theologians of the east: he introduced into the west a great deal of their thought (notably in his great theological work *On the Trinity*), and the rich and profound tradition of Scriptural interpretation which they inherited from Origen. He seems to have been a man of most kindly and charitable disposition, though an extremely vigorous controversialist in defence of Catholic truth. His relics are still venerated in the great Romanesque church which bears his name in the city of Poitiers. His feast appears in the Anglican as well as the Catholic calendar, and has given its name to the legal and university 'Hilary term' in England.
January 14th

HILDA † 688
A relative of St Edwin, king of Northumbria, Hilda was abbess of the double monastery of Whitby, where the great synod of 664 was held (*see* St Wilfrid). Her success in her office is recorded in Bede's *Ecclesiastical History*, which tells us that Hilda was consulted by kings and princes. Caedmon was a servant at Whitby Abbey and became a monk on St Hilda's advice.
November 17th

HILDEGARD 1098–1179
Builder and abbess of the Benedictine monastery of Rupertsberg, near Bingen on the Rhine, Hildegard was one of the most striking characters produced by the twelfth century and a very remarkable woman. A mystic who recorded her visions in a work she called the *Scivias* (i.e. 'Know the Ways [of the Lord]'), she was also a musician, an intelligent student of medicine and natural history, a prophet, and a moralist who was afraid neither of archbishop nor emperor should their conduct seem worthy of rebuke.
September 17th

HILDEGUND † 1183
Daughter of Count Herman of Lidtberg and mother of Bd Herman and Bd Hedwig. When her husband Lothair died, she converted her castle near Cologne into a convent, became its prioress and caused it to flourish greatly.
February 6th

HILDEGUND † 1188
When she accompanied her father on a pilgrimage to Ierusalem, she was dressed as a boy for greater safety. When her father died on the return journey, she made her way back and became a Cistercian novice at Schönau. Not until her death was her sex discovered.
April 20th

HILDELITHA † c. 717
An Anglo-Saxon princess, she became a nun in France, and returned to guide St Ethelburga in her foundation at Barking where she succeeded her as abbess.
September 3rd

HIMELIN Eighth Century
After visiting Rome, this Irish priest was taken ill at Vissenaecken in Brabant and died there after miraculously turning water into wine. His shrine in this town is much honored by pilgrims, but no reliable account of his life really exists.
March 10th

HIPPARCHUS and his Companions — the Seven Martyrs of Samosata † 297 or 308?
Hipparchus and Philotheus, magistrates of Samosata, were not present at a public thanksgiving for the successes of the emperor. He became suspicious, and they and five other friends were arraigned before him and crucified for denying the Roman gods.
December 9th

HIPPOLYTUS, *see* Timothy, Hippolytus and Symphorian.

HIPPOLYTUS Third Century
There are at least three candidates for this title, of whom two have a feast day on August 13th and another a feast day on August 22nd.

The St Hippolytus of legend was St Laurence's jailer. He was converted and baptized by St Laurence, became his disciple and assisted at his funeral. For this he was brought before the emperor, who ordered him to be flogged. His nurse (St Concordia) and the nineteen members of his household were beaten to death, but the saint himself was spared this punishment in order that he should be torn to pieces by horses. What is suspicious about this legend is that the word 'Hippolytus' means 'loosed horse', and there is a well-known Greek legend about Hippolytus, the son of Theseus, who suffered the same fate as the saint is alleged to have suffered. It is easy to see how the saint became patron of horses and their riders.

It is more likely that the saint whose feast is kept on August 13th was a priest and theologian who lived in Rome during the first part of the third century. He composed a number of works, all in Greek, then the official language of the church of Rome, of which few survive. Among these is the *Philosophoumena* in which he attacks contemporary heresies, affiliating them to various pagan philosophies. In his honor his disciples erected a statue which was discovered headless in the sixteenth century. On his chair a list of his books is inscribed. He drew up a table for calculating the date of Easter which was proved, however, almost immediately to be incorrect. Among his many commentaries on Scripture, one survives, the oldest extant Christian commentary on a book of the Bible, a commentary on Daniel in which he seeks to calm fears or destroy excited anticipations of the Second Advent by proving that the world must last 6,000 years, 300 more than the date of writing. Though he did not condemn it, Pope Callistus looked askance at Hippolytus's theology of the Divine Word which continued an undeveloped and ill-formulated theology tending to regard the Word as a subordinate Deity. When Callistus was chosen pope in 217 Hippolytus revolted and set himself up as anti-pope. He also denounced what he regarded as Callistus's laxities; nor did he shrink from personal slander. For his followers' use he drew up a book of directions, chiefly liturgical, called the *Apostolic Tradition*. Soon forgotten in the west, it long survived, variously modified, in eastern churches. It is our sole authority for the canon of a Roman mass earlier than the fourth century, though his canon was not intended to be a formula verbally fixed. When in 235 the Emperor Maximin revived the persecution of Christians, Pope Pontian and the anti-pope Hippolytus were banished to the Sardinian mines; Hippolytus surrendered his papal claim and invited his followers to submit to the legitimate pontiff. Both soon died, victims of this concentration camp, and when the persecution ceased their bodies were brought back to Rome for burial (August 13th). Though Hippolytus's conduct was not saintly, his private life had always been austere, and his death was a martyrdom.

His tomb on the Tiburtine Way was honored as a martyr's, but his true story was quickly forgotten, and the Roman liturgy presents him as St Laurence's jailer.

The St Hippolytus whose feast is kept on August 22nd is usually considered to have been bishop of Porto, who was martyred under the Emperor Alexander. In the Roman Martyrology he is referred to as a 'man greatly renowned for his learning', but he would seem to be the same person as the St Hippolytus referred to above.
August 13th and *August 22nd*

HOMOBONUS † 1197
A merchant of Cremona, he was outstandingly just and charitable, seeking out the poor in order to help them. He is the patron of tailors and clothworkers.
November 13th

THE HOLY INNOCENTS
In the second chapter of St Matthew's gospel will be found the story of the three wise men who came to Jerusalem seeking the king of the Jews. Herod took alarm at the news of the birth of a possible rival, and ordered his men to slay all the male children in Bethlehem and its neighborhood of two years old and less.

Estimates of the number of children killed by Herod vary from six to 144,000. In fact, it is unlikely that there would have been more than about twenty-five or thirty boy babies under two in a place as small as Bethlehem at any one moment. These children have been commemorated as martyrs by the church since the fifth century; in England their feast used to be known as Childermas.
December 28th

HONORATUS † 429
Born in Gaul of a distinguished Roman family, he became a Christian and a hermit on the isle of Lérins, near Antibes, where he founded a celebrated monastery. He died soon after his consecration as bishop of Arles.
January 16th

HONORATUS of AMIENS *Sixth Century*
The cult of Honoratus, bishop of Amiens, became widespread in France after 1060. He is the patron saint of bakers and confectioners, and the Faubourg Saint-Honoré in Paris is named after him.
May 16th

HONORIUS of CANTERBURY † 653
A Roman monk, he was chosen by St Gregory the Great for the English mission. In 627, he succeeded St Justus as archbishop of Canterbury, being consecrated by St Paulinus of York.
September 30th

HOPE, *see* Faith, Hope, Charity and Wisdom.

HORMISDAS † 420
A nobleman, he was made to look after camels because he was a Christian. He is reputed to have died a martyr.
August 8th

HORMISDAS † 523
A widower, he was elected pope in 514 and spent much of his time in dealing with the attempt of Acacius in Constantinople to reach agreement with the Monophysites. His son, St Silverius, also became pope.
August 6th

HUBERT † 727
Legend makes Hubert, like St Eustace, a huntsman converted by a stag that turned and, with a cross between its antlers, bade him mend his ways or end in Hell. What we do know for certain is that Hubert was bishop of Tongres-Maastricht-Liège from 705 to 727 and worked hard to convert eastern Belgium, most of which was covered in forest and still pagan.
November 3rd ILLUSTRATION: page 223

HUGH of BONNEVAUX † 1194

A nephew of St Hugh of Grenoble, he became abbot of Bonnevaux, and in 1177, acted as mediator between Pope Alexander III and the Emperor Frederick Barbarossa.
April 1st

HUGH of CLUNY † 1109

He succeeded St Odilo as abbot of Cluny. *See* The Cluny Saints.
April 29th

HUGH of GRENOBLE 1052–1132

Born in Dauphiné at Châteauneuf near Valence, he was elected bishop of Grenoble at the age of twenty-eight to purge the diocese of its disorders, and he occupied the see until his death fifty-two years later. He granted St Bruno the site for his monastery in the mountains of the Chartreuse, and his part in founding the Carthusian order is discussed in the article on St Bruno.
April 1st

HUGH of LINCOLN 1140–1200

The child who became St Hugh was born at Avalon in Burgundy. His mother died when he was eight, and his father, a knight who had longed as a boy to enter religion, gave his two elder sons their share of the family inheritance and took the small Hugh with him into the house of the Canons Regular of St Augustine at Villars-Benoît. At an age when modern children are scarcely out of the nursery, Hugh dedicated himself to God. At fifteen he took his first formal vows. Full grown, he visited with his prior the Grande Chartreuse, remote in the mountains, where a man might concentrate himself entirely upon contemplative prayer. After some struggle he went there, twenty-three years old, and in that corporate solitude 'made his soul'. He was ordained priest. He was appointed procurator, administering the monastery farms, helping the poor, and receiving guests who spoke to him of places as far away as England, where, at forty, he was to be used to serve the outside world.

Henry II, hearing that he 'carried the whole human race in his heart', asked that he should be made Prior of the Charterhouse, which had been founded not very successfully in Somerset to expiate the royal share in the guilt of St Thomas of Canterbury's murder. Obedient but reluctant, Hugh was sent. He proved just, wise and loving in his relationships with his own community and with others, with his capricious and temperamental patron, and with the frightened, hostile, local people who had been dispossessed of their lands to endow the monastery and for whom he arranged compensation. At forty-six he was made bishop of Lincoln, and commanded by the general of his order to accept the office.

He carried out his task admirably, even though much of the prayer that irradiated his work had to be made on horseback, riding about his enormous diocese. He maintained church rights against the encroachments of the crown, and established several constitutional precedents against unlawful taxation. He defended individuals oppressed by the cruel and powerful royal foresters. In his ceaselessly busy life he made time to bury the neglected dead, and to tend stinking, suppurating lepers, not denying them the human warmth of a caress. He healed people spiritually and physically diseased.

Fearless charity and considerable humor marked his dealings with the alarming Plantagenet kings, and at the risk of his own life he protected the Jews in the fierce racial riots of 1190 and 1191. He was loved not only by such as had good reason to love him, but also by infants, animals and even wild birds, among them the swan with which he is often p ainted. His contemporary, Giraldus Cambrensis, describes him as 'full of talk and fun... brusque, enthusiastic, and a strict disciplinarian'. He was accustomed to say that to be a true Christian a man must have purity of life, love in his heart, and truth on his lips.

He died in 1200, in London, at the bishop of Lincoln's Inn, where three centuries later law, justice, humor, sweetness, and the love of God were combined again in Henry VIII's Chancellor, St Thomas More.
November 17th   ILLUSTRATION: page 224

HUGH of ROUEN † 730

Although a pluralist, holding the sees of Rouen, Paris and Bayeux, as well as being abbot of Fontenelle and Jumièges — probably due to his close relationship with the dukes of Burgundy — he used his income to improve the churches under his jurisdiction.
April 9th

HUGH or LITTLE HUGH of LINCOLN † 1255

Nine-year-old Hugh of Lincoln was alleged to have been tortured, crowned with thorns and crucified by Jews on Friday, August 27th, 1255. The accusations of ritual murder made against the Jews in the middle ages are discussed in the life of Simon of Trent.
August 27th

HUMILITY † 1310

After the death of her two sons, she entered the monastery of St Perpetua at the age of twenty-four and later withdrew into a more complete solitude, where she practiced severe mortifications, eating little, sleeping on her knees and wearing a shawl made of bristles. After twelve years she became abbess of the first Vallombrosan nunnery.
May 22nd

HUMPHREY or HUNFRID † 871

A monk of Prüm Abbey in the Eifel, he became bishop

of Thérouanne where the terror of the Northmen was at its height. Encouraged by Pope Nicholas I, he kept his flock together until better times. He was also made abbot of Saint-Bertin.

March 8th

HUNNA or HUVA   *Seventh Century*

Although of the reigning house of Alsace, and married to a nobleman, she earned the nickname of the 'Holy Washerwoman' by doing the washing of poor neighbors.

April 15th

HYACINTH, *see* Protus and Hyacinth.

HYACINTH   1185–1257

The Apostle of Poland was born at Kamler near Breslau. He studied at Cracow, Prague and Bologna, was ordained and then appointed to a canonry of Cracow by his uncle, the bishop. Many of the details of his life come from an unreliable account which ;ays that in 1216 he went with his uncle to Rome, where he met St Dominic, and became one of the first members of the newly formed order of the Dominicans. We do know that he returned to Poland in 1222 at the head of a Dominican mission, which founded many houses of the order and spread into Prussia, Danzig, Lithuania, Russia and even into the Balkans.

St Hyacinth is credited with many miracles, including one of restoring a dead person to life, and another of having walked across the waters of the Vistula. He died in 1257 on the feast of the Assumption, and before three years had elapsed his tomb had become a place of pilgrimage. He was canonized in 1594 by Clement VIII.

August 17th

HYACINTHA MARISCOTTI   † 1640

She made herself so disagreeable when she was passed over in marriage in favor of her sister, that her family forced her to enter the convent of Viterbo. There she indulged in every means of evading the rule; and, even when successfully exhorted to reform, she soon lapsed after a short period of exaggerated fervor.

Yet, in the end, she became a wise and understanding novice-mistress, severe only to herself and celebrated for the studied moderation of her advice.

January 30th

HYGINUS   *Second Century*

Although he appears in the Roman Martyrology, there is no evidence for his martyrdom. During his rule as pope, however, the church in Rome was much troubled by gnostic heresiarchs.

January 11th

HYPATIUS   *Fifth Century*

After much wandering, he set up a monastery near Chalcedon and was vehement in denouncing Nestorius.

June 17th

I A   *Sixth Century*

According to legend, she floated from Ireland on a leaf and landed at what is now St Ives (Port Ia), in Cornwall, where she established a hermitage.

February 3rd

IA and her Companions   † c. 360

Martyred during the persecution of King Sapor II of Persia, St Ia was supposed to have been a Greek who was singled out from her nine thousand companions for especially prolonged tortures.

August 4th

IBAR   *Fifth Century*

Little is known of this early missionary in Ireland, except that he had a monastic school on the island of Beggery or Beg-Eire (Little Ireland) – so-called because, although he was banished by St Patrick from Ireland with the words, 'Thou shalt not be in Erin', St Ibar replied, 'Erin shall be the name of the place in which I shall be'.

April 23rd

IDA of HERZFELD   † 825

Brought up at the court of Charlemagne, and becoming a widow while still young, she devoted herself to her religion and to the care of the poor.

September 4th

IDESBALD   † 1167

In middle-age, he joined the monastery of our Lady of the Dunes which had been established on the sand hills near Dunkirk and of which Idesbald later became abbot.

April 18th

IGNATIUS of ANTIOCH   *First Century*

Ignatius, bishop of Antioch, martyred at some date in the reign of Trajan (98–117) was devoured by wild beasts in the arena. Our knowledge of him is derived from seven letters written on his journey to Rome where, as he writes, he was taken in the custody of a guard 'bound to ten leopards (that is, a company of soldiers) who become more brutal for kind treatment.' Nevertheless, so illogically sporadic was the persecution, that delegations from churches on or near his route, headed by their bishops, came to greet him, sending delegations back to his widowed church.

From Smyrna, Ignatius wrote letters to the churches of Ephesus, Magnesia, Tralles and Rome, from Troas to the church of Philadelphia and back to the church of Smyrna and to its bishop, the future martyr, St Polycarp. Recurrent themes in these letters are thanks for the kindness shown by the delegations, insistence on obedience to the bishop and under him to the presbyters and deacons – 'no Eucharist is valid unless celebrated by the bishop or a presbyter delegated by him' – and warnings against the Docetist heretics who denied the reality of our Lord's body. In this connection the real presence of our Lord's body in the Eucharist is emphatically asserted. The Docetists 'abstain from the Eucharist ... because they do not confess that the Eucharist is the flesh of our Saviour Jesus Christ'. For the first time we hear of 'The Catholic church' in the memorable saying, 'Where Jesus is, there is the Catholic church'. The presence of Jesus, in fact, not only in the church but in the individual Christian is a *leitmotif* with Ignatius, who calls himself 'Theophoros' – the God bearer. Polycarp is encouraged, as a younger man, to persevere in the excellent conduct of his episcopal office.

The letter to the church of Rome is unlike the others. Here alone no mention is made of the bishop or other clergy. On the other hand the supremacy of the church of Rome, the church of 'St Peter and St Paul', is recognized not only by Ignatius's language of deference but explicitly when he speaks of 'the church which ... in the land of the Romans has the presidency'.

The letter is an urgent plea that the Roman Christians may not attempt, by employing what influence they possessed with the government, to obtain the writer's pardon. Ignatius longs to consummate his union with Jesus by sharing his passion: 'Suffer me to be eaten by the beasts through whom I can attain to God. I am God's wheat and I am ground by the teeth of wild beasts that I may be found pure bread of Christ ... I long for the beasts that are prepared for me ... let there come on me fire and cross and struggles with wild beasts ... mangling of limbs, crushing of my whole body ... may I but attain to Jesus Christ. I am learning in my bonds to give up all desires ... for my desire (*eros*) has been crucified, and there is in me no fire or love for material things; but only water living and saying to me from within, "Come to the Father".'

February 1st   ILLUSTRATION: page 257

IGNATIUS of CONSTANTINOPLE   † 877
Of royal birth, he was confined in a monastery on the deposition of his father. He became patriarch of Constantinople in 846, but because of his uncompromising denunciation of vice and support for the rights of the church, he was exiled in 858. He was restored to office in 867.

October 23rd

IGNATIUS of LACONI   1701–1781
He joined a Franciscan friary near Cagliari, and worked as a weaver for fifteen years. In 1741 he was sent out to beg for alms, an occupation he discharged with conspicuous success for forty years.

May 11th

IGNATIUS of LOYOLA   c. 1491–1556
Don Inigo Lopez de Recalde was born about 1491 in the Basque hill country near the village of Azpeytia. He was the youngest of eleven children of an ancient noble family. He was christened Inigo, after a Spanish Benedictine saint, but later took, and towards the end of his life always used, the name of Ignatius out of devotion to St Ignatius of Antioch. As a youth he entered the service of a noble friend of his family called Juan Velasquez, and after Velasquez's death that of the duke of Najera, viceroy of Navarre. He received only a superficial education in youth. His interests at that time were in gaming, in affairs of gallantry and above all in feats of military prowess. In the war between France and Spain in May 1521, the French crossed the Pyrenees and laid siege to Pampeluna. Others of the defenders were for surrender, but Ignatius insisted that they hold out. In the storming of the fortress his thigh was fractured by a cannon-ball. He was taken to the Castle of Loyola, where it was discovered that the bone had been badly set. It had to be broken and re-set. He bore the pain with fortitude and it was during his long subsequent convalescence that, finding no other literature, he passed his time in reading the lives of the saints. Their example fired him to emulation. 'Supposing', he said, 'I were to do what St Francis and St Dominic have done?' He resolved to become a knight in the service of God.

In 1522, when he was recovered, he made his way to the shrine of our Lady of Montserrat. There he made a three-day confession, gave his knightly apparel to a beggar, hung his sword upon an altar of our Lady, and going to the neighboring town of Manresa, took service in a hospital there. There was a danger for a time that he might fall into an extravagance of asceticism, but from this he was saved by his utter obedience to his confessor. It was at Manresa that he received that divine illumination by which the rest of his life was guided. He composed there the *Spiritual Exercises*, in which he lays down the principles by which a Catholic ought to 'regulate his life', so as to attain his end which is 'to praise the Lord His God, to reverence and to serve Him, so that he shall be saved'. He sketches out his doctrine of 'election', and his demand that all shall always be done, *ad majorem Dei gloriam*: 'to the greater glory of God'.

He remained for about a year at Manresa and thence made a pilgrimage to Palestine, stopping on the way at Rome. After he had venerated the Holy Places in Palestine, he returned to Barcelona. There, though now over thirty, he went to school, sitting on the bench beside the little children, in order to repair the gaps in his education, until he was fit to proceed to the universities at Alcala and Salamanca. At both of these places he was delated to the Inquisition and had to spend some days in the cells. But his doctrine was finally vindicated, and in 1528 he left Salamanca for Paris and the Sorbonne. He spent seven years in Paris, and it was there that he collected his first six disciples. On the Feast of the Assumption, 1534, at St Denis's in Montmartre these seven solemnly dedicated themselves to the service of God, taking vows of poverty and chastity. Their design at that time was to proceed to Jerusalem and devote themselves to the salvation of souls in infidel countries. Ignatius returned to Spain and later in 1536 the company, which had by then grown to ten, met at Venice, intending there to embark for their journey. They found that it was impossible, owing to the disturbed state of the eastern Mediterranean. The rest of the company went therefore instead to Rome, leaving Ignatius behind in Venice. The pope, Paul III, received them with high favor, and they returned to Venice, bringing with them a special papal authorization for the ordination to the priesthood of Ignatius and six of his companions. When, after another year, it still proved impossible to sail to the Holy Land, Ignatius concluded that it was not the will of God that they should make that journey. Instead he put his Company, under the title of the Society of Jesus, at the disposal of the Holy See. They moved to Rome, and Ignatius said his first mass there on Christmas Day 1538, at Sta Maria Maggiore. He drew up the constitutions of his new order and presented them to Pope Paul III, who exclaimed on seeing them, 'The finger of God is here,' and in his bull *Regimini Militantis Ecclesiae* of September 1540 gave formal recognition to the order. The order added to the three customary vows of poverty, chastity and obedience a fourth of special obedience to the pope.

In its first constitution the order was limited to sixty members. Ignatius, in spite of his own protest, was unanimously elected general on April 7th, 1541. The rule limiting the Society's members to sixty, was revoked by a second papal bull on March 15th, 1543. Ignatius hardly left Rome for the rest of his life, but the expansion of the Society in all parts of the world under his generalship was little short of miraculous, and by the time of his death on July 3rd, 1556 it numbered twelve provinces, a hundred and one houses and nearly a thousand members.

St Ignatius was canonized on March 12th 1622.

July 31st   ILLUSTRATION: facing page 225

IGNATIUS of ROSTOV   † 1288

As bishop of Rostov, Ignatius had to contend with the Tartar oppression, the quarrels of nobles, and false accusations which were made about him to the archbishop of Kiev.

May 28th

ILDEPHONSUS   † 667

Highly honored in Spain, he is particularly associated with devotion to the Virgin Mary which he encouraged by his work on her perpetual virginity *(De virginitate perpetua sanctae Mariae)*. He was abbot of Agli near Toledo before succeeding his uncle, St Eugenius, as archbishop of Toledo.

January 23rd

ILLTUD or ILLTYD   c. 425–c. 505

Said to be a cousin of King Arthur, he was born about 425, probably in Brittany. As is the case for most of the Welsh saints, our knowledge of him comes from a biography written centuries after his death, but it seems certain that he was a knight, and married, when he decided to renounce the world; his wife, too, decided to seek the religious life. Illtud, the knight, has some claim to be identified with the Sir Galahad of Arthurian legend, but it is beyond dispute that Illtud, the monk, was the principal founder of Welsh monastic life. He was ordained by St Germanus of Auxerre, and through him perhaps acquired knowledge of the monastic movement in Gaul.

It is stated in the (much earlier) *Life* of St Samson that Illtud's first monastery was on a small island, and this has sometimes been identified with Caldey, off the coast of Pembrokeshire, which certainly has a venerable monastic history. More probably the 'island' was a secluded place in the Vale of Glamorgan, known now as Llantwit ('Llan-Illtud'). Here Illtud established a great monastery which became the center of the religious and intellectual life of South Wales. His subjects included Samson, Gildas and possibly David. Illtud's renown as a scholar is always emphasized in the lives of the Welsh saints; he is described as 'the most learned of the Britons in the Old and New Testaments, and in every kind of philosophy'. His monastery is said to have had hundreds of monks, but this probably includes the many pupils who lived there. Llanilltud seems to have been a great monastic school, from which monks went out on those missionary journeys which were always the mark of Celtic monasticism.

Not much is definitely known of the details of Illtud's life and work, but of his influence there can be no question. Even legends for which there is no sure foundation can bear witness to a saint's special vocation. Illtud's achievement in regulating monastic life was a great advance on the holy anarchy that seems up to his time to have been characteristic of the Celtic hermits. The combination of manual work and intellectual study fostered the apostolic but practical zeal of his pupils. Illtud is said to have died in Brittany, about 505, and his relics are venerated at Dol.

Illtud is honored in many Welsh church dedications, and it has been suggested that the mysterious 'Aldate' is in fact Illtud under a variant name. In Brittany, too, there was a cult of Illtud, who like so many Welsh saints seems to have been equally at home in 'Lesser Britain'. A ninth century cross at Llantwit has an inscription referring to Illtud, and some scholars have interpreted an inscription on an Ogham stone at Caldey as also honoring Illtud. If this were so it would provide some proof for Illtud's connection with that island.

November 6th

INDRACTUS and DOMINICA   *Eighth Century*

This brother and his sister were treacherously murdered by Saxons in England when they were on their way from Ireland to Rome. Their bodies were said to have been buried in Glastonbury Abbey.

February 5th

IÑIGO, *see* Eneco.

INNOCENT I   † 417

Born at Albano, near Rome, he succeeded St Anastasius I as pope in 401 and reigned for sixteen years. He was a firm upholder of papal supremacy, supporting St John Chrysostom and confirming the condemnation of Pelagianism by the African bishops.

July 28th

INNOCENT of TORTONA   *Fourth Century*

Although his parents were exempt from persecution, he was sentenced to the stake soon after their death, but escaped to Rome, and eventually became bishop of Tortona, his birthplace.

April 17th

IRENAEUS   *Second Century*

srenaeus was born in Asia Minor in the first half of the Iecond century. All we have to date him by is his statement in a letter to Florinus, that he remembered old Polycarp vividly, though he himself was young at the time. Polycarp died in 155, so 130–135 would not be far out as the date of Irenaeus's birth. When he came west is uncertain, but we find him at Lyons as a priest in 177. We do not know when he became bishop of that city, but we see him in that role in 199, taking an important part in the settlement of the controversy between Rome and Asia Minor about the date of Easter. There is a respectable tradition, from Gregory of Tours, the pseudo-Justin, and Jerome, that he died a martyr.

But the man about whom we know so little historically shows us much of himself in his writings – more than is generally the case with ancient writers. In the long and rambling treatise *Against Heresies* we sense a man blessed and permeated with a rare vision. The disciple of Polycarp, who was himself the disciple of St John the Evangelist, he is still within the circle of light whose center is the love between John and Christ. This human love gave to John's mystic vision a wholly unique quality, saving it from the element of fantasy which is never entirely absent from mystic writings. The vision is whole, and lovingly contains the world which it utterly transcends; and while the Christian tradition can

never die, the tradition of the beloved disciple could not but lose its original savor, which belongs to heaven not earth. Of this tradition, Irenaeus is the last representative. He enjoyed that vision, characteristic of the first generations of Christians, of the world in its beginning and in its end, which is, in the best sense of the word, optimistic. This had none of the illusion that always goes with optimism. The world had just shown its evil as never before or since, and the blood on the cross was still fresh in the Christian memory.

This vision of the world provoked, inevitably, a reaction. The separation of spirit from body that is far older than Christianity received a new impulse from the challenge, and made a desperate bid to convert the new faith into its own ways. The dynamic element in the gospel was divorced from the world-affirming element, and so lent itself to an orgy of world-denial. It was to these 'gnostics', as they were called, that Irenaeus undertook to show the true vision, the Christ who is, as opposed to the Christ about whom the sectaries are for ever proclaiming, 'Lo, he is here, he is there'. If it is true that a polemical work has its scope defined by the nature of the challenge it answers, Irenaeus's work was able to be more catholic than is generally the lot of such writings. The gnostics gave a challenge to which the Christian could answer with his deepest and widest conviction.

It was above all in the Eucharist that Irenaeus saw this Christian answer, and his statements about it are among the most precious of the *Monumenta Christiana*. He sees the splendor of the Eucharist in terms wider than other eucharistic writing: it lies, for him, not only in the fact that the consecrated elements are the body and blood of Christ, but in the fact that bread and wine are able to yield to these divine realities. In this fact the whole creation is necessarily involved, and Irenaeus expresses this poetically by relating the eucharistic consecration to the whole natural process that has produced the bread and wine: 'Christ counselled his disciples to offer to God first fruits from his creatures, when he took bread which is from the creature and gave thanks, saying: "This is my body". And in the same way with a cup, which also is from this world of ours: this he declared to be his blood, and taught the new oblation of the new covenant' (*Against Heresies* 3, 11, 5). 'And on what basis can it be affirmed among the gnostics that the consecrated bread is the body of their Lord and the cup is his blood, if they will not admit that he himself is the Son of the world's maker – His Word, that is, through whom the wood blooms and the fountains flow and the earth gives first the blade, then the ear, then the perfect grain in the ear?' (*Ibid*, 4, 18, 3). In other passages, a more detailed relation of the elements with the cosmic process leads him on to the resurrection which is its culmination: 'And the stock of the vine is bent down to earth and bears fruit in its proper time, and the grain of wheat falls into the earth, is dissolved, and rises manifold through the Spirit of God who holds all things together; and afterwards, brought by providence to the use of man, these receive the word of God to become Eucharist, which is the body and blood of Christ: so our bodies which the Eucharist has nourished, buried now and dissolved into the earth, shall rise in their appointed time, when the Word of God gives it to them to rise in the glory of God the Father.' (Ibid, 5, 2, 3).

What Irenaeus is saying is that in the Eucharist we see the world as God sees it, and that this vision involves, as we have seen, a reverence for the elements even in their natural state, since this is their potentiality to become the divine mysteries. We find this attitude in the primitive liturgies, above all in the Roman canon when the bread and wine are referred to as 'these holy and unspotted sacrifices' (haec sancta sacrificia illibata). It has been lost in the heat of a later and far less catholic polemic, as has also the serene vision of which it is the sign. There is no primitive writer who points the way back to this vision as surely as does Irenaeus.
June 28th

IRENAEUS and MUSTIOLA   *Third Century?*
This Irenaeus was a deacon who was martyred for giving Christian burial to St Felix at Sutril. Mustiola, a noblewoman, was beaten to death for looking after St Irenaeus and other Christian prisoners.
July 3rd

IRENAEUS of SIRMIUM   † 304
Bishop of Sirmium, he was tried during Diocletian's persecution by Probus, governor of Pannonia, now Mitrovica, of which Sirmium was the capital. Resisting the entreaties of his family, he refused to worship idols and was beheaded.
March 24th

IRENE, *see* Agape, Chionia and Irene.

IRMINA and ADELA   *Eighth Century*
St Irmina († 710) was nun and a zealous supporter of St Willibrord. St Adela († 734), who became a nun after her husband's death, was the grandmother of St Gregory of Utrecht.
December 24th

ISAAC, *see* Sapor and Isaac.

ISAAC JOGUES, *see* the Martyrs of North America.
          ILLUSTRATION: page 161 (c)

ISAAC of CONSTANTINOPLE   *Fifth Century*
A hermit who was imprisoned for prophesying the downfall of the Arian Emperor Valens, he found favor with his successor, Theodosius. He founded a monastery in Constantinople, later named the Dalmatian monastery after St Dalmatus, one of his disciples.
May 30th

ISAAC of CORDOVA   † 852
Isaac was a Christian of Cordova who mastered Arabic and worked for the Moorish government. He became a monk and in a religious disputation with the principal magistrate of the city he denounced Mohammed so bluntly that he was arrested and put to death.
June 3rd

ISAAC of SPOLETO   *Sixth Century*
Through persecution by the Monophysites, he left Syria for Italy, where he lived as a recluse on Monte Luco, near Spoleto.
April 11th

ISAAC or SAHAK I   † 439
Having become a monk after his wife's death, he succeeded his father, St Nerses I, as katholikos of the Armenians. Once he had established the primacy of his see, he set about reforming the Armenian church, forbidding the marriage of bishops and promoting monasticism. He was responsible for the development of Armenian as a literary language by causing the Bible to be translated into it.
September 9th

ISAIAS of ROSTOV   † 1090
From the abbacy of St Demetrius in Kiev, his native city, he was promoted in 1077 to the bishopric of Rostov.
May 15th

ISCHYION, *see* Chaeremon, Ischyion and their Companions.

ISIDORE of ALEXANDRIA   † 404
A desert ascetic, ordained by St Athanasius and appointed governor of the Alexandrian hospital, he was unjustly condemned by St Jerome for origenist heresy and excommunicated by Bishop Theophilus. He died in Constantinople under St John Chrysostom's protection.
January 15th

ISIDORE of CHIOS   *Third Century*
An officer in the Roman Army, he was denounced at Chios as a Christian and, proving obdurate, his tongue was cut out and he was beheaded.
May 15th

ISIDORE of PELUSIUM   *Fifth Century*
Abbot of a monastery near Pelusium. Two thousand and twelve letters written by him and still extant, all outstandingly well expressed, account for the reverence in which he was held by St Cyril, St Chrysostom and other prelates.
February 4th

ISIDORE of SEVILLE   † 636
Born about the middle of the sixth century, Isidore was

the brother of three saints – St Leander, his predecessor in the see of Seville, St Fulgentius and St Florentina. His noble family was related to the royal house of Visigothic monarchs whose conversion from Arianism to Catholicism occurred during his lifetime. As Isidore's *Life* is late and untrustworthy we cannot be sure of detailed events. Early an orphan, he was educated by his elder brother Leander, severely but with great success; for his erudition was truly remarkable, covering every branch of knowledge (including Hebrew and Greek). He was indeed a walking encyclopedia, and it was not surprising that he was chosen to succeed his brother as archbishop of Seville, an office he held for some forty years. The duties of his episcopate did not stop the output of his amazingly prolific pen. He wrote a dictionary of synonyms, a treatise of astronomy and geography, biographies of illustrious men and of biblical characters, and a history of the Goths, our only source book for much of Visigothic history. His most comprehensive and influential work was in fact an encyclopedia, his *Etymologies*, summarizing the knowledge of his age. In a period of encroaching barbarism this work of preserving the surviving inheritance of antiquity was urgent and indispensable.

Though never himself a monk, Isidore composed a monastic rule. He explained, developed and codified the Mozarabic Liturgy. He labored to eradicate the remnants of Arianism and crushed the heresy of the Acephali, a Spanish off-shoot of the Monophysite heresy, which may have originated much earlier in the east as their Greek name suggests. The Monophysites taught that Christ was one divine-human nature. By example and legislation Isidore provided schools for the education of his countrymen, their curriculum as comprehensive as his own studies. Influential at court, he took a prominent part in a council at Toledo in 610, presided over the second council of Seville in 618 or 619, and the fourth council of Toledo in 633.

Honesty, however, compels us to admit that the glory of Isidore's achievements is smirched by his encouragement of, or at least acquiescence in, anti-Semitic canons enacting severe penalties against Jews who refused to pretend to believe in the Christian faith.

Isidore died a saintly death in 636. His relics were later translated to Leon. Benedict XIV proclaimed him a doctor of the church.

April 4th

ISIDORE THE HUSBANDMAN   † 1130

A Spanish peasant, he was yet able to give freely to the poor, living with his wife a life of such piety that both are venerated as saints. He is the patron of his birthplace, Madrid.   ILLUSTRATION: page 258

May 15th

ITA   *Sixth Century*

St Ita was born of Christian parents towards the end of the fifth century. She belonged to the noble tribe of the Decii in County Waterford. All her early biographers favor the pleasant metaphor describing her as the 'Brigid of Munster'. Actually the differences were more striking than the resemblances between those two foremost women saints of the Celtic church (*see* St Brigid). Brigid's effective life as a nun was spent in continual movement. When she had made a success of one convent settlement, she moved off to found another. Organization was her bent. Ita did just the opposite. Instead of entering one of Brigid's convents, she founded another in a district where there was none, at Killeedy, County Limerick. There she remained all her life, courting retirement. Again, there is an emphasis on austerity in Ita's life not found in Brigid's. Ita's mortifications were on a par with those of the greatest contemporary missionaries.

A strongly individualistic character is glimpsed in the legends of Ita. When she decided to settle in Killeedy, a chieftain offered her a large grant of land to support the convent. But Ita would accept only four acres, which she cultivated intensively. The convent became known as a training school for little boys, many of whom later became famous churchmen. One of these was St Brendan, whom Ita accepted in fosterage when he was a year old and kept until he was six. The great Navigator revisited her between his voyages and always deferred to her counsel. He once asked her what were the three things which God most detested, and she replied: 'A scowling face, obstinacy in wrong-doing, and too great a confidence in the power of money'. St Mochoemoc, whom because of his beauty she called 'Pulcherius', was another great personage of the Celtic church she fostered in infancy.

Ita died on January 15th, which is now kept as her feast, about the year 570. There is a strong local cult of her in Munster, particularly in Waterford and Limerick, and her name is a popular one for Irish girls. In the middle of the nineteenth century a new move was made in Ireland for the development of her cult, when Bishop Butler of Limerick obtained from Pope Pius IX a special office and mass for her feast.

January 15th

ITHAMAR   *Seventh Century*

A native of Kent, he was the first Englishman to hold an English bishopric, that of Rochester.

June 10th

IVO

He is supposed to have been a Persian bishop who, after much travelling, settled in the fen-country of England.

The town of St Ives in Huntingdonshire is named after him.
April 24th

IVO of CHARTRES   *c.* 1040–*c.* 1116

We do not know St Ivo's exact date of birth or death. He was born about 1040 near Beauvais, the child of a wealthy landowner. Educated in a church school in Beauvais, he spent some time studying in Paris, which was just beginning to be a famous center of learning, and then went to Bec, where he was a pupil of Lanfranc and met St Anselm. He did not become a monk but a canon regular at Nesles in Picardy. In 1078 he was summoned to rule over a house of Augustinian canons which had recently been founded in honor of St Quentin at Beauvais, and under his rule it became a model community. It was there that Ivo began to teach theology and to earn his reputation as one of the foremost theologians of his day. Fourteen years later, the bishop of Chartres was deposed for simony and Ivo elected to succeed him. The archbishop of the province was opposed to this election, and Ivo had to go to Pope Urban II for consecration.

In 1092 the French king contracted an uncanonical marriage and Ivo opposed him, an act which cost him several months imprisonment. On his release he continued to oppose the king. The affair dragged on, and each time a French see fell vacant there was a struggle over the succession, since the king sought to obtain a bench of bishops who would accept his marriage. This sad business continued until 1104. The French king was excommunicated more than once but at last repented, agreed to separate from his lady and made his peace with the church. By this time the papacy was involved in a quarrel over the propriety of lay rulers investing bishops with the pastoral staff and ring, which to the pope symbolized spiritual things and to the lay ruler their title to the prelate's civil obedience. The pope, Paschal II, was somewhat rash and extreme, and Ivo, although his conduct had shown him zealous for papal authority and opposed to any improper lay intervention in episcopal elections, fell under a cloud for insisting that the lay ruler had some rights which deserved recognition. He proposed that lay rulers should give up investiture by ring and staff but that they should still receive the new bishop's homage and fealty. In 1107 this formula was adopted by the pope to settle his quarrel with the English and French kings.

Ivo was, in his day, something of a 'new' theologian. He knew not only sacred texts, but was also one of the first students of Justinian's civil law, besides being tolerably well acquainted with the Latin classics. He was indeed one of the earliest of the humanist teachers of the twelfth century renaissance, many of the most famous of whom were associated with his cathedral school at Chartres. In everything he did, his love for the church and his charity for her members were obvious. When he died *c.* 1116, although he was at loggerheads with the canons of his cathedral, they seem to have had no doubt of his sanctity, and he has been revered as a saint ever since.
May 23rd

IVO of KERMARTIN   † 1303

Ivo Hélory, from Brittany, went to Paris and became a successful lawyer. He became judge in the ecclesiastical courts at Rennes, then at Tréguier. He was ordained in 1284 and abandoned legal practice three years later, devoting himself to the care of the poor and innocent. The patron saint of lawyers, he is the subject of an amusing and probably contemporary Latin rhyme which, freely translated, goes:

> St Ivo was a Breton,
> A lawyer and an honest man:
> How strange!

May 19th

JAMES and MARIAN   † 259

In the reign of the Emperor Valerian edicts were issued striking at the heart and organization of the Christian communities. Private Christian worship was not forbidden but, by methods sufficiently familiar to us, it was attempted to make it impossible in practice by attacking the bishops, priests and deacons, and then the laymen of rank and position.

The passion of James and Marian is told to us by one of their fellow Christians who was himself arrested with them but, under the provisions of the edicts, later released. He relates that they were travelling in Numidia and had reached the outskirts of the city of Cirta, where the persecution was particularly fierce. James and Marian both believed that they had been brought to this place, where so many of their fellows were suffering, by divine direction; and indeed after two days a band of soldiers followed by a crowd came to their dwelling-place and took them off to prison. There they were tortured, James confessing boldly that he was a deacon. Marian was only a 'reader' in the church, but his tortures were the worse for that, as his persecutors were determined to make him confess that he too was a deacon. When these extreme cruelties were found to have no effect he was returned to the prison with James and their companions in faith and suffering. In the prison, waiting for what should come, Marian had a marvellous dream in which he saw Cyprian, the bishop of Carthage who had been martyred in the previous year. And James, too, then recounted a dream of great beauty and joy which he had while on the journey to Cirta.

They were brought into open court and seen by the governor, who sent them on to Lambesa, and here they were sentenced to death. During the night James received a visit in a dream from his friend, the martyred Bishop Agapius, who showed him that he and Marian and their companions would soon be in that place which Agapius had already reached. The very next day the clergy in prison were taken out to a small valley with a river running through it, the slopes on either side providing seats for spectators as in a theatre. And there were so many to die that they were drawn up in rows so that the executioner could pass from one to another with his sword. Their eyes were blindfolded, but notwithstanding this many of them saw a vision as it were of horses in heaven being ridden by young men clothed in white. And Marian prophesied aloud of the calamities that would follow this shedding of the blood of the righteous. Then the executioner did his work so that 'the river drank of the blood of the blessed.' When all was over, Marian's mother, who was called Mary, took the body of her son and embraced it, rejoicing in him and kissing his wounds. 'O Mary, rightly named!' says the writer, 'O mother, blessed both in thy son and in thy name.'
April 30th

JAMES INTERCISUS † *c.* 421
Because he was in high favor at the Persian court, he did not at first openly profess his Christian faith. When he did so, the king sentenced him to have his limbs chopped off, one by one—hence his surname *intercisus*, which means 'cut to pieces'.
November 27th

JAMES KISAI, *see* Martyrs of Japan.

JAMES of NISIBIS † 338
A leading personage in the Eastern church, he was the first bishop of Nisibis in Mesopotamia and attended the council of Nicaea in 325.
July 15th

JAMES of the MARCH 1394–1476
Born at Montebrandone in the March of Ancona, he joined the Observant branch of the Franciscans and preached many missions throughout Europe. In 1426, he and St John of Capistrano were appointed inquisitors against the Fraticelli, whom they punished with the utmost severity. St James, however, was more lenient to the Hussites at the council of Basle. He himself was arraigned for heresy in 1462, but the pope forebore to give a decision.
November 28th

JAMES THE GREATER *First Century*
Like his brother, St John the Evangelist, James occupied a prominent position among the Twelve. Coming second or third to Peter in the official lists (*see* references in James the Less), he was also singled out, with Peter and John, to be a privileged witness of the raising of the daughter of Jairus, the Transfiguration, and the Agony in the Garden (Mark 5:37; 9:2; 14:33). A fisherman of Bethsaida, of a family, perhaps, of more than ordinary means – his father, Zebedee, could afford hired men (Mark 1:19–20), and his brother was personally known to the High Priest (John 18:15–16) – James shared with John the nick-name Boanerges, 'Sons of Thunder'. This title, bestowed by Christ (Mark 3:17), suggests that the brothers were impetuous and hot-tempered, and we may see this exemplified in different ways in the two incidents described in Luke 9:54 and Mark 10:35–41.

James was put to death by the sword at the command of Herod Agrippa (Acts 12:2), probably in the year 42. Towards the end of the second century, Clement of Alexandria, relying on the information of 'those before him', states that the apostle's accuser was himself converted, and suffered at the same time as James.

Tradition asserts that James brought the gospel to Spain, but because of the early date of his death, this claim is quite untenable. In the Acts of the Apostles it is Paul who is depicted as the pioneer missionary, and James was dead before Paul's activity began. Moreover, there is a constant tradition that the sole western church of apostolic foundation was that of Rome – in 416, we find Pope Innocent I making an authoritative statement to this effect. Finally, the universal silence of Spanish authors of the first seven centuries, particularly when they are engaged in extolling the glories of the Spanish church, is, to say the least, disconcerting.

In fact, the tradition only appears in written form for the first time in the seventh century, arising from a Greek source of doubtful historical credentials, but it was a century later, when a star miraculously revealed what was claimed to be the tomb of James, that popular belief spread. This shrine at Compostella (probably derived from Campus stellae: the field of the star) rivalled Rome as a center of pilgrimage.

Although we may not believe that St James visited Spain, this does not dispose of the claim that the relics at Compostella are his. ILLUSTRATION: page 259
July 25th

JAMES THE LESS *First Century*
The only direct information which the New Testament provides about the second apostle who bore the name James is that he was the 'son of Alphaeus' (Matthew 10:3; Mark 3:18; Luke 6:15; Acts 1:13). In these circumstances, it is not surprising that attempts have been made

to identify him with one, or more, of the several people so named elsewhere in the New Testament. The most outstanding of these is James, 'the brother of the Lord', who is thus described by St Paul (Galatians 1:19; *cf. also* 2:9 and 12). He is probably to be identified with the recipient of a vision of the Risen Christ (1 Corinthians 15:7), and is, doubtless, the same James who is depicted as the leading Christian of the church of Jerusalem (Acts 12:17; 15:13; 21:18). Finally, it seems natural to identify him with the Lord's brother of that name mentioned in the Gospels (Matthew 13:55; Mark 6:3). It was the opinion of St Jerome – an opinion for a long time generally accepted – that James, son of Alphaeus, and James, the Lord's brother, are the same person; but the tendency among biblical scholars nowadays is to distinguish between the two, and to be content with regard to this apostle, as we have to be content in the case of others of the Twelve, with the bare mention of his name.

The term 'brethren of the Lord' is used by New Testament writers to designate a group of persons distinct from the Twelve (*cf.* 1 Corinthians 9:5; Acts 1:13 and 14). In their few appearances in the Gospels, they are show as incredulous with regard to Christ's preaching, even positively opposed to him; and this at a time when the Apostolic College was already constituted (*e.g.* John 7:3-5; Mark 3:21 and 31-36). While no completely convincing argument can be found, it would appear more probable that neither James nor any other of the brethren was a member of the Twelve.

Similarly, if one keeps in mind the pre-eminent position occupied by James, the Lord's brother, among the Jewish converts at Jerusalem, he would appear the most likely author of the Epistle of James, a letter addressed primarily to the convert Jews of the Dispersion.

Early Christian tradition agrees with Josephus in stating that James, the Lord's brother, was put to death by the Jewish authorities (probably in the year 62). Hegesippus, writing in the second century, describes James as an ascetic—'wine and strong drink he drank not, nor did he eat meat; he neither shaved his head, nor anointed himself with oil ... and the skin of his knees was hardened like a camel's through his much praying.' He was held in high repute for his sanctity, but gradually incurred the envy and enmity of the scribes and pharisees because of his sway over the people, and this culminated in their stoning him to death within the temple precincts, while he was addressing the crowd.

The very large and involved question of the relationship between Christ and 'his brethren' can only be touched on here. In the first place there can be no doubt that the Greek word in the original texts means 'brother'; at the same time one should remember that, as used in the New Testament, *viz* to designate a well-defined group of people (*e.g.* 1 Corinthians 9:5), the term must have taken its rise among the Aramaic-speaking first Christians; that, therefore, our Greek term is merely a translation of the current Aramaic word. Consequently, it is permissible to argue that, as in several verifiable instances in the Old Testament, so here, 'brother' does not necessarily mean full-brother, nor even half-brother, but may be used to designate remoter degrees of kinship, including cousins, since neither Hebrew nor Aramaic had a word for 'cousin'. If, then, Christ did have cousins, the only suitable word in Aramaic to describe them would have been 'brethren'. Catholic belief in the perpetual virginity of Mary, while resting largely on the basis of a firm tradition, still finds some support in the nuances of Scripture: Mary's implied vow of virginity (Luke 1:34); the family life of Mary and Joseph, as told by Luke, makes no mention of other children; Christ alone is 'son of Mary'; the otherwise hardly comprehensible action of Christ in confiding his mother to St John's care. The theory which would make the 'brethren' sons of Joseph by a previous marriage, likewise, has no Scriptural foundation. Conversely, the view which holds them to be Christ's cousins by being the children either of a sister of his mother, or of a brother of St Joseph, has only conjectural value.
May 11th

JANUARIUS, *see* Faustus, Januarius and Martius.

JANUARIUS   *Fourth Century*
St Januarius has acquired fame, not so much because of his life and death, but because of the periodic liquefaction of the relic of his blood which is preserved in Naples.

The history of his martyrdom is somewhat obscure, as there are no references to him in the early Roman martyrologies, the present entry being derived in all probability from the writings of Bede in 733. It is believed, however, that Januarius was bishop of Benevento in Italy at the time of Diocletian and, hearing of four Christians imprisoned for the faith, went to visit them. Informers subsequently denounced him and he also was imprisoned together with his companions. Accounts of his death vary; it appears that he and his companions were exposed to the wild beasts in the amphitheatre at Pozzuoli, but the animals did not touch them. The saint was then beheaded in 305. The body was first kept at Benevento, but later, because of the threat of war, it was removed to Monte Vergine and finally to Naples. The earliest reference to the saint appears to be that of Uranius (431), who attributed the staying of the eruption of Vesuvius to his intercession.

Such was the background of the devotion to St Januarius until about the fifteenth century, since which time the relic of his blood preserved in the cathedral at Naples has attracted increasing and world wide attention. The relic is contained in a flagon-shaped flask about four inches high and two and a quarter inches in diameter, the flask itself being enclosed in a glass reliquary on a jewelled stand. There are thus two thicknesses of hermetically sealed glass between the relic and the atmosphere. The relic itself consists of a solid mass of a dark, opaque substance which half fills the flask. About eighteen times a year, in the presence of a large congregation, the relic is exposed before another relic believed to be that of the martyr's head. After a period varying from a few minutes to several hours, during which the priest repeatedly inverts the flask and invocation is made to heaven for the miracle to take place, the solid mass is seen to liquefy, becoming bright red in colour, and on occasions it has bubbled and frothed.

In attempting to assess the significance of this event, let it be immediately said that the facts as described occur without fraud or deception. Testimony to this has been given by numerous people including many sceptics, scientists and others frankly hostile. There is, however, no such unanimity about the explanation of the phenomenon. Many declare it is miraculous, while others say that a natural explanation has not been excluded. The matter is still not proven, but some relevant points are worth mentioning. The relic appears to vary in volume, at one time filling only half the flask, while at another it occupies two-thirds or more. This variation may, however, be more apparent than real, for there is no means of telling whether the mass is solid throughout, or whether empty space is enclosed within a solid crust thus accounting for the apparent variation in volume. A greater difficulty is that the weight of the relic has been found to vary at different times by as much as twenty-seven grammes. It has been suggested that the liquefaction is due to the heating which must occur when the relic is brought out into the densely packed cathedral. Observations have shown, however, that at a temperature of 86° F, two hours have elapsed before liquefaction has taken place, whereas at 66° F, it has occurred within fifteen minutes. On the other hand, failure to liquefy occurs more frequently in December than in the summer months. One further point of importance is that on seven occasions, when a jeweller has been repairing the casket, the specimen has liquefied.

These are the facts about the relic, and from them we must attempt to draw some conclusion. From the scientific point of view it cannot be said that there has been an adequate investigation of the phenomenon. Weighing the whole reliquary, random observations on the general temperature of the air when liquefaction occurs, and even spectroscopic observation which has shown that the specimen is probably blood, are not enough. Subjecting the flask to successive temperatures under conditions of varying humidity, ascertaining whether there is a partial vacuum within the flask, removal of a portion of the specimen for analysis and attempting to reproduce the phenomenon under controlled conditions, are only a few of the requirements for a satisfactory scientific analysis. These have not been fulfilled hence we can only form a judgment on the basis of circumstantial evidence.

The points which do seem worthy of stress are that the specimen on occasion froths and bubbles, which suggests that under appropriate conditions it may pass from solid through liquid to the gaseous state; in other words, it may boil like any other substance given the correct conditions. The variable temperature at which the phenomenon occurs is not a stumbling block to a physical explanation, for the temperature of liquefaction will vary according to the pressure within the flask, and we have no knowledge of the pressure changes which may be occurring. A very important fact is that liquefaction has occurred during repair of the casket, a circumstance in which it seems highly unlikely that God would work a miracle. Moreover, the frequency with which the phenomenon occurs is unlike the miraculous, which in general is a rare event. There is something unusual about Naples in this regard, for this relic is not unique in the city, for since the fifteenth century the number of liquefactions has been steadily increasing, until now there are several relics including one which is alleged to be the blood of St John the Baptist.

It would seem, therefore, that the production of this phenomenon is not beyond the bounds of a physical explanation, and the inability to advance a completely satisfactory explanation at the present time may be a measure only of the incompleteness of the scientific investigation.   ILLUSTRATION: page 260
September 19th

JARLATH   *Sixth Century*
Not to be confused with his namesake who was a disciple of St Patrick, he founded a monastery at Cluain Fois, near Tuam, of which he was abbot-bishop.
June 6th

JASON   *First Century*
He seems to have been the Jason mentioned in Acts 17: 5–9 at whose house St Paul stayed in Salonika. In legend, he is venerated as an evangelist and a martyr.
July 12th

JEREMY, *see* Elias, Jeremy and their Companions.

JEROME   *c. 342–420*
Jerome was born about 342 at Stridon near Aquileia, in the border area between Dalmatia, Pannonia and Italy. His full name was Eusebius Hieronymus Sophronius. He seems to have belonged to a well-to-do family, and he received a very good literary and rhetorical

education, of the sort usual for young men of the upper classes in the ancient world, first at Stridon and then under the famous grammarian Donatus at Rome. This education left a deep mark upon him. He learnt to write an admirable, pure and vigorous Latin, and acquired a passionate love for the Classics which never left him, though he came to regard it as a temptation, as his account (in a letter to Eustochium) of a dream he had while lying ill at Antioch shows; in it he was dragged before the divine judgement-seat, accused of being a Ciceronian, not a Christian, and severely beaten. The rhetorical training which he received (we do not know under what masters) after he left Donatus also left its mark upon him. Most of the Fathers and other Christian writers of the ancient world had the same sort of education in rhetoric and consequently acquired a persistent tendency to rhetorical exaggeration and the oversharpening of controversial points; but the effect of this kind of training on a person of Jerome's explosive temperament was particularly unfortunate. He would, perhaps, have had less trouble in life, have made fewer enemies, and kept more friends, if he had not so thoroughly acquired a skill in polemical rhetoric based on a deep study of those masters of abuse and insult, the great Roman orators and satirists.

Jerome was brought up as a Christian, and seems always to have taken his religion seriously. He was not baptized till he was in his nineteenth year (on Easter Day, 366, at Rome), but this, at that period, was not at all unusual. When visiting Trier, after he had finished his studies at Rome, he gained some knowledge of the ascetic way of life (perhaps brought there by the exiled St Athanasius), and decided that this was where his vocation lay. He joined an informal community of priests and laymen at Aquileia in 370. This broke up after a few years as the result of some dispute whose details we do not know, and in 374 Jerome, with a group of friends, went east to the original homelands of Christian asceticism, and after staying for some time in Antioch went to live as a hermit in the desert of Chalcis, at that time a popular, and even perhaps a little over-crowded, eremitical resort. Here, where he had 'no other company but scorpions and wild beasts', he suffered greatly from ill-health and still more from temptations so strong that 'in my mind I often found myself among groups of dancing girls', and he lamented that 'before a man thus prematurely dead in his flesh still raged the fires of lust'. To control his imagination, when his bodily austerities failed to do so, he set himself to learn Hebrew, so starting on his real life-work as a scholar devoted to the interpretation of the Scriptures.

He returned to Antioch in 378 and went on to Constantinople to study the Scriptures under the great Greek theologian and preacher St Gregory Nazianzen.

In 382 he went to Rome and became secretary to Pope Damasus. It is this episode in his life that misleadingly causes him to be represented in pictures as a cardinal; a papal secretary at that time was not a Cardinal Secretary. Here he started his serious work on the Scriptures by revising the existing Latin versions of the Gospels and the Psalms. He also vigorously encouraged the movement towards the ascetic life which was then developing among some of the great ladies of Rome. This aroused opposition among some of the Roman clergy, whom he attacked, with their lady friends, in the most picturesquely intemperate language: 'What are rouge and paint doing on the face of a Christian? These poultices of lust are signs of an impure mind. How can a woman be said to weep for her sins when her tears make furrows on her painted cheeks? What can she expect from Heaven when, in supplication, she lifts up a face that its creator wouldn't recognize?' In consequence of such rebukes he became extremely un-popular, and after the death of St Damasus in 384 retired again to the east.

A group of Roman ladies who had been living the religious life under his direction followed him, headed by St Paula and her daughter St Eustochium, and they settled down in a group of convents near the Basilica of the Nativity at Bethlehem. Here Jerome spent the rest of his life as happily and peacefully as was possible for him. He engaged in frequent and vigorous contro-versy: one of his controversies, that over the teaching of Origen, led to a permanent break with his oldest and closest friend Rufinus. But the great work of his later life was that for which he had prepared himself in the desert of Chalcis and which he had already begun at Rome, the preparation of his Latin version of the Scriptures. It is on this that his authority in the Catholic church rests, and it is this that provides the best evidence for his holiness: for to produce a great translation of the Bible which is lastingly acceptable to Christians needs a deep spirituality and an utter devotion to God and his Word as well as profound and wide-ranging scholarship.

The whole of the Latin Bible called the Vulgate was either translated or worked over by St Jerome, with the exception of the books of Wisdom, Ecclesiasticus, Baruch, and the two books of Machabees. He made a second revision of the Psalms besides that already mentioned which he made at Rome, and it is this second revision which is included in the Vulgate and generally used in the Divine office. The Vulgate has been adopted by the Catholic church as her official text, but this does not imply that it is to be preferred to the original or that other versions are excluded.

St Jerome died peacefully at Bethlehem on September 30th, 420. St Paula and St Eustochium had died before him. His body was buried with theirs under the church of the Nativity, but was afterwards taken to Rome and is now in St Mary Major's.

September 30th   ILLUSTRATION: facing page 256

JEROME EMILIANI   1481–1537

Founder of the Clerks Regular of Somascha, he was ordained in 1518 after serving in the Venetian army. He devoted himself to the care of orphans, of whom he is the patron, and is said to have been the first to teach doctrine by means of set questions and answers.

July 20th

JOACHIM

The husband of St Anne (*q.v.*) and father of our Lady.

August 16th   ILLUSTRATION: facing page 273

JOACHIMA DE VEDRUNA   1783–1854

At the age of thirty-three, after seventeen years of married life, Joachima was left a widow with six children; but by 1826 she had founded the Carmelites of Charity to teach the young and nurse the sick. Before she died, foundations were made throughout her native Catalonia. She was canonized on April 12th, 1959.

August 28th

JOAN ANTIDE-THOURET   1765–1826

The life of Joan Antide Thouret spans the French Revolution, and her life's work consisted principally in re-endowing the church in France with sisters of charity. The daughter of a tanner, she went at the age of twenty-two as a novice to the Sisters of Charity (founded by St Vincent de Paul). The revolutionaries closed the house and suppressed the order before she could take her vows (she was chased over the convent wall by a militiaman who broke her rib with a blow from his rifle butt), and she returned home where she undertook nursing of the sick and managed to organize worship in secret, enabling priests to say mass and administer the sacraments. For a time she had to take refuge in Switzerland but, with the coming of better days, returned to Besançon where she opened a free girls' school.

Slowly the work developed, and she found herself at the head of a religious establishment which grew gradually into a Congregation of nuns. She was called to Naples to take charge of a hospital (known as Regina Coeli) with a thousand beds; with this foothold in Italy her Congregation spread rapidly there. The archbishop of Besançon was by no means pleased that the little Congregation was no longer merely a diocesan one, and, with the intention of keeping the Besançon houses entirely under his own jurisdiction, cut them off from their foundress and forbade her to have anything to do with them; the sisters were not even allowed to communicate with her.

Mother Thouret endured this trial with great patience and forbearance, and in the last three years of her life busied herself over Italian foundations; at her death,

which occurred in Naples, the 'Daughters of Charity under the Protection of St Vincent de Paul' already possessed one hundred and twenty-six Italian houses.

August 25th

JOAN ELIZABETH BICHIER des AGES   1773–1838

One of a group of saints who worked for the revival of religion in France after the Revolution, Joan Elizabeth Bichier was born at the Château des Ages in Poitou in 1773; she was thus in her seventeenth year on the outbreak of the French Revolution. She gave herself to a life of prayer and good works, looking after the poor and relieving suffering of all kinds in those troublous times. During the Terror religion went underground, and Joan Elizabeth held secret meetings at her house for prayer and religious instruction of the neighboring peasants, doing the best she could in the absence of a priest. It was thus that she met St Andrew Hubert Fournet, who was ministering in secret in the neighboring villages. Under his direction she collected together a few companions and, with the coming of better times, they all took the religious vows. Serene in manner, forthright yet humble, always busy yet always at peace, she transformed what had been intended as a local undertaking for charitable work and education of the poor into an important congregation with several houses. At the death of the foundress, in 1838, there were ninety-nine houses, and, at the present time, the Sisters of St Andrew (as she liked to call them after St Andrew Hubert Fournet's patron) or the Daughters of the Cross (their official title) are to be found all over the world.

August 26th

JOAN FRANCES de CHANTAL   1572–1641

She was born Joan Françoise Fremyot on January 23rd at Dijon, the daughter of a president of the parliament of Burgundy. She was the active and capable housekeeper of a great household before she became the founder and superior of an order of contemplative nuns.

At twenty she was married to a local nobleman, the Baron de Chantal. He was good and kind, and the marriage was a happy one; she had the distinction and presence of a great lady, and she possessed intelligence and good humor too. Though she performed her rôle in the society of the neighborhood her mind was elsewhere. Though she would entertain on her husband's behalf, she received visitors with reserve during his absences and was observed to wear dresses which were noticeably less fine. Then she would devote herself to prayer and to exploring the disturbing feeling that God had chosen her life for some great service.

After eight years of marriage she lost her husband in a hunting accident. Her only desire now was to live a life of prayer, but everything seemed to be in the way of it. There were her four children to bring up; she was the guest of a difficult father-in-law; or else she was acting as hostess for her father in Dijon. Also she had put herself in the hands of a tyrannical and obtuse director who wearied her flesh and spirit and would not let her seek advice elsewhere. She dreamed of a perfect and understanding director and at last she found one in St Francis of Sales; she attended his sermons at Dijon in 1604; they were introduced at the house of her brother. It was as if Francis too had found someone he was seeking; he had had a vision of a new order of nuns which would be led by a widow.

Francis found a great soul whose splendid simplicity did not realize how far she had progressed in the life of contemplation. Later when Mme de Chantal experienced the full influence of the mysticism of the Spanish Carmel through Mother Mary of the Trinity and others met in Dijon, she found that they had little to teach her: they could only explain the privileges that she had been granted by God.

Francis moved with sympathy and discretion. He wanted to be absolutely sure of the vocation of his charge. They met again at St Claude in his diocese; then after a decisive interview at Annecy in June 1610 the Congregation of the Visitation was founded. It was intended to meet the needs of those who desired a religious life but were not physically or temperamentally able to withstand the stringent demands of contemporary enclosed orders. At first its aims included tending the poor and the sick; but under the inspiration of its foundress it moved naturally towards a more strictly contemplative form of life, and its charter was revised to this end in 1615.

St Joan de Chantal is a saint of prayer; she speaks of 'that pure capacity to receive the spirit of God which suffices for all method'; but because she attained to the high flights of Mary through a hard apprenticeship to the duties of Martha she is an inspiration to all who labor at reconciling practical life and devotion. She was canonized in 1767.

August 21st

JOAN of ARC   1412–1431

Joan of Arc was born at Domrémy, in Champagne, in January 1412, the youngest of five children born to Jacques d'Arc, who, though a peasant, farmed his own land. She was a child like any other, taught by her mother the skills a woman needed, but untroubled with book-learning; remarkable only for her early and intense love of prayer, which yet did not prevent her playing the usual children's games round the village 'fairy tree'. She grew up against the chaotic background of the wars between France and the English and Burgundian alliance,

and though Domrémy lay alongside Burgundian territory it had always been loyal to the French. When she was about thirteen there came the first of those experiences which she was afterwards to call her voices: to begin with, it was a voice only, but later, light, and later still, presences manifested themselves whom she knew to be St Michael, St Margaret and St Catherine. Like St Teresa of Avila, she was reluctant to talk of these things. Little by little her apparently preposterous mission was defined, and by May 1428 she was fully persuaded that she must now act in the king's affairs, and that, initially, this meant tackling Robert Baudricourt, who commanded at Vaucouleurs nearby. Her reception was coldly hostile, and he sent her packing to her father, suggesting a whipping for good measure.

At home again, the summer wore on; and the worse the war went for France the more insistently the voices pressed her; so back to Vaucouleurs she came in the New Year, and persisted until at last Baudricourt let her go to try her luck at Chinon where the Dauphin lay with his court. Frivolously, Charles disguised himself to fox her, but it was at his feet that she knelt without hesitation on entering. She had come, she announced, to raise the siege of Orleans and to get him crowned at Rheims; Charles, excusably, hesitated and despatched her to Poitiers for ecclesiastical examination, but after rigorous inquiry it was agreed that there was nothing heretical in her claims. Back at Chinon, she chose her standard – a figure of God the Father, with fleur-de-lys and the words 'Jesus Maria' superimposed – and wearing boy's clothes she went off to Blois with the Duc d'Alençon, de Boussac, de Retz, La Hire and de Xantrailles; her men, she insisted, were to confess and to prepare themselves spiritually before battle, and so, to the chant of the *Veni Creator*, she marched on Orleans and entered it on April 30th. By May 8th the English had lost the ring of forts around the city and the siege had been raised, though Joan herself had been wounded by a stray arrow. Her idea was to consolidate these gains with the swift coronation she felt to be essential, but in Chinon she found Charles laggard and the archbishop of Rheims and La Trémouille, the favorite, openly hostile. It was at least decided that the French forces should attack along the Loire and a succession of quick assaults culminated in the brilliant victory of Patay, and so laid open the road to Rheims. On July 16th, 1429, Charles was solemnly crowned there, with Joan standing near grasping her standard for, as she justly observed, since it had endured the tribulation, it was only fair that it should share the honor.

Joan advised in advance on Paris, but the king continued to vacillate and gave the English time to build up their defences; the half-hearted attack was unsuccessful, Joan herself was wounded and the battle called off. The psychological effect was bad, for her invincibility was now in question, and the struggle dwindled into an armistice with the Burgundians; Joan, sadly, laid her arms upon the altar of St Denis and went away. But at the end of March 1430 she was around Compiègne, skirmishing with the English forces, and here, just as her voices had foretold, she was taken prisoner when her retreat was cut off. Her actual captor was Jean de Luxembourg, who would have accepted a ransom, but Charles made no effort to free her; and after one desperate effort to escape she was eventually handed over to the English: in Rouen she was guarded night and day by English soldiers – never alone and no other woman near.

The English could hardly execute her for defeating them in battle, so they contrived to have her tried for heresy by one of their supporters, Cauchon, bishop of Beauvais. He cross-examined her daily, but her replies were made always with an epic simplicity and an orthodoxy as unshakable as it was docile. Since she was on trial for heresy, none of the consolations of religion were permitted – no mass, no sacraments – and there is a story that on her return one day from the pitiless inquisition she knelt weeping outside a church she was not allowed to enter. The trial itself was a mockery, with the judges urged to hurry up and earn their reward and the result a foregone conclusion. Joan held out heroically, refusing to betray her mission and her voices, with an almost miraculous wisdom, but in the end they wore her down and some kind of retraction was obtained; but almost at once she withdrew it, dressed herself like a boy again, and was finally condemned by thirty-seven judges on May 29th as a relapsed heretic and handed over to the secular arm for sentence. On May 30th she was at last allowed to make her confession and receive communion, and then hustled to the stake in the market place of Rouen. She asked for a cross – one was roughly made from the faggots and on this she fixed her gaze until she died, calling upon the name of Jesus until the last: an English soldier standing by said, 'We have burned a saint.' With the utmost haste her ashes were thrown into the Seine before nightfall, lest there should be more trouble.

The French, who had done nothing to help, attempted no intervention, and Charles appeared conveniently to have forgotten her. All seemed over. Yet by February 1450 the now triumphant Charles had, from Rouen, ordered an inquiry to be made into the Maid's trial, on the grounds that it was invalid both in law and equity. This inquiry, and a second, two years later, both came to nothing, though both pronounced favorably; but a third, initiated by Callixtus III, opened in November 1455 in Paris at Notre Dame, and it proceeded until, in February 1456, it issued its findings that the previous sentence was 'full of fraud and deceit, totally contrary to both law and equity' and that it was now 'broken and annulled'. Joan was completely rehabilitated by both church and state; and she was declared Blessed in April 1909, and was canonized by Pope Benedict XV in 1920. Her feast is on May 30th, and the second Sunday in May is kept as the 'Fête Jeanne d'Arc' in France, whose secondary patron she is.

Joan of Arc, like Francis of Assisi, is a saint who has been extravagantly romanticized, and mostly for the wrong reasons, though the romance is certainly there. Here was this very young girl, called out of her pastoral solitude by supernatural voices to get her king crowned and lead his armies to victory; her defeat, martyrdom and final triumphant rehabilitation all bear the marks of the forlorn hope that sets the heart afire, but the important thing is that the final apotheosis was due, not to the victory, but to the simplicity of her burning love of God. 'It is a pity', wrote Jean Anouilh, 'but that's how it is.'   ILLUSTRATION: page 261
May 30th

JOAN of LESTONNAC   † 1640
A niece of the essayist Montaigne, Joan de Lestonnac joined the Cistercians after the death of her husband. The life was too hard for her, and she eventually founded the Congregation of Notre Dame, mainly to educate girls and counteract the Calvinism rife in her native Bordeaux.
February 2nd

JOAN of VALOIS   1464–1505
Joan, the second daughter of Louis XI, King of France, and Charlotte of Savoy, was born on April 23rd, 1464. At the age of two months she was betrothed to Louis, Duke of Orleans, and the marriage took place in 1476. There is no doubt that it was invalid, for Louis of Orleans married her in fear of his life if he did not comply with the king's orders to do so. Joan was by no means a prepossessing figure: she was hunch-backed, lame and pock-marked. On her husband's succession to the throne he obtained a declaration that the marriage was invalid. Joan, therefore, was not to be queen of France; she was given instead the title of Duchess of Berry. 'If so it is to be, praised be the Lord,' was her remark on this occasion. And there, really, is the basis of her holiness and the spiritual testament that she left in the Order of the Annunciation which she founded; by her choice of name for her nuns she emphasized the parallel between our Lady's 'Be it done to me . . .' and her own 'If so it is to be . . .'

All her life she met with opposition and countered it with such gentle words as these. There were difficulties without number. The pope seemed unwilling to give his approval, though Louis XII approved readily enough, thinking perhaps that Joan, bound by vows, would be less likely to upset the verdict given in the suit of nullity; his fears were groundless, and in any case directly after the verdict he had married Anne of Brittany. There were difficulties arising from Joan's character; she was inclined to be autocratic with her nuns, impatient at their slow progress. The foundation was made at Bourges, and the remains of the house may still be seen there. At the time of the French Revolution there were fifty 'Annonciade' convents in France; now there are but two, and one in England.

Joan died at the age of forty-one, on February 4th, 1505. Misfortune followed her after her death; the Huguenots ransacked the monastery at Bourges; her body was burned. It would be interesting to study the parallel between the romantic poetry of the period and the terms employed by Joan in her writings, which breathe a knightly spirit. The statutes of the Annonciades are quite chevaleresque in tone, and it may be recalled that the annunciation figured on Joan of Arc's banner. It was a theme dear to the Valois.

After all these years it is to be wondered how this unhappy, deformed woman, a pawn in the intrigues of Louis XI, rejected by Louis XII, so much the woman of another very different age, can have any significance for our own. One lesson of her life may be emphasized: her insistence on patience and peace. Both are obvious all through her life; her devotion to peace is found exemplified in the means that she adopted to propagate it, a confraternity, 'the Order of Peace', attached to the order of nuns. She lays down in its rules how its members, with peace in their hearts, on their lips, and working for it among those who are at enmity, shall themselves establish it. Above all they must pray for peace, and here is another echo from Charles of Orleans:

> Pray for peace, the true treasure of joy,
> Pray, you prelates and men of good life . .

St Joan of Valois was canonized in 1950.
February 4th

JOANNICUS † 846
Born in Bithynia, he was a soldier until the age of forty, when he retired to Mount Olympus. He became a monk at Eraste, near Brusa, was a fearless opponent of the iconclastic emperors, and trained many famous monks, including St Euthymius the Thessalonian.
November 4th

JOHN, *see* Antony, Eustace and John.

JOHN, *see* Cyrus and John.

JOHN I † 526
He succeeded St Hormisdas as pope in 523. His lack of success on a mission to the Emperor Justin I at Constantinople aroused the suspicions of Theodoric the Goth (who was then ruling Italy), and John was imprisoned at Ravenna.
May 27th

JOHN III, *see* Alexander, John III and Paul IV.

JOHN and PAUL *Fourth Century*
Their relics are housed in the church of SS Giovanni e Paolo on the Coelian Hill in Rome, which is alleged to have been built on the site of their house. We know little more than that they were Romans and martyrs, although it is alleged that they were brothers and officers attached to the royal household.

Excavations beneath the church have revealed the rooms of an ancient house, a chapel containing the tomb of a martyr or martyrs, and frescoes painted in the fifth century, depicting the martyrdom of two men and a woman and other scenes difficult to interpret.
June 26th

JOHN BAPTIST de la SALLE 1651–1719
This saint is the patron of teachers, his great achievement having been to provide a system of education for the common people at a time when the poor were grossly neglected; not merely by founding charity schools, a thing which had been attempted countless times before only to end in repeated failure, but by creating a body of trained teachers, and thus setting them on the only possible basis which guaranteed success.

It was not by inclination, but solely by chance that he was led to take up this work. Indeed his family background and early training seemed hardly to have prepared him for it. Born in Rheims on April 30th, 1651, the eldest son of an aristocratic family, he inherited the rank and fortune of his parents, which set a gulf between him and the teeming masses of the poor. At sixteen, while he was pursuing a course of classical studies at the Collège des Bons Enfants, he became a canon of Rheims, and seemed to be marked out for a successful career in the church. He subsequently studied at Saint Sulpice and the Sorbonne for the priesthood, and was ordained at the age of twenty-seven. Up to this point nothing denoted what his mission was to be, and he himself had no inkling of it. But it was shortly after this that he was asked to co-operate in establishing some charity schools in his native town, and this led him to take charge of the teachers, to bring them into his own home and to train them. Little by little he became further involved in the work until he began to realize that everything pointed to his being the chosen instrument of Providence for the creation of a system of Christian education for the poor, whose ignorance and depravity were the disgrace of this 'splendid century', so remarkable for its achievements in every other sphere.

As he had made the will of God the guiding principle of his life, he decided to give himself up completely to this task, resigning his canonry and giving away his fortune in order to be on the same footing as the teachers with whom he lived. In so doing he aroused the anger of his relatives and incurred the derision of his class-minded compatriots, but this in no way made him alter his resolution. In 1684 he transformed his group of schoolmasters into a religious community, under the name of Brothers of the Christian Schools, and this was the origin of the order which continues to this day and is spread all over the world. So that his order might confine itself solely to the work of teaching, he laid down that no brother might become a priest and that no priest might join the order. This rule is still observed. The first years were marked by poverty and hardship, but these were cheerfully endured, thanks to the example of self-abnegation and extraordinary power of leadership shown by de la Salle, who vowed that he would live on bread alone, if necessary, rather than abandon the work he had begun.

The religious and professional training of his brothers became his chief care, but he saw that he would never be able to satisfy all the requests he received for teachers unless he undertook the formation of secular school-masters as well, so he organized a training college for some forty youths in Rheims in 1687; the first instance of such an institution in the history of education.

After opening schools in a number of neighboring towns, in addition to those in Rheims itself, he went to Paris in 1683 to take over a school in the parish of St Sulpice, and there he established his headquarters. In the capital his work spread rapidly, and before long the brothers were teaching over 1,100 pupils. In Paris, too, he founded another training college, with a charity school attached, and organized a Sunday academy, or continuation school for youths already employed. When the exiled monarch, James II, entrusted fifty Irish youths to his care, he arranged for special courses to be given them to suit their needs.

The scope of his work was now such that it aroused the bitter antagonism of the writing masters and the teachers of the Little Schools, who saw their fee-paying pupils drifting into his free schools, and they brought law-suits against him. His schools were pillaged, and he found himself condemned and forbidden to open training colleges or charity schools anywhere in the Paris area. As a result he was excluded for a time from the capital, but by now his brothers were established in other localities, notably in Rouen, Avignon and Chartres, so that the decrees against him failed to ruin his work. Indeed from this time on, his communities multiplied all over France: in Marseilles, Calais, Boulogne, Mende, Grenoble, Troyes and other places. In Rouen he founded two important institutions: a fee-paying boarding school for the sons of bourgeois, who desired an education superior to that of the primary school but more practical than that of the 'classical' colleges; and a reformatory school for youthful delinquents and young men detained under *lettres de cachet*. Both proved very successful, and were significant forerunners of modern institutions of a similar kind.

In 1709 he established a third training college, at St Denis, but this lasted only a couple of years, after which it had to be closed as a result of an unfortunate law-suit.

De la Salle spent the last years of his life in Rouen, completing the organization of his institute, writing the Rule of the brothers in its definitive form, and composing *Meditations* and a *Method of Mental Prayer*. On Good Friday, April 9th, 1719, he died.

His brothers, already established in twenty-two towns of France and in Rome, now expanded their work rapidly. In 1725 they received a bull of approbation of their institute from the pope and letters patent from the king granting them legal recognition. The Revolution ruined their work in France, but they were by now established in Switzerland and Italy, so that they were able to survive this catastrophe and returned to France when more favorable conditions prevailed under Napoleon. Today they number over 15,000 and conduct educational institutions of every kind all over the world. In the United States alone there are some 2,000 brothers in five different Provinces.

De la Salle's pedagogical system is outlined in *The Conduct of Schools*, which he composed in 1695, and which is now considered an educational classic. It shows clearly his practical turn of mind and his essentially religious approach to the education of children. He wrote also several school manuals, notably *The Rules of Good Behaviour* and *The Duties of a Christian*, which proved very popular and went through over a hundred editions.
May 15th ILLUSTRATION: page 262

JOHN BAPTIST ROSSI   1698–1764
Born at Voltaggio near Genoa, as a priest in Rome he worked for forty years among the poor, and especially among cattle-drovers and homeless women of all kinds. He was in great demand as a confessor, and he once said that the shortest road to Heaven lay in guiding others thither through the confessional.
May 23rd

JOHN BERCHMANS   1599–1621
The son of a shoemaker, he was born at Diest in Brabant, joined the Society of Jesus – walking from Antwerp to Rome to do so – and was only twenty-two when he died. Although he died in Rome and was hardly known to his fellow countrymen, well over twenty-four thousand copies of his portrait were published in Flanders within a few years of his death. He was canonized in 1888.
November 26th

John Melchior Bosco was the son of peasant parents of Piedmont. He was born on August 16th, 1815, just on two months after the battle of Waterloo, into a Europe that was still bleeding from the results of the Napoleonic wars and at the same time beginning to feel the consequences of the industrial revolution. These two factors were largely the cause of most of the evils of his period, and his life was devoted to remedying them, particularly in so far as they affected the young. His early days were spent at Becchi, his birthplace, a small hamlet near Chieri and some twelve miles east of Turin, on the small farm run by his mother with the help of her sons, after the death, in 1817, of his father, Francis Bosco.

He was a devout boy. At the age of nine he experienced a dream which was to affect him for the rest of his life. It was in fact the first of several which, occurring at intervals until shortly before his death, were distinguished by their vividness and prophetic nature. This first dream in which he saw wild beasts turned into gentle lambs and unruly disobedient children becoming well behaved, showed him what he must do in life. Ever afterwards he was convinced that he must work for boys as priest and educator. He obtained his schooling at Chieri, working in his spare time to provide board and lodging, and, after a seminary course during which his considerable intellectual talents and astounding memory were revealed, he was ordained priest.

At the hospice known as the 'Convitto Ecclesiastico', where he now went for a course in pastoral theology, he was taught by St Joseph Cafasso, and was not uninfluenced by St Joseph Cottolengo, both of whom – the first by the provision of an educated and zealous clergy, the second by the foundation of a large hospital for the poor and needy – were endeavoring to cope with the urgent problems of the times and place. Visits to the local gaols, at the instance of Don Cafasso, showed Don Bosco the magnitude of the problem represented by the many youths whom destitution, the absence of home influence and religious instruction brought rapidly to their present sorry plight.

Don Bosco was not only aware of these youths, others in the city sought him out, as boys were to do all his life long, and he began first at the Convitto and then elsewhere the Sunday meetings which grew into the 'festive oratories' at which religion and recreation, instruction and worship were so blended that none of it was unattractive. It was a full-time occupation for numbers were continually increasing. Many youths were coming into the city to find work at the extensive building then going on, and families were moving in from the country, attracted by the opportunities to be found in the expanding capital.

On leaving the Convitto, Don Bosco, after a short time as chaplain at a girls' orphanage, was able to give his whole time to the service of these lads. After overcoming numerous difficulties he was able to purchase a small house in the quarter of the city known as Valdocco, and there he founded the Oratory of St Francis of Sales – a hostel for apprentices and schoolboys. Soon the hostel had become a training center and a school – the apprentices and boys no longer went out to work or class; they were taught under Don Bosco's roof. A church was built, the buildings were enlarged, a great basilica of our Lady, Help of Christians, rose up to dominate the whole of that part of Turin. In the meantime Don Bosco had founded the Salesian Congregation and later, in collaboration with St Mary Mazzarello, a Congregation of nuns to do similar work for girls. With the gradual expansion of the Salesians he undertook work in France and Spain and sent some of his men as missionaries to the Indians of Patagonia. When he died he had under his charge some seven hundred boys in Turin, numerous houses in Italy, all with their 'festive oratories' in addition to other educational work, together with houses abroad. But it was no longer boys out of prison that were being dealt with; Don Bosco's efforts were preventing their being sent there by training them to earn their livings and in the practice of Christianity.

John Bosco is one of those saints who seem to disappear behind their immense achievements; we seek the man and find only what he has done. What was his secret? He possessed the common attributes of the saint – the practice of heroic virtue, assiduous prayer and the rest – but the secret of much of his work, in one sense the modality of his holiness, was his love of youth. Boys took to him because they sensed immediately that he loved them. Of his educational system he himself says that he had none, that he improvised as he went along. That is true, but his guiding principle was love and respect for the boy as a person, with the consequence that he evolved a system of 'preventive' rather than repressive discipline; he insisted, too, long before St Pius X's decree, on frequent communion but left it to each boy's conscience and attraction, and rigidly excluded 'general communions' and the like where children are almost herded to the sacraments.

He was beset by urgent tasks of all kinds, preaching, running his Congregation, the constant need to raise money, the difficulty of contending with official (both lay and ecclesiastical) opposition, delicate negotiations with an anti-clerical government on behalf of the Holy See; yet he was never put out, never impatient, always smiling, ready to help a boy, hear a confession, go to a sick bed. He never slept more than five hours a night, and often less; but the real secret of his calm, unhurried method of dealing with the many problems that beset him was the realist approach to life that he derived from his peasant origins and his great trust in Providence. 'What you have to do,' he once remarked, 'is to take the burden fairly and squarely on your shoulders; it will soon settle down and you will hardly feel it.' The miracles with which he is credited, and some are certainly authentic, were all due to that trust of his in Providence: it never failed him.

His penance he found in daily life – the constant interruptions and obstacles to be overcome, the daily discomfort of varicose veins, eczema, failing sight. Not long before his death he stumped France to obtain funds for his good works and soon afterwards went to Spain. He died in Turin in 1888; he was quite worn out. His body rests in the great basilica that he built beside those of St Dominic Savio, his pupil, and St Mary Mazzarello, his collaborator.   ILLUSTRATION: page 263
January 31st

JOHN CALYBITES   *Fifth Century*
He left his wealthy family to enter the monastery at Gomon on the Bosphorous founded by St Alexander. The legend concerning him seems to have been confused with that of St Alexis.
January 15th

JOHN CASSIAN   *c. 360–433*
A Rumanian, he became a monk on a visit to Palestine, and lived as a solitary in the Egyptian desert. He moved on to Constantinople, becoming a disciple of St John Chrysostom, and then to Marseilles, where he founded two communities. He introduced into western Europe the ideals of eastern asceticism, and the influence of his writings on St Benedict of Nursia was very considerable.
July 23rd

JOHN CHRYSOSTOM   *c. 347–407*
John Chrysostom was born at Antioch in Syria; his father was a commander in the imperial army, but he died soon after the boy's birth. His devout mother saw to it that John had a good education, and the young man felt himself increasingly drawn to a life of prayer and solitude; on his mother's death he withdrew into the desert, where he remained for some years. His health began to fail under the austerities of this regime, and he returned to Antioch ready for whatever he might be called upon to do.

In 381 he was ordained a deacon, and in 386, priest; and he began his preaching. He gave hundreds of sermons and homilies, a good number of which have come down to us, and he gained widespread influence. In an age when the spoken word had the power which the printed word has acquired in the modern world, Chrysostom gave his hearers books full of instruction, information, advice, warning, consolation. His sermons covered many fields, and often were highly topical:

if some great event, disastrous or happy, was engrossing the citizens of Antioch they would flock to hear John's commentary on it. Perhaps much of his power may be ascribed to the directness of 'attack' that kept his learning or advice always alive and immediate: 'Please listen to me – you are not paying attention. I am talking to you about the Holy Scriptures, and you are watching people lighting the lamps.'

In 398 Chrysostom was consecrated archbishop of Constantinople. Constantinople was a city of extraordinary passions, turbulence, intrigue and corruption. Chrysostom continued his sermons, drawing the moral when the city had proved itself more than usually hotheaded, inveighing especially against the misuse of riches and the evil habits of the wealthy, of which Constantinople exhibited some striking examples. He set himself to purify the archbishop's household, tainted by too much concern with dignity and pomp; he dealt firmly with irregularities among the clergy, and firmly too with heretics of whom, especially Arians, there were many, though he remained adamant on the point that a heretic must never be put to death. The money that he saved on his own household went to the founding of hospitals and to the needs of the poor. But his many good works were brought to an end by the contemporary curse of political and ecclesiastical faction.

The Empress Eudoxia, vain and spiteful, wished to revenge herself on the archbishop for some fancied slights, and she allied herself with the party of Archbishop Theophilus of Alexandria; they managed to obtain, from the Emperor, Chrysostom's banishment. He was sent first to Cucusus in Armenia, where the local bishop gave him glad hospitality. Pope St Innocent I sent a delegation to Constantinople to arrange a council to consider the business, but its members were insulted and thrown into prison, and orders were given that Chrysostom should be removed farther away. He was by now an old man, and he was hurried on the journey in all weathers with no pity. At last his strength gave out, he collapsed and was taken to the chapel of St Basiliscus near Comana in Cappadocia. And here, having received the Holy Mysteries, he died. In 438 the body of St John was brought back in solemn procession to Constantinople, the new Emperor and his sister doing penance for the sins of their parents.

'Chrysostom' signifies golden mouth, and it is for the eloquence and glory of his preaching that St John received this title. His name is also inextricably linked with the liturgy (that is, the mass) of St John Chrysostom, which is the one most commonly in use in the east; but to what extent, in fact, he shaped or developed it is a matter of some doubt. This in itself may have a certain significance; because St John Chrysostom is remembered even more as a person than as a preacher. He was a great figure, a living influence in his own time; and through his sermons, which often enough reveal a human impatience and excitement, his writings, and especially through his letters, we receive today a vivid impression of the man.

Cardinal Newman in his *Historical Sketches* said of him: 'I consider St Chrysostom's charm to lie in his intimate sympathy and compassionateness for the whole world, not only in its strength but in its weakness; in the lively regard with which he views everything that comes before him ... I speak of the discriminating affectionateness with which he accepts everyone for what is personal in him and unlike others.'

January 27th   ILLUSTRATION: page 264

JOHN CLIMACUS   *Seventh Century*

A learned abbot and great spiritual director he was a monk of Mount Sinai. Because of his notable work *The Ladder (Klimax) to Paradise*, which described the thirty degrees to religious perfection, his artistic attribute is a ladder.

March 30th

JOHN DAMASCENE   *c. 690–c. 749*

Brought up at the court of the Mohammedan ruler of Damascus, he succeeded his father as what might be called chancellor of the exchequer to the Caliph. He subsequently resigned to become a monk at Mar Saba near Jerusalem, John was a great opponent of the Iconoclasts, a poet and hymn-writer, and the author of a famous treatise, *Of the Orthodox Faith*, comparable to the *Summa* of St Thomas Aquinas.

A dubious legend relates that, while still in the service of the Caliph, he was falsely accused of treachery, and his right hand was cut off. It is for this reason that the Gospel of the man with the withered hand is used at his mass.

March, 27th

JOHN de BRÉBEUF, *see* Martyrs of North America.
ILLUSTRATION: page 161 (A)

JOHN de BRITTO   1647–1693

Nobly born, and highly favored by King Pedro II of Portugal, he became a Jesuit missionary in southern India.

Sir W. W. Hunter has this to say of these early Jesuit missionaries in his *Imperial Gazetteer of India*: '(they) became perfect Indians in all secular matters, dress, food, etc., and had equal success among all castes, high and low ... They brought the old Christian settlements of the Syrian rite into temporary communion with Rome.'

St John was martyred at Oriur near Ramuad, by order of the Rajah Raghunatha and was canonized in 1947.

February 4th

JOHN EUDES   1601–1680

St John Eudes was one of the outstanding figures of the counter-reformation in France. Born at Ri, near Argentan, he attended the Jesuit college in Caen, studied for the priesthood at the Paris Oratory and was ordained in 1625. His first labors as a priest took place among the victims of the plague that was then ravaging his native Normandy. He was much influenced by Bérulle, founder of the French Oratory and 'Apostle of the Incarnate Word', but left the Oratorians in 1643 to establish the Society of Jesus and Mary, a congregation of secular clergy familiarly known as the Eudists, whose special task was to be the education of priests and the giving of missions. A great preacher himself (during the course of his life he preached well over a hundred missions all over France), Eudes had recognized the people's need for good pastors. He had already (1641) founded the women's congregation of our Lady of Charity of the Refuge, for the spiritual care of fallen women. From this foundation the Good Shepherd order subsequently sprang.

But of all his activities the one that has perhaps had the most widespread influence in the church as a whole is his foundation of the public devotion to the Sacred Heart, an achievement which until the early years of this century was attributed principally to St Margaret Mary Alacoque, the Visitation and the Society of Jesus. The obscurity which for more than two centuries surrounded Eudes's priority in this field is attributed by Bremond in his magistral *Histoire littéraire du sentiment religieux en France* to the nefarious activities of the Jansenists, whose hostility Eudes incurred by his steadfast opposition to their harsh and narrow conception of a Christ who dies only for a small number of predestined elect. The Eudists as a whole were never tainted with Jansenism and did much to combat its influence. Eudes composed the mass and office of the Sacred Heart in 1668–9, and a feast of the Sacred Heart was first celebrated by Eudist communities on October 20th, 1672; the first of St Margaret Mary's revelations at Paray did not occur until December 27th, 1673, and the mass said in the Dijon Visitandines' chapel at their first public celebration of the Sacred Heart is clearly based on Eudes's mass. In the Beatification decree Pius X declared that John Eudes must be regarded as the father, doctor and apostle of the devotion to the Sacred Heart of Jesus and of its precursor, the devotion to the heart of Mary (Eudists celebrated a feast of the Holy Heart of Mary as early as 1648). The devotions founded by St John Eudes and St Margaret Mary have since merged into one, but it is possible to discern at the beginning differences of emphasis; for example, by 'the love of Jesus' Eudes understands above all the love of Jesus for his Father, while the Paray devotion was concerned primarily with the love of Jesus for men.

Bérulle tried to give theocentric mysticism a specifically Catholic color by making it Christocentric; his disciple Eudes moves one step further on, from contemplation of the person of Jesus as a whole to contemplation of the ultimate source of love in that person: the heart. All Eudes's ideas are already present in his *Royaume de Jésus* (1637). His vernacular style (he wrote several devotional works) tends to be rhetorical and diffuse; his best writing is to be found in the Latin of his office of the Sacred Heart. He died on August 19th, 1680, was beatified in 1909 and canonized in 1925.

August 19th

JOHN FISHER 1469–1535

John Fisher, born at Beverley, Yorkshire, was the son of a prosperous mercer who died in 1477. About 1482 the boy's mother sent him to Cambridge University where he distinguished himself as a scholar. He was ordained in 1491 on the title of his Fellowship of Michaelhouse (now incorporated in Trinity College). After studying theology for ten years, he took his D.D. in 1501, and was later recognized as one of the leading theologians of Europe.

His university soon discovered his gifts as an administrator; he held in turn the offices of proctor, vice-chancellor and chancellor, and in 1514 he received the unique distinction of being elected chancellor for life. It was in the course of his university duties that, in 1494, he first met the Lady Margaret Beaufort, mother of Henry VII. He became her confessor and advised her on the charitable uses of her great wealth. It was at his suggestion that a preachership was endowed at Cambridge and Readerships in Divinity in both universities. He was largely responsible for her decision to refound and endow Godshouse as Christ's College, and, after her death in 1509, he carried out her wishes in founding St John's College, to which he transferred lands given to him by the Lady Margaret.

He was made bishop of Rochester in 1504, and he ruled that poorest of sees for thirty years; he was a truly pastoral bishop, encouraging his priests by his manner of life and by his interest in their welfare. He was a noted and assiduous preacher, and he did all he could to provide well-instructed priests who could preach to the people.

It was due to his influence that Erasmus was brought to Cambridge as lecturer in Greek. He and Sir Thomas More became close friends of John Fisher, and there is a record of the three being together at Rochester in 1516. Sir Thomas More became High Steward of Cambridge University in 1525. He and John Fisher had been drawn closer together at this period by the call to combat the Lutheran heresy. The bishop wrote his *Confutatio* (1523) in Latin, a book for theologians by a theologian, which had a wide circulation on the continent; the layman wrote his *Dialogue Concerning Heresies* (1528) in English for the common reader. It may be noted that in his sermons and writings against heretics, John Fisher never used the abusive language of contemporary controversy; he relied on reason and persuasion to bring back the prodigals.

The year 1527 was fateful to England, for it was then that Henry VIII took the first steps towards seeking the annulment of his marriage with Catherine of Aragon. She had married his elder brother Arthur in 1501; he died six months later. Catherine always maintained that the marriage had not been consummated. A papal dispensation allowed Henry VIII to marry his brother's widow in 1509. The lack of a male heir turned his thoughts to the dissolution of his marriage; he argued that the papal dispensation had no validity. Cardinal Wolsey was instructed to seek the opinion of John Fisher, whose prestige as a man of holy life and of great learning gave exceptional weight to his views. After studying the problem thoroughly he came to the conclusion that the papal dispensation was valid, and therefore that Henry and Catherine were man and wife in the eyes of the church. From that position he never moved in spite of the pressure brought to bear on him by king and cardinal. He was not content with passive opposition, but in the legatine court set up to try the issue, and from the pulpit, he defended the queen, although he knew that Henry regarded opposition to his will as a form of treason.

An attempt to implicate John Fisher in the fate of the Nun of Kent failed; she had prophesied against the king. A more certain weapon was provided by the Act of Succession of 1534. This declared the king's marriage to Catherine void, and his subsequent marriage to Anne Boleyn to be lawful; the succession was settled on her children. All had to take an oath accepting the whole Act. When the oath was tendered to John Fisher he refused to take it; so did Sir Thomas More. Both were prepared to accept the succession as determined by Parliament, but not that part of the Act which implied a denial of the pope's authority, inasmuch as it declared the papal dispensation invalid.

On April 17th, 1534 Bishop John Fisher and Sir Thomas More were committed to the Tower. They were kept apart.

John Fisher was sixty-five years of age when he was imprisoned; he was suffering from a wasting sickness and was clearly nearing his end. Nothing shows the king's vindictiveness more than his relentless persecution of this aged man stricken by a fatal disease. On May 20th, 1535, the pope created John Fisher Cardinal-priest of the title of St Vitalis. This so infuriated the king that he hurried forward the proceedings against the new cardinal.

The Supremacy Act and a new Statute of Treason were passed while John Fisher and Sir Thomas More were in the Tower. Treason was now made to cover anything said against the king's titles, so that to refuse to recognize him as Supreme Head of the church of England became treason. Neither of the prisoners would give him that recognition, for to do so was to deny the authority of the pope. Each, however, was careful not to put that refusal in words that could be used against them; they begged to be excused. Many attempts were made to get them to say the fateful words. At length Richard Rich, the solicitor-general, visited John Fisher in the Tower and told him that the king 'for the satisfaction of his own conscience' wished to know the bishop's opinion on the Supremacy; Rich assured the prisoner that whatever he said would not be used against him but would remain private to the king. Thereupon John Fisher declared 'that the King was not, nor could be, by the law of God, Supreme Head of the church of England.' As a priest he could not refuse to answer a question of conscience, but he had fallen into a trap, and the words he had spoken were used against him at his trial on June 17th, 1535. In spite of his protest at this breach of trust, he was condemned as a traitor.

He was beheaded on Tower Hill on June 22nd, 1535. His naked corpse was left on the scaffold all day until it was hastily buried without ceremony in the nearby churchyard of All Hallows. His head was displayed on London Bridge until July 6th when it was thrown into the Thames to give place to the head of his fellow martyr. Sir Thomas More was buried within the church of St Peter ad Vincula within the Tower; at the same time the remains of John Fisher were removed to the same resting place.

John Fisher and Thomas More were beatified in 1886 and canonized in 1935. Their feast is kept jointly.

July 9th   ILLUSTRATION: page 265

JOHN FRANCIS REGIS   1597–1640

Although his work and fame are local, St John Francis Regis is one of the great figures of the counter-Reformation. Born in Languedoc, at Fontcouverte on January 1st, 1597, he was admitted to the Society of Jesus at Toulouse on November 8th, 1616. He spent almost all his short life preaching the faith in the wild, mountainous country of the Velay and Vivarais. This region, in common with the area further to the south, had suffered much in the wars of religion, and there had been many conversions to protestantism.

John Francis, a man of great austerity of life, adapted his apostolate to the needs of his time. In the words of Goyau, he preached 'from farm to farm . . . to souls one by one when he could not gather them into groups'. Like his great compatriot, St Vincent de Paul, he was not content with verbal preaching alone. He practised the corporal works of mercy to a heroic degree. His room was always full of clothes, furniture, odds and ends of all kinds which he had collected for the poor. One of the causes dearest to his heart and for which he worked unceasingly was the reclamation of prostitutes.

His forthrightness, intrepidity and courage inevitably raised up enemies against him. There were those who took scandal at his unusual methods; there were those of evil life who resented his condemnation of their ways. Even among the clergy of the Vivarais, those whom he reproached for infidelity to their vocation, banded together to impede his apostolate. He was delated to the bishop of Viviers and for a time he was 'under a cloud'.

But this trial was only temporary. In obedience to his religious superiors before whom he had laid plans for a great extension of his work – at one time he wished to join his fellow Jesuits of the Canadian mission – he continued his evangelization of the Vivarais. He never spared himself. During the last four months of his life, he heard ten thousand confessions. Exhausted by such labors, he died at La Louvesc on December 12th, 1640. He was beatified by Clement XI in 1716 and canonized by Clement XII in 1737.

A basilica was built above his tomb, which soon became and has ever since remained one of the great French centers of pilgrimage. Among the thousands who have come to this church high up in the mountains of the Ardèche, none is so well-known as St John Vianney, who at the grave of St John Francis prayed during a period of crisis in his own life.

The burning apostolic spirit of this great Jesuit still broods over the mountains and scattered villages of the land he reclaimed for the church. His work has endured, and the faith remains firm and secure in the Ardèche. His spirit lives on also in religious institutes which, although not founded by him, are inspired by his ideals and methods. Mention should be made in particular of the Nuns of the Cenacle, whose mother-house is at La Louvesc, and whose work for the instruction and education of the laity is so well known.

The problems of the apostolate in our own time are not dissimilar to those John Francis faced, and his combination of preaching and the corporal and spiritual works of mercy is as essential in the twentieth century as it was in the seventeenth.

June 16th

JOHN GOTO, *see* Martyrs of Japan.

JOHN GUALBERT   † 1073

Son of a Florentine nobleman, he set out to avenge his brother's murder. He met the murderer at last in a passage from which escape was impossible. With crossed arms, the man awaited his death, but, touched by the

image of the cross, John spared his life. He founded the Vallombrosan Benedictines, an austere congregation which still exists, at a place called 'Vallis Umbrosa' near Fiesole.
July 12th

JOHN JOSEPH of the CROSS　　　1654–1734
Born near Naples of prosperous parents, Carlo Gaetano Calosirto joined the Franciscans of the Alcantarine reform at the age of sixteen, taking the name of John Joseph of the Cross. He led an extremely ascetic life, was three times superior of the monastery of Piedimonte di Alife and finally provincial of the Italian Alcantarines. He is said to have worked many miracles during his lifetime.
March 5th

JOHN LALANDE, *see* Martyrs of North America.

JOHN LEONARDI　　　　　　　† 1609
Born at Lucca and inspired by the reforming zeal of the Counter-Reformation, St John was assisted by SS Philip Neri and Joseph Calasanctius to form a new order of secular priests to work among the sick and imprisoned. The order which is mainly confined to Italy is known as 'The Clerks Regular of the Mother of God'.
October 9th

JOHN NEPOMUCEN　　　　　　† 1393
He was vicar-general to the archbishop of Prague at the accession of King Wenceslaus IV. This king wanted to found a new bishopric at Kladrau by confiscating the revenues of the Benedictine abbey there, as soon as the old abbot was dead. He was forestalled by John Nepomucen, and, in his rage, the king killed him with his sword. There is no authority for believing the traditional story that the king killed him because he refused to break the seal of the confessional.
May 16th

JOHN of BERGAMO　　　　　† *c.* 690
Bishop of Bergamo, he was a vigorous opponent of the Arians.
July 11th

JOHN of BEVERLEY　　　　　† 721
St John was a Yorkshire youth of noble family. He was born some time about the middle of the seventh century and was sent to Canterbury to be educated in the remarkable circle surrounding Archbishop Theodore. He returned to the north where he became a monk of Whitby; he himself became a teacher and, in 687, bishop of Hexham. He later taught Bede and ordained him.

　　The see of Hexham had been carved out of the diocese of the Northumbrians during St Wilfrid's first exile; and, while Wilfrid's expulsion was undoubtedly unjust, the division of the vast diocese was necessary, so that John was forced to oppose Wilfrid's more extreme claims. John later became bishop of York, and thus laid himself open to the charge of usurpation by Wilfrid. John, however, retained the see. He founded a monastery at Beverley, where he retired in 718. He died there in 721, and his persistent reputation for sanctity caused his canonization in 1037.
May 7th

JOHN of BRIDLINGTON　　　　† 1379
An Augustinian of Bridlington, his shrine was famous in the middle ages, and he was one of the saints to whose intercession Henry V attributed his victory at Agincourt.
October 21st

JOHN of CAPISTRANO　　　　1386–1456
He joined the Franciscans at the age of thirty, after having been governor of Perugia and having married a daughter of one of its chief citizens. He was given a hard novitiate, but within ten years of his ordination in 1420 he was assisting St Bernardine of Siena to compose the differences between the party of reform and the opposition within the Franciscan order. He gained great renown as a preacher and in 1451 was sent to Bohemia to combat the Hussites. He died a few years later as a result of his exertions in the successful defence of Belgrade against the Turks.
March 28th

JOHN of CHINON　　　　*Sixth Century*
A Breton, he lived in Neustria, and he is also known in France as St Jean du Moustier, or Jean de Tours.
June 27th

JOHN of EGYPT　　　　　　† 394
He spent his last fifty years walled up in rocks above his birth-place, Lycopolis, now Asyut. His asceticism, his counsel, and his prophesies, particularly those concerning Theodosius I, enjoyed wide fame.
March 27th

JOHN of GOD　　　　　　† 1550
After a dissolute youth in the army John was stung by remorse and settled down in Granada to sell objects of piety. He was so affected by a sermon given by John of Avila that he was carried off to a lunatic asylum. Eventually he decided to devote himself to the care of the poor and the sick, and carried out this task with enthusiasm and surprising efficiency, founding the Brothers Hospitallers.
March 8th

JOHN of KANTI or CANTIUS　　1390–1473
Lives of John of Kanti (Kanti is near Oswiecim in Poland) are many but not entirely dependable. Nevertheless we have record of him as a holy and learned man who was both a distinguished university teacher and a benefactor of the poor. He came from a family of good position, and was sent to the University of Cracow,

where he did well. He was ordained priest, and appointed to a lectureship in the University. His academic life was however interrupted when jealous rivals managed to get him removed from his teaching post, and he was sent to labor as a parish priest. This caused him much distress, as he was both unused to this kind of work and weighed down by the feeling of its heavy responsibility. But he gradually won the love of his parishioners, who wept when, after some years, he left them to return to the University of Cracow as professor of Scripture. This post he held for the rest of his long life; and he became increasingly famous for his teaching, his humble and austere way of living and his spontaneous generosity to those in need. Perhaps his best lesson for us, especially in these days of increasing communication, lies in one of his favorite sayings to his pupils: 'Fight all false opinions, but let your weapons be patience, sweetness and love. Roughness is bad for your own soul and spoils the best cause.'

When he died St John was greatly mourned, and was already accounted a worker of miracles; but he was not canonized until 1767.
October 20th

JOHN of MATERA   † 1139
Born at Matera in the kingdom of Naples, he wandered through Italy to find a suitable place to settle as a hermit. After many trials, including charges of keeping hidden treasure and of heresy, he founded the Benedictine monastery of Pulsano.
June 20th

JOHN of MATHA   † 1213
A native of Provence, he was founder of the Trinitarians, whose original object was the redemption of Christians held captive by the Mohammedans. The further details of his life given in the traditional biography are almost certainly fictitious, as are the accounts of a reputed co-founder, St Felix of Valois, who never existed.
February 8th

JOHN of MEDA   † 1159
It is said, but with little authority, that this secular priest organized one of the orders of the Humiliati in Milan, adapting the Rule of St Benedict for laymen who, while living in the world, devoted themselves to penance and good works.
September 26th

JOHN of NICOMEDIA   † 303
Supposed to have torn down the decrees of Diocletian when they were displayed in his city, he was burned to death.
September 7th

JOHN of PANACA   Sixth Century
He came to the west while Monophysites were trou-

bling Syria. He founded an abbey at Spoleto, where he became abbot, and another near Pesaro.
March 19th

JOHN of REOMAY   Sixth Century
Summoned from Lérins to his native Langres to found Reomay Abbey, now Moutier-Saint-Jean, he was one of the pioneers of French monasticism.
January 28th

JOHN of SAHAGUN or of ST FACUNDO
† 1479
Ordained in 1445, John made a reputation as a preacher in Salamanca. After a severe operation he joined the Augustinians, and eventually became prior of the Salamanca house, maintaining its celebrated discipline by example rather than severity. He healed many feuds in society, and in his sermons was no respector of birth or position. He is said to have been poisoned by a woman whom he had denounced for living with some one else's husband.
June 12th

JOHN of the CROSS   1542–1591
Juan de Yepes was born at Fontiveros, near Avila, Spain, on June 24th 1542. His father worked as a weaver, having been cast off by his family of prosperous merchants for marrying beneath him. His mother was a saintly woman; left a widow soon after John's birth, she settled in Medina del Campo, where John went to school and worked in a hospital. He entered the Carmelite order there in 1563 and the following year was sent to the university at Salamanca. In 1567 he was ordained and, at Medina, first met St Teresa of Avila, who persuaded him to introduce her reform among the friars. This he did at the end of 1568. For several years he was engaged in this work and in acting as confessor to the nuns at Avila. The reform met with opposition and unreformed friars twice kidnapped him and locked him up, the second time for nearly nine months in Toledo, where he wrote some of his poetry. He escaped, and for several years ruled and founded reformed communities in the south of Spain. In 1588 he attended the first general chapter of the reformed friars in Madrid and was appointed prior of Segovia. Three years later he was deprived of his offices and moved south to Ubeda, where he died shortly afterwards.

John of the Cross is more renowned for his writings than for his life, which, apart from the sufferings inflicted on him by his cantankerous brethren in religion, and apart from his holiness and extraordinary sweetness of nature, is unremarkable. His books, which all deal with the development of mystical experience in the soul, have the peculiarity that they are written as prose commentaries on his poems. He is a remarkable prose stylist: clear, simple, acute, subtle, constantly illustrating his text with Scripture (a great part of which he must have had by heart). He is one of the three or four greatest lyrical poets of Spanish literature, though his output is small. His inspiration may not have been entirely original (this is controversial), but the finished product is unsurpassed. It is sometimes said that his poetry is merely the poetry of human love, but close study of the text convinces that human love is being used as the analogue of the action of the Holy Spirit on the soul truly seeking God. The fundamental contribution of John of the Cross to the doctrine of the spiritual life is, first, his exact treatment of the earliest stages of infused ('mystical') contemplation and, second, his clear, coherent exposition of the whole course of the interior life.

In *The Ascent of Mount Carmel*, he deals in detail with the ascetic purification of the soul which all who seek union with God must effect. By the use of his famous diagram of the ascent of Mount Carmel, he bids us always prefer 'not the thing which is easiest but that which is hardest, not the most pleasant but that which is least pleasant ... desiring to be stripped and emptied of everything the world can offer and to be poor for Christ's sake,' promising the soul which sincerely pursues this course great consolation soon, provided it is pursued with method *and discretion*. He prescribes rules for prayer in a section which is a treatise on faith, for the soul comes close to God by allowing faith to govern the imagination and the intellect in all its dealings with God. At first imagination and intellect must be worked to the full in what is called meditation; then comes a time, when the soul is habituated to this discipline, when it is enough to turn the attention serenely to some aspect of the matter of previous meditation (a scene from the life of Christ, a thought concerning God, a text or a few words which have, in some way, come to 'convey' God to us). Soon, the spiritual life may rest entirely on this second kind of prayer, called contemplation, sometimes 'acquired contemplation'. John, and other writers also, use the word to signify a closer union of the soul with God by passive or mystical prayer. St John explains that during the first, acquired, contemplation, God may begin this mystical prayer in the soul, but his action on it will be unfelt, and there is no certainty that the soul will be led from there into higher degrees of union with God. In the *Ascent*, II, XIII, three rules are given by which the soul may know when it is time to give up working hard with the mind at prayer and rest in this acquired contemplation, which corresponds to St Teresa's 'recollection'.

In *The Dark Night of the Soul*, John of the Cross deals with mystical contemplation, a prayer which is passive, a direct action by God on the soul, and entirely without words, thoughts or mental imagery. He gives (I, IX) three signs by which the soul may know that this action

has begun, before it becomes so strong as to be unmistakable and felt. *The Spiritual Canticle* and *The Living Flame of Love* trace the development of this prayer to its culmination when the soul is transformed, as much as in this life it can be, into God. It is sometimes thought that St John's teaching is only accidentally Christian and could be reconstructed independently of the person of Christ; this is a mistake, as a close study of his writings from this point of view would show.

In the popular mind, John is perhaps best known for his austerity, his stress on *nada* ('nothing', his catchword to drive home the principle that the soul that desires God must eliminate every other desire), not to be understood in any sense of annihilation of personality. There must be no question of diminishing the saint's insistence that God cannot enter the soul if its attention is on something else, but the terrifying aspect of it has been a little overdone. The saint himself could enjoy things of beauty and even has a place for them as incitements to the love of God, and he was gentle and affectionate in his personal relations. The positive aspect of *nada* is to be filled with God, and this is brought about by and brings about absolute submission to his will, an easier approach, perhaps, in our times, to John's ascetic teaching. He is specially penetrating and scathing about the religiosity that consists in emotional attachment to the externals of religion and about the subtle forms of self-love to be found even among the genuinely devout. John of the Cross has a special appeal to the twentieth century mind. Modern man, even without religion, understands the meaning of 'Love one another', expects poverty in those who would win him to God, and, in a world of extraverted progress, is haunted by the longing for an interior life. John, in his life and in his doctrine, brings him just this.

John died at Ubeda on December 14th, 1591, was canonized in 1726 and was made a doctor of the church in 1926.
November 24th

JOHN 'of the GRATING'   *Twelfth Century*
He was called 'De Craticula' from the grating around his tomb. Born in Brittany, he became a Cistercian under St Bernard of Clairvaux. Later abbot of Buzay, one of his many foundations, he was appointed bishop of Saint-Malo.
February 1st

JOHN of the GOTHS   *Eighth Century*
When in 761, the bishop of the Goths was promoted to the see of Heraclea for supporting the emperor's iconoclastic policy, he was succeeded by St John who helped to re-establish orthodoxy. As a result of the Khazar invasion, John died in exile.
June 26th

JOHN THE ALMSGIVER   *Seventh Century*

A rich widower of Amathus, he was appointed patriarch of Alexandria and thereafter devoted his life to the poor. He emptied the treasury of his church of its 80,000 pieces of gold in order to relieve the poor, and answered protests by telling of a vision he had had. A beautiful woman had appeared to him representing Charity: 'I am the oldest daughter of the King,' she had said, 'if you will be my friend, I will lead you to him'.

January 23rd

JOHN THE BAPTIST   † *c.* 30

He was the son of SS Elizabeth and Zachary and from early childhood had been aware of the extraordinary happenings which had attended his conception and birth.

Since early manhood he had lived an austere and solitary life in the regions south-west of Jerusalem, known as the desert of Judea. He was clothed in a garment of camel's hair, with a leather girdle about his loins, and his food was locusts and wild honey. Such a way of life was not unusual in those days for there were several hermits living in that desert and along the banks of the Jordan, but there the resemblance ended; here was a hermit who broke silence in no uncertain terms. Between October and December of the year 27 A.D. the voice of the last and final prophet was heard: 'Repent, he said, the kingdom of heaven is at hand.' (Matthew 3:2). He demanded two rites of those who came to him: an open confession of their sins, and a physical ablution as an outward sign of their change of heart. Even in this he was not going beyond the general pattern of Jewish worship; his originality lay in the fact that these rites were demanded as a preparation for the imminent coming of one far greater, whose shoes he was not worthy to carry (*cf.* Matthew 3:11).

From Jerusalem and the neighboring towns of Judea men flocked to hear him. He made no extravagant demands, yet many, impressed by his example, joined him in his austere way of life and became his disciples.

God had revealed to him that 'the man who will baptize with the Holy Spirit is the man on whom thou wilt see the Spirit come down and rest'. (John 1:33). Always he was on the watch, and when, eventually, he caught sight of Jesus of Nazareth in the crowd, preparing to be baptized, he had some premonition that this was his kinsman, the Messiah, even before the predestined sign had been given. John would have restrained him. 'It is I,' he said, 'that ought to be baptized by thee, and dost thou come to me instead?' (Matthew 3:14). Jesus overcame John's reluctance and was baptized; then 'suddenly heaven was opened, and he saw the spirit of God coming down like a dove and resting upon him. And with that, a voice came from heaven, which said,

'This is my beloved Son, in whom I am well pleased.' (Matthew 3:16 and 17).

Then Jesus departed, as unostentatiously as he had come, and John continued his work, and still men flocked to him, but now from as far away as Galilee.

Forty days later Jesus returned to the river bank and John caught sight of him in the crowd. Pointing him out to two of his disciples he said, 'Look, this is the Lamb of God.' (John 1:29). These two disciples, Andrew and John, understood and followed Jesus, but so great was John's personal attraction that despite his exhortations, many of his other disciples refused to leave him.

A few weeks later, probably in May, while he was still trying to convince them that it was Jesus whom they must follow, he was snatched from them.

King Herod Antipas had won the affections of his brother's wife, Herodias, who had left her husband, Herod Philip, in Rome, and come to Palestine with her daughter Salome.

John the Baptist denounced this scandal, and Herod had him imprisoned in the Machaerus, a sumptuous fortress on the borders of his territory; but as he held John in awe he treated him well and allowed his disciples to visit him. Through his disciples John was able to follow the progress of Jesus's ministry, and the news did nothing to calm his spirit, restless for the consummation of his mission: the solemn manifestation of the Messiah. Jesus was working miracles but he had not proclaimed himself as the Messiah; until that great moment his own mission would, he felt, remain unfulfilled, and his disciples would remain unconvinced. What could he do to hasten this longed-for moment?

He sent two of his disciples to ask Jesus publicly a question so framed as to require an explicit declaration of his Messianic nature. 'Is it thy coming that was foretold, or are we yet waiting for some other?' (Luke 7:19).

But Jesus would not allow John to force his hand; the time for this formal declaration had not yet come. He did no more than point to the evidence of his miracles, miracles which Isaiah had predicted would characterize the Messianic age, and with this John and his disciples had to rest content.

Between February and March of the year 29 A.D. Herod held, in the Machaerus, a celebration in honor of his birthday; it was an occasion designed to impress his provincial guests with the splendor of his court, and it was an occasion which served the murderous schemes of Herodias.

The company, bemused by good food and wine, were well prepared for the climax of the evening's entertainment. Salome, educated in Rome, was an accomplished dancer, and now she came forward and performed before the guests with a grace and charm beyond anything they, in the provinces, had ever seen.

They were enchanted and Antipas was so delighted by her success that he called her to him and promised, on oath, that he would give her anything she asked.

Salome hastened out to ask her mother's advice; when she returned her request was a terrible one.

'My wish is that thou shouldst give me the head of John the Baptist; give it me now, on a dish.' (Mark 6:25).

Herod's remorse did not prevent him from fulfilling his rash promise; at once he sent one of his guards to execute John in his cell, and St Jerome tells us that when Salome took the dripping head to her mother, Herodias gave vent to her hatred by thrusting a bodkin through the tongue as Fulvia had done with the head of Cicero. (*Adv. Rufinum.* 3, 42).

The martyr's disciples were allowed to give his body fitting burial and he has been venerated ever since as the greatest saint of the Old Dispensation; but the memory of his victim haunted Herod, and played upon his conscience to the end of his days.

ILLUSTRATION: facing page 304
June 24th: his Nativity; August 29th: his Beheading

JOHN THE DWARF   *Fifth Century*
One of the famous saints of the Egyptian deserts, he was remarkable for his simplicity and absent-mindedness. *October 17th*

JOHN THE EVANGELIST
St John the Evangelist, like Shakespeare, has something about him which irresistibly attracts the crank, and probably more books have been written and more wildly fantastic theories advanced about his writings and their authorship than about any other writer who ever lived. The reason may perhaps lie in the strange two-sidedness of his character. How, says the critic, can works so profound have been written by a mere Galilean fisherman? How can the author of the Johannine epistles, with their message of love and brotherhood, be the fire-breathing visionary of the Apocalypse? Or how can the 'Son of Thunder' who wanted Christ to call down fire from heaven upon the inhospitable Samaritans (Luke 9:54) be identified with the gentle 'disciple whom Jesus loved' and to whom he bequeathed the care of his Blessed Mother? Yet no theory of multiple authorship will fit the facts, for all these different St Johns are intimately and inextricably mingled in all the Johannine writings. The unlearned fisherman is there – in the extreme simplicity of syntax and vocabulary. The mystical theologian is there – in the Prologue (John 1:1ff.) the Discourse in the upper room (John 13 to 17) and the First Epistle. The Son of Thunder is there – in the truculent speeches of Jesus and in St John's own denunciation of 'Antichrist' (1 John 2:18ff). The differences between the Apocalypse and the other writings are balanced by equally striking similarities. Even in the anecdotes of St John's old age, preserved by second-century writers, we find the same contrast. The aged bishop of Ephesus, who condensed all Christian teaching into the one imperative, 'Little children, love one another', was the same St John who refused to enter a public bath-house where Cerinthus the heretic was known to be, for fear lest fire from heaven should destroy the very building (fire from heaven again!). In short, we are still in the same position as those priests who interrogated St John after Pentecost (Acts 4:13) and who, 'discovering that Peter and John were simple men, without learning, were astonished.' Astonishment: that is what everyone must feel who comes to close quarters with St John.

It is as well to remember, of course, that at least fifty years – half a century of prayer and meditation, of teaching and debate – separate St John the Apostle from St John the Evangelist. As a very young man he had listened to John the Baptist, and when the Baptist pointed to Jesus and said 'Behold the Lamb of God' he had transferred his allegiance to our Lord. A few months later, when he and his elder brother James were helping their father with his fishing, Jesus called to them, 'and they, leaving their father Zebedee in the boat with the hired men, turned aside after him' (Mark 1:20). Thereafter these two, with Peter, became the closest and most constant companions of Christ. They alone were with him at the raising of Jairus's daughter, at the Transfiguration and in Gethsemane. After the resurrection they became, along with James son of Alphaeus, the 'pillars of the Church' (Galatians 2:7) in Jerusalem; but after his elder brother had been beheaded by Herod (*c.* 44 A.D.) St John seems to have left Palestine, and it is James the Less who is bishop of Jerusalem at the time of St Paul's last visit (*c.* 57 A.D.). Of St John's own movements between then and his exile on the island of Patmos we know nothing. Even the date of that exile is uncertain, depending on whether we take the wicked emperor of the Apocalypse to be Nero or Domitian. But all authorities agree that he spent his later years at Ephesus, acting as patriarch to the churches of Asia; that he died there at a great age, about the end of the century; and that it was only in these later years that he consented, under pressure from his disciples, to commit his Gospel to writing.

Everything that St John ever wrote could be contained in quite a small booklet, yet so rich is the vein that one is embarrassed to know how best to sample it in such a brief note as this. Should one concentrate on the famous 'Logos-doctrine' – that Christ was the 'Word' of God, the word by which he created all things and by which he spoke to Moses and the prophets? Or should one discuss St John's insistence on Faith – by which he meant not only belief in the divinity of Christ but also an absolute and boundless trust? He certainly abhorred all heretics, especially those who denied the actual, earthly, fleshly reality of God-made-man in this world. Or should one concentrate on John the contemplative, the spiritual father of all Christian monks and nuns? Or on the visionary of the Apocalypse? Or on the poet of the Gospel prologue?

St John himself would probably have said that the whole of him is summed up in the single sentence of his first Epistle (1 John 4:8), that 'God is love.' It was love which had brought God down to earth in the person of Jesus, and it is only by love – of God and of his fellowmen – that a man can join himself, through Christ, to God. And this union with God – for the body in the Blessed Sacrament, for the mind and will by faith and good works – is the only thing that matters. It is life and light and victory and bliss, here and everywhere, now and forever. But it can all be summed up and bound together by the one word 'love'. Love of God implies faith and trust and obedience. Love of our neighbor implies all that is meant by 'right conduct'. All goodness, all happiness, all wisdom is included in that single word.

'And he who sat on the throne said, Behold, I make all things new. I am Alpha, I am Omega, the beginning of all things and their end; those who are thirsty shall drink – it is my free gift – out of the spring whose water is life. (Revelation 21:5).

Jesus had promised that water to Nicodemus (John 3:5), to the Samaritan woman (John 4:13) and to all the world (John 7:37), but it is St John who most simply and clearly shows us where the well of it is to be found. 'God', says St John, and he was the first to say it, among all the philosophers, prophets and saints of the world, 'God is love', and only in his love can the thirst of all the world be quenched.   ILLUSTRATION: page 266
December 27th

JOHN THE GOOD   † 660
Other than that he was strenuously opposed to the Monothelites, little is known of this bishop of Milan. He attended the Lateran Council in 649.
January 10th

JOHN THE IBERIAN   † c. 1002
He entered the monastery on Mount Olympus in Bithynia, where he was joined by his son St Euthymius. They later retired to Mount Athos, and were persuaded to found the monastery of Iviron there for their fellow-countrymen, with first St John, and then his son as superior.
July 12th

JOHN THE SILENT   454–558
At the age of eighteen, he built and ruled over a monas-tery being chosen bishop of Colonia in Armenia ten years later. After nine years, he left for Jerusalem and applied to be admitted to the monastery of St Sabas, where he performed the most menial tasks cheerfully and silently. His identity was only discovered after several years, when St Sabas judged him fit to be ordained. St John was allowed to go on living in retirement and died at the age of 104.
May 13th

JOHN VIANNEY (The 'Curé d'Ars')   1786–1859
Although all the saints belong to the universal church there is a sense in which they have a special local significance. John Vianney is known throughout the world as the 'Curé d'Ars'; that title with its undertone of affection is sufficient description of his special mission, which was in the first place to give an example to the priests of France immediately after the horrors and persecution of the revolution, when, despite many who were fervent, many others had fallen by the wayside or regarded themselves as merely functionaries. His work of transformation in the almost godless village of Ars was therefore an example for all France, but his work for individual souls was to spread his fame throughout the world.

John Mary Vianney was born at Dardilly, some eight miles north-west of Lyons, in 1786. His peasant parents were among those who remained faithful Catholics during the revolution, giving hospitality to visiting priests. John Vianney was present at mass said in secret in the woods or in a barn. After his first communion (at the age of thirteen) he made up his mind to be a priest, but it was only at the age of seventeen that he felt that he could tell his father. He obtained his consent two years later. His education was rudimentary; he had no Latin. Abbé Balley, of Ecully, received him among the pupils taught at the presbytery but found considerable difficulty in teaching him anything. Meanwhile owing to an error he was called up for service in Napoleon's army in 1809. Another misunderstanding caused him to be posted as a deserter until in 1810 a general amnesty allowed him to return home.

A year at Verrières for his philosophy proved him a model seminarist but with no aptitude for learning, and the seminary at Lyons where he went for his theology was obliged to send him away because he could derive no profit from the lessons delivered in Latin. Abbé Balley took him in once more, taught him sufficient theology from a French manual and presented him for ordination in 1815. He was accepted principally on account of his devout life.

Such was his preparation for a life's work which, after a short period as curate to his tutor in Ecully, was wholly given up to the evangelization of the parish of Ars and

JEROME: painting by Antonello da Messina (*fl.* 1446 – 1479). (*National Gallery, London*)

PLATE 9

IGNATIUS of ANTIOCH (with mitre), with Julian (central figure) and other saints: detail from predella by Fra Angelico (1387–1455). (National Gallery, London.)

ISIDORE the HUSBANDMAN, lithograph by R. A. Hook, showing the saint ploughing with the help of an angel

JAMES THE GREATER: detail from the left shutter of 'The Last Judgment' by
Hieronymus Bosch (c. 1640 – 1518). (*Acad. Fine Arts, Vienna.*)

JANUARIUS: sculpture by Cosimo Fanzaga (1591 – 1688). *(Duomo, Naples.)*

JOAN of ARC: sculpture by François Rude (1784–1855). *(Louvre, Paris.)*

JOHN BAPTIST de la SALLE: engraving by Scotin after portrait by Pierre Leger (1716).
(From a Biography of the Saint by Canon Blain, 1730.)

JOHN BOSCO: a photograph

JOHN CHRYSOSTOM: miniature on reliquary
(eleventh century). *(Museo Cristiano, Vatican.)*

JOHN FISHER: drawing by Hans Holbein (1497–1543). *(British Museum.)*

Imago aequilae

JOHN THE EVANGELIST: MS illumination from the Lindisfarne Gospels (eighth century).
(*British Museum.*)

Photo: Exclusive News Agency

JOHN VIANNEY (the 'Curé d'Ars'): sculpture

JOSEPH: detail of fresco 'Marriage of the Virgin' by Giotto (1266 – 1337).
(Cappella degli Scrovegni all' Arena, Padua.)

JOSEPH BENEDICT LABRE: painting by Antonio Cavalucci (1752 – 1795).
(Galleria Nazionale de' Arte Antica, Rome.)

JOSEPH of ARIMATHEA: detail from 'Descent from the Cross' by Rogier van der Weyden (1399 – 1464). *(Mauritshuis, Hague.)*

JUDE: relief figure in alabaster, painted and
gilded. English (fifteenth century). *(Victoria and
Albert Museum, London.)*

KEVIN or COEGMEN:
ceramic relief by Cathal Sean O'Maodhchain (b. 1936.)

JOACHIM (*left*) with Sabinus: detail from a sixth century mosaic.
(*Ch. di San Apollinare Nuovo, Ravenna*)

PLATE 10

to dealing with the many who soon came to seek his help. The basis of his personal approach to his work consisted in the two means taught by our Lord – prayer and fasting. Whenever no duty required his presence elsewhere he was to be found in church; his meals and sleep were reduced to a minimum. His sermons at first were preached to a few old women, but gradually as his influence was felt, drunkenness, Sunday work, the dancing, which kept people from church, all disappeared. None of this was accomplished without great cost to the parish priest: calumny of his good name was circulated in the neighborhood, his colleagues criticized him, he was denounced to the bishop, Monsignor Devie, who having made inquiry about his life and conduct offered him as an example to his colleagues.

John Vianney had to endure too those preternatural manifestations sometimes ascribed to poltergeists: rappings, moving of furniture, voices, his bed catching alight and other characteristic phenomena rendered his presbytery almost uninhabitable. He bore it all calmly enough and after a time was troubled no more in this way. By this time the pilgrims were already beginning to crowd into Ars. At first a few notable sinners from the surrounding countryside were converted by the fame and example of the parish priest of this little village. Then others came from further afield. Soon a special booking-office in the station at Lyons was issuing tickets for pilgrims – they were eight-day tickets, because it was impossible to be certain of seeing the parish priest and return home in less time than that. A regular coach service connected Ars with the nearest station for Paris. For years John Vianney worked a twenty-hour day, the greater part of which was passed hearing confessions.

About one in the morning he would walk the thirty yards from his presbytery to the church, and ring the angelus, thereby announcing that he was ready for the penitents. He was busy with them until he said mass at seven; after his thanksgiving he returned to the confessional, and there for the greater part of the day he remained, emerging only at eleven to give a catechism lesson and then go to his dinner (which took only a quarter of an hour); after a visit to the sick he was back in the confessional, coming out again only in the evening for night prayers. He then retired to the presbytery and shut himself up in his room for his short night of three hours or so – how much of it was spent in sleep we shall never know.

Such a life, endured for thirty years, was one of the greatest miracles of Ars; there were others in abundance, all ascribed by John Vianney to the prayers of St Philomena. Sinners were converted, the sick healed, vocations settled, men and women set on the straight path to holiness, with a sentence or two from that tired quiet voice behind the grille. He could read people at a glance and often foretold their future with startling accuracy.

Three times he tried to resign his post and retire to a monastery; he was prevented on each occasion by his bishop or his parishioners. He was haunted by the notion that he must prepare himself for death far from the crowds that thronged round him, clipping pieces off his cassock, his white hair, pulling his breviary from under his arm in their desire for relics, importuning him for his blessing, for a cure, for a conversion of friend or relative. He was torn in two between his desire for a contemplative life and his zeal for the conversion of souls; it was no question of personal preference but the desire merely for the better service of God. But he died in harness on August 4th, 1859 at the age of seventy-three. Reputed a saint in his lifetime, he was canonized by Pius XI in 1925 and made patron of the pastoral clergy.
August 9th   ILLUSTRATION: page 267

JOHN ZEDAZNELI and his Companions † *c.* 580
St John was the head of a party of thirteen Syrian monks who went to evangelize Georgia. They are celebrated there as 'the fathers of the Iberian church'.
November 4th

JONAS, *see* Barachisius and Jonas.

JOSAPHAT, *see* Barlaam and Josaphat.

JOSAPHAT KUNCEVIC of POLOTSK
                                    c. 1580–1623
Born in 1580 or perhaps 1584, in Vladimir, the capital of Volynia in the Ukraine, then a Polish province, he was baptized John. Though of noble family, his father had gone into trade with some success, and had even become a town councillor. Josaphat was apprenticed to a merchant in Vilna in Lithuania, with whom he worked until 1604, when he became a monk in the Basilian house at Vilna. The Ruthenian and Ukrainian Christians, the vast majority of whom were of the Byzantine rite, were deeply divided, since the reunion of their church with Rome had been proclaimed by most of their bishops at Brest-Litovsk in 1596. The patriarch of Constantinople had done his best to prevent this important secession from Orthodoxy, and named a special exarch to Ruthenia for this purpose. Nor was it popular with the local grandees, who saw it as another threat to their autonomy; but it had the complete support of the Polish monarchy and central government. Although, throughout his life, St Josaphat remained loyal to the Holy See, his spiritual and liturgical outlook were Byzantine. He had learned the whole slavonic service book by heart as a child; he strictly kept the fasts of the Byzantine calendar, which are much more rigorous than those of the Latin one; and the prayer to which he had most recourse was the 'Jesus Prayer', the devotion

favored by many oriental Christian ascetics and mystics. The mixed motives of the partisans of Orthodoxy and Papacy, and the pull of opposing political loyalties were meaningless to Josaphat. He could not believe that the traditional devotions and customs of his people, and indeed of the whole Orthodox world, were in any way incompatible with loyalty to a church united under the Holy See.

In his order he distinguished himself by his severe austerities, which his Jesuit teachers thought excessive, as well as by his intellectual attainments. He was ordained in 1609 and soon acquired a great reputation as a spiritual director; he also wrote several works of controversy about this time (*On the Baptism of St Vladimir, On the Falsification of Slav Books*). In 1617 he was consecrated bishop of Vitebsk with the right of succession to the archbishopric of Pskov, which he exercised in 1618. While devoted to his people, he was intransigent towards schismatics, disapproving even of such concessions as the central Polish government was prepared to make. In 1623, while visiting Vitebsk, he was attacked by a nationalist crowd, cut down and shot. His body was taken back to Pskov, and on its journey received much reverence, even from his enemies.

His martyrdom assured the survival of the Catholic Slavonic church. Its members have different customs, canons, liturgy and language from the Poles, who are Latin Catholics, while they are independent of Moscow and the Russians because of their allegiance to Rome; they have, therefore, become an important focus of the Ruthenian nationalist movements in recent times.

The cause of St Josaphat was begun by Pope Urban VIII in 1628, when the tomb was opened and the body found incorrupt. He was beatified in 1643 and canonized in 1867.
November 14th

JOSEPH

Singularly little is known about St Joseph. If it is true that Matthew 1 and 2 is dependent upon a source which ultimately stems from St Joseph (as Luke 1 and 2 is based upon one stemming from our Lady), Matthew in the event tells us as little about him as Luke. The genealogy in both Gospels places him in the line of David. At the beginning of our era this royal descent was no longer a title to rank or riches, and everything we know about Joseph (e.g. the substitute offering made at the Presentation in Luke 2:24) suggests that he was one of the unprivileged poor. His family belonged to Bethlehem in Judea (Luke 2:4), but he had removed to Nazareth in Galilee to take up there the occupation of builder (the word used in Matthew 13:55 is wider than is suggested by the translation 'carpenter'). There is no reason to suppose that he was above the normal age of twenty to twenty-four when he married Mary, who would herself be between fifteen and twenty. Matthew mentions the annunciation to Joseph of Mary's miraculous conception, the visit of the Magi, the flight to Egypt and the return to Nazareth. Luke fills in the intermediate details of the birth, the circumcision, the presentation, and the temporary loss of the child in Jerusalem at the age of twelve. From this time Joseph disappears from the Gospel pages, and since there is no mention of him with Mary during the public ministry of Christ, it is probable that he died in the interval.

With their concern to provide the information demanded by popular curiosity and piety, the apocryphal Gospels are more than usually liberal in their treatment of Joseph, and expatiate on the children of his first marriage, the death of his wife, his long years of widowhood, his winning the guardianship of Mary in competition against other suitors, the ordeal by which his chastity is proved, the circumstances surrounding the birth of Christ, and finally his protracted death and the consolation given him by Jesus and Mary. While some of these details have great poetic beauty, others betray their origin and purpose too clearly to be mistaken for history. Thus, Joseph's former marriage has been invented to give some explanation of the 'brothers and sisters' of Jesus (Matthew 12:46; 13:55, etc.), and his death at the age of 111, based on that of his Old Testament namesake, is an attempt to compensate and account for his early disappearance from the Gospels.

The Gospels remain therefore as the only reliable source of information about Joseph. Yet with all their reticence they have left a sharp outline of his character. Even if it is unsafe to argue from the mere fact that they record no word of his, it is clearly their purpose to present him as the patient instrument of God, who does what is required of him with unquestioning faith. His pious observance of the Jewish Law, his faithful protection of the family in his charge, his willing acceptance of hardship, his prompt obedience to the demands of God, his constancy under trial, his calm dignity at all times, these mark him out as the 'just' or godly man, who can be proposed as a model to all Christians, and to Christian working men in particular. Christ's own attractive human character, with its forthrightness, courage and deep charity, was developed under the example and upbringing he received from Joseph. Yet Joseph's true greatness lies at a deeper level, and the customary description of him as the putative or foster-father of Jesus may here be a little misleading. The term suggests a purely metaphorical relationship to Christ, the merely extrinsic exercise of parental authority. It would be more accurate to say that Joseph was, in every way short of generation, the true father of Christ, a term which the Gospels do not hesitate to use constantly. Jesus was truly the fruit of the marriage in which Joseph played an indispensable rôle. If his fatherhood was virginal it was not thereby something less than physical fatherhood; by its spiritual nature it was an earthly reflection of the paternity of God himself. The relationship of the Virgin Father to Christ is therefore analogous to that of the Virgin Mother. Both Mary and Joseph are integral parts of the mystery of the incarnation; and in so far as this mystery is extended through time in the mystical body of the word made flesh, Joseph continues his rôle of fostering, protecting and guiding the church, not by any mere extrinsic title, but by the very nature of things.

The reticence of the Gospels has helped to obscure this true dignity of Joseph. The cult which grew up in the east in connection with the fourth century account of his happy death, and which only slowly spread to the west through the middle ages, was not acknowledged universally until the seventeenth century, and did not receive its final crown until 1870, when Pius IX proclaimed Joseph as the Patron of the Universal Church. This fact is commemorated annually on March 19th. In 1955 Pius XII added a second feast of Joseph the Worker, to be celebrated on the traditional Labor Day of May 1st.

March 19th and *May 1st*   ILLUSTRATION: page 268

JOSEPH BARSABAS   *First Century*
He is referred to in the New Testament (Acts 1:21–22) and seems to have been one of the seventy-two disciples, continuing as a missionary after their dispersal.
July 20th

JOSEPH BENEDICT LABRE   1748–1783
This is the story of a social misfit who finally found his niche in heaven by not having one on earth. Benedict Joseph Labre was born at Amette near Boulogne in 1748, the eldest of a family of fourteen. He was educated by an uncle, a priest, and quite early in life decided that he had a vocation to the monastic state. For one reason or another he was unable to remain in a monastery; in vain he tried with the Cistercians, with the Carthusians, with the Cistercians again, and on each occasion despite his fervor was obliged to leave on account of the severe spiritual trials that befell him in the noviciate.

Still craving solitude, Benedict sought it on the road as a pilgrim, and so found his vocation. He avoided inns and travelled by unfrequented routes. He slept under a hedge, in a barn; rarely would he enter a house, never would he accept more than sufficient for his immediate needs. And so he reached Rome. Dirty, not from choice but because the poverty he felt he was called to compelled it, without settled lodging, never knowing where his next meal was coming from, always meek and grateful, sheltering in bad weather in a nook in the wall, spending hours in church – so he passed his time in the capital of Christendom. Then he was on the road again,

on pilgrimage to Compostella, to the shrines of Germany, Poland, then back to Rome where, if the term can be used, he settled, but went yearly on a pilgrimage to Loretto. He died in Rome in 1783, and hardly had he done so than the children were running through the streets shouting, 'The saint is dead! The saint is dead!' He was thirty-three.

To the modern mind his life is an enigma and a stumbling-block, but it must be seen as an unconscious protest against the social evils, the poverty and injustice then prevalent in Europe. He is also, surely, the patron of displaced persons, the thousands who are herded about Europe and confined in camps, and forgotten – the misfits caused by the mistakes of politicians.

April 16th   ILLUSTRATION: page 269

JOSEPH CAFASSO   1811–1860
Born at Castelnuovo d'Asti, Piedmont, the son of a peasant, he went to Turin after ordination, and became lecturer in moral theology at the institute attached to the church of St Francis of Assisi, of which he was later rector. He did much work among the convicts of Turin, and was also the spiritual director of St John Bosco.
June 23rd

JOSEPH CALASANCTIUS   1556–1648
Joseph Calasanctius was born at Peralta de la Sal in the province of Aragon of parents who were among the richest in the country. After he was ordained priest in 1583, he threw himself into the work of religious reform, which he did so successfully that he was appointed vicar-general of the diocese of Urgel at the age of thirty-four. He felt, however, impelled to go to Rome, and resigning his appointments, went to that city, where he lived for five years as a humble pilgrim. During this time, St Joseph came to see the misery and vice which existed among the poor. He was convinced that these conditions were caused by religious ignorance and, as he was now possessed of a considerable fortune through the death of his father, he set up a number of free schools for the poor. He followed this up by founding the order of Clerks Regular of Religious Schools under the patronage of the Mother of God, an order of which St Joseph was made general in 1622. Schools, under his direction, continued to multiply and his work spread to Germany, Bohemia and Poland.

As St Joseph grew older, he became the victim of intrigue, and it was suggested by his assistants that he was too old to continue. At the age of eighty-six he was subjected to all the indignities of an official inquiry from which he emerged triumphant. In 1648 he died of a fever aged ninety-two, and he was canonized in 1767.

In 1948 he was made the Apostle of Education and patron of all Christian schools. His mass reminds us of the qualities necessary in all who teach: 'Suffer the little children to come to me, and forbid them not, for of such is the Kingdom of God.'

August 27th

JOSEPH COTTOLENGO † 1842

He opened a small hospital for the poor in Turin, which was moved to the outskirts during a cholera epidemic in 1831, and grew rapidly. It was named Piccola Casa, or Little House of Divine Providence, and his helpers were formed into the Brothers and Daughters of St Vincent.

He kept no accounts, for he made no investments; when money came in, it was spent, and when he was pressed by his creditors he prayed for help – it always came. His method of providing for the future was to found religious societies. These included the Daughters of Compassion and the Daughters of the Good Shepherd for women, and the Hermits of the Holy Rosary and the Congregation of Priests of the Holy Trinity for men.

He died worn out by his efforts aged fifty-six and was canonized in 1934.

April 29th

JOSEPH of ARIMATHEA First Century

The legend of St Joseph of Arimathea grows out of the references to him in the Gospels, for it was he who took away the body of Jesus and, with the help of Nicodemus, prepared it for burial and placed it in the sepulchre. In the apocryphal *Gospel of Nicodemus* we are told that the Jews shut Joseph up in a windowless cell, from which he was released by four angels and transported to his native city of Arimathea.

It was left to the monks of Glastonbury, whose abbot claimed to take precedence over all other English abbots, to develop the legend in the interests of their foundation. In 1184, this great abbey was burned down and its position as a place of pilgrimage gravely imperilled; it may have been nothing more than a fortunate coincidence that after this disaster the monks were able to produce not only the bodies of King Arthur and his queen Guinevere, but also the discovery, never before recorded, that in the year 63 St Joseph of Arimathea had been sent to England by St Philip, the Apostle, and, at the bidding of the archangel Gabriel, had built a church of wattles at Glastonbury in honor of our Lady, thirty-one years after the passion of our Lord, and fifteen after the Assumption. This was the first church to be built in England, and it was dedicated to our Lady by our Lord himself. The historian, William of Malmesbury, writing before the fire, did not know of this, and the first mention is to be found in an introduction by another hand to his *The antiquity of the church of Glastonbury*, on the strength of which later monastic historians produced their developments of the legend. The claim that the legend has a pre-Norman source is based upon the *Prophecy* of Melkin, a document enigmatic in character and difficult to date.

It was further asserted that Joseph possessed two cruets which were filled with the blood and sweat of the Lord and that these were buried with him at Glastonbury. This was probably intended as a counterblast to the less edifying legend of the Holy Grail in which the sacred cup of the Last Supper was brought to England by Joseph, passed on by him to a line of kings, lost, and then sought by King Arthur and his knights of the Round Table.

Although the monks would not accept the Holy Grail, they were quite willing to associate Joseph with King Arthur, and it was said that Joseph had married the daughter of Longinus, the spearman of the Crucifixion and natural son of Julius Caesar, and that Igerne of Cornwall (mother of King Arthur) was a descendant of this marriage.

Such legends not only supported Glastonbury's claim to precedence but ante-dated the claims of the British over the French and Spanish churches – a fact which led to incidents at the councils of Pisa (1409), Constance (1417), Siena (1424) and Basle (1434). Glastonbury might indeed call herself the second Rome, and although in the first flush of the Reformation later historians were inclined to cite this title as evidence against the primacy and authority of the Roman see, they came to fear that 'the leaven of monkery had swollen and puffed up the circumstances'.

Certain facts, however, remain to be accounted for: an existing building made of wattles was roofed over in wood by St Paulinus in 625; and Glastonbury was persistently identified with Avalon – the burial place of the Celtic kings, the isle of Avallac and Glast, the gods of the underworld – where King Arthur was taken to be healed of his wounds. Recent excavations have established that the original church was built of wattles in the first century, and also that it was built on the site of a pagan sanctuary. Although it is possible, therefore, to see in the legend of Joseph of Arimathea nothing more than an effort by misguided piety to take advantage of such traditional veneration for the greater glory of God – and of Glastonbury – the fact of Glastonbury's being a sacred place in pre-Christian times would account for its early settlement by Christian missionaries; and the St Joseph legend both helps and hinders the elucidation of the facts.   ILLUSTRATION: page 270

March 17th

JOSEPH of COPERTINO 1603–1663

Joseph Desa of Copertino was born on June 17th, 1603. His home was miserably poor; he was sickly, and extremely dull. He was refused admittance into one convent after another, or dismissed for clumsiness, ignorance or absent-mindedness. At last he was accepted as a servant by the Conventual Franciscans of Grotella and, against all probability, was ordained in 1628. At once the 'abnormal' side of his life began.

In 1645 the Spanish ambassador to the Holy See, the High Admiral of Castile, having spoken for some time with him in his cell at Assisi, said that his wife too would like to meet him. The Father Guardian told him to go down to the church: Joseph said he would obey but did not know whether he would be able to speak to her. He entered the church, saw a statue of our Lady over the altar and straightway flew some twelve paces above the onlookers to its feet, and after a while, 'uttering his customary shrill cry', returned to the floor and then his cell, having said nothing to the Admiral, his wife and their large retinue. Instances could be multiplied up to the last month of Joseph's life.

What strikes us immediately is that his miracles kept drawing such crowds that not only was he up before the Inquisition, but his desperate Superiors sent him from convent to convent. Once the Inquisition removed him to a Capuchin friary, where he was kept in strict enclosure and forbidden even to write or receive letters – to his own bewilderment: 'Must I go to prison, then?' he said. Yet, at Assisi, the duke of Brunswick and Hanover, after visiting him, abjured Lutheranism and became a Catholic; Urban VIII, having seen him in ecstasy, said that should Joseph die first, he himself would give evidence of what he had seen. Most important, Prosper Lambertini did his best, as Promotor Fidei ('Devil's Advocate'), to discredit him, yet afterwards (as Benedict XIV) published the decree of Joseph's beatification in 1753 and, in his classical work on Beatification, alluded to the 'eye-witnesses of unchallengeable integrity' who witnessed to Joseph's 'upliftings from the ground and prolonged flights'. It is difficult to see how, if we reject this evidence, we shall ever find any historical evidence acceptable. In considering saints whose lives record abnormal phenomena, such as 'levitation' certain general principles need to be established. To start with, it is best to avoid the words 'mysticism' and 'mystic', which it is preferable to keep for what concerns a specially close union with God: this need not connote any abnormal phenomena.

No believer in God can exclude the possibility of 'miracles'; but in this context a miracle does not have to be described as a defiance of the laws of nature: a stone, left to itself, lies where it is; but if other forces, directed by the intelligence, lay hold of it, it may find itself the capital of a pillar in a cathedral: but quarryman, architect, sculptor will all have obeyed *their* laws, else the fabric would collapse. Secondly, when an abnormal event is observed, every test known to science should be applied to it. But we must recall that even if such an event escapes from every scientific test (as do, for example, some cures at Lourdes), the investigator is not asked to assert that it is a miracle: indeed, the church herself cannot define the miraculous character of such an event as a 'truth of faith'. The church's approbation is in essence negative: she says that there is nothing in, for example, the story of Fatima, contrary to faith or morals, and that if, after prudent inquiry, an investigator thinks the story is credible, he is not forbidden to believe in it and to affirm his belief in public. Naturally, few are able to make a personal inquiry, but a man would be rash to disregard the verdict of the experts who have done so.

We must avoid two extremes: that of the greedy for miracles, who rush ahead alike of church and science; and that of those who refuse, *a priori*, to admit the possibility of a supernatural element in some abnormal event. Once, when a case of stigmatization was being investigated, several doctors were asked if a profound lesion of the tissues, lasting for years, without either treatment or gangrene, could be produced by auto-suggestion only: all except two said 'Yes'. They were asked if any of them had met with an instance of this. None had. On the other hand, the body can undergo astonishing de-formations, as is illustrated by the case of Mlle Jahenny, an ecstatic. On September 27th, 1880 she exhibited the following phenomena (and others) in the presence of a doctor, a priest, and four other 'persons of credit': her head shrank downwards so that her shoulders protruded 'notably' above it; each shoulder successively seemed to stand at right angles to the collarbone; the right side of her body was so dilated from arm-pit to hip that on the left of her torso practically nothing could be felt. Such 'elongation' or distortion cannot do much good either to the patient or the onlooker in whom it would, rather, exite alarm or repulsion, as was urged by the Promotor Fidei ('Devil's Advocate') in the case of Sister Veronica Laparelli (died 1620), whose beatification was hoped for but not granted.

Levitation, however, can at least have a symbolical value, as representing the 'heavenward' aspiration of the soul. If, then, there is good evidence for a 'levitation', no appeal to hysteria or self-suggestion seems possible, and we must look elsewhere. 'Stigmatization' is discussed in the life of St Gemma Galgani, and the reader is advised to consult *The Physical Phenomena of Mysticism*, by H. Thurston (1951), and *Levitation*, by O. Leroy (1928).

St Joseph of Copertino was canonized in 1767, fourteen years after his beatification.
September 18th

JOSEPH of LEONESSA   1556–1612
An ascetic Capuchin friar from Leonessa in Umbria, he

was a great preacher. He went as a missioner to the Christian galley-slaves near Constantinople, and because he preached to the Mohammedans, the Turks imprisoned, tortured and banished him. He died in Leonessa.

February 4th

JOSEPH of PALESTINE † *c.* 356

Assistant to the Jewish patriarch, Rabbi Hillel, Joseph was present when the rabbi was secretly baptized on his death-bed. Moving gradually towards Christianity, he was detected reading the Gospels, and was beaten up by his suspicious fellow-Jews. This decided him to be baptized, and the rest of his life was spent in spreading the Gospel, especially among the Jews.

July 22nd

JOSEPH ORIOL † 1702

A priest in Barcelona, of the utmost selflessness, he was a powerful though severe spiritual director, and so gifted with healing powers that he gained overwhelming fame.

March 23rd

JOSEPH PIGNATELLI 1737–1811

A nobleman, born at Saragossa, he became a Jesuit and left Spain when the society was banished in 1767. In 1773 the society was completely suppressed, and St Joseph retired to Bologna. He worked assiduously to keep a nucleus of Jesuits in being, and, in 1804, he was allowed to form a province in Naples. He later became provincial for Italy, but it was not until three years after his death that the Society of Jesus was completely restored. Pope Pius XI called him 'the restorer of the Jesuits'.

November 28th

JOSEPHA ROSSELLO 1811–1880

Born at Albisola Marina on the Ligurian coast in Italy, she was the daughter of a potter and founded the order of the daughters of our Lady of Pity. Its purpose was to instruct poor girls – particularly those who were strange to city life – and to save and care for fallen ones. Her community, which had begun with three sisters, a sack of potatoes and four shillings, had developed by the time of her death into some sixty-eight separate convents.

December 7th

JOSSE, *see* Judoc.

JOVITA, *see* Faustinus and Jovita.

JUDAS QUIRIACUS, *see* Cyriacus.

JUDE *First Century*

This apostle is referred to by various names – Thaddeus (Matthew 10:3; Mark 3:18, meaning probably 'deep-chested') and Jude (Luke 6:16; Acts 1:13).

Can we identify him with the author of the canonical epistle, who describes himself as 'Jude, the servant of

Jesus Christ and brother of James' (Jude verse 1)? If we could accept unreservedly our English rendering of Luke 6:16 which reads 'Jude, brother of James', an affirmative answer might be given. However, the Greek original simply has 'Jude of James', and while it is not grammatically impossible for this to mean 'brother of', the normal meaning of the construction is 'son of James'. In addition, the author of the epistle seems (verse 17) implicitly to segregate himself from the group of Apostles. The most natural interpretation of the title of the epistle is to recognize here the Jude and James who were 'brethren of the Lord' (Mark 6:3). This would provide a further reason for differentiating the two Judes, since 'the brethren', in all probability, were not members of the Twelve (*see* St James the Less). Nor does it lessen the authority of the epistle. The 'brethren' are shown to be in close association with the Apostles, James, in particular, enjoying great authority in the primitive church (Acts 15:13). What more natural than that Jude should associate himself with his brother's labors, and, like him, confirm the infant Christian communities by letter?

Post-scriptural tradition asserts that Jude, the Apostle, preached in Mesopotamia and there suffered martyrdom. In time, St Jude came to be regarded as the special patron of 'hopeless cases', possibly because it was felt that devotion to him had hitherto been neglected, through his having the same name as the traitor. A Little Office of St Jude appeared and, in abbreviated form, the main prayer reads: 'Most holy apostle, most faithful friend and servant of Jesus Christ, Judas Thaddeus, who ... art invoked as the special advocate of those who are in trouble and almost without hope ... pray for me that by thy merits, I may receive consolation in my tribulations and difficulties ... and finally, with thee and all the elect, I may love and bless God eternally. Amen.'

October 28th　　　　ILLUSTRATION: page 271

JUDITH, *see* Salome and Judith

JUDOC or JOSSE † *c.* 668

Chaucer's wife of Bath swears 'by God and by Saint Joce'. He was the son of Juthael, king of Brittany, and a famous hermit. It is said that Charlemagne gave his hermitage at Saint-Josse-sur-mer as a hospice for cross-channel travellers.

December 13th

JULIA *Sixth Century*

Patroness of Corsica and Leghorn, Julia was probably martyred in the sixth or seventh century by Saracen pirates, but legend makes her a Carthaginian maiden of the fifth century.

May 22nd

JULIAN, *see* Besas, Cronion and Julian.

JULIAN, *see* Caesarius and Julian.

JULIAN, *see* Theodulus and Julian.

JULIAN, BASILISSA and their Companions † 304?
We have no certain evidence that this husband and wife existed. According to the ancient martyrologies, they devoted their lives and their house to the relief of the poor. Basilissa died after severe persecution, and Julian, with several others, was martyred later.
January 9th

JULIAN of ANTIOCH
A Cilician from Anazarbus, he was widely venerated in the fifth century and eulogized by St John Chrysostom at Antioch. After enduring much torture, he was sown into a sack of scorpions and vipers and drowned.
March 16th

JULIAN of BRIOUDE   Third Century
Supposed to have been a soldier in Gaul, he fled from Crispin, the persecuting governor of Vienne, but was discovered and beheaded.
August 28th

JULIAN of LE MANS
No certain facts remain, but this first bishop of Le Mans was honored in England, probably through the influence of Henry II, who was born in Le Mans.
January 27th

JULIAN of TOLEDO   † 690
As archbishop of Toledo, he gained for his see supremacy over all Spain. Among his writings his *Life* of the Visigothic king, Wamba, whom he baptized, has great historical interest.
March 8th

JULIAN SABAS   † 377
A celebrated hermit, he lived in a cave by the Euphrates in Edessa, Mesopotamia. When refuting accusations of Arianism in Antioch, during Emperor Valens' reign, he worked great miracles which revived the dying faith there.
January 17th

JULIAN THE HOSPITALLER
His legend tells us that he was a young nobleman who left his parents, because he had been told that he would one day murder them. His parents sought for him and at last came to the castle where he lived. His wife received them in his absence and placed them for the night in his own bed. On the morning she went to church and, whilst she was away, her husband returned to discover strangers in his bed. Thinking that his wife had been unfaithful to him, he slew them with his sword; but, later, when it was brought home to him what he had done, he built a hospital for poor people by a river and, as a penance, gave up the rest of his life to their care.

He has become the patron of boatmen, travellers and innkeepers.
February 12th

JULIANA   Fourth Century?
This virgin and martyr was honored at Cumae and Naples, but all we know about her is from a popular medieval story of her struggles with the Devil while she was in prison.
February 16th

JULIANA FALCONIERI   1270–1341
Juliana was the child of noble, wealthy Florentine parents, and on the death of her father was educated under the direction of St Alexis Falconieri, her uncle. Refusing to marry she entered the Servite Third Order and was instrumental in founding its conventual branch, of which she became superior. She showed great devotion to the eucharist. On the day of her death being unable to take food she was deprived of communion, and a host was placed at her request on her breast; it miraculously penetrated into her body, enabling her, says tradition, to be nourished with the sacrament of Christ's body. There is a reference to this in the collect recited on her feast day. She died in Florence in 1341.
June 19th

JULITTA, *see* Cyricus and Julitta.

JULITTA   † c. 303
An edict of the Emperor Diocletian deprived Christians of the protection of the laws, and St Julitta, a widow of Caesarea in Cappadocia, was deprived of her estates before being burned to death.
July 30th

JULIUS I   † 352
The son of a Roman, he succeeded Pope St Mark in 337. He supported the exiled St Athanasius in his claim to the see of Alexandria, insisting that any deposed bishop had the right to appeal to the pope.

St Julius built what is now the Church of the Twelve Apostles in Rome, besides many other churches in that city.
April 12th

JULIUS and AARON   † 304?
Said to have been martyred at Caerleon in Monmouthshire under Diocletian.
July 3rd

JULIUS and his Companions   † c. 302?
A veteran legionary, St Julius was martyred with three other soldiers (Pasicrates, Valentio and Hesychius) at Durostorum in Lower Moesia (Silistria in Bulgaria).
May 27th

JUSTA and RUFINA   † 287?
That these two Spanish women were Christians was

made public when they refused to sell objects for use in heathen ceremonies in their pottery shop. When challenged they refused to sacrifice to the gods and were cruelly executed.
July 19th

JUSTIN MARTYR † c. 165
The first important Christian apologist whose works are extant, Justin was martyred at Rome in the reign of Marcus Aurelius, thanks probably to the enmity of a Cynic philosopher whom he had defeated in a public disputation.
April 14th

JUSTINA, see Cyprian of Antioch and Justina.

JUSTINA
St Venantius Fortunatus, bishop of Poitiers, tells us that St Justina was the glory of Padua, where a church was built in her honor in the sixth century.
October 7th

JUSTUS and PASTOR † 304
These boys, aged thirteen and nine respectively, presented themselves to Dacian, governor of Spain, when he was conducting a trial of Christians. Angered by their lack of awe for his authority, he had them whipped and put to death.
August 6th

JUSTUS of BEAUVAIS
He was executed in Gaul by Rictiovarus during the persecutions of Diocletian. His *Acta* are, however fictitious.
October 18th

JUSTUS of CANTERBURY † 627
St Justus is a shadowy figure from the first generation of English Christianity. He was sent to England by Gregory the Great in 601 to join St Augustine of Canterbury, who made him the first bishop of Rochester in 604. It is disputed whether he was a monk or not, although it is likely that he was. During the pagan reaction in Kent he fled to Gaul, from where he was soon recalled by the repentant Kentish king. In 624 he became the fourth archbishop of Canterbury. He consecrated and despatched St Paulinus on his mission to Northumbria. He died in 627.
November 10th

JUSTUS of LYONS † c. 390
The bishop of Lyons, whose zeal and firmness against heresy gained the respect of St Ambrose, delivered up a lunatic who had assaulted passers-by to the authorities on condition that his life should be spared. Nevertheless he was lynched, and St Justus, scrupulous about his part of the affair, retired to a monastery in Egypt.
October 14th

JUSTUS of URGEL *Sixth Century*
Brother of the bishops of Valencia, Egara and Huesca, he was the first known bishop of Urgel and attended the councils of Toledo and Lerida.
May 28th

JUTTA † 1260
Born at Sangerhausen in Thuringia, she married young and, after the death of her husband, wandered through Europe barefoot, and died in Prussia, of which she is patroness.
May 5th

JUVENAL † 376
Bishop of Narni, he saved the city from the Ligurian and Sarmatian invaders – so the legend says – by calling down a great thunderstorm.
May 3rd

JUVENTINUS and MAXIMINUS † 363
Called 'pillars of the church' by John Chrysostom, they were distinguished officers under Julian the Apostate during his wars on Persia. They were beheaded at Antioch for condemning the persecution of Christians.
January 25th

KENELM † c. 812
An unlikely legend says that he succeeded to the Mercian throne at the age of seven, and that his envious sister caused Ascebert, his tutor, to murder him. The real Kenelm of Mercia reached manhood and died during the lifetime of his father.
July 17th

KENNETH, see Canice.

KENTIGERN or MUNGO *Sixth Century*
The name of Kentigern, more commonly known as Mungo, is still widely heard in the great modern city of Glasgow. For, although it has seen many metamorphoses, Glasgow is an ancient city, and owes its very origins to the saint who founded his monastery on the site before the year 540.

Kentigern seems to have come from East Lothian, on the other side of Scotland, and to have been of royal stock, his name meaning 'Lord and master'. He was compelled to leave his home at an early age and was brought up by a hermit called Serf who lived on the further side of the wide sea estuary of the Firth of Forth. It was Serf who first called him Mungo, a name signifying 'the well beloved'. Going west, he founded his monastery where Glasgow stands today. He was made a bishop, adopting Glasgow as his see. The enmity of a local ruler drove him out of Scotland, and he took refuge with St David in Wales. Here he founded the

important monastery afterwards called after his disciple, St Asaph. He later returned to Glasgow where he died at the age of about eighty-five, it is thought either in the year 603 or in 612. Six hundred years later, the magnificent Gothic cathedral, still Glasgow's finest building, was built over his shrine.
January 14th

KENTIGERNA, *see* Fillan.

KESSOG   *Sixth Century*
Scotland's national patron before St Andrew. Of royal Munster stock, he became itinerant bishop in Scotland and evangelized the country round Loch Lomond. The place and occasion of his martyrdom are uncertain, but he was buried at Luss.
March 10th

KEVIN or COEGMEN   *Seventh Century*
This name means 'well-begotten', and he is said to have been born at Leinster of royal descent. He founded the monastery of Glendalough, is one of the principal patrons of Dublin, and is the subject of many beautiful legends.   ILLUSTRATION: page 272
June 3rd

KEYNE   *Sixth Century?*
It is expressive of the state of our knowledge of St Keyne that it has been suggested that the saint was a man, not a woman. It seems on the whole unlikely; tradition is too strong that she was a virgin dedicated to the Lord, and the fourteenth century life, although not a reliable historical document, cannot be entirely ignored. The reason, however, given for that suggestion is significant. Her name is found in many places in south Wales, on the Welsh border, in Somerset and Cornwall, in the latter most notably at St Keyne in the Looe valley, where we find the once famous and still not completely forgotten holy well. She is, then, said to have travelled over these parts doing missionary work and founding churches, and the suggestion that Keyne may have been a man is based on the dangers and hardships inherent in such work. But Keyne would only have been doing that which is common work to missionaries at any time, and following the pattern of extensive journeying set by so many of the Celtic saints. She resembles them too in that she survives in folklore as well as in geography. The story goes that she turned vipers into snake-like stones in the place in Somerset where she first chose to live as a solitary; and the odd shaped fossils which are to be found in the quarries of nearby Keynsham are even today locally associated with this wonder.
October 8th

KIERAN, *see* Ciaran.

KIERAN of SAIGHIR, *see* Ciaran of Saighir.

KILIAN   *Seventh Century*
An Irishman, he went as a missionary to Artois. His legend tells us that he arrived at the house of Count Eulfus, asked for a drink and was refused. When the count came in from hunting, he found that every single cask of wine was empty. Realising the cause of this, he sent for St Kilian and apologised. The wine returned to the casks.
November 13th

KILIAN and his Companions   † *c.* 689
An Irish monk and bishop, Kilian set out with Colman and Totnan to preach in Germany. They aroused the hostility of Duke Gosbert's wife by denouncing his marriage to his brother's widow, and were murdered.
July 8th

LADISLAUS of HUNGARY   † 1095
He succeeded to the Hungarian throne in 1077 and supported the cause of Gregory VII against the emperor. Although he gave full liberty to Jews and Muslims, he was chosen to lead the First Crusade, but he died before it began.
June 27th

LAETUS, *see* Donatian, Laetus and their Companions.

LAISREN, *see* Laserian or Molaisse.

LAMBERT of LYONS   † 688
He left the court of King Clotaire III to enter the abbey of Fontenelle, of which he later became abbot, and succeeded St Genesius as archbishop of Lyons.
April 14th

LAMBERT of MAESTRICHT   *c.* 635–705
The principal patron of Liège, he succeeded his tutor, St Theodard, as bishop of Tongres-Maestricht, although four years afterwards he was banished by a palace revolution and retired to the monastery of Stavelot. He was reinstated in 682 and assassinated in 705.
September 17th

LAMBERT of VENCE   † 1154
A monk of Lérins, he became bishop of Vence in 1114, and ruled for forty years.
May 26th

LANDELINUS   *Seventh Century*
Brought up by St Autbertus, he took to a life of crime, in atonement for which he became a recluse at Lobbes. This hermitage soon became a large abbey, so he left it in the charge of St Ursmar and tried again to live a solitary life; but his settlement at Crespin also became a great monastery, and he agreed to rule as abbot.
June 15th

LANDERICUS or LANDRY   *Seventh Century*
Bishop of Paris in 650, he founded the city's first hospital, later famous as the Hôtel-Dieu.
June 10th

LANDOALD and his Companions   *Seventh Century*
According to an untrustworthy tenth century *Life*, they were missionaries in Holland and Belgium, assistants to St Amand. They included St Amantius, a deacon, St Adeltrudis, St Bavo's daughter, and St Vindiciana, Landoald's sister. They settled at Winterhoven and strengthened the faith around Maestricht.
March 19th

LANDRY, *see* Landericus.

LASERIAN, LAISREN or MOLAISSE   † 639
A monk of Iona, he was said to have been ordained at Rome by St Gregory the Great, and to have returned to Ireland. After the unsuccessful synod of White Fields, to settle the controversy over the date of Easter, he was sent to Rome where he was consecrated bishop of Leighlin by Pope Honorius, returning as papal legate for Ireland and managing to settle the Easter dispute.
April 18th

LAURENCE   † 258
Of all the Roman martyrs he has been the most popular. Alone, outside apostles, he has been honored from the fourth century by a vigil, one of the few retained under the recently revised rubrics. The Leonine Sacramentary (sixth century) assigns him no less than fourteen masses, and in the middle ages there were at least thirty-four Roman churches dedicated to him. He became in fact Rome's third patron.

How are we to account for these exceptional honors? It is a puzzle to which the key has been lost. Were the story of his fourth century Passion true, the story accepted by the Roman liturgy and well known throughout the Catholic world, the answer would be clear.

Archdeacon to St Sixtus, Laurence met the pope under arrest and reproached him for not having permitted him to share his crown. Sixtus promised that within a few days a more painful martyrdom would be his and bade him distribute the property of the church among the poor. A report of these words reached the Emperor Decius, who placed him under arrest. He converted his gaoler Hippolytus. Brought before the prefect Valerian he was commanded to surrender the church treasures. Granted three days' respite to collect them he distributed the property among the poor and, at the end of the three days, presented these poor folk to Valerian as the church's wealth. The prefect, infuriated, bade him sacrifice to the gods, and, on his refusal after a series of tortures, he was roasted to death on a gridiron. On this deathbed he taunted Decius, now in personal superintendence: 'One side has been roasted, turn me over and eat it.'

Unfortunately this Passion as it stands is incredible. Not only does the writer confuse the persecutions of Decius and Valerian, making the latter emperor prefect of the former, but he contradicts implicitly the certain fact that Pope Sixtus was not led off to trial and execution but beheaded on the scene of his arrest. Many critics, therefore, for example the Bollandist Père Delehaye, believe that Laurence suffered the decapitation of his fellow deacons. It is, however, generally accepted that he was Sixtus's seventh deacon and suffered in this persecution of 258.

But the question presses for an answer. If Laurence shared the fate – simple decapitation – of the pope and his fellow deacons, why did he receive his unique cultus? It may be replied that until his Passion was composed he did not receive any exceptional cultus. Even if this be true, we must still wonder why, of the seven deacons martyred contemporaneously, Laurence alone was made the hero of a sensational Passion.
August 10th   ILLUSTRATION: page 305

LAURENCE JUSTINIAN   1381–1455
Laurence was born of noble parents, at Venice. His mother was left a widow at the age of twenty-four with five children to bring up. From the start Laurence was distinguished by his serious and devout life, and his mother feared that the mortifications to which he subjected himself might undermine his health. She accordingly arranged an attractive marriage for him with a beautiful and wealthy girl; but Laurence decided to join the community to which his uncle already belonged, the canons of St George of Alga.

He continued to practise great austerities. In summer, he denied himself the pleasure of walking in the gardens of the community, and in winter he kept away from the fire. He suffered lack of sleep, he went thirsty, he would allow himself to be falsely accused and refused to reply in his defence, and he would walk about Venice with a sack on his back begging for alms. On one occasion, the place in which the community stored its food was burned down and, on hearing a member lament its loss, St Laurence replied, 'Why lament? We have vowed poverty, and God has granted us this blessing that we may feel it.'

He was made a priest in 1406, and, in 1433, much against his will, he was made bishop of Castello. His predecessors had inspired jealousies and conflict which were soon put down by the example given by the new bishop to his flock. He restored churches and monasteries, lived with his customary austerity, refusing to have silver upon the dining table or to keep any of the state customary to bishops. In 1451, Pope Nicholas V united the sees of Castello and Venice, and appointed St Laurence to be the first patriarch of Venice. No better archbishop could have been found, for Venice was at the height of its prosperity and achievement.

At first the Venetians were suspicious of the political consequences of St Laurence's appointment, but they were soon won round by his great humility. On one occasion, the Doge reproached him for his attacks upon women who were too fond of fashion and cosmetics, but Laurence explained himself so well that the Doge burst out laughing and said, 'You are an angel not a man. You are the only person I have ever met with whom I would be willing to change souls.'

When the fever of which he died came upon him, he refused the bed that had been prepared for him, preferring to lie upon straw. After his death on January 8th, 1455, his body remained incorrupt for two months. He was canonized in 1690.
September 5th

LAURENCE of BRINDISI   1559–1619
Cesare de Rossi born at Brindisi, was educated in Venice and became a Capuchin Franciscan in Verona. He worked among the Jews, and then in Central Europe to counter the spread of Protestantism. He became minister-general of his order; the rest of his life being spent in missionary work and diplomacy.
July 23rd

LAURENCE of CANTERBURY   † 619
He went to England with St Augustine of Canterbury, whom he succeeded as archbishop. He was so discouraged by the depraved behavior of King Ethelbald that he decided to return to France, but was rebuked and flogged by St Peter in a dream. By remaining at his post, he succeeded in converting the king.
February 3rd

LAURENCE of SPOLETO   † 576
One of a party of three hundred Catholics driven from Antioch by the heretical patriarch Severus, he became bishop of Spoleto in Italy. He was called 'the Illuminator' because of his ability as a peacemaker. He died at the monastery of Farfa, of which he was founder and abbot.
February 3rd

LAURENCE O'TOOLE   1128–1180
Lorcan O'Toole, whose name has been anglicized Laurence, was born near Castledermot, County Kildare. His father, Maurice, was a Leinster chieftain who in the course of time was reduced to a subordinate position by the encroachments of a rival great family, the MacMurroughs. The moment came when Maurice O'Toole was compelled to hand over to the Mac-Murroughs his youngest son, Laurence, aged ten, as hostage for his loyalty.

At first the boy was kept in the MacMurroughs' stronghold and treated like a member of the family. But when Maurice O'Toole again became suspect of what the MacMurroughs called treachery, Laurence was taken far away and imprisoned in a herdsman's hut 'in a desert, stony place', where he was given barely enough food to keep him alive. Two years passed before his father's overtures to relieve him were successful. The abbot of Glendalough was appointed mediator between the two families and allowed to take the boy into sanctuary. When at last Maurice O'Toole arrived in Glendalough for Laurence, he announced somewhat portentously that he intended one of his four sons to enter religion and that he would draw lots to decide which of them it should be. At this, Laurence burst out laughing, for he had long been sure of his religious vocation. No lots had to be drawn.

He remained in Glendalough and eventually became its abbot. When he was thirty-two, he was forced to leave this retreat on his appointment as archbishop of Dublin, the first native-born Irishman ever to fill that see. His elevation marked the end of Scandinavian domination in Dublin.

At a period when a precarious peace was being patched up between the MacMurroughs and the O'Tooles, Laurence's sister was given in marriage to Dermot Mac-Murrough. This classical villain of history treated her badly and later eloped with Dervorgilla, wife of Tiernan O'Rourke, prince of Breffni, an event commonly accepted as prelude to the Anglo-Norman invasion. Laurence was thus deeply implicated in the national disaster. He was at the storm centre of the conflict. When Dermot MacMurrough died, his daughter, Eva (who was Laurence O'Toole's niece), was married to Richard, earl of Pembroke, called 'Strongbow', the leader of the invasion from England. The archbishop remained in Dublin through two sieges and a famine. During the first siege, he was actually negotiating peace terms with the Normans outside the gates, when some of the soldiers treacherously broke into the city and ran amok among the civilians. Ever the father of his people, Laurence had to rush from the peace talks to save the citizens from being massacred.

In all the subsequent vicissitudes of the Anglo-Norman invasion, Laurence kept steadfastly on the side of the Irish. He went twice to King Henry II as ambassador of peace. On his second embassy in 1180, Henry refused to see him in England, and Laurence followed the king to his court at Bures, near Bayeux, in Normandy. The weeks of strain and travel told heavily on the archbishop, and by the time he reached the abbey of St Victor at Eu, he was mortally ill. Someone suggested that he should make his will, and he answered: 'God knows, I have not a penny under the sun to leave anyone.' The plight of his people in Dublin troubled his death-bed and his last words revealed his thoughts: 'Alas, you poor, foolish people, what will you do now? Who will take care of you in your trouble? Who will help you?'

He was an ascetic. Even when archbishop, he continued to live in community as a canon regular of Arrouaise. He wore a hair shirt, never ate meat, and fasted every Friday on bread and water. But when he thought it his duty to entertain, nothing customary was lacking from his table, and he drank water colored to look like wine so as not to spoil the feast. To have had to leave Glendalough remained ever a personal sorrow. Every Lent he returned to that lovely valley to make a forty days' retreat in St Kevin's cave on a precipice of Lugduff mountain over the Upper Lake. He was thus the medieval link with the Celtic saints.

It was Ireland's good fortune that St Laurence O'Toole died abroad. His *Life* was written shortly afterwards by a contemporary in Normandy, and thus his record was saved from the later upheavals in which so many precious Irish documents were lost. Fitting honor, too, was paid to his memory: a French sea port was called after him and a great Gothic church dedicated to him in Eu. Most significant of all, he was canonized only forty-five years after his death. One may safely assume that this would not have happened had he died in his own war-riven country.
November 14th

LAURENTINUS, *see* Pergentinus and Laurentinus.

LAURUS, *see* Florus and Laurus.

LAZARUS   *First Century*
The brother of Martha and Mary, whom Jesus brought back to life, he was widely honored in the early church. The relics of Lazarus were supposed to be at Marseilles, owing to a confusion with a fifth century bishop of Aix called Lazarus, but there are some grounds for believing that he may have been bishop of Larnaka (Kition) in Cyprus and that he was buried there.
December 17th

LAZARUS   *Fifth Century*
Bishop of Milan during the Gothic invasions, he is said to have introduced Rogation days with processions, litanies and fasts as a means of invoking God's protection; but it is doubtful if he was the first to do this.
February 11th

LEANDER   † 596
Of distinguished Cartagenian family, brother of SS Fulgentius, Isidore and Florentina, this bishop of Seville was the close friend of St Gregory the Great. He converted the Visigoths from Arianism, and reformed the Spanish liturgy. He introduced the recitation of the Nicene Creed in the mass, and is honored in Spain as doctor of the church.
February 27th

LEBUIN or LIAFWINE or LIVINIUS   † *c.* 773
A monk of Ripon, he went to Germany, worked under St Gregory of Utrecht, and founded a church at Deventer. He is most probably the same person as that St Livinius who was supposed to have been an Irish bishop martyred at Eschen, near Alost.
November 12th

LEGER, *see* Leodegarius.

LELIA   *Sixth Century?*
She was probably great-granddaughter of Prince Cairthenn who was baptized by St Patrick.
August 11th

LEO I (THE GREAT)   † 461
The date of St Leo's birth is not known, nor the place certainly, although it seems probable that it was Rome. We have record of him as deacon in positions of responsibility under Celestine I and Sixtus III, and he himself became pope in 440. His work was so great and so manifold that it does it much less than justice to summarize it, but it took four chief forms: control of heresy in the west, intervention in doctrinal controversy of profound importance in the east, the defence of Rome itself against barbarian invasion, and his work as pastor and teacher.

Leo took measures against no less than three heresies. The laxity which was permitting Pelagians to receive communion was done away with, and explicit confession of faith demanded before admittance to full church membership. Manichaeism had been brought to Rome by refugees from Vandal attacks in Africa, and Leo saw to it that the clandestine community was brought into public light. He also gave vigorous support to the bishops in Spain and Africa in their work against Priscillianism. The doctrinal disputes which were engaging the church in the east concerned the nature of our Lord himself. The two original protagonists were Eutyches an abbot in Constantinople and St Flavian, patriarch of Constantinople, who during the struggle received such physical ill-treatment from the supporters of Eutyches that he died. In 451 a general council of over six hundred bishops was convened at Chalcedon, and to this gathering Leo's letter on the two-fold nature of our Lord was read. 'Peter has spoken by Leo!' was the decision of the bishops. This famous letter has become a classic, setting forth the church's teaching on the nature of Christ.

There is something most spectacular about Leo's confronting of the barbarians. In 452 the Huns lead by Attila poured into northern Italy and leaving desolation in their path, marched on Rome. The terror-struck citizens, and even the General and the Emperor, could look only to Leo. He with his clergy went out from the city and held open parley with Attila, who consented to spare the city on the payment of an annual tribute. Genseric, the leader of the Vandals three years later, was less amenable to the great pope; but even then Leo's influence was so remarkable as to make the Vandals stop short at looting the city, and refrain from murdering its people and setting it on fire.

In all these ways Leo showed himself a great and wise upholder of the office he held, of its authority in matters of doctrine and its right and duty to protect the church from spiritual and, in so far as it is possible, even from physical enemies. He was also a great pastor, preaching systematically and diligently, and carrying on a remarkable correspondence with all parts of the empire; we may still read many of the letters written by him. He was declared a doctor of the church in 1754.

April 11th   ILLUSTRATION: page 306

LEO II   † 683
He succeeded St Agatho as pope in 681 and confirmed the findings of the sixth general council which had condemned Monothelism.
July 3rd

LEO III   † 816
Leo III is known only in his acts, his personality is quite lost. He became pope in 795 at a time when Rome and, often enough, the papal elections were dominated by local and aristocratic factions. The fact that Leo seems to have been of humble origin suggests a more than usual ability and sanctity for him to have been elected at all – and he was elected unanimously – under these circumstances. Unfortunately faction persisted and a number of the principal papal ministers, relatives of the last pope, attempted to force Leo to resign. They kidnapped him and attempted to put out his eyes and cut out his tongue – had they succeeded, the pope, of course, would have been unable to fulfil his duties. Leo escaped and fled for aid to Charlemagne, the king of the Franks.

For fifty years the Frankish kings, with papal encouragement, had been building their power in northern Italy, and by the last years of the eighth century, the Frankish kings had replaced the Byzantine emperors as the principal temporal support of the papacy. Charlemagne heard the pope's complaint and came, late in 800, to Rome to see for himself. Here he sat in judgment on the pope – although the fiction was maintained that the pope voluntarily chose to clear himself of the charges against him – and the pope's enemies were utterly confounded. The best men of the time, Alcuin for instance, were entirely on Leo's side, so that there is little doubt that his case was good. On Christmas day, Charlemagne entered St Peter's and his crown was placed on the altar. The pope later ceremonially replaced

it on his head, and, allegedly unknown to Charlemagne and against his wishes, the congregation hailed him with the imperial *laudes* as emperor of the west. So was the Roman Empire 'renewed' in the person of a barbarian Frankish king and at the hands of a pope; neither party can have had the least idea of the terrible and long-drawn-out consequences of this ceremony.

Leo lived until 816. He was noted as having begun the rebuilding of Rome and for having checked the long decay of the city. He also attempted to prevent the Frankish church from adding the *filioque* clause ('and the Son') to the Creed, because he was anxious to preserve unity with the Byzantine church.
June 12th

LEO IV   † 855
In 847 he succeeded Sergius II as pope, and had immediately to organize the defence of Rome against Saracen attacks. He faced all his problems – including the political and schismatic intrigues of his opponents – with determination and vision.
July 17th

LEO IX   † 1054
Although a deacon, he went to Italy with Emperor Conrad II as a military leader. While there, he was chosen bishop of Toul, and he introduced the Cluniac reform into the monasteries of the diocese. In 1048 he was chosen as pope by his kinsman the Emperor Henry III. With the help of Hildebrand he proved to be an energetic reformer, strenuously opposing simony and relaxations of the rule of celibacy, visiting and travelling and, on one occasion, assembling an army which he commanded in order to maintain the church's prerogatives. He also instituted the rule vesting the election of popes solely in the college of cardinals.
April 19th

LEO and PAREGORIUS
After Paregorius' martyrdom at Patara in Lycia, his friend Leo was apprehended by Lollian, the Lycian governor, for condemning idolatry. As he persisted, he was dragged over stones to his death.
February 18th

LEO KARASUMA, *see* Martyrs of Japan.

LEO or LYÉ   Sixth Century
At Mantenay, where he was born, Leo joined a monastery of which he later became abbot. The date of his death is said to have been revealed to him in a vision.
May 25th

LEO THE GREAT, *see* Leo I (The Great).

LEOBINUS or LUBIN   Sixth Century
A peasant's son he became a monk after hard study, and on St Avitus's advice entered an abbey near Lyons. He

was later abbot of Brou and a zealous bishop of Chartres.
March 14th

LEOCADIA † 304?
The patroness of Toledo, she is said to have died there, imprisoned for her faith during the persecution of Diocletian.
December 9th

LEOCRITIA or LUCRETIA † 859
Converted to Christianity during Moorish rule in Cordova, she was confined by her parents, but escaped to the protection of St Eulogius. She was discovered, and both saints were executed.
March 15th

LEODEGARIUS or LEGER *c.* 616–679
He was brought up in the court of Clotaire II, became bishop of Autun in 663, and was forced into political intrigue on behalf of the king against Ebroin, the mayor of the palace. In 676 the tide turned against Leodegarius who was captured, blinded and eventually murdered.
October 2nd

LEONARD of NOBLAC *Sixth Century?*
According to an eleventh-century account, which is by no means trustworthy, he was the founder of the monastery of Noblac on the site of what is now the town of Saint-Léonard in France, and he was especially venerated during the late middle ages. He was supposed to have been the godson of Clovis I, to have ensured by his prayers that the queen was safely delivered of her child, and to have been promised by Clovis that any prisoner he visited should be released. Because of these stories he was regarded as the patron of women in childbirth and of prisoners of war.
November 6th

LEONARD of PORT MAURICE 1676–1751
Born on the Italian Riviera at Porto Maurizio, he became one of the greatest missionaries of the Riformella (Reformed) branch of the Franciscans. During his missions he particularly advocated the practice of the Stations of the Cross, exposition of the blessed Sacrament, and devotion to the Sacred Heart and to the Immaculate Conception; and he is largely responsible for popularizing these devotions in the church.
November 26th

LEONARD of VANDOEUVRE † 570
St Innocent, bishop of Le Mans, became a patron of this wandering hermit and helped him to found a monastery at Vandoeuvre, of which King Clotaire later became a patron.
October 15th

LEONIDES † 202
This Christian philosopher was the father of seven sons of whom the eldest was Origen. He suffered martyrdom at Alexandria during the persecution under Severus.
April 22nd

LEONTIUS of ROSTOV † 1077
He came from Constantinople to live as a monk in the Caves of Kiev. He was appointed bishop of Rostov, where he was so ill-treated that he is regarded as a martyr.
May 23rd

LEOPOLD of AUSTRIA 1073–1136
This prince was offered and refused the imperial crown. Of his many religious foundations those at Heiligenkreuz, Klosterneuburg, and Mariazell still exist.
November 15th

LESIN, *see* Licinius.

LEU, *see* Lupus.

LEUTFRIDUS or LEUFROY † 738
Born near Évreux, he wandered far in search of instruction before returning to his birthplace and founding the monastery later known as La Croix-Saint-Leufroy.
June 21st

LEWINA
She is supposed to have been martyred by the Saxons in England before their conversion to Christianity.
July 24th

LIAFWINE, *see* Lebuin.

LIBERATA, *see* Wilgefortis.

LIBERATUS and his Companions † 484
Liberatus was the abbot of a monastery in North Africa, during the persecution of Huneric the Vandal. With six other monks, Boniface, Servus, Rusticus, Rogatus, Septimus and Maximus, he was summoned to Carthage and martyred.
August 17th

LIBERT, *see* Lietbertus.

LIBORIUS *Fourth Century*
This bishop of Le Mans is invoked against gravel, and his commemoration was added to the Calendar by Pope Clement XI, who suffered from this complaint.
July 23rd

LICINIUS or LESIN *Seventh Century*
A cousin of Clotaire I, and created count of Anjou, he became a monk and subsequently bishop of Angers.
February 13th

LIDWINA of SCHIEDAM 1380–1433
Although she has been the subject of many distinguished biographies by Thomas à Kempis and others, and is regarded as being in a special sense the patroness of all

those unknown people who lead a life of intense and prolonged suffering, Lidwina has never been formally canonized. Her cultus was recognised by Pope Leo XIII in 1890, and she is usually referred to as St Lidwina, but her inclusion in this Dictionary may be justified by the light her life throws upon one of the most interesting physical aspects of mysticism: prolonged fasting.

Lidwina was born of humble parents at Schiedam in Holland. At the age of fifteen she met with a skating accident in which she broke a rib. Complications developed until she could find no relief from the pains which afflicted every part of her body. The doctors said she could not recover, and Lidwina who had until this time been an attractive and healthy girl bitterly resented her fate; but – with the encouragement of the parish priest – she began to meditate upon the Passion, and gradually came to see her suffering as a vocation, which she now enthusiastically embraced to such an extent that she added to her mortifications by sleeping on a wooden bed.

Her beauty disappeared to be replaced by the most horrible disfigurements, her body began to putrefy; yet this life of suffering was to last nearly forty years. She soon became unable to take solid food, existing at first on wine, then on water, and finally for the last nineteen years of her life on little else than Holy Communion. In 1421 the municipality of Schiedam drew up a declaration in which it attested that 'within the seven years last passed she (Lidwina) has used no food or drink at all nor does use any at present.'

The modern reader may find such a claim quite impossible to accept, but Herbert Thurston, S.J., in *The Physical Phenomena of Mysticism* shows that the ability to live without eating is not confined to saints – as the inmates of Belsen and Dachau discovered during the last war. Evidence from cases which have been observed by sceptical and even hostile witnesses under modern conditions certainly seems to suggest that prolonged fasting from solid food is possible, but what is disputable is whether people can survive for longer than fourteen days without drinking. Illness often forces fasting upon sufferers who cannot take food without vomiting. Such was the case of Mollie Fancher of Brooklyn, New York. A Protestant, born in 1848, she was prevented by illness from eating more in thirteen years than the quantity eaten by a healthy man at a single meal. A much more controversial case is that of the Catholic, Theresa Neumann of Konnersreuth, who – it is alleged – has been fasting since September 30, 1927. She is still alive and was visited by many thousands of American and Allied soldiers during the last war.

Complete abstinence from food cannot, however, be regarded as a certain sign of supernatural intervention – as Pope Benedict XIV made quite clear in his work on the beatification and canonization of saints. Furthermore, it is much harder to establish that there has been *complete* fasting than earlier authorities realised, and no case has yet been observed in a manner which would satisfy a scientist; for there is always the risk of a person's being in such a condition that he or she is not aware of having eaten and is therefore convinced quite sincerely of having fasted completely. And as long as these prolonged fasts have their origin in a bodily disease or, as in the case of a trance, are attended by a suspension of normal bodily activities, we need not presume any supernatural interference, although modern scientists are no longer satisfied with the explanation that satisfied Benedict XIV. He believed that as long as the mind was at rest, as in the case of mystic, ecstatic or other trance-like conditions, the nervous system was nourished at the expense of the muscular tissues: the organism was living on its capital. This explanation is no longer entirely acceptable to modern biologists, so that when – as in the cases of SS Nicholas von Flüe and Catherine of Genoa – all the usual daily tasks of walking about, working, and talking are fully discharged, then we are most certainly obliged to talk of powers outside the natural order.

Lidwina's claim to sanctity, however, is based not upon her prolonged fasting or even her visions, but upon her intense and horrifying suffering nobly borne. *April 14th*

LIETBERTUS or LIBERT   † 1076
Nephew and star pupil of Bishop Gerard of Cambrai, he succeeded him in 1051. After failing to reach Jerusalem in pilgrimage, he built the monastery of the Holy Sepulchre at Cambrai.
June 23rd

LIMNAEUS, *see* Thalassius and Limnaeus.

LIOBA   † 780
Lioba came from a good Anglo-Saxon family and received her education at the abbey at Wimborne in Dorset. She became a nun there, and was sent out to Germany with a group of other nuns at the request of St Boniface of Crediton, the great Anglo-Saxon missionary to the Germans, who was a relation of her mother's. Lioba's nunnery became a center for good works of all kinds, and a motherhouse for many others, thus doing invaluable work in the conversion and civilising of the heathen Germans.

Lioba was a great abbess, and, for the times, highly educated. She ordered her community in the true traditions of Benedictine monasticism with its combination of manual and intellectual work; allowing no extreme austerities to interfere with the corporate and sane life laid down by the Rule; busy, but always with leisure

to be consulted by her own nuns, to succour the needs of the local people outside her abbey walls who turned to her on every occasion of distress, or to discuss weighty affairs with dignitaries of church and state. She was a close friend of St Boniface, who looked to her and to her nuns for continuous spiritual support in the missionary labours of his monks. Lioba survived his martyrdom many years, and finally died in retirement at an advanced age, having taken loving farewell of her friend Hildegard, wife to the Emperor Charlemagne. She was buried in the abbey church at Fulda near the tomb of St Boniface.
September 28th

LINUS
First Century

He succeeded St Peter as pope and is referred to by St Paul in his second letter to Timothy (4:21).
September 23rd

LIPHARDUS and URBICIUS
Sixth Century

A successful lawyer of Orleans, St Liphardus became a monk in middle-age and later, with St Urbicius, he retired to a secluded place which developed into a great monastery at Meung-sur-Loire.
June 3rd

LITTLE HUGH of LINCOLN, *see* Hugh.

LIUDHARD
Seventh Century

He may have been that bishop of this name who accompanied Princess Bertha, daughter of King Charibert of Paris, when she married the then heathen Ethelbert, king of Kent.
May 7th

LIVINIUS, *see* Lebuin.

LOMAN
Fifth Century?

He accompanied his uncle, St Patrick, to Ireland. After a chance meeting with Fortchern, son of the chieftain Fedelmid, Loman converted the royal household and was appointed bishop of Trim.
February 17th

LONGINUS
First Century

Legend describes him as being that centurion who, standing by the Cross, pierced Christ's side with his lance. Converted to Christianity, he was martyred either at Caesarea, or, according to the Mantuans, at Mantua.
March 15th

LOUIS BERTRAND
1526–1581

Born in Spain at Valencia, he joined the Dominicans at the age of eighteen. From 1562 to 1569 he preached the gospel in Spanish America, where his enthusiasm led him to make conversions in numbers which reflect the age's belief in the importance of the mere act of baptism and sometimes made difficulties for his successors. For instance, in the Santa Marta mountains he is said to have baptized fifteen thousand persons. He was much distress-

ed, and often impeded in his efforts, by the attitude of the Spanish colonists towards the natives. For most of his life, however, Louis Bertrand was novice-master at Valencia, an office which he discharged with his natural strictness and lack of humor, but not unkindly. He is one of the patron saints of Colombia.
October 9th

LOUIS IBARKI, *see* Martyrs of Japan.

LOUIS IX, KING of FRANCE
1214–1270

To think of St Louis is to experience afresh the concept of chivalry; it is also to make acquaintance with one of the most accessible of the saints. So accessible, indeed, is he that we are tempted to forget his claims to sanctity, among his other virtues. Louis was a brave, though not a very successful, soldier; he was an excellent administrator; he exercised his kingship with a rare nobility. These are the virtues, however, of a medieval monarch, not of a saint. Where did he show himself, then, at his most exceptional?

In order to answer that question, it is necessary to divide his life into its two main parts, and then to see where the king blends into the saint. He was born on April 25th 1214, the son of Louis VIII and Blanche of Castile, herself half English. He acceded to the throne when he was only twelve years old, and at nineteen he married Marguerite, daughter of the count of Provence, by whom he had a numerous family. By the time he assumed full power – his mother having acted as regent during his minority – he had already experienced his fill of troubles. The nobles of France, with Henry III of England in the background, were always embarking on seditious projects against the throne, and within his own household the young king had to contend with the jealousy of his strong-willed Spanish mother at the expense of his wife. It is on record, for instance, that at Pontoise, where the king and queen had rooms the one above the other, their only chance of meeting in private was on the staircase, while servants were posted to give warning of his mother's angry approach.

The first serious test of Louis's ability to rule came when Hugh of Lusignan rebelled against him, with the support of Hugh's stepson, Henry III. After defeating the English at Taillebourg in 1242, Louis, who was above all a man of peace, made the first of two settlements designed to remove all causes of war between England and France – a vain but honorable hope. Two years later, after an illness, he set in motion preparations for his first crusade, which, after the initial success of taking Damietta, in the Nile delta, came to disaster in April 1250, when he was captured with the remainder of his army. Only the subsequent overthrow of the Sultan saved his life, and made possible his release against a large ransom. He went on to the Latin kingdom of Jerusalem, until the death of his mother recalled him to France. Ten years later he announced a second crusade, in the teeth of much opposition, and, in July 1270, he embarked with his army from Aigues-Mortes for Africa. A few weeks later, in Tunis, he sickened of typhus and died. He was canonized in 1297.

So far his life gives little indication of sanctity; but behind the façade of the Christian ruler there was a striking personality at work. Perhaps its presence can best be felt in the two buildings with which his name is peculiarly associated: the Sainte Chapelle in Paris (built to accommodate the Crown of Thorns) and the abbey of Royaumont, near Chantilly. Royaumont was partly destroyed after the French Revolution, but enough of the original structure remains to show the apt combination of peace, devotion and splendor which made it one of the chief shrines of Europe for over five hundred years. Here, by the quiet waters of the Oise, and under the shade of the great forests which stretch from north and south towards the abbey buildings, it is easy to reconstruct the image of the saint superposed upon that of the king. For he was above all a saint of action, and so, although we have record of his conversing with St Thomas Aquinas and other doctors of the church, and although his personal piety was exceptionally pure, it is by his actions that he has earned his second crown.

In an age of violence, he gave a noble example of justice and mercy. He loved his people only less than he loved his faith. Of great personal simplicity, he knew how to assume the majestic trappings of royalty whenever it was fitting. Through the delightful memoirs of the Sieur de Joinville, one of his closest companions in war and in peace, we have innumerable anecdotes of his daily life – anecdotes which range from his rebuke to some overbearing bishop, to the charming story of his intervention during an argument between Joinville and Robert de Sorbon, founder of the theological institution which later became the Sorbonne. Sorbon was getting the worst of the discussion and the king strongly intervened on his side. Later, however, he took Joinville apart and whispered that he had been in the right. 'But', he said, 'I saw poor Master Robert so confused and ill at ease that he sorely needed me to come to his help.'

This warm humanity sometimes took an almost childish form. When he had been ransomed from the Saracens and was returning by boat to Acre, he complained that his brother, the count of Anjou, never kept him company on board – so much so that one day, catching him at dice with Gautier de Nemours, he lost his temper, threw over the table and cast the dice into the sea. The chronicler comments, 'It was Nemours who had the best of it, since he seized the occasion for stuffing all the coins on the table into his pocket.'

In fact, as writers through the centuries have pointed

out, it is the strength of St Louis that he was a man very like the rest of us, liable to lose his temper, apt to share the common errors of humanity, and yet ever ready, in confidence and simplicity, to carry out to the highest of his ability, and in full consciousness of the eye of Heaven fixed upon him, the tasks which lay in his path. It is not so much the sixty-five miracles established at his canonization which mark his path, it is the touching devotion and kindliness with which his short life is so constantly embellished. If St Louis has not the magical fire which surrounds the name of that other great saint of France, St Joan, he has the gift, not less ennobling, of transmuting ordinary things to instruments of a high purpose.
August 25th   ILLUSTRATION: page 307

LOUIS MARY of MONTFORT   1673–1716
Louis Grignion, founder of the Missionaries of the Company of Mary and of the Daughters of Wisdom, was ordained in 1700. Appointed chaplain to the hospital at Poitiers, he introduced improvements which aroused opposition and was forced to leave the diocese. He returned from a visit to Rome as official 'missionary apostolic' and spent the rest of his life giving missions in his native Brittany. His methods seem to have been emotional but successful. He wrote the treatise *True Devotion to the Blessed Virgin*.
April 28th

LOUIS of ANJOU   1274–97
At the age of fourteen he was sent to Barcelona as hostage for the release of his father, Charles II of Naples. He spent seven years in captivity, and on his release became a Franciscan. He was only twenty-three when he received a papal dispensation to become both a priest and bishop of Toulouse.   ILLUSTRATION: page 308
August 19th

LOUISE de MARILLAC   1591–1660
Louise de Marillac was born in the Auvergne district of France in 1591, but becoming a Parisian by her marriage with Antoine Le Gras, she remained one after his death by devoting her whole life to the poor and sick of the city. She was the foundress and the first superior of the Sisters of Charity, 'the servants of the poor', to whom, at St Vincent de Paul's request, she gave the initial training for their work. Vincent, it can be said, 'groomed' her for the position and his task, though different from hers, was equally difficult; he had to overcome her scrupulosity and impulsiveness, and try to imbue her with some of his own calm deliberation and trust in God. The work grew from parochial associations of visitors of the sick poor into a world-wide congregation of nuns. In those days, which could not conceive of nuns without cloisters and enclosure, they were a novelty. Most of them were illiterate peasants who by force of circum-

stances and under obedience were obliged to become nurses, schoolmistresses, charity organisers. They wore the peasant costume of the day and though in our own this has become a distinctive dress, in the seventeenth century it enabled the sisters to pass unremarked in the streets of Paris. Their convent, Vincent told them, was to be the house of the sick; their cloister, the city streets; their chapel, the parish church; their veil, modesty. When Louise died in 1660 the Sisters of Charity already had several houses – in Angers, Poland and Madagascar. Her body is preserved at the mother house which she established at the rue du Bac in Paris and is there exposed to the veneration of the faithful.
March 15th

LUAN, *see* Moloc.

LUBIN, *see* Leobinus.

LUCIAN and MARCIAN   † 250?
Martyred at Nicomedia under the edict of Decius, they were supposed to have been magicians who were converted to Christianity by the failure of their arts upon a Christian girl.
October 26th

LUCIAN of ANTIOCH   † 312
A noted theologian from Samosata in Syria who revised the Old and New Testaments. For some time he supported the heretic, Paul of Samosata, but entered the Catholic communion before his martyrdom at Nicomedia under Diocletian's persecution.
January 7th

LUCIAN of BEAUVAIS   *Third Century*
A Roman apostle in Gaul, he was possibly a companion of St Dionysius of Paris or of St Quentin. He was martyred with two companions, Maximian and Julian, by Julian, governor of Gaul.
January 8th

LUCILLIAN and his Companions   † 273
Formerly a pagan priest in Numidia, Lucillian was arrested and imprisoned in a hot oven, from which – according to an unreliable legend – he emerged unharmed to encourage his fellows prisoners, Claudius, Hypatius, Paul and Dionysius. They were eventually executed, as was Paula, a Christian woman who had tended them in prison.
June 3rd

LUCIUS, *see* Montanus, Lucius and their Companions.

LUCIUS, *see* Ptolemaeus and Lucius.

LUCIUS   *Second Century?*
At the beginning of his *Ecclesiastical History*, the Venerable Bede states that in the year 156, Lucius, a British king, wrote a letter to Pope St Eleutherius asking for missionaries to be sent to make him a Christian. The authenticity of this statement remains to be proved, as does the existence of St Lucius. The view usually accepted is that this story arose from a mistaken reading of a document referring to King Lucius Abgar of Edessa. The phrase 'Britium Edessenorum' (the Edessan fortress) was thought to refer to Britain (Brittania).
December 3rd

LUCIUS   † 350
He succeeded Eutropius as bishop of Adrianople, but like him was banished to Gaul for condemning Arianism. He tried to return, but was arrested and exiled again.
February 11th

LUCIUS I   † 254
Almost immediately after his accession as pope, he was exiled; and although he was allowed to return to Rome, he reigned for only eight months. The manner of his death is uncertain, but he was reputed to be a martyr.

Although he is buried in St Cecilia's, Rome, his relics are claimed by Bologna and Roeskilde, the ancient capital of Denmark, of which city he is the patron.
March 4th

LUCRETIA, *see* Leocritia.

LUCY   *Fourth Century*
Devotion to this Sicilian saint can be traced back to the fourth century, and although she is honored in the canon of the mass and as one of the chief virgin martyrs it is impossible to separate her real identity from the legends about her. According to these, she was born of noble parents in Syracuse, made a vow of virginity, and was reported to the governor by a rejected suitor for being a Christian. She was tried and executed by a sword.

As the name, Lucy, derives from 'lux' or 'light', she has become associated with festivals of light and with invocations against afflictions of the sight. Additions to her legend occurred in which she was blinded by her persecutors, and the church of San Giovanni Maggiore at Naples even claims to possess her eyes.
December 13th   ILLUSTRATION: page 309

LUCY FILIPPINI   1672–1732
Sent from Tuscany to an educational institute in Montefiascone, under Bd Rose Venerini she became a most successful and beloved promoter of education. In Rome, she started the Maestre Pie, an institute of immense importance in the education of Italian women.
March 25th

LUDAN   *Thirteenth Century?*
By tradition, a Scottish prince, he gave his wealth to charity and died on a pilgrimage to Rome, receiving his last communion from an angel. His relics were honored at Scheerkirche, near Hispheim.
February 12th

LUDGER † 809

A Frisian, he was educated at Utrecht and then under Alcuin at York. He was given spiritual charge over five Frisian provinces by Charlemagne. As bishop of Münster he evangelized Heligoland and Westphalia, and founded many religious buildings.

March 26th

LUDMILA 860–921

When her husband, Duke Borivoy of Bohemia who was converted by St Methodius, died, she supervised the upbringing of her grandson St Wenceslaus. Before he could come to the throne, she was murdered by those who resented her influence.

September 16th

LUDOLF † 1250

A Premonstratensian canon regular before becoming bishop of Ratzeburg. He was banished after brutal persecution by Duke Albert of Sachsen-Lauenberg, and died as a result, at Wismar in Mecklenburg. He founded the Rehna convent.

March 29th

LUFTHILDIS *Ninth Century*

No contemporary account exists of this saint's life, but legend says that she was persecuted by her stepmother for persistently giving to the poor, and that she later became a hermit.

January 23rd

LUGHAIDH, *see* Molua.

LUKE THE EVANGELIST

St Luke, the author of the third Gospel and the Acts of the Apostles, was the largest single contributor to the New Testament. He was also, as his writings show, one of the best educated of the early Christians. Yet so extreme were his modesty and self-effacement that even the little we do know about him has to be read between the lines with a magnifying -glass. We focus it first upon the 'we-sections' of the Acts (where St Luke, by using 'we' instead of 'they' admits his own presence on the scene). We shift it to the sparse references in St Paul ('Demas and Luke, who share my labours,' 'the beloved Luke, my doctor,' 'only Luke is with me'). We search out the subjects about which he seems especially well-informed (like the geography and administration of the empire and, of course, medical matters). We examine his choice of language and the use he made of earlier Christian writings. And gradually, as in a developing-dish, the latent image of St Luke emerges.

He was a Greek, not a Jew, by birth; but since all the great cities of the near east were Greek, in language and civilization, he may have been born in any of them. A second century writer, however, whose word there is no reason to doubt, says that he was a native of Antioch in Syria, and at all events he seems to have been living there in the forties of the first century and to have been one of the earliest Gentile converts. By profession he was a doctor, and the most likely university for his studies would be Tarsus. It is therefore possible that he had some previous acquaintance with St Paul. To St Paul, at any rate, he attached himself, and he emerges into the light of his own writings as a member of St Paul's mission through Asia Minor into Europe about 49 or 50 A.D. When the party reached Philippi, however, St Luke stayed there – not as the bishop of the newly-founded church, for he never seems to have taken holy orders, but rather as what we should call a 'leading layman'. Moreover, he seems already to have cast himself for the part of an historian – a rôle for which his education and training well suited him. Careful observation and precise description were the watch-words of the Greek medical schools, and St Luke's writings show that he knew how to apply them in the field of history. He had already kept exact notes of what he had himself observed, and he evidently kept in touch, by correspondence, with St Paul and his companions.

In about 57, however, St Paul returned from Corinth through Macedonia on his way to Jerusalem, gathering 'legates' from different churches as he went, and St Luke joined him. From then onwards he was never far from his master's side. He witnessed the attempted lynching of St Paul by the Jews and his rescue by the Roman police. When St Paul set sail for Rome, after two years of imprisonment at Caesarea, St Luke was with him. They were shipwrecked together in Malta and arrived together in Rome. But at Rome St Luke found another task awaiting him. Rome was the see of Peter, and St Peter's spokesman, St Mark, was engaged on (or had already published) his written Gospel. But there were in existence other memoirs, written or oral, fragmentary or complete, of our Lord's life on earth. St Luke decided that the mission to the gentiles needed a new Gospel, written in more 'literary' Greek than Mark's, so as not to offend the taste of educated pagans, and not addressed so exclusively to Jews as Matthew's, so as to present in a coherent form the most authentic material available on the life of Christ. The composition of this book and its sequel, the Acts, appears to have been completed in Rome between 61 and 70 A.D., but St Luke escaped the persecution of the Christians by Nero, in which SS Peter and Paul perished (*c.* 66 A.D.) and spent the latter part of his life in Greece. 'Serving the Lord faithfully,' writes our second-century authority, 'unmarried and childless, he died at the age of eighty-four in Boeotia, full of the Holy Spirit.'

St Luke has always been a very popular saint. This is partly, perhaps, because we understand him so well. He is a layman, a European, inheriting the culture of classical

Greece. He is 'one of us'. But still more is it due to his gentle and engaging character. All his writings are full of human interest, human sympathy, concern for the poor, chivalry towards women; and he was obviously attracted by, and avidly collected for his Gospel, the record of Christ's countless works of mercy. Indeed, one might almost find fault with him for dimming out the sterner side of our Lord's character and teaching. But the doctors, whose patron saint he is, have every reason to be proud of him, for surely no physician ever surpassed him in that 'love of mankind' which Hippocrates enjoins. And the rest of us can be grateful to him as well, for it is to him that we owe the parable of the barren fig-tree (13:6), of the prodigal son (15:11) and of the good Samaritan (10:30). We also owe him the story of the repentant thief and all the five joyful mysteries of the Rosary. But above all we owe him the *Ave Maria*, the *Magnificat*, the *Benedictus* and the *Nunc dimittis* with more than half the story of Christmas day; and it is here that his self-effacing modesty most tantalizes us.

Did St Luke get the story from the Mother of God herself? He does not tell us, but it is quite possible. After the crucifixion, we know, she was cared for by St John, and there is certainly evidence of contact between these two evangelists. Incidents in their Gospels (especially St Luke's account of the transfiguration, with its Johannine words 'They saw his glory') and similarities of language in the early part of Acts, strongly suggest it. Moreover, if St Luke was baptized at Antioch in the early forties of the century it would have been natural for him to seek out St John in Jerusalem. Our Lady, at that time, would have been no more than seventy years old, or less. There is thus no reason why St Luke may not have heard the story from her own lips. But even if it came to him more indirectly we still owe him eternal gratitude for preserving it; and when we sing our carols or when we gaze, in churches or museums, at pictures of the Annunciation, Visitation or Nativity it would be a gracious gesture to one of the most gracious of saints to send him up a little prayer of thanks.
October 18th

LUKE THE YOUNGER   *Tenth Century*
Son of a farmer in Thessaly, he was a youth of remarkable holiness and charity. When he sowed the fields for his father, he made sure that half the seed fell on the lands of the poor. After overcoming many difficulties, he became a hermit on Mount Joannitsa in Corinth.
February 7th

LULL   † 786
A monk of Malmesbury, he went to Germany to work as a missionary under St Boniface, whom he succeeded as bishop of Mainz.
October 16th

LUPICINUS, *see* Romanus and Lupicinus.

LUPUS or LEU   † 623
This bishop of Sens was banished by King Clotaire on a false charge but was very soon reinstated.
September 1st

LUPUS or LOUP   † 478
He separated from his wife to become a monk of Lérins. Elected bishop of Troyes, he maintained his monastic way of life and accompanied St Germanus of Auxerre to Britain in 429.

Later on, he was taken hostage by Attila the Hun and, although his intervention had saved Troyes from pillage, he was banished from his see for two years because of the groundless rumor that he had collaborated with his captor.
July 29th

LUTGARDIS   † 1246
Because she had no dowry and was unlikely to find a husband, she entered a Benedictine convent at the age of twelve; but after a vision of our Lord she changed her way of life and became a mystic. Later she moved to the Cistercian house of Aywières.
June 16th

LUXORIUS, CISELLUS and CAMERINUS
                                                     † 303?
Luxorius, a Roman soldier and a convert, was stationed at Sardinia when the persecution of Diocletian began. With two young boys, Cisellus and Camerinus, he was executed by order of the prefect Delphius.
August 21st

LYÉ, *see* Leo.

Macaire, *see* Macarius of Ghent.

MACANISIUS   *Fifth Century?*
Many extraordinary stories about this Irish saint are preserved, but no facts. He is supposed to have been the founder and first bishop of the diocese of Connor.
September 3rd

MACARIUS of ALEXANDRIA   *Fourth Century*
An Alexandrian confectioner who departed to the Lower Egyptian deserts, he became a celebrated leader of anchorites. Himself a rigorous ascetic, he made silence and fasting so important in his rule that the story is told that on being given a present of a bunch of grapes, he passed them on to a sick monk, who in turn passed them on to another monk until, eventually, the grapes found their way back to Macarius.
January 2nd

MACARIUS of JERUSALEM † c. 335

According to tradition he miraculously discovered Christ's Cross in Jerusalem and was entrusted by Constantine with the construction of a church on the site of the holy sepulcher. As bishop of Jerusalem he was noted for his staunch opposition to Arianism.
March 10th

MACARIUS or MACAIRE of GHENT † 1012

Although his cult is popular in Flanders, where he is invoked against all epidemics, little is known about this saint.
April 10th

MACARIUS THE ELDER † 390

A cow-herd of Upper Egypt, at an early age he became a hermit. He was falsely accused by a woman of having assaulted her, and, as he suffered her accusations in silence, he was dragged through the streets and beaten for his hypocrisy. Still he suffered in silence, sending the woman money against the day when her child would be born. At last the woman confessed, and Marcarius withdrew into the desert where he presided over the many anchorites drawn to him by his reputation. Although his austerities were great – he usually ate once a week – he never gave way to spiritual conceit. 'Fasting pleases when men see you,' he once said, 'but it seems intolerable when the craving for esteem cannot be gratified because you are by yourself.'
January 15th

MACARIUS THE WONDER WORKER
† c. 830

Abbot of Pelekete and famous for his miraculous cures of the sick, he was banished for his anti-iconoclastic attitude to the island of Aphusia, off the coast of Bithynia, where he died.
April 1st

MACARTAN Sixth Century

Very little is known of him, but he is said to have been a great teacher, and was possibly consecrated bishop by St Patrick.
March 26th

MACCUL, see Maughold.

MACEDONIUS Fifth Century

Theodoret, whose mother was cured by this Syrian ascetic, relates many tales of his great healing powers. He lived on bread and water until he was ninety.
January 24th

MACHABEES † 168 B.C.?

One of the rare instances in which saints of the Old Testament have been commemorated in the liturgy of the western church. These martyrs take their name from Judas Machabeus, son of Mathathias, the original leader of the Jewish revolt against Antiochus Epiphanes of Syria. They were put to death at Jerusalem for defying the attempt by Antiochus to convert them forcibly from Jewish to Pagan beliefs. The Machabees, of whom one of the most prominent was an old man called Eleazar, a leading Scribe, have been honored among Christians from the earliest times, perhaps because their sufferings anticipated and closely paralleled those of the first Christian martyrs. (*See* 2 Machabees ch. 6 and 7).
August 1st

MACHAR Sixth Century

An Irish missionary, he accompanied St Columba to Scotland and was probably the first bishop of Aberdeen.
November 12th

MACRINA THE ELDER Fourth Century

Grandmother of St Basil the Great, who attributed his doctrinal purity to her careful instruction; she and her husband lived in constant danger and discomfort from religious persecution.
January 14th

MACRINA THE YOUNGER 330–379

Daughter of St Basil the Elder and St Emmelia, she helped to bring up her younger brothers, including SS Basil the Great, Peter of Sebaste and Gregory of Nyssa. On her mother's death, she gave all her goods to the poor.
July 19th

MADELEINE SOPHIE BARAT 1779–1865

Under the guidance of her brother Madeleine Sophie Barat became at an early age proficient in Latin, Greek, Spanish and Italian. The brother, nine years her senior, was a stern disciplinarian. If her work was bad, she was punished – sometimes by a box on the ears – but if she did well, no word of praise was uttered. She was never allowed to relax from this discipline – even walks were forbidden unless they were strictly necessary for exercise; and when, in a moment of mistaken tenderness, she gave her brother a present, he threw it on the fire. She was ten when the French Revolution occurred in 1789. Afterwards, and still under the influence of her brother, she met Father Varin who desired to found a female counterpart of the Jesuits which should do for girls' education what they did for boys'. On November 21st, 1800, Madeleine with three companions dedicated herself to the Sacred Heart and so the New Congregation was begun. From the first house at Amiens it was to spread in the lifetime of its foundress all over Europe and to Africa and America, and its boarding schools have become famous.

Madeleine's energy in extending the work was seconded by her reliance on God which enabled her to succeed in times of great difficulty. 'Too much work is a danger to an imperfect soul,' she said, 'but for one who loves our Lord it is an abundant harvest.'

May 25th ILLUSTRATION: page 310

MADELGISILUS or MAUGUILLE
Seventh Century
He crossed to England from Ireland with St Fursey, and, after his death, lived as a recluse near the monastery of Saint-Riquier or Centula.
May 30th

MADRON or MADERN *Sixth Century?*
Nothing is known of this saint who has given his name to a parish in Cornwall, but great interest was aroused in the seventeenth century, when a cripple named John Trelille was cured by bathing three times in the stream which flowed through the baptistery of the church.
May 17th

MAEDOC, *see* Aidan of Ferns.

MAELOR, *see* Maglorius.

MAELRUBHA, *see* Malrubius.

MAFALDA or MATILDA † 1252
The daughter of King Sancho I of Portugal, her marriage at the age of eleven to King Henry I of Castile was annulled because of their consanguinity. She then joined the Benedictine house of Arouca, which she persuaded to change to the Cistercian rule.
May 2nd

MAGENULF or MEINULF † *c.* 857
Charlemagne's godchild, he became a priest and devoted his wealth to founding a nunnery on his estate at Bödoken.
October 5th

MAGLORIUS or MAELOR *Sixth Century*
Said to have been the son of St Umbrafael, he was educated by St Illtyd and became the companion in Brittany of St Samson, whom he succeeded as abbot and bishop of Dol. He founded a monastery on Sark to which he retired.
October 24th

MAGNERICUS † 596
Educated by St Nicetius, bishop of Trier, he went with him into exile, and, six years after their return, became his successor.
July 25th

MAGNUS † 1116
In the early centuries of Christianity in Britain, the Christian peoples suffered constantly from the raids of the pagan Vikings of Norway, who were in possession of many of the Scottish islands. The Viking earl of Orkney in the eleventh century had a son, Magnus, who sailed in the service of the king of Norway on many bloodthirsty raids. But, during a fierce battle off the Welsh island of Anglesey, Magnus refused to fight, saying that the battle was unjust and cruel. This was an act of great disgrace in Viking eyes, and Magnus had to escape. He lived for a time at the Scottish court of Malcolm III. Then he and his cousin, Haakon, were made joint earls of Orkney. Haakon soon became jealous of Magnus, who was much loved for the justice and clemency of his rule, and Haakon picked a quarrel with him. He invited Magnus to come alone to the little island of Egilsay to settle their differences. Magnus came with one or two friends, but soon they saw that Haakon was treacherously arriving with a fleet of armed longships. Magnus went into the little church on Egilsay to pray, and then came out to meet his death.

Magnus was one of the most popular pre-Reformation saints in Scotland. His nephew, St Ronald, who became earl of Orkney, had a splendid cathedral built, which still stands intact at Kirkwall in the Orkneys. A famous London church, St Magnus the Martyr, was also dedicated to him.
April 16th

MAHARSAPOR † 421
One of the first Persian martyrs, this nobleman was walled up in a cistern after three years of suffering.
October 10th

MAIMBOD *Ninth Century*
An Irish missionary in France, he was killed by pagans while preaching near Kaltenbrunn in Alsace.
January 23rd

MAJOLUS or MAYEULE † 994
Abbot of Cluny – *see* the Cluny Saints.
May 11th

MAJORICUS, *see* Dionysia, Majoricus and their Companions.

MALACHY 1095–1148
Malachy O'More was the son of a professor in the Armagh School. Although plundered and burned nine times by the Ostmen, it was still functioning strongly and had lost none of its prestige as the leading ecclesiastical school in Ireland.

Generally speaking, however, the destruction of the Celtic monasteries by the Vikings had deprived the Irish church of an indispensable spiritual and cultural influence. In many parts of the country, Christian people were then forced to mingle with the heathen, and, in the words of an ancient writer, there followed a period of 'deathly barbarism'. By the twelfth century, Ireland was largely cut off from Rome with the result that many abuses had crept into church organization. One of the worst of these was that laymen held abbacies and bishop-rics by right of hereditary succession, collecting the revenues and appointing priests to carry out the spiritual duties.

Malachy decided to be a priest, and he had the good fortune to find teachers, first in Armagh and later in Lismore, who had experience in other countries of strict church discipline and knew the need for reform in Ireland. Malachy's own family provided an illustration of the prevalent abuse. His uncle, a layman, inherited the abbacy of Bangor, once a famous Celtic monastery, but at this time a forlorn ruin, although still richly endowed. After Malachy's ordination, the uncle resigned from Bangor in his favor. Immediately Malachy struck a blow for reform and set a headline to the Irish church by accepting the office and the ruined site, while he handed on to another all the lands and revenues. He went to live in the derelict abbey and began the work of restoration by sawing up with his own hands timber for the construction of huts to house students. Soon he was joined by a band of disciples, all eager to restore monastic life. Such was Malachy's influence, he was made bishop of Down and Connor a year later, and five years afterwards he was appointed archbishop of Armagh, so that here, too, he might break the evil tradition of hereditary succession. There was a rival claimant, however, and for three years Malachy refused to accept Armagh, having no wish to increase the strife and bloodshed fomented by his rival's supporters.

Finally installed in Armagh, he carried on the fight for reform at the source of authority in the Irish church. When order was restored, he resigned the primacy but continued to work at the reorganisation of the church. Late in the year 1139, he set out for Rome to obtain papal approval of the newly created archdiocese of Cashel as well as for his work in Armagh. On his way through France, he visited St Bernard in Clairvaux, and the two saints became close friends at their first meeting. Malachy was charmed with Clairvaux, where he saw the realization of all his monastic ideals.

On reaching Rome, he asked the pope to allow him to retire to Clairvaux, but instead Innocent II made him papal legate to Ireland. On his return journey, Malachy left four of his companions to be trained at Clairvaux. A few years later, he established at Mellifont in Louth the first of a series of Irish Cistercian foundations, which were an invaluable asset to the church in Ireland.

Malachy travelled the country for another eight years, bringing the people back to the sacraments and restoring the liturgical life of the church. Dressed in a plain habit, he preferred to travel on foot and mingle with the people, who were greatly attracted by his mortified ways. When he had reorganized the Irish church, he completed its unification by presiding over a national council of the hierarchy.

Then he left Ireland once more to secure the approval of Pope Eugenius III, who was then in France, but who had left that country again before Malachy could reach it. The disappointed papal legate arrived at Clairvaux seriously ill and died a few days later in the arms of St Bernard. It was the feast of All Souls in the year 1148. He was fifty-four. His tomb was placed beside the high altar in the abbey church.

St Bernard immediately wrote Malachy's *Life*, thus saving his friend's memory from the flood of ruin which was to overwhelm the Irish church in later centuries. It is mostly thanks to St Bernard's biography, his letters and his two sermons on the same theme, that full recognition was given to Malachy as the greatest reformer of his century, that he was so speedily canonized in the year 1190, and that his name is prominent in European literature.

November 3rd

MALCHUS   *Fourth Century*
St Jerome is our authority for the story of St Malchus whom he met as a very old man near Antioch. As a young man, Malchus had been a desert monk who, on the death of his father, had set off home to look after his mother. On the journey, the caravan to which he belonged was attacked, and he was taken off into slavery together with a young woman whom his captor insisted on his marrying. Threatened with death if he disobeyed, Malchus agreed, but the couple lived as brother and sister and went through many adventures together. Of the woman, Malchus told Jerome that although he loved her as a sister, he never entirely trusted her as a sister; but she insisted on living near him, even after they had managed to escape and Malchus had rejoined his monastery.

October 21st

MALLONIUS or MELLON   *Fourth Century*
He was the first bishop of Rouen, but there is a village in Wales called after him, and he may have been a Welshman by birth.

October 22nd

MALO   *Seventh Century*
A Welsh monk, he evangelized Brittany and the port of St Malo stands on the site of the headquarters of his diocese.

November 15th

MALRUBIUS or MAELRUBHA   † 722
He became a monk at the abbey of Bangor, and crossed to Scotland, where as abbot of Applecross, his piety and learning were famous.

April 21st

MAMAS † c. 275

A shepherd, he was martyred at Caesarea in Cappadocia.
August 17th

MAMERTUS   *Fifth Century*

Elder brother of the poet Claudian, and bishop of
Vienne, he began the custom of penitential processions
during the three Rogation days before the Ascension.
May 11th

MANECHILDIS   *Sixth Century?*

According to an unreliable legend, she was the youngest
of a family of seven girls, all of whom received the veil
from St Alpinus and became saints.
October 14th

MAPPALICUS and his Companions   † 250

Mappalicus, a confessor, was one of eighteen Carthagin-
ians who, in April 250, died of torture or starvation
during the persecution of Decius.
April 17th

MARCELLA   † 410

Widowed soon after marriage, she devoted herself to
charitable works with St Jerome as her spiritual adviser.
He referred to her as the glory of Roman ladies, and
she established several communities for other Roman
ladies who followed her example.
January 31st

MARCELLIAN, *see* Mark and Marcellian.

MARCELLINA   † c. 398

Her father was prefect of the Gauls and her brother was
St Ambrose of Milan. In 353 she took a vow of chastity
and spent the rest of her life in prayer and mortification.
July 17th

MARCELLINUS, *see* Cletus and Marcellinus.

MARCELLINUS   † 413

Friend of St Augustine and secretary of state to the
Emperor Honorius, he was sent to Carthage to judge
between the Catholics and the Donatists. In revenge for
his adverse judgement and subsequent repression, the
Donatists accused him and his brother Apringius of
complicity in Heraclian's rebellion, and they were
executed without trial.
April 6th

MARCELLINUS and PETER   † 304

Marcellinus was a well-known priest in Rome, and
Peter is said to have been an exorcist. They suffered
martyrdom during the reign of Diocletian, and are
commemorated in the canon of the Mass.
June 2nd

MARCELLINUS of EMBRUN   *Fourth Century*

With St Vincent and St Domninus, he was an active
evangelist in France, and became the first bishop of
Embrun. Through the persecution of the Arians, he
died in exile.
April 20th

MARCELLUS I   † 309

He succeeded St Marcellinus as pope in 308 but reigned
for only a year as he was banished by Maxentius for his
severity against apostates and lapsed Christians. His body
lies under the high altar of the church in Rome which
bears his name. The account of his alleged martyrdom
is unreliable and conflicts with earlier evidence.
January 16th

MARCELLUS AKIMETES   † c. 485

The Akoimetoi monks ('the non-resters') were so called
because, by taking turns, they sang the divine office
through day and night without a break. Their monastery
was situated on the opposite shore of the Bosphorus to
Constantinople, and Marcellus became its third abbot.
He ruled for forty-five years, besides helping to establish
other foundations of which the most celebrated was the
monastery founded in 463 at Constantinople.
December 29th

MARCELLUS and APULEIUS

They are said to have been converted by St Peter, and
to have been martyred at Rome.
October 7th

MARCELLUS and CASSIAN   † 298

The best known of the saints called Marcellus was a
centurion in the reign of the Emperor Diocletian.
Christians were soldiers in the Roman legions; but,
during the feasting and merrymaking at Tangier that
accompanied the celebration of the emperor's birthday,
Marcellus found he could be one no longer. He dropped
his soldier's belt, the sign of his allegiance, by the
standards of the legion, and threw down his cane – his
symbol of authority as an officer – and his arms. 'I serve
Jesus Christ, the eternal king,' he said, 'from now on I
serve your emperors no more.' The soldiers seized him
and reported the matter to their commander, who
ordered Marcellus to be imprisoned.

When the festivities were over Marcellus was brought
before the commander, who interrogated him carefully
and not without fairness. Marcellus stated plainly that
on the day in question he had said in public that as
a Christian his only allegiance was to the Son of God
the Father almighty. The commander said, 'I can't
overlook your rash behavior. I must report this to
Caesar.' And he referred the case to Aurelius Agricolan,
the deputy for the perfects of the guard. Marcellus
was brought before Agricolan in court and the charge
was read: he had thrown off his belt of allegiance,
and, saying that he was a Christian, pronounced

public blasphemies against the gods and against Caesar. Agricolan questioned Marcellus about his mad actions, and Marcellus boldly affirmed that he had indeed done those things which had been reported of him. 'I did throw my arms,' he said, 'for it is not right for a Christian who serves the Lord Christ to serve also the demands of the world.' It would seem that Marcellus, in the midst of pagan merrymaking and no doubt the customary paying of divine worship to the Emperor, had seen clearly the entanglements in which his post as an officer of the Roman army was gradually ensnaring his soul. His call was not unlike that which takes men from positions of importance and authority to monastery or hermitage: the acute sense of being increasingly smothered by the affairs of the world, and the essential need to get back to the heart of life. But with Marcellus it was sudden and overwhelming. Agricolan took strong disciplinary action, and Marcellus was condemned to death. 'God bless you,' said Marcellus. And he was taken out of the court and beheaded.

There is appended to the very trustworthy account of the martyrdom of St Marcellus one also of the death of St Cassian. According to this he was a shorthand writer at the trial of Marcellus, and was so outraged by Agricolan's sentence that he could not restrain his feelings. He made common cause with Marcellus and himself suffered martyrdom soon afterwards. Unfortunately the report of this, which is vivid and lively enough, is of doubtful authenticity, although there seems certainly to have been a Cassian martyred in Tangier. *December 3rd (Cassian); October 30th (Marcellus).*

MARCELLUS and his Companions † 287?
These martyrs, who comprised a whole Christian community, were beheaded either at Oxyrynchus in the Egyptian Thebaid or in Moesia (Rumania).
August 27th

MARCELLUS and VALERIAN † c. 178
They escaped from the massacre at Lyons of St Pothinus and his companions in 177, but were martyred very soon afterwards.
September 4th

MARCELLUS of APAMEA † c. 389
As bishop of Apamea in Syria, he personally superintended the destruction of many heathen temples. One of these, however, was strongly defended, and Marcellus was killed by the defenders; for this he is accounted a martyr.
August 14th

MARCELLUS of PARIS † c. 410?
He succeeded Prudentius as bishop of Paris, and the suburb in which he is buried is still called Saint-Marceau.
November 1st

MARCHELM † 762
An Englishman, he was inspired by the example of St Willibrord to undertake missionary work in the Low Countries. He died at Oldenzaal.
July 14th

MARCIAN, *see* Lucian and Marcian.

MARCIAN, *see* Nicander and Marcian.

MARCIAN † c. 387
A Syrian patrician, he was a hermit of such distinction that, much to his dismay, his fame became wide-spread, his followers multiplied, and there were quarrels as to who should have his body. His nephew Alipius even went so far as to build a chapel for its reception while Marcian was still alive.
November 2nd

MARCIAN † 471
Born of a distinguished Roman family in Constantinople, he was ordained priest by the Patriarch Anatolius. His strict morality and fervent endeavors to assist the poor brought him high dignity in the church.
January 10th

MARCIAN or MARIAN Fifth Century
He entered a monastery at Auxerre as an exile from Bourges, then held by the Visigoths. He looked after the farm animals and seems to have had a special power over all animals, for there are many stories about the care and protection he gave them.
April 20th

MARCIANA Fourth Century
A Christian from Rusuccur in Mauritania, she was bitterly persecuted under Diocletian for spurning idolatry. Her chastity miraculously remained inviolate, but she was finally killed by wild animals in the amphitheatre at Caesarea.
January 9th

MARCULF or MARCOUL Sixth Century
Of noble family, he set out as a missionary but retired to found a monastery at Nanteuil. He was looked upon as the patron of skin diseases, and the French King was supposed to have derived from him the power of healing known as 'touching for the king's evil'.
May 1st

MARGARET MARY ALACOQUE 1647–1690
St Margaret was born on July 22nd, 1647 at Lhautecour in the Charolais district of Burgundy. She was the fifth child of Claude Alacoque, a royal notary.

When she was eight years old, her father died, and her troubles began in earnest. Her mother fruitlessly tried to collect bad debts he had left in the countryside.

Mother and daughter were obliged to share the farm with relations-in-law, envious, rapacious and coarse, who were glad to have the refined Alacoques at their mercy. Margaret was cured from a wasting sickness at fourteen, after making a vow to our Lady that she would one day be one of her daughters. In June 1671, after many struggles, she entered the Visitation convent of Paray-le-Monial among forty aristocrats, some of whom had no vocation.

In the retreat before her profession, our Lord said, 'Behold the wound in my side, wherein thou art to make thine actual abode, now and for ever.' She was professed on November 6th, 1672, and made assistant to the kindly but brisk and practical infirmarian who had small use for ecstasies.

The first of the four great visions in which Christ revealed his Sacred Heart to her took place soon after Christmas on the feast of St John the Evangelist, 1673. He said, 'My divine Heart is so inflamed with love for men, and for thee in particular, that being unable any longer to contain within itself the flames of its burning charity, it must spread them abroad by thy means.'

In the second great vision, 'He assured me that we must honour the heart of God under the figure of this heart of flesh.'

The third great vision took place on a first Friday of some unspecified month. Christ especially enjoined her to communicate on the first Friday of each month.

These revelations brought all manner of physical infirmity to her which she welcomed joyfully.

In the autumn of 1674, God promised to send her a servant of his to confirm her in her way. 'My faithful servant and perfect friend,' Père Claude la Colombière made his final vows at Lyons in February 1675, and immediately afterwards, to the surprise of everybody who had followed his brilliant career in Paris, he was sent to be superior of the Jesuit house at Paray. A shrewd intellectual, he never knew ecstasies by personal experience, but was content to love Christ in 'a cloud of unknowing'. When he saw Margaret, he was inspired to say to Mère Saumaise: 'She is a chosen soul.' He confirmed her in her way.

The greatest vision of all took place within the octave of Corpus Christi in the year 1676. Before the Blessed Sacrament exposed on the altar, she heard these tremendous words: 'Behold this Heart which has so loved men, that it has spared nothing, even to exhausting and consuming itself in order to prove its love to them.' And then Christ asked her that the Friday after the octave of Corpus Christi should be set apart for a special feast to honor his heart; Communion was to be received on that day and reparation made by a solemn act.

Père la Colombière told her to commit all her visions to writing before he left for London.

The terrible persecution from the community came to a head on November 20th, 1677. Our Lord commanded Margaret to offer herself as a victim to divine justice, to expiate the sins of the community against charity. When she knelt down to do so, they all began to think she had gone out of her mind. The night that ensued is almost unbelievable. She said that all the sufferings of her life put together would not compare with what she endured that night. Afterwards, one of the nuns affirmed on oath: 'She knew that the said sister Alacoque had suffered all that one could suffer by contempt, contradictions, rebukes, insults, reproaches, without complaining, and praying for those by whom she was ill treated.'

Mère Saumaise, her superior, left on Ascension Day 1678, and on June 17th came forty-four year-old Mère Greyfié, providentially sent to sift the evidence, to put the saint to the test and to guard her exquisite humility. Mère Greyfié decided that Margaret's complete cure from her ills, for a specified time, would be the proof that her visions were authentic.

In 1684 Mère Greyfié left Paray. A new generation of young nuns was springing up. Soon after, Margaret was appointed novice mistress. On her feast, St Margaret's Day, July 20th 1685, which fell that year on a Friday, Margaret told her novices that, instead of presents, she would prefer them to offer to Christ's heart all the honors they had intended for her. So they prepared a little altar for her on the morning of her feast, having placed on it a crude, naïve drawing of the wounded Heart surrounded by flames and a crown of thorns. By June 1686 the nuns were doing honor to a miniature of the Sacred Heart in choir. On September 7th, 1688, the first chapel in the garden was consecrated to the Sacred Heart.

Her work done, Margaret fell ill on October 8th, 1690. She whom Abbé Bremond movingly calls 'so fragile and so lofty, so dolorous and so exquisite' was soon to become the inheritor of all the graces of the Sacred Heart. She died in an ardent transport of love on 17th October. She was forty-three years of age.

The nuns noticed how beautiful she had become. Outside in the street could be heard the voices of children crying out: 'The saint of the Holy Maries is dead.'

She was beatified in 1864 and canonized in 1920.
October 17th

MARGARET of CORTONA   1247–1297

She was born at Laviano in Umbria, of a poor peasant family. Brought up by a stepmother who hated her, she grew into a girl of unusual beauty, and at seventeen she was seized and carried off by a young nobleman. She lived with him for the next nine years, and had a son. In 1273 her lover met a tragic and mysterious end – according to tradition, Margaret was guided by his dog to find his murdered body in a forest – and she set out for home with her son. Refused admission by her triumphant stepmother, she turned to the Franciscans of Cortona; but they told her she was too young and pretty to be admitted.

The Moscari, a kindly family of the neighborhood, took in Margaret and her child; and for several years she lived with them, earning her own living by looking after children, and atoning for her past by penances whose severity alarmed the town. Hating her own beauty, she wanted to disfigure her face with a razor, but her confessor forbade this. Eventually she was received as a Tertiary (member of the lay order) of St Francis, and in 1277 the Moscari gave her a private cell near their home.

Here she lived for some years, devoting to the poor all the strength left her by her extravagant penances. She founded a hospital, bestowing on it any gifts she received; she organized a confraternity of Franciscan Tertiaries to look after prisoners, who might otherwise perish of neglect; she gave counsel to the ever-growing crowd of penitents, who besieged her as her fame for sanctity spread. Her son became a Franciscan friar. He seems to have been an unhappy one; but Margaret received the assurance of Christ that he would be saved.

Tireless as she was in good works, her vocation was contemplation; she wanted nothing but to enjoy Christ in solitude. In 1288 she obtained the bishop's permission, over the heads of the reluctant friars, to retire to a little retreat on the top of Mount Sant-Egidio. Here she gave herself up completely to contemplation, passing through all the stages of mystical experience, and entirely alone except for the visits of her priest. She died on February 22nd 1297. At the moment of her death a nun some distance away had a vision of her soul entering Heaven and acclaimed as Christ's new Magdalene; and miracles took place immediately, though she was not canonized until 1728.

Like St Mary Magdalene, she turned from a life of sin to become the friend of Christ. Whatever came between her and him – her beauty, her friends, her own son – she shut out of her life completely. Such a renunciation is hard for us to understand, but those who are called to forsake the world completely, have sometimes to renounce its human affections as well. They will not recover their friends till they meet them in Heaven; as Margaret was seen by the mystic, surrounded by the souls she had helped to save.

February 22nd   ILLUSTRATION: page 311

MARGARET 'of ENGLAND'   † 1192

By tradition she was an Englishwoman, but she may have been a Hungarian. After accompanying her mother on a pilgrimage to Jerusalem and Bethlehem, she went alone to shrines in Spain and France. She died in the Seauve Bénite nunnery.

February 3rd

MARGARET of HUNGARY   1242–1270

Margaret was the daughter of Bela IV, king of Hungary and champion of Christendom, at a time when the Tartars were threatening to engulf central Europe. She was brought up in the care of Dominican nuns from the age of three, and at twelve years old she made her profession in the convent built for her by her parents on an island in the Danube. From that time on she lived a life of the most extreme austerity. Conscious, perhaps, of the difference her sisters in religion would have liked to make for her, a princess, she not only embraced all the normal tasks of the conventual life but took upon herself the lowliest, most menial and most unpleasant that were to be done. She accompanied this by the most rigorous mortifications, imitating the poverty-stricken not only in their toil, their hunger and their shortage of sleep, but even in their lack of cleanliness – a form of penance practised at the time. She had implicit faith in the power and efficacy of prayer, and many miracles and wonders were attributed to her intercession.

After her death the process of her beatification was begun almost at once, and as we still have the depositions we can read eye-witness accounts of these miracles and of her way of life, expressive of her overpowering desire to allow no created thing to stand between herself and God. However, in spite of this immediate recognition of her holiness, the process of beatification was not completed, and it was only in 1943 that she was canonized.

January 26th

MARGARET of SCOTLAND   c. 1045–1093

Margaret was born about the year 1045. Her father, the English Prince Edward, son of Edmund Ironside, was in exile and had married a German princess, probably a niece of the wife of St Stephen, king of Hungary. It was in the Hungarian court that Margaret was brought up, and there she must have gained that insight into just and saintly rule that was to be the mark of her own sanctity. When she came to England at the age of about twelve it was to the court of another saint, Edward the Confessor. With the Norman Conquest in 1066, Margaret and her mother, with her brother and her sister, were again exiled, and sought refuge in Scotland. Although he was at the time at war with their own country, the Scottish King, Malcolm Canmore, received the exiles kindly.

Malcolm Canmore, whose name means 'The Great Ruler', was a powerful and able king. He fell in love with the gentle Margaret and eventually, for her wish had been to enter a convent, persuaded her to marry him. Their life together is described in some detail in a memoir, probably written by Margaret's confessor, Turgot, later bishop of St Andrews. It is an enchanting story of the impact of a young woman of wisdom and holiness upon a husband whose background was altogether rougher and less educated, but who aspired towards the holiness manifest in his wife.

Margaret spent much of her time and money on works of charity, herself attending on the poor, the aged, the orphans and the sick. She supervised the making of vestments and fine things for the church. She was an admirable mother. She solved the problem facing the church in the Scotland of her day. Cut off by pagan invasion, the Celtic church had come to differ on points of procedure with Rome, and it was Margaret's personal achievement to reconcile the conflicting elements by bringing the Celtic church in Scotland back to conformity. This she did in such a way as to avoid schism or bitterness. Similarly, her efforts to introduce European culture into Scotland were markedly successful. Whereas in England the Norman Conquest left a legacy of bitterness, the comparatively peaceful infusion of medieval culture into Scotland under Margaret and her sons was effected in such a manner as to bring a veritable golden age to Scotland, that lasted for two hundred years after Margaret's death. She died in Edinburgh Castle, and died, like so many saints, at a time when all that she had worked for seemed lost; her husband was killed in battle and rebel forces were attacking Edinburgh. But three of her sons succeeding to the throne in turn, their mother's work was reinforced and brought to fullness.

Margaret was canonized in 1250. Her feast is kept in Scotland on November 16th.
June 10th

MARGARET or MARINA
Although she was one of the Fourteen Holy Helpers and enjoyed great popularity, her story is entirely fictional. That she was supposed to have been swallowed by a dragon who found her indigestible and brought her up, may account for the fact that she is the patron saint of women in childbirth.   ILLUSTRATION: page 312
July 20th

MARGARET THE BAREFOOTED   † 1395?
After she was released from an unhappy marriage by the death of her husband, she continued to imitate the poor, whom she aided, by going barefoot. She is buried at San Severino.
August 27th

MARI, *see* Addai and Mari.

MARIAN, *see* James and Marian.

MARIAN, *see* Marcian.

MARIAN of QUITO   1618–1645
Mariana Paredes y Flores, 'the Lily of Quito', was an orphan of a noble Peruvian family and died at the age of twenty-six. Besides practising the conventional mortifications of hair-shirts, and prolonged fasting, she used each Friday to don two crowns – one of thorns, the other of spikes – and to spend that night in a coffin.
May 26th

MARINA, *see* Margaret.

MARINA
'Marina' is the Latin version of 'Pelagia', and this saint's legend seems to echo that of St Pelagia, a girl who lived disguised as a monk for many years.
February 12th

MARINUS   *Fourth Century?*
Nothing certain is known of this saint. According to legend he was a stonemason, who began his career as a recluse in order to escape a woman who claimed that he was her absconding husband. The site of his hermitage is in the present state of San Marino, which is named after him.
September 4th

MARINUS and ASTYRIUS   *Third Century*
Marinus, a soldier of noble blood from Caesarea, Palestine, was just about to be promoted centurion for his distinguished military service, when a rival objected, saying that he was a Christian. The governor asked if this were true and, on being told by Marinus that it was so, gave him three hours to think over it. At the end of this period, Marinus again professed his faith and was led away to execution. The martyrdom of Astyrius, a Roman senator, is generally assumed to have occurred at the same time, since he saw Marinus die and buried the body.
March 3rd

MARIUS, MARTHA, AUDIFAX and
ABACHUM   *Third Century*
A newly converted family, pilgrims to Rome when Claudius was persecuting the church there. Marius and his sons were beheaded and Martha was drowned for burying Christians burned in the amphitheatre.
January 19th

MARIUS or MAY   *Sixth Century*
According to dubious evidence, he was a monk of prophetic gifts from Orleans, who founded the abbey of Bodon in Sisteron, and became its first abbot.
January 27th

MARK, *see* Martin.

He became pope in 336 in succession to St Silvester.
October 7th

MARK and MARCELLIAN   *Third Century*

Twin brothers and deacons of the Roman church, they
were imprisoned at the beginning of the reign of
Diocletian. Thirty days were allowed to elapse between
sentence and execution to give them time to recant, but
during that time they succeeded in converting their
relatives and some of their captors. Their story is
probably fictitious, but they were authentic Roman
martyrs and are buried in the catacomb of Balbina.
June 18th

MARK of ARETHUSA, *see* Cyril of Heliopolis and Mark.

MARK THE EVANGELIST   *First Century*

'Mark, who had been Peter's interpreter, wrote out carefully, though not in sequence, as much as he remembered
of the Lord's deeds and sayings.' These are the words of
'John the Elder', who lived in the Apostles' time (*cf.*
Eusebius, *Historia Ecclesiastica*, iii.39.15). Who was this
Mark? He was certainly not one of the twelve Apostles.
But there is no doubt that a man named Mark was
widely known in early Christian circles, not only as a
companion of St Paul but also as a dear friend of Peter
when in Rome (Colossians 4:10; 1 Peter 5:13; 2 Timothy
4:11). It is natural enough to identify this Mark with the
Mark of whom 'John the Elder' spoke; but this is not all.
Three times in the Acts of the Apostles a 'John, also called
Mark' is mentioned (Acts 12:12, 25; 15:37) as an intimate friend of Barnabas. Now the Mark of Colossians 4:
10 is there described as the cousin of Barnabas. Scholars,
therefore, are generally agreed that the Mark spoken of
in the Epistles, the 'John Mark' of the Acts, and the
author of the second Gospel, are one and the same person.

Granted this identification, the following summary
of the evangelist's career may be offered. He was the son
of Mary, a Jerusalem widow prosperous enough to
employ a maidservant and to own a house sufficiently
large for Christian gatherings. Peter chose this house as
a refuge after his escape from prison in 43 (Acts 12:
12–17). Mark must therefore have been familiar with
Peter's reminiscences from his early days. Two years
later, in 45, we find Mark with Barnabas and Paul
on the latter's first missionary journey; but he refused
to follow them when they travelled north of Taurus,
and went back home (Acts 13:13). St Paul was not
pleased. He declined Barnabas's proposal to take Mark
with them on the second journey (in 50), but Barnabas
sided with his cousin and sailed with him to Cyprus,
Barnabas's native land (Acts 15:36–39).

We hear nothing more of Mark until 61, when he was
in Rome with Paul – the quarrel was evidently mended
(Colossians 4:10). It is not known whether he then
journeyed to Colossae in south-western Asia Minor to
receive the welcome Paul asked the Colossians to give
him. In any case Mark was in Rome three years later
(64), since St Peter sends his greetings along with his
own, affectionately referring to him as 'my son Mark'
(1 Peter 5:13). This was the year of Peter's martyrdom. It was now, or very shortly after, that Mark wrote
the Gospel – in Rome, as it seems, though some early
authorities declare for Alexandria. In 67 the evangelist
was in Ephesus since Paul, writing a few months before
his own death, asked Timothy to bring Mark with him
to Rome (2 Timothy 4:11). The old wound had
completely healed.

So much for the New Testament evidence; we have
henceforth to rely on a fluctuating tradition. That Mark
preached in Alexandria after Peter's death is probable
but not certain; that he was founder and first bishop of
that church is altogether uncertain (Clement, fl. 200,
and Origen, fl. 203, the great Alexandrian doctors, do
not mention it). There is no very reliable authority to
support the statement of the *Chronicon Pascale* (of
uncertain date: fourth? seventh? century) that Mark
became bishop of Alexandria and was martyred by
burning in Trajan's reign (98–117 A.D.).

The physical appearance of the saints is of no great
consequence. This is just as well since all we know of
Mark's (the evidence is early and reliable) is that he was,
in the Latinized Greek of our source, *colobodactylus* –
which is to say 'stumpy-fingered'. And that is no great
aid to devotion. But to the amateur physiognomist at
least it suggests the opposite of the 'artistic temperament'
and this conclusion, if not its premises, is exact, as we
shall see.

If it is true that we may judge a writer's temperament
from his style, we know Mark very well indeed. One
preliminary qualification must however be made: the
vital, vivid quality of the second Gospel betrays an eye-
witness which is Peter and not Mark. (Though Mark
possibly witnessed our Lord's arrest: it is conjectured
rather boldly by many modern commentators that he
is to be identified with the anonymous young man who
'ran away naked'; *cf.* Mark 14:50ff). Nevertheless, Mark
is no mere gramophone playing Peter's records: he is
an author drawing on Peter's reminiscences, and his own
hand is discernible throughout. It shows him as a man
of few words (673 verses to Matthew's 1068) and of
unpolished style (he casually mixes his verb-tenses, over-
works the conjunction 'and' as a simple story teller will,
makes astonishingly free use of the rather vulgar Historic
Present – the dignified Luke in a gospel twice as long
uses it only ten times to Mark's one hundred and fifty!).
One would judge him impatient, or incapable, of literary

elegance. And yet, if these are defects, Mark enjoys the corresponding quality: a massive sincerity. He stubbornly refuses to tone down awkward facts or even to explain them. For example: that the Apostles were slow of understanding is concealed by none of the evangelists, but St Mark goes out of his way to underline it: 'so dulled were their hearts', he says (6:52). In this place St Matthew keeps a discreet and charitable silence. Nor will Mark disguise their discreditable ambition (9:34). Peter himself is not exempted from this straightforward treatment: he, too, is slow of wit (9:6; Matthew omits this!). But perhaps the most striking proof of Mark's unimpeachable honesty is that, in the interests of faithful report, he is prepared to risk an appearance of self-contradiction. It is beyond doubt that Jesus is for him the Son of God in the fullest sense of the term (he is above the angels, 13:32, forgives sins, 2:10ff., etc.) and yet Mark alone of all the evangelists does not hesitate to say of our Lord at Nazareth that 'he could not do any wonderful works there' (6:5). Nor does he hide the fact that our Lord's own relatives suspected him of imprudence or worse (3:21), or that Christ's expectations in the matter of the fig-tree were disappointed (11:13). Details of this kind leave Mark's title intact ('The Gospel of Jesus Christ, Son of God'), but they wear an appearance of difficulty which he disdains either to conceal or to remove. With a historian of this caliber we are in safe hands.

Under the high altar of San Marco in Venice lies, it is said, the body of the evangelist, martyred in Alexandria, there venerated, and brought to San Marco by Venetian merchants in the ninth century. There is no reason to doubt the story's substance, though the identity of the piously stolen body depends on the solidity of the Alexandrian tradition. A granite pillar in the adjoining piazzetta carries Mark's emblem: a lion – for the majestic desert voice of the Baptist opens his Gospel. The saint would like none of this publicity. Of all evangelists the simplest, the model of all who work for God unnoticed, he would rather have from us the devotion of reading and meditating what he has written; and we can hear him saying in his own blunt way: 'Don't look at me, look at Him.'   ILLUSTRATION: page 313
April 25th

MARO   † 433
A recluse near Cyrrhus who followed the example of his master St Zebinus by continual prayer and mortification. Besides training many holy men, he built monasteries and exercised his great healing powers.
February 14th

MARTHA   *First Century*
Sister of Mary of Bethany (see Mary Magdalene) and Jesus's hostess. She busied herself preparing a meal for her guest while her sister sat listening at his feet (Luke 10) when Martha complained of Mary, our Lord defended her sister's choice of 'the best part'. Henceforward she will typify the active, as her sister the contemplative, life. When Jesus returned to Bethany to raise Lazarus (John 11), Martha plays once more her active role. While Mary sits indoors, she hurries out to meet him and again to expostulate: had he been there, as he could have been had he come when first informed of her brother's illness, Lazarus would not have died. In reply Jesus elicits an act of faith in his power as the resurrection and the life to raise from death to life.

Martha received little recognition and no cult until about the year 1200. Another Martha, a Persian nun martyred near Hazza on June 6th, 347, whose relics were preserved at Tarascon in Provence, was identified with her; and she was credited, as probably had been her Persian namesake, with delivering the countryside from a destructive dragon, the Tarasque. Her feast finally found a place in the Roman Missal and Breviary.
July 29th   ILLUSTRATION: page 314

MARTHA of PERSIA   † 347
She was one of a group of Persian martyrs, nuns, who suffered near Hazza on June 6th 347. Her martyrdom was shared by four others, Thecla, Enneim and two Marys. Their relics found their way to southern Gaul, where Martha was finally identified with Martha of Bethany, the two Marys with Mary the mother of James and Mary Salome. Another Persian martyr, Sara, who suffered December 10th, 352, became identified with a maidservant of Mary Magdalene and Martha (see St Martha).
September 23rd

MARTIAL, see Faustus, Januarius and Martial.

MARTIAL   *Third Century*
He was sent from Rome to evangelize the Limousin, and became the first bishop of Limoges. There are stories of his being baptized by St Peter, and in the diocese of Limoges he is regarded as the founder of the local church.
June 30th

MARTIN I   † 656
Martin, who had been papal legate at Constantinople, was elected pope in 649. The Emperor Constans II, to whom the pope was politically subject, had just issued a doctrinal decree, the 'Type', in which he placed the Monothelite heresy, that Christ had only one will, on a level with the Catholic doctrine by forbidding anyone to speak of one or two energies or wills in Christ. In October 649, at a council assembled at the Lateran, Pope Martin condemned the 'Type'.

He paid for his courage. On June 17th, 653, the

Emperor's representative in Italy, Calliopas, the exarch of Ravenna, arrested the pope in his cathedral. He was accused of complicity in a revolt of the former exarch Olympius. He was taken by sea to Constantinople, where he arrived on September 17th. Though the victim of gout, he had been ill-used on the voyage, deprived of sufficient food, forbidden even to wash, and on arrival he was kept in prison until December 20th, when at a mock trial in the emperor's presence he was degraded and sentenced to death. Remitted to prison, he suffered acutely from the intense cold; a kindly woman gave him her own bed and bedclothes, and the dying patriarch of Constantinople, afraid of divine judgment, persuaded Constans not to put his prisoner to death. But he was banished to Cherson in the Crimea, where he died as the result of his privations, probably on April 13th, 656.

Since the ninth century, the feast of St Martin of Tours, November 11th, has attracted the feast of Pope Martin to the following day, 12th November. This St Martin is the last of the popes to be venerated as a martyr.

November 12th

MARTIN de AGUIRRE, *see* Martyrs of Japan.

MARTIN of BRAGA   † 579

An eminent scholar who wrote several important works. His zealous preaching converted Galicia in Spain from the Arianism which had been thriving under the Suevi, and he became bishop of Dumium and then of Braga.

March 20th

MARTIN of TOURS   c. 315–397

Our knowledge of Martin is derived from his friend and biographer Sulpicius Severus. The many and striking miracles he ascribes to his hero provoked incredulity at the time and still provoke it today. But he asseverates his veracity in tones which carry conviction, and, when allowance is made for inaccurate reporting, mal-observation and misinterpretation, the miracles are incredible only to one who denies the existence of a spiritual world. Substantially we can trust Sulpicius.

Martin, born about 315 at Sabaria in Pannonia (now Hungary), was the son of an officer in the army. Both parents were pagans, but, when he was still a boy, he had himself enrolled as a catechumen. As a soldier's son he was a conscript. As an officer at Amiens he shared his military cloak with a beggar, and, the following night, he saw our Lord wearing the halved cloak. In consequence he was baptized but remained reluctantly in the army. Two years later barbarians invaded Gaul. Martin asked leave of his commander, probably Constantius, to resign his commission. 'I am a soldier of Christ, it is not lawful for me to serve.' Charged with cowardice he offered to stand unarmed in the forefront of battle. The barbarians however surrendered without a fight. Martin was then permitted to leave the army (probably in 339).

The bishop of Poitiers, St Hilary, ordained him an excorcist. He spent the ensuing years in various places and was for some time a hermit in an island off the Italian coast. He converted his mother and was flogged for public opposition to the Arians. He rejoined St Hilary when that bishop returned from exile and founded at Ligugé, near Poitiers, a hermitage which soon expanded into a community of hermits.

He was elected bishop of Tours for the repute of his holiness, though perhaps still more for the miracles which attested it. An influential minority, however, of his future flock and some of the bishops who assembled for his consecration – noblemen or landowners – objected to a bishop who was not a gentleman: 'a man so contemptible with dirty clothes and unkempt hair'. He was consecrated on July 4th, 371.

He did not abandon his monastic life, but made his headquarters a monastery of the eremitical type, which he founded outside Tours. Having clothed a beggar with his tunic Martin sang mass in a rough garment flung down by his irate archdeacon. When he blessed the people five members of his congregation saw a ball of fire surround his head. At prayer he encountered demons, often under the guise of heathen deities, and Satan disguised on one occasion as our Lord. Satan once taunted him with admitting as monks men guilty of grievous sin. 'If you, yourself,' he replied, 'would, even now, repent of your misdeeds, I have such trust in the Lord Jesus Christ that I would promise you mercy.' He conversed with angels and was often visited by SS Peter and Paul. Questioned by Sulpicius and his friends about an indistinct conversation overheard in his cell, he admitted that 'Agnes, Thecla, and Mary' had been with him. Thrice Martin raised to life a man dead or apparently dead. He cured a woman with an issue of blood, a leper by a kiss, a paralytic by pouring oil into his mouth. A troop of soldiers beat up Martin when his uncouth figure made the mules shy which were dragging their waggon. His companions bore him off unconscious, but the mules would not budge. The soldiers discovered their victim's identity and, when they had begged his pardon, the mules moved forward.

Martin was the apostle of the country districts, forcibly destroying sanctuaries venerated by the pagan rustics. He once accepted a challenge to stand where a sacred tree he had ordered to be felled must crush him in its fall: it swerved aside, and the marvel produced wholesale conversions. A pagan's sword raised to behead Martin fell down powerless. When violent opposition prevented his demolition of a temple, he saw in prayer two protecting angels. He returned to the village and there was no further interference. Helen, the saintly wife of the usurping Emperor, Maximus, waited humbly on him at table. At the instigation of his courtier bishops,

Maximus put the heretic Priscillian to death though he had promised Martin to spare his life. Martin refused to communicate with these bishops, and yielded only to obtain the recall of a tribune dispatched to Spain for further executions. He over-awed Count Avitianus into the release of a batch of prisoners he had destined to torture and death.

Martin fell mortally ill at Candes, a village in his diocese where his services were required as peacemaker. As he lay dying his disciples implored him not to leave his flock at the mercy of wolves, the powerful section of opponents whose victory he foresaw (*see* Brice). He made the immortal reply of the good shepherd: 'Lord, if thy people still need me, I will not shirk the toil. Thy will be done.' The sacrifice was not asked, for he died on November 8th 397. Three days later, on his present feast day, he was buried at Tours. He was the first neither martyr nor reputed martyr, to receive the cult of a saint. His shrine became the most venerated Gallic sanctuary.

November 11th   ILLUSTRATION: page 315

MARTIN of VERTOU   *Sixth Century*

Nothing authentic is known of this saint, who is sometimes confused with St Martin of Braga, beyond the fact that he was born at Nantes, became a hermit in the forest of Dumen in Brittany and evangelized the district around the Sèvre.

October 24th

MARTIN or MARK   † *c. 580*

St Gregory in his *Dialogues* tells us all that we know of this hermit and his miracles. St Benedict reproved him for one of his more extravagant austerities, which was to chain himself to the rock, by saying, 'If you wish to serve God, do not bind youself by an iron chain, but by the chain of Christ'.

October 24th

MARTINA

Although she is ranked among the patrons of Rome and was alleged to have been martyred in the reign of the Emperor Alexander (222 to 235), it is by no means certain that she existed. Her acts make many ridiculous claims, including one that at her martyrdom milk flowed from her body instead of blood.

January 30th

MARTINIAN, *see* Processus and Martinian.

MARTINIAN and Companions and MAXIMA   † 458

St Martinian and his brothers were Vandal slaves who were converted by their fellow slave, the virgin Maxima. For this they suffered martyrdom under the Arian king, Genseric. Maxima, after many trials, was allowed to go free and became abbess of a large convent.

October 16th

MARTINIAN THE HERMIT

It is quite probable that Martinian never existed. Legends of his temptations by women are almost certainly borrowed from the stories of other saints. The final temptation occurred when he was alone on a desert island. The sole survivor from a shipwreck turned out to be a woman whom he was obliged to rescue; but so concerned was he over the consequences that he swam across to the mainland immediately, leaving the woman behind to imitate his penitential way of life – which she did.

February 13th

MARTIUS or MARS   *Sixth Century*

A hermit who attracted disciples, he founded the abbey of Clermont in the Auvergne.

April 13th

MARTYRIUS, *see* Sisinnius, Martyrius and Alexander.

The MARTYRS in PERSIA   † *c. 345*

Over one hundred in number, including nine virgins and many priests, they are said to have died at Ctesiphon in the reign of King Sapor II after refusing to worship the sun.

April 6th

The MARTYRS of GORKUM, *see* Nicholas Pieck and his Companions.

The MARTYRS of JAPAN   † 1597

Franciscans: PETER BAPTIST, MARTIN de AGUIRRE, FRANCIS BLANCO, FRANCIS-of-ST-MICHAEL, Spanish; PHILIP de las CASAS, Mexican; GONSALO GARCIA, Indian? (Possibly India's only canonized saint.) *Jesuits:* PAUL MIKI, JOHN GOTO, JAMES KISAI, Japanese. *Japanese Franciscan Tertiaries:* CAIUS FRANCIS, soldier; FRANCIS of MIAKO, physician; LEO KARASUMA, Korean; LOUIS IBARKI, ANTONY DEYNAN and THOMAS KASAKI, altar boys; and eleven others.

In 1597, forty-five years after St Francis Xavier had evangelized much of Japan, Hideyoshi, a powerful official spurred on by a Spanish captain's foolish boast that the missionaries were preparing the way for the conquest of Japan by the Spaniards and Portuguese, martyred these twenty-six saints. Tortured and killed near Nagasaki, they were canonized in 1862.

The main period of persecution in Japan extended from 1617 to 1632. The aim was to extirpate Christianity, and two hundred and five martyrs produced at this time were beatified in 1867. They have not yet been canonized.

February 5th

JOHN THE BAPTIST : painting by Leonardo da Vinci (1452 - 1519). (*Louvre, Paris*)

PLATE 11

LAURENCE: detail painting by Bernardo Daddi (*fl. c. 1320 – 1457*). (*Ch. di S. Croce, Florence.*)

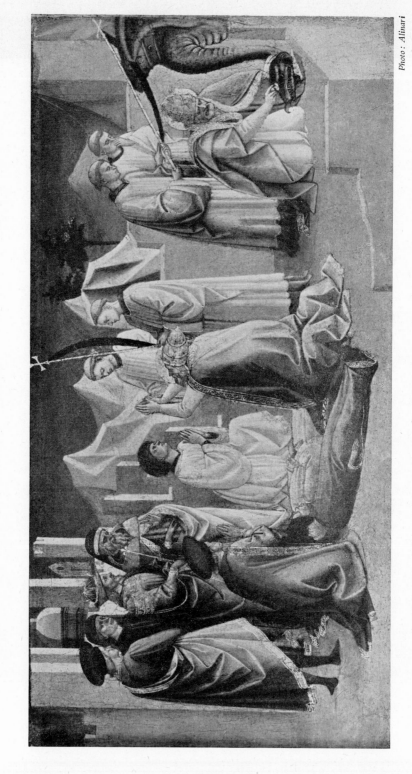

LEO I (THE GREAT): painting by Francesco Pesellino (1422 – 1457). (*Palazzo Doria, Rome.*)

LOUIS IX, KING of FRANCE: detail from predella by Simone Martini (1283 – 1344). (*Museo Nazionale, Naples.*)

LOUIS of ANJOU: detail of painting on wood (fifteenth century). *(Louvre, Paris.)*

LUCY: sculpture by Luca della Robbia (1400 – 1482). (*Ch. di Sta Lucia, Florence.*)

Photo: Alinari

MADELEINE SOPHIE BARAT: from the portrait by Savinien Petit (nineteenth century).
(Sacré Cœur, Amiens.)

MARGARET of CORTONA: painting by Martinetti (1901)

MARGARET or MARINA: French limestone figure (sixteenth century).
(Victoria and Albert Museum.)

MARK THE EVANGELIST: sixth century mosaic.
(Ch. di San Vitale, Ravenna.)

313

MARTHA: detail from painting by Velazquez (1599 – 1660). *(National Gallery, London.)*

MARTIN of TOURS: sculpture on façade (thirteenth or fourteenth century). *(Duomo, Lucca.)*

MARY MAGDALEN dei PAZZI: engraving.

MARY MAGDALENE: fresco by Giotto (c. 1266 – 1337). (Cappella degli Scrovegni all' Arena, Padua.)

MATTHEW, APOSTLE and EVANGELIST: painting by Rembrandt (1606 – 1669). (Louvre, Paris.)

Photo: Hulton Picture Library

MATTHIAS: terracotta relief by Luca della Robbia (1400 – 1482). *(Ch. di Sta Croce, Florence.)*

MENNAS: ivory pyxis (sixth century), probably Egyptian. *(British Museum.)*

MARY THE BLESSED VIRGIN painted by Luke: by Rogier van der Weyden (*c*.1400 - 1464).
(*Museum of Fine Arts, Boston*)

PLATE 12

The MARTYRS of MAR SABA † 796

Monks of a monastery between Jerusalem and the Dead Sea, they were killed by marauding Arabs. Most of them were smoked to death in a cave in which they had taken refuge.
March 20th

MARTYRS of NAJRAN, *see* Aretas and the Martyrs of Najran.

The MARTYRS of NICOMEDIA † c. 303

The legend has it that 20,000 Christians were burned to death in a church at Nicomedia by Diocletian. There was certainly fierce persecution in Nicomedia in 303.
December 25th

The MARTYRS of NORTH AMERICA

Seventeenth Century

SS RENÉ GOUPIL († 1642); JOHN LALANDE and ISAAC JOGUES († 1644); ANTONY DANIEL († 1648); JOHN de BRÉBEUF and GABRIEL LALEMANT († 1649); CHARLES GARNIER and NOEL CHABANEL († 1649).

As early as 1608 two Jesuits had been sent to Nova Scotia, but their work suffered from the wars with England, and it was not until 1632, when Canada reverted to France, that a mission center could be permanently established by the Jesuits at Quebec. In 1633 the Superior, Paul le Jeune, was joined by John de Brébeuf, an aristocrat of Norman birth and soldierly bearing, Antony Daniel and Ennemond Massé. The difficulties of these pioneers are typified by Le Jeune's experiences when he accompanied a party of Algonquins on a hunting expedition: his efforts to preach to them were frustrated by roars of ribald laughter, because the Indian who had taught him the language had – for a joke – palmed off the foulest words as the equivalent for the vocabulary of Christian belief; and Le Jeune also began to taste the four worst aspects of Indian life: cold, heat, smoke and dogs. Of these he found smoke by far the worst. It filled the hut in which men, woman and dogs slept together round the fire, and prolonged exposure to it usually brought blindness in the end, a fact which caused Le Jeune to remark: 'Unhappy infidels, who spend their lives in smoke, and their eternity in flames.'

Le Jeune decided that no mission could hope to succeed unless it were directed to the settled tribes; and the Hurons who lived on what is now the eastern shore of Lake Huron in Simcoe County, Ontario, were chosen as the main focus of the mission. In 1634, Brébeuf, Daniel and Davost succeeded in establishing themselves among this nation of twenty thousand people who lived in thirty villages, each of which contained about seven hundred dwellings.

The missionaries found the Indians polite but distant, and apart from babies and the dying almost impossible to convert to what they regarded as merely a white man's religion. 'Do you hunt in Heaven?' they asked, 'or make war, or go to feasts?' 'No,' they were told. 'Then we will not go,' they replied; 'It is not good to be lazy.' The missionaries, realising that what opposed them was a complete way of life with its trial marriages, tortures and cannibal feasts, resolved to concentrate upon building up settlements ruled by themselves and peopled by their converts, for they did not treat the Indians as aliens but encouraged and even hoped for intermarriage with French settlers. To Le Jeune, at least, their pattern was the Jesuit utopia, that was being developed in Paraguay.

The wisdom of this decision was confirmed by the experiences resulting from the plague of 1638 which coincided with the arrival of five more missionaries, including Isaac Jogues – a scholar and an athlete who could outrun the Indians – and Charles Garnier. The Indians began to revile the Jesuits as sorcerers who had brought a curse upon their nation, and when their long, black soutanes were seen outlined against the snow as they approached some lonely Indian village, the children ran screaming to their mothers that Famine and Pestilence had come in person to make away with them. It was at this time that Jean de Brébeuf had his vision of a gigantic cross approaching from the quarter where lay the dreaded enemy of the Hurons – the Iroquois. When asked what it was like, he replied, 'Large enough to crucify us all'.

The Iroquois had been nursing their resentment since their defeat by the French thirty years before, and the scale of their attacks had been growing steadily. In August 1642, Jogues, Goupil (who had joined the mission as a layman and worked as a medical orderly) and a party of Indians were returning from Quebec with much needed food and stores for the mission and the starving Indians. They were attacked and captured by the Iroquois who gnawed at their fingers like mad dogs, tore out their nails and made them run the gauntlet in every village they passed through. The refinements or 'carresses', as the Indians called them, of their torture were yet to come: hot coals, knives, mutilations – always to a background of banter and pleasantry, the more hideous for the suavity of the manner in which such taunts were made. Death, the climax of what was more of a diabolic rite than a mere display of cruelty, was usually by burning, the body afterwards being divided and eaten.

Goupil was saved the worst – he was killed on 29th September, 1642 by a tomahawk blow for daring to baptize a child – but Jogues was kept for many weeks under perpetual sentence of death. Towards the end of 1643 he was able with the help of some Dutch traders to escape by boat to France; but he was back on the mission by 1644 and was sent by the Governor of New France as an envoy to the Iroquois during a brief period of truce. Encouraged by the results of this visit, Jogues returned, taking with him another lay assistant, John Lalande; but their success was short-lived: a bad harvest, a suspicious box belonging to Jogues which the Indians believed to contain a plague, and the two men were captured, tortured and eventually murdered on October 18th, 1644.

Although most Hurons were beginning to accept the Christian faith their morale as a nation was suffering under the persistent Iroquois attacks; and the next martyrdom occurred on July 4th, 1648, when their principal fortress, St Joseph, a village of two thousand people, was destroyed by the Iroquois. Antony Daniel, who had been their priest for four successful years had just finished mass. When he realized that the defenders were overwhelmed, he urged them to flee, saying, 'I will stay here. We shall meet again in Heaven.' Still clad in his vestments, he walked towards the Iroquois. For a moment they paused in amazement, and then let fly a volley of arrows; afterwards they stripped their victim, bathed their faces in his blood and flung his body into the blazing church.

In the following spring, the Iroquois redoubled their efforts to exterminate the Hurons, and, in an attack of 1,000 braves upon the village of St Louis, they captured John de Brébeuf and Gabriel Lalemont. Because of his defiant bearing, Brébeuf – the Ajax of the mission – was tortured so severely that he died within four hours: a necklace of red-hot tomahawks was hung round his neck and he was baptized by an apostate Huron in boiling water. As he lay dying, the crowd drank his blood that they might become as valiant as he; the privilege of eating his heart they reserved for their chief.

Lalemont, who was of a weak and sickly constitution, survived seventeen hours of torture before he, too, expired on March 17th, 1649.

Two further martyrs were claimed by these Turks of the Indian church when the terror spread into the Tobacco nation living in the valleys of the Blue mountains. On the attack on St Jean, in December 1644, Charles Garnier was killed as he strove to give absolution to a dying Indian – the son of a wealthy Parisian, he had lived off roots and acorns during the famine and would walk thirty or forty miles in the summer heat over enemy country just to baptize a dying Indian. His colleague, Noel Chabanel – who so disliked the conditions of the mission that he bound himself by an oath to stay there for life –, was killed by an apostate Huron who believed the new religion to have been responsible for the fate which had afflicted his country.

Thus ended the mission to the Hurons for whom the way to Christian faith proved hard indeed; only in desolation, despair and dispersion as a nation were they able to discover the inadequacies of the traditional beliefs which had seemed to sanctify their way of life. Yet the influence of the mission extended beyond that of its converts to produce over the years a change in the lives of the Indians – prisoners were still killed, but no longer tortured so deliberately or eaten after death – and although they remained savages, they ceased to be devils.
September 26th   ILLUSTRATION: page 161

The MARTYRS of SEBASTE † 320
Forty young Roman legionaries of various races, they were exposed naked on a frozen pond outside the gates of Sebaste (Sivas in Turkey) in the reign of the Emperor Licinius. An interesting document, still extant, known as 'The Testament of the Forty Martyrs of Christ' has now been authenticated as written by one of their number.
March 10th

The MARTYRS of the SERAPEUM † 390
They were killed by insurgents in the temple of Serapis in Alexandria during riots caused by the conversion of a temple of Dionysius into a Christian church.
March 17th

The MARTYRS of UTICA † c. 258?
Their numbers and the manner of their death are unknown. The poet Prudentius has a story of three hundred martyrs burned to death in a limekiln, but this seems to be pure fancy.
August 24th

The MARTYRS under the DANES *Ninth Century*
Many killed in the Danish raids are reckoned martyrs, since especial cruelty was shown to those regarded as representatives of Christianity. Among those killed were Beocca, abbot of Chertsey, Abbot Hedda and eighty-four monks of Medeshamstede (Peterborough) and all the religious of Bardney, Ely, Croyland and Thorney.
April 10th

The MARTYRS under NERO † 64
Uncounted victims of the first Roman emperor to persecute Christians, they were made scapegoats by Nero for the great fire that devastated Rome in July 64. Tacitus tells us that no one believed them guilty of the crime, but they were put to death with wanton cruelty, some being smeared with pitch and used as torches at an entertainment given by Nero.
June 24th

MARUTHAS † c. 415
Bishop of Maiferkat between the Tigris and Lake Van, he was able to influence King Yezdigerd of Persia in

favor of the Christians and reorganized the Persian church.
December 4th

MARY, *see* Flora and Mary.

MARY
This Mary is sometimes described as the slave of a Roman official but in fact nothing at all is known about her.
November 1st

MARY di ROSA   1813–1855
Mary di Rosa devoted herself to social work from the age of seventeen, worked in the hospital at Brescia during the cholera epidemic of 1836, and in 1840 began to organize the Handmaids of Charity, a religious society whose purpose was to look after the spiritual as well as the material needs of the sick. Its houses are mainly in Italy.
December 15th

MARY EUPHRASIA PELLETIER 1796–1868
In 1825, at the age of twenty-nine, she became superior of the Convent of the Refuge in Tours, and convinced of the necessity for central organization, she founded the Institute of our Lady of Charity of the Good Shepherd in 1835. At her death it consisted of 2,760 nuns.
April 24th

MARY FRANCES of NAPLES   1715–1791
Anne Mary Rose Nicolette Gallo, a Neapolitan, took the name of Mary-Frances-of-the-Five-Wounds when she became a Franciscan tertiary in 1731. At first she lived at home, but for the last thirty-eight years of her life kept house for a secular priest. She was a mystic who used to experience the pains of the Passion during Lent and was granted many visions.
October 6th

MARY GORETTI   1890–1902
She was born to poor, illiterate peasant parents in the province of Ancona, Italy, on October 16th, 1890. Shortly afterwards, owing to extreme poverty, the family migrated to a small village in the neighborhood of Anzio.

Her father went into partnership and shared a house with another man, one of whose two sons, a young man of twenty, developed a passion for Mary Goretti, who would appear to have been an exceptionally beautiful child.

About a month before the final tragedy, the young man, Alessandro Serenelli, made serious sexual advances, which the child rebuffed, upon which Alessandro assured her that he would quite certainly kill her if she mentioned the matter to her mother (her father had died rather more than a year previously).

The crisis came on July 5th, 1902, when Alessandro had engineered that they should be alone in the house. He made a passionate assault upon the child, threatening her with death if she refused to gratify his desire. Mary's answer was: 'No, no, no! God does not wish it. If you do that you'll commit a sin, you'll go to hell.' Alessandro was as good as his word: in his frenzy, he stabbed the poor child no less than fourteen times, both back and front. The surgery of the time was unable to save her life; and, after great suffering, she died a day later, having specifically forgiven her murderer, after admission to membership of the Children of Mary, and reception of the Last Sacraments.

She was beatified on April 27th, 1927, and canonized on June 24th, 1950. Her murderer was sentenced to thirty years' imprisonment, but by 1910 he had repented, and is now working as a gardener in an Italian monastery.

What reason is there for canonizing a peasant girl who met her death, as the result of a *crime passionel*, before she reached the age of twelve? It is possible to object that Mary Goretti acted almost reflexly in a state of acute panic to the kind of situation which she had been conditioned to regard as the most terrible that could be imagined, and that no heroic virtue could possibly have been realized. This is not borne out by the facts: it will be remembered that Alessandro made advances to Mary on two previous occasions, and on the third time gave her plenty of time to choose between death and rape. Moreover, even one's least reflective conduct at any given moment depends upon the dispositions that have been laid down in the past; in other words, 'virtue' is much more a matter of habit than an isolated instance. People like Mary Goretti – and martyrs for purity, even those who are willing to experience a little momentary emotional discomfort on its behalf, are few and far between – have an ever-present realization that lightly to surrender one's bodily integrity, even to the most compelling needs of the moment, upsets the whole rhythm of the universe.

Perhaps that is the chief reason why the canonization of Mary Goretti at the height of the splendors of the last Holy Year strikes one as being particularly significant and timely. It came as a clarion call of protest against the hopeless dreariness of base personal standards: this saint was canonized for our benefit, not for hers.
July 6th

MARY MAGDALEN dei PAZZI   1566–1607
A member of an illustrious Florentine family, St Mary Magdalen became a Carmelite nun at the age of seventeen. She lived an ascetic life, often experiencing long spells of spiritual barrenness, but also many exceptional graces in the form of visions and raptures.
May 29th   ILLUSTRATION: page 316

MARY MAGDALEN POSTEL   1756–1846

Mary Magdalen Postel is yet another modern French saint whose life work was the restoration of religion after the French Revolution. She was born in Normandy, and throughout her life displayed characteristic Norman thoroughness and industry. After rudimentary schooling at Valogne she returned home and opened a school in her native village. The Reign of Terror revealed her great qualities – she continued giving religious instruction, sheltered priests and, entrusted with the blessed Sacrament, was able to give holy communion to those in hiding.

After the Revolution she was given charge of a school and then, seeing the great need for nuns to teach poor children, founded the Sisters of the Christian Schools. She was now in her fiftieth year, but had little need to make her own life more mortified as a nun: for years past, for instance, she had subsisted on one meal a day in order to have something to spare for the poor. The new Congregation went through the many trials which are almost common form if a religious foundation is ultimately to prosper: in them all Mother Magdalen gave evidence of confidence in God, faith, courage and perseverance. She died on July 16th, 1846.

July 17th

MARY MAGDALENE   *First Century*

When our Lord was the guest of Simon the Pharisee, *an unnamed sinner* obtained pardon by the love she displayed, anointing his feet and drying them with her hair (Luke 7).

Mary from Magdala, a Galilean village, exorcised by our Lord (Luke 8), was among the ministering women who followed him on his journeys. Present on Calvary, she was among the women who brought spices to his tomb. She first informed the Apostles that it was empty. Returning at once to the garden she saw and spoke with angels in the sepulcher. She finally recognized her risen Lord, mistaken at first for a gardener (John 20).

Mary of Bethany, sister of Martha and Lazarus, sat at Jesus's feet listening while Martha prepared his meal. She thus chose the best part, contemplation (Luke 10). When Jesus came to raise Lazarus from the dead she played a similar part, sitting quietly at home until Martha summoned her to meet 'the Master'. A few days later she anointed him (Matthew 26).

Though the Gospels do not warrant identification of these three woman and the opinion of the Fathers is divided, the western Church from the sixth century has identified them, and the identification finds expression in the liturgy. A spiritual or mystical identification, favored by certain fathers, is rich in significance and instruction. And with this understanding we may read and appreciate Philip de Greve's hymn of exquisite and haunting beauty, 'Collaudemus Magdalenae' which was used in the Sarum Breviary, where it is divided into three parts. A translation of two of these may be found in the *English Hymnal*.

According to tradition, Mary Magdalene died and was buried at Ephesus. In 899 the Emperor Leo VI translated her alleged relics to a monastery at Constantinople. It was not until the tenth century that devotion to Mary Magdalene, the composite saint, took root in the west.

About 1050 the monks of Vézelay, an abbey recently reformed and affiliated to Cluny, began to claim her body, brought, they related, from the Holy Land either by a ninth-century saint, Badilo, or by envoys despatched by their founder. A little later a monk of Vézelay believed that he had detected in a crypt at St Maximin in Provence, carved on an empty sarcophagus, a representation of the unction at Bethany. The monks of Vézelay pronounced it to be Mary Magdalene's tomb from which her relics had been translated to their abbey. Thus the erection of one of the finest examples of Romanesque architecture was made possible by pilgrims to a spurious relic.

The Provençals, however, took full advantage of this development and outstripped Vézelay by pilgrimages to three places henceforward associated with Mary Magdalene. One of these was St Maximin, where the crypt still contains sarcophagi attributed to the Magdalene, St Maximin and St Sidonius. The representation of the anointing (?) has, however, disappeared. Another is the Sainte Baume, a grotto in the face of a cliff, where Mary Magdalene is said to have spent long years of penance and ecstatic contemplation, whose detail was suggested by the life of the penitent Mary of Egypt. The third is a church on the coast, built and fortified against pirates in the twelfth century. Dedicated originally to St Mary (our Lady) of the Sea, its title became The Three Marys of the Sea – 'Les Saintes Maries de la Mer'. A legend originating about the year 1200 informs us that Mary Magdalene, driven out to sea by the Jews, landed here together with Mary, mother of James, Mary Salome, her sister Martha, their maid Sara, Lazarus, Maximin, one of the seventy-two disciples, and Sidonius, the man born blind. In fact Maximin and Sidonius were saints of Auvergne, the latter being the fifth century man of letters and bishop; Lazarus was a fifth century bishop of Aix; Martha, the two Marys and Sara were Persian martyrs of the fourth century whose relics were brought later to southern Gaul (*see* Martha).

In legend and artistic representation Mary Magdalene, at once sensuous and spiritual, made a powerful appeal to the Baroque mentality, and she became a typical figure of Baroque devotion, literature and art.

July 22nd   ILLUSTRATION: page 317

MARY MAZZARELLO　　　　1837–1881
Born of a peasant family at Mornese in the south of Piedmont, she began teaching after an illness which prevented her from helping the family in the fields. As a member of a Marian sodality, she first met St John Bosco when he visited her village to see about founding a boys' school. She was twenty-eight. A building was constructed but it was used, instead, as a school for girls with St Mary as its head-mistress. It was run by a staff who became the nucleus of a new congregation the daughters of our Lady Help of Christians, otherwise the Salesian Sisters.

After many trials, thirteen other houses were established in St Mary's lifetime; and there are now over 800.
May 14th

MARY MICHAELA DESMAISIÈRES 1809–65
Born in Madrid, she was the sister of the Spanish ambassador to Paris and Brussels. In order to care for the destitute and for prostitutes in particular, she founded the Handmaids of the Blessed Sacrament and of Charity, becoming their mother general in 1859.
August 25th

MARY of CEREVELLON　　　　† 1290
For the reasons given in the life of St Peter Nolasco, it is impossible to verify the claim that when the Order of our Lady of Ransom was formed to help the victims of the Moors, Mary of Cerevellon became its first nun. Known in Spain as Mary of Help, she is the patroness of sailors in danger.
September 19th

MARY of CLEOPHAS　　　　*First Century*
The Roman Martyrology says 'Blessed John the Evangelist calls (her) sister of the most holy Mary, Mother of God, and relates that she stood with her by the cross of Jesus'; but her relationship to our Lady is uncertain.
April 9th

MARY of EGYPT　　　　*Fifth Century?*
The medieval legend of this saint derives from a story in the life of St Cyriacus. Repenting her life as a prostitute in Alexandria, she spent forty-seven years wandering alone in the desert. Just before her death, she was discovered by a monk named Zosimus.
April 2nd

MARY THE BLESSED VIRGIN　　*First Century*
'When the fullness of time was come, God sent his Son, made of a woman' (Galatians 4:4). Here is the central and vital event of history: 'The Word was made flesh' (John 1:14). The angel had told Mary that the holy spirit would come upon her, and therefore the Holy One to be born would be called the Son of God (Luke 1:35). The lowly 'handmaid of the Lord' is Mother of God. From that follows all her greatness.

The Gospels show her humble, obedient, candid and prudent at the Annunciation, a poet and prophet in her Magnificat, generous and kind in the visit to Elizabeth, and at Cana, silent and contemplative, for 'she kept all these words in her heart' (ibid 2:19, 51). 'Blessed is the fruit of thy womb ... and blessed art thou who hast believed,' said Elizabeth to Mary, and in a passage which forms the Gospel of her mass, Jesus heightened a woman's praise of her by adding: 'Still better, blessed are they who hear the word of God and keep it,' (ibid 1:42, 45; 11:28). Her motherly heart must have shared the aims and sufferings of the son who offered himself to his Father for men. She bore him in abandonment and poverty to be the joy of angels and shepherds. She offered him in the temple and was told that a sword would pierce her soul (ibid 2:35). The first gentiles found him in her arms. After that brief glory, came flight into Egypt and retirement to despised Nazareth. When Jesus reached boyhood, he left her and Joseph and was found in his Father's house (ibid 2:48ff.). Yet he cannot but have been the perfect son, and in the home he was subject to them. Then he had to go from her to the men whom, with a detached but tender allusion, he called his relations (Matthew 12:50, *cf.* Luke 1:38). In face of an apparent refusal (perhaps given with a smile), she gained her trustful wish, and for her sake alone, he worked his first miracle (John 2:1–11). As her influence is decisive when he thus 'manifests his glory', so at the last she is standing erect by the Cross. When Jesus said, 'Woman, behold thy son,' and to the beloved disciple, 'Behold thy Mother,' he was as a loving son providing for her. But at that moment when the second Adam accomplished all Scripture, his use of the title 'Woman' seems to recall Eve, the 'mother of all the living' (Genesis 3:20); and Catholic teaching, with Origen (*In Joann.*, 1, 6), sees here the recognition of Mary as the spiritual Mother of all Christians.

Mother of Jesus, she was present when the infant church was brought forth at Pentecost (Acts 1:14; 2:1), and according to tradition, she lived another eleven years. She must have been for Luke, at least indirectly, the source of what he says in his Gospel about our Lord's infancy, and she doubtless helped John by her companionship after the Crucifixion to develop into the apostle of Love. When, in the Apocalypse (ch. 12), he saw the woman clothed with the sun, who brought forth a man-child to rule the nations and whose enemy was the ancient serpent, the figure, although a symbol of the church, cannot but suggest the mother of the Messiah and of the rest of his seed, the second Eve.

Already in the second century Christian writers from all over the ancient church were recognizing Mary's freely accepted part in the Redemption as repairing Eve's part in the Fall. 'Eve,' says St Irenaeus, who represents Asia Minor, Rome, Gaul and a tradition coming from St John himself, 'was disobedient, and so brought death upon herself and upon the whole human race . . . Mary was obedient, and so became the cause of salvation both for herself and for the whole human race . . . The knot formed by the disobedience of Eve was untied by the obedience of Mary,' and 'thus the Virgin Mary became the Virgin Eve's advocate,' (*Adv. Haer.*, 3, 22, 4; 5, 19, 1). St Justin of Palestine speaks similarly (*Dial. with Trypho*, 100), while, from Africa, Tertullian writes: 'Eve believed the serpent; Mary believed Gabriel. The fault which the one committed by her belief, the other by her belief blotted out.' (*De Carne Christi*, 17). It early became a proverb: Death through Eve, life through Mary.

The assertion that devotion to Mary derived from worship of the pagan goddess, the Great Mother, contradicts Christian theology and history. Mary was never worshipped as a goddess. Christians have always understood the infinity between creatures and God. The council of Nicaea (325) defined that God the Son is consubstantial with the Father, above all creatures. But that showed the dignity of the mother whose son he deigned to become. When therefore Nestorius, bishop of Constantinople, attacked the title 'Mother of God', he disclosed the flaw in his own belief in the Incarnation. Against him, the council of Ephesus (431) defined the unity of Christ's person, and so the rightness of calling Mary 'Mother of God'. After that, Christian thought and poetry recognized ever more clearly her place in the Incarnation.

The Greek Fathers realized that God must have prepared Mary to be the mother of the Redeemer and that her rôle as Second Eve involved her immaculate conception. She was the daughter of her father and mother, but she never incurred original sin, being always one with her son. Eve was created immaculate, Mary was so conceived. Eve's descendants are deprived by the original sin of that state of grace which they should have inherited, and there is consequent disorder in their natures. Mary was ceaselessly in God's grace, and this the Greek Fathers found also expressed in the angel's greeting: 'Hail, full of grace.' The Gospel Greek will bear their interpretation.

So when, in 1854, Pius IX defined that Mary's Immaculate Conception had been revealed by God, he was not adding an extraneous dogma to the deposit of faith. Why then was it so long in being proclaimed? It had met difficulties in the minds of western theologians. Against the heresy of Pelagius, which denied original sin, the church had insisted on the universal need for redemption. Mary was not exempt, although the great champion of grace, St Augustine, had declared that for the honor of our Lord, he wished there to be absolutely

no question of sin in her case (*De Nat. et Gratia*, 36, 42). The feast of her Conception (early introduced in England) was opposed even by St Bernard and St Thomas Aquinas. But when, at Oxford, Duns Scotus published the distinction – Christ did redeem his mother, but so that he kept all sin from her – the way opened for the theological development summarized in Pius IX's definition. And so the church glorified her whom the poet Wordsworth so finely calls 'our tainted nature's solitary boast'. But Mary's privilege does not separate her from our race. It gives a mother who loves without a shadow of selfishness.

In 1950 Pius XII defined that after her mortal life 'the Immaculate Mother of God was assumed, body and soul, to heavenly glory.' The doctrine of Mary's Assumption does not rest upon legendary accounts. It rests upon the traditional, living belief of the church, and upon her motherhood and immaculate conception. Death and corruption are consequences of original sin. Christ, though sinless, accepted death to effect our redemption; but not corruption. He rose with body incorrupt, and thereafter associated with himself the immaculate mother from whom he received the flesh which redeems us. What value had the definition? In an age of materialism and despair, it gave certainty to our hopes that our heavenly mother is already enjoying the eternal beatitude of soul and body which we must strive to attain.

It is Catholic faith that Mary was perpetually virgin. This is the ancient tradition which Scripture supports, as is shown in the discussion of 'the brethren of the Lord' in the life of St James the Less. Difficulties may suggest themselves from the title 'first-born' given to Jesus and from the statement that Joseph did not know her 'until' she brought forth her son, Jesus (Matthew 1:25). But 'first-born' was a technical term for the first male child, even if there were no others, and 'until' was used (e.g. 2 Kings 6:23) without implying a future change.

In her Magnificat Mary prophesied: 'From henceforth all generations shall call me blessed.' In the *Hail Mary* every age repeats Elizabeth's salutation: 'Blessed art thou amongst women'.

Principal feasts:

February 2nd	Purification
March 25th	Annunciation
July 2nd	Visitation to St Elizabeth
August 15th	Assumption
August 22nd	Immaculate Heart
September 8th	Birthday
September 12th	Most Holy Name
September 15th	Seven Sorrows
October 7th	Holy Rosary
October 11th	Motherhood
November 21st	Presentation in the Temple
December 8th	Immaculate Conception

Feasts commemorating appearances of St Mary:

February 11th   our Lady of Lourdes
                (*see* Bernadette Soubious)

July 16th   our Lady of Mount Carmel
                (*see* Simon Stock)

August 5th   our Lady of the Snows, or Dedication
                of St Mary Major

(the legend is that our Lady caused snow to fall upon the spot on which St Mary Major is built and appeared to the patrician John and his wife telling them to build there this first church dedicated to her in Rome)

September 24th our Lady of Ransom
                (*see* Peter Nolasco)

ILLUSTRATION: facing page 321

MATERNUS   *Fourth Century*

As bishop of Cologne, he was invited to Rome to become one of the judges in the dispute between the Catholics and Donatists of North Africa. He was also present in this connection at the synod of Arles in 314.
September 14th

MATHURIN, *see* Maturinus.

MATILDA, *see* Mafalda.

MATILDA   † 968

Wife of Henry 'the Fowler', son of the Saxon Duke Otto. After his death she suffered much from the dissensions of her sons Henry and Otto ('the Great'). She founded four religious houses.
March 14th

MATRONA

Three saints called Matrona are commemorated on the same day, but the Roman Martyrology notes only the Christian servant of a Jewess in Thessalonica, who was beaten to death when her faith was discovered.
March 15th

MATTHEW, APOSTLE and EVANGELIST
First Century

Few people love the tax-collector. Even in these days when the relation between taxer and taxed is, no doubt, scrupulously correct, his name strikes cold. Much more was this so in the Palestine of the first century, when it was in his interests to bully and harry and falsify. But even the mild and honest tax-collector was not acceptable to official Judaism: he did business with the gentile and handled his money; he was legally impure, socially outcast. A Jewish Rabbi would be bold indeed to invite him to join his inner circle of disciples: it would be a gesture of defiance to the established prejudice. And so the formula 'publicans and sinners' slipped even into the phrase-book of the evangelists and, quaintly enough, into the Gospel of Matthew the publican. This term

'publican', by the way, does not accurately describe Matthew's profession but flatters it. The Roman *publicanus* was a wealthy farmer of State taxes, not a humble collector (*portitor*). On the other hand, we should not picture Matthew going from door to door. He had his office in Capharnaum, Peter's home town and the headquarters of our Lord's Galilean ministry. The place naturally had its custom house, since it lay on the road that leads from Damascus just where, at the north-west corner of Lake Galilee, that road passed from the territory of Herod Philip to the domains of his brother, Herod Antipas. Not customs only but road-tolls would be calculated and exacted here, according to a vague tariff that would leave a certain lucrative freedom to the customs officer himself. The Pharisees might despise it, but the trade was a profitable one and much sought after: whether it was to be pursued honestly or dishonestly would depend on the character of the officer.

'And as Jesus passed further on, he saw Levi, the son of Alphaeus, sitting at work in the customs-house and said to him, 'Follow me'; and he rose up and followed him' (Mark 2:14). That this was a call to the apostolate there is no doubt – its terms too closely match those of the call of Simon and Andrew, to be otherwise (*cf.* Mark 1:16ff.). Yet 'Levi' does not appear in any list of the Twelve (Mark 3:16ff.; Matthew 10:3ff.; Luke 6:14ff.; Acts 1:13). Now the vocation of the tax-collector is reported in the first Gospel too, but there he is called 'Matthew' (Matthew 9:9ff.), thus identifying him with the Matthew who appears in all the apostolic lists. The widely accepted and most natural explanation is that Matthew and Levi are one person with two Semitic names (not unprecedented; *cf. e.g.* the Machabee brothers in 1 Machabee 2:2–5). It may be that our Lord himself gave him the name Matthew (*Mattai*, 'gift of God', in Aramaic) as he gave *Kepha* to Simon.

This Matthew, then, got up from his registers and henceforth – at our Lord's suggestion – took a lesson from the lilies and the birds who never did a day's calculation in their lives (Matthew 6:25ff.). His master was no longer Antipas, the shrewd 'fox' (Luke 13:32), but one who, unlike the foxes, had not even a home (Matthew 8:20). The change destroyed all Matthew's worldly prospects: Simon and Andrew might return to their fish, waiting for them in the lake, but Matthew had thrown over a coveted business and could never recover it. He left it gladly, it seems, and completely – at least it was not he but Judas who kept the accounts for the apostolic group (John 13:29).

Matthew's new style of life (he would have called it 'improvident' once) must have wrenched his careful temperament sorely, but this temperament was to have its almost humorous revenge as we shall shortly discover. After the incident of his call Matthew disappears from the New Testament except as a name in the apostolic lists. What became of him? We have a sentence from a book by Bishop Papias of Hierapolis who was born about 70 A.D., and who published his *Explanation of the Oracles of the Lord* about 125. 'Matthew wrote an ordered account of the oracles (of our Lord) and each interpreted these oracles according to his ability' (Eusebius, *Historia Ecclesiastica*, iii.39). That Matthew wrote in Aramaic for converted Jews appears from other authorities of the second and third centuries. Time had had its revenge. When the need for a written gospel record began to be felt, upon which of the Apostles would the choice fall? Upon one who was used to the pen, no doubt. Poor Matthew was back where he started, but this time with an eager will and a high purpose. In Palestine, some time between the years 40 and 50, this ex-civil servant produced not the lively and artless Gospel of a St Mark but the orderly, almost ledger-like, treatise which we know as 'The Gospel according to St Matthew'. For if we are to judge from our surviving Greek edition of it, whose substantial identity with its Aramaic original there is no reason to doubt, Matthew's mathematical temperament has re-asserted itself with a certain arithmetical neatness. Hence the seven parables of the Kingdom, the seven woes for the Pharisees, seven invocations of the Lord's Prayer, the probable number of seven Beatitudes. So, too, with the number five: five disputes with the Pharisees, the five loaves, five talents and above all the five books into which the body of his Gospel is clearly divided. And then, as we might expect, a sign of special knowledge on the financial side. Thus the 'denarius' of Mark and Luke becomes 'the coin of the tribute' – a customs officer has his own way of looking at these things. So also, though Mark and Luke omit it, we find the incident of the Temple tax in the first Gospel complete with its little technicalities of indirect tax and poll tax, its 'didrachmas' and its 'stater'.

And so Matthew's old trade entered a new service: the accountant became an evangelist; the ledger turned into a Gospel. It is not surprising that he alone records his Master's words: 'Every scholar whose learning is of the kingdom of heaven . . . knows how to bring both new and old things out of his treasure-house' (13:52). For there is no poor tool of ours that God's service will not perfect and dignify.

The first Gospel, the church's favorite, is Matthew's memorial: the rest of his apostolic work is lost in the mists of contradiction. That he preached the gospel to the Jews in Palestine for perhaps fifteen years after the crucifixion is fairly sure (Eusebius, *Historia Ecclesiastica*, iii.24.265), but confusion of his name with that of Matthias (Acts 1:26) has left us with a varying tradition: Ethiopia, Parthia, Macedonia are all mentioned and even

an apostolate among the cannibals. It is commonly but not unanimously affirmed he died a martyr's death; but we know for certain that he lived a martyr's life – and tha is enough. And for us he will always be the man who knew what money was and what it was not.
September 21st   ILLUSTRATION: page 318

MATTHIAS   *First Century*
The only reliable information about St Matthias comes from the Acts of the Apostles. He accompanied Christ from the time of his baptism by St John the Baptist, and he was elected one of the twelve apostles in the place of Judas.

According to the Greeks, he brought Christianity to Cappadocia and was crucified at Colchis. His body was alleged to have been kept in Jerusalem and afterwards taken by St Helen to Rome.
February 24th   ILLUSTRATION: page 319

MATURINUS or MATHURIN *Fourth Century?*
Born at Larchant, he converted his parents, became a priest and made a reputation as an exorcist.
November 1st

MAUDEZ, *see* Mawes.

MAUGHOLD or MACCUL   *Fifth Century*
An outlaw converted by St Patrick, he lived as a penitent on the Isle of Man until the death of the two missionaries already there, when he was chosen bishop of the island.
April 27th

MAUGUILLE, *see* Madelgisilus.

MAURA, *see* Timothy and Maura.

MAURA and BRIGID   *Fifth Century?*
A legend says that they were Northumbrian princesses who were murdered at Balagny-sur-Therain when returning from a pilgrimage. They are sometimes identified with the virgins Maura and Britta who are venerated in Touraine.
July 13th

MAURA of TROYES   *c. 827–850*
The subject of a funeral oration by St Prudentius, bishop of Troyes, she died at the age of twenty-three after a life of consistent austerity.
September 21st

MAURICE, CANDIDUS and their Companions
† 287?
According to the legend, SS Maurice and Candidus were officers of a Roman legion which, composed entirely of Christians, refused to sacrifice to the gods and was surrounded and slaughtered by the orders of Maximian near Agaunum (St Maurice-en-Valais). That Maurice, Candidus and some companions were martyred at

Agaunum seems certain; that a whole legion was massacred is unlikely.   ILLUSTRATION: page 78
September 22nd

MAURICE of CARNOËT   † 1191
He entered the Cistercian abbey of Langonnet in his native Britanny. He became abbot of Langonnet and then the first abbot of Carnoët, which had been founded by Duke Conan IV at his suggestion.
October 13th

MAURILIUS   † 453
A Milanese who came to Touraine and was ordained by St Martin of Tours, he was bishop of Angers for thirty years.
September 13th

MAURUNTIUS   † 701
Son of St Adalbald and St Rictrudis, he was educated at the court of King Clovis II, but retired to the monastery of Marchiennes. He founded the abbey of Breuil, and became its abbot.
May 5th

MAURUS   *Sixth Century*
Gregory the Great, the only trustworth authority, states that St Maurus trained at Subiaco and succeeded St Benedict as superior there. He is said to have walked miraculously over water to rescue a drowning boy.
January 15th

MAWES or MAUDEZ   *Sixth Century?*
This monk was famous in Cornwall and especially in Brittany where he established a community on an island off the coast of Léon.
November 18th

MAXELLENDIS   *Seventh Century*
Her parents insisted on her marriage, although she had taken a vow of virginity. She was killed by her impatient fiancé, Harduin of Solesmes, who was striken with blindness until he had repented of his act.
November 13th

MAXENTIA
An Irish princess, she fled to Gaul rather than marry a pagan, and was killed by her rejected suitor near Senlis.
November 20th

MAXENTIUS   *Sixth Century*
Brought up by St Severus, he avoided the fame which his piety had brought him by entering a monastery in Poitou, and changing his name from Adjutor to Maxentius. He became abbot of this community in 500.
June 26th

MAXIMA, *see* Martinian and his Companions and Maxima.

MAXIMIAN, *see* Bonosus and Maximian.

MAXIMILIAN   *Third Century*
Sent by Pope St Sixtus II to evangelize Noricum, he established a see at Lorch, where he eventually suffered martyrdom.
October 12th

MAXIMILIAN of THEVESTE   † 295
The law of the later Empire obliged a son to follow his father's profession. Maximilian, therefore, as a soldier's son, was brought before the proconsul Dion on March 12th, 295, for compulsory enlistment. We are fortunate in possessing a contemporary report of the proceedings. Maximilian refused outright to serve in the army: 'I cannot enlist for I am a Christian. I cannot serve. I cannot do evil. I am a Christian'. Dion: 'You must serve or die.' Maximilian: 'You can cut off my head, but I will not be a soldier of this world, for I am a soldier of Christ . . . My army is the army of God, and I cannot fight for this world. I tell you I am a Christian.' Dion: 'There are Christian soldiers serving our rulers.' Maximilian: 'That is their business. I also am a Christian, and I cannot serve.' Dion: 'But what harm do soldiers do?' Maximilian: 'You know well enough.' Dion: 'If you will not do your service, I shall condemn you to death for contempt of the army . . . Your impiety makes you refuse military service, and you shall be punished . . . as a warning to others.'

He then read the sentence: 'Maximilian has refused the military oath through impiety. He is to be beheaded.' The sentence was duly executed. Maximilian was a little over the age of twenty-one. Since his body was taken to Carthage for burial, it is thought that the scene of his trial and death may be near that city, and that Theveste is a copyist's faulty reading.
March 12th

MAXIMINUS, *see* Juventius and Maximinus.

MAXIMINUS   *Fourth Century*
He was educated under St Agrecius whom he succeeded as bishop of Trier. He was host to St Athanasius of Alexandria and St Paul of Constantinople when they were in exile, and it was he who called the synod at Cologne which condemned the Arian Euphratas.
May 29th

MAXIMINUS of AIX   *Fifth Century*
According to an unsubstantiated legend he was one of the seventy-two disciples who left Palestine after the Ascension; he evangelized Provence and became first bishop of Aix. *See* Mary Magdalene.
June 8th

MAXIMUS, *see* Tibertius, Valerius and Maximus.

MAXIMUS † 250
A businessman in a small way he suffered martyrdom either at Ephesus or Lampsacus during the persecution of the Emperor Decius. The official *acta* still survive.
April 30th

MAXIMUS of RIEZ *Fifth Century*
Born near Digne in Provence, he succeeded St Honoratus as abbot of Lérins in 426 and later became bishop of Riez.
November 27th

MAXIMUS of TURIN *Fifth Century*
As bishop of Turin, he attended a synod at Milan in 451, and a council at Rome in 465. He was a prolific writer, and many of his sermons, homilies and treatises survive.
June 25th

MAXIMUS THE CONFESSOR *c.* 580–662
He resigned his post as secretary to the Emperor Heraclius and retired to the monastery of Chrysopolis, of which he became abbot. He headed the opposition to the Monothelite heresy; for this he endured banishment, and, at the age of eighty-two, he was silenced by the loss of his tongue and right hand.
August 13th

MAY, *see* Marius.

MAYEULE, *see* the Cluny Saints.

MECHTILDE, *see* Gertrude the Great and Mechtilde.

MECHTILDIS of EDELSTETTEN † 1160
At the age of five, her parents sent her to be educated in the double monastery they had founded. She later became abbess, but was asked by the bishop of Augsburg to take over the convent of Edelstetten which was badly in need of reform. She agreed and ultimately had great success.
May 31st

MÉDARD *Sixth Century*
A native of Picardy, he was ordained at the age of thirty-three, and became bishop of Vermandois. He was the subject of various invocations, – against toothache, for a good harvest, for a good vintage – and he even had some connection with the weather.
June 8th

MEDERICUS or MERRY *Seventh Century*
Born at Autun, he became a monk and then abbot of the local monastery.
August 29th

MÉEN or MEWAN *Sixth Century*
He crossed from Cornwall to Brittany and built the monastery of Gael. In the middle ages, a fountain at the abbey attracted many pilgrims because it was thought to heal skin diseases.
June 21st

MEINGOLD *Ninth Century?*
According to the most plausible of many legends attached to his name, he was a belligerent count of Huy, in Belgium. He repented his ways, but was killed soon afterwards by former enemies.
February 8th

MEINRAD † 861
A hermit near Zürich who moved southwards to escape the fame of his holiness. The celebrated Swiss abbey of Einsiedeln, built forty years after Meinrad was murdered, still stands on the site of his last hermitage. He was killed by two robbers to whom he had given food and shelter.
January 21st

MEINULF, *see* Magenulf.

MEL and MELCHU *Fifth Century*
Nephews of St Patrick whom they accompanied as missionaries to Ireland. Melchu was probably a bishop with no fixed see, but may have succeeded Mel as bishop of Ardagh.
February 6th

MELAINE *Sixth Century*
A Breton monk, he became bishop of Rennes in succession to St Amand, and took a leading part in the council of Orleans in 511.
November 6th

MELANGELL or MONACELLA
The daughter of an Irish or Scots king, she fled to Powys to avoid marriage and, after fifteen years in hiding, became abbess of a community which grew up on land given her by the Prince of Powys.
May 27th

MELANIA THE YOUNGER 383–439
Granddaughter of St Melania the Elder, she was forced into marriage against her will at the age of fourteen to Valerius Pinianus. Only after her two children had died in infancy was she allowed to pursue a religious life. Her vast estates were divided among the poor, and at the Gothic invasions, she moved with her husband to Africa, and then to Palestine, where she was a great friend of St Jerome. After the death of her husband, she became the head of a convent on the Mount of Olives.
December 31st

MELAR, *see* Melorus.

MELCHIADES, *see* Miltiades.

MELCHU, *see* Mel and Melchu.

MELETIUS † 381

Born of a distinguished family in Melitene, Lesser Armenia, his meekness made him greatly beloved, but he was constantly troubled by Arians, both when bishop of Sebaste and when archbishop of Antioch.
February 12th

MELEUSIPPUS, *see* Speusippus, Eleusippus and Meleusippus.

MELITO *Second Century*

As bishop of Sardis, he addressed an Apology for Christianity to the Emperor Marcus Aurelius. His oratory and writings were well known.
April 1st

MELLITUS † 624

He was head of the second group of missionaries sent from Rome in 601 by Pope St Gregory, and the first bishop of London. He retired to France when the East Saxons reverted to paganism, but returned in 619 to succeed St Laurence as archbishop of Canterbury.
April 24th

MELLON, *see* Mallonius.

MELORUS or MELAR or MYLOR

Supposed to have been the son of Melianus, duke of Cornouaille, he was placed in a monastery by his usurping uncle Rivoldus. When he became famous for his piety, his uncle had him beheaded, and his relics were later taken to Amesbury in Wiltshire, where the church was dedicated to him.
October 1st

MENNAS

An Egyptian who was probably a Roman soldier, he was beheaded for professing his faith in Egypt during Diocletian's persecution. His tomb with the shrine built over it at Bumma, near Alexandria, was a great place of pilgrimage, and, as recently as 1943, his intercession was regarded by the orthodox patriarch of Alexandria as having been responsible for saving Egypt from German invasion. ILLUSTRATION: page 320
November 11th

MENNAS, HERMOGENES and EUGRAPHUS

This is the entirely legendary story of Mennas and his assistant, Eugraphus, who on an imperial mission to Alexandria, declared themselves Christians. They were arrested, but converted their judge, Hermogenes, and all three were beheaded.
December 10th

MENNAS of CONSTANTINOPLE † 552

Born in Alexandria, he was patriarch of Constantinople from 536 until his death.
August 25th

MENODORA, METRODORA and NYMPHODORA † 304?

They are supposed to have been orphans and sisters who were put to death in Bithynia during the persecution of Diocletian.
September 10th

MERCURIUS

According to a worthless legend he was a high-ranking army officer, who, after winning a battle for the Emperor Decius, refused to sacrifice to the gods and was executed. Mercurius acquired considerable posthumous celebrity as the heavenly executioner of Julian the Apostate.
November 25th

MERIADOC *Sixth Century*

A Welshman, he went to Brittany via Cornwall, probably with St Gwinear, and may have been a regionary bishop.
June 7th

MERRY, *see* Medericus.

MESROP † 441

A learned Armenian bishop, he assisted St Isaac. His native alphabet was almost non-existent before he revived it and made possible a translation of the Syriac Bible into Armenian. He established a school for similar work in Georgia.
February 19th

MESSALINA, *see* Felician and Messalina.

METHODIUS, *see* Cyril and Methodius.

METHODIUS I, PATRIARCH of CONSTANTINOPLE † 847

He left the monastery he had built at Chios and went to Constantinople in order to support the patriarch, Nicephorus, during the iconoclastic persecution. When Nicephorus was deposed, Methodius went to Rome, but returned to Constantinople in 821, only to be scourged, exiled and imprisoned. The persecution ended in 842, and Methodius became patriarch.
June 14th

METHODIUS of OLYMPUS † *c.* 311

He appears to have been a bishop of Lycia and is reputed to have died a martyr; otherwise he is only known through his writings, especially the *Banquet of the Ten Virgins*.
September 18th

METRODORA, *see* Menodora, Metrodora and Nymphodora.

METROPHANES *Fourth Century*

He may have been nephew of the Emperor Probus. He became the first bishop of Byzantium, ruling from 306 to 313 or 316 and dying before the foundation of Constantinople.
June 4th

MEWAN, *see* Meen.

MICHAEL

The Jews regarded Michael as the special protector of Israel, and in Christian usage he has become the protector of the church. In the prayers after low mass, he is accordingly invoked to be 'our safeguard against the wickedness and snares of the devil', and is referred to as the 'captain of the Heavenly Host' because of what St John tells us about him in the Apocalypse (12:7 to 9): 'And there was war in heaven. Michael and his angels fought against the dragon . . . And the great dragon was cast out, that old serpent called the Devil and Satan, which deceiveth the whole world: he was cast out into the earth, and his angels were cast out with him.'

In the offertory anthem of the mass for the dead, Michael is charged with the care of all departed souls that he 'the holy standard bearer (may) introduce them to the holy light, which thou didst promise of old to Abraham and to his seed'.

The main feast is, of course, on Michaelmas Day (September 29th), but on May 8th a lesser feast is observed to commemorate the appearance of St Michael on the summit of Mount Gargano in Apulia during the time of Pope Gelasius (492–6).

See also Angels and Archangels.
September 29th and *May 8th* ILLUSTRATION: page 353

MICHAEL de SANCTIS   c. 1590–1625

From his youth his imagination was captured by St Francis of Assisi, and as soon as he was able, he joined the Trinitarian friars, and later the reformed branch of that Order. He was twice superior of the house at Valladolid.
April 10th

MICHAEL GARICOÏTS   1797–1863

The Garicoïts family were Basque peasants from the French side of the Pyrenees, and Michael, their eldest son, was born in 1797. After spending his early youth as a shepherd boy, on his reiterated desire to be a priest and with the bishop's encouragement, he was accepted by the diocese of Bayonne and ordained in 1823. His ecclesiastical career as a curate and later as parish priest, seminary professor and finally rector was marked by his efforts to revive religion after the evil effects of the French Revolution and to stamp out the last remaining traces of Jansenism: to do this he relied principally on preaching devotion to the Sacred Heart and in 1838 established a society of priests for home missions under the title of 'Society of Priests of the Sacred Heart of Betharram' (where he was then parish priest). On the appointment of a new bishop of the diocese he encountered some opposition, but finally by the middle of the century the congregation was firmly established.

St Michael Garicoïts seems to have possessed an immense capacity for work and the gift of suffering all sorts of trials in silence, but his outstanding characteristic was his great missionary zeal. With St Andrew Hubert Fournet and St Joan Elizabeth Bichier des Ages (with whom in the last years of her life he was in touch), he forms one of a group laboring in France for the renewal of religion, though his work spread eventually far beyond that country.
May 14th

MICHAEL of CHERNIGOV and THEODORE
† 1246

Michael, duke of Chernigov, and Theodore, one of his noblemen, are popular Russian heroes who gave themselves up to the Tartar leader in order to divert his cruelty from the general populace to themselves. For this they are accounted martyrs.
September 21st

MILBURGA and MILDGYTHA   *Eighth Century*

Sisters of St Mildred: Milburga, endowed with great spiritual and healing powers, founded the convent of Much Wenlock in Shropshire, and became its abbess; Mildgytha, a nun, was honored for the miracles worked at her tomb.
February 23rd

MILDRED   *Seventh Century*

Her mother, St Ermenburga, founded the abbey of Minster-in-Thanet on the land given to her as a penance by King Egbert of Kent, who had killed Ermenburga's brothers. After an education at Chelles in France, Mildred returned to England and succeeded her mother as abbess.
July 13th

MILTIADES or MELCHIADES   † 314

An African, he became pope in 311. During his reign Constantine became emperor, and religious freedom was assured to Christians. The Donatist schism also began at this time: it arose over the appointment of Caecilian as bishop of Carthage.
December 10th

MIRIN   *Seventh Century?*

An Irish missionary in Scotland, he is variously described as abbot of Bangor and as regionary bishop.
September 15th

MOCHOEMOC   *Seventh Century*

Brought up by his aunt, St Ita, he entered the Bangor monastery in County Down, and later established a settlement at Liath-mor where SS Dagan and Cuanghas studied under him.
March 13th

MOCHTA † 535?

After crossing to Ireland, he came under the influence of St Patrick and was sent by him to Rome where he was supposed to have been made a bishop. When he retired to Louth his followers soon formed a large community.
August 19th

MOCHUDA, *see* Carthage.

MOCIUS, *see* Mucius.

MODAN Sixth Century

The abbot of his monastery and patron of the High Church at Stirling, he is said to have preached in places along the Forth, especially at Falkirk.
February 4th

MODESTUS, *see* Vitus, Modestus and Crescentia.

MODOALDUS Seventh Century

Modoaldus was bishop of Trier between c. 622 and c. 640.
May 12th

MODOMNOC Sixth Century

He left Ireland to study under St David in Wales, and is said to have introduced bees into Ireland. The bees he tended in Wales refused to leave him and made the journey to Ireland in his company.
February 13th

MODWENNA Seventh Century?

There is much confusion between this Modwenna, and other saints with similar names and equally obscure origins. A saint of this name was certainly venerated at Burton-on-Trent, and it is possible that she was a solitary who lived on an island in the river Trent.
July 6th

MOLAISSE, *see* Laserian or Laisren.

MOLING † 197

The abbey he founded at Aghacainid was named Teghmolin after him, and the town of St Mullins, Co. Carlow, now stands on its site. He succeeded St Aidan as bishop at Ferns in Leinster.
June 17th

MOLOC or LUAN Sixth Century

Probably a Scotsman, educated in Ireland under St Brendan, he returned to Scotland as a missionary in Argyll and the Isles, and seems to have become a bishop.
June 25th

MOLUA or LUGHAIDH † 608

A monk at Bangor, he was sent by St Comgall to found other houses, of which Clonfertmulloe, or Kyle, was the most famous. He told his monks to cultivate their land so that they might always have enough to eat and drink; from such sufficiency came stability and from such stability would come true religion.
August 4th

MOMMOLINUS Seventh Century

A monk of Luxeuil, he made foundations at St Omer and at St Peter's at Sithiu. In 660, he became bishop of Noyon and founded the abbey of Saint-Quentin.
October 16th

MONACELLA, *see* Melangell.

MONEGUNDIS † 570

After the death of her two daughters, she retired to a cell at Chartres. When she removed to Tours a community grew up around her which became the convent of St Pierre-le-Puellier.
July 2nd

MONICA 332–387

St Monica, the mother of St Augustine, was born, probably, at Thagaste in Numidia, where she married and lived the greater part of her life. She was of Berber stock and her name is Berber. Practically everything we know of her life comes from her son's writings, particularly Book IX of his *Confessions*. She was well, but rather strictly, brought up by the old nurse of the family, who, among other things, would never allow her to drink between meals. Perhaps in reaction from this she developed the habit of taking unauthorised drinks, which grew larger as time went on, when she was sent by her parents to draw wine from the barrel; but when one of the household slaves taunted her with being a drunkard she was ashamed and gave it up. She was married young to Patricius, a short-tempered, but by no means bad or unlikeable, man, with an old mother who was at first violently hostile to her. She managed both husband and mother-in-law excellently, so that the old lady was completely won over and St Monica, unlike many of her married friends and neighbors whose husbands were supposed to be better tempered, never had any marks of ill treatment from her husband to show; her own account of the matter was that Patricius kept his hands off her because she kept her tongue off him.

Her relationship to her brilliant son was a miracle of perseverance and unwearying affection. She probably never fully understood his intellectual difficulties and vagaries, and was profoundly distressed by his Manichaeism. Augustine, on his side, during his Manichaean period, seems to have found his mother, with her uncompromising Catholicism, rather a nuisance: at any rate, when she decided to accompany him to Rome (Patricius had died some years before, leaving her free to devote herself to her son) he gave her the slip and went off without her. But she followed and caught him up in Milan, where she found to her joy that he was no longer a Manichee: from this time onward they were on the best of terms. She soon came to know St Ambrose, who had the highest regard for her, and she for him. He even persuaded her to give up some of her North African pieties of which he disapproved or which were not in accordance with Milanese custom, such as holy picnics at the graves of the martyrs and fasting on Saturdays.

At last in 386 she had the supreme joy of seeing her son's conversion, which he himself attributed to her prayers and tears more than to any other human agency. She shared his retreat at Cassiciacum, and was present at his baptism by St Ambrose. Then, in 387, she started back for Africa with St Augustine and his friends. At Ostia she shared with her son that great exaltation of spirit of which he tells in the tenth chapter of Book IX of his *Confessions*: as they talked about the life of heaven, he says, they were raised in thought above all created things; they entered into their own minds and passed them, and came at last to touch directly, for a moment, the eternal Wisdom and Word of God. After this St Monica said, 'My son, for my part, I have no more pleasure in anything in this life. I do not know what I am still to do and why I am here, now my hope in this world is finished. There was one thing because of which I wanted to stay a little while in this life, to see you a Catholic Christian before I died. God has given me this and much more, in letting me see you despise earthly happiness and devote yourself to his service. What am I doing here?' Soon after, she fell ill and died at Ostia, at the age of fifty-six.

She had always been very anxious to be buried with her husband, but now when she was asked if she would mind leaving her body so far from her native city, she answered, 'Nothing is far from God; and there is no fear that he will not know where to raise me up from at the end of the world.' And her last words to her sons were, 'Lay this body anywhere; don't worry about that. I only ask you to remember me at the altar of the Lord wherever you may be.' St Augustine certainly never forgot her; nor will anyone who has read about her in his *Confessions*. She was buried at Ostia. Her body is supposed to have been translated to Rome in 1430, and to be now in the church of St Agostino.

May 4th   ILLUSTRATION: page 354

MONTANUS, LUCIUS and their Companions
† 259
Eight disciples of St Cyprian of Carthage, they were arrested after an uprising in Carthage against the procurator Solon. After a long period in prison, during which they deliberately starved, they were beheaded.
February 24th

MORAND   *Twelfth Century*
A nobleman educated at Worms, he became a monk of Cluny after having stayed there during a pilgrimage. St Hugh sent him to found a monastery in Alsace.

He is the patron of vine-growers because he is supposed to have existed through Lent on a single bunch of grapes.
June 3rd

MOSES   † 251
A priest in Rome, he died in prison during the persecution of Decius.
November 25th

MOSES   *Fourth Century*
An Arabian hermit at Rhinoclura, he was appointed bishop among the Arabs by a treaty between their queen and the Romans. He succeeded in converting many of the tribes in the Arabian desert.
February 7th

MOSES THE BLACK   † c. 405
A renegade slave who became a bandit, his strength and ferocity were remarkable. After his conversion, he lived as a desert monk, was ordained, and perished in a Berber raid.
August 28th

MUCIUS or MOCIUS   † 304
He was a priest who suffered martyrdom during the persecution of Diocletian at Constantinople.
May 13th

MUNCHIN   *Seventh Century*
Called the 'Wise'. Though it is doubtful whether he was ever bishop of Limerick, he is the patron of that diocese, and honored on his feast day throughout Ireland.
January 2nd

MUNGO, *see* Kentigern.

MUNNU, *see* Fintan of Taghmon.

MURTAGH or MUREDACH   *Sixth Century*
He seems to have been a bishop at Killala, although it is not known exactly when.
August 12th

MUSTIOLA, *see* Ireneaus and Mustiola.

MYLOR, *see* Melorus.

NABOR and FELIX   *Fourth Century*
Moorish soldiers stationed at Milan, they are said to have been executed at Lodi.
July 12th

NAPOLEON

St Napoleon is the only saint who was a logical fiction. The baptismal name of Napoleon was much used by certain pious Italian families so that it was assumed that there must have been a saint Napoleon at some time and in some place. The question became acute after the Emperor Napoleon restored the Catholic religion in France, and a new feast to replace the traditional national celebration of St Louis's day was needed. So the Emperor's birthday was substituted, thinly disguised as St Napoleon's day. This happened to fall on the day following the feast of the Assumption, and one of Napoleon's ministers made the tactful suggestion that the new saint and his day would aquire more tone if the day were moved to August 15th. The Emperor enthusiastically agreed; and the celebration of St Napoleon was joined to the Assumption for the rest of his reign with a collect and other prayers of commemoration at lauds and mass.

It was now necessary to furnish St Napoleon with a *Life* and this the cardinal-legate undertook to provide. He identified St Napoleon with an Egyptian martyr, Neopolus, who suffered under Diocletian and whose name, without any biographical details, is preserved in some ancient martyrologies. The cardinal supplied St Neopolus with exquisite tortures bravely borne and a noble ancestry; unfortunately it has now been shown that Neopolus was the name of a place, not a martyr. However, the cult was abolished by Louis XVIII and it was not revived even by Napoleon III. A number of icons of St Napoleon survive, all suspiciously like the Emperor, and a masonic lodge was dedicated to him. Otherwise it cannot be said that the cult of St Napoleon has made headway among the devotional habits of French Catholics.

NARCISSUS of JERUSALEM   *Third Century*

He was already an old man before he became bishop of Jerusalem. A false accusation led to his voluntary exile, but he returned, and, with St Alexander to help him, continued to rule until his death at the age of about 120.
October 29th

NATALIA, *see* Adrian and Natalia.

NATALIA, *see* Aurelius, Natalia, Felix and their Companions.

NATHALAN   † 678

A Scots nobleman who took to farming, this saint is the subject of an interesting legend. When a sudden storm interfered with his harvest he murmured against God. Later on, when he realized what he had done, he bound his right hand to his leg with an iron lock and key, threw the key into the Dee and vowed never to free his arm until he had made a pilgrimage to Rome.

He fulfilled his vow and arrived in Rome. There he met a boy who offered him a fish for sale. He bought it, and in its belly discovered the key which he had thrown into the river back in Scotland. On hearing of this wonder, the pope sent for Nathalan and made him a bishop on the spot. He returned to Scotland. Although some churches bear his name, he remains a legendary figure.
January 19th

NATHANAEL, *see under* Bartholomew.

NATHY and FELIM   *Sixth Century?*

Felim was the first bishop of Kilmore. Nathy was a priest and is mentioned in the life of St Attracta.
August 9th

NAZARIUS and CELSUS

Nazarius was the son of a Roman army officer and of a Christian mother. He went off with Celsus to preach the Gospel, and they were martyred at Milan. Their bodies were discovered by St Ambrose in 395 and the relics translated to the church of the Apostles.
July 28th

NECTAN   *Sixth Century*

Possibly a missionary from Ireland, who may have been murdered by robbers, he was widely venerated in Devon and Cornwall. His tomb is at Hartland, North Devon.
June 17th

NECTARIUS   † 397

Praetor of Constantinople, he was recommended to succeed St Gregory Nazianzen as archbishop although he was apparently still unbaptized. The Emperor Theodosius chose him from the list submitted, and he ruled for sixteen years.
October 11th

NEMESIAN and his Companions   † 257

A bishop of Numidia, he was the leader of a large group of Christians, including nine bishops, who were imprisoned in North Africa under the Emperor Valerian.
September 10th

NEMESIUS, DIOSCORUS and their Companions   † 250

In the persecution under Decius, Nemesius was wrongfully arrested at Alexandria for theft. He was discharged but immediately rearrested for being a Christian, and executed. Arsenius, Heron and Isidore were tortured and executed in the same persecution. Dioscorus, a boy of fifteen, was released after torture.
December 19th (Nemesius); *December 14th* (his Companions)

NEON, *see* Claudius, Asterius, Neon, Domnina and Theonilla.

NEOT   *Ninth Century?*

Details of the life of St Neot are extremely uncertain. Coming from supposedly royal Anglo-Saxon parentage he is said to have been a monk in the monastery of Glastonbury. He longed however for the truly solitary life and travelled into Cornwall to settle in the place that is now known as St Neot. He made a pilgrimage to Rome, and on his return he followed the Pope's recommendation and founded a college of clergy which ministered to the needs of the Cornish people round about. King Alfred – to whom by some accounts he was closely related – visited him there; and it is told that, on the night before the victory over the Danes at the battle of Aethundune, Neot came to Alfred in a dream.

Neot's relics were removed from Cornwall and enshrined in the place now known as St Neots in Huntingdonshire. Some say this was commanded by Neot himself in a vision, but there is a story of the guardian of the Cornish shrine removing them secretly with the approval of no less than two bishops and one king. St Neot remains a living if obscure figure to us, if only for the odd circumstance that Asser's famous *Life of King Alfred* quotes the original story of Alfred burning the cakes from a life of St Neot, which has not survived. And his 'history' is interesting as indicative of connections between Saxon and Celt: an Anglo-Saxon monk leaving his name as a Cornish saint.
July 31st

NEREUS, ACHILLEUS and DOMITILLA
First Century?
The church containing their relics on the Via Ardeatina in Rome was thrice rebuilt, and although the full story of their martyrdom may be fictitious their cult is very ancient. It now seems likely that there were two Domitillas, one of whom was niece to the Emperor Domitian and Titus. Nereus and Achilleus were soldiers who, on their conversion, deserted the Imperial Army.
May 12th

NERSES
Fourth Century
An official of the Armenian king, he was ordained after his wife's death and, in 363, became chief bishop of Armenia. He was poisoned by King Pap whom he had excommunicated.
November 19th

NERSES KLAIËTSI
† 1173
Succeeding his brother Gregory as katholikos of the Armenians in 1166, he worked for the re-union of the Greek and Armenian churches with Rome.
August 13th

NERSES LAMPRONAZI
1153–1198
Son of a Cilician prince and nephew of Nerses Klaiëtsi, he was educated at the abbey of Skeyra and became in 1176, archbishop of Tarsus. He was instrumental in bringing most of the Armenian church back temporarily to the rule of Rome.
July 17th

NERSES of SAHGERD and his Companions   † 343
Nerses, bishop of Sahgerd, and his disciple Joseph were among those who suffered martyrdom at the time of King Sapor II of Persia.
November 20th

NESTABUS, *see* Eusabius, Nestabus, Zeno and Nestor.

NESTOR, *see* Eusabius, Nestabus, Zeno and Nestor.

NESTOR
† 251
This bishop of Magydus was crucified during the persecution by Decius. He was so beloved that when, from the cross, he exhorted the crowd to pray, the pagans knelt with the Christians.
February 26th

NICANDER and MARCIAN
Fourth Century
They were supposed to have been Roman soldiers who were beheaded in Moesia for refusing to sacrifice to the gods.
June 17th

NICARETE
Fifth Century
A woman of good family, she came from Nicomedia to live in Constantinople, and helped to nurse St John Chrysostom through an illness.
December 27th

NICASIUS and his Companions
Fifth Century
Tenth bishop of Rheims, St Florentius, his deacon, St Jucundus, his lector, and St Eutropia, his sister were among those slaughtered during a barbarian occupation of the city.
December 14th

NICEPHORUS
Nicephorus – a layman living in Antioch – quarrelled with his friend Sapricius, a priest. Three times he tried to become reconciled, but Sapricius was unyielding; and then Sapricius was taken before the governor for refusing to sacrifice to the gods. He was condemned, and on his way to execution was stopped by Nicephorus who, yet again, asked forgiveness. Sapricius refused. The time came for his execution. But as the sentence was about to be carried out, Sapricius yielded – to the governor. He would sacrifice to the gods. He had apostatized. Immediately Nicephorus stepped forward, confessing his faith and claiming to be executed in his place. His wish was granted. It seems probable, unfortunately, that this story was concocted as a moral lesson upon the virtues of faith, humility and charity; but it could also be regarded as an early manifestation of anti-clericalism.
February 9th

NICEPHORUS of CONSTANTINOPLE † 828
The son of a brave Christian, he was appointed patriarch, while still a court official. Throughout his administration he was troubled by the iconoclasts led by the emperor, who eventually managed to depose him. He left many written works.
March 13th

NICETAS † 824
After the death of his mother, his father brought him up in a monastery. Later he became a monk of Medikion on Mount Olympus, of which he was abbot at the time of the iconoclastic persecution under Leo V. At first he submitted, but later retracted and spent six years in a dungeon. On his release he lived as a hermit until his death.
April 3rd

NICETAS of CONSTANTINOPLE
Ninth Century
A relative of the Empress Irene, during the iconoclastic persecutions of Leo V he retired to the monastery of Khrysonike in Constantinople. After the persecutions he was obliged to go to Katisia in Paphlagonia.
October 6th

NICETAS of NOVGOROD † 1107
Against the advice of his superiors he withdrew from the Caves monastery, of which he was a monk, to solitude. There he succumbed to the temptation to give up prayer for reading, and through constant study of the Old came to despise the New Testament. The monastery's prayers saved him; he turned once again to prayer, rejoined his community and eventually became bishop of Novgorod.
January 31st

NICETAS of PEREASLAV † 1186
An unpopular collector of taxes near Rostov, he entered a monastery where he lived in great austerity. He was killed when robbers mistook the iron links of a penitential shirt he wore next to his skin for silver.
May 24th

NICETAS of REMESIANA *Fifth Century*
A friend of St Paulinus of Nola, he worked among the Bessi, a race of brigands, and became bishop of Remesiana, now Bela Palenka in Serbia. He may have composed the *Te Deum*.
June 22nd

NICETAS THE GOTH † 375
A priest living on the banks of the Danube, he was burned for his faith during the persecution of Athanaric.
September 15th

NICETIUS or NIZIER of BESANÇON
Seventh Century
A friend of SS Gregory the great and Columbanus, he was a vigorous enemy of heresy. After his election as bishop, he restored to Besançon its episcopal see, which had been transferred to Nyon on Lake Geneva.
February 8th

NICETIUS or NIZIER of LYONS † 573
Of a noble Burgundian family, he lived humbly with his mother even after his ordination. His uncle St Sacerdos, on his deathbed, nominated him his successor as bishop of Lyons
April 2nd

NICETIUS of TRIER † 566
An abbot of Limoges, he was chosen bishop of Trier by King Theoderic I in preference to the popular St Gallus of Clermont. He was, nevertheless, an outspoken critic of royal infidelities and excommunicated King Clotaire.
December 5th

NICHOLAS I † 867
Brought up in the papal household, he was elected pope in 858. His rule was short but outstandingly just, and he strongly upheld the sanctity of marriage, refusing on two occasions to confirm episcopal licenses for royal divorce. Throughout his life he was engaged in negotiations with Constantinople.
November 13th

NICHOLAS of BARI *Fourth Century*
St Nicholas of Bari is one of the most popular and revered saints of the church; but the details that are known of his life are few in the extreme. His birthplace was probably Patara in Asia Minor, and he became bishop of Myra, the capital of the province. He is said to have been imprisoned during the persecutions of Diocletian, and to have been one of those who condemned Arianism at the council of Nicaea. He died at Myra and was there buried in the Cathedral. Over the centuries his fame spread widely and his shrine became a center of pilgrimage. But in the eleventh century the Saracens came into possession of Myra, and the relics of St Nicholas were speedily and secretly removed to Bari in Italy. Here his renown even increased, his tomb becoming so famous and much visited that the saint is known commonly as Nicholas of Bari. The miracle of the 'manna of St Nicholas', a sort of sweet-smelling 'myrrh' exuded by the body of the saint and with health-giving properties, is said still to take place today.

Of all the countries to which the fame of St Nicholas has extended it is Russia that honors him most. He and St Andrew the apostle are the patrons of Russia, and before the revolution Russian Orthodox pilgrims came to Bari in great numbers. In the popular imagination he became the heir of Mikoula, the god of harvest, 'who will replace God, when God becomes too old'.

He is patron also of Greece, Apulia, Sicily and Lorraine. In the east he is looked to especially as protector of sailors and in the west of children. This latter seems to have developed from the popular story of how he secretly and anonymously provided dowries for three girls whose father could not afford to arrange marriages for them, and the very much less likely tale of the children who were murdered by an inn-keeper and put in a brine-tub, only to be brought to life again by the saint. In the Netherlands, Germany and Switzerland he is the giver of presents on his feast day. Here, of course, he remains the bishop, St Nicholas; but the transformation of St Nicholas into Santa Claus and so into the Father Christmas of America and England is a curious development.

In medieval England Nicholas was as popular as in the rest of the Christian world. A great number of churches were dedicated to him, and in tiny sea ports we find the typical little chapel built on an eminence and looking out to sea. These dedications survived the Reformation, the saint's fame did not. Santa Claus is very much part of the so-called traditional English Christmas, and it might be thought that he was a memory of St Nicholas lingering down the years. In fact Santa Claus came to England from America, and that not so many years ago. Dutch Protestants had begun the process of taking the 'sting' out of the Catholic saint while retaining him as a popular children's figure, and, in New Amsterdam, they introduced this idea to America. It needed only time, the growth of commercial advertisement and the genuine romance and geniality of the conception to produce the Santa Claus of today.

December 6th   ILLUSTRATION: page 355

NICHOLAS of TOLENTINO   c. 1245–1305
Nicholas was born about 1245 to childless parents of middle age who had invoked the prayers of St Nicholas of Bari. His birthplace was in northern Italy, at Sant' Angelo in Pontano. Devout from childhood, he received a canonry in boyhood, and, when still a youth, he joined the Augustinian friars. For many years, he was sent from convent to convent preaching; but the last thirty years of his life he spent at Tolentino, from which he takes his name. His preaching, mostly in the open air, was highly successful, producing a multitude of conversions and reconciling bitter feuds. To preaching Nicholas added visits to the sick and captives. Though uncritical and credulous biography has exaggerated his miracles, he undoubtedly effected many cures and obtained divine aid for those who sought his prayer.

Nicholas's rigorous fasts damaged his health. His superiors pressed him to take more nourishment. Torn between obedience and abstinence, he was encouraged by a vision of our Lord and he recovered from his illness, by eating on our Lord's instructions a piece of bread signed with the cross and soaked in water. Henceforward he used such bread to cure the sick and in his honor it is blessed by the Augustinians to this day.

He died in ecstatic joy on September 10th, 1305. When a pious thief cut off the arms of the corpse, the body was concealed and lost. The severed arms remain and are said to bleed when a great calamity is about to befall the church. Nicholas was canonized in 1446.
September 10th

NICHOLAS PIECK and his Companions   † 1572
These men, known as the Martyrs of Gorkum, were martyred by Dutch Calvinists and were captured at the Franciscan convent of Gorkum, near Dordrecht. They were eleven Franciscans, including Nicholas Pieck, the guardian, Jerome Weerden, the vicar; three secular priests, Leonard Vechel, Nicholas Janssen, Godfrey van Duynen; John van Oosterwyk, an Augustinian canon; John van Hoornaer, a Dominican; the Premonstratensians Adrian van Hilvarenbeek and James Lacops; and Andrew Wouters, a secular priest. Together with the ninety year-old Antony van Willehad and Nicasius van Heeze, they were hanged at a deserted monastery at Ruggen near Briel.
July 9th

NICHOLAS STUDITES   † 863
He entered the Studite monastery in Constantinople, and at the end of a period of persecution and banishment by the iconoclastic emperors, became its abbot. He remained loyal to the deposed patriarch of Constantinople, St Ignatius, in his dispute with the emperor.
February 4th

NICHOLAS THE PILGRIM   † 1094
He wandered through Italy clad in a shirt, carrying a cross and chanting the Kyrie until he died at Trani. He was canonized by Pope Urban II because of the miracles which were wrought at his tomb.
June 2nd

NICHOLAS von (of) FLÜE   1417–1487
Had Nicholas not been a saint, or had he eaten and drunk like other saints, Switzerland with all it has meant for peace and humanity would probably not exist today. For Nicholas's entire life was ordained in view of his vocation to save his country.

Nicholas von Flüe was born on March 21st, 1417 in the Canton of Unterwalden on the lake of Lucerne, a citizen of a peasant democracy and a farmer's son. As he grew up he proved himself a capable farmer, and the ability he displayed in the local parliament, of which every male citizen was a member, led to his election at an early age as councillor and judge. He also proved himself a capable commander of troops. In the war against the duke of Tirol he persuaded his compatriots to respect a convent of nuns. Though willing to perform his military service, Nicholas condemned as immoral, wars of aggression and the slaughter of non-combatants inevitable in any major modern war. About the age of thirty he married a farmer's daughter, Dorothy Wiss, and built a farmhouse to receive her. The couple had ten children and descendants survive to this day.

Nicholas had thus approved himself to his countrymen as a thoroughly capable man, as farmer, military leader, member of the assembly, councillor, judge and father of a family – also a man of complete moral integrity. All the while, however, he led a life of contemplative prayer and rigorous fasting. He was the subject of symbolic visions and a diabolic assault.

After some twenty years of married life, in 1467 Nicholas received a compelling call to abandon his home and the world and become a hermit. Though she had just borne his tenth child his wife heroically consented. His neighbors, however, even his older children, regarded his action as indefensible, unbalanced, immoral and irresponsible. He set out for Alsace, where he intended to live. Had he carried out his intention his vocation would have been missed. A storm, however, symbolically interpreted, and friendly advice not to settle where the Swiss were detested made him turn back from the border. At the same time he became incapable of eating or drinking – a condition which continued for the rest of his life. As an act of obedience to a bishop he once ate with acute agony a piece of soaked bread. (The problem of prolonged fasting is more fully discussed in the account of St Lidwina of Schiedam.)

He returned to his native canton, passing the first night undiscovered in the cow-shed of his farm and settled in a hermitage at Ranft within a few miles of his home. It was no temptation to return home, as he never felt the least desire for his former life. Symbolic visions continued to be a feature of his contemplation, and when, after a month's strict surveillance, his countrymen were convinced that his fast was genuine, they recognised his sanctity and vocation, and he became a spiritual guide whose advice was widely sought and followed. Pilgrims came from distant parts to consult him. He acquired influence with Duke Sigismund of the Tirol, whom he confirmed in his neutrality when the Swiss confederacy met and defeated Charles of Burgundy. Everything was ready for the climax of Nicholas's life: the accomplishment of his unique vocation.

The victorious cantons were at loggerheads. The rural cantons opposed inflexibly the demand of Zurich and Lucerne that Freiburg and Soleure be admitted to the confederacy. A conference held at Stans, December 1481, failed to reach agreement. Next day the delegates would disperse and a civil war ensue which would presumably have destroyed the confederacy. The parish priest, once Nicholas's confessor, hurried to Ranft and laid the matter before the hermit. During the night Nicholas dictated suggested terms of agreement. The priest returned in time to persuade the delegates to give a hearing to the proposals of a man so widely respected for his well tried practical abilities and so widely venerated for his holiness. The terms suggested – the conditional admittance of Freiburg and Soleure – were unanimously accepted and embodied in the agreement of Stans. Switzerland had been saved.

Nicholas survived his achievement almost six years, universally revered, visited and consulted. On March 21st 1487, his seventieth birthday, he died, apparently of his first illness. One is glad to know that his wife and children attended his deathbed. After all, she had never lost her husband completely. Honored by Swiss Protestants, venerated by Swiss Catholics, Nicholas's cult, uninterrupted since his death, was officially sanctioned by Clement IX (1667-9). In 1947 he was canonized by Pope Pius XII.   ILLUSTRATION: page 356

March 22nd

NICODEMUS   *First Century*

In the year 415, we are told that a priest living in Jerusalem called Lucien was led by a dream to find the relics of St Stephen, the first martyr, together with those of SS Nicodemus, Gamaliel and Abibon.

Nicodemus is mentioned by St John (chapter 3) as coming to visit Jesus in the night – a rich man and a senator or member of the Sanedrin, but courteous, prudent, open-minded yet timid – too frightened to accept our Lord's invitation to be 'born-again', but not too frightened to remain silent when Jesus was accused. Then he spoke in his defence (John 7:50), while after the Crucifixion he assisted Joseph of Arimathea in embalming the body. The rest is legend, and there is no foundation for believing that Nicodemus was baptised by the apostles John and Peter or that he was hounded out of Jerusalem by the Jews.

August 3rd   ILLUSTRATION: page 357

NICOMEDES

This Roman martyr was buried in a catacomb on the Via Nomentana which was discovered in 1864.

September 15th

NIKON 'METANOEITE'   † 998

From Pontus, he retired to the monastery of Khrysospetro, whence he went as a missionary to Crete. His surname 'Metanoeite' means 'repent', the word with which he invariably began his sermons.

November 26th

NILUS of ROSSANO
c. 910–1004

He became a monk on the death of his wife and daughter, and after living in several different monasteries became abbot of St Adrian's, near San Demetrio Corone. In 981 he and his monks were forced to flee from the Saracens, and for a time were housed at Monte Cassino. He died just before the building of the permanent home of the community, at Grottaferrata.
September 26th

NILUS THE ELDER
Fifth Century

The traditional story is of a court official who retired to Mount Sinai and wrote two letters to the Emperor Arcadius at Constantinople attacking his treatment of St John Chrysostom. But it is possible that this official has been mistakenly identified with a monk of Ancyra in Galatia.
November 12th

NINIAN
Fourth Century

St Ninian was the first of the great Scottish missionaries, and as such has always been held in particular honor and esteem in his own country. In pre-Reformation days his shrine was an important place of pilgrimage and was visited by many Scottish kings. Today, again, pilgrimages are made every year to the cave which was his hermitage on the Galloway coast, in the south-western corner of Scotland.

Ninian was born about the year 360, the son of a chieftain of Galloway who had been converted to Christianity. As a young man he journeyed to Rome, where he was kindly received and assisted in his education by the pope of the time, St Damasus. After fifteen years, Pope St Siricius made him a priest and a bishop and sent him back to preach the faith in his own country. It was probably while he was making his journey home that Ninian visited St Martin of Tours, where he must have stayed for a while, making himself acquainted with the way of life of the monks living in their separate cells on the banks of the Loire. Then Ninian continued his journey homeward to Galloway. He arrived at Whithorn on the Galloway coast, where he built his *Candida Casa*, the White House, the first stone-built church ever to be seen in Britain. We know the year of its building because before it was finished the news reached him of the death of his friend and mentor, St Martin of Tours, to whom he then dedicated his own church. This was in the year 397. Only in 1949, excavations carried out among the ruins of the later Premonstratensian church (dating from 1150) revealed the very foundations of *Candida Casa*, still with traces of white lime on its walls.

Although Ninian established a community of monks at Whithorn, he spent much of his time travelling far into Scotland, preaching Christianity to the Picts. He substantially converted the Southern Picts, those who lived to the south of the River Forth. But he did not limit his labors to such comparatively accessible country. He founded churches far up the east coast, and even sailed to the Orkneys and perhaps to the Shetlands as well. When we consider the state of the country at the time, and how little men knew of the petty kingdoms beyond their own, we must marvel at the journeyings of Ninian, marked out to this day by place-names throughout so many parts of Scotland. Ninian blazed a trail that others were to follow. These were the missionaries not only of the Pictish church that he founded but of the Celtic church with whom after a period of reversion to paganism, St Columba triumphantly revived Christianity in Scotland. St Ninian was over seventy when he died.
September 16th

NINO
Fourth Century

Taken as a captive into Georgia, she converted the king by her example and miraculous cures.
December 15th

NIZIER, *see* Nicetius of Besançon.

NIZIER, *see* Nicetius of Lyons.

NOEL CHABANEL, *see* Martyrs of North America.

NON or NONNITA
Sixth Century

The legend runs that she was a Welsh nun, violated by a local chieftain called Sant, and that as a result she became the mother of St David. She was formerly honored in Wales and in Brittany, where she seems to have spent her last years.
March 3rd

NONNA
† 374

A Cappadocian, she was the wife of St Gregory Nazianzen the Elder – whom she had converted – and her three children were St Gregory Nazianzen, St Gorgonia and St Caesarius.
August 5th

NONNITA, *see* Non.

NORBERT
c. 1080–1134

Norbert was born at Xanten in about 1080 and was brought up at the imperial court where, despite the fact that he had embraced an ecclesiastical career and had been ordained subdeacon, he lived a life of great worldliness. Thrown from his horse during a thunderstorm he underwent a spiritual experience which has been compared to St Paul's on the road to Damascus. He was ordained priest and devoted his life to popular preaching, living poorly and humbly on a pittance and giving the balance of his considerable revenues to the needy. At Prémontré (a solitary spot near Soissons) to which he had retired, he brought into being his order of Canons Regular (Premonstratensians or Norbertines – also sometimes called White Canons from the color of their habit) whose function was to live in community and combine the monastic life with the canonical, that is, the service of the church and the administration of the sacraments.

In 1126 Norbert was made archbishop of Magdeburg; henceforward his influence on the affairs of the church at large was considerably increased. He was a friend of St Bernard's and helped him in his struggle against the anti-pope Anacletus; he successfully opposed Tanchelin's heresy concerning the eucharistic presence, and he effected a great renewal of religion in his own diocese. He died, worn out by his labors, in 1134.

June 6th   ILLUSTRATION: page 358

NOTBURGA   *c. 1265–c. 1313*
She was dismissed from her job as kitchen-maid in the household of Count Henry of Rattenberg, because she persisted in giving the food left over from each meal to the poor. She was later reinstated as housekeeper, and is recognized as the patroness of peasants and servants.
September 14th

NOTHELM   *Eighth Century*
He assisted the Venerable Bede in the composition of his *Ecclesiastical History* and succeeded St Tatwin as archbishop of Canterbury in 734.
October 17th

NUNILO and ALODIA   † 851
These sisters, who lived at Huesca, had too great a reputation for Christian piety to escape the notice of the persecuting Abdur Rahman II, and they were beheaded.
October 22nd

NYMPHA, *see* Trypho, Respicius and Nympha.

NYMPHODORA, *see* Menodora, Metrodora and Nymphodora.

ODHRAN, *see* Otteran.

ODILIA or OTTILIA   *Eighth Century*
It is impossible to distinguish fact from legend in the life of this saint. Born blind, she was rejected by her father and brought up in the convent of Baume-les-Dames near Besançon. She received her sight after her baptism by St Erhard. Her parents then accepted her, and she founded a convent at Niedermünster.
December 13th

ODILO, *see* Cluny Saints.   † 1049
January 1st

ODO of CANTERBURY   † 959
Born in East Anglia, he became bishop of Ramsbury and afterwards archbishop of Canterbury, in which position he encouraged St Dunstan to persevere in his monastic reforms.
July 4th

ODO of CLUNY   † 942
See the Cluny Saints.
November 18th

ODULF   *Ninth Century*
Born at Oorschot in Brabant where he was a priest, he went with St Frederick to evangelize Friesland. He built his main church and monastery at Stavoren.
June 12th

OENGUS or AENGUS   *Ninth Century*
An Ulsterman of royal birth, he was celebrated for his learning and known as the 'culdee' or God's vassal because of his austere life. At first a monk of Clonenagh at Leix, he retired to a hermitage at Dysartenos. Later on he entered the community at Tallaght, near Dublin, concealing his name and asking to do the most menial tasks. Eventually he was discovered by the abbot, St Maelruain, who insisted on freeing him for other work. After St Maelruain's death, Oengus returned to Clonenagh where he became abbot.
March 11th

OIDILWALD THE HERMIT, *see* Ethelwald.

OLAF   *c. 995–1030*
Olaf was born in or near 995, a very minor member of the East Norwegian royal family. He followed the traditional career of the Viking, a delinquent apprenticeship in looting and murder. As a mature warrior of fourteen he joined the most famous Viking of his age, Thurkell the Tall, in an expedition against the English in the unhappy reign of Ethelred the Unready. In 1012 the Vikings seized St Alphege, then archbishop of Canterbury, and brutally murdered him. Thurkell went over to the English service in disgust, but Olaf, who was still pagan, remained with the main Viking force. At the age of eighteen he was baptized at Rouen, and he probably joined the exiled King Ethelred, for his return to England from exile in Normandy in 1014. Olaf seems to have remained faithful to his new English lord and he may have fought for him against the new Viking leader, Canute (Knut); at any rate he never seems to have entered Canute's service, although in 1016 Canute became king of the English as well as of the Danes, and a powerful patron. Instead, Olaf returned to his native Norway, now largely under the sway of Denmark. But the principal Danish warriors were with Canute in England, and Olaf, not yet twenty-one, rapidly made himself king of Norway.

He fought his battles under the sign of the cross, and his vigor in stamping out pagan practices among the nominally Christian Norwegians lost him powerful support. Canute of England and Denmark, although he represented himself as the pattern of Christian kingship, did not scruple to make use of the dissident pagan Norwegian princelings, whom he bribed with money and promises against their Christian ruler. Olaf rapidly lost support – his own rashness was partly to blame – and was forced into exile in Russia. In 1030 he returned, and met his death in a battle which took place during a total eclipse of the sun on August 31st. Although his opponents were for the most part Norwegians and Christians, Olaf was regarded after his death as the champion of Norwegian independence and strict Christianity. His cult was immediate and enduring. Even the Danish rulers of Norway were forced to allow the translation of his incorrupt remains to his new Cathedral of Nidaross (Trondhjem), and churches dedicated to St Olaf sprang up all over Western Europe, but especially in districts opposed to the Danes.

Olaf, dead, achieved what he had failed to achieve while alive. Opposed by his name and reputation, Danish power began to collapse all over the north. In 1035, Olaf's son regained Norway, and Canute, now on his deathbed, barely survived his empire. St Olaf is not easy to understand. He was a warrior, often brutal and a man of loose life; but his reputation for sanctity was immediate on his death, and his cult cannot be entirely explained on political grounds. He was undoubtedly a great man, and it seems that in some ways he must have been a good one. Certainly his Christianity was less political than Canute's, and he might well have saved his throne and his life had he been prepared to compromise only a little with paganism.
July 29th

OLDEGAR, *see* Ollegarius.

OLGA   † 969
Widow of Igor, grand-duke of Kiev, she was one of the first Russians to be baptized, but her efforts to spread Christianity in Russia were not very successful.
July 11th

OLLEGARIUS or **OLDEGAR**   † 1137
Dedicated to God by his noble parents while Saracens were ravaging Catalonia, he became bishop of Barcelona, then archbishop of Tarragona. He was charitable to the poor, a zealous disciplinarian, and the organizer of a successful crusade against the Moors.
March 6th

OLYMPIAS   *c. 361–c. 408*
Born in Constantinople of a distinguished family, she was an orphan who married a prefect of that city.

She was soon widowed and, refusing to marry again, founded a community of widows and virgins which soon came under the patronage of the bishop, St John Chrysostom. Soon Olympias and her community were responsible for a hospital and an orphanage, but when Chrysostom was exiled in 404, their work was disbanded and they were persecuted. Olympias died at Nicomedia worn out by her sufferings.
December 17th

OMER, *see* Audomarus.

ONESIMUS   *First Century*
A slave of Colossae in Phrygia, often confused with Onesimus of Ephesus, he robbed his Christian master Philemon. In his flight he met St Paul who converted him, entrusted him with a letter to his master (the Epistle to Philemon), and subsequently made him a bishop.
February 16th

ONUPHRIUS   *Fifth Century?*
This hermit is supposed to have lived alone in the desert for seventy years until he was found by an abbot, Paphnutius. They prayed together all night, and Onuphrius died on the following day. The Christian name, Humphrey, is derived from his name.
June 12th

OPPORTUNA   *Eighth Century*
She received the veil from her brother, bishop of Séez, at a Benedictine convent near Almenèches, of which she became abbess.
April 22nd

OPTATUS and his Companions and ENCRATIS
                                                          † 304
Optatus and seventeen others were victims of the persecution of Diocletian at Saragossa. Encratis is described as a living martyr, since she seems to have survived her tortures horribly maimed.
April 16th

OPTATUS of MILEVIS   *Fourth Century*
As bishop of Milevis in Numidia, he was foremost in combating the schism of the Donatists by publishing in 370 a treatise on the universality of the church.
June 4th

ORSIESIUS   *Fourth Century*
A disciple of St Pachomius, he was quite a young man when he was made abbot of the monastery of Khenoboski in the Egyptian desert. His strictness caused such opposition that he had to be replaced for a time by St Theodore.
June 15th

OSBURGA   † 1016
Little is known of her life. She may have been the first abbess of a nunnery founded by King Canute in

Coventry, and she was formerly much honored there.
March 30th

OSMUND   † 1099
Osmund came over to England with the Normans and in 1078 was appointed bishop of Salisbury. Perhaps his most important work was his reorganization of the liturgical books of Salisbury, a work which produced the 'Sarum use' employed in England until the reign of Mary.
December 4th

OSWALD of NORTHUMBRIA   † 642
He became king of Northumbria after St Edwin, his uncle, was killed in battle in 633. A year later Oswald regained his kingdom by defeating Cadwallan, the Welsh King, at a battle near Hexham. How Oswald then enlisted the help of St Aidan in converting his countrymen to Christianity is told in the life of St Aidan.

Oswald married Cyneburga, who was the daughter of Cynegils, the first king of Wessex to become a Christian. Oswald's power became so great that the other kings recognized him as their overlord, and he did much to spread the Christian faith not merely by means of his influence as king but also by his devout life.

In 642 he went off with a small force to oppose the pagan king of Mercia, Penda, but was defeated and killed in a battle near Oswestry.

Devotion to St Oswald was widespread during the middle ages, extending from Ireland to Bohemia and Italy; and Bede says that his relics were thought to assist the cure of the sick.
August 9th

OSWALD of WORCESTER   † 992
Oswald was the son of a pagan Viking settled in the English Danelaw, but he was brought up a Christian. His uncle, Odo, became archbishop of Canterbury in 942. Odo was deeply influenced by the new reformed monasticism which was then spreading all over France from the abbey of Cluny (*see* the Cluny Saints), and, under his guidance, Oswald became a monk and tried to reform a small community of clerks at Winchester. The clerks proved incorrigible, so Oswald left Winchester for the newly reformed abbey of Fleury, where the body of St Benedict himself was then alleged to be buried. Here Oswald learnt at first hand what life in a fully monastic community meant and he remained with the community until 959, when he was summoned to the deathbed of Archbishop Odo. Oswald arrived too late to see his uncle, but he was recommended to St Dunstan, who, in 960, left the see of Worcester for Canterbury and persuaded the new king, Edgar, to appoint Oswald to succeed him at Worcester. In 963 another disciple of Dunstan, Ethelwold, was made bishop of Winchester, and the time was felt to be ripe for a determined attempt to revive true Benedictine monasticism on a great scale.

Oswald had already founded a tiny monastery at Westbury on Trim, but it was necessary to gain royal permission and royal help to withdraw ancient monastic endowments from the possession of secular clerks, many of them married and related to local great persons, before true monks could be established. At a great synod held at Easter 964, King Edgar authorized the expulsion of the secular clerks and their replacement by monks. At Christmas of the same year Oswald expelled all the married clerks from the cathedral of Worcester and began to convert the community into a full Benedictine monastery. So long as the Worcester clerks would live a communal, celibate life, Oswald was prepared to impose the full regimen of the monastic rule gradually. Certainly at his death in 992 he left a flourishing cathedral monastery at Worcester.

Oswald remained bishop of Worcester until his death, but from 973 he was also archbishop of York. He fulfilled his episcopal duties well, and he was one of the most businesslike of medieval bishops; but he was equally the zealous monk, and he founded or revived seven monasteries in the midlands, of which the most famous was Ramsey. He also rebuilt the cathedral of Worcester on a much bigger scale and rededicated it to St Mary. Associated with St Dunstan and St Ethelwold for most of his public life – when he died popular veneration joined his name with theirs – he has been revered ever since as one of the three saints who revived English monasticism.   ILLUSTRATION: page 359
February 28th

OSWIN   † 651
He was brought up in Wessex after his father, King Osric of Deira, had been killed in battle. He returned to his throne in 642 and ruled wisely and well, being the patron of St Aidan. He was murdered at the instigation of his cousin, Oswy of Bernicia.
August 20th

OSYTH   *Seventh Century*
According to legend she was the daughter of a Mercian chieftain, who was married against her will to Sighere, king of the East Saxons. She soon left him and founded a convent on the East Coast, where she was subsequently murdered by pirates.
October 7th

OTGER, *see* Wiro, Plechelm and Oteger.

OTTERAN or ODHRAN   † 563
He accompanied St Columba to Iona, having been an abbot in Meath, and died soon after his arrival.
October 27th

OTTILIA, *see* Odilia.

OTTO of BAMBERG † 1139
Chancellor to the Emperor Henry IV, he was the imperial nominee to the bishopric of Bamberg, but delayed his consecration until he had received it from Paschal II. His attempts to mediate between the papacy and the emperor culminated in the concordat of Worms. Besides launching a successful missionary campaign in Pomerania he founded twenty monasteries.
July 2nd

OUEN, *see* Audoenus.

OUTRIL, *see* Austregisilus.

OYEND, *see* Eugendus.

PACHOMIUS † 348
Converted to Christianity while serving as a conscript in the imperial army, he lived in the desert with a hermit named Palaemon. He built a monastery on the banks of the Nile known as Tabennisi, followed by six other monasteries for which he drew up a written Rule, the first of its kind.
May 9th

PACIAN Fourth Century
A prolific writer, greatly respected by St Jerome. Little is known of this bishop of Barcelona, though his reply to a Novatian heretic is famous: 'My name is Christian, my surname Catholic. The one puts me in a class, the other gives me a character. The second is a testimonial, the first is a label.'
March 9th

PACIFICO of SAN SEVERINO 1653-1721
An orphan at the age of five, he was brought up by an uncle who treated him as a domestic servant. He became a Friar of the Observant branch of the Franciscans, and was noted for his patience, austerity and gift of prophecy.
September 24th

PADARN or PATERN Fifth-Sixth Century
He founded a monastery in Cardiganshire at a place which was later called Llanbadarn Fawr (the great church of Paternus) where he was both abbot and bishop.
April 15th

PAIR, *see* Paternus.

PALLADIUS † 432
Sent by Pope Celestine as a missionary bishop to Ireland, he founded churches at Cilleen Cormac near Dunlavin, Tigroney on the Avoca, and Donard in Wicklow. He was not very succesful, however; but the claim that he went to Scotland and died at Fordun, near Aberdeen, is probably of patriotic origin.

Those writers who hold that Ireland was converted by two SS Patrick identify Palladius with St Patrick the Elder as distinguished from the celebrated St Patrick the Younger, author of the *Confession*.
July 7th

PAMBO † c. 390
One of the early generation of monks who spent their lives in the Egyptian Thebaid, he was a disciple of St Antony the Abbot and was visited by St Melania the Elder. He spent six months in meditation upon the text: 'I will take heed to my ways, that I sin not with my tongue: I will keep my mouth with a bridle.' But when he did speak, it was with effect: 'There are other ways of becoming perfect besides being a monk . . . Purpose never to offend your neighbor, and you will be saved.'
July 18th

PAMMACHIUS † 410
A Roman senator, he married Paulina, a daughter of St Paula, and was a devoted friend of St Jerome. With St Fabiola, he founded a hospice for pilgrims at Porto.
August 30th

PAMPHILUS and his Companions † 309
A native of Berytus (Beirut) in Phoenicia he studied at Alexandria, and settled at Caesarea, where he was renowned as a scholar. In company with Paul of Jamnia, Valens and Seleucus, he was beheaded; other Christians who expressed sympathy with them were also executed.
June 1st

PAMPHILUS of SULMONA Seventh Century
Bishop of Sulmona and Corfinium, he aroused the hostility of his clergy by his habit of rising just after midnight and insisting upon singing his mass shortly afterwards.
April 28th

PANCRAS † 304?
He was supposed to be an orphan who came to Rome, was converted and suffered martyrdom at the age of thirteen. ILLUSTRATION: page 360
May 12th

PANCRAS of TAORMINA First Century
He was supposedly a native of Antioch who was sent to evangelize Sicily and became the first bishop of Taormina. He is reckoned a martyr, since he was stoned to death by bandits.
April 3rd

PANTAENUS Second Century
Probably a Sicilian, he was a celebrated teacher of philosophy and doctrine at Alexandria.
July 7th

PANTALEON † c. 305
Pantaleon is said to have been martyred in Nicomedia

under Diocletian about the year 305 and the legends about him bear out his name, which is derived from the Greek, meaning 'all-merciful'. He was born in Nicomedia and brought up in the Christian faith by his mother. As a young man he studied medicine with success, and was appointed physician to the Emperor Galerus Maximinian in Nicomedia. But the temptations of the pagan court were too much for him, and he fell away from the faith. Some time later he was reconverted by a friend and, thereafter, devoted his whole life to caring for the sick and poor in his capacity as a doctor. Denounced as a Christian by his brother physicians he was put to torture and finally beheaded.

It is said that milk, instead of blood, flowed from his veins, nevertheless alleged relics of his blood are preserved at Constantinople, Madrid, and Ravello in south Italy; and on his feast day, the blood liquefies, as the present writer can testify, having witnessed the strange phenomenon at Ravello. Here the relic is kept in a glass phial encased in a silver reliquary between two bronze grills, which are embedded in the wall and immovable, above a side altar in the main church of the village. For the greater part of the year it is a black mass at the bottom of the phial, covered with a white fatty substance that looks as if it well might have been milk. On the vigil of the feast day, this black mass suddenly begins to increase in volume and to become a translucent red, the colour of freshly shed blood. On the feast day itself the liquefaction is complete, and the relic remains in this state for some weeks, only gradually returning to its former condition. It is said that the same happens to the other relic kept at Madrid.

During the last century, before the relic was enclosed between grills, a canon was showing it to a visitor, when it suddenly began to liquefy. In order that his friend might observe the phenomen more clearly the canon held the candle close up to the phial so that the glass cracked with the heat, and the blood began to escape. Horrified at what he had done, the good man threw himself on his knees and implored the saint to stop the liquefaction, promising him a silver statue if he did so. The liquefaction promptly ceased, and now a small silver statue of the saint adorns the reliquary. But the crack remains for all to see, and so does the dried blood that escaped through it down the glass of the phial. On the feast day this dried blood liquefies but does not run. See also the account of the liquefaction of the blood of St Januarius for a description of this phenomenon from a scientific point of view.

July 27th

PAPHNUTIUS THE GREAT † c. 350?
One of the monks of the desert, he became bishop in the Upper Thebaid. He suffered greatly under the Emperor Maximinus but survived to oppose the Arians and to defend St Athanasius of Alexandria. Although himself a celibate, he opposed clerical celibacy, and it is owing to his influence that in the Eastern church a married man may still continue to live with his wife after ordination.

September 11th

PAPYLUS, *see* Agathonica, Papylus and Carpus.

PAREGORIUS, *see* Leo and Paregorius.

PARISIO † 1267
Born in Treviso, he entered the Camaldolese order at the age of twelve. He became spiritual director to the nuns of St Christina, and lived to be one hundred and seven.

June 11th

PARTHENIUS, *see* Calocerus and Parthenius.

PASCHAL I † 824
This pope did much for religious buildings during his rule, and endeavored to help orthodox Catholics against the iconoclasts. He was accused, despite his protestations to the contrary, of having been responsible for the murder of two papal officials, and when he died, the Romans refused him burial in St Peter's.

February 11th

PASCHAL BAYLON 1540–1592
Paschal was born at Torre-Hermosa in Aragon in 1540 on Whitsunday, called by his compatriots Pascua, whence his name Paschal. From childhood he displayed an extraordinary devotion to the blessed Sacrament. At the age of nine his parents found him before the tabernacle absorbed in prayer, and when he later became a shepherd lad, he spent his solitary hours with his flock in fervent prayer, approaching as often as he could a shrine of our Lady.

About the age of twenty he sought admittance to a Franciscan friary of the reformed observance lately instituted by St Peter of Alcantara. Refused at first, he found employment in the neighborhood, and his behavior gave such edification that he was not only admitted to the community but offered the position of a choir brother. Humility made him choose to be a lay brother, and such he remained till death. His mortifications exceeded even those of his fellows in the first fervor of the reform. But he preferred obedience. Hard on himself, he was gentle and affable to others and always cheerful. On one occasion a friar surprised him in the refectory dancing before our Lady's image. What time he could spare from his duties he spent in prayer before the blessed Sacrament, and he could never serve too many masses.

Sent to France with a messsage to the minister general

he was several times stoned or set upon by the Huguenots, against whom he defended intrepidly his Catholic faith. A wound in his shoulder caused him pain for the rest of his life. He died at the friary of Villa-Real near Valencia, on May 17th, 1592, on Whitsunday, the festival of his birth, and drew his last breath as the bell announced the Elevation. For two centuries, it is said, knocks were heard from time to time proceeding from his tomb, portents of things to come.

His biography was written by a former superior, Father Ximenes, and he was canonized in 1640. In 1897, Leo XIII proclaimed him the patron of Eucharistic Congresses and fraternities of the Blessed Sacrament.
May 17th

PASCHASIUS RADBERTUS   *Ninth Century*
Abandoned as a child, he was brought up by the monks of St Peter in Soissons. He joined the abbey of Corbie, and later became abbot. He resigned after seven years. A voluminous writer of some distinction he made the schools of Corbie famous, and his views are still quoted in theological works. His most celebrated book is the *De Corpore et Sanguine Christi*.
April 26th

PASTOR, see Justus and Pastor.

PATERN, *see* Padarn.

PATERNUS of ABDINGHOF   † 1058
A Scot or Irishman, he journeyed to Germany and lived as a solitary in the abbey of Abdinghof in Westphalia. He perished in a fire which he himself predicted, through refusing to break his vow of seclusion and to leave his cell.
April 10th

PATERNUS or PAIR   † 564
Often confused with St Padarn, he retired from the monastery of Ansion in Poitou to lead a solitary life near Coutances. He became abbot of the community which grew up around him, and at the age of seventy he was chosen bishop of Avranches.
April 16th

PATIENS of LYONS   *Fifth Century*
A bishop of Lyons, he dealt successfully with the problems raised by the Gothic invasion of Burgundy.
September 11th

PATRICIA
Accounts of her life, which are probably fictitious, say that she was a member of the imperial family, who went from Constantinople to Rome to make a vow of virginity. Although she returned to Constantinople, she died in Naples.
August 25th

PATRICK of IRELAND   † 492
It is fortunate that we possess in *The Confession of Saint Patrick* a document of unquestioned authenticity. It gives a living portrait of the writer compared with which the present controversies over the accepted chronology of his life pale in significance, although one eminent scholar has gone so far as to say: 'Only two events in Patrick's life can be dated, and these only approximately, namely his coming to Ireland *c.* 461, and his death *c.* 492.' (*The Two Patricks* by Thomas F. O'Rahilly; *see also* the account of St Palladius.)

In the *Confession* St Patrick himself tells us briefly the facts of his life. His father's name was Calpurnius. He was a Roman decurion, that is, a collector of the imperial taxes and member of the council ruling a Roman settlement. He lived with his family on a farm near the village of Banavem Taberniae, a place which scholars have agreed to situate near the mouth of the Severn in Wales. This district was raided by pirates when Patrick was sixteen; he was captured with hundreds of others, carried off to Ireland and there sold as a slave. The boy's head was closely shaved to mark his new status, and his clothes exchanged for the sheepskin tunic and sandals always worn by slaves. Henceforth his main occupation was herding droves of swine on the slopes of a mountain traditionally identified as Slemish in Antrim.

It was a searing experience for the boy reared in comfort and with an innate sense of superiority. But he held on tenaciously to the Christian training he had received. In his solitude on the mountain he learned to pray. Hitherto an average, careless boy, he soon acquired a precocious gravity.

Six years passed during which his character was reformed by prayer and asceticism. He began to plan his escape. Twice he was instructed by a clear inner voice: once to console him that he was soon to return to his fatherland, and a second time to tell him that his ship was ready. Carefully choosing the moment, he set off on foot for the south-east coast. When he had covered two hundred miles, he came upon a ship about to sail and succeeded in boarding it. After many adventures with the heathen crew, he got back to his parents in Britain. Some time later, he left them again in order to study for the priesthood in Gaul. He rose to the rank of bishop and was entrusted with the mission to Ireland, in succession to St Palladius, who had preceded him there and had just died.

Ireland had always been in his thoughts, because of a dream he had in which he saw an angel named Victor arriving with many letters, out of which he selected one for Patrick. It was inscribed with the words *The Voice of the Irish* and, as he was unfolding it, he heard Irish voices crying to him to come back to them. It was an experience that shook him profoundly because he knew the very voices.

The *Confession* goes on to tell about the tensions of his

life. At first his superiors were unwilling to give him charge of the mission to Ireland. They doubted his competence. Some of his colleagues even imputed unworthy motives to Patrick's persistence, saying that he was really out for promotion for himself and not the evangelization of Ireland. He experienced, too, a terrible disillusionment in friendship. It seems that before his ordination he had been troubled in conscience and had confided to a student friend some sin he thought he might have committed before he was fifteen, that is, before his capture in the pirate raid which was the turning-point of his life. At the time the friend had succeeded in reassuring him. Later the same friend ardently supported Patrick's nomination as bishop. But at the second ecclesiastical conference to discuss Patrick's promotion, the same friend suddenly turned against him, discovered reasons against his appointment and even publicly betrayed that ancient confidence of student days, urging it as an argument against him. The result was that Patrick underwent a severe spiritual crisis. He was nearly overwhelmed by a temptation to despair. Discussing it many years after the event, even the memory of it was still painful: 'I am grieved for my dearest friend . . . a man to whom I had even entrusted my soul! How could he bring himself to put me to shame publicly before everyone . . .'

St Patrick calls this writing *My Confession before I die,* so that one assumes he wrote it towards the end of his life when he believed he had not much longer to live. He had before his eyes the success of his work. The whole island was almost entirely linked up, even to its remotest parts, with churches and monastic foundations, to which flowed a strong tide of conversions. A vigorous native clergy was in possession; a native bishop had been nominated to succeed him.

In view of such results, the humility of the *Confession* is almost disconcerting, especially the classical opening: 'I, Patrick, the sinner, am the most illiterate and the least of all the faithful, and contemptible in the eyes of very many.'

Elsewhere he says: 'I was like a stone lying in the deep mire; and he that is mighty came, and in his mercy lifted me up, and verily raised me aloft and placed me on the top of the wall.'

Later again, he calls himself 'a fool, the abhorred of this world', and he returns frequently to the subject of his academic ignorance: 'I blush and am exceedingly afraid to lay bare my lack of education; because I am unable to make my meaning plain in a few words to the learned.'

While it is true that the conversion of Ireland is a golden page in Christian history, the ease of the transition from paganism to the faith has been somewhat exaggerated. If there was no organised persecution of the Church, there was much local hostility. The *Confession* incidentally reveals a man of great physical courage: 'On occasion I used to give presents to the kings, besides the hire that I gave to their sons who accompanied me; and nevertheless they seized me with my companions. And on that day they most eagerly desired to kill me; but my time had not yet come. And everything they found with us they plundered, and me myself they bound with irons. And on the fourteenth day the Lord delivered me . . . Daily I expect either slaughter, or an unfair attack . . .'

While the legendary stories may not be trustworthy in points of fact, they are wholly consistent in confirming the self-portrait of the *Confession*: a man of St Paul-like qualities, who never again deviated from the asceticism learned in his first years of slavery, 'undeterred by hunger or cold', a mighty toiler, completely selfless, accessible to the meanest of his converts.

He who had escaped from slavery to the Irish surrendered himself again to be their slave in a new sense. He admits that he used to long to revisit his kinsfolk in Britain and, even more keenly, his old friends in Gaul; but his solicitude for the Irish would not allow him to leave them even for a short time: 'I fear to lose the labor which I began . . . Let it not happen to me from my God that I should ever part with his people which he purchased in the ends of the earth . . .'

The Irish people have responded with a depth of human affection undiminished by the passage of centuries. On March 17th they celebrate his feast all over the world with a fervor which makes his cult perhaps the most living one of all fifth century saints.
March 17th

PATROCLUS   *Third Century?*
Buried at Troyes and greatly honored after the discovery there of his Acts, he was evidently a man of outstanding charity and holiness. He was martyred during the persecution of the Emperor Aurelian.
January 21st

PAUL, *see* Thea, Valentina and Paul.

PAUL
Paul of Tarsus is not everybody's saint. Many good Christians (especially, perhaps, among women) feel antagonistic towards him, finding him harsh, difficult, uncompromising. It is therefore somewhat consoling to find that his contemporaries felt the same way about him – not merely his former associates among the Jews (who tried to murder him) but also the saints of the church. St Peter, St Mark, St Barnabas, they all had rows with St Paul at one time or another, and even the gentle St James suggested to him that he ought to be more tactful. Yet they all, in the end, came to regard

him with reverence and affection; and this is the common experience of those who, starting with feelings of antagonism towards St Paul, take the trouble to get to know him, in his epistles and in the Acts of the Apostles. He was so indomitable, so loyal, so full of deep affection for his friends. Sooner or later he disarms all criticism and the rugged shell dissolves to reveal both the humanity and the holiness beneath.

He was born at Tarsus, a rich university city in southern Asia Minor, and his parents were evidently of good standing, being Roman citizens. He was brought up as a strict Pharisee and instructed in Jewish theology by the famous Rabbi Gamaliel. Everyone, no doubt, expected great things of this brilliant young man when he went up to Jerusalem a year or so after the crucifixion, and their expectations were, though in an unexpected way, fulfilled. As all the world knows, Saul of Tarsus was present at the martyrdom of St Stephen and heard him pray for his murderers. That prayer was answered. Not very long after, on his way to Damascus, Saul had that blinding vision of the risen Christ which turned him from a persecutor into a leader of the Christians.

Yet there was a delay before the train then fired exploded its mine. Immediately after his baptism St Paul retired for two years of meditation in the desert, after which he returned to Damascus. It was not until three years had passed that he went up to Jerusalem to confer with the Apostles, and after that he retired once more to Tarsus. There is thus a period of about ten years (34–44 A.D.) during which St Paul is almost lost to our sigh,oand it must have been then that his powerful intelctlet with God's help, wrought that bridge between Judaism and Christianity, Hebrew and Gentile, which is his greatest gift to the world.

Not that he was the first, of course, to baptize a gentile. Peter had christened Cornelius, Philip had evangelized Samaria and baptized the Ethiopian eunuch; but systematic preaching to non-Jews only began at Antioch in the early 40's of the century, and St Barnabas, commissioned by the Apostles to investigate the situation, whole-heartedly approved of it. But he did more. He bethought him of St Paul, living forgotten at Tarsus, and he went there to seek him out. Paul returned with him to Antioch and from that time onwards devoted himself wholly to missionary work and propaganda. He laid down the rôle of Mary and took up that of Martha. The scholar and contemplative became the teacher and preacher.

There is no need to follow in his unresting footsteps as, in journey after journey, he evangelized Cyprus, Asia Minor, Macedonia and Greece. Wherever he went there was a storm – of enthusiasm on one side and of execration on the other. He was imprisoned, stoned, beaten, ship-wrecked, attacked by illness and even by fits of despondency; but on he went. And wherever he went he talked – in synagogues, quoting Scripture, or in public places, quoting classical poets – and wherever he talked there sprang up a little center of Christianity. It was like an acolyte going swiftly to and fro lighting candles. And in a dozen years or less (45–57 A.D.) he had changed what had been (humanly speaking) little more than a Jewish sect into the embryo of a world-religion.

Then, in 57, he returned to Jerusalem. His friends implored him not to. They knew how bitterly he was hated by the Sanhedrim and how little the church could do to protect him. But he pressed on, undaunted, and for a week or so all seemed well. Then came the inevitable riot, and only the intervention of the Roman garrison saved Paul from being lynched. Two years of imprisonment followed (quite unjust, but the Roman governor was hoping for a bribe) during which St Paul took, or made, every possible opportunity to preach his doctrines to any and every audience – greatly alarming the governor, Antonius Felix, with the prospects of a future life for the unjust and incontinent, and 'almost persuading' Herod Agrippa 'to turn Christian'.

On Felix's supersession by Festus, however, Paul's appeal to the Emperor was attended to and he was sent with Julius, a centurion of the Augustan cohort, to Rome. Everyone knows how the ship was caught in a storm and wrecked on the coast of Malta, but the way in which St Paul took charge of things in the emergency shows his inborn qualities of leadership. It was not until the spring of the next year (60 or 61) that the party at length reached the capital, where St Peter was already established, and thereafter St Paul once again fades into the shadows. About his further travels, probably to Spain and certainly back to the near East, we have scant information. Even the date and manner of his martyrdom are uncertain. Tradition, supported by some internal evidence, speaks of a second and more rigorous imprisonment under Nero (the first emperor to make Christianity a crime) and tells us he was beheaded at Tre Fontane about 66 A.D. But the New Testament itself is silent.

Yet the historical instinct of his companion St Luke, who ends the story with their arrival at Rome, was sound. St Paul had been injected, like a vaccine, into the bloodstream of the civilized world at Damascus. He had travelled along its veins and arteries, bearing the healing medicine of Christ to one organ and ganglion after another. But at Rome he had reached its heart. Thenceforward the quickening grace could be left, pumped along the arteries of commerce and administration, to find its own way to the empire's remotest corners and beyond.

What exactly, though, was the serum that he carried?

The church of Rome was already founded, as St Paul's own epistle to it proves. The chief of the Apostles was established there. The sacraments were being administered, the gospel preached – perhaps already put into writing by St Mark. What was St Paul's particular contribution?

First, his fiery zeal and the example which it set. To see and hear St Paul in action made others feel that they themselves were woefully timid and tepid. But mainly he brought intellectual stiffening to the church – oaken ribs of closely reasoned thought to strengthen the Fisherman's barque against the storms ahead. For he was a man who detested all vagueness and who worried out every logical consequence and implication. To speak of 'Pauline doctrines' is not strictly accurate. St Paul did not originate doctrines. But he unravelled them – wrung them out, as it were, from the gospel which he had received. Thus, from the bare statement that 'Jesus is the Christ' he squeezed out a completely new interpretation of the Old Testament, with the church as a new Israel, Grace taking the place of the Mosaic Law, and with Christ as a new Adam, the perfect 'Image' of God (a doctrine closely akin to St John's 'Logos-doctrine', but using a visual instead of an aural metaphor). From the words 'Saul, Saul, why persecutest thou me?' he developed the doctrine of the Mystical Body: 'There is nothing but Christ in any of us' (Colossians 3:11), and from the parable of the laborers in the vineyard, or of the king whose invited guests were replaced by chance-met strangers from the highways and hedges, he deduced the end of the old Israel and the old Jerusalem to be replaced by a new Jerusalem, where there is 'no more gentile and Jew, barbarian or Scythian, slave or free'.

And perhaps it was this last doctrine, this bold and uncompromising acceptance of the church's *Catholicity*, which was the most typically Pauline contribution of him who called himself the Apostle to the Gentiles. St Peter had been timid on this issue, but St Paul would have no compromise, and it was he more than any other man who showed how and why the church must be Catholic, universal, and what that Catholicity implies. *June 29th*   ILLUSTRATION: page 361

PAUL I   † 767
Educated with his brother, Stephen III, at the Lateran school, he succeeded him in the papacy. He ruled firmly and vigorously for ten years.
June 28th

PAUL IV, *see* Alexander, John III and Paul IV.

PAUL AURELIAN   *Sixth Century*
A chieftain's son from southern Wales, trained at a monastic school with St David, he took twelve companions and sailed to Brittany. Guided by an angel, he established communities at Ushant, Ploudalmézeau and Batz, before becoming bishop of Léon.
March 12th

PAUL MIKI, *see* Martyrs of Japan.

PAUL of CONSTANTINOPLE   † 350 or 351
Secretary to Bishop Alexander, he was raised by him to the diaconate, and nominated his successor; but he spent most of his life in exile through the opposition of the Arians, and was murdered at Cucusus in Armenia.
June 7th

PAUL of CYPRUS   † c. 760
Martyred during persecution by the Emperor Constantine Copronymus for refusing to trample upon the crucifix, he was pressed between boards, torn with combs and then burned alive.
March 17th

PAUL of LATROS   † 956
He was induced by his brother Basil to live as a hermit on Mount Latros, near the monastery of Karia, where his example attracted so many disciples that he moved to the isle of Samos.
December 15th

PAUL of NARBONNE and his Companions
Third Century
Missionaries sent from Rome to Gaul, SS Saturninus of Toulouse and Dionysius of Paris were martyred, but SS Trophimus of Arles, Martial of Limoges and Gatian of Tours, with Paul as their illustrious leader, survived danger and founded many churches.
March 22nd

PAUL of the CROSS   1694–1775
There is little picturesque incident to chronicle in the life of Paul Francis Danei; practically his whole life was taken up with prayer, penance and devotion to the Passion of our Lord, which he was instrumental in propagating far and wide by the religious congregation which he founded (the Passionists). He was born at Ovada in north Italy in 1694 of devout middle-class parents. Although his life until the age of fifteen was all that a Christian's should be, at this period he underwent a kind of conversion which caused him to devote his whole life to prayer and penance: he spent many hours on his knees, practised great austerities, such as sleeping on the ground and continual fasting, and so acquired an influence over his contemporaries which resulted in several of them entering the religious life or the secular priesthood.

At the age of twenty an attempt to join the Venetian army to fight in defence of Christendom against the Turks showed him conclusively after a period in the ranks that his vocation was elsewhere. He returned to his life of prayer and penance.

A further six years passed and it was only when he was twenty-six that his future course was clearly shown to him in a series of visions; there he learned that he was to found a congregation that was to be specially devoted to the Passion. He at once began the life that was to be that of the Passionists, drawing up the rule and submitting it to Rome for approval which, after a little difficulty, was obtained in full. He and his brother, John Baptist, who had joined him, now settled on Monte Argentaro and there received the first novices. Benedict XIV was obliged to temper to some degree the austere life of these first Passionists who, in addition to the severity of a strict monastic life, wore themselves out preaching in the surrounding countryside. Paul was an ardent missionary, preaching the Passion everywhere and obtaining many conversions. The latter years of his life were passed in establishing a Congregation of enclosed Passionist nuns; he was now popularly acclaimed as a saint and wherever he went was obliged to bear with the thronging crowds, anxious to obtain a piece of his habit as a relic, to touch him or to request the cure of some malady or other favour. He died on October 18th 1775, at the age of eighty and was canonized a little less than a century later in 1867.

It seems curious that this Italian saint, who never left the country of his birth, should have been preoccupied with the conversion of England, about which he knew very little. 'England is always before my eyes,' he said, 'and if ever again it becomes Catholic the benefit to the church will be immeasurable.' Although in person he was never able to take any active steps to help forward this cause, it is worth recalling that sixty-five years after his death a Passionist, Fr Dominic Barberi, came to England and was instrumental in reconciling with the church John Henry Newman and many others, thus contributing to the revival of Catholicism in that country.
April 28th

PAUL THE FIRST HERMIT *Fourth Century*
This saint is known as the first hermit and was born of a rich family in Upper Egypt. He lost his parents when he was fifteen years old and fled into the desert in order to avoid the horrors of persecution. He discovered a cave at the foot of a mountain and, nearby, a palm-tree and a spring of pure water. Here he lived for ninety years without speaking to anyone.

He was discovered by St Antony the Abbot, who had been commanded by God in a vision to search for him. The search lasted three days. When the saints at last met, St Antony was ninety and St Paul over a hundred. Legend tells us that during the time the two men were together in the desert a number of miracles occurred. A crow, which had brought bread each day to

St Paul, arrived with double the usual amount the day after St Antony's arrival.

After a night spent praying together, St Paul told St Antony that he would shortly die and asked him to bring him a cloak which St Athanasius of Alexandria had given St Antony. The saint obeyed and went off to fetch the garment. On his return journey, as he neared the cave, he saw the soul of St Paul rising into Heaven. At the mouth of the cave he found St Paul's body, which he wrapped in the cloak that had belonged to St Athanasius. The saint died at the age of 113 and was buried in a grave dug by two lions.   ILLUSTRATION: page 362
January 15th

PAUL THE SIMPLE   *Fourth Century*
He had been a laborer all his life until, at the age of sixty, his wife's infidelity caused him to seek St Antony the Abbot in the Egyptian Thebaid. He asked to become a monk but Antony rejected him as too old, yet still St Paul persisted. In order to discourage him, St Antony put his obedience to the test. He was made to stand outside in the heat and to pray until he was told to stop; he was then brought to make mats which, after he had made fifteen, were condemned, so that he was told to take them to pieces and begin all over again. He was invited to a meal, told to sing psalms instead, and then ordered to sit beside the food until nightfall. Once he was made to gather up some honey from the ground without picking up any dust.
March 7th

PAULA   347–404
Of an illustrious Roman family, this widow gave all to charity and with one daughter accompanied St Jerome on a pilgrimage. In Bethlehem they founded a convent, which Paula ruled with intelligence and discretion.
January 26th

PAULINUS of AQUILEIA   † 804
An Italian farmer's son, he became a celebrated professor and was much honored by Charlemagne. During his illustrious career as patriarch of Aquileia he encouraged missionaries, strongly opposed the Adoptionist heresy, and wrote a number of books.
January 28th

PAULINUS of NOLA   c. 353–431
Paulinus was born at Bordeaux about 353. His father was praetorian prefect, he was educated by the rhetorician and poet Ausonius, and he inherited large estates in Gaul and Italy. He won renown at the bar and was consul in 378. Marriage to a Spanish lady, Therasia, brought him a dowry of estates in Spain. About 389 he was baptized at Bordeaux. Baptism began a new life. To Ausonius's dismay and his family's wrath, he and his wife, living henceforward in continence, sold their

estates one after another and gave the proceeds to the poor. He wore poor clothes and fasted rigorously.

In 394 or 395 he was ordained priest at Barcelona under pressure of popular clamor. Shortly afterwards he settled at Nola in southern Italy, where he still possessed lands, and became head of an informal monastery. Devoted to the local martyr, Felix, he paid him a yearly tribute of verse and built a basilica in his honor, adorned with mosaics whose meaning was explained by accompanying inscriptions. He also erected a guest house for poor pilgrims, himself occupying the upper storey. Visited by St Nicetas and St Melania the Elder, Paulinus corresponded with the leading churchmen: St Jerome, St Augustine, who addressed to him his treatise on Care for the Departed, and St Martin's biographer, Sulpicius Severus. He had been St Ambrose's guest. In 409 he was chosen bishop of Nola. His death in 431 is described by an eye-witness, Uranius. From his death bed he celebrated Mass with two episcopal visitors. Thirty-two poems from his pen, and fifty-one letters, survive.
June 22nd

PAULINUS of TRIER † 358
Educated in Poitiers and a disciple of St Maximus, he was one of those bishops who supported St Athanasius against the Arians. For this he was deposed and died an exile.
August 31st

PAULINUS of YORK † 644
Sent to England by Pope Gregory I, he was made bishop of York when Ethelburga of Kent went to marry King Edwin of Northumbria. He converted the king and many of his people, but when Edwin was killed and Northumbria overrun by the pagan Mercians, Paulinus returned to Kent with Ethelburga and died as bishop of Rochester.
October 10th

PEGA *Eighth Century*
A recluse, sister of St Guthlac, she lived near Croyland in Northamptonshire where Peakirk (Pega's church) is called after her. She died while a pilgrim in Rome, and her relics worked many miracles.
January 8th

PELAGIA of ANTIOCH *Fourth Century*
When a party of soldiers came to arrest her, this fifteen year old girl jumped from the top of the house and was killed.
June 9th

PELAGIA of TARSUS † 304?
Hers is the story – probably fictional – of the Christian virgin who suffered martyrdom rather than marry a pagan.
May 4th

PELAGIA THE PENITENT
A famous actress and courtesan named Margaret, she was converted and baptised by St Nonnus. Dressed as a man she retired to the Mount of Olives in Jerusalem where she lived as a monk.
October 8th

PELAGIUS or PELAYO † 925
Left as a hostage in the hands of the Moors in Cordova, this thirteen year old boy refused to abandon his faith and was terribly mutilated in the course of his martyrdom.
June 26th

PELEUS and his Companions † 310
The Egyptian bishops, Peleus and Nilus; Elias, a priest; and Patermuthius, a layman were burned to death at Phunon, near Petra, for celebrating Mass during the persecution of Firmilian, the governor of Palestine.
September 19th

PEREGRINE LAZIOSI 1260–1345
As a youth at Forli he was an active anti-papalist, but he was so impressed by St Philip Benizi's meek behavior at a violent political meeting that he became a Servite. He went to Siena and later founded a new community of the order at Forli.
May 1st

PEREGRINE of AUXERRE *Third Century*
He became the first bishop of Auxerre and suffered martyrdom when he appealed to the citizens of Intaranum to give up idolatry.
May 16th

PERGENTINUS and LAURENTINUS † 251
These brothers, patron saints of Arezzo, were said to have been students there during the persecution of Decius. Although only reprimanded when they were first arrested, they were beheaded when they persisted in their faith. It is probable, however, that their story is a fiction which developed from the mis-reading of church dedication to St Laurence (Laurentius).
June 3rd

PERPETUA and FELICITY *Third Century*
Perpetua and Felicity and the friends who died with them at Carthage in 203 are specially vivid figures among primitive martyrs. Of all such victims of pagan persecution we may feel what St Augustine felt of these, that 'we too are the fruits of their labor.' But these African martyrs are among the few early ones of whom there are detailed authentic records which bring home to us their experiences and their personalities. We have a contemporary document which includes a diary by Perpetua herself, a page or so by another martyr, and a concluding narrative by a first-hand witness who may have been Tertullian.

Vibia Perpetua was a girl of twenty-two, of distinguished family, married and with a baby son. Felicity was a married slave. Under the anti-Christian edict of 202, these two were arrested with three men, Saturninus, Secundulus and Revocatus; they formed a group of young converts still 'under instruction' with a layman called Saturus, who later joined them voluntarily in prison. They were guarded first in a private house, and were baptized there; then they were moved to the common prison of Carthage, where they suffered from heat, darkness and rough handling, but were visited and helped by two deacons, Tertius and Pomponius.

One day the whole group was hurried off to the forum to be tried by the Roman procurator, Hilarian. Perpetua's pagan father made a desperate effort here to shake her resolution, and implored her for her child's sake to sacrifice to the gods. Perpetua, like her friends, declared herself a Christian and refused to sacrifice. All were then condemned to the beasts and returned to prison rejoicing.

They were to be killed at the games on March 7th, the feast of Geta Caesar. In the interval, Secundulus died, perhaps beheaded. Felicity was pregnant, and feared that for that reason she would be forbidden to face the beasts on the same day as her friends. They all prayed, and an eight-months child was born, a girl. The delivery had been very painful, and a gaoler, hearing her groan, asked her what she expected to do in the worse ordeal with the beasts. She answered: 'My sufferings here are my own; there, another will be in me, suffering for me as I for him.' The adjutant of the prison, Pudens, was converted.

During their imprisonment, Saturus and Perpetua were consoled by visions. Saturus saw himself and his friends taken after martyrdom into the presence of an Apocalyptic figure worshipped unceasingly with the cry of 'Holy, holy, holy.' The martyrs were lifted by angels to kiss the divine face; they exchanged the kiss of peace themselves, then entered a heavenly rose-garden where they made peace between a bishop and priest who had unedifyingly quarrelled.

Perpetua saw first a ladder raised heavenwards, guarded by a dragon and edged with swords and knives. She trod on the dragon's head and climbed up to a great garden where our Lord as Good Shepherd was tending his sheep. Welcoming her, he offered her a morsel of curd which she received sacramentally.

Her next vision concerned a brother, Dinocrates, who had died when he was seven. She saw him first in a place of pain, thirsting for water he could not reach. She awoke and prayed for him for some days, then saw him again, in happiness.

Her last vision came on the day before the contest. She saw herself in the amphitheater, wrestling with a hideous Egyptian and trampling him underfoot. 'Thus I saw that my contest would be not with beasts but with the devil, but I knew that the victory was mine.'

On this same day the martyrs contrived to celebrate the Agape, or love-feast, in prison. On the morning of the games they entered the amphitheater confidently and cheerfully. When the beasts were turned upon them, Revocatus and Saturninus were mauled at once; Saturus twice escaped unhurt. The two girls were charged by a mad cow. Perpetua was tossed first; she sat up, smoothed her torn dress over her thigh, pinned up her dishevelled hair; then, seeing Felicity on the ground, went over and helped her up. The crowd was satisfied for the time and let them return to the entrance. Here Perpetua seemed to come out of a trance; she asked when she and Felicity were to be thrown to the cow, and would not believe this had already happened till she looked down and saw how she had been mauled.

Saturus meanwhile had been gravely wounded by a leopard; he had time to call the convert soldier, Pudens, from whose hand he took a ring, dipped it in his blood and returned it as a relic. 'Farewell; remember the faith and me.' (A martyr called Pudens was commemorated at Carthage on April 29th.)

The martyrs, having survived the beasts, were now to be beheaded. For the last time they gave each other the kiss of peace, then moved to the point where the crowd desired to watch their death. Saturus was first, Perpetua last. When the executioner came to her, his hand slipped (he was new to the trade, and perhaps was frightened of this commanding, aristocratic girl); the point entered her body, and she screamed; then guided the man's hand to her neck.

The martyrs' bodies were enshrined in the Basilica Maiorum at Carthage; the lettered stone which had covered them was excavated in 1907. From the fourth century their names have stood in the Roman Martyrology, and Perpetua is daily named in the canon of the mass, though the Felicity who precedes her is probably the Roman martyr of 162 A.D. The feast of our saints, originally on March 7th, is now on March 6th. St Augustine, who preached in their honor at least three times, says of the whole group of martyrs: 'In this noble company there were men as well, most courageous men, who suffered and overcame, but it was not these who gave their names to the feast.'

March 6th   ILLUSTRATION: page 363

PERPETUUS   *Fifth Century*
Bishop of Tours for more than thirty years, his life was shortened by the Gothic invasions and the spread of Arianism. Unfortunately, the interesting document which purports to be his will was a seventeenth century forgery.
April 8th

SEBASTIAN: painting by Mantegna (1430-1 - 1506). (*Louvre, Paris*)

PLATE 13

MICHAEL: painting by Hans Memlinc (1430-35–1494).
(Wallace Collection, London.)

MONICA: painting by Bennozo Gozzoli (c. 1421 – 1497). (Ch. di S. Agostino, San Gioniguiano.)

Photo: Hulton Picture Library

NICHOLAS of BARI: thirteenth century medallion showing him rescuing sailors in a tempest.
(Jerusalem Chamber, Westminster Abbey.)

Photo: Schweizerisch Landesmuseum

NICHOLAS von (of) FLÜE: painting on wood by unknown
artist (1492). *(Private Collection, Sachseln, Unterwalden.)*

NICODEMUS: early sixteenth century beechwood carving, south Germany. *(Staatliche Museum, Berlin.)*

NORBERT: 'St Norbert preaching against the heresy of Tanchelin', painting by Jan Bruegel (1568 – 1628). (K.G.H. Galerie, Brussells.)

OSWALD of WORCESTER: stained glass window by John the Glazier (mid-fifteenth century).
(All Souls' College Chapel, Oxford.)

PANCRAS: brass rubbing from tomb of Thomas Nelond, Prior of Lewes (1433). *(Cowfield, Sussex.)*

Photo: National Gallery, London

PAUL: detail from altarpiece, painted on wood, ascribed to Master of the
Pala Sforzesca (*c.* 1495). *(National Gallery, London.)*

PAUL THE FIRST HERMIT with Antony the Abbot, being fed by a raven: Limoges enamel by Leonard Limousin (1536). (British Museum.)

PERPE   TUA

FELICI   TAS

PERPETUA and FELICITY: sixth century mosaic. *(Archbishop's Palace, Ravenna.)*

PETER: detail from 'The Descent from the Cross' by Rogier van der Weyden (1399–1464).
(Mauritshuis, The Hague.)

Photo: Hulton Picture Library

PETER CANISIUS: mosaic made for Heiligtumsfeier at Aachen (1930).

Photo: *By courtesy of Edition Notre Dame des Anges, Paris*

PETER MARY CHANEL: sculpture.

PETER of ALCÁNTARA: painted wooden figure by Petro de Mena (seventeenth century).
(*Barcelona Museum.*)

PHILIP BENIZI: detail from painting by Girolomo Romanino (1484-7-c. 1562). (National Gallery, London.)

THOMAS AQUINAS: detail of Strozzi altarpiece by Andrea Orcagna (*c.*1308 - 1368).
(*Ch. di S. Maria Novella, Florence*)

PLATE 14

PETER, *see* Marcellinus and Peter.

PETER † 64?

Simon Peter, of Bethsaida (on the east bank of the Jordan), was by trade a fisherman. He was brought to Jesus by his brother Andrew, and later both were called 'to be fishers of men'. At that date they appear to have shared a house at Capharnaum, and Simon was a married man (possibly a widower?). Among the twelve apostles, Simon, who had been called 'Peter' by Jesus, has an eminence which is plainly evidenced not only in the Acts of the Apostles but in the Gospels, where his name heads the apostolic lists, and he appears as the usual mouthpiece of the Twelve in their intercourse with their Master. The church teaches that this leadership has been inherited by the successive bishops of Rome, who are thus endowed with universal jurisdiction and with infallibility in doctrinal definition. In support of this doctrine of the Roman primacy tradition has appealed especially to three Gospel texts.

(1) Matthew 16:17–19. This passage, centrally placed in Matthew, and another in Matthew 18:17, are the only sayings attributed to Jesus in which the word 'church' (Greek *ecclesia*) occurs. Various opinions about Jesus having been mentioned, he has asked the disciples: 'And what of you? Who do you say that I am?', and Simon Peter has answered: 'Thou art the Christ, the Son of the living God.' In reply Jesus congratulates Simon on having learned this cardinal truth not by human means ('flesh and blood') but by divine revelation. Then, echoing the pattern of Simon's words, he goes on: '(As thou hast said that I am the Christ, the Son of the living God, so) I in my turn tell thee, that thou art Peter . . .' The parallelism indicates that, just as 'Christ' in Simon's statement was not a name but a title, so 'Peter' here is not just a personal name but a name denoting a function or office, the nature of which is at once made clear: '(Thou art Peter) and upon this rock I will build my church.' The Greek word for 'Peter' is *Petros* (masculine); that for 'rock' is *petra* (feminine). But Jesus will have been speaking in Aramaic, and in Aramaic (as can be seen from St Paul's epistles) the original of the name 'Peter' was *Kepha*, identical with the Aramaic word for 'rock'. So Jesus in fact said: 'Thou art Rock, and upon this rock I will build my church'. Simon then is to have the function of being the firm substructure (not just a foundation-stone, but the rock on which the foundation-stones will rest) of the church which Jesus is going to 'build': '. . . upon this rock I will build my church, and the gates of hell' (i.e. the powers of mortality or evil) 'will not prevail against it,' cf. Matthew 7:24–27. Thus the church will have a stability superior to the worst assaults, and the source of this stability will be the rock on which it is to be built, Simon Peter, but Simon Peter

considered not as a fallible man (Simon) but as endowed with a function (Peter).

The next clause of the text ('and I will give to thee the keys of the kingdom of heaven') should be compared with Isaiah 22:19–22, whence it appears that, in the earthly anticipation of the post-historic Reign of God, Peter is to have the supreme authority as the temporal representative of the eternal King. Finally Peter is told that his decisions ('and whatever thou shalt bind on earth etc.') will have divine sanction. It is sometimes argued that, as the 'binding and loosing' promise is also made to all the Twelve in Matthew 18:18, this promise gives nothing peculiar to Peter. But as Peter's function as rock-foundation and his office as 'grand vizier' are special to himself (a house is not built on several rocks, nor is a kingdom ruled by several viceroys), so too this third promise may be thought to give Peter a unique jurisdiction.

(2) John 21:15–17 ('. . . Feed my sheep'). For the metaphor of the flock we may specially refer to a passage from this same Gospel (ch. 10) where the unity of Christ's flock is emphasized: 'There shall be one flock and one shepherd', viz. Christ. From this it seems that in our passage Jesus, now that his visible presence is to cease, is handing over his flock to Peter as his vice-regent. The Ephesian elders (Acts 20:28) and the elders addressed in 1 Peter 5:2 are also described as shepherds. But if 'one flock' requires 'one shepherd' there will be need, above the subordinate level of local pastors, of one supreme shepherd of the flock of Christ. It is not enough that Christ in heaven remains the divine pastor of the flock, since if it were enough there would indeed be no need of a supreme vice-pastor, but no need either of such local pastors as those mentioned in Acts and 1 Peter.

(3) Luke 22:32 ('. . . it is for thee to be the support of thy brethren'). This passage looks like an injunction to Peter to carry out the stabilizing task assigned to him in Matthew 16.

We may add (4) that Mark 9:33–37 seems to turn a general warning to all the apostles (cf. the parallel in Matthew 18:1–5) into a special admonition to the 'first' (cf. Matthew 10:2) of the Twelve: 'If anyone wishes to be first, he shall be the last of all and the servant of all' – servant of the servants of God.

After the Ascension Peter's leadership of the Twelve seems to have been unquestioned. It is he who, before Pentecost, tells the assembled brethren that the place left vacant by Judas's fall should be filled. He is the spokesman to the crowd gathered at Pentecost. He 'visits the saints (i.e. the Christians) everywhere' and takes the crucial step of admitting the Gentile Cornelius to baptism. When Herod found the Jews pleased by the execution of James, the brother of John, 'he went further and laid hands on Peter also'. The author of the Acts relates

Peter's escape from prison, and promptly tells the story of Herod's fatal illness. At the council of Jerusalem Peter takes Paul's side in the discussion on circumcision, as also does James, who by now appears to be the head of the local church of Jerusalem and therefore the leader of Jewish Christianity. In the Acts no further mention is made of Peter. But we know from Galatians that Peter visited Antioch (possibly before the Council of Jerusalem), and from 1 Peter we may infer that he visited many churches in Asia Minor. It is just possible that when Paul (Romans 15:22) explains his own delay in visiting Rome by his reluctance to 'build on the foundation another man had laid' he is thinking of Peter, who may have visited Corinth (cf. 1 Corinthians 1:12) *en route* for Rome.

According to the main stream of Christian tradition Peter's powers and prerogatives passed to the bishops of Rome. Onwards from the mid-third century at least we have documentary proof that the bishops of Rome were claiming to be the successors of Peter, and no record exists of any other city of the early Christian world claiming to possess either Peter's tomb or the effective succession to his powers. It was accepted without question that Peter had suffered martyrdom in the capital city.

Neither literature nor archaeology affords quite explicit proof of Peter's residence and death at Rome. But it may at once be stated that both texts and material remains have come down to us which indicate, by their implications and the natural inferences to be drawn from them, that both these fundamental points in the Petrine tradition were accepted by the Christian world of the late-first and second centuries. The tradition can, in fact, be traced back to a period which is little, if at all, later than the lifetime of persons who had known Peter; and it is not easy to explain the circumstances in which the whole story of his association with the imperial capital could have been invented and successfully propagated within so short a span.

The early literary texts, prior to *c.* 200, supporting the tradition, are as follows: (1) the reference (recorded by Eusebius) made by the late-second-century Roman priest Gaius to 'trophies' of Peter and Paul that could be seen in Rome in his time; (2) the allusion to Peter and Paul as preaching and suffering martyrdom in Rome in the letter sent *c.* 170 to the Romans by Dionysius of Corinth; (3) the description of Peter and Paul as 'commanding' the Roman Christians in the letter sent to Rome in the second century by Ignatius of Antioch; (4) the claim that Peter and Paul were the principal recent martyrs 'among us' put forward by Clement of Rome, at the end of the first century, in a letter to the Corinthians; (5) the First Epistle of Peter penned from 'Babylon', which can hardly be other than a sobriquet

for Rome. (For a detailed discussion of these texts, see Jocelyn Toynbee and John Ward Perkins, *The Shrine of St Peter and the Vatican Excavations*, 1956, pp. 127–34).

Archaeological evidence for the existence of the Roman Petrine tradition by the middle of the second century at least has been furnished by the recent excavations beneath the Vatican Basilica. These researches have brought to light, directly below the papal altar of the present church, a small niched shrine, or Aedicula. This Aedicula was made in the wall of a tomb as it was actually being built and it is, therefore, exactly contemporary with it; and as that wall is dated to *c.* 160 by brick stamps in an associated drain, the shrine can be assigned securely to that time. It seems that the workmen in digging the foundations for the tomb-wall cut through a burial, the disturbed bones from which were discovered just under, and sealed by, the floor of the niched shrine; and it would appear that the shrine was built to mark the place where those bones reposed. The shrine shows no sign of ever having changed hands; it underwent a series of successive embellishments between the time of its erection and the end of the third century; it was a place of Christian pilgrimage in the early fourth century, as inscriptions prove; and it was made the focal point of Old St Peter's by Constantine (*c.* 330) at the cost of a most elaborate and difficult engineering operation and in the teeth of the families whose richly-adorned and well-cared-for mausolea he destroyed for this purpose. The implications of these discoveries are that this Aedicula was Christian from the first and was built by mid-second-century members of the Roman church to identify a place that they connected intimately with Peter and probably believed to be his actual grave. In that case the bones sealed beneath the shrine were presumably regarded as being his. (For the details of these excavations, see Toynbee and Ward Perkins, *op. cit.* pp. 135–67, 182–6).

In the light of this evidence, literary and monumental, there is a strong case for holding that Peter did visit Rome and transmitted his primacy to its first bishop personally, before undergoing martyrdom during Nero's persecution of the Roman Christians. Of his activities and domicile in Rome we know nothing. The familiar stories are all derived either from local legends or from relatively late and unreliable documents.

Against the doctrine of the Roman Petrine primacy it has been objected that, as the Second Coming was expected to be imminent, Jesus would not have provided for a succession to St Peter. But if Jesus was 'the Christ, the Son of the living God', no error about the date of the Second Coming will have vitiated his provision for his church, which was to continue 'until the consummation of the world' (Matthew 28:20) and has in fact continued for nearly two thousand years. Jesus received from his Father, and transmitted, a transmissible authority; and if a 'vicar' of Christ was needed for the first Christian generation, it can hardly be supposed that the need died out with the death of St Peter.

June 29th, Peter and Paul
February 22nd, Peter's Chair at Antioch
January 18th, Peter's Chair at Rome
August 1st, Peter's Chains   ILLUSTRATION: page 364

PETER ARBUES   c. 1440–1485

In 1484, he was appointed head of the Inquisition in Aragon, and although no acts of cruelty or injustice can be proved against him, his activities aroused enough emnity to provoke his assassination.

September 17th

PETER BALSAM   † 311

A Christian from Eleutheropolis in Palestine, he was tried by Severus the governor during the persecution by Maximinus. He gladly suffered crucifixion rather than endure eternal pain by renouncing God.

January 3rd

PETER BAPTIST, *see* Martyrs of Japan.

PETER CANISIUS   1520–1597

This doctor of the church is often called the second Apostle of Germany. Both Holland and Germany claim him as their son, for Nijmegen, where he was born, May 8th, 1521, though a Dutch town today, was at that time in the ecclesiastical province of Cologne and had the rights of a German city. His father, a Catholic and nine times burgomaster of Nijmegen, sent him at the age of fifteen to the University of Cologne, where he met the saintly young priest, Nicolaus van Esch. It was he who drew Canisius into the orbit of the loyal Catholic party in Cologne, which had been formed in opposition to the archbishop, Hermann von Wied, who had secretly gone over to the Lutherans. Canisius was chosen by the group to approach the emperor, and the deposition of the archbishop which followed averted a calamity from the Catholic Rhineland. Shortly afterwards Peter Canisius met Bd Peter Faber, one of the first companions of St Ignatius, and made the *Spiritual Exercises* under his direction. During this retreat he found the answer to the question he had put to himself: how best could he serve God and assist the stricken Catholic church in Germany?

He was inspired to join the Society of Jesus, and, after his ordination in 1546, soon became known by his editions of works of St Cyril of Alexandria and of St Leo the Great. In 1547 he attended the council of Trent as procurator for the bishop of Augsburg, where he became still further imbued with the spirit of the Catholic Counter-Reformation. His obedience was tested when he was sent by St Ignatius to teach rhetoric in the comparative obscurity of the new Jesuit college at Messina,

but this interlude in his public work for the church was but a brief one.

Recalled to Rome in 1549 to make his final profession, he was entrusted with what was to become his life's work: the mission to Germany. At the request of the duke of Bavaria, Canisius was chosen with two other Jesuits to profess theology in the University of Ingolstadt. Soon he was appointed rector of the University, and then, through the intervention of King Ferdinand of the Romans, he was sent to do the same kind of work in the University of Vienna. His success was such that the king tried to have him appointed to the archbishopric. Though he refused this dignity, he was compelled to administer the diocese for the space of a year.

It was at this period, 1555, that he issued his famous *Catechism*, one of his greatest services to the church. With its clear and popular exposition of Catholic doctrine it met the need of the day, and was to counter the devastating effect of Luther's *Catechism*. In its enlarged form it went into more than four hundred editions by the end of the seventeenth century and was translated into fifteen languages.

From Vienna Canisius passed on to Bohemia, where the condition of the church was desperate. In the face of determined opposition he established a college at Prague which was to develop into a university. Named Provincial of southern Germany in 1556, he established colleges for boys in six cities, and set himself to the task of providing Germany with a supply of well-trained priests. This he did by his work for the establishment of seminaries, and by sending regular reinforcements of young men to be trained in Rome.

On his many journeys in Germany St Peter Canisius never ceased from preaching the word of God. He often encountered apathy or hostility at first, but as his zeal and learning were so manifest great crowds soon thronged the churches to listen. For seven years he was official preacher in the cathedral of Augsburg, and is regarded in a special way as the apostle of that city. Whenever he came across a country church deprived of its pastor he would halt there to preach and to administer the sacraments. It seemed impossible to exhaust him: 'If you have too much to do, with God's help you will find time to do it all,' he said, when someone accused him of overworking himself.

Another form of his apostolate was letter writing, and the printed volumes of his correspondence cover more than eight thousand pages. Like St Bernard of Clairvaux he used this means of comforting, rebuking and counselling all ranks of society. As the needs of the church or the individual required, he wrote to pope and emperor, to bishops and princes, to ordinary priests and laymen. Where letters would not suffice he brought to bear his great powers of personal influence. Thus at the conference between Catholics and Protestants held at Worms in 1556, it was due to his influence that the Catholics were able to present a united front and resist Protestant invitations to compromise on points of principle. In Poland in 1558 he checked an incipient threat to the traditional faith of the country; and in the same year, he earned the thanks of Pope Pius IV for his diplomatic skill in healing a breach between the pope and the emperor. This gift of dealing with men led to his being entrusted in 1561 with the promulgation in Germany of the decrees of the council of Trent.

Shortly afterwards he was called on to answer the *Centuries* of Magdeburg. This work, 'the first and worst of all Protestant church histories', was a large-scale attack on the Catholic church, and its enormous distortions of history would have required more than one man to produce an adequate answer. Yet Peter Canisius showed the way by his two works, *The History of John the Baptist*, and *The Incomparable Virgin Mary*.

From 1580 until his death in 1597 he labored and suffered much in Switzerland. His last six years were spent in patient endurance and long hours of prayer in the college of Fribourg, now that broken health had made further active work impossible. Soon after his death, December 21st, 1597, his tomb began to be venerated, and numerous miracles were attributed to his intercession, He had the unique honor of being canonized and declared a doctor of the church on the same day, June 21st, 1925.

April 27th　　　　　ILLUSTRATION: page 365

PETER CELESTINE, *see* Celestine V.

PETER CHRYSOLOGUS　　　　　*c.* † 450
Archbishop of Ravenna, he rooted out the remains of paganism in his diocese. His sermons (hence his name 'Chrysologus', 'of the golden words') won him in 1729 the title of doctor of the church.

December 4th

PETER CLAVER　　　　　1581–1654
St Peter Claver was born in 1581, or as some authorities maintain 1583, at Verdu in Catalonia. Both his parents were impoverished members of ancient and distinguished families, pious without ostentation.

Peter Claver graduated with distinction from the Jesuit College at Barcelona, entered the Jesuit novitiate at Tarragona in 1602 and took his final vows on August 8th 1604. While he was studying philosophy at Majorca, Alphonsus Rodriguez, the saintly door keeper of the college, urged him 'to go to the Indies and save millions of these perishing souls.' Claver obeyed, and in 1610 landed in Cartagena, a port in the Caribbean Sea. Cartagena was the principal slave market in the New World, and a thousand slaves were landed there every month.

Father Claver met every slave ship on its arrival, bringing with him biscuits, brandy, lemons and tobacco which he had collected on a house-to-house visitation. 'We must,' he said, 'speak to them with our hands before we try to speak to them with our lips.'

About one Negro in three died on the voyage, and Father Claver's first task was to baptize the dying. Many of his African interpreters could not endure the stench and fainted when they tried to penetrate into the dark bowels of the slave ship through which Father Claver moved serenely. It was said that his person was sometimes illumined with the rays of glory as he passed through the hospital wards of Cartagena, and perhaps the dying Africans saw a face illumined with love, as they felt the deft movement of kind hands easing their tortured bodies and his lips meeting their filthy sores in a kiss.

From the moment that he landed in Cartagena to the day of his death forty-four years later, Father Claver dedicated his every waking thought to the Negroes, of whom he baptized more than three hundred thousand. He trained up a group of African interpreters to act as catechists in the many African languages represented among the slaves.

Claver accepted slavery as an inevitable though regrettable element in the social system. It was with the slaves as victims of that social system rather than with the system itself that he was concerned. His life was dedicated to reforming the individual rather than to reforming the system. His heroic predecessor at Cartagena, Father Sandoval, combined Claver's love for the individual slave with Wilberforce's hatred of slavery. He collected all the relevant facts about the slave trade and wrote a book which is one of the most effective attacks on this infamous traffic and is still an invaluable source book for historians of slavery.

Claver, on the other hand, was concerned not with the institution of slavery but with the slaves. That was his vocation, just as the abolition of slavery was Wilberforce's, and it is no belittlement of Wilberforce to point out that it is easier to hate slavery than to love slaves. Any man with an appreciation of natural justice would inevitably be led to the conclusion that slavery was unjust, but the love which Father Claver lavished on the slaves was something which transcended the natural order.

Once when he was summoned to hear the confession of a Negro, so ulcerous and infected that he had been thrown into a remote corner to save others from his insupportable presence, Father Claver recoiled when he saw and smelt this miserable man. Then overwhelmed with remorse he kissed the wounds and the repulsive sores. This was no stunt. He felt that it was necessary to restore self-respect to those whose very presence inspired normal people with disgust, and the extravagance of such oft repeated gestures as kissing leprous wounds, may have helped to convince the ulcerous lepers and infected Negroes that man is made in the image of God, and that the most degraded of lepers is infinitely precious in the eyes of God.

In the second place, Claver was fighting the battle which never ended between his higher and his lower nature, and he knew that his instinctive shrinking from disgusting sights and smells could only be conquered by drastic means. The note of the supernatural is as evident in his humility as in his love. When he signed himself 'Slave of the slaves for ever' he meant exactly what he said. On his missionary journeys he placed a Negro in control of the party. Once, when Father Claver was invited to give a mission in a particular place, he replied that he would come if the Negroes consented. The Negroes did not consent and Father Claver did not come.

Father Claver's activities were not confined to the Negroes, but proud Spaniards who sought him out had to be content with such time as he could spare from his ministrations to the slaves. Some ladies complained that the smell of the Negroes clung tenaciously to the confessional which they had used, could they not confess to him elsewhere? 'I quite agree,' said Father Claver with the disarming simplicity of the saint, 'I am not the proper confessor for fine ladies. You should go to some other confessor. My confessional was never meant for ladies of quality, it is too narrow for their gowns. It is only suited to poor Negresses.' But it was to Father Claver that they wished to confess and to no other. 'Very well, then,' said Father Claver meekly, 'but I am afraid you must wait until all my Negresses are absolved.' In the sight of God the white man and the Negro might be equal, but in the sight of Father Claver the Negro had precedence every time.

On one occasion during Holy Week Father Claver noticed a lady in the congregation whose dress did not satisfy his somewhat exacting standard of Catholic modesty. He descended from the pulpit and pointed out that the dress was not only inappropriate to Holy Week but most unsuitable in view of the lady's age. It was this maladroit allusion to her age which infuriated the good lady. The Father Rector, who happened to arrive at this moment, rebuked Father Claver, who fell on his knees, kissed the feet of his Superior and asked for the severest possible penance. The lady herself was so impressed that she resolved there and then to profit by Father Claver's admonition. Many people took advantage of Father Claver's humility. Ignorant Negroes often treated him with insolence, but their insults, we are told, 'had an inexpressible charm for him. He hearkened to them with joy that appeared in his countenance.'

Father Claver died in 1654. He was beatified on July 16th 1850 by Pius IX, and canonized on June 15th, 1888, by Leo XIII.

St Peter Claver has a special message for the modern world, which so often forgets the individual in schemes for changing his environment. Much of what now passes for pity is inspired by ambition or self-importance, or by that creative instinct which finds expression not only in art and literature but also in organization and in the planning of a welfare state. 'The world and its future,' wrote H. G. Wells, 'is not for feeble folk any more than it is for selfish folk. It is not for the multitude but for the best.' Modern humanitarianism is often pitiless in its attitude to the misfits, and if you want a man who is prodigal of love for 'feeble folk', you had better advertize for a saint.

September 9th

PETER DAMIAN   † 1072

Luminary of the eleventh century church, Peter was born at Ravenna. His mother, driven to despair by a large family and insufficient means to support it, threw her new born child out to die, but a priest's concubine restored her to more maternal sentiments. Soon an orphan, the boy was starved and ill treated by a married brother. Another brother, however, intervened and educated Peter, who, in gratitude, added to his own his brother's name of Damian. His brilliant success as a student and professor proves that his later objection to the humanities was at least not the envy of ignorance. Peter joined the monastery of Fonte Avellana, a semi-eremitical community, akin rather to the Carthusians than the Benedictines they styled themselves. His austerities outdid even those of the monks. Twice his abbot despatched him to reform other monasteries. In 1043, under obedience, he became abbot.

Such was the repute of his holiness that successive popes employed him in the urgent task of reform, and, in 1057, Stephen IX compelled him to enter the Curia as cardinal bishop of Ostia. Never was reform more necessary, and in the highest quarters. Peter, however, opposed to vice a puritanism which took scandal when a bishop played chess. Moreover, when at Sutri in 1046, the Emperor Henry III deposed two popes and substituted a worthy nominee of his own, Peter welcomed this Erastian method of reform and congratulated Henry. Later however he supported the archdeacon Hildebrand who, as Gregory VII, would shake off the imperial yoke and effect a papal reform. Peter spent his later days in retirement at Fonte Avellana, though his solitude was broken by diplomatic missions on which the popes employed him. A diet of coarse bread and stale water, an iron girdle, frequent and severe flagellations: such fasting and self-torture did not prevent him reaching the age of eighty-three, when he died in 1072. His beautiful hymn on the joys of Paradise and a charming letter to the Empress Agnes display a side of his character more attractive today. He is a doctor of the church.

February 23rd

PETER FOURIER   1565–1640

Peter Fourier was born at Mirecourt in the Vosges; at the age of twenty he joined the Canons Regular of St Augustine at Chamousey; he was ordained in 1589 and after supplementary studies at Pont-à-Mousson was appointed parish priest at Mattaincourt, a stronghold of Protestantism. His priestly zeal and the influence of his holiness made it a model parish. With Bd Alix Le Clerc he was the founder of a Congregation of Canonesses devoted to the free education of girls. St Peter died in 1640 and was canonized in 1897.
December 9th

PETER, GORGONIUS and DOROTHEUS
                                   † 303

Important officials in Diocletian's residence at Nicomedia, Asia Minor. Hearing reports of their Christianity, the Emperor ordered them to worship idols but, undaunted by torture, they refused and were killed.
March 12th

PETER MARTYR of VERONA   † 1252

Born at Verona in 1205. Although his parents were Albigensians, he grew up an orthodox Catholic and received the habit from St Dominic himself. He became a successful preacher in Lombardy and was made inquisitor general for the Milanese territories by Pope Gregory IX in 1234. His zeal in this office aroused hostility, and he was assassinated while on a journey from Como to Milan in 1252. His murderer repented and died as a Dominican lay-brother.
April 29th

PETER MARY CHANEL   1803–1841

He was born in 1803 in the diocese of Belley, and although he joined the missionary order of the Marists in 1831, he was not able to undertake the missionary work he had set his heart upon until 1836, when he sailed to the Pacific Islands.

In November 1837 he landed on the tiny island of Futuna, a few miles north of Samoa and Fiji. He was made welcome, but as his influence grew, friendship turned to suspicion; and the chief, on hearing that his son had become a Christian, caused Fr. Chanel to be assassinated.

April 28th   ILLUSTRATION: page 366

PETER MORONE, *see* Celestine V.

PETER NOLASCO   *c.* 1189–1258

The two orders founded for the redemption of captives held by the Moors – the Mercedarians and the Trinitarians – both labor under the difficulty that their first members left no written records; consequently the lives of their founders are very largely unknown to us, and the legends that have grown up around their names depend on documents (proved to be spurious) which were fabricated in the sixteenth century, some three hundred years after their deaths.

Peter Nolasco was a Spaniard, born probably at the end of the twelfth century, when Spain was at grips with the Moorish invasion. He was pre-occupied with the problem of Christians taken prisoner by the infidels and founded the Order of our Lady of Ransom (the Mercedarians) for the ransoming of these captives; at their profession, members of this order add a fourth vow of personally carrying out the redemption of captives. The title of the order is derived from the claim that our Lady appeared simultaneously to St Peter Nolasco, to the king of Aragon, and to St Raymund of Penafort assuring them of her patronage if they persevered in their efforts to ransom those whom the Moors held captive. The evidence for these visions is, however, late and dubious, although the feast of our Lady of Ransom is observed on September 24th.
January 28th

PETER of ALCÁNTARA   1499–1562

Pedro Garavito was born at Alcántara, Spain, in 1499. His father, a lawyer, was governor of Alcántara and died while Peter was still at school. From childhood, Peter was given to the practice of prayer. He spent two years studying law at Salamanca. At the age of sixteen he joined a particularly strict house of Observant Franciscans at Manjaretes. He was ordained in 1524. Thereafter his life is uneventful except for some thirteen years of apostolic work among the people (he was noted for his preaching on the Old Testament), and for his efforts to lead a more and more retired and penitential life. He attempted first to make his province still stricter in observance and then, that failing, to establish new provinces of ever more severe rule: first in 1540, when he started a small group of Franciscan eremitical communities, and again in 1554, when the bishop of Coria allowed him to start another eremitical settlement, after his own minister had refused.

St Peter went to Rome in this year to secure papal approval. The General of the Observants withheld his support, and Julius III, in authorizing the saint to build a convent on his new plan, placed him under the Conventuals. St Peter returned and founded his new house at Pedrosa in 1555, thus starting what came to be called the Alcántarine Franciscans, who survived till 1897, when Leo XIII amalgamated all the Observants into one group. The reform spread, by means of new foundations and by absorption, and in 1561 Pius IV erected it into a province and returned it to the general jurisdiction of the Observants.

St Peter's main points were extreme poverty, so that the friars were not even to accept stipends for saying mass; extreme simplicity, symbolized by that favorite counter-reform austerity of going barefoot; as close an approximation to the hermit ideal as the council of Trent allowed, expressed by keeping the number in each community down to eight; and an extreme insistence on the contemplative aspect of the Franciscan vocation, expressed by the provision of three hours daily to be given by rule to mental prayer. All St Peter's life was spent in the southern border area of Extremadura, between Spain and Portugal. Its chief characteristic is its stern penitential practice, especially the custody of the eyes (concerning which many stories are told of him) and his incredible vigils: he told St Teresa of Avila that for forty years he had not slept for more than an hour and a half every night. In various of her writings she tells us much about him. He was instrumental in the realization of her first foundation of the Carmelite reform, writing on her behalf to the bishop of Avila. The letter he wrote to St Teresa herself about the degree of poverty to be observed by her new convent is characteristic: 'Perfection of life must be discussed only with those who live the life of perfection', he tells her, 'because, normally, no one has a clearer conscience or a better feeling for good than is given by what he himself practises.'

St Peter was a great contemplative and guided St Teresa in about 1555 over 'intellectual' visions. He compiled a short book on the subject of prayer: *A Treatise on Prayer and Meditation*. It consists of two series of seven meditations on the Last Things and the Passion of Christ, together with advice to the soul seeking God in prayer. The meditations are not without literary grace, but the book is most notable for its breadth of view and for the writer's desire not to confine the soul to a rigid system. St Peter in part greatly reduces a much longer book by Luis de Granada (whose work he acknowledges), but the spirit and the practical counsels are all his own.

St Teresa described St Peter in a famous sentence in her *Life* (chapter 27): 'He was a very old man when I knew him and so extremely thin that he looked like nothing so much as if he were made of the roots of trees.' She adds: 'With all this holiness he was very k ndly, though spare of speech except when asked questions, and then he was delightful, for he had a keen understanding.' Popular devotion to the saint is largely owing to St Teresa's vision in which, she says, our Lord told her 'that nothing I asked him for in his name would be unheard.' This has been understood as applying to everyone and is sometimes so translated.

He is often adopted as a patron for night watchmen because of his own vigils. It is worth noting that in his book he is careful to say on the subject of sleep that one must not 'deny the body what is due to it, that the body itself may not hinder what is due to the soul.'

St Peter died at Arenas on October 18th, 1562, and was canonized in 1669.   ILLUSTRATION: page 367
October 19th

PETER of ALEXANDRIA † *c.* 311
He succeeded St Theonas as bishop of Alexandria in 300 and was put to death by Maximinus Daia. He was the last martyr executed by public authority in Alexandria.
November 26th

PETER of ATROA 773–837
Trained under St Paul the Recluse whom he succeeded as abbot of St Zachary's monastery in Atroa. Though chiefly celebrated for his miracles and spiritual insight, he was also a wise superior, and preserved the monks during several persecutions.
January 1st

PETER of BRAGA *Fourth Century*
He was supposed to have been the first bishop of Braga in Portugal and to have suffered martyrdom at the hands of the local king, whose daughter he had baptized.
April 26th

PETER of CAVA † 1123
Appointed bishop of Policastro on his return from Cluny Abbey in France, he resigned and became abbot of the Cava monastery, founded by his uncle St Alferius. The strictness he had learnt at Cluny at first made him unpopular, but the monks came to appreciate its value, and the foundation prospered.
March 4th

PETER of CHAVANON 1003–1080
After serving for many years as priest in his native parish of Langeac in Haute-Loire, he founded a convent for Augustinian canons at Pébrac in Auvergne.
September 11th

PETER of LAMPSACUS † 251
and his Companions
He was beheaded at Lampsacus on the Hellespont for refusing to sacrifice to Aphrodite.

At Troas two other Christians, Andrew and Paul, were also condemned. Dionysia, a girl of sixteen, had protested at the recantation of a third Christian, Nicomachus. She was beheaded.
May 15th

PETER of MOUNT ATHOS *Eighth Century?*
Supposed to have been led to Mount Athos by a vision, he lived there as a hermit before the famous monastery was built.
June 12th

PETER of SEBASTE † 391
A learned writer, son of St Basil the Elder and youngest of an entire family of saints. He was educated by his sister St Macrina, and he succeeded his brother, St Basil, as abbot of the monastery founded by their mother,

St Emilia. Later St Peter became bishop of Sebaste.
January 9th

PETER of TARENTAISE † 1175

From the monastery of Bonnevaux, to which he had attracted many relatives, he moved to be superior of a new Cistercian house at Tamié in the Alps, where he built a hospice. In 1142 he was elected archbishop of Tarentaise, and he did much to remedy the damage done by the slackness of his predecessor. He was famous as a mediator, and died on a mission to restore peace between Louis VII of France and Henry II of England.
May 8th

PETER ORSEOLO 928–987

He was born in 928, and while still a young man successfully commanded the Venetian fleet and succeeded the murdered Doge, Candiani IV. After ruling for two years with great wisdom, he suddenly retired to France to the Cuxa abbey in Rousillon, and later became a hermit.
January 10th

PETER REGALATUS † 1456

At the age of thirteen he entered the Franciscan friary in Valladolid, and later moved to the house at Tribulos, of which he became the head. His name, Regalatus, derives from his strict enforcement of the rule.
May 13th

PETER THOMAS 1305–1366

A Carmelite, he spent much of his life as a papal diplomat. In 1359 he was sent to Constantinople as 'Universal Legate to the Eastern Church', more or less in command of a large body of troops, and he died seven years later from wounds received in an assault on Alexandria.
January 28th

PETER THE VENERABLE, *see* the Cluny saints.

PETROC *Sixth Century*

St Petroc was a famous saint in his time, and he is commemorated by church dedications in north Cornwall, Devon, Wales and Brittany. Our knowledge of his life is derived first of all from a medieval account of the saint which was probably originally composed in Bodmin priory. This is an engaging document, combining some reputable history with many legends. According to this, Petroc, the son of a Welsh king, became a monk and together with some of his friends went to study in Ireland. Then they sailed to Cornwall, and settled in a Celtic monastic establishment by the river Camel; the place is now known as Padstow – Petroc-stow. After living there for thirty years he made a pilgrimage to Rome and the Holy Land, and even spent some time, in a manner common among Celtic monks, on an islet in the Indian Ocean. Many tales of his goodness are told of him after he returned to Cornwall: how he healed the sick, and not only sick people but even a dragon which

had a splinter in its eye; how he saved a stag from the hunters. A later version of the same *Life* says that Petroc retired to the 'wilderness' of Bodmin Moor; and, finally, realizing that his life was coming to its close, set out to say farewell to his communities. He died while he was on the journey.

An incident of a kind not untypical of the irresponsibilities of medieval religious fervor shows Petroc's great popularity. The monastery of Petroc's foundation had moved to Bodmin taking Petroc's body with it. In 1177 the relics were stolen by one of the canons of the Augustinian priory and presented to the abbey of Saint-Méen in Brittany. The prior of Bodmin appealed to King Henry II, who stepped in, and the abbey of Saint-Méen had to yield up the relics to the prior, who brought them back amid public rejoicing, thereby apparently inaugurating an annual remembrance in Bodmin which, like so many customs, survived the Reformation in a distorted form whose meaning has been obscured.

Petroc was undoubtedly one of the outstanding figures in the great tradition of Celtic monasticism. The Celtic saints live for us not only in their written lives but embedded, as it were, in those countries where they journeyed, preaching, converting and founding churches, and leaving their names and renown behind them. The custom of keeping the 'feast' of a town or village, that is the feast day of its saint, has survived in Cornwall and been adopted by very varying Christian denominations, and in Bodmin Petroc is popularly commemorated by a fair. In Brittany, of course, the tradition received no dislocation from the Reformation. In Loperic, for instance, Petroc is revered as a 'local' saint in a straightforward way that need not call academically on history, studies in folklore, or half remembered customs as its support. The post-Reformation Catholic churches at Padstow and Bodmin are both dedicated to St Petroc.
June 4th

PETRONAX *Eighth Century*

Pope St Gregory II in 717 persuaded him to make a pilgrimage to the tomb of St Benedict on Monte Cassino. He found a few hermits among the derelict buildings, who elected him their superior; and it was he who was responsible for the refounding of the abbey.
May 6th

PETRONILLA *Third Century*

Probably a Roman martyr, she was most certainly not the daughter of the Apostle St Peter, as certain traditions have alleged.
May 31st

PETRONIUS *Fifth Century*

Bishop of Bologna, he repaired many of the churches destroyed by the Goths.
October 4th

PHARAÏLDIS
Eighth Century

Her legend says that in spite of cruelty from her husband, whom she married against her wish, she kept herself a virgin. She is called Varelde in Belgium, and is celebrated for her many miracles, being frequently invoked against children's diseases.

January 4th

PHILADELPHUS, *see* Alphius, Cyrinus and Philadelphus.

PHILASTRIUS
Fourth Century

He left his home, travelled through Italy, combating heresy as he went, and became bishop of Brescia. He even went so far as to denounce as heretical the giving of unscriptural names to stars.

July 18th

PHILEAS
† 304

He was converted to Christianity and appointed bishop of Thmuis in Egypt, his birthplace. During the persecution by Maximinus, he was tried and beheaded for refusing all compromise with idolatry. Philoromus, a Christian tribune who supported him, died also.

February 4th

PHILEMON and APOLLONIUS
Fourth Century

The legends which have gathered around these saints were probably inspired by the fact that Philemon was a musician and a jester. They were martyred during Diocletian's persecution.

March 8th

PHILEMON and APPHIA
First Century

A wealthy citizen of Colossae in Phrygia, he was converted to Christianity by his friend St Paul. Apphia was probably his wife and is referred to in St Paul's Epistle to Philemon. In the East, they are venerated as martyrs.

November 22nd

PHILIBERT
608–685

Son of the bishop of Aire, he entered the abbey of Rebais of which he became abbot. His lack of success, however, led him to leave, and, in 654, he founded the abbey of Jumièges. Other foundations followed and he became responsible for a number of communities.

August 20th

PHILIP BENIZI
1233–1285

He was born of a distinguished Florentine family on August 15th, 1233. He spent five or six years at the University of Paris and then, at his father's wish, studied medicine at Padua, although he would have preferred to read theology. When he returned to Florence in 1254, he gave up the prospect of a brilliant medical career in order to become a lay brother of the Order of Servites. Against his wish he was ordained priest in 1259 and made General of the Order at the age of thirty-four in 1267.

Despite the political troubles which unsettled Italy and the uncertain support of succeeding popes, the Servite order had fifteen houses in Italy and had spread into France and Germany. Later on, under Philip's guidance, it was to spread into Poland, Hungary and India; but despite his important position reached at so early an age, Philip continued to remain humble. The story that he had given his cloak to a leper and that the leper had become cured of his leprosy spread through Italy, and it may have been responsible for his being proposed as a candidate for the papacy in 1269. When he heard the news, Philip fled into the mountains and remained in hiding until all chances of his being elected pope had passed.

He was a great worker for peace and was largely responsible for reconciling the Guelphs (supporters of the pope) to the Ghibellines (supporters of the emperor), whose quarrels had rent Italy. Philip's prayers are said to have caused a man who had insulted him publicly to repent and, ultimately, to join the Servite order (*see* St Peregrine Laziosi). On another occasion, Philip was accosted by two prostitutes. He spoke to them gently and gave them money on condition that they would live honestly for three days. The impression he made upon them was so great that they became the first members of the order of cloistered Servite nuns which Philip founded at Todi.

As he lay dying, Philip asked for the little ivory crucifix which he had had from boyhood. 'There,' he said, pointing to the crucifix, 'is my book. From it I have learned the Christian life and the road to Paradise.' The collect of his mass reminds us of the marvellous example of his humility.   ILLUSTRATION: page 368

August 23rd

PHILIP of HERACLEA
† 304
and his Companions

When the persecuting edicts of Diocletian were published at Heraclea, St Philip was bishop, Severus a priest and Hermes a deacon. They were imprisoned by Bassus the governor; and Justin, his successor, moved them to Adrianople where they were burned to death.

October 22nd

PHILIP de las CASAS, *see* Martyrs of Japan.

PHILIP NERI
1515–1595

Philip was born in Florence in 1515, and there passed his boyhood and adolescence. His friends called him 'Good Pippo', and he seems to have been a boy of deep unobtrusive piety, as good-humored as he was good-hearted. He learnt the faith from his parents, and from the Dominician friars of St Mark's, among whom he came and went familiarly.

In 1533 he left home to join an uncle near Naples, who had a thriving business, but no heir. Philip left after a matter of months, sure he was not called to such a life. He walked to Rome, which he entered without plan or provision, and it was in Rome that he was to live and die.

A Florentine gave him a room, on condition that Philip should spend some little time teaching his sons. He did so, and for the rest he prayed and studied in solitude, eating once a day a meal of bread, water, and olives; sleeping a few hours on the floor, and hanging a few clothes on a cord across the room.

He wandered in the catacombs and around the churches in prayer. At Pentecost, 1544, while he was praying to the Holy Spirit, what seemed to him a ball of fire entered into his heart, causing him paroxysms of fervor and a swelling, though no pain. When his body was examined, after death, two ribs over his heart were found broken, and arched to leave more space within.

After several years, he began to work for souls other than his own. He moved among young men in the squares and shops and banks, using his natural as well as his supernatural powers of attraction, and asking them when they meant to begin doing good. So infectious were Philip's cordiality and good spirits that they accepted the challenge, and many gave to God that place in their lives which is his by right, but which had been denied him before.

At last, Philip's confessor persuaded him to become a priest. In 1551 he was ordained, and soon became known as an apostle of frequent confession and communion. Realizing that if young men and boys might be kept from idleness, they would be spared much temptation, Philip opened his own room to them, and there they would pray, talk and hear discourses on the Gospels, singing and laughing, so that Philip's room came to be known as 'the home of Christian mirth'. When this room proved too small, they used a larger one, which they called 'the Oratory' (i.e. place of prayer).

Philip fought the vices of the time in a humorous way. He showed up vanity by making people into laughing-stocks. Undue introspectiveness and self-preoccupation – there was Luther to show how dangerous these faults might be – he treated in the same way: when an over-earnest penitent asked Philip for permission to wear a hair shirt, Philip said, 'Certainly, provided you wear it outside your clothes.'

When letters arrived from Francis Xavier describing his mission in the East, Philip was tempted to join him and shed his own blood for Christ. But a Cistercian monk advised him otherwise, saying, 'Your Indies are in Rome'. So Philip persevered, becoming the 'Apostle of Rome', and when he was canonized in 1622, there was canonized with him Francis Xavier, 'Apostle of the Indies.'

In 1575 Philip's friend, Pope Gregory XIII, gave him and the priests who followed him a church of their own, which they rebuilt and called the New Church; and, to this day, the New Church is the home of the Roman Oratory. Philip was made Superior of the new community, and so the Congregation of the Oratory was founded. Philip would not found an order – there were plenty already, he said. He directed that the community should live as secular priests without further vows, bound together only by mutual love and common purpose, working for souls by prayer, preaching and the sacraments. He made few rules, but asked that those few be kept; and there are now some forty or fifty oratories whose members strive to bring souls and God together in St Philip's way.

Towards the end of his life, Philip's habit was to say mass in a private chapel, alone but for the server. Just before the Communion, the server would withdraw, leaving Philip alone with our Lord for two hours or more, until the saint was ready to finish the mass.

Early in 1595, Philip, never strong, grew unwell. He said mass and heard confessions as usual on May 25th, but in the early hours of the next day he had a severe haemorrhage, and having blessed the assembled community with a feeble movement of his hand, he closed his eyes in death. As is usual, this day, May 26th, is his feast day, and the opening words of his mass – 'The charity of God is poured forth in our hearts, by his Spirit dwelling within us' – recall not only the miracle mentioned earlier, but also the motive of Philip's whole life – a burning desire to bring souls to God and God into souls.

Philip had come to Rome to find church and city deeply stained by indifference and downright wickedness. He lived there sixty years, not withdrawing from the world, not condemning it, scarcely even criticising it; he fought the mischief by the counter-attractions of holiness, purity, truth, and innocent gaiety. He walked the streets in a shabby cassock, armed with unaffected humility and unpretending love; or he sat in his little room, talking and laughing with all comers. The reform of the Catholic church owed much to the reformer of Rome, its center. Philip's followers, whether as members of the religious orders, or as parents, or as cardinals, or as Oratorians, were a much-needed leaven.

Of all those who have experienced the attraction of St Philip, none can be better known than John Henry Cardinal Newman, who, shortly after his conversion to the Catholic church, went to Rome to study for the priesthood, and there came to know the Oratory and St Philip. He saw in St Philip one who, like himself, was opposed to all imposture and humbug; he saw in him that 'choicest of priests' of which St Philip's Litany speaks; a priest who spoke in his heart with God and was able to speak from his own heart to the hearts of all who heard him – as Newman had done as an Anglican in his Oxford Sermons, and as he was to do again as a Catholic. Newman joined the Oratory, and returned to England with the pope's commission to found a house there, which he did, in Birmingham, in 1848. From there, in the following year, he founded a second English Oratory in London, sending Father Faber and others there for the purpose.

May 26th   ILLUSTRATION: page 401

PHILIP of ZELL   *Eighth Century*
After a pilgrimage to Rome, where he was ordained, this Englishman settled in the Rhineland as a hermit. His *Life* is, however, neither contemporary nor certain.

May 3rd

PHILIP THE APOSTLE   *First Century*
The Gospels of SS Matthew, Mark and Luke tell us nothing of Philip except our Lord's choice of him as an Apostle. St John, however, in youth his fellow towns-man at Bethsaida, and in old age his neighbor in Asia Minor, tells us more of him. It was he of whom Jesus asked how sufficient bread could be provided to feed the five thousand, and who replied that 'two hundred silver pieces could not buy enough.' The Greeks who wished to see Jesus approached Philip, and, at the Last Supper, it was he who asked to be shown the Father.

It is often suggested that Philip the Apostle may be identified with Philip the Deacon, and this is discussed in the life of that saint.   ILLUSTRATION: page 402

May 11th

PHILIP THE DEACON
(surnamed THE EVANGELIST)   *First Century*
He was one of the seven deacons appointed to superin-tend the distribution of relief among the poor Christians of Jerusalem (Acts 6). Shortly afterwards he preached the gospel for the first time in Samaria, where he worked miracles and made many converts whom he baptized, among them Simon Magus (Acts 8). At the bidding of an angel he journeyed to the road running through the desert from Jerusalem to Gaza, where he met, converted and baptised the treasurer of the Ethiopian Queen Candace (*ibid*). Led by the spirit to Azotus he settled at Caesarea, where more than twenty years later St Paul was his guest. 'He had four daughters, unwedded maids who possessed the gift of prophecy' (Acts 21).

These are the biblical data about Philip the Deacon, surnamed the Evangelist, because of the zeal with which he preached the faith. It is possible to suggest that he and Philip the Apostle are identical although this is not the common opinion; but from early times the identification was made by some Christian writers. Was it confusion?

Polycrates, a second century bishop of Ephesus, in-forms us that Philip, 'one of the twelve', was 'buried at Hierapolis along with his two aged virgin daughters' and that a third daughter, who 'lived in the Holy Spirit', i.e. was a prophetess, was buried at Ephesus. It is unlikely that two Philips had daughters and no sons, four prophetesses in one case, at least one prophetess in the other. That Polycrates makes no mention of a fourth daughter is explicable, if she had died or left home before her father left Palestine. An early Roman tradition (third century) places the evangelist and his daughters at Hierapolis, and the Tralles of a variant tradition about him may have been the city only fifteen miles from Hierapolis. Hierapolis, moreover, is close to Ephesus, where St John wrote the Gospel in which Philip is prominent. St Luke, it is true, tells us that the Apostles, the twelve, refused the financial work for which the deacons were chosen; but we cannot expect meticulous accuracy from an ancient historian. If eleven of the twelve stood apart from the deacons and their work, but one, for a special reason, took it up, St Luke need not have felt obliged to mention the fact. Such a reason existed. The question addressed by our Lord to the Apostle Philip about the provision of food suggests that he had a special interest in the supply of provisions and a gift for it, which was precisely the deacons' work. Moreover the institution of deacons was the result of a complaint made by the Greek-speaking Christian Jews. It was Philip, the apostle, to whom the Greeks applied for access to our Lord. He could probably speak Greek, because, as his name suggests, he was possibly of gentile descent: John Hyrcanus had convert-ed forcibly many Gentiles in Galilee. As such he would be designated for the delicate task of mediating between the Christians of Greek and Aramaic speech; but a simple deacon would hardly have taken the initiative of preaching to the Samaritans and baptizing a gentile proselyte. That he did not confirm his Samaritan con-verts but left the imposition of hands to Peter and John can be explained by the Apostles' decision to set this seal of approval on the admission of Samaritans to the church.

Is it merely fanciful to detect in Apostle and Evangelist a strain of experimental, mystical, even ecstatic religion? The Apostle would see God, exhorts Nathaniel to come and see for himself who Jesus is, and, according to one tradition, has a prophetic daughter. The Evangelist receives an angel's command (an illumination, surely, during prayer), is rapt by the Spirit, and transmits this aptitude to prophetic daughters. Surely the Apostle and the Evangelist are the same man.

June 6th

PHILOGONIUS   † 324
In 319 while still a layman – he had been a successful lawyer – he was made bishop of Antioch.

December 20th

PHILOMENA or PHILUMENA *Second Century*
On the strength of the discovery of the skeleton of a girl of about fourteen in a cavity in the catacombs of St Priscilla in Rome and of the inscription on the tiles enclosing the cavity, it was thought that the body of a second century virgin martyr of the name of Philomena had been brought to light. This occurred in 1802. What was the evidence for this inference? The inscription *Lumena Paxte Cum Fi* was understood to have been intended for *Pax Tecum Filumena* ('Peace be with you, Filumena'), the presence in the tomb of a phial with traces of blood was thought to provide evidence of martyrdom, and the symbols on the tiles (arrows, a palm and a flower) were taken to provide further evidence to the same effect.

Archaeology has since proved conclusively that the presence of these phials in tombs is no evidence of martyrdom and that there is a strong possibility that the tiles were re-used for the tomb discovered in 1802; in other words, they refer not to the body they then enclosed but to that of one Philomena in a previous tomb. The consequence of all this is that we know nothing whatever of St Philomena, where her relics are, when she suffered and if indeed she was a martyr. Her veneration was popularized by St John Vianney, 'the Curé d'Ars', who ascribed to her intercession the marvellous answers to his own prayers, and it is likely that without his championing of her little would have been heard of her existence outside Mugnano, where a sumptuous shrine has been built for the bones discovered in 1802, and publicity given to a *Life* of her written on the strength of some valueless private revelations of an Italian nun of the nineteenth century.
August 10th

PHOCAS of ANTIOCH
He is probably that St Phocas, 'the Gardener', buried at St Michael's in Antioch. Such was his triumph over the Old Serpent, that touching his basilica was said to cure snake-bites.
March 5th

PHOCAS THE GARDENER
Phocas, a gardener, lived at Sinope on the Black Sea, and was a martyr. The legend is that he entertained those who had been sent to execute him without their knowing his identity, that they revealed their purpose to him, and that he promised to bring them to Phocas in the morning. That night he labored in his garden for the last time, by digging his grave and quietly making everything ready for the morrow. Next morning he presented himself to his guests and told them who he was, urging them to do their duty. He was beheaded.
September 22nd

PHOEBE *First Century*
In St Paul's Epistle to the Romans, she is mentioned in the last chapter and appears to have been the bearer of the letter from Cenchrae in Corinth, where she was a deaconess, to Rome.
September 3rd

PHOTINA and her Companions
A Samaritan woman, her two sons and six companions were said to have been martyred for confessing their Christianity. Nothing is certainly known of them.
March 20th

PIERIUS † *c.* 310
Sometime head of the catechetical school in Alexandria, he lived through the persecution of Diocletian, and ended his days at Rome.
November 4th

PIONIUS *Third Century?*
A priest and eloquent preacher in Smyrna, he was martyred with Sabina and Asclepiades during the persecution by Decius. They resisted all attempts to weaken their faith, but Pionius was racked, torn and finally burned alive. An eyewitness said that when the fires were put out, Pionius's body showed no signs of torture or burning.
February 1st

PIRAN *Sixth Century*
He was so long mistakenly identified with Kieran of Saighir that his own acts were obscured. Many places in Cornwall bear his name, and tin-miners in the mid-eighteenth century still kept his feast.
March 5th

PIRMINUS † 753
The Moorish invasion of Spain drove him into Germany, where, in 724, he founded the first German Benedictine abbey at Reichenau. Exiled for political reasons, he established the abbeys of Murbach in Alsace and Amorbach in Lower Franconia and became a regionary bishop.
November 3rd

PIUS I *Second Century*
He may have been born a slave. It is certain that he succeeded St Hyginus as pope.
July 11th

PIUS V 1504–1572
He was born on St Antony's day 1504 at Bosco near Alessandria in north Italy, the son of Paolo and Domenica Ghisleri, and baptized Antony. His family was poor, and he was put out to tending sheep; as a richer neighbor offered to pay his fees, however, he was sent to the Dominican school at Bosco and entered the convent at the age of fourteen, taking the name of Michael. He was professed at Vigevano near Milan in 1521 and or-

dained in Genoa in 1528. For some years he was lecturer in theology and philosophy in the Dominican house at Pavia. In 1543 his presence at a general chapter of the province of his order is recorded, where he was noted for his defence of an extreme position in regard to the authority of the Holy See. He was appointed commissary of the Inquisition, first for the Pavia diocese, and later for Bergamo and Como. His activities were extremely unpopular and a great deal of resentment was voiced, and he was even physically molested. An appeal against a confiscation of a large quantity of allegedly heretical books was lodged in Milan and referred to Rome, where the saint won his case and first met and favorably impressed Cardinal Caraffa. In 1551, on that Cardinal's recommendation, he was summoned to Rome by Pope Julius III to become commissary-general of the Inquisition. In 1551 the irascible Cardinal Caraffa became Pope Paul IV and, during the next year, appointed Michael Ghisleri bishop of Sutri and Nepi. He was already a high official of the province of his Order as well as of the Inquisition, but he was reluctant to accept the episcopate, which the pope said would 'attach a chain to his feet, to prevent his creeping back into the cloister'. The next year he was created a cardinal, and the year after grand inquisitor. The pope was now becoming increasingly morose and violent, and it was the inquisitor who was sometimes constrained to modify his more extreme directives, such as those against heretical books. By contrast the next pope, Pius IV (a Medici), was so worldly that the saint retired to his second bishopric, Mondovi in Lombardy. But in 1565 the pope died, and, owing largely to the influence of St Charles Borromeo, Cardinal Ghisleri was elected pope during a conclave singularly free from outside interference, and took the name Pius V.

The election was largely unexpected though not unwelcome to the emperor and the king of Spain, and was definitely a victory for the reforming party: whatever his dignities the new pope had always lived as much like a simple friar as he could, keeping a small household, walking in preference to riding, acknowledging his humble origins. He was not a first popular with the Roman people. But his assiduity in attending liturgical functions, his evident personal piety, his habit of visiting the seven basilicas of Rome on foot, his small entourage, his refusal to push any member of his family, the disbanding of most of the papal army, generous almsgiving: all these served to make him both a familiar and a popular figure.

The reforms recommended by the council of Trent were taken up by Pius V almost immediately on election. The breviary and missal were overhauled, while the Vulgate and the Greek New Testament were revised. A new edition of the works of St Thomas Aquinas was prepared, and the Tridentine catechism was translated into many languages. The residence of bishops as well as that of the lower clergy was enforced, all traces of simony removed from the still corrupt Roman curia, the congregation of the Index was established, and a clean sweep of moral abuses was attempted: severe canonical penalties were even imposed on those attending bull-fights. In Rome, itself, an attempt was made to stamp out prostitution, but it caused such ruin to trade in general that the attempt had to be modified; heavy punishments, however, were imposed for adultery and blasphemy.

By the standards of his time Pius was neither obscurantist nor violently fanatical. He was not insensible to the arts, and was the patron of Vasari, della Porta, and Vignola, as well as the sponsor of sensible recommendations regarding church music; the public burning of heretics (auto-da-fé) became increasingly rare. But in political matters he had little flair; he even considered handing the whole matter over to a committee of cardinals. Recommendations such as that to a French commander fighting the Huguenots, to give no quarter sounded definitely barbarous even at the time, and created an unfortunate impression. The affairs of Mary Queen of Scots and the excommunication of Queen Elizabeth were not handled with particular foresight. But Pius would not let political considerations interfere with matters of principle or with the administration of justice: the case of the unfortunate Bartolomeo Carranza, archbishop of Toledo, condemned as a heretic by the Spanish inquisition, worried him enormously. Against the insistent protests of King Philip II, the archbishop was brought to Rome for re-trial, and Pius seemed to have become convinced of his innocence, though the case was still pending when the pope died.

In spite of his unworldliness, he was successful in his chief political aim. The league against the increasingly menacing Turkish sea-power between himself, the king of Spain and the Venetian Republic was signed in May 1571, and a combined fleet under Don John of Austria defeated the Turks at Lepanto, crushing their sea-power, which never recovered.

Pius is said to have seen a vision of the battle as it was taking place, and after receiving the news of victory, felt that his life's work was done. He died some months later, on May 1st, 1572.

This six-year pontificate made the reforms recommended by the eighteen-year council of Trent a reality, and gave a complexion to church government which did not alter materially for 250 years. He was beatified by Clement X in 1672, canonized by Clement XI in 1712, and his relics are venerated in the Dominican church at Bosco, which he founded.

May 5th ILLUSTRATION: page 403

In the first confident years of the twentieth century a peasant was elected to the papacy for the first time since the middle ages. No pope since the council of Trent had had so full an experience of the pastoral life of the church; nor has any pope since then left a more personal stamp upon it. *Instaurare omnia in Christo:* to give history its fulfilment by resuming everything in Christ: in the encyclical *E Supremi Apostolatus* of October 4th, 1903, two months after his election, Pius X proclaimed his purpose in the phrase with which he had proclaimed it as patriarch of Venice. The preparation of children at an early age for the reception of the holy Eucharist, and its frequent reception all through life, were his most earnest recommendations; we have come to take them for granted now, but they were not taken for granted then. The encyclical *Acerbo Nimis* of April 15th, 1906, *(On the Teaching of Christian Doctrine)* called for the systematic catechetical instruction of everyone, adults as well as children, as a second fortification. He was the defender of the integrity of the faith, seeing with holy simplicity the significance of those tendencies in theology and philosophy which came to be known collectively as modernism, and condemning them in the decree *Lamentabili* of July 1907 and the very long encyclical *Pascendi* of September 8th, 1908, the substance of which has to be publicly professed to this day by those who teach in Catholic seminaries. In a hundred ways his hand was felt in dioceses and parishes, seminaries and religious houses all over the world. He reformed the Calendar and the Breviary. He reformed church music with his *Motu Proprio* of November 22nd, 1903, calling for the universal use of the Gregorian chant; he founded Institutes in Rome for musical and biblical studies; he initiated the immense work of codifying canon law.

Born on June 2nd, 1835, Giuseppe Melchiorre Sarto was the second and eldest surviving son of the ten children of the parish clerk of the Venetian village of Riese. Margherita Sanson was a seamstress, half the age of Giovanni-Battista Sarto when she married him. Giuseppe was not yet seventeen when his father died; his mother was left in even greater poverty than before, but she would not listen to his suggestion that, in order to maintain the family, he should abandon the vocation of which he had been certain since his confirmation at the age of ten. When he was eleven he had been given a place in the high school at Castelfranco, five miles away; for four years he had walked the distance twice a day, usually barefoot. By the time his father died he had already been attending the seminary at Padua for two years. He was ordained priest at Castelfranco on September 28th, 1858, when he was twenty-three. There followed seventeen years in country parishes in the diocese of Treviso – nine as a curate, eight as a parish

priest; years spent very close to the poor, for whom he was constantly devising ways of escape from financial difficulty as well as from ungodliness. That was the vocation he believed to be his; in a private letter he described as 'a misfortune' the summons to Treviso in 1875, to become all at once chancellor of the diocese, rector of its seminary, a canon and a domestic prelate.

In 1884, Leo XIII, whom he was to succeed, appointed him bishop of Mantua, and he immediately encountered that resistance from secular authority which he was to experience again on his appointment to be cardinal patriarch of Venice, in 1893, as well as in the conclave at which he was elected pope, ten years afterwards. It was nearly six months before he could take possession of the see of Mantua, and more than a year before he could go to Venice. In the conclave of 1903 the prince-bishop of Cracow, Cardinal Puzyna, informed the Cardinals that the Austrian Emperor claimed a veto, against Cardinal Rampolla, who had been Leo XIII's secretary of state. At the first scrutiny, in the morning of August 1st, Cardinal Sarto had received only five votes; the American Cardinal Gibbons, with others, persuaded him not to veto himself, and at the seventh scrutiny, on August 4th, he received fifty votes out of sixty-two. As pope he made it clear, in the Constitution *Commissum Nobis*, that no political attempts to influence future conclaves could be tolerated. He set himself also to ease the relations between the church and the Italian kingdom. He re-opened the way to Catholic participation in the political life of Italy, giving the bishops permission to suspend at their discretion the decree of the Holy Office which forbade the faithful to vote in elections; and when he set himself completely to reorganize the Congregations and Tribunals of the Roman Curia, in the Constitution *Sapienti Consilio* of 1908, it was a sign that the loss of the states of the church was accepted; there was no longer any need for the framework of a civil government. The French had gone out of their way to make it plain that they would never again uphold the patrimony of Peter, and the pope was stern when the Napoleonic Concordat was repudiated in 1905, accepting a complete separation of church and state in the knowledge that poverty for the church in France was to be preferred to the proposed dependence.

Amid all these and many other intricate matters, Pius X never felt himself really at home. He was 'a prisoner in the Vatican' not because the Papal States had been lost but because he belonged in the cooler air of the Venetian Plain. Once he burst into tears on meeting a friend from the old days, exclaiming, 'Look how they have dressed me up!' There are many such stories. His sisters, who had begun to keep house for him when he was a parish priest, moved to Rome to do his laundry and mending;

when he was ill his priest-nephew, son of the inn-keeper of Riese, was summoned to give him holy Communion. He brought his chaplains and his cook from Venice, to keep about him as much of the old life as he could, with his Venetian friend, Lorenzo Perosi, to look after the music. He lived frugally at the Vatican, because that was the only way he knew how to live. He swept away much petty ceremony, broke with many traditions of formality, not only from humility but to make himself less ill at ease; he carried a large nickel watch instead of asking his attendants to tell him the time, and when he died they found in the pockets of his white soutane what might have been found in the pockets of a school-boy: a pen-knife and a stump of pencil. It was 1914. On the eleventh anniversary of the pope's election Europe had gone to war; on August 8th he became ill; he said his last mass on the feast of the Assumption and died on August 20th, his heart broken, it was said, at the agony of mankind. His cause was introduced only nine years later; he was beatified on June 3rd, 1951 and canonized on May 29th, 1954; only one other Pope since the thirteenth century has been canonized.

September 3rd   ILLUSTRATION: page 404

PLACID   *Sixth Century*
The son of a Roman patrician, Placid was entrusted as a child to the care of St Benedict at Subiaco. His wisdom and virtue made him dear to St Benedict, and he proba-bly accompanied his master to Monte Cassino, which is said to have been given to St Benedict by Placid's father, Tertullus.

October 5th

PLATO   † 814
He entered the monastery of Symboleon on Mount Olympus in Bithynia, and in 770, at the age of thirty-six became abbot. When he visited Constantinople in 775, he refused many honors, but he agreed eventually to become abbot of the Sakkudion. He was persecuted by the Emperor for opposing his divorce, and he was not entirely freed from imperial persecution until three years before his death.

April 4th

PLECHELM, *see* Wiro, Plechelm and Oteger.

PLUTARCH, POTAMIAENA   † 202
  and their Companions
Members of a catechetical school presided over by Ori-gen at Alexandria, they were martyred in the persecu-tions of Severus. Plutarch, because he was well-known, suffered first. Heraclides, Hero and Serenus were be-headed, while Herais, a young maiden, was burned. Marcella and Potamiaena were mother and daughter, Potamiaena being lowered into a cauldron of boiling pitch. Afterwards one of the guards, Basilides, received baptism and was beheaded.

June 28th

POEMEN   *Fifth Century*
With his brothers he retired to the desert of Skete in Egypt where they lived in characteristic austerity. After the death of his elder brother, he governed the small community in the wanderings enforced upon it by hostile tribes.

August 27th

POLLIO   † 304
A lector in the church of Cybalae in Lower Pannonia (now Mikanovici in Yugoslavia), he was burned alive for refusing to sacrifice to the gods.

April 28th

POLYCARP of SMYRNA   † *c.* 155
St Polycarp was bishop of Smyrna and a personal disci-ple of St John the Evangelist. We can still read the letter written to him by the martyr St Ignatius of Antioch, St Polycarp's own letter to the Philippians, and a con-temporary account of Polycarp's martyrdom; so that centering in Polycarp we have precious documents of the earliest days of Christianity.

He had been the revered bishop of Smyrna for many years when, during the persecutions of the Emperor Marcus Aurelius, he was betrayed. The chief of the police and his son at first treated the old bishop gently, and took him into their own chariot to try to persuade him to be reasonable. But Polycarp was firm, and when they came to the public place of trial he was pushed roughly out, and brought before the proconsul. The proconsul tried bullying and threats of the wild beasts, but Polycarp remained adamant, offering indeed to instruct the proconsul in the doctrines of Christianity. When it was proclaimed that 'Polycarp has confessed he is a Christian' the crowd howled with rage, demand-ing that a lion should be set on him, but this could not be done as the games were officially closed. So they rushed to get fuel that Polycarp might be burned. But when the fire was lit the flames made a sort of arc meeting above his head, and not apparently harming him. So he was stabbed to death. It was thought prudent to burn the body of the saint; but afterwards the Christians came and gathered up his bones and bore them away.

January 26th

POLYEUCTUS   † 259
During persecution at Melitene in Armenia, this newly-converted soldier, undeterred by the desperate appeals of his wife Paulina and his family, confessed his Christianity and was beheaded. He was the inspiration for Corneille's great tragedy, *Polyeucte*.

February 13th

POMPILIO PIRROTTI   1710–1756
Teaching was his vocation, and he worked devotedly in Italy as one of the clerks regular of the Religious Schools.
July 15th

PONTIAN   *Third Century*
Succeeding St Urban I as pope in *c.* 230, he was banished together with the anti-pope, Hippolytus, to Sardinia during the persecutions of Maximinus. He is reputed to have suffered martyrdom there. *See* St Hippolytus.
November 19th

PONTIUS   *Third Century*
Deacon to St Cyprian of Carthage, whom he accompanied into exile at Curubis, he is known solely for his *Life of Cyprian.*
March 8th

PONTIUS   *Third Century*
Supposed to have been the son of a Roman senator, he converted the Emperor Philip, after whose death he was arrested at Cimella, now Cimiez, near Nice, and beheaded. But even his very existence is dubious.
May 14th

POPPO   978–1048
A Flemish monk, he advised the emperor, St Henry II, reformed various monasteries for the great reformer Richard of Saint Vanne, and finally became abbot-general of several monasteries in Lotharingia.
January 25th

PORCARIUS and his Companions   † *c.* 732
St Porcarius was the abbot of Lérins when it was attacked by Moorish raiders. Having foreseen the raid, he sent as many as possible to safety, and met his death with the remainder.
August 12th

PORPHYRY   † 420
A monk of Skete, then a hermit in Palestine, his patient devotion during a long illness in Jerusalem was rewarded by a miraculous cure. He became bishop of Gaza while it was still heathen, but he eventually gained the emperor's consent to the destruction of the temples and images. His *Life*, written by Mark the deacon, is an important source of information about paganism in the Christian east.
February 26th

POSSIDIUS   *Fifth Century*
A pupil of St Augustine at Hippo, he became bishop of Calama. After many struggles against the Donatists and Pelagianism, he died in exile.
May 16th

POTAMIAENA, *see* Plutarch, Potamiaena and their Companions.

POTAMION   *Fourth Century*
Bishop of Heraclea and an opponent of the Arians, he was badly maimed in 310, in the persecution under Maximinus Daia. Thirty years later he was again persecuted (by the Arian Emperor Constantius) and beaten to death.
May 18th

POTHINUS and his Companions   † 177
The reign of the Emperor Marcus Aurelius is marked by the widespread persecution of Christians, a persecution which he himself, philosopher and just man though he was in many ways, saw fit to encourage. The letter from the churches of Vienne and Lyons, written after a violent outburst of persecution in that district in 177, is addressed to the churches of Asia and Phrygia, and it gives a detailed description of the sufferings of the martyrs under the leadership of Pothinus, bishop of Lyons, and Sanctus, deacon of the church at Vienne.

Of Pothinus himself we are told that he was over ninety and already very ill when he was brought before the tribunal. Nevertheless he stoutly 'bore witness' and for his recalcitrance, was treated with every indignity, the people in the court hitting and kicking him or throwing at him anything they could lay their hands on: 'all thinking that anyone was guilty of great offence and impiety if he was behindhand in brutality towards him.' Pothinus died two days later in prison. This frenzy of hatred and insane conviction that was felt to be fulfilling the words of our Lord – 'the time is coming when anyone who puts you to death will claim that he is performing an act of worship to God' – was intensified by the repetition of the common reports that Christians ate their own children and indulged in similar perversions. Every effort was made to induce the sufferers to deny their faith, with little effect. Sanctus endured manifold torments. Biblias had given way, but suddenly seemed to come to herself, denied her own denial and 'was added to the company of the martyrs.' Among those who suffered were Vettius Epagathus, Alexander, Maturus, Attalus, Ponticus, Blandina, and many other martyrs whose names we do not know.
June 2nd

PRAEJECTUS or PRIX   † 676
Under his charitable, wise and diligent rule as bishop of Clermont, religious fervor became general. Later however he was thought to be involved in the death of Hector, *patricius* of Marseilles, and was assassinated with the abbot St Amarin.
January 25th

PRAETEXTATUS or PRIX   † 586
During his thirty-five years' rule as bishop of Rouen, he became embroiled in the complicated feuds of Clotaire I's

sons and their associates. He was banished, reinstated and finally assassinated.

February 24th

PRAXEDES

She was thought to be the sister of St Pudentiana, but although she is buried near her in the catacomb of Priscilla it is unlikely that the legend of the two sisters is true.

July 21st

PRIMUS and FELICIAN   † *c. 297*

Patrician brothers of Rome, they escaped persecution for some time, but when Primus was eighty they were arrested, tortured and executed. They were buried in the Via Nomentana, outside the walls of the city, and the translation of their relics by Pope Theodore in 640 to a basilica in Rome was the first case of its kind.

June 9th

PRISCA, *see* Aquila and Prisca.

PRISCA

A virgin and martyr, she was the subject of an early cult in Rome, and is said to be buried in the catacomb of Priscilla.

January 18th

PRISCILLA   *First Century*

Probably wife of the martyr Manius Acilius Glabrio and mother of St Pudens. Though she was foundress of the most ancient and important Roman catacomb, little is known of her.

January 16th

PRISCUS or PRIX   *Third Century*
and his Companions

Priscus and Cottus were natives of Besançon, who in the persecution of Emperor Aurelian fled to Auxerre, only to suffer martyrdom there with a number of others.

May 26th

PRIX, *see* Praetextatus.

PRIX, *see* Praejectus.

PROBUS, *see* Andronicus, Tarachus and Probus.

PROCESSUS and MARTINIAN

These two martyrs are buried in the south transept of St Peter's, Rome. The legend asserting that they were the gaolers of SS Peter and Paul and were converted by them is probably untrue.

July 2nd

PROCLUS   † *446*

Although many thought him the best person to succeed Atticus, the archbishop of Constantinople, he had to remain a by-stander and critic of a number of unworthy occupants of the see before he was himself elected in 434. He showed a tactful gentleness in dealing with heretics which reconciled many of them to the church.

October 24th

PROCOPIUS   † *303*

There is a celebrated account of this martyr by Eusebius, bishop of Caesarea. He was the first of the Palestinian martyrs persecuted by Diocletian.

July 8th

PROCULUS 'THE SOLDIER'   † *c. 304*
and PROCULUS of BOLOGNA   † *542*

St Proculus 'the Soldier' seems to have been an officer in the army of Diocletian who suffered martyrdom at Bologna. Another Proculus, a native and bishop of the city, also suffered martyrdom there at the time of Totila the Goth.

June 1st

PROSPER of AQUITAINE   *Fifth Century*

A native of Aquitaine, he engaged in the Pelagian controversy on the side of St Augustine, and became secretary to St Leo the Great. He was a layman.

June 25th

PROSPER of REGGIO   *Fifth Century*

Little is known beyond the name and approximate date of this bishop of Reggio.

June 25th

PROTASE, *see* Gervaise and Protase.

PROTERIUS   † *457*

He was elected patriarch of Alexandria in 451, when the city was plagued by Eutychian heretics led by Timothy 'the cat' and Peter 'the croaker'. They constantly threatened his life, and when finally he was driven to take sanctuary, the mob broke in and stabbed him.

February 28th

PROTUS and HYACINTH

In 1845, the tomb of St Hyacinth was discovered at St Hermes or Basilla on the Old Salarian Way. The condition of his remains showed that he had been martyred by burning, but we know nothing else for certain. Protus was buried nearby.

September 11th

PRUDENTIUS of TROYES   † *861*

Elected bishop of Troyes, he was a well-known theologian, and became engaged in a controversy on predestination.

April 6th

PTOLEMAEUS and LUCIUS   *Second Century*

Ptolemaeus, a Roman, converted a dissolute woman to Christianity and persuaded her to separate from her pagan husband. The disappointed husband reported Ptolemaeus to the magistrates, and he was condemned for being a Christian. For expressing sympathy with him at his trial, a bystander, Lucius, was also martyred.

October 19th

PUBLIA
Fourth Century

A rich widow of Antioch, where she established a community of widows and virgins, she became involved in a dispute with Julian the Apostate.
October 9th

PUBLIUS
Fourth Century

Son of a senator in Zeugma on the Euphrates. He became first a hermit and then gathered a large community which he ruled in severe asceticism and intense devotion. He is chiefly honored in Greece.
January 25th

PUDENTIANA and PUDENS
First or Second Century?

St Pudens was supposed to have been a Roman senator, and father of Pudentiana, both of whom suffered martyrdom.
May 19th

PULCHERIA
399–453

At the age of fifteen she was made to share the throne with her brother, Theodosius II, because he was so ineffective a ruler. When Theodosius married, his wife secured Pulcheria's banishment, but on his death in 450 Pulcheria became empress and nominated as emperor a general, whom she married on condition that he allowed her to retain her vow of virginity.
September 10th

QUADRATUS
Second Century

This bishop of Athens had been a disciple of the Apostles, and when Emperor Hadrian visited Athens, Quadratus read a treatise to him in defence of Christianity. Modern scholars, however, doubt the identification of the apologist with the bishop, or of either with the disciple.
May 26th

QUENTIN or QUINTINUS

He is reputed to have left Rome with St Lucian of Beauvais on a missionary journey to Gaul. He settled in Amiens, where he was later imprisoned and taken to Augusta Veromanduorum (the present St Quentin) to be tortured and beheaded.
October 31st

QUIRINUS
† 308

As bishop of Siscia, now Sisak in Croatia, he was arrested under the edicts of Diocletian and was taken to Sabaria (now Szombathely in Hungary), where he was drowned. His body was later transferred to the catacomb of St Sebastian in Rome.
June 4th

QUITERIA
Fifth Century

She is invoked against dog bites and is supposed to have been the daughter of a Galician prince who fled rather than marry a pagan. She was overtaken at Aire and beheaded by her father's agents.
May 22nd

RADBOD
† 918

Of royal blood, he was educated by his uncle bishop Gunther of Cologne, and became bishop of Utrecht.
November 29th

RADEGUND
518–587

St Radegund, queen and foundress of the monastery of the Holy Cross at Poitiers, stands out as a figure of radiant, supernaturally human and humane goodness among the monstrous savagery of her Frankish royal relations. She was born in 518, probably at Erfurt in Thuringia, the daughter of King Berthaire. By murder and war she came into the hands of Clotaire I, king of Neustria, son of Clovis, the first Christian king of the Franks. Clotaire, who was outstanding even among Frankish royalties for sensuality and cruelty, eventually married her (possibly polygamously); but when he murdered her brother she left him and went to Poitiers, where she founded her abbey (refusing to be the first abbess herself but appointing her friend Agnes instead). Here she lived a most holy and charitable life, praying, encouraging learning, and doing all she could to promote peace in a world full of meaningless wars.

She was very austere to herself and very kind to her nuns; among other things she used to clean their shoes for them. She had a great love of cleanliness, installed baths in the convent, and on one occasion cured a sick nun by giving her a hot bath (her contemporaries thought this was a miracle). The great event in the life of the abbey was the arrival from Constantinople, of a relic of the Holy Cross, sent by the Emperor Justin. For its reception Radegund's friend Venantius Fortunatus wrote the hymn *Vexilla Regis*, which is still sung in the Passiontide Office. She died peacefully in 587, and her tomb, in the church dedicated to her at Poitiers, is one of the great places of pilgrimage of France.
August 13th

RAINERIUS of PISA
† 1160

After a dissolute youth, his repentence was so great that he wept for three days and became blind. His sight was restored, and although he never joined any religious order he was living in the monastery of St Vitus at Pisa when he died.
June 17th

RALPH or RAOUL † 866

Son of Count Raoul of Cahors, he was educated by the abbot of Solignac, and in 840 became archbishop of Bourges. He founded several religious houses, wrote a book of Pastoral Instructions, and encouraged daily communion by the laity.

June 21st

RAPHAEL THE ARCHANGEL

Raphael was one of the seven archangels who stood before God. His name signifies 'God has healed', and this healing function is brought out by his rôle in the story of Tobias, where he restores sight to the old man and guards the young one in his journey. In the mass of his feast the Epistle is taken from the Book of Tobias, and in the Gospel Raphael is identified with the angel who moved the healing waters of the pool near Jerusalem – 'and he that went down first into the pool after the water had been moved was healed of his infirmity' (John 5:1–4).

See also Angels and Archangels.

October 24th　　　ILLUSTRATION: page 405

RAYMUND, *see* William, Stephen, Raymund and their Companions.

RAYMUND NONNATUS 1204–1240

For the reasons given in the life of St Peter Nolasco, the traditional account of St Raymund's life cannot be regarded as reliable. He was supposed to have been born at Portel in Catalonia in 1204, and to have been called non-natus (not born) because he was taken from his mother's body after her death in labor. For this reason, St Raymund has been taken as the patron saint of midwives.

From an early age, he was determined to work among those Christians who had fallen into the hands of the Mohammedans, and he joined, therefore, the Order of our Lady of Mercy (the Mercedarians) which had been founded by SS Raymund of Penafort and Peter Nolasco. He was sent to Africa, where he devoted all his resources to ransoming those Christians who were imprisoned by the Mohammedans. When his resources were exhausted, St Raymund offered himself as a hostage for those whom he could ransom in no other way; and he succeeded not only in strengthening the faith of the Christian captives, but in converting some of their Mohammedan jailers. This was too much for the infidels, for it was a crime punishable by death to talk of religion to a Mohammedan; and they proceeded to put St Raymund to the torture. As they were unwilling to kill him for fear of forfeiting his ransom, his lips were pierced by a red-hot iron and padlocked, the governor, himself, keeping the key and only allowing the padlock to be unlocked at meal times. St Raymund was kept in this condition for eight months, until St Peter Nolasco sent his ransom and orders for him to return. Soon after his return to Spain the saint was made a Cardinal, but he still refused to live in any but the most humble and austere way. Thereupon the pope summoned him to Rome. He obeyed but again insisted upon travelling as a poor man. He was never to reach the pope, for he died on the way, near Barcelona in 1240 at the early age of thirty-six. In the collect of his mass, God is asked to deliver us from the slavery of sin as St Raymund delivered 'thy faithful held in bondage by the infidels.'

August 31st　　　ILLUSTRATION: page 406

RAYMUND of PENAFORT 1175–1275

Born at Penafort in Catalonia, at twenty he was already teaching philosophy at Barcelona. He became a succesful lawyer, but it was not until he was forty seven that he joined the Dominicans and compiled at their request the first collection of cases of conscience. He preached the war against the Moors, and in 1230 was summoned to Rome to become Pope Gregory IX's confessor. Here he compiled his five books of papal and conciliar decrees, *The Decretals*, which had been commissioned by Pope Gregory and were approved in 1234. Elected third master general of the Dominicans in 1238, he resigned after two years and spent the last two years of his long life converting the Moors.

St Raymund is often held to have been one of the founders of the Mercedarian order, and this claim is discussed in the article on St Peter Nolasco.

January 23rd　　　ILLUSTRATION: page 407

RAYMUND of TOULOUSE † 1118

After his wife's death, he built an almshouse for thirteen destitute priests and became a canon of the church of St Sernin.

July 8th

REGINA or REINE

She was supposed to have been tortured and beheaded in Autun by the prefect Olybrius for refusing to marry him.

September 7th

REGULUS or RIEUL Third Century

He was probably first bishop of Senlis, and he is patron of that city; but all certain knowledge of him perished when Senlis Cathedral and its archives were burned.

March 30th

REINELDIS † c. 680

The daughter of St Amalberga, she lived, according to her legend, at Saintes, with a subdeacon called Grimoald and Gundulf, her servant. They were killed in a raid and are accounted martyrs.

July 16th

REINOLD   *Tenth Century*

A monk of St Pantaleon in Cologne, his zealous supervision of building operation antagonized the workmen, who killed him with hammers. He is, nevertheless, honored as patron of stone masons.
January 7th

REMACLUS   † *c.* 675

The first abbot of the monastery founded at Solignac by St Eligius, he was successively abbot of Cugnon in Luxembourg and of Stavelot and Malmedy. He may have been a missionary bishop.
September 3rd

REMBERT   † 888

A monk of the Torhout monastery near Bruges, his birthplace, he succeeded St Anskar as archbishop of Hamburg and Bremen. He began the work of converting the Northern Slavs, and redeemed many of their slaves.
February 4th

REMIGIUS   † *c.* 530

Bishop of Rheims, possibly the seventeenth, Remigius (Remi) owes his fame to the fact that he baptized the Frankish king, Clovis. Our earliest knowledge of him is a letter from St Sidonius Apollinaris, flattering his literary talent. When, probably in 482, Clovis became king of the Franks, Remigius wrote him a letter of advice which proves that Clovis was already favorable to the Catholic church. The king's conversion, however, was delayed until his prayer to the God of his Catholic wife defeated the Alamanni – probably 497. A little later, the exact date is unknown, Remigius solemnly baptized Clovis in his cathedral.

We possess two other letters written by Remigius; and the shorter version of his will is substantially genuine. After an episcopate of at least seventy years he died about 530.
October 1st

RENÉ GOUPIL, *see* Martyrs of North America.

REPARATA

She may have been martyred at Caesarea during the persecution of Decius.
October 8th

RESPICIUS, *see* Trypho, Respicius and Nympha.

RESTITUTA of SORA   *Third Century*

Many incredible stories are recounted about this high-born Roman girl who may have been martyred at Sora.
May 27th

RHIPSIME, GAIANA   † *c.* 312?
  and their Companions

These, the first martyrs of the Armenian church, were supposed to have been members of a Roman community of consecrated virgins. A most unlikely legend has it that Diocletian wanted to marry Rhipsime, and that the community moved with her when she was obliged to flee from such unwanted attentions. Their martyrdom came when Rhipsime similarly refused King Tiridates of Armenia.
September 29th

RICHARD, 'KING'   † 720

Father of SS Willibald, Winebald and Walburga, he died at Lucca on a family pilgrimage to Rome. His fictitious name and title were piously invented by the people of Lucca to match the veneration in which he was held.
February 7th

RICHARD of ANDRIA   *Twelfth Century?*

This Englishman may have been bishop of Andria in Apulia during the papacy of Adrian IV, another Englishman.
June 9th

RICHARD WYCHE   *c.* 1200–1253
  or RICHARD of CHICHESTER

Richard was born about 1200 at Wyche (the present Droitwich) of a family that had seen better days. After managing to set the family estates in order – even working as a ploughman to do so – he showed signs of a vocation for the priesthood and some intellectual promise, so he was sent to Oxford as a poor scholar. There he had a brilliant academic career and became one of the first chancellors of the University. He was a close friend of an Oxford contemporary, St Edmund of Abingdon.

In 1244 he was elected bishop of Chichester. His election was opposed by the king, but the pope consecrated him in 1245 and forced Henry III to accept him under threat of excommunication. He was a model bishop, austere in his personal life and exacting in the standard of conduct he expected from his clergy.

He was one of the earliest English bishops to patronize the new order of Preachers, and his confessor was a Dominican who wrote his biography after his death in 1253.
April 3rd

RICHARDIS   *Ninth Century*

This daughter of the count of Alsace became Empress of the Holy Roman Empire by her marriage to Charles the Fat. When her husband suspected her of infidelity, legend relates that she claimed the ordeal by fire and passed through it unscathed. She separated from her husband and eventually retired to a convent, she had herself founded at Andlau.
September 18th

RICHARIUS or RIQUIER   *Seventh Century*
Born near Amiens, he was converted by two Irish priests and studied in England. Later, he retired from the monastery he had founded at Celles, to live as a recluse.
April 26th

RICHIMIR   *Eighth Century*
Little is known of him except that he settled with his followers in the Loire valley, and later built a monastery at Saint-Rigomer-des-Bois, which he ruled until his death.
January 17th

RICTRUDIS   † 688
Of a noble Gascon family, she married St Adalbald of Ostrevant, and their children, Mauruntius, Eusebia, Clotsind and Adalsind were all later revered as saints. After the murder of Adalbald, she founded the double monastery of Marchiennes, where she was succeeded as abbess by Clotsind.
May 12th

RIGOBERT of RHEIMS   *Eighth Century*
Abbot of Orbais, he became archbishop of Rheims until he was banished to Gascony by Charles Martel. He was later recalled. He endured all tribulations with the greatest patience and unimpaired religious devotion.
January 4th

RIQUIER, *see* Richarius.

RITA   1381–1457
The standard works of reference are generally a little guarded about St Rita of Cascia, since the first biography of her appeared 150 years after her death. Nevertheless she is widely venerated as 'the saint of the impossible', 'the advocate of desperate causes', and those who come across her image, whether it be a battered little effigy in St Philippe du Roule in Paris or a splendid altar in Santo Spirito in Florence, do so with the sense of gratitude appropriate to so necessary and irreplaceable a vocation as that to which her name has been given.

She was born of peasant stock in 1381, and according to the story, her wish to enter the Augustinian convent at Cascia was frustrated by her parents' order that she should marry. The husband chosen for her turned out to be a dissolute boor, who terrorized her and her children for eighteen years, until at last his heart was touched by her exemplary patience. Too late, however; for shortly after, he was killed in a brawl, under circumstances which made her two sons vow to avenge him. She prayed that they might die rather than carry out their purpose, and her prayers were answered. Furthermore, we are told that they died forgiving; and thus left the way plain for St Rita to return, for the last twenty-

five years of her life, to the convent which she was at last permitted to enter, and in which her charity was only equalled by the austerity of her life.

We are to consider her an emblem of patient obedience; and we are to remember that her flower is the rose. Her reality, indeed, like the scent of the rose, is something easier to perceive than to analyze. But it has persisted like the rose she asked for when she lay dying. Blossoming in winter, it achieves the impossible.
May 22nd

ROBERT BELLARMINE   1542–1621
This bishop and doctor of the church is venerated as one of the greatest Catholic apologists of all time. He was the third son of Vincenzo Bellarmine, chief magistrate of the little Tuscan town of Montepulciano, where he was born October 4th, 1542. His mother was Cynthia Cervini, sister of Pope Marcellus II. As a pupil at the Jesuit college in his native town, Robert gave promise of a brilliant career, and was destined by his father for the profession of medicine. When, however, he entered the Society of Jesus in 1560 it was with his father's consent.

Indifferent health during his course of philosophy at the Roman College did not hinder his being recognized as the outstanding student of his year. From Rome he was sent to teach boys for four years in the Jesuit colleges at Florence and Mondovi. He now mastered Greek by being set to teach it to his classes. He was frequently invited to preach in famous pulpits although he was not yet a priest, but from the outset he showed that he was a born orator. He studied theology first at Padua and later at Louvain, where he was ordained priest in 1570. Courses of sermons which he preached at Louvain had striking success. Protestants came over from England to hear him, and there were many conversions. His audiences were attracted by a compelling spiritual quality and intellectual maturity which offset his unimpressive appearance: he was a little man, and used to stand on a stool in the high pulpits of Flanders.

As a professor of theology at the Jesuit college in Louvain, he was noted for his devotion to the writings of St Thomas Aquinas. In his lectures he conducted an effective but charitable campaign against the doctrines of the Louvain theologian Michael Baius, from whose teaching Jansenism later originated. Robert also inspired his students with a love for the study of Hebrew, and wrote a simplified Hebrew grammar for their use. His vast reading at this time in the works of the Fathers of the church and other ecclesiastical writers bore fruit in his celebrated work *On Ecclesiastical Writers* (1623).

By the end of his Louvain period he was equipped to fill the difficult post of Professor of Controversy at the Roman College. This lectureship had been founded by the Jesuits to provide an answer in the language of the day to Protestant attacks. These were directed chiefly against the nature and authority of the church and the sacraments. For eleven years, Robert labored at this course with conspicuous success. Many of his students were destined to become missionaries in England and Germany, and some of them were to shed their blood for the Catholic faith in England. The lectures were first published at Ingolstadt, 1586–1593, under the title *Disputations on Controversies of the Christian Faith against the Heretics of this Time*. There were twenty editions of this great work during the author's lifetime, and many later. They were the most complete defense of the Catholic faith that the church possessed, and for three centuries were the armory of preachers and writers. Popes and bishops praised them repeatedly. In the divine office for his feast St Robert's leading rôle in the defense of the see of Rome is specially noted. The *Controversies* were so remarkable for the fairness and courtesy with which they presented the Protestant position that some Catholic voices were raised in protest; but the Protestants in England and Germany organized special courses of lectures and sermons to answer Bellarmine.

Other important tasks which occupied St Robert about this period were the revision of the great *Commentary on the New Testament* of his fellow Jesuit, Salmeron, and work on the commissions for the revision of the Roman ritual and of the Vulgate Bible. He also gave much help to Pope Sixtus V in his edition of the works of St Ambrose.

As theologian to Cardinal Gaetani, papal legate in France in 1589, St Robert proved that he was an able diplomat as well as a scholar. The legation endured great hardships during the siege of Paris, but the hardest trial which Robert had to endure at this time came from an unexpected quarter. The great champion of papal authority heard that Pope Sixtus V had determined to place the first volume of the *Controversies* on the index. He was dissatisfied with Robert's teaching, which was by no means new, that in temporal matters papal authority is not immediate and direct, but flows only indirectly from his spiritual authority. Before he could put his decision into force Sixtus died, and his successor revoked the condemnation. Bellarmine's opinion is, today, common Catholic teaching. In spite of this trial it was Robert who contributed most to the correction of the faulty Sixtine edition of the Vulgate, and wrote the preface to the new edition issued by Pope Clement VIII, in which a charitable veil is drawn over the editorial shortcomings of Pope Sixtus.

Robert was successively spiritual father and rector of the Roman College, and later provincial of Naples. In Rome he guided the young Jesuit saint, St Aloysius Gonzaga; and in Naples he himself was acclaimed as a saint by another Jesuit who was destined to be canonized, St Bernadino Realino.

Compelled to accept the office of cardinal in 1599 he was occupied henceforward with ecclesiastical affairs, notably with the case of Galileo and the dispute on grace between the Dominicans and the Jesuits.

Three happy years were spent as archbishop of Capua, and, then, in 1605, Robert was summoned to Rome to take up his pen once again in defense of the church. In turn he disposed of Fra Paolo Sarpi of Venice, King James I of England and the Gallican writer William Barclay.

Robert died on 17th September, 1621, was canonized in 1928, and made a doctor of the church in 1931.

May 13th ILLUSTRATION: page 408

ROBERT of CHAISE-DIEU † 1067

A canon of the church of St Julian at Broude, he went to Rome on pilgrimage, and on his return, with the help of a penitent knight named Stephen, he founded the abbey of Chaise-Dieu, which had soon 300 monks following a reformed Benedictine Rule.

April 17th

ROBERT of MOLESME † 1110

St Robert of Molesme was born near Troyes in Champagne some time early in the eleventh century and died at his monastery of Molesme in the year 1110. Very little is known of his family and early life, but it is certain that he became a monk at the monastery of Moûtier-la-Celle when he was sixteen years old. After taking vows he became prior of his monastery and then, some time later, abbot of St Michael of Tonnerre. While he was abbot of Tonnerre some hermits, living in the forest of Colan, asked him to become their superior and show them how to live according to the Rule of St Benedict, but this his community would in no wise consent to his doing. Nevertheless he left his monastery very soon afterwards and returned to his mother house. The good hermits of Colan were not to be so easily thwarted; they applied to the Holy See, and in answer to their petition the pope commanded the abbot of La Celle to send them Robert as their superior. In the year 1075, as the number of his monks began to grow, he moved the whole community from the forest of Colan to a more suitable site at Molesme. At first they had to suffer great privations, but very soon their fame spread, and they became prosperous from the donations of the devout. As their riches grew so their fervor waned, until at last Robert left them in disgust and betook himself to a poor community of hermits in the neighborhood. But he did not remain there long, for in response to an appeal from his monks, who found that their prestige had suffered by his departure, he returned to Molesme after little more than a year's absence.

In the meantime two of his best monks, St Alberic

and the Englishman, St Stephen Harding, had left Molesme and set up as hermits in the neighborhood of Bar-sur-Aube, only to move again, when the bishop of the diocese commanded them to return to their monastery, to a more remote site known as Cîteaux about fifteen miles south of Dijon. Very soon after his return to Molesme, Robert was again in difficulties, and in despair of ever being able to rule the community as he wished, he set out to join Alberic and Stephen at Cîteaux, accompanied by twenty monks. With the help of the duke of Burgundy and his vassal, the viscount of Beaune, a church was soon built, and on March 21st in the year 1098 Robert was formally installed as the first abbot. But he was not to be left in peace for long; within a year after his arrival at Cîteaux orders came from the Holy See through Hugh de Die, archbishop of Lyons, commanding him to return forthwith to Molesme. The archbishop threatened him with severe penalties should he 'with his usual inconstancy', ever attempt to leave his monastery again. It is interesting that, with an eye to Robert's reputation, his early biographers did not scruple to change the word 'inconstancy' to 'constancy' in the document of the archbishop commanding his return to Molesme. So Robert's wanderings came to an end: in obedience to the Holy See he remained abbot of Molesme until his death in the year 1110, but his heart was always with his monks at Cîteaux.

Although Cîteaux became in due time the mother house of a great reform and of an order spread throughout the world that has endured to our own day, there is no evidence at all that Robert ever intended to become a reformer or to found a new order; he seems never to have wished for anything else than to be allowed to live in peace, according to the letter of the Rule of St Benedict. The archbishop of Lyons referred to his inconstancy, but in this desire of his to live according to the letter of the Rule he never wavered. He wandered from one monastery to another, but his purpose always remained the same. Perhaps he lacked the born leader's gift of inspiring others with his own ideals, perhaps he was impatient of human infirmity, yet nevertheless by his courageous perseverance in his ideal he helped to found the mother house of the Cistercian Order and, thereby, to achieve something greater than he could possibly have conceived.
April 29th

ROBERT of NEWMINSTER † 1159
A Yorkshire Benedictine of Whitby, he joined a band of monks who founded what was later known as Fountains Abbey. He left to become abbot of another Cistercian house, at Newminster.
June 7th

ROCK † *c.* 1378
The only facts that can be verified about him are that he came from Montpellier and worked among plague victims in Italy.
August 16th

RODERIC and SOLOMON † 857
St Eulogius, an eye-witness, states that Roderic was betrayed by his Mohammedan brother during the Moorish oppression of Spain, and thrown into prison with another Christian, Solomon. Both were beheaded, and the guards threw even the blood-stained stones into the river to prevent the Christians from obtaining any relics of the two martyrs.
March 13th

ROGATION, *see* Donatian and Rogation.

ROMANUS † 258
An unknown Roman martyr, his legend is that he was martyred the day before St Laurence, whose example had led him to become a Christian.
August 9th

ROMANUS *Sixth Century*
A monk in a monastery near Subiaco, he settled St Benedict in a remote cave and brought him food. According to an unreliable legend, he left Italy at the approach of the Vandals, and settled near Auxerre in France, where he founded the abbey of Fontrouge.
May 22nd

ROMANUS and LUPICINUS *Fifth Century*
These two brothers lived as hermits in the Jura Mountains. They became joint abbots of the two monasteries founded there for their followers, ruling with compassion but great austerity.
February 28th

ROMANUS of ANTIOCH † 304
A deacon of Caeserea, he was arrested at Antioch for encouraging Christian prisoners. His tongue was torn out, and after a long and painful imprisonment he was strangled.
November 18th

ROMANUS of ROUEN *Seventh Century*
A courtier of King Clotaire II, he became bishop of Rouen. In his honor, the chapter of Rouen had the privilege, until the Revolution, of securing the release annually on the feast of the Ascension of one prisoner condemned to death. Before his release, the prisoner had to listen to two sermons and to carry the shrine of the saint in procession.
October 23rd

ROMANUS T̶H̶E̶ ̶M̶E̶L̶O̶D̶I̶S̶T̶   *Sixth Century*
The most celeb̶r̶a̶t̶e̶d̶ ̶o̶f̶ ̶G̶r̶e̶e̶k̶ hymn-writers, he is
venerated as a s̶a̶i̶n̶t̶ ̶i̶n̶ ̶t̶h̶e̶ ̶e̶a̶s̶t̶e̶r̶n̶ church.
October 1st

ROMAR̶I̶C̶   † 653
A courtier̶ ̶o̶f̶ ̶K̶i̶n̶g̶ ̶C̶l̶o̶t̶a̶i̶r̶e̶ ̶I̶I̶, he entered the monastery
of Luxev̶i̶l̶.̶ ̶l̶a̶t̶e̶r̶ ̶h̶e̶ ̶f̶o̶u̶n̶ded on his estates the abbey of
Remi̶r̶e̶m̶o̶n̶t̶ ̶(̶R̶o̶m̶a̶r̶i̶c̶'̶s̶ hill) of which St Amatus was
the̶ ̶f̶i̶r̶s̶t̶ ̶a̶b̶b̶o̶t̶ ̶a̶n̶d̶ ̶R̶o̶m̶aric the second.
D̶e̶c̶e̶m̶b̶e̶r̶ ̶8̶t̶h̶

R̶O̶M̶B̶A̶U̶T̶,̶ ̶s̶e̶e̶ ̶R̶umold.

R̶O̶M̶U̶A̶L̶D̶   *c.* 950–1027
A̶ ̶m̶e̶m̶b̶e̶r̶ ̶o̶f̶ ̶t̶h̶e̶ family of the dukes of Ravenna, he
f̶o̶u̶n̶d̶e̶d̶ ̶m̶a̶n̶y̶ ̶m̶onasteries, among them one at Camal-
d̶o̶l̶i̶ ̶n̶e̶a̶r̶ ̶A̶r̶e̶z̶z̶o̶ in Tuscany. Camaldoli is a collection
o̶f̶ ̶f̶i̶v̶e̶ ̶o̶r̶ ̶s̶o̶ ̶hermitages which gave its name to a new
c̶o̶n̶g̶r̶e̶g̶a̶t̶i̶o̶n̶ of Benedictines, the Camaldolese, whose
m̶e̶m̶b̶e̶r̶s̶ ̶w̶e̶ar a white habit and live as hermits, but in
a̶ ̶c̶o̶m̶m̶u̶n̶i̶ty.
f̶e̶b̶r̶u̶a̶r̶y̶ ̶7̶t̶h

R̶O̶M̶U̶LA and her Companions   *Sixth Century*
S̶S̶ ̶R̶omula, Herundo and Redempta lived together in
R̶o̶m̶e. St Romula contracted paralysis and although
s̶h̶e̶ ̶w̶a̶s̶ the youngest was the first to die.
J̶u̶l̶y 23rd

R̶OMULUS of FIESOLE   *First Century*
A Roman, he was converted by St Peter, became the
first bishop of Fiesole and was martyred during the
persecution of Domitian. This is the account provided
in an eleventh-century fiction; but there is, however,
some evidence for supposing Romulus to have been a
deacon of Fiesole.
July 6th

ROSALIA   † 1160?
Possibly a nun of a Greek convent, she is said to have
lived in a cave on Monte Pellegrino in Sicily.
September 4th

ROSE of LIMA   1568–1617
Not all saints are for our imitation; some are for our
admiration only. We can venerate and admire their
holiness, but are not to seek to follow them in the
particular way in which they achieved it. St Rose belongs
to this category. She is important because she is the first
saint of the New World to be canonized and is thus a
witness to the fact that, amid the injustice and inhu-
manity inseparably bound up with the Spanish conquest
of America, the leaven of Christianity was still at work.

Rose was born at Lima in 1568. Her short life of
thirty-one years, passed entirely in that city, was wholly
given over to voluntary penance and prayer, the former

of a nature so extreme as to appear inhuman. Her parents,
Caspar del Flores and Maria del Oliva, of Spanish
middle-class extraction, brought up their daughter in
accordance with the customs of their nationality, class
and period. In addition to depriving herself of sleep and
food Rose was at pains, it seems, to humble herself by
methods that would impair her great natural beauty and
render her unattractive. Told by visitors that she was
beautiful, she rubbed pepper on her cheeks to produce
a blotchy complexion; her delicately made hands she
steeped in lime and as a result so injured herself that she
was incapacitated for a whole month; when her mother
placed a garland of flowers on her daughter's head, Rose
impaled it there so firmly with a sizeable pin that it
could be removed only with great difficulty, besides
being painful to a degree.

When her parents fell on hard times Rose contributed
to their support by heavy work in the garden and by
doing needlework. In all things, however, including her
voluntary penances, she showed herself obedient to her
parents and confessor, though, as was her right, she
persisted for upwards of ten years in her refusal to marry
at the former's behest. She joined the third order of
St Dominic, took a vow of chastity and choosing as her
patroness St Catherine of Siena endeavored to model
her life on hers, though it requires to be said that Rose
possessed neither the intellectual caliber nor the forceful
personality of that great Dominicaness.

As the price of her mystical experiences, and in
addition to her voluntary penances, Rose had to suffer
the persecution, misunderstanding and interior darkness
and temptation that appear to be the common lot of the
saints. She bore it all with humility and resignation. The
latter portion of her life was passed in a hut in the
garden, where until three years before her death, she
lived as a recluse. In 1614 she was taken under the
protection of Don Gonzalo de Massa and his wife, who
gave her shelter and care during the long illness that
preceded her death in 1617.

Rose's life, as was pointed out, is not necessarily for
our imitation, and in modern times we may even find it
difficult to admire. During her life an ecclesiastical
commission examined her and pronounced that the
mystical phenomena she experienced were of divine
origin. Nowadays, even these we might postulate as
having at least in part a pathological cause (*see* SS Joseph
of Copertino *and* Gemma Galgani). But the lives of
some saints require to be regarded as a protest against
prevailing evils: in this context Rose's appears in sharp
contrast with the materialist outlook engendered by
prosperity in the Spanish American dominions and as a
witness to the things of the spirit at a period which
seems wholly concerned with those of this world.
August 30th   ILLUSTRATION: page 409

ROSE of VITERBO † 1252?

During Frederick II's campaign against Pope Gregory IX, Rose, then twelve years old, preached in Viterbo against submission to the emperor, for which ultimately her family were banished from the city. The convent of St Mary of the Roses, to whom she applied for admittance on her return, refused to accept her; although, as she had prophesied, she was buried in its church when she died at the age of about seventeen.
September 4th

ROSENDO, *see* Rudesind.

RUADAN of LOTHRA Sixth Century

A pupil of St Finian of Clonard, he founded the monastery of Lothra in what is now Tipperary.
April 15th

RUAN, *see* Rumon.

RUDESIND or ROSENDO † 977

Appointed bishop of Dumium when eighteen years old, he ruled with remarkable wisdom until he retired to the Celanova monastery of which he was founder and abbot. He may also have been bishop of Compostella for some ten years.
March 1st

RUFINA, *see* Justa and Rufina.

ILLUSTRATION: page 410

RUFINA and SECUNDA † 257?

Daughters of a Roman senator, they fled during the persecution under Valerian, after their fiancés had apostasized. They were taken, however, and beheaded.
July 10th

RUFINUS, *see* Valerius and Rufinus.

RUFUS and ZOSIMUS † c. 107

Companions of St Ignatius of Antioch in his martyrdom, their names and deeds are mentioned in a letter from St Polycarp of Smyrna to the Christians of Philippi in Macedonia.
December 18th

RUMOLD or ROMBAUT † c. 775

An Englishman or Irishman, he went on a pilgrimage to Rome, where he was made a bishop. He afterwards engaged in missionary work in the Low Countries where he apparently died a martyr.
July 3rd

RUMON or RUAN Sixth Century?

He may have been a monk of Glastonbury and the brother of St Tudwal, bishop at Tréguier. He is sometimes mistakenly identified with the Breton, St Ronan.
August 30th

RUMWALD Seventh Century?

We are told that he was born in Northamptonshire of royal parents, made his own confession of faith, delivered a sermon to his parents, and died at the age of three days.
November 3rd

RUPERT, *see* Bertha and Rupert.

RUPERT Eighth Century

He was bishop of Worms before undertaking missionary work in Bavaria. Supported by Duke Theodo, he established Christianity there, built churches and helped to civilize the country. As bishop of Juvavum, which he renamed Salzburg, he did much to develop the salt-mines.
March 29th

RUSTICUS, *see* Dionysius.

RUSTICUS, *see* Eleutherius and Rusticus.

RUSTICUS of NARBONNE Fifth Century

Son of a bishop, he himself became bishop of Narbonne in 427, and a letter survives written to him by Pope St Leo I dissuading him from resigning his see.
October 26th

SABAS 439–532

Born in Cappadocia in 439, at the age of eight Sabas ran away to a monastery, where he spent happy and fervent years. At eighteen, attracted by the hermit's life, he went to Jerusalem and entered a monastery of the semi-eremitical type. At the age of thirty he obtained leave to pass five days a week in a cave. With one other monk he shared St Euthymius's annual Lenten retreat into the wilderness of our Lord's Temptation. He spent four years alone in the desert. In 478 he settled in a gorge of the Cedron, in a cave high on the face of a cliff. After five years' solitude, disciples gathered and he founded a monastery close by, whose abbot he became. The monks inhabited separate cells. In 491 Sabas was ordained priest against his will, so that his community of 150 might no longer lack a priest. With funds inherited from his mother he built a hospice at Jericho. He was appointed superior general of all the hermits in Palestine, whether solitary or gathered in communities, and he also founded several monasteries in Palestine.

From time to time he left his monastery to live in complete solitude. On one occasion a lion sought to eject him, but at his request departed peaceably. Sabas was much involved as a champion of Catholic orthodoxy in the struggle against the Monophysites. He was sent with other abbots to Constantinople to protest against the imperial persecution of Catholics. On his return he undertook a preaching tour against the Monophysites. His persistent efforts obtained the abolition of an oppressive and unjust tax. At the age of ninety-one he went once more to Constantinople on a mission to the Emperor Justinian.

He died at the age of ninety-three, December 5th 532. Our knowledge of his life is derived from a trustworthy biography. His monastery, Mar Saba in a gorge of the Cedron, survives to this day and is among the oldest monasteries still inhabited.
December 5th

SABAS THE GOTH † 372
St Sabas was one of the Goths in eastern Europe who were converted by their Christian prisoners. At the beginning of one persecution, he openly declared his faith, but was released. He was again arrested and although his guards offered to let him escape, he insisted that they carry out the sentence – death by drowning.
April 12th

SABINA
It is not certain that she existed, although, according to an unreliable passion, she was a widow who was converted by her servant Serapia. Both were martyred.
August 29th

SABINIAN
Venerated as the first martyr of Troyes, he was martyred there during one of the earliest of the Roman persecutions.
January 29th

SABINUS and his Companions † 303?
The following story seems purely legendary. In the persecution under Diocletian, Sabinus, a bishop, had his hands cut off, while his deacons, Marcellus and Exsuperantius, died under torture. Sabinus himself was beaten to death at Spoleto, but not before the governor, Venustian, and his family had been converted.
December 30th

SABINUS of CANOSA Sixth Century
Bishop of Canosa, his birthplace in Apulia, he was the friend of St Benedict, while Pope St Agapitus I entrusted him with important missions. In old age he became blind, and he was renowned for his charity and prophetic gifts.
February 9th

SABINUS of PIACENZA † 420
A learned opponent of Arianism and a close friend of St Ambrose, this bishop of Piacenza was reputed to have stayed the flood water of the Po river by casting in a written order.
January 17th

SADOTH Fourth Century
He succeeded the martyred bishop of Seleucia and Ctesiphon, St Simeon Barsabae. This bishopric – the most important in Persia – suffered most during Sapor II's persecution. When he, too, was apprehended, Sadoth strengthened his Christian companions through their fearful tortures until they were all finally beheaded.
February 20th

SAHAK I, *see* Isaac.

SAIRE, *see* Salvius.

SALABERGA and BODO Seventh Century
St Salaberga was cured of blindness by St Eustace of Luxeuil. Her second husband, Blandinus, and two of their five children, Bauduin and Anstrudis, are also honored as saints. She persuaded her brother, St Bodo, to enter the double monastery she had founded at Laon, and he later became bishop of Toul.
September 22nd: Salaberga; *September 11th*: Bodo

SALOME and JUDITH Ninth Century
Salome was supposed to have been an English princess who entered the monastery of Ober-Altaich in Bavaria. She was joined by the widow Judith, a close relative, and both lived as solitaries. It is possible that one was Edburga, the daughter of Offa of Mercia, who fled after having poisoned her husband in mistake for someone else.
June 29th

SALVATOR of HORTA † 1567
Venerated as a saint while he lived but not canonized until 1938, he was a Franciscan at Horta in Tortosa and later at Barcelona. His austerity was such that he fasted frequently, scourged himself daily and never wore shoes.
March 18th

SALVIUS of ALBI † 584
A magistrate, he retired to a monastery of which he later became abbot. He was appointed bishop of Albi in 574.
September 10th

SALVIUS or SAIRE Sixth Century?
Often mistaken for St Salvius of Albi or St Salvius of Amiens, he was a recluse who lived in the forest of Bray in Normandy.
October 28th

SALVIUS or SAUVE Seventh Century
After succeeding Ado as bishop of Amiens, he ruled during the reign of Theodoric II.
January 11th

SALVIUS or SAUVE and SUPERIUS Eighth Century
This missionary bishop and his disciple were murdered in Valenciennes, and their bodies thrown into a pit. The

disciple's body was found lying on top of his master's, and as his identity was not known, he was called *superus* or *superius*.
June 26th

SAMONAS, *see* Abibus, Gurias and Samonas.

SAMSON   *c. 485–565*
Samson, abbot and bishop, and one of the greatest of the Welsh saints, was the son of Amwn of Dyfed and Anna of Gwent. The pupil of St Illtud, he was ordained by St Dyfrig and succeeded St Pŷr as abbot of Ynys Bŷr, which is usually identified with Caldey, the island off the coast of Pembrokeshire. He visited Ireland, where he left two foundations, Ballygriffin, near Dublin, and Bally Samson in Wexford. He then returned to Dyfed, where he lived for some time as a hermit in the cave near Stackpole Elidyre. Then, having been consecrated bishop by St Dyfrig, on February 22nd, the feast of St Peter's Chair, he crossed to Cornwall, where his principal foundation was at Southill. He made foundations also at Padstow and Fowey, and appears to have visited the Scilly Isles. From there he crossed over to Brittany.

His personality and influence are strikingly indicated by his successful visit to Chilebert, the son of Clovis, to secure the release of the young Breton prince, Iudual. This tireless traveller, great ascetic and fearless monk died in a ripe old age at Dol. At the council of Paris (*c.* 557) he had signed his name, 'Samson, sinner and bishop.'

Samson was Wales's greatest gift to Brittany. When Brittany gave Wales Geoffrey of Monmouth, Samson was given an exalted rôle in Geoffrey's saga. On expelling the English from York, King Arthur makes the saint archbishop of York, and there a church, dedicated in consequence to the saint, yet stands; for great names are essential to great fiction.
July 28th

SAMSON of CONSTANTINOPLE
                                                   Fifth Century
A wealthy man, Samson is said to have been a doctor as well as a priest and to have founded at his own expense a hospital for the sick poor of Constantinople.
June 27th

SANCHIA, *see* Teresa and Sanchia of Portugal.

SANCTIUS or SANCHO   † 851
When still young, he was captured by the Moors who took him to Cordova. For refusing to abandon his faith, he was impaled upon the ground.
June 5th

SAPOR and ISAAC   † 339
Two bishops who suffered in the persecution under King Sapor II of Persia. Isaac was stoned to death, and Sapor died of his torture. Three others were martyred with them: Mahanes, Abraham and Simeon.
November 30th

SATURNINUS   † *c.* 309
He may have been a Carthaginian priest who came to Rome and suffered martyrdom on the Salarian Way, where he was buried.
November 29th

SATURNINUS, DATIVUS,
    and their Companions   † 304
Under Diocletian's persecution, Saturninus, a priest of Abitina in Africa, and forty-eight other Christian men, women and children, were sent for trial to Carthage. They strongly defended their faith, and all died in prison.
February 11th

SATURNINUS or SERNIN   *Third Century?*
The first bishop of Toulouse, he was martyred – it is said – by an angry mob of pagans before whose gods he had refused to sacrifice. He was tied to a bull which was then driven down a hill, dragging the saint with it. His relics are in the basilica of St Sernin at Toulouse.
November 29th

SATURUS, *see* Armogastes, Archinimus and Saturus.

SATYRUS   *c. 340–c. 379*
After his father's death, he went with his brother and sister, SS Ambrose and Marcellina, to Rome. He qualified as a lawyer, and, as a layman, helped his brother to administer the diocese of Milan. Yet he remained a mere catechumen until a shipwreck, from which he escaped with the Blessed Sacrament secured in a scarf about his neck, frightened him into baptism shortly before his death.
September 17th

SAUVE, *see* Salvius.

SAUVE, *see* Salvius and Superius.

SAVA   1174–1237
Younger son of Stephen I, founder of the Nemanydes dynasty and of the independent Serbian state, he became a monk of Mount Athos. In 1219 he was ordained bishop of the Serbs and in 1222 archbishop. For fifty years he consolidated Christianity among the Serbs, established Serbian bishops and richly earned his title as Serbia's patron.
January 14th

SAVIN   *Fifth Century?*
Supposed to have been born in Barcelona, he became a

monk at the monastery of Ligugé. He eventually settled as a hermit in the Pyrenees.

October 9th

SCHOLASTICA   *Sixth Century*

Scholastica was the sister of St Benedict, the patriarch of western monasticism. She is alleged, on no very certain authority, to have been his twin. What little we know of her life is contained in St Gregory the Great's second *Dialogue*, which gives an account of St Benedict and of his miracles. She must, like her brother, have been born in the Sabine township of Nursia, and her parents were presumably of good country stock. The tradition which connects the family with the wealthy patrician family of the Anicii is quite unsound. At some time, possibly when she was still quite a young girl, Scholastica took the veil, and in her later years we find her living close enough to Monte Cassino to meet her brother once a year. She died shortly before him, and they were buried in the same tomb. Even this fact does not fix the date of her death with any certainty, because St Benedict's own dates are still disputed, but the year may have been 547.

Scholastica is the heroine of one of the most charming legends in the *Dialogue*. St Gregory tells us that on one occasion when she had, as usual, spent the day with her brother, enjoying the 'mutual comfort of heavenly talk', she implored him to continue the conversation through-out the night. St Benedict, perhaps rather sternly, refused, on the grounds that to spend a whole night outside his monastery would be a breach of the Rule. Thereupon his sister buried her head in her hands and began to weep. As she wept, a sudden storm arose, with such a violent downpour of rain that neither St Benedict nor his companions could set foot out of doors. The great abbot was inclined to be annoyed. 'God Almighty forgive you, sister,' he said, 'what is this that you have done?' She replied: 'I prayed you to stay, and you would not hear me; I prayed to Almighty God, and He heard me!' So St Benedict was forced against his will to stay. St Gregory comments on this incident: 'No wonder if at that time a woman were more powerful than he . . . For according to the saying of St John "God is love", and with good reason she was more powerful who loved more.' It is not often that great saints have been given little lessons in charity by their sisters.

Three days later St Benedict saw a vision of Schol-astica's soul leaving her body and ascending to heaven in the form of a dove. Whereupon, 'rejoicing much in her great glory', he sent for her body and buried it in his own tomb, where he was soon to join her. Her bones are said to have been brought to Fleury-sur-Loire by the same party of monks who removed St Benedict's relics towards the end of the sixth century, but the story has

given rise to a controversy which is unlikely ever to be resolved. Scholastica's feast is celebrated on February 10th and she has always been regarded as a special patroness of Benedictine nuns.   ILLUSTRATION: page 411

February 10th

SEBALD   *Eighth Century*

After living as a hermit at Vicenza, he went with St Willibald to Germany where he resumed his eremitical life. He is patron of Nuremberg.

August 19th

SEBASTIAN   *Third Century*

According to his fictitious acts, Sebastian, a captain in the Praetorian Guard, lived in Diocletian's palace and favor. When the Emperor discovered his Christian faith he ordered him to be shot to death with arrows. Left for dead, he was found by a Christian widow, Irene, and nursed back to health. Returning to the palace he accosted Diocletian and reproached him with his perse-cution of Christians. The enraged Emperor had him cudgelled to death and his body thrown into a sewer. A Christian lady, Lucina, buried it at a place called Ad Catacumbas, where his basilica stands today.

All we know of Sebastian is the fact of his martyrdom in Rome at a date unknown, his burial ad Catacumbas and a connection of unknown nature with Milan. It was at a comparatively late period that artists, desirous of painting the nude, depicted him so frequently as a youth almost naked, pierced with arrows.

January 20th   ILLUSTRATION: facing page 352

SEBBE   † *c.* 694

One of the two rulers of the East Saxons, he remained faithful at a time when, as a result of a plague, many of his subjects had apostasized. He later gave up his throne to enter a monastery.

September 1st

SECHNALL, *see* Secundinus.

SECUNDA, *see* Rufina and Secunda.

SECUNDINUS or SECHNALL   † 447

With Auxilius and Iserninus, he crossed from Gaul to help St Patrick as a bishop in Ireland, where he is remembered as a hymn-writer.

November 27th

SEINE, *see* Sequanus.

SENAN   *Sixth Century*

No Irish saint of the golden age is in greater need of rehabilitation than St Senan of Iniscathy, who flourished about the middle of the sixth century. Between historians, antiquarians and the purveyors of silly legends (not to mention the whimsical bard, Thomas Moore, who pandered to the frivolous), he has been misrepresented as misanthropic and a woman-hater, vindictive and gloomy, as well as fiercely possessive about property titles. In reality he was an original, who pioneered the founding of monasteries on coastal and river islands, where the contemplative life was fostered by isolation and by the beauty of nature; a virile character, austere certainly like all his compeers; a teacher who won the love of his pupils, he was remarkable, too, for his compassion with human griefs and for immense hospitality.

He was born in Moylough, near Kilrush, County Clare, and was educated by St Natalis in Kilmanagh, County Kilkenny. Here he also took his turn herding the cattle of the monastic farm and grinding corn for the community's use. After ordination, he, too, became one of the great monastic founders of the era, displaying an extraordinary predilection for islands, especially those situated in the mouths of rivers. He is said to have set up churches on an island in the river Slaney in Wexford; on Great Island in Cork harbor and on Iniscarra in the river Lee; on Inismore, Low Island and Iniscunla in the mouth of the river Fergus; on Mutton Island and Bishop's Island off the Clare coast; and on Inisluinge and Iniscathy (anglicized Scattery) in the river Shannon. He died at Iniscathy, where his grave is still venerated. This island, strikingly situated in the mouth of the river Shannon, is famous today for its splendid group of ecclesiastical remains of various ages and a near-perfect round tower.

The riddle of Senan's wonderful island itinerary has never been adequately explained. The suggestion has been put forward that pagan Ireland, worshipping fire and water as the primal sources of life, had enthroned the Druidic river god on the islands later selected by Senan, who overthrew the false gods and supplanted them with Christian altars. Hence the scenic background to this saint's name is always the panorama of river meeting sea with its distinctive silvery light and its color range of grey, green and blue.

Even in the twentieth century his local cult is strong in Ireland. There is a wealth of living lore centered around the numerous holy wells dedicated to him throughout Munster. A pilgrimage entailing at least three hours of prayer takes place to the hilltop cemetery of Moylough on two pattern days every year; the first on his feast day, March 8th, and the second on June 29th.
March 8th

SENATOR   † 475
With St Abundius, he was sent as legate to Constantinople after the condemnation of St Flavian. He later became bishop of Milan.
May 28th

SENNEN, *see* Abdon and Sennen.

SENOCH   † 576
After his conversion, he went from his native Poitou to live as a hermit in Touraine.
October 24th

SEQUANUS or SEINE   † 580
This Burgundian lived in seclusion until he founded and governed a monastery in the forest of Segestre, near the source of the Seine.
September 19th

SERAPHINA, *see* Fina.

SERAPHINO   1540–1604
A Capuchin lay-brother, he was born at Montegranaro in 1540.
October 17th

SERAPION   † c. 212
Bishop of Antioch, he was celebrated for his theological erudition.
October 30th

SERAPION   *Fourth Century*
Called 'the Scholastic' for his great learning, he left Alexandria, became a desert recluse and was befriended by St Antony the Abbot. When later appointed bishop of Thmuis, he successfully opposed prevailing heresies until Emperor Constantius banished him. His most important work extant is the liturgy of his see, the *Euchologion*.
March 21st

SERENICUS and SERENUS   *Seventh Century*
Brothers, natives of Spoleto, they entered the Benedictine community at Rome. They moved to France, where Serenicus founded a monastery and Serenus lived as a hermit.
May 7th

SERENUS THE GARDENER or
    CERNEUF of BILLOM   *Fourth Century*
A hermit living at Sirmium, in the present Yugoslavia, he rebuked the wife of an Imperial guard for walking in his garden. He was asked if he were a Christian. He willingly confessed and was beheaded.
February 23rd

SERF or SERVANUS   *Sixth Century?*
This bishop was closely associated with Culross in Fifeshire and was buried there. Although we know little for certain about him, *see* Kentigern.
July 1st

SERGIUS I   † 701
A compromise candidate, he was canonically elected to the papacy against a background of bribe and counter-bribe. He had to oppose the autonomous action of a large group of eastern bishops who at the Concilium 'Quinisextum' drew up a series of disciplinary canons

with a markedly anti-western bias. Sergius had many contacts with the English church, through SS Caedwalla and Willibrord.
September 8th

SERGIUS and BACCHUS † 303?
Roman officers of the Syrian frontier-guard, they were arrested for refusing to sacrifice to the gods and taken to Rosafa in Mesopotamia, where they were executed.
October 7th

SERGIUS and GERMANUS of VALAAM
These monks founded the monastery of Valaam on an island in the Finnish lake of Ladoga, possibly in 1329.
June 28th

SERGIUS of RADONEZH *c.* 1315-1392
A hermit who founded the monastery of the Holy Trinity at Makovka, Sergius was consulted by bishops and princes. He encouraged Dmitry Donskoy, Prince of Moscow, to challenge his Tartar overlords and is regarded as one of the greatest of Russian saints.
September 25th

SERNIN, *see* Saturninus.

SERVAIS, *see* Servatius.

SERVANUS, *see* Serf.

SERVATIUS or SERVAIS † 384
An Armenian, he was a supporter of St Athanasius and bishop of Tongres.
May 13th

SERVULUS *Sixth Century*
Crippled with palsy he was obliged to become a beggar, yet he was never heard to complain, spending his time in prayer and in committing passages of the Bible to memory, since he could not read. He was buried in the church of St Clement in Rome where, each day, he had been carried to the porch to beg for alms.
December 23rd

SETHRIDA, *see* Ethelburga, Ercongota and Sethrida.

SEURIN, *see* Severinus.

The SEVEN FOUNDERS of the SERVITE ORDER *Thirteenth Century*
SS Bonfilius, Alexis, Amadeus, Hugh, Sostenes, Manettus and Buonagiunta were seven young Florentines who joined a confraternity of the Blessed Virgin and were inspired by a vision of our Lady to withdraw from the world. They settled eventually on the slopes of Monte Seranio, where they built a church. After a visit by the bishop, who advised them to adopt a rule of life, they received another vision of our Lady, in which she advised them to follow the rule of St Augustine. She carried in her hand a black habit, and an angel at her side held a scroll with the title 'servants of Mary'. This happened on April 13th, 1240, and from that day the group were known as the Servites (viz, the servants of Mary).
February 12th

The SEVEN HOLY BROTHERS, *see* Felicity and the Seven Holy Brothers.

The SEVEN MARTYRS of SAMOSATA, *see* Hipparchus and his Companions.

The SEVEN SLEEPERS of EPHESUS
According to this hagiological version of the Rip van Winkle story, seven Christian men went to sleep in a cave near Ephesus during the persecution of the Emperor Decius (249-251), and woke up again in the reign of Theodosius (379-395). After a visit from the bishop and the emperor before whom they successfully established their identities, they fell once more asleep – for good. This myth crops up in different forms in many lands.
July 27th

SEVERIAN † 453
The heretic Theodosius took the see of Jerusalem by force from Juvenal and began a rule of bloodshed. Severian, bishop of Scythopolis, strongly condemned him, and was killed.
February 21st

SEVERINUS † 507
It now seems unlikely that Severinus was abbot of Agaunum. He performed many miraculous cures, including that of King Clovis, and died at Château-Landon. Saint-Séverin in Paris is named after him.
February 11th

SEVERINUS BOETHIUS *c.* 480-524
A member of one of the most important Roman families, he was born about 480, and by the age of twenty was already beginning to make his reputation as a scholar. His chief service was to translate the major philosophers of antiquity into Latin, and it was by this means that the works of Plato and Aristotle became familiar to the medieval scholars.

He followed his father into the service of the great Ostrogoth, Theodoric, ruler of Italy, hoping to apply Plato's dictum that philosophers ought to accept the responsibilities of office. He was made a consul by Theodoric in 510, and for twelve years rose in his service; but the king became suspicious of a plot to overthrow him, and Boethius was cast into prison. There he wrote his *Consolation of Philosophy* which was one of the most popular books in the middle ages. The fact that it makes no reference to the consoling power of Christianity has given rise to persistent comment. Dr Johnson went so far as to say that 'it was very surprising that upon such a subject, and in such a situation, he should be *magis philosophus quam Christianus* ('more of a philosopher than a Christian').

But Boethius' execution in 524 was traditionally regarded as martyrdom, and his cult was confirmed by Pope Leo XIII in 1883.
October 23rd

SEVERINUS of NORICUM   *Fifth Century*
This hermit came from the East and, until his death, travelled throughout Austria establishing monasteries, preaching, healing and assisting the people. Heathens as well as Christians sought his advice, and to those who besought him to be their bishop he replied that he had given up his solitude for their benefit and that this must be sufficient.
January 8th

SEVERINUS of SEPTEMPEDA   *Sixth Century*
Often confused with Severinus of Noricum, this saint was bishop of Septempeda and brother of St Victorinus. He gave his name to San Severino in the Ancona Marches.
January 8th

SEVERINUS or SEURIN
He was bishop of Bordeaux and a zealous opponent of Arianism.
October 23rd

SEXBURGA   *Seventh Century*
The daughter of Anna, the East Anglian king, she married King Erconbert of Kent. She founded a convent on the Isle of Sheppey; there her daughter Ermenilda succeeded her as abbess when she herself took the place of her sister Etheldreda at Ely.
July 6th

SHENUTE   *c. 334–c. 452*
One of the early desert monks of Egypt, he succeeded his uncle as abbot of a community at Atripe in the Thebaid in 385. He was one of the first to enforce a definite rule and this he did with a firmness amounting to severity. He lived to a great age, becoming in effect the superior of all the desert communities modelled upon his own.
July 1st

SIDONIUS APOLLINARIS   *c. 430–c. 479*
Celebrated for his letters and poems, he was born at Lyons, and married the daughter of the Emperor Avitus. He frequented the court and wrote panegyrics on the successive Emperors, but in 472 he was elected bishop of Clermont. He proved himself to be, militarily and spiritually, an excellent leader of his people against the Visigoths.
August 21st

SIGEBERT III of AUSTRASIA   †656
Son of Dagobert I of France and brother of Clovis II, he ruled Austrasia for eighteen years and founded twelve monasteries. He died at the age of twenty-five.
February 1st

SIGFRID   †690
Elected co-adjutor to St Benedict Biscop at Wearmouth when St Esterwine died, he was afflicted with a lung-disease which caused his premature death.
August 22nd

SIGFRID   *Eleventh Century*
He was probably a missionary bishop who went from York to Norway, and then into Sweden where Christianity was weak. As bishop of Växjö he converted King Olaf with many of his subjects, and he is honored as Sweden's apostle.
February 15th

SIGIRAMNUS or CYRAN   *Seventh Century*
He retired from the court of King Clotaire II to lead a religious life, founding monasteries at Méobecq and Longoretum.
December 5th

SIGISMUND of BURGUNDY   †524
Although his father, Gundebald, the Vandal ruler of Burgundy, was an Arian, Sigismund was converted to Catholicism shortly before he came to the throne. In repentance for killing his son in a fit of rage, he refounded the abbey of St Maurice at Agaunum. He prayed for punishment, and it came when he was captured and executed by King Clodomir.
May 1st

SILAS or SILVANUS   *First Century*
He may have been St Peter's secretary (1 Peter 5:12), but he was certainly one of the brethren (Acts 15:22) and accompanied SS Paul and Barnabas to Antioch. He went with St Paul on his second missionary journey, sharing his imprisonment at Philippi. He died in Macedonia.
July 13th

SILVERIUS   †537
He was the nominee to the papacy of the Ostrogothic king of Italy in succession to St Agapitus I. His father, St Hormisdas, had also been pope. Silverius soon became involved in the intrigues of the Empress Theodora, was deposed, exiled and probably murdered on an island off Naples.
June 20th

SILVESTER I   †335
Silvester succeeded St Miltiades as pope in 314 soon after Constantine had freed Christianity by the Edict of Milan. Silvester is supposed to have baptized Constantine and

cured him of leprosy, and it was probably to Silvester that Constantine gave the Lateran palace.

December 31st   ILLUSTRATION: page 412

SILVESTER GOZZOLINI   1177–1267

Born in 1177 of a noble family at Osimo, of which city he later became a canon at the age of fifty, he resigned his canonry and became a hermit, giving to his disciples the Rule of St Benedict in its strictest form and building them a monastery. This was the origin of the Silvestrine Benedictines, who have remained separate from the other congregations ever since. They wear a blue habit.

November 26th

SILVIN   *Eighth Century*

Just before his marriage, Silvin left the court of Childeric II and Thierry III, and became a priest. He was probably a regionary bishop in northern France where he preached with great success and ransomed many slaves from the barbarians.

February 17th

SIMEON   *First Century*

This is the Simeon who took the child Jesus in his arms in the Temple at the time of his presentation. No more is known of him than is recorded in St Luke's Gospel.

October 8th   ILLUSTRATION: page 413

SIMEON BARSABAE and his Companions † 341

Bishop of Selucia and Ctesiphon, he was one of many who were martyred in the persecution under King Sapor, including the priests Abdechalas and Ananias, Usthazanes the king's tutor, and Pusicius, overseer of the king's workmen.

April 21st

SIMEON METAPHRASTES   *Tenth Century*

An early collector of saints' lives surnamed Metaphrastes, or 'the reteller', he was probably an official of the imperial court.

November 28th

SIMEON of JERUSALEM   *First Century*

The son of Cleophas (St Joseph's brother), his mother may have been our Lady's sister, and he is referred to in St Matthew's gospel (ch. 13) as one of our Lord's brethren. St James the less – whose life should be consulted for a discussion of the relationship between Christ and his brethren – was his brother, and Simeon succeeded him as bishop of Jerusalem. He survived the destruction of Jerusalem and many persecutions, but he was eventually arrested – some say at the age of 120 – during Trajan's persecution and was crucified.

February 18th

SIMEON of SYRACUSE   † 1035

This Sicilian monk of Mount Sinai was sent by his abbot to Normandy and was captured by pirates. He escaped

but arrived too late to fulfil his mission. After other adventures, he was once more permitted to live as a hermit near Trier.

June 1st

SIMEON SALUS   *Sixth Century*

This saint went to such lengths to humble himself that the Syrians, among whom he lived at Emesa, called him 'salos', which is Greek for mad. He was obviously subject to periodic bouts of insanity, yet he maintained a heroic love of God; and his life is therefore of particular consolation to those similarly afflicted who are able to retain their love for God.

July 1st

SIMEON STYLITES   † 459

Simeon's life of extraordinary austerity is guaranteed by the testimony of friends and disciples. A Cilician shepherd lad, born about 390, Simeon entered a monastery at the age of thirteen. Ten years later he moved to another remarkable for its austerity, where he outfasted monks who ate only once a day by eating only once a week. A rope of palm leaves which he wore twisted around his body was betrayed by a stinking sore. It could be removed only by excisions which left him unconscious. The abbot expelled him. Living now in a hermitage, below a mountain, he began a custom, continued for at least twenty-six years, of passing Lent without food or drink. At the end of three years he retired to the summit, where he built an enclosure open to the sky.

To remove himself from the throng of visitors by whom he was increasingly beset, for he had become a miracle worker, Simeon decided to live on the top of a pillar raised progressively in height from about ten to about sixty-seven feet. Its diameter did not exceed six feet, and as it was without a seat, his sole relaxation from standing upright was to stoop or lean. He made constant bows of reverence and wore an iron collar.

The neighboring abbots and bishops suspected that he had adopted such mortifications from pride, but when he prepared to obey an order to descend, they encouraged him to remain on his pillar. Far from being an uncouth fanatic he showed unruffled patience, gentleness and kindness to all. Yet in his last years he suffered from a secret ulcer in his foot. Friends and disciples attest his miracles and predictions. He died on July 22nd or September 2nd, 459.

Though the first, Simeon was by no means the last Stylite – from the word 'stulos', a pillar. He was followed in oriental Christendom by a succession of pillar saints extending over many centuries.

To us, a life of self-torture, such as the fakir's, is repellent. But it suited the mentality of its environment and made Simeon a successful and far-reaching evangelist of

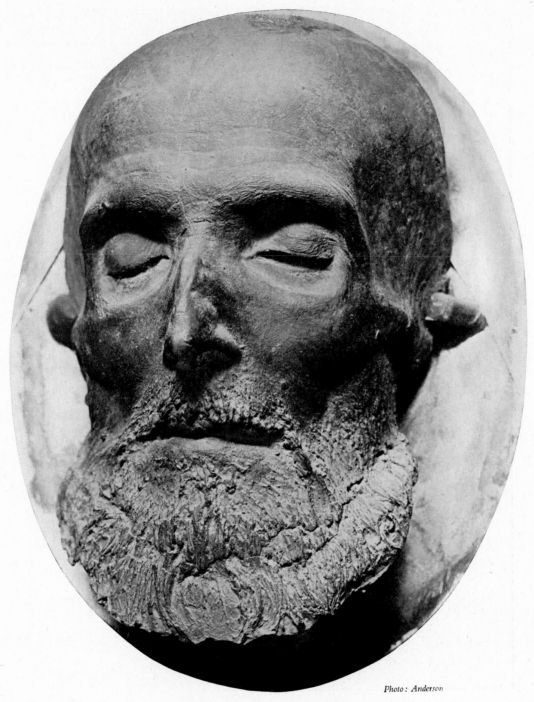

PHILIP NERI: death mask. *(Ch. dei Gerolomini, Naples.)*

PHILIP THE APOSTLE: sculpture by Nanni di Banco (1373 – 1421).
(Ch. di Or S. Michele, Florence.)

PIUS V: monument by Leonardo da Sarzana, sixteenth century. *(Basilica di Sta Maria Maggiore, Rome.)*

PIUS X: photograph.

RAPHAEL THE ARCHANGEL with Tobias: painting from the school of Andrea del Verocchio (1435–1488). *(National Gallery, London.)*

RAYMUND NONNATUS: painting by Sarlo Caraceni (1585–1620).
(Ch. de S. Adriano, Rome.)

RAYMUND of PENAFORT: painting by Ludovico Carracci (1555–1619).
(Ch. S. Domenico, Bologna.)

ROBERT BELLARMINE: engraving.

ROSE of LIMA: painting by Tiepolo (1696–1770).
(Ch. dei Gesuati, Venice.)

RUFINA, painting by F. Zurbaran (1598–1663). *(Fitzwilliam Museum, Cambridge.)*

SCHOLASTICA: detail from 'Crucifixion' by
School of Master of Liesborn (*fl. c.* 1465).
(National Gallery, London.)

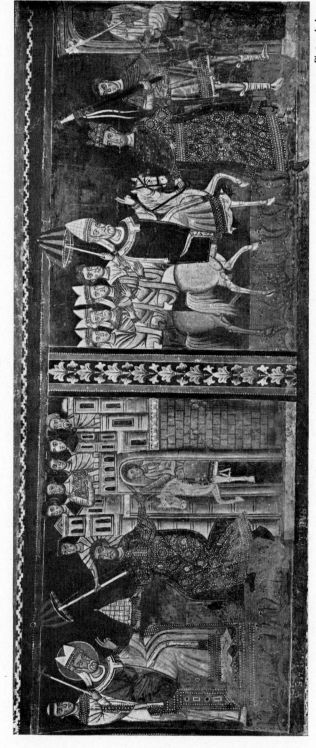

SILVESTER I: detail from mid-thirteenth century fresco. (*Ch. di SS Quatro Coronati, Rome.*)

SIMEON: detail from painting by Luca Signorelli (*c.* 1441 – 1523). *(National Gallery, London.)*

SIMEON STYLITES: painting by Frank Brangwyn (1867 – 1956).
(Galleria Internazionale d' Arte Moderna, Venice.)

SIMON: sculpture by Luca della Robbia (1400–1482). *(Ch. di Sta Croce, Florence.)*

SIMON STOCK: ceiling canvas by Tiepolo (1696 – 1770). *(Brera, Milan.)*

Christian faith and morality. He preached daily to crowds. The Bedouin from the surrounding deserts flocked to hear him. Persians, Armenians, Georgians thronged around him. A delegation arrived from an Egyptian village. He bade the villagers share the irrigation waters justly. Emperors consulted him and asked his prayers. The Emperor Marcian visited him incognito. He persuaded the Empress Eudoxia to abandon the Monophysites. To St Geneviève, remote in the far west, he sent greetings and a request for prayers. The Stylite thus proved himself God's messenger to an age so different from our own.   ILLUSTRATION: page 414
January 5th

SIMEON STYLITES THE YOUNGER

c. 517–592

After the death of his father, he left his native Antioch and was brought up in a remote place by a stylite named John. From the age of ten he lived for forty-five years on the top of a pillar in the monastery he established.
September 3rd

SIMEON THE ARMENIAN   † 1016

After a pilgrimage to Jerusalem, this Armenian went on to Rome, wandered through Italy, and then retired to the Cluniac monastery of Padilirone.
July 26th

SIMON   *First Century*

Apart from listing him among the Twelve, the New Testament furnishes no further information directly referable to this Apostle. He is distinguished from Simon Peter by the name of 'the Zealot' (Luke 6:15; Acts 1:13), which does not mean that he was a member of the fanatical Jewish sect of that name, but simply indicates his zeal for the Law. As the Aramaic word for 'zeal' is 'Kana', this could serve also to explain the title given him by the other Synoptics, 'the Cananean' (Matthew 10:4; Mark 3:18). This latter title, however, has been taken by some to indicate that he was a native of Galice; and the tradition arose that Simon was, in fact, the bridegroom of the marriage-feast at Cana. One early martyrology describes Simon witnessing Christ's miracle, and then 'leaving the wine and the marriage-feast to follow Christ and be numbered among the Apostles' – unfortunately, no historical evidence can be found for this dramatic scene of renunciation.

As with James the Less, the possibility arises of identifying Simon with one of the 'brethren of the Lord' (Mark 6:3); but the reasons which suggested the exclusion of James from the Twelve apply with equal force here, and therefore, one cannot identify the Apostle with the St Simon (or Simeon), who, tradition asserts, succeeded his brother James as bishop of Jerusalem.

Similarly, we can glean nothing certain from tradition

concerning Simon's apostolic labors or death. Those accounts which tell of his missionary activity in Africa and in the British Isles can be rejected as totally lacking in foundation. Inherently less unlikely, though still wanting in firm evidence, is the tradition which assigns him to Egypt and, finally, Persia. Though there is fairly general agreement among the extant sources that it was in Persia that Simon suffered martyrdom, there are fewer witnesses to the tradition that he died along with St Jude; and since none of the sources rests firmly in antiquity, it would be hazardous to pronounce with certainty on the place or circumstances of the Apostle's death.
October 28th   ILLUSTRATION: page 415

SIMON OF CRÉPY   † 1082

Although he wanted to enter a monastery, he was prevented by William the Conqueror, a relative by marriage, who wanted him to marry his daughter Adela. Eventually, however, he managed to escape to the monastery of Saint-Claude in the Jura.
September 30th

SIMON of TRENT and   † 1475
WILLIAM of NORWICH   † 1144

Simon of Trent was only two and a half when he was killed by a Jewish doctor, who admitted his crime after he had been tortured, and twelve year old William of Norwich was also killed by Jews. It was alleged that the murders were committed to procure blood for Jewish paschal rituals, and such charges of ritual murder occur throughout the middle ages – the first recorded being in 415. They are entirely without foundation, as there is no place in the Jewish liturgy for blood sacrifices of this kind – how, then, did the belief arise?

Blood was used in certain magical rites and the children could have been killed by magicians, who may have happened to be Jews. Another explanation is that, as Christian persecution of the Jews reached a climax at Easter (the time of the Jewish pasch), some Jews may have been goaded to take retaliation upon the only defenceless Christians they could find, children like Simon of Trent and William of Norwich.
March 24th

SIMON PETER, *see* Peter.

SIMON STOCK   *Twelfth Century*

It is usually stated that Simon the Englishman (as he was known in early times) was born in Kent in or about 1165 of noble parents, that from the age of twelve he lived as a hermit in the trunk of a tree (hence, it is said, the surname Stock), and that after twenty years of solitary life he joined the Carmelites when they arrived in England in 1241. Another tradition says, with more probability, that he went on a pilgrimage to the Holy Land and having joined the Order at the monastery of

Mount Carmel came to England with the first colony of hermits to reach the country. There are many difficulties in the first legend. The Carmelites came to England in 1241, but according to the legend Simon must have joined them nearly half a century before their arrival. It is said also that he died a centenarian in 1265.

One of the few facts that we possess about Simon is that he died in Bordeaux in 1265 and that, for the previous twenty years, he worked energetically for the establishment of the Carmelites in Europe. The Carmelites were a small group of European hermits living on Mount Carmel in the Holy Land, who came to Europe as a result of the collapse of the ill-fated kingdom of Jerusalem established by the Crusaders, and the hostility of the Saracens. At the chapter held at Aylesford in 1247 Simon was elected general of the order and at once set about reorganizing and adapting it to its new circumstances. He obtained from Rome a modification of the Rule, he journeyed about founding houses, taking care to establish as many as possible near the university towns. He travelled as far afield as Gascony and Sicily. In all this he encountered opposition not only from within the order but from outside, a consequence of the rapid development for which he was responsible; he met it energetically and was busy on the affairs of his office when he died at Bordeaux in 1265. His achievement can be summarized by saying that elected to govern a small congregation of hermits whose fate under new circumstances in Europe was at least doubtful, he transformed it within the space of twenty years and, at his death, left it well on the way to becoming a great order of friars on a somewhat similar pattern to the Dominicans and Franciscans. This was hardly the work of a man in his eighties and nineties, but, as so often, the truth is far more impressive than the legend.

Simon's name is also connected with the legend according to which it is asserted that our Lady appeared to him, proffering the habit of the order and telling him that all who died wearing it would be saved. From this grew the confraternity, associated with the Carmelites, whose members wear the small scapular which represents the Carmelite habit; this confraternity has spread all over the world. It must be pointed out that the historical evidence on which the legend is based is by no means satisfactory, but it is to be remembered that the legitimacy and authenticity of the devotion depend on the approval of the church, which it possesses, and not on the legendary account of its origins.

Simon's body, which was buried at Bordeaux, was in 1951 translated to the restored Carmelite house at Aylesford in Kent – the house at which in 1247 was held the chapter which elected him general of the order. St Simon has never been canonized, but his feast is kept by the Carmelite order and in certain English dioceses.

The proper mass authorized for his feast mentions, in the collect, the scapular devotion, praying that as through him we have obtained a sign of such special protection, so we may lay hold of the rewards eternally stored up for us.   ILLUSTRATION: page 416

May 16th

SIMPLICIAN   † 400
Bishop of Milan and friend of St Augustine, Simplician's example helped to convert that great saint to Christianity.
August 13th

SIMPLICIUS   † 483
He succeeded St Hilarius as pope at one of the most difficult periods for the church in Italy. Odoacer occupied Rome, Arians and pagans were devastating the land; but undeterred, Simplicius zealously endeavored to relieve the widespread misery, convert the heathen and oppose the Monophysite policy of the Byzantine emperor.
March 10th

SIMPLICIUS   *Fourth or Fifth Century*
He was bishop of Autun towards the end of the fourth century.
June 24th

SIMPLICIUS, FAUSTINUS and BEATRICE
Legend says that the brothers Simplicius and Faustinus were thrown into the Tiber for refusing to sacrifice, and that their sister Beatrice was martyred seven months afterwards. Their relics were translated to St Mary Major's in Rome.
July 29th

SIRICIUS   † 399
He succeeded St Damasus as pope in 383 and was the first pope to enforce clerical celibacy.
November 26th

SISINNIUS, MARTYRIUS and ALEXANDER
                                                       † 397
These Cappadocians came to live in Milan, where they attracted the attention of St Ambrose who sent them as missionaries to the Tyrolese Alps. Their success aroused so much enmity that the heathen beat them to death.
May 29th

SISOES   † c. 429
Living as a recluse in the desert, first at Skete, and then across the Nile, he modelled his life on that of St Antony. He has a namesake and contemporary, St Sisoes the Theban, also a solitary.
July 6th

SIXTUS or XYSTUS I   *Second Century*
At about the time of Trajan he succeeded St Alexander I as pope, reigning for about ten years. He is honored as a martyr.
April 3rd

SIXTUS II, FELICISSIMUS, AGAPITUS
and their Companions † 258
On August 30th, 257, under the shadow of Valerian's persecution, Sixtus was consecrated pope in succession to Stephen I. 'A good and peaceable priest,' as St Cyprian's deacon Pontius terms him, he averted a threatened schism by leaving local churches free to follow their established customs as regards the rebaptism of heretics (*see also* Cyprian of Carthage *and* Stephen I).

A year later Cyprian is passing on the news that 'Sixtus has been put to death on the night of the Ides of August (August 6th), and with him four deacons.' The Roman Christians had been surprised by the police at a celebration of mass in the catacomb of Callistus. The house titles could no longer be used for worship. To prevent wholesale arrests Pope Sixtus offered himself to the death prescribed on identification for members of the clergy. He was beheaded in his episcopal chair and with him four of his seven deacons – Januarius, Magnus, Vincent and Stephen. Two others, Felicissimus and Agapitus, were arrested and decapitated the same day in the catacomb of Praetextatus. His death for his sheep in such striking circumstances assured Sixtus a popular cultus. Buried in the papal crypt in the catacomb where he was put to death, his relics were transferred, probably by Leo IV (847–855), to the church where they are still venerated, the Old Church of St Sixtus. He is mentioned in the canon of the Roman mass.

August 6th ILLUSTRATION: page 449

SIXTUS or XYSTUS III † 440
Elected to succeed St Celestine as pope in 432, he restored and dedicated many Roman churches, including St Mary Major and St Peter ad Vincula.

August 19th

SMARAGDUS, *see* Cyriacus, Largus and Smaragdus.

SOCRATES and STEPHEN
According to an unreliable source they were British Christians who suffered martyrdom at Monmouth in the persecution of Diocletian.

September 17th

SOLA † 794
He crossed from England to Germany and became a disciple of St Boniface. His hermitage became the abbey of Solnhofen, near Eichstätt.

December 3rd

SOLANGIA † 880
This daughter of a poor family of Villemont near Bourges took a vow of chastity, and was killed in defense of it.

May 10th

SOLOMON, *see* Roderic and Solomon.

SOPHRONIUS Seventh Century
Born in Damascus, he was called 'the Sophist' for his aptitude in Greek philosophy. After a long pilgrimage with the hermit John Moschus, he was elected patriarch of Jerusalem and was particularly notable for his opposition to monothelism.

March 11th

SOTER and CAIUS † 174 and 296
St Soter succeeded Anicetus as pope, and St Caius succeeded St Eutychian. The manner of their deaths is not certain.

April 22nd

SOTERIS † 304
An Italian of noble birth, she set no value on her great beauty and wealth but devoted herself to God and was martyred under the persecutors Diocletian and Maximian.

February 10th

SOZON
His legend states that he was a shepherd who was led by a vision to destroy a pagan idol. The bravery with which he endured his torments greatly impressed the magistrate, but Sozon refused to accept his pardon and was burned to death.

September 7th

SPERATUS and his Companions, the Scillitan
Martyrs † 180
At Scillium, in what is now Tunisia, twelve Christians were arrested – Speratus, Nartzalus, Cittinus, Veturius, Felix, Aquilinus, Laetantius, Januaria, Generosa, Vestia, Donata, and Secunda. They were taken to Carthage, where they refused to sacrifice to the gods or to acknowledge the deity of the emperor, and all were beheaded.

July 17th

SPEUSIPPUS, ELEUSIPPUS and
MELEUSIPPUS Second Century
According to the Roman martyrology, they were triplets martyred with their grandmother Leonilla, at Langres in France. They probably originated as a pious story which was later taken to be true.

January 17th

SPIRIDION Fourth Century
Although bishop of Tremithus near Salamis, he remained a simple shepherd, married and with a family. His unsophisticated directness often foiled errors cloaked in fine words.

December 14th

STANISLAUS KOSTKA 1550–1568
The son of a Polish senator, he wished to become a

Jesuit, but his father violently opposed him, so he set off on foot, walking 350 miles through Germany to Rome where St Francis Borgia received him. He died after nine months in the novitiate, aged eighteen.

November 13th

STANISLAUS of CRACOW   1030–1079

St Stanislaus is chiefly remembered as patron of the Polish city of Cracow, whose bishop he was, and where his relics are kept in the cathedral. There is no good contemporary account of the saint, and the details of his life are not entirely clear. He is said to have been born of a noble family, to have been brought up by his parents in habits of devotion and to have been well educated. He was ordained priest and attached to the cathedral at Cracow, where he soon became famous for his preaching and his own good example. When the bishop died, Stanislaus was chosen as his successor both by the enthusiasm of the people and the decree of Pope Alexander II.

He was most generous to the poor and needy, but he was also courageous and strict in discipline and the defense of morality, and he came face to face with the king of Poland, Boleslaus II. In a cruel and wicked career, he had finally outraged his people by the abduction of the wife of one of his noblemen. But the nobles and court prelates kept silent. Stanislaus however upbraided the king to his face, and threatened him with the censure of the church. The king failed in his attempt to discredit the bishop by slander, as – according to the biographers – a key witness returned from the dead to vindicate him; but Stanislaus was at last driven to excommunicate the king, who became so enraged that he sought out the bishop and killed him while he was saying Mass. Stanislaus was canonized in 1253 by Innocent IV in the basilica of St Francis at Assisi; and a relic of the saint, sent from Cracow in the following year, is still preserved there. ILLUSTRATION: page 450

May 7th

STEPHEN, *see* Socrates and Stephen.

STEPHEN, *see* William, Stephen, Raymund and their Companions.

STEPHEN I   *Third Century*

Stephen succeeded St Lucius I as pope in 257, at a time when the pagan persecutions were temporarily suspended. Unfortunately the Christians took advantage of the lull to persecute each other, and a fierce controversy raged over the validity of baptism administered by heretics. Stephen found himself opposed to no less a person than St Cyprian of Carthage, who had behind him the African bishops and their congregations. Cyprian insisted that heretics should be baptized upon becoming Catholics, while Stephen insisted that this was unnecessary and that the laying on of hands was quite sufficient.

Stephen seems to have been inflexible in his conduct of the dispute, for he refused to meet a delegation from the church in Africa, threatened those who disagreed with him with excommunication, and declared, 'No innovation must be introduced, but let that be observed which tradition has handed down.'

It is often said that Stephen was martyred during the persecution of the Emperor Valerian, but there is not sufficient evidence for this to be certain.

August 2nd

STEPHEN HARDING   † 1134

St Stephen Harding was born in Dorset some time early in the latter half of the eleventh century, and he died at the abbey of Cîteaux in the year 1134. While still quite a child he was offered as an oblate by his parents to Sherborne Abbey, but on reaching manhood he sickened of the monastic habit and set out to see the world. While on his way back from a pilgrimage to Rome he visited Molesme Abbey and remained there to become a monk. Here he fell under the influence of the abbot, St Robert, and his zeal for reform. Not long afterwards Robert, in despair of ever bringing his monks round to his own point of view, departed from Molesme to live for a short time with some hermits in the neighborhood, leaving his prior, St Alberic, and Stephen, to face the fierce opposition of their brethren. It is not perfectly clear what happened after this; one account says that Alberic and Stephen left Molesme soon after Robert's departure, to live as hermits in the diocese of Langres, and that on being told by the bishop to return to their monastery, they moved to a site a few miles south of Dijon known as Cîteaux, where they were joined by Robert and about twenty monks from Molesme; another account says that they both returned to Molesme in obedience to the bishop and left again some time afterwards, accompanied by Robert, who himself had come back to Molesme in the meantime.

Whichever account is true, it is certain that in the year 1098 Robert, Alberic, Stephen, and a group of about twenty other monks from Molesme founded a new monastery at Cîteaux, where they lived a simple and austere life according to the letter of St Benedict's Rule. Within little more than a year, Robert returned to Molesme, leaving Alberic in his place, and, on the death of Alberic in 1108, Stephen was chosen as abbot. For all his austerity Stephen seems to have been a man of great charm and a scholar of the first rank. Soon after becoming abbot he set about revising the text of the Latin Bible, calling in Jewish rabbis to explain the Hebrew of the Old Testament. But the first years of his rule were not easy, hardly any novices were able to endure the stern life, and the numbers of the community fell to as low as seventeen or eighteen monks. The whole venture seemed in jeopardy, but Stephen would not mitigate in the smallest degree the high ideals with which it had started, in fact he made things more difficult by forbidding the duke of Burgundy, a great benefactor, to hold his court in the monastery.

Then in the year 1112 the tide changed with the arrival of St Bernard and thirty companions. In an amazingly short time after this, Cîteaux became the mother house of a rapidly spreading monastic order. As it turned out, Stephen was quite able to cope with this sudden new development; in the year 1119 he summoned all the abbots of the newly founded houses to Cîteaux and presented them in chapter with the famous constitutions known as the *Carta Caritatis*, which has remained ever since the framework of the whole order. Yet in spite of his colossal achievement in impressing his austere personality on the whole order and giving it the character by which it was enabled to withstand the shocks and accidents of time and survive to our own day, Stephen remains a shadowy figure. Perhaps it is inevitable that a man of his retiring disposition should have been eclipsed in popular estimation by the dramatic appeal of his brilliant disciple, St Bernard, and that in an order which has been recruited since the reformation largely in France, his rôle in the formation of it should not have received, until quite lately, all the attention it deserves. Old and nearly blind, Stephen resigned his office at the general chapter of the order in 1133, and died in the following year on March 28th. His feast day is observed in the order on July 16th.
April 17th

STEPHEN of HUNGARY   *Eleventh Century*
Stephen was the son of Geza, duke of Hungary, and was baptized when he was ten years old, at a time when many of the Hungarian nobility were turning to Christianity. When he was twenty-two years old he succeeded his father as governor of the Magyars, and began a number of wars to unite the country. At the conclusion of his campaigns, he asked Pope Silvester II to establish a proper hierarchy in the country and to grant him the title of King, in order that he might better be able to protect his people and the church. The pope agreed to these proposals, and King Stephen was crowned by the first archbishop of Hungary, St Astrik, in 1001.

Stephen completed the establishment of the monastery of St Martin begun by his father, and saw to it that, as Magyar priests became available, churches were set up throughout his country. He required by law that every tenth town should build a church and support a priest.

Stephen took a particular interest in the poor. One day he was distributing alms to a crowd of beggars, who grew so clamorous that the king was swept off his feet and thrown to the ground. He was not angry at the incident but laughed it off, saying that he would always continue to give alms to anyone who asked him. His religious actions had their political consequences, for his popularity with the poor insured that the nobles would never become too powerful. As he grew older, Stephen hoped to delegate his sovereignty to his son, but unfortunately the prince was killed in a hunting accident, and Stephen's last years were made hideous by frequent disputes over the succession. He died at the age of sixty-three in 1038 and is buried in the Church of our Lady at Buda.
September 2nd

STEPHEN of MURET   † 1124
He was founder and abbot of a monastery near Limoges in the Muret valley, which was later transferred to Grandmont. This was the origin of the Order of Grandmont which lasted for less than a century. St Stephen refused to write a rule, forbade his monks to leave their enclosure, and put the administration of the community into the hands of the lay-brothers.
February 8th

STEPHEN of OBAZINE   † 1154
With another priest, Stephen became a hermit in the Obazine forest, and was later consecrated abbot of the monastery founded for their numerous disciples. The community had no written rules, for Stephen's austere example sufficed; but before he died he sent to Dalon, a dependency of Cîteaux, to ask for monks to instruct his community in their rule, and he himself became a Cistercian.
March 8th

STEPHEN of PERM   † 1396
A monk of Rostov, he set out to evangelize in the east of Russia, translating the scriptures into the language of the Zyriane (a people living to the south-west of the Urals), and inventing an alphabet for them. In 1383 he was made the first bishop of Perm in recognition of his work.
April 26th

STEPHEN of RIETI   *Sixth Century*
An abbot of a monastery near Rieti. St Gregory the Great mentions his great patience and speaks of his rude speech but cultured life.
February 13th

STEPHEN of SUROSH   *Eighth Century*
This native of Cappadocia was archbishop of Surosh in the Crimea when he was exiled in the iconclastic persecution under Leo III, returning in 740.
December 15th

STEPHEN of SWEDEN *Eleventh Century*
He was probably a monk of New Corbie in Saxony. Consecrated a regionary bishop, he did missionary work in Sweden and was martyred by pagans whose worship of Woden he had suppressed.
June 2nd

STEPHEN PECHERSKY † 1094
A disciple of St Theodosius in the monastery of the Caves at Kiev, he succeeded him on his death. Later he built the monastery of Blakhernae at Klov, and in 1091 became bishop of Vladimir.
April 27th

STEPHEN PROTOMARTYR † *c.* 35
It is a pity we do not know more about St Stephen. As one of those Greek-speaking Jews of the Dispersion, reared and educated in Graeco-Roman civilization, and also as the forerunner of St Paul, he has a special significance in the early history of the church. There is some evidence that he was educated at Alexandria. Perhaps he was one of those 'Greeks' who sought out our Lord in his last days on earth (John 12:20). If so, he abundantly proved in his own person the words which Jesus then spoke – that the grain of wheat cannot bear fruit unless it falls to the ground and dies.

He first appears in history as one of the seven deacons whom the Apostles ordained (Acts 6) to assist them in administration, but he seems to have applied himself from the first to preaching and apologetics – directed especially towards the Greek-speaking synagogues – and it was one of these, that of the 'Freedmen', which denounced him to the Sanhedrim as a heretic. They accordingly arrested Stephen and put him on trial.

The speech in which he defended himself is reported by St Luke at considerable length and is apt to seem dull to a modern reader. What is it but a résumé of Old Testament history? Why should it reduce the assembled pundits of Judaism to inarticulate rage? Because of the twist he gave to it. Because of the interpretation which, explicitly or implicitly, he put upon the story. He made two main points: first, that God was to be found not only in the Temple, or in Jerusalem, or even in Palestine, but anywhere. God had been with Abraham in Chaldea, with Joseph in Egypt, with Moses in Sinai, with the Israelites in the desert, with David before ever the Temple was built. And his second point was this, that the official leaders of Judaism had habitually rejected the accredited messengers of God. The patriarchs had sold Joseph into slavery, their descendants in Egypt had exiled Moses; in the wilderness Aaron had led them away from the Law into idolatry. Again and again the Jewish leaders had rejected, stoned and persecuted the prophets of God; and now, to crown all, they had murdered Messiah, the Just One, the Son of Man. But He, Jesus, was now standing on the right hand of God in Glory.

The Sanhedrim were convulsed with hysterical rage. They hustled Stephen off to a place outside the city and stoned him to death. As he died he prayed for them, 'Lord, do not count this sin against them,' and the prayer was heard – not only by God but by Saul of Tarsus. Saul had been present at all this. He knew that he was witnessing a revolting crime. He could not bring himself to join in the stoning; but he held the coats of those who did. Afterwards, he tried to smother his conscience by furiously persecuting other Christians, but it was hard for him to kick against the goad. Not long afterwards he set out on that journey to Damascus which led him, in the end, to a martyrdom like Stephen's. In the words of St Augustine, 'If Stephen had not prayed, the Church would not have gained Paul'. The Feast of the finding of his body is commemorated on August 3rd.
December 26th ILLUSTRATION: page 451

STEPHEN THE YOUNGER † 764
A monk and later an abbot of St Auxentius near Chalcedon, he retired to a more austere life, but was disturbed when the iconoclastic Emperor Constantine Copronymous sought his approval. This he refused to give, and after a lengthy persecution he was eventually beaten to death.
November 28th

STREMOINE, *see* Austremonius.

STURMI † 779
A disciple of St Boniface, he left the abbey of Fritzlar in Bavaria, where he was educated, and, in 744, became the first abbot of the monastery of Fulda, which he modelled on Monte Cassino, obtaining for it freedom from episcopal control. This led to a controversy with St Lull, the bishop of Mainz, in which the fidelity of the monks to their superior was decisive.
December 17th

SULIAU, *see* Tysilio.

SULPICIUS II or SULPICE † 647
The devotion, the miraculous powers and especially the inexhaustible charity of this second bishop of Bourges rendered him so beloved that, at his death, the vast crowds of people made it almost impossible for the officiating clergy to carry out the burial service.
January 17th

SULPICIUS 'SEVERUS' † 591
This bishop of Bourges is often confused with his successor Sulpicius 'Pius', and with the writer Sulpicius Severus. Gregory of Tours admired him greatly, but it is not certain that he was ever canonized.
January 29th

SUNNIVA and her Companions   *Tenth Century*
Sunniva was an Irish princess who, to escape offers of marriage, fled with her followers and settled in caves on an islands off the Norwegian coast. The inhabitants, suspecting them of cattle-stealing, tried to attack them, but were prevented by a landslide which sealed the caves.
July 8th

SUPERIUS, *see* Salvius or Sauve and Superius.

SUSANNA, *see* Anne.

SUSANNA   *Third Century?*
The niece of Pope St Caius, she possessed not only beauty but learning and was so highly regarded that the Emperor Diocletian wished her to marry his son-in-law, Maximian. She not only refused to accept this offer, preferring to remain celibate, but succeeded in converting to Christianity two of the officers whom the emperor had sent to find out the cause of her refusal.
    She was eventually beheaded, together with her father, in their house at Rome.
August 11th

SWITHBERT   † 713
An English missionary under St Willibrord in Lower Germany, he was so successful, particularly in Hither Friesland (which included Southern Holland) that he was consecrated regionary bishop. He is highly honored in the places he evangelized, and is invoked against angina.
March 1st

SWITHUN   † 862
St Swithun died in 862 as bishop of Winchester. It is not known when he was born, but he was a secular clerk with something of a reputation for virtue and learning. He was attached to the West Saxon court and was one of King Egbert's principal advisers. He was given the king's son, Ethelwulf, the father of Alfred the Great, to educate; and to him must go some of the credit for the strongly religious tone of the West Saxon court under Ethelwulf and his sons.
    He was consecrated bishop of Winchester in 852, and as bishop was something of a builder. He may also have been one of the first contributors to the *Anglo-Saxon Chronicle*. A number of agreeably humble miracles were attributed to him – he was said to have restored a basket of eggs dropped by an old market woman when crossing a bridge. His great reputation for sanctity is, however, largely owing to the cult which sprang up at Winchester a hundred years after his death, in the time of St Ethelwold and the monastic reformation, when his body was translated. His shrine was splendid, but when it was looted by Henry VIII in 1538 its gold and jewels were found to be false.

When he died he was buried at his own request in the churchyard, in order that the passers-by would walk over his grave and the rain fall upon it. It is always said that if it rains on his feast day, it will rain for forty days after, but it is not known how St Swithun came to be associated with the weather. Similar stories are told of SS Médard, Gervase and Protase in France.
July 15th

SYAGRIUS   † 600
Elected bishop of Autun in about 560, he seems to have been distinguished for his mildness and reluctance to take any drastic action.
August 27th

SYMMACHUS   † 514
He succeeded Anastasius II as pope in 498 and was immediately faced with a pro-Byzantine anti-pope. He did much to enrich and restore the churches of Rome.
July 19th

SYMPHORIAN, *see* Timothy, Hippolytus and Symphorian.

SYMPHOROSA and her Seven Sons
Whether the seven martyrs Crescens, Julian, Nemesius, Primativus, Justin, Stacteus and Eugenius were in fact her sons is doubtful. According to legend they were all killed in different ways under the Emperor Hadrian, thus joining their mother and father, St Getulius, in martyrdom. *See* Felicity and the Seven Holy Brothers, of which this story may be a doublet.
July 18th

SYNCLETICA   *Fourth Century*
Though beautiful and wealthy, she retired with her blind sister to serve God in the seclusion of a disused burial chamber. She lived in extreme penance, influencing many women by her example and wise words, until she died of cancer.
January 5th

T ANCO or TATTO   † 808
A missionary to Germany, he succeeded St Patto as abbot of Amalbarich abbey and later as bishop of Verden. He was a great preacher, but condemned vice so strongly that an angry crowd killed him.
February 15th

TARACHUS, *see* Andronicus, Tarachus and Probus.

TARASIUS   † 806
Elected patriarch of Constantinople while still a layman, he was zealous, charitable and ascetic; he refused to

connive at the emperor's desire to divorce his wife in favor of one of the maids of honor.
February 25th

TARCISIUS   *Third Century*
A Roman, he was killed when carrying the Blessed Sacrament, preferring death to surrendering it into unworthy hands.
August 15th

TASSACH, *see* Asicus.

TATIAN DULAS   *Fourth Century?*
He was tried by Maximus, prefect of Cilicia, and died of the prolonged tortures applied to make him renounce his faith.
June 15th

TEILO   *Sixth Century*
Of St Teilo much has been written, yet little is known. What is certain is that he flourished in the sixth century, and that his memory was cherished and his intercession sought in south Wales and Brittany for more than a millennium after his death. Indeed Erasmus Saunders, writing in 1721, in his *State of Religion in the Diocese of St David's* complains that the country folk still invoked our Lady and St Teilo 'as if they had hardly yet forgotten the use of praying to them.' His principal monastery was at Llandeilo Fawr. The tradition which associates him with St David is almost certainly sound.

He was a principal leader in the great revival of religion which came from south-west Wales, and which carried the influence and names of David and Teilo, through Breconshire, Radnorshire and Monmouthshire up to the Wye, thus fortifying the earlier work of Dyfrig, Cadoc and Illtud. The influence of the revival spread to Brittany, and the tradition that he spent some years there in person may well be true.

We are probably nearer to his authentic tradition at the isolated little church of Llandeilo Gresynni, near Llannarth in Monmouthshire, than at Llandaff. The church marks the spot where the Welshmen stood in battle against the pagan English, and where, like Moses of old, the saint stood to pray for his countrymen and to turn the battle against the heathen.
February 9th

TELEMACHUS, *see* Almachius.

TELESPHORUS   *Second Century*
By birth a Greek, he was the seventh pope; succeeding Sixtus I, he died a martyr.
January 5th

THE TEN MARTYRS of CRETE   † 250
The edict of Decius against Christianity set off a persecution in Crete. The most famous of the martyrs were Theodolus, Saturninus, Euporus, Gelasius, Eunician, Zoticus, Cleomenes, Agathopus, Basilides and Evaristus. They are known as the ten martyrs of Crete and were executed at Gortyna.
December 23rd

TERESA and SANCHIA of PORTUGAL
                                          † 1250 and 1229
Teresa was the eldest of the three daughters of King Sancho I. When her marriage to her cousin was declared invalid, she retired to her estate at Lorvão and replaced the Benedictine abbey there by a Cistercian convent, in which she resided. Sanchia never married, and impressed by her sister's example, also converted an Augustinian convent which she had founded at Cellas to the Cistercian rule.
June 17th

TERESA MARGARET REDI   1747-1770
Born in Arezzo, she is especially honored at Florence where she spent the last five years of her short life in St Teresa's convent as a Carmelite nun. Her body has remained incorrupt to this day.
March 11th

TERESA of AVILA (or JESUS)   1515-1582
Teresa Sánchez de Cepeda y Ahumada was born, probably at Gotarrendura, near Avila, in Spain, on March 28th, 1515. She was of partly Jewish descent, and grew up in a strictly religious home of the upper middle class, one of a large family. Her mother's death in 1528 made a deep impression on her. She was a boarder in a convent school in Avila for about two years. In 1536 she took the Carmelite habit at the convent of the Incarnation there, and was professed a year later. In 1538 her health broke down, and she left the convent for nearly two years, following various cures. During this time she came under the influence of an uncle, who introduced her to Francisco de Osuna's *Third Spiritual Alphabet*, which led her to the practice of mental prayer. For the next fifteen years, according to her own account, her spiritual life was tepid, but about 1556 she had a second conversion and began to experience mystical prayer sometimes accompanied by visions and voices. She was greatly helped at this period by a number of Dominican and Jesuit confessors.

About 1558 she began to think and speak of reforming the unrecollected life led by the community of the Incarnation, and she was possibly influenced in this by St Peter of Alcántara whom she had first met in 1555. Soon this idea took the form of returning to the primitive Carmelite rule, and in 1562 she founded the convent of St Joseph at Avila. Thereafter, her life was filled with the activities attendant upon her sixteen foundations and in writing her books. The reform spread to the friars (*see* St John of the Cross) and many of her first nuns made foundations abroad, from one of which in Belgium sprang the convent for English nuns at Antwerp. The Carmelite nuns in the U.S.A. can trace their foundation back to this convent. St Teresa met with great opposition from clerics of various kinds both because of her mystical experiences (there was in Spain during her lifetime a vivid recollection of some notorious false mystics of the fifteenth century) and her reforming zeal. But by persistence and force of character she overcame them all. By her Carmelite reform St Teresa inaugurated a reform in the organized religious life of women and in the framework of spirituality in general that has had immense influence throughout the church. If it could be examined afresh and re-applied with an eye to twentieth century conditions, it is possible that the influence could be extended yet further in the future. The nature of this reform was not at all concerned with gross abuses, but can be summed up by saying that her whole aim was to re-organize Carmelite life with a view to intensifying the practice of mental prayer. Her complaint about the convent of the Incarnation was that it had too many nuns (130), lady boarders and visitors were too numerous, there were economic differences between the nuns (who retained their property) and, as a result of all this, the organization, material and spiritual, had fallen into confusion (e.g. in the last years before its reform, only bread was supplied to the nuns; for proper meals they had to go daily to their parents or relatives). St Teresa's reforms are directly related to these shortcomings: strict enclosure, complete poverty, great austerity, small numbers (twenty-one), many hours of solitude daily, and two hours daily of mental prayer prescribed by rule. To make room for these innovations, the long choir office was shortened, and monotone was substituted for singing.

As a writer, Teresa is even more renowned than as a reformer. Her books fall into two categories: autobiographical and mystical works. In the *Life*, she relates her early life and spiritual experiences and gives an account of the early stages of prayer; in the *Interior Castle* (or *Mansions*) she traces the development of mystical prayer through seven stages. Her observation and description are exact and minute. Although not attaching undue importance to visions and so forth, she gives much space to them and discusses them more than St John of the Cross. This is natural since she was herself a visionary, while, so far as we know, St John's life was less rich in these phenomena. Her account of the mystical experience coincides with that of St John, despite their different approach – hers a record of psychological interest and drawing distinctions between the different phases; his the exploration of the theological implications

of the gradual development of a fundamentally single and unitary experience. As a stylist St Teresa is greatly admired in Spanish-speaking countries. She is natural, spontaneous, vivacious, scrupulously exact, and writes the unliterary language of mid-sixteenth century upper class Avila with perfection. But her tendency to digression, and other faults of composition, make her difficult to read and almost impossible to translate. Nevertheless, there is never any doubt about her meaning on important matters.

In the countries of Hispanic tradition the appeal of Teresa has been potent since the sixteenth century, and the Carmelite reform, particularly the nuns', has flourished to this day. Abroad, specially in France and Italy, the saint has also been greatly venerated, although in France the extreme Spanish quality of her spiritual tradition has, from the beginning, been somewhat modified. For the last century or so, the appeal of St Teresa, especially outside the Hispanic tradition, has been different: she has been admired as a powerful personality, a pioneer feminist and a literary figure who has made a great contribution to our knowledge of human psychology. Most people who approach her writings succumb to her enchantment. Her contemporary appeal is probably greatest in the human authenticity of her personality; her faults are revealed to us in her writings without pretence – her over-determination, her excessive drive, her imperfect judgment of human beings, her too great, if unconscious, reliance on the strength of her personality and charm; but the great character built up over long years and in the face of many difficulties, interior and exterior, is revealed also, and her overwhelming love of God and devotion to the inner life. In an age dominated by personality and too easily seduced by charm, she is a saint admirably suited to draw us on to the ideal of good character and the overcoming of self.

Teresa died at Alba de Tormes on October 4th, 1582, and she was canonized in 1628.

October 15th ILLUSTRATION: page 452

TERESA of LISIEUX 1873–1897

St Teresa of the Child Jesus and of the Holy Face was born at Alençon (France) on January 2nd, 1873 and received at baptism the names of Marie Françoise Thérèse. She was the ninth and last child of Louis Martin and Zélie Guérin. Her parents had at one time intended to serve God in the cloister, but their wish was to be fulfilled only by proxy; their five surviving daughters embraced the religious life, four of them in the Carmelite convent of Lisieux.

St Teresa entered Carmel at the age of fifteen years and three months (in 1888). She became a novice one year later, and a professed Carmelite on September 24th,

1890. For three years she was given menial employments in the convent, cleaning, dusting, mending linen and such like. At seventeen she was put in charge of the sacristy and at twenty was appointed 'Companion of the novices' under Mother M. de Gonzague. The first signs of the tuberculosis that carried her away three years later appeared in June 1894. She continued in her usual occupations without any relaxation until the end of Lent 1896, and she died soon after in the infirmary on September 30th, 1897.

During the nine years she had spent in that little provincial convent of Normandy, she had apparently never done anything remarkable, spectacular or even noticeable, so that, during her last illness, some nuns wondered what the prioress could find to say in the short biographical notice that was sent to Carmelite convents after the death of members of their order. This uneventful life, however, has attracted more attention than that of many great men or women; her biography went through a record number of successive editions. Preliminary steps towards Teresa's beatification were taken barely twelve years after her death, and her canonization occurred fourteen years later, on May 17th, 1925. She has now long been the most popular saint of modern times.

If we endeavour to trace the causes of this astounding popularity, we may think at once of the happy wording of the promises made by her on her deathbed ('I will let fall a shower of roses – I will spend my heaven doing good upon earth'); but these promises would have meant nothing had they not been fully realised by miraculous cures, conversions, favors of every kind granted through her intercession. The part taken by Mother Agnès in her sister's canonization, in rendering assistance at every step of the cause, cannot be exaggerated. Her correspondence with various Roman prelates comprises thousands of letters. This had been foreseen by St Teresa herself, when she said 'She will be busy watching the letter box'. To Mother Agnès also we owe the publication of the *Story of a Soul*, which was the means of making her sister known to the Catholic world. She rearranged and rewrote most of the book, and, in her anxiety for her sister's glory, modified or left out of the story some passages that might have given a wrong impression (just as she had her sister's photographs improved later on). Nevertheless, in the autobiography, the story, the thought and even the style remained in essentials what they were in Teresa's original manuscript.

The publication of a facsimile of this manuscript was resisted successfully by Mother Agnès during her lifetime. It only took place in 1956. It will oblige future biographers to make some little alterations to the portrait of St Teresa as a child. Let us add that the style of the autobiography, generally emotional, and sometimes melodramatic, discourages the fastidious but is a sheer delight to the many and has contributed not a little to the extraordinary success of the book.

When all is said and done, these are only contributory causes and would have long ago ceased to influence the popularity of the saint were it not for her heroic virtues. She never had any visions or revelations; she never worked any miracle in her lifetime, but in the obscurity of the cloister, in ordinary and commonplace circumstances, she found all the materials she needed to build her sanctity and reach perfection.

This was no easy task, for she had a difficult nature to conquer. Even in her first childhood her pride and obstinacy were already much in evidence. Céline, her sister, noted this carefully. In her childhood she had resolved to be a saint. She was under the impression she had never done her own will and at thirteen that she had already reached perfection. The fact was that she had yet a long way to go, and a hard struggle to wage before she became the humble, obedient, uncomplaining, smiling young saint one discovers later on in Carmel. Her greatest handicap, however, was a neurotic condition against which she had to fight all her life long. In childhood it manifested itself when she was four and a half years old, by an extreme timidity and a distressing propensity to tears, at ten by a severe nervous breakdown with hallucinations, delusions, catalepsy etc., at twelve by a state of scruples, which eight years later still afflicted her sorely. Meanwhile she was subject to black moods, to days of depression without any apparent cause, and during the last eighteen months of her life to an obsession, that of religious doubts, apparently causeless also. We must see in this neurosis the main element of those sufferings to which she alludes constantly, and 'which were all the more painful to bear because she was the only one who knew of them'. In fighting this distressing condition, she showed a persistent and admirable courage. After her 'Christmas conversion' she began to grapple with her tendency to tears, and continued to try and overcome her scruples all the time, keeping to herself the secret of her trials, unruffled apparently and always deceptively smiling. There is no doubt that her 'Little Way', her complete surrender to the love and power of God, was her method of approach to the problem of scruples. For her it could not be solved by obedience and authority, but only by her way of trust and absolute self surrender to the love of God. In a similar way she put her obsession of doubts 'which she could not explain' to the service of her perfection. She had never wavered, never surrendered to her haunting doubts, and she did not falter at the end. Now in the face of death, gathering all her faith, all her love, she voiced with her last breath her vehement protest that the silence of God had neither touched her faith nor diminished her love, and her last words were 'Oh! I love him. My God, I love you.'

Her long continued fight against her scruples and her religious doubts ended in making perfect her faith and hope in God, and in fact set the final seal on her sanctity and her greatness.   ILLUSTRATION: page 453
October 3rd

TERNAN   *Fifth or Sixth Century*
He seems to have been prominent in the conversion of the Picts, and was one of their first bishops.
June 12th

THAÏS
According to legend she was a celebrated Egyptian courtesan, who was converted by St Paphnutius, and as a penance, lived for three years on bread and water in a tiny cell which no one was allowed to enter.
October 8th

THALASSIUS and LIMNAEUS   *Fifth Century*
They are mentioned in *Philotheus* by Theodoret who knew them both. Thalassius was a hermit near Tillima in Syria, and Limnaeus was his disciple. Limnaeus lived alone on top of a mountain in a shelter without a roof for thirty-eight years. He cured himself of a snake-bite by prayer and built two hostels for the blind near his cell.
February 22nd

THALELAEUS   *Third Century*
He was a physician who was known as the 'Merciful', because he did not charge for his treatment. He is said to have undergone martyrdom at Aegae in Cilicia.
May 20th

THALELAEUS THE HERMIT   *Fifth Century*
A recluse of Cilicia, known to Theodoret, he lived near Gabala beside a heathen shrine and converted many of its worshippers. For ten years he lived cramped in a small cage, weeping almost continually.
February 27th

THARSILLA and EMILIANA   *Sixth Century*
These sisters were the maiden aunts of St Gregory the Great, and lived a retired life in their father's house.
December 24th

THEA, VALENTINA and PAUL   † 308
Put to death at Gaza by the governor of Palestine in the reign of Maximinus II.
July 25th

THECLA   *First Century?*
Supposed to have been a convert of St Paul's and once held in high honor all over Christendom, Thecla may never have existed. Her fame rested on a second-century romance known as the *Acts of Paul and Thecla*. She is also sometimes identified with the Thecla who shared the martyrdom of St Martha of Persia.
September 23rd

THECLA, *see* Timothy, Agapus and Thecla.

THECLA of KITZINGEN   *Eighth Century*
A nun of Wimborne, she went to Germany to help St Boniface and became abbess of Ochsenfurt and then of Kitzingen.
October 15th

THECUSA, *see* Theodotus, Thecusa and their Companions.

THEOBALD of ALBA   † 1150
He gave up the prospects of material success promised by his position as the son of wealthy parents to become a cobbler, a calling he considered to be more in keeping with the teachings of Christianity.
June 1st

THEOBALD of MARLY   † 1247
A Montmorency, Theobald joined the Cistercians of Vaux-de-Cernay in 1220 and became their abbot in 1235.
July 27th

THEOBALD or THIBAUD of PROVINS † 1066
Son of Count Arnoul of Champagne, he lived with another hermit in the forest of Pettingen in Luxembourg. There, their fame troubled them, and they travelled to Italy, where they both ended their days.
June 30th

THEOCTISTA
Most probably a pious fiction, this is the tale of a girl from Lesbos who was captured by Arabs, but escaped on the island of Paros where she lived as a recluse, until a man named Simon discovered her and brought her Communion, after which she died.
November 10th

THEODARD   † 670?
This bishop of Tongres-Maestricht was murdered when on his way to Childeric II to defend ecclesiastical rights.
September 10th

THEODARD of NARBONNE   † 893
As a young lawyer, in Toulouse, he attracted the attention of Archbishop Sigebold of Narbonne, who ordained him, made him his archdeacon, and named him as his successor.
May 1st

THEODORA and DIDYMUS   † 304?
Theodora was supposed to have been sentenced to be kept in a brothel in Alexandria for refusing to sacrifice to the gods, and was rescued by Didymus who changed clothes with her. Didymus was detected and beheaded, while Theodora died of shock.
April 28th

THEODORA of ALEXANDRIA

Supposed to have been the wife of the prefect of Egypt, she lived disguised as a monk in the desert.
September 11th

THEODORE, *see* Michael of Chernigov and Theodore.

THEODORE and THEOPHANES † 841 and 845

Monks of the St Sabas monastery at Jerusalem, these brothers were twice exiled in the iconoclastic persecutions. On the second occasion they were brought before the emperor at Constantinople, who ordered that twelve lines of verse should be tattooed on their foreheads. As one of the brothers was known to be a poet, the emperor apologised for the literary shortcomings of the verses, but a courtier interjected, 'Sire, they are not worth better verse.' The inscription described the men as having been born in the city (Jerusalem) where the incarnate word of God first walked; exiled as apostates, they fled to Constantinople, and now bore the marks of their impieties upon their faces as common criminals.
December 27th

THEODORE, DAVID and CONSTANTINE
Fourteenth Century

St Theodore the Black († 1299) was duke of Yaroslav and Smolensk; David and Constantine were his sons by his second marriage. Wise and merciful rulers, their relics were enshrined in 1464.
September 19th

THEODORE of HERACLEA

A saint highly honored in Greece, and now thought to be the same person as Theodore of Amasea. He was probably a Christian in the army of Licinius by whom he was martyred.
February 7th

THEODORE of SYKEON † 613

A native of Sykeon in Galatia, he became a monk and a priest when on pilgrimage to Jerusalem. Although a recluse, he founded several monasteries, and had to be forced to accept the see of Anastasiopolis, which he held for only ten years before retiring again to a solitary life.
April 22nd

THEODORE of TARSUS † 690

In 664 the synod of Whitby effectively secured the union of the Celtic and Roman sees in England under the primacy of the archbishop of Canterbury. Almost immediately after the synod, Canterbury fell vacant, and the new unity of the English church was shown when the Kentish and Northumbrian kings co-operated in choosing a new archbishop, whom they sent to Rome for consecration, where he died very shortly after his arrival. The pope decided to provide an archbishop to succeed him, and he chose an African monk, Hadrian, who however insisted on his unworthiness, and the succession passed to a most extraordinary choice, an aged Greek monk living in Rome, Theodore of Tarsus. Although the English church as a whole had only just passed into the Roman obedience and although there were already serious divergences of custom and ill-feeling between Greek and Latin Christians, the pope nevertheless chose Theodore, though sending with him Abbot Hadrian to see that he introduced no Greek perversities into England.

In 669, Archbishop Theodore, then nearly seventy, arrived in Kent. He immediately began a visitation of the whole English church with a view to filling the sees emptied by a terrible outbreak of plague. In Northumbria he was faced with the first clash between church and state in newly converted England. After Whitby, St Wilfrid had been appointed bishop of Northumbria and gone to Gaul for consecration, but in his absence a monk, St Chad, or Ceadda, had been appointed in his place, and irregularly consecrated into the bargain. Theodore acted with firmness; he deposed Chad, regularized the consecration and later made him bishop of the Mercians, and insisted on Wilfrid's reinstatement. By 672 order was so far restored that he could hold the first general synod of the whole English church at Hertford. Not only was this the first English ecclesiastical council, it was also the first all-English assembly of any kind whatsoever.

It was apparent that Theodore's main administrative task was to secure fixed sees – the English tribal kingdoms were perpetually at war with one another, and their kings expected the boundaries of their sees to fluctuate accordingly – and to secure the creation of new sees to meet the needs of the growing church, a problem which also required great tact and diplomatic skill. Theodore succeeded in solving both these problems, and the sees of Hereford, Worcester and Lindsey were created by him. His most difficult task was the subdivision of the Northumbrian see, which he was able to do only in Wilfrid's absence, at the cost of some injustice to that stormy prelate. In 679 another English council was held at Hatfield, and, for the first time, the English church participated in a concern of the whole church: the heresy of Monthelitism was condemned at papal request. In 680 Theodore was reconciled with St Wilfrid and endeavored to secure such restitution for him as was compatible with the preservation of church order in the north; and he secured Wilfrid's temporary restoration at York before his death in 690.

Theodore is a dim figure who is known to us mainly by his work. But his work was outstanding. He secured a reasonable system of episcopal government in a most

difficult situation, he effectively maintained for Canterbury a prestige above that of any tribal bishopric. He preserved the idea of a united English church in an England which had no other kind of unity. He had also an intellectual importance. His decisions in cases of conscience were so respected that collections of them called penitentials were made soon after his death and, carried to the continent by the English missionaries, became the foundation of the western penitential system. He seems to have taught some Greek, and his cathedral school, together with that of Aldhelm at Malmesbury and Bede at Jarrow, were the sources of that English but ecumenical culture which is so conspicuous a feature of the English church in the eighth century.
September 19th

THEODORE THE SANCTIFIED   314–368
Born in the Upper Thebaid, he joined St Pachomius in the desert at Tabenna, and was later ordained by him. He became abbot of Tabenna *c.* 347.
April 27th

THEODORE THE STUDITE   † 826
In 794 he succeeded his uncle, St Plato, as abbot of the monastery built on the family estate at Sakkoudion. Exiled when they expressed their disapproval of the emperor's adultery with their kinswoman, Theodota, they were able to return in 797 when the emperor was dethroned.

Theodore is one of the foremost monastic legislators, and he developed the abbey of Studius, of which he became abbot *c.* 799, into a community of a thousand monks. During the iconoclastic persecution of Leo V, he suffered imprisonment at Bonita and Smyrna for seven years. He was under sentence of death when he was released at the accession of Michael the Stammerer in 820, but was not reinstated.
November 11th

THEODORE TIRO   † 306?
He was martyred at Amasea for his uncompromising profession of faith while still a recruit *(tiro)* in the Roman army.
November 9th

THEODORET   † 362
He was a priest in Antioch who was beheaded when he refused to give up the valuables of his church to the prefect, Julian, uncle of Julian the Apostate.
October 23rd

THEODORIC or THIERRY   † 533
After persuading his wife to release him from his obligations, he became a priest and founded the monastery of Mont d'Or, near Rheims.
July 1st

THEODOSIA, *see* Apphian and Theodosia.

THEODOSIA   † 745
A nun of the Anastasias at Constantinople, she accidentally killed an official while he was about to destroy an image of our Lord on the order of the emperor. Her subsequent execution was considered a martyrdom by those who propagated her cult, but she does not appear in the Roman martyrology.
May 29th

THEODOSIUS of PECHERSK, *see* Antony of Pechersk.

THEODOSIUS THE CENOBIARCH   423–529
He was born at Garissus in Cappadocia in 423, and became a hermit near Bethlehem. He was soon so famous that his disciples filled a spacious monastery at Cathismus. To this monastery were attached three hospitals: for the sick, the aged, and the insane. This last hospital contained many who had lost their reason as a result of the extravagant practice of asceticism. Though banished later on by the heretical emperor, Anastasius, Theodosius was recalled by Justin.
January 11th

THEODOTA   † 304?
Theodota and her three sons were – it is said – denounced as Christians because she refused to marry the prefect Leucatius. They were martyred in Bithynia.
August 2nd

THEODOTA of PHILIPPOPOLIS   † *c.* 318?
She was supposed to have been a prostitute who, having repented of her sins, let herself be stoned to death at Philippopolis in Thrace rather than give up her faith.
September 29th

THEODOTUS, THECUSA and their Companions   † 304?
A pious fiction, this is the story of an inn-keeper of Ancyra in Galatia who was beheaded for rescuing the bodies of seven Christian girls drowned in a pond for refusing to be robed as pagan priestesses.
May 18th

THEODULUS, *see* Agathopus and Theodulus.

THEODULUS, *see* Alexander, Eventius and Theodulus.

THEODULUS and JULIAN   † 309
At Caesarea in Palestine, Theodulus, an official in the household of the governor Firmilian, was peremptorily crucified for encouraging imprisoned Christians. Julian, a catechumen, gladly suffered death by fire for honoring the bodies of SS Elias, Jeremy and their companions.
February 17th

THEONILLA, *see* Claudius, Asterius, Neon, Domnina and Theonilla.

THEOPHANES, *see* Theodore and Theophanes.

THEOPHANES THE CHRONICLER   † 817
Author of a chronography or history of the world. When his wife entered a convent, he left Constantine V's court, founded two monasteries and became abbot of that on Mount Sigriana. He died of maltreatment after the iconoclast, Leo the Armenian, had imprisoned him.
March 12th

THEOPHILUS of CORTE   1740
Only son of noble parents, he became a Franciscan, and was a reader in theology at Civitella of which he later became guardian or superior. He founded similar houses in which the rule was strictly kept in Corsica and Tuscany.
May 21st

THEOPHILUS THE PENITENT
His story, which is entirely fictitious, enjoyed great popularity. According to it, this devout, humble man became embittered, made a pact with the Devil but finally won divine forgiveness.
February 4th

THEOPHYLACT   † 845
Appointed bishop of Nicomedia by St Tarasius under whom he had trained, his charitable rule was short. He was in prison until he died for condemning the Iconoclast, Leo V, and prophesying his violent death.
March 7th

THEOTONIUS   † 1166
An archpriest of Viseu, he is highly honored in Portugal. He died as abbot of the new monastery for Canons Regular at Coimbra.
February 18th

THEUDERIUS or CHEF   *Sixth Century*
A monk of Lérins, he returned to his native Dauphiné and founded a monastery near Vienne, although he himself lived as a recluse.
October 29th

THIBAUD, *see* Theobald of Provins.

THIERRY, *see* Theodoric.

THOMAS AQUINAS   1225–1274
St Thomas Aquinas was born in the castle of Roccasecca near Naples about the year 1225. He was educated at the nearby abbey of Monte Cassino and then at the University of Naples; it was while he was an undergraduate there that he decided to become a Dominican. The order was not yet thirty years old, and his family were shocked at the idea of a nobleman's becoming a mendicant friar; besides, they had hoped he would do something to restore their fortunes by returning to Monte

Cassino as its abbot. They kidnapped him and shut him up in the family castle until he should come to his senses. But in the end his firmness prevailed, and he was allowed to return to the order. It was the one outwardly dramatic event of his life; there were thirty years of intense activity before him, but the battles he was now to fight were intellectual ones. Henceforth all his energies were directed to teaching, explaining and defending the Catholic faith.

St Thomas lacked the universal interests of his master St Albert; he was, for instance, not much concerned with the thirteenth century revival of experimental science that Albert fostered. But in philosophy and theology he achieved a depth of understanding and an ease of exposition unequalled even in that century of genius. From his early studies in Naples, and later from St Albert, he quickly realized the importance of the new knowledge of Aristotle that came through the new translations made first from Arabic versions and later (largely on Thomas's insistence) from the original Greek. To theologians bred in the Platonist tradition that was St Augustine's heritage to Christianity, Aristotle was deeply suspect: they felt about him much as a modern theologian might feel about Marx – he seemed to lay all the emphasis on material things. Matters were made worse by the insistence of certain contemporary philosophers on just those aspects of Aristotelianism that conflicted with the Catholic faith. These men were often sincere Christians who could yet see no way of reconciling their faith with what they had learned of Aristotle through the great Arabian philosopher Averroes. Reason seemed to be proving conclusively that the world has existed eternally that God has no knowledge of individual persons or things, and that our souls are not immortal. On the one hand St Thomas had to persuade these Averroists, as they were called, that better reasoning could show where Aristotle was mistaken; on the other he had to persuade the over-cautious that much of Aristotle was sound and invaluable for the theological task of seeking to understand the truths of faith. By his single-minded devotion to truth, and by his own personal charm, he eventually gained the sympathies of even his most determined opponents, just as he had won over the secular masters of Paris who were jealous of the recognition gained by himself and the other mendicant professors at that University.

All this time he was turning out a volume of writing very large by modern standards: commentaries on Aristotle, on the scriptures, treatises on special philosophical and theological questions, and two complete systematic treatises of theology. The second of these, the *Summa Theologica*, is a masterly synthesis of the Latin and Greek patristic traditions, illuminated by the use of philosophical reasoning drawn from Aristotle and Plato.

The ordering of the material shows the originality of his mind, particularly in the middle section on Christian morality, which breaks entirely fresh ground. He had realised that the deeply reasonable order of man's return to the creator, in whose image we are made, harmonized the manifold variety of human action into a single moral pattern. If we are tempted to see in Thomas merely the busy university professor, ever engaged in the affairs of church and order, these works provide the corrective. Their clarity and penetration in the solution of most complex questions could only come from an inner life spent in contemplation of God. The source of his intellectual achievement was his life as a religious. In his own well-known words, 'communicating one's contemplations to others is a greater thing than merely contemplating' (S.T. 2-2. 188.6). Contemplation comes first, and it will flow naturally into activity. There is no sign in St Thomas of that tension between the religious and the intellectual life which is given expression in the *Imitation of Christ,* and which so many modern Catholics seem to feel. His sanctity was achieved in and through the main work of his life, his intellectual activity. There is no need to repeat here the stories that have survived of his humility and devotion. It is in his works that we find the best evidence of that total cleaving to God which is sanctity. The medieval convention and his own self-effacement give them at first sight an air of impersonality, but anyone who studies them comes to know their author no less intimately than does, say, the student of Newman. He comes to see the characteristics of Thomas's mind, its strongly empirical bent, its refusal to speculate where evidence is lacking, its refusal to play down the natural in favour of the supernatural; he learns to face new difficulties as Thomas would have faced them.

In 1272 St Thomas was recalled to Naples as regent of studies in the Dominican priory. The productive part of his life was nearly over. He had had ten years in Italy, partly at the papal curia, and in 1269 had returned to Paris to teach theology. But now at the end of 1273 an experience as he was saying mass convinced him that he could write no more, 'since all that I have written seems to me like so much straw compared with what I have seen and what has been revealed to me' (*Processus informativus,* Naples 1317, no. 79). He was soon after summoned to take part in the council of Lyons, but he died on his way there at the Cistercian abbey of Fossanova. He was not yet fifty years old.

He was canonized in 1323, and he was declared a doctor of the church in 1567. Leo XIII made him patron of all catholic schools, and indeed his teaching has come to occupy a unique position in the church as the basis of theological studies in the majority of seminaries.

March 7th ILLUSTRATION: facing page 369

THOMAS KASAKI, *see* Martyrs of Japan.

THOMAS MORE 1478–1535

Thomas More died as he had lived – shrewdly, even wittily and with deliberation. Born in London on February 6th, 1478, he was, in his own words, 'of no famous family, but of honest stock', yet for two generations at least there had been eminent lawyers in his family. At the age of twelve, he went as a page to Cardinal Morton, archbishop of Canterbury, who two years later sent him to Canterbury College, Oxford, where his father helped him to concentrate on his studies by keeping him so short of money that he could not afford to pay for his shoes to be repaired. At sixteen he left Oxford for London and the Inns of Court. Three years later, in 1493, he met the Dutch scholar Erasmus, then making his first visit to England. More combined his legal studies with the testing of his religious vocation by living for four years at the London Charterhouse. There he began those austerities he maintained throughout his life; for, even as lord chancellor, he rose at 2 a.m., studied until 7 a.m., and, much to his daughter-in-law's amusement, wore a hair shirt.

More decided that his vocation was not for the religious life, and that he would marry. His way of choosing a bride was highly characteristic, because, although the second daughter of the family of his choice was the 'fairest and best favoured, yet when he considered that it would be both grief and rare shame also to the eldest to see her younger sister in marriage preferred before her, he then of a certain pity framed his fancy towards her.'

His wife lived only for four years and, within a year of her death he married a wife who bore him no children but acted as a mother to the three girls and a boy he already had. 'Neither a pearl nor a girl' was his description of her, but despite her forthright, even truculent, manner, the marriage was highly successful; for More was no spoiled priest, and his children, especially the girls, received an education at their home in Chelsea which was far in advance of what was then customary. Nor should the idyllic picture of his family life be allowed to obscure the skill with which he overcame the potential sources of disharmony: for him sanctity began at home.

His reputation as a lawyer soon brought him to the attention of King Henry VIII, who pressed him to join his service. More agreed and prospered: he was knighted, and, in 1523, was made speaker of the House of Commons.

Henry's wife, Catherine of Aragon, had failed to provide a male heir, and by 1527 he was determined to bring the marriage to an end. Such a proposal may have originated in Henry's conscience – as he claimed; but it may have been put to him either by Wolsey – to spite the Queen's nephew, Charles V – or by the woman who refused to be his mistress because she was determined to become his wife: Anne Boleyn. The legality of Henry's marriage to his brother's widow and of the pope's dispensation which made it possible does seem to have been genuinely disputable, and opinions were solicited from various bishops, including St John Fisher. From the start, More disliked the business, but this did not deter the king in 1529 from making him lord chancellor when Wolsey failed to produce the pope's consent to the divorce.

Although some years before, More had said of the king, 'If my head would win him a castle in France it should not fail to go,' he was twelve years his senior and may have hoped – with Wolsey out of the way – to take the king's mind off the divorce. Perhaps he remembered what he had said in his book *Utopia* (1515): 'That which you cannot turn to good, so to order that it be not very bad.' The king, for his part, may have believed More to be more pliant than he was. His discretion was so complete that he mortified his tongue as rigorously as his body, but a reputation for silence can sometimes seem to promise future consent.

When the pope finally pronounced against the divorce, Henry was too angry to see the difference between a moral decision and a political manoeuvre, nor did those clergy and laity who subsequently accepted him as supreme head of the church of England in 1532 see the distinction any more clearly. After four hundred years the issues seem clear enough – almost too clear – but at the time it required the insight of a saint to pierce the fear and confusion aroused by the king's behavior; and even for St Thomas More such insight had come slowly. When Henry had rushed to the defense of the pope against Luther in 1521, More had reminded him, 'The Pope is a prince as you are, and in league with all the other Christian princes,' and one has only to look at the behavior of the Renaissance popes to understand why it took More, on his own admission, ten years to see the pope as more than a man-made authority.

When Henry required the clergy to submit to him, More resigned; but the time had come when he was to achieve a greatness far exceeding that of the 'holy and righteous' lord chancellor who liked to serve the parish mass and carry the cross in processions.

Henry was determined to secure unconditional support for his policy, and in April 1534 More was brought before the commissioners at Lambeth and asked if he would take the oath recognizing the heirs of Anne Boleyn as lawful; since the oath also contained a repudiation of the pope's authority, he refused and was imprisoned. Now begins that battle of wits between a despot determined to destroy his opponents by due

force of law and one of the most able lawyers of his time – how able, can be seen from the simplicity and originality of his defense. More would not say, even to his beloved daughter Margaret Roper, why he refused to swear the oath. He asserted that to be silent was not a crime but a right, and that to refuse to say that the king was supreme head of the church of England was not a capital charge. What was capital was to assert that he was not. A never-ending series of interrogations was begun, to trap its victims into this denial. All but More succumbed. Accustomed as he was to mortification, he seemed able to take imprisonment in his stride, and such apparent contentment provoked his wife to a famous outburst, to which he merely replied: 'Is not this house as nigh Heaven as mine own?'

After the verdict was given against him, More rounded on his judges: what right had they to make laws against Christ's universal Catholic church, when it was from Rome that they had received the faith? 'And therefore am I not bounden to conform my conscience to the Council of one realm against the general Council of Christendom.' That was the climax of the years of prayer, study and mortification, and it is a claim that we in this dissension-torn century are more willing to accept than were those who stood at the threshold of four successful centuries of nationalism.

St Thomas More was executed on July 6th, 1535, and his bearing on the way to the block once again revealed the strength and subtlety of his character. He was offered wine but refused it, saying, 'My Master had easell and gall, not wine, given him to drink.' He jested with the executioner. But with his last words he stated clearly and finally the reason for his death: 'I die the King's good servant, but God's first.'

July 9th   ILLUSTRATION: page 454

THOMAS of CANTERBURY   1118–1170

He was born in the city of London in 1118. His family name of Becket was rarely used by his contemporaries, to whom he was Thomas of London or Archbishop Thomas. His father was a Norman knight, Gilbert, who had become a prosperous merchant in London; his mother was also Norman, and he had at least two sisters, one of whom later became abbess of Barking. To his mother he owed his early piety, a devotion to our Lady, and generosity to the poor. From boyhood upwards he was richly endowed by nature. He was tall, handsome and vigorous, with dark hair, pale complexion and a prominent nose; his sight and hearing were unusually keen, he had a remarkably retentive memory, and he was a master of extemporary speech and debate. As a boy he was devoted to field sports and as a young man his energy, his practical ability and his initiative were more evident than his wisdom or his judgment. After a schooling at Merton priory and Paris he became, at twenty-one, financial clerk to a relative in the city, but after three years he was taken into the household of Theobald, the Norman monk-archbishop of Canterbury. The young Thomas gradually made his way upwards by his charm, his generosity and his adaptability. He was ambitious, and refused no opportunity of advancement or preferment, he enjoyed display and activity, but all are agreed that his life both then and at all times was absolutely pure. The archbishop gave him the post of archdeacon, and he seemed to be following the normal career of an able ecclesiastic when, at the age of thirty-six, he was recommended by Theobald to the young King Henry as chancellor.

Henry II was a man of very great ability and energy with a genius both for leadership and for organisation; at the same time he was self-willed, imperious, and passionate, wholly unspiritual and bent on gaining control of every power in his kingdom. Thomas the chancellor, who then and always had a personal affection for Henry, devoted all his efforts to serve and please the young king. Accepting all the wealth that came his way he spent it lavishly on entertainments, on rich clothes and plate and on hunting, hawking, and even on martial exploits, but he never failed to work hard and prudently in the king's interest, and there is evidence that he felt a secret dissatisfaction with himself and his worldly life.

In 1163 Theobald died, and the king secured the election of his friend, confident that he would serve all his interests. Thomas resisted, and warned the king that he might regret his choice. Then he accepted the office, and with what seemed a sudden change he became an austere and spiritual man, devoted to the interests of the church, the faithful servant of the pope. It was not long before the clash with the king occurred. Henry was resolved to reassert all the rights which had been claimed and exercised fifty years before by the Conqueror and his sons. Since that time, however, the papacy had established the claim of the church to control matters such as the trial of clerics and the excommunication of offenders, and had asserted its right to hear appeals and decide all cases. Again and again the archbishop and his king were in conflict, and affairs reached a crisis when the king demanded assent to the Constitutions of Clarendon (1164), which were an assertion of all the customs of the past that were now contrary to the law of the church and the practice of the papacy. Thomas hesitated, and for a moment gave way, thus breaking the solidarity of the bishops in their resistance. Then, at a council at Northampton in 1164 he reasserted his opposition and in face of threats of death or imprisonment, broke away by night and crossed to France to seek the pope.

For the next six years the archbishop was in exile in France, while he and the king and Pope Alexander III wrangled and discussed in an endeavor to settle the controversy and restore peace to the church in England. The issue was clouded for contemporaries by the mistakes and even the faults of the archbishop, by the ability and plausibility of the king, who had in some respects a strong case, and by the unwillingness of the pope to go to extremities with a powerful monarch. Meanwhile Thomas, at the abbey of Pontigny and elsewhere, gave himself to penance and devotion in what may be called a 'second conversion' from piety to sanctity. Finally, after a war of denunciations and excommunications, and a series of abortive conferences, an uneasy peace was patched up in the last months of 1169 and Thomas returned in triumph to Canterbury. Almost at once, the king in France, exasperated by the archbishop's refusal to withdraw some censures, let slip words which were taken to be a command, or a permission, to kill the archbishop as a traitor. Four knights crossed the Channel, and on the afternoon of December 29th appeared in the archbishop's hall intent on picking a quarrel. Thomas met them with dignified argument, but refused to budge from what he declared was justice and obedience to the pope. The knights retired in fury and donned their armor, while the archbishop entered the cathedral, refusing to allow the doors to be locked. The four knights rushed upon him in the north aisle and tried to drag him from the church. He resisted, and they cut him down with their swords. His last words were: 'I accept death for the name of Jesus and for the Church.'

The murder shocked the conscience of all Europe; miracles were announced immediately at the tomb; the archbishop was canonized as a martyr by Alexander III in 1173; the king did public penance at his tomb, and much of what St Thomas had striven for was secured by his death. Canterbury became a place of pilgrimage second only to Rome and perhaps Compostella, and churches were dedicated to St Thomas in all countries, even in the remote Iceland. That Thomas gave his life for the freedom of the church is certain; more than four centuries later, another Henry, another St Thomas, and another archbishop of Canterbury, drew the moral in their different ways. That he was a man to whom all would apply the word 'great' is also clear. He was no doubt a son of his age – the age of crusades and of the Norman conquerors – alike in his magnificence, his carriage and his austerities, but those who have seen in him only an ambitious, violent and headstrong prelate have failed to allow for the gentleness and devotion that were always part of his character, and for the real and profound conversion of his later years. Had he died a natural death in 1170 he would not perhaps have been acclaimed as a saint, but in his last years and months he prepared himself by his fortitude and zeal for truth and justice, for the heroic assertion of the rights of the spiritual power which led to his martyrdom.

December 29th   ILLUSTRATION: page 455

THOMAS of DOVER   † 1295

Although never formally canonized, Thomas of Hales has always been popular near Dover, where as a monk of St Martin's priory he was killed by French raiders for refusing to disclose the whereabouts of the church valuables.

August 2nd

THOMAS of HEREFORD   1218–1282

A member of one of the most powerful families in the country, Thomas Cantelupe became chancellor of Oxford in 1262, and, after the defeat of Henry III, chancellor of England. He became bishop of Hereford in 1275, ruling his diocese with such strength of justice that it was said that either the devil was in him, or he was over familiar with God.

October 3rd

THOMAS of VILLANOVA   1488–1555

Thomas was an ideal bishop in sixteenth-century Spain, and among the patrons of almsgiving, in every respect a father in God. He was born in 1488. Son of a mother remarkable for her charities, from boyhood he could not refuse an alms. His luncheon for school, clothes, shoes, and supplies from his parents' store, all were given. Having taken his degree at the University of Alcala and now a master of theology, in 1516 he joined the Augustinian hermits, was professed in 1517 and ordained priest in 1518. He became Provincial of Andalusia, and later of Castile. His sermons, moving by their fervent conviction and by the contemplative's experience of God, won him an extensive reputation; and he preached at court before the Emperor Charles V and his son Philip.

In 1544 the archbishopric of Valencia became vacant. Save for a few years recently there had been no resident archbishop since 1455. The emperor, intending to appoint a friar from the order he particularly favored, the Hieronymites, ordered his secretary to prepare a brief in his favor. The secretary returned with a brief made out in the name of Thomas. 'That', exclaimed the astonished emperor, 'was not the name I gave you.' 'I swear to your Majesty,' the secretary replied, 'I distinctly heard you name Thomas of Villanova.' Charles, seeing God's hand in the mistake, refused to have it corrected. Thomas did all he could to escape the episcopate, but a command from his prior general, Seripando, obliged him to yield. Consecrated at Valladolid, where he was prior, he reached his diocese so poorly attended that the prior of the Augustinian house

outside Valencia could not at first credit his identity. He was enthroned on January 1st or 2nd, 1545. His episcopate was a lavish outpouring of money for every kind of need, his expenditure far exceeding his revenue yet never failing. For himself shabby, even threadbare, clothing, and a minimum of food and furniture, were good enough. But his tailor, who condemned him as a skinflint, thought otherwise when he provided his daughters with dowries and a further sum to furnish their homes. Impoverished noblemen forbidden by the social code to work were assisted. Though the Spanish church was wealthy its funds were badly distributed. The secular clergy were for the most part poor, and Thomas was their generous benefactor. Exposure of unwanted babies on the doorsteps of churches was common, and Thomas encouraged poverty-stricken parents to dump their babies at night outside his palace door. They were placed in orphanages prepared for their reception, which he visited at regular intervals. These were equipped with a staff of nurses. He told his nurses, 'The King of Heaven has entrusted his children to me, and on his behalf I entrust them to you.' For the medical service of the poor he provided a pharmacy, two doctors and a surgeon. The flour he distributed during a period of scarcity outlasted the natural supply, and on another occasion, when three widows asked for assistance, his granary, which that morning had been empty, was found to be full of corn. Witness of this miracle was a servant who must have known had any corn been brought in. Daily alms were distributed to a crowd of poor folk, and many were established in trade. A cripple who could no longer practise his trade as a tailor was cured.

Thomas struggled valiantly to re-establish clerical discipline, and in particular to abolish concubinage. His success was far from complete. Concubinage was too wide spread and was tolerated by public opinion. Prayer, however, and tact, heartfelt pleading, often the sight of penance on his own body, converted many offenders.

To avenge his brother's murder a priest broke the seal of confession. Thomas, informed by an illumination at prayer that the convicted murderer was preparing to meet death in defiant despair, investigated the case and, having proved the priest's guilt, rescued his victim and punished the offender with exemplary severity.

His attempts, on the other hand, to compel the nominally converted Moors to abandon Mohammedan worship and practice the Catholic religion failed: not even a saint could undo the effect of forcible 'conversion'.

Thomas dispatched his coadjutor bishop and another visitor to visit the country parishes and bestow alms everywhere. A thief who stole their alms-purse restored it and confessed, when he found his path blocked by the apparition of a bishop wearing a religious habit.

In an age of unblushing nepotism, though he welcomed his poor relations, he would give them nothing beyond that supply of genuine need which he gave to others. This charity was supported by contemplative prayer. One Ascension Day Thomas was rapt in an ecstacy which lasted eleven hours.

For many years he had suffered from ill health, a complication of different maladies, and, oppressed by a sense of insufficiency, he begged the emperor to release him from the burden of his episcopate. Charles returned an evasive answer and did nothing. A voice from his crucifix comforted Thomas: 'Do not trouble yourself, on my mother's birthday you shall come to me and rest'. He prepared for death. During his last illness he insisted that everything he possessed must be given away that he might die a pauper. He even gave away the bed on which he lay, accepting it as a loan. Our Lady's birthday came on Sunday September 8th, 1555, and, while hearing mass, he died. Amid the lamentations of the entire city, he was buried in the church of the Augustinian priory. He was canonized in 1658. His office contains two special antiphons: 'Rich are his alms to the needy; still his bounty abides in memory'; 'Wherever faithful men are met his alms deeds will be remembered.'

September 22nd

THOMAS THE APOSTLE   *First Century*

The Apostle St Thomas (also called Didymus, 'twin') is the subject of a masterly character sketch in St John's Gospel. It is important because he is not unlike many well-meaning people of today who have received a technical education and nothing else, and believe only what they can see and touch. He comes to notice when, against the protests of the frightened disciples, Jesus insists on returning to Judaea to raise Lazarus from the dead. Thomas, loyal and pessimistic, enlists the others to go too, 'that we may die with him' (John 11:7-16). Then, at the Last Supper, when Jesus tells his disciples that he is about to leave them and that they know the way where he is going, this same common-sense Thomas, evidently under great strain, cries, 'Lord, we do not know where you are going; and how can we know the way?' Jesus treats him to the sublime answer: 'I am the way ... No one goes to the Father save through me.'

The shattering blow of the crucifixion was followed by 'women's tales' of a resurrection. Poor Thomas, who had not died with him after all, was away, perhaps hiding his head in sullen bitterness, when Jesus appeared to the rest. He met their enthusiastic testimony with obstinate disbelief which became neurotically brutal: 'Unless I see in his hands the mark of the nails, and put my finger in the place of the nails, and put my hand into his side, I will not believe.' A sad, lonely week must have followed for him, with the others so happy. Then he rejoined them in his loyal way, although the doors were still shut for fear of the Jews. Only Jesus could convince him, and he came specially to give him the proof he demanded: 'Bring your finger here and see my hands; and put forth your hand and place it in my side; and be not unbelieving, but believing.' Thomas needed no more and burst into the great cry which is the climax of St John's Gospel and Christianity's age-long confession: 'My Lord and my God.' Peter and Thomas are the first two disciples mentioned as present when Jesus manifested himself at the sea of Galilee. Thomas would not be left out again.

Jesus said to Thomas: 'Have you believed because you have seen? Blessed are they who have not seen and yet believe.' Here is encouragement to those who receive God's gift of faith with the simplicity of a child. But Jesus never said men should shut their eyes, and St Gregory remarks that Thomas's doubt helps us more than the faith of others. Faith is above reason, but reason leads to faith, for the things men see and touch point beyond themselves. To deny this brings neurotic conflict. St Thomas's feast on December 21st is fittingly near the day when we celebrate the Incarnation. A strong, early tradition makes him the Apostle of India.

December 21st   ILLUSTRATION: facing page 448

THORFINN   † 1285

He was not honored until his body was discovered fifty years after his death at Ter Doest near Bruges. A man of exceptional kindness and generosity, he was driven by King Eric from his Norwegian bishopric of Hamar, and he eventually found refuge in the abbey of Ter Doest.

January 8th

THORLAC   † 1193

An Icelander, Thorlac Thorhallsson was ordained at eighteen, and, after some years of study in Paris and Lincoln, returned to Iceland in *c.* 1161. He established a monastery at Thykkvibaer of which he became abbot and, in 1178, he became bishop of Skalholt. Five years after his death he was canonized by the Icelandic Parliament (the Althing) which had – after due debate – accepted Christianity as the official religion of Iceland in the year 1000.

December 23rd

The THREE WISE MEN   *First Century*

Little is known for certain about the Magi, or the three wise men, who came with their gifts to the stable at Bethlehem. The tradition that there were three of them is extremely ancient, but other traditions – for example, their regal status and their names – Balthasar, Melchior and Caspar – are much later. It is only since the fifteenth

century that one of them has been depicted as a Negro. Relics supposed to be the bones of the three kings have lain in Cologne Cathedral since 1164 and were much venerated in the middle ages.
July 23rd

TIBBA, *see* Cyneburga, Cyneswide and Tibba.

TIBURTIUS   *Third Century?*
A Roman deacon, he was beheaded on the Via Labicana and buried at a place called The Two Laurels.
August 11th

TIBURTIUS, VALERIUS and MAXIMUS
The bodies of these martyrs have been found in the Catacomb of St Callixtus in Rome. Their names were linked with that of St Cecilia, but nothing is known for certain about this connection.
April 14th

TIGERNACH   † 549
He was supposedly of royal blood and was baptized by St Conleth with St Brigid for his godmother. He was captured by pirates and taken to Britain, where he was freed. He founded the abbey of Clones and succeeded St Macartan as bishop of Clogher.
April 4th

TIGRIUS and EUTROPIUS   † 404
Accused of revenging St John Chrysostom's banishment by arson, Tigrius, a eunuch priest at Constantinople, formerly a slave, was tortured with Eutropius, a reader, by the idolatrous prefect Optatus. Tigrius was banished to Mesopotamia, but Eutropius died.
January 12th

TILBERT, *see* Alcmund and Tilbert.

TILLO   *Eighth Century*
By birth a Saxon, he was made a captive in the Low Countries, but being redeemed from captivity, he was ordained priest by St Eligius. He became a successful missionary in the Low Countries, and is still particularly honored at Courtrai.
January 7th

TIMOTHY   *First Century*
The son of a Greek father and a Jewish mother, Timothy was converted to Christianity about the year 47 A.D., during St Paul's first missionary visit to his native town of Lystra in Asia Minor, in a persecution so fierce that Paul had been stoned and left for dead (Acts 14:6–19). During a second visit in the year 50, Paul chose him as a travel companion to replace St Mark (who had baulked at the dangers of these journeys, Acts 13:13; 15:38), and to assist Silas and himself in the work of evangelizing the middle east (Acts 16:1ff.). Timothy thus witnessed the first preaching of the gospel in Europe

(Acts 16:9ff.). From this time he is mentioned frequently in the Acts of the Apostles and in the Epistles as one of the 'apostles' or emissaries of Paul, left behind in or sent back to the various Christian communities to watch over the growth of the faith planted there. About the year 51 he countersigns Paul's letters to Thessalonica, and himself journeys from Corinth to take them to the recently converted community. In 57 he makes a return journey to deliver the second Epistle to the Corinthians, and in the following year he is again with Paul in Corinth, sending greetings to the church in Rome. When Paul finally goes to Rome himself, in chains, Timothy is still at his side, adding his name to the letters sent about the year 62 to Philemon, Colossae and Philippi ('I have no one else here who shares my thoughts as he does, no one who will concern himself so unaffectedly with your affairs ... without his own interest at heart, but Christ's.' Philippians 2:20).

In the year 63 Paul seems to have been released from his captivity and to have taken the opportunity to realize his project of evangelizing the western world. In his absence from the east, he gave some of his former associates the more permanent function of presiding over the Christian communities, although they were not attached to any one of them in the manner of the bishops of a few decades later. Timothy was given such an appointment over Asia, and stationed at the capital of Ephesus. Here he received the two Pauline letters that have been preserved in the New Testament, one from Macedonia about the year 65, and the other about two years later from Rome, where Paul had been imprisoned a second time.

It is from these letters that we learn most about Timothy. They are mainly concerned with the danger that faced the Asian churches (a form of the early Gnosticism and compromise with Hellenism, against which Paul had warned the community at Colossae a few years previously); but in passing they throw much light on the character of the man Paul had left to fight the danger. Apparently diffident and nervous in temperament, he is yet enthusiastic enough in his work to need a warning to look after his health. He is a man who knows well enough the sufferings he will have to undergo to guard the faith committed to him ('persecution is inevitable for those who are determined to live really Christian lives'. 2 Timothy 3:12), and Paul's repeated exhortations (many of which have passed into the liturgy) are inspired less by a fear of Timothy's defection than by the certainty that his own end is near, and that the helpers he had picked with such care must soon shoulder the burden alone. In his last will and testament to Timothy, he can only remind him of all that he has taught him, 'in firm resolve, in patience, in love, in endurance' (2 Timothy 3:10); and his final appeal, asking him to come and comfort his last hours, stands as the most eloquent monument to one whom he has called constantly 'my well beloved son'.

The New Testament contains one further reference to Timothy (if indeed the same person is meant) in Hebrew 13:23, where mention is made of his release from an otherwise unknown imprisonment about the year 67, and of the author's hopes to accompany him on a visit to Jerusalem. Beyond this nothing is known for certain. A tradition asserts that he remained at Ephesus as bishop until his death. The fourth century 'Acts of Timothy' describe his death by stoning and clubbing, and the unusual sobriety of the account indicates that it may be derived from a genuine source. Constantinople claims his relics (the Timothy who is buried by St Paul in Rome is a fourth century martyr who was later confused with the companion of the Apostle), and his memory is celebrated on January 24th, in connection with the feast of his master on the following day.
January 24th

TIMOTHY, AGAPIUS and THECLA
Fourth Century
Palestinians, they were martyred during the persecution of Diocletian. Timothy's remains were enshrined in a basilica at Gaza.
August 19th

TIMOTHY and MAURA
Third Century
They had been married less than three weeks when, under the edict of Diocletian, they were commanded to give up their holy books to be burned. When they refused they were tortured and left nailed to a wall; they took nine days to die.
May 3rd

TIMOTHY, HIPPOLYTUS and SYMPHORIAN
This St Timothy was martyred *c.* 303 during the persecution of Diocletian. St Hippolytus, bishop of Porto, is discussed in the article on St Hippolytus. St Symphorian was martyred at Autun *c.* 200.
August 22nd

TITUS
First Century
A gentile, he was converted by St Paul and became his secretary. We learn from Paul's letters to the Corinthians that he twice sent Titus from Ephesus to Corinth to deal with church matters there. When St Paul went to Crete, he ordained Titus bishop that he might complete the work which St Paul had begun.
February 6th

TORQUATUS and his Companions
First Century?
Torquatus was supposed to have been the head of a party sent by the Apostles Peter and Paul to evangelize Spain. Each became bishop of a district and all seem to have

suffered martyrdom. The entire story is, however, unsupported by any evidence and is a medieval fabrication.
May 15th

TRIPHYLLIUS
Fourth Century
A law student, he became a disciple of St Spiridion, went with him to Cyprus and became bishop of Nicosia.
June 13th

TROND, *see* Trudo.

TROPHIMUS
Third Century?
The first bishop of Arles, he has been frequently but falsely identified with that Trophimus who was taken to Jerusalem by St Paul (2 Timothy 4:20).
December 29th

TRUDO or TROND
Seventh Century
A missionary in his native Brabant, he founded a church and a monastery on his own land, and a nunnery near Bruges.
November 23rd

TRUMWIN
Seventh Century
From his see at Abercorn on the Firth of Forth, this English bishop ruled the Southern Picts until they rebelled and drove out the English. Trumwin was forced to flee and retired to Whitby Abbey.
February 10th

TRYPHO, RESPICIUS and NYMPHA
Four martyrdoms occurred at Nicaea during the persecution of Decius, and relics belonging to three martyrs were preserved in several Roman churches, among them St Trypho. From these and other unrelated facts a highly unreliable legend of Trypho, Respicius and Nympha seems to have been constructed.
November 10th

TUDWAL
Sixth Century
A Welshman, he went to Brittany and became the first bishop of Tréguier.
December 1st

TURIBIUS of ASTORGA
Fifth Century
This bishop of Astorga was known for his stout defence of Catholicism against the heresy of the Priscillianists which had become widespread in Spain.
April 16th

TURIBIUS of LIMA
1536–1606
When a bishop is canonized it is customary for the name of his see to figure in his title as saint; it is peculiarly fitting in the case of St Turibius, for just as St Thomas of Villanova stands out as a pattern for bishops in the Old World so does St Turibius in the New. He was born at Mayorqa in Spain in 1536, and studied law at Salamanca, being afterwards appointed judge of the Inquisition court at Granada. When the see of Lima fell

vacant in 1578 there was not a little surprise that the appointment should be given to Turibius, a layman: he was consecrated and took possession of his see in 1581, proceeding at once to justify his suitability for the post by wearing himself out in the service of his flock for the next quarter of a century.

He travelled throughout his diocese on foot, often unaccompanied, braving the equatorial climate, wild animals, tropical diseases and other dangers, in order to reform the clergy and preach the faith to the people scattered over the huge territory in his care. He founded a seminary (the first in the American continent); he baptized and confirmed nigh on a million people (he confirmed St Rose of Lima). By the example of his life he showed the natives that Christianity was something other than what was displayed to them in the dissolute lives of many of their Spanish conquerors, not excluding some of the clergy; he took the trouble to master their language and opposed all attempts to justify the Spanish way of treating them, quoting to his critics the words of Tertullian, 'Christ said, "I am the Truth", not "I am the custom".' He remained in harness to the end. At the age of sixty-eight, far from home and sensing the approach of death, he dragged himself to the church at Santa to receive viaticum, and there he died in 1606.
April 27th

TUTILO
Tenth Century

Principal of the cloister school at the Saint-Gall monastery. Though greatly admired by all, particularly by King Charles the Fat, for his exceptional artistic talents, he shrank from all praise. Few of his works survive.
March 28th

The TWELVE BROTHERS

Possibly martyrs of southern Italy or Africa, they were venerated at Benevento at least as early as the sixth century. Their relationship is posthumous and due to the wishful thinking of early hagiographers (*see* St Felicity and her seven sons).
September 1st

TYCHON
Fifth Century?

The patron saint of vine-growers in Cyprus, he was an early bishop of Amathus, the present Limassol.
June 16th

TYRANNIO, ZENOBIUS and their Companions
† 304 and 310

Eusebius, an eye-witness, relates how these Egyptian Christians in Palestine and Tyre were beheaded after wild beasts in the arena had miraculously left them unharmed. Their companion Tyrannio, bishop of Tyre, and Zenobius, a priest, were martyred later under Maximinus.
February 20th

TYSILIO or SULIAU
Seventh Century?

Abbot of Meifod in Montgomeryshire, he was exiled by his brother's widow when he refused to marry her and take up his brother's principality in Powys. He ended his days in Brittany.
November 8th

UBALD of GUBBIO
† 1160

Ubald Baldassini, an orphan, was brought up by his uncle, bishop of Gubbio, and after his ordination, was made dean of the cathedral. He was allowed to refuse the see of Perugia, but he succeeded his uncle at Gubbio in 1128.
May 16th

ULPHIA
Eighth Century

She was a solitary, probably under the guidance of St Domitius, and in later years she formed and directed a community at Amiens.
January 31st

ULRIC of AUGSBURG
890–973

Educated at St Gall, he succeeded his uncle, St Adalbero, as bishop of Augsburg. He was canonized by John XV in February 993: the first recorded papal canonization.
July 4th

ULRIC of ZELL
c. 1029–1093

He left the service of the Empress Agnes for that of his uncle, the bishop of Freising. In 1052 he became a monk at Cluny, but spent much time in making other foundations, becoming abbot of the one at Zell in the Black Forest.
July 14th

ULTAN
† 686

With his brothers, St Fursey and St Foillan, he went to East Anglia, where they founded an abbey in Burgh Castle, a roman fort near Yarmouth. After a pilgrimage to Rome, he became abbot of Fosses, built on land given to him by St Gertrude. He was also abbot of Péronne, where he died.
May 2nd

ULTAN of ARDBRACCAN
† 657

A bishop, possibly of Ardbraccan, he wrote a life of St Brigid.
September 4th

UNCUMBER, *see under* Wilgefortis.

URBAN I
† c. 230

This pope is buried in the cemetery of St Callistus on the Via Appia, and he has often been confused with a martyr, also called Urban, who is buried on the same road bank in the cemetery of Praetextatus.
May 25th ILLUSTRATION: page 456

438

URBICIUS, *see* Liphardus and Urbicius.

URSICINUS   *Seventh Century*
A disciple of St Columbanus, whom he followed in exile from Luxeuil to Metz, Ursicinus established a small community in Switzerland at the foot of Mont Terrible, where now stands the town of Saint-Ursanne.
December 20th

URSMAR   † 713
He was perhaps already a bishop when he became abbot of Lobbes in Belgium. As well as founding other monasteries, he was also an active missionary in Flanders.
April 19th

URSULA and her Companions
As an authentic inscription informs us, in the fourth, or at the latest, early fifth century, Clematius, a man of consular rank, in consequence of visions rebuilt a ruined basilica at Cologne on the tomb of virgin martyrs. Of names, number or date we are told nothing.

This is the nucleus of fact underlying preposterous elaborations of legend beginning in the ninth century. Ignorance of Latin epigraphy mistook eleven for 11,000, a mistake however which suggests that the martyrs were in fact eleven. Names were added, Ursula being taken from the tombstone of an eight year old girl of that name. At least as early as St Dunstan, the Cologne martyrs were associated with Britain: the result, one might suggest, of confusing with them martyrs, probably nuns, who assisted the Anglo-Saxon mission to Germany and suffered death in the Low Countries. The excavation in the Twelfth Century of the cemetery surrounding the church of the Virgins provided relics of this multitude of martyrs. The identifications were supported by 'revelations' supplying names and corroborative detail.

Thus took shape the legend of a British King's daughter visiting Rome with 11,000 virgins together with married associates and their children (to explain bones dug up in the cemetery) and their martyrdom on their return journey at the hands of the Huns, together with a nonexistent Pope Cyriacus and equally non-existent bishops.
October 21st   ILLUSTRATION: page 457

V

VAAST, *see* Vedast.

VALENTINA, *see* Thea, Valentina and Paul.

VALENTINE   † c. 269
The custom of sending 'valentines' on February 14th has made St Valentine one of the most popular names in the church and outside it; but there is no direct connection, not even by way of legend, between this saint and this custom. What appears to have happened is that that date was commonly supposed to be the one on which the birds begin to pair, hence young men and girls would formally choose each other then, or at least send each other greetings; as, in the church's calendar, the day was the feast of St Valentine so the custom was, as it were, put under his protection.

What we know of St Valentine is slight enough. He was apparently a priest; and he was beheaded in Rome on the date of his feast, during the persecutions under the emperor known as Claudius the Goth, about the year 269. He was buried on the Flaminian Way, and his tomb there became a center of considerable popular devotion. There is a complication in the fact that a second martyr, Valentine, a bishop, is also commemorated on the same date. He too is said to have been beheaded, but at Terni near Rome. Whether the traditional accounts have made two people out of one is a matter for discussion; it is certainly quite possible.
February 14th

VALENTINE   *Fifth Century?*
An abbot and afterwards a missionary bishop in Rhaetia (i.e. Eastern Switzerland and the Tyrol), he was buried in Mais in the Tyrol, but in 768 his remains were transferred to Passau.   ILLUSTRATION: page 458
January 7th

VALERIA, *see* Vitalis and Valeria.

VALERIAN, *see* Marcellus and Valerian.

VALERIAN and other Martyrs in Africa
                        Fifth Century
Victims of the Vandal persecutions. Valerian was an eighty-year-old bishop who refused to hand over the sacred vessels belonging to his church. He was therefore forbidden to lodge in any house or field and was obliged to sleep by the roadside.
December 15th

VALERIUS, *see* Tiburtius, Valerius and Maximus.

VALERIUS and RUFINUS   *Third Century*
Probably missionaries sent from Rome to evangelize Gaul, they suffered martyrdom near Soissons.
June 14th

VALERIUS of SARAGOSSA, *see* Vincent and Valerius of Saragossa.

VALERY, *see* Walaricus.

VANNE, *see* Vitonus.

VARUS, *see* Cleopatra and Varus.

VEDAST or VAAST   † 539
A solitary living at Toul he was ordained priest and chosen to accompany King Clovis I to his baptism at Rheims. Miracles wrought on this journey and when

he was instructing the Franks converted large numbers of people. He was made bishop of Arras.
February 6th

VENANTIUS · *Third Century?*
An alleged martyr of Camerino he seems to owe his cult to the fact that Pope Clement X was for many years bishop of that diocese.
May 18th

VENANTIUS FORTUNATUS · *c. 535–605*
Born in about 535 at Treviso, he was educated at Ravenna and left Italy when he was thirty for France, where he was ordained. He is particularly remembered for his ability as a poet, and he wrote the hymns *Vexilla regis prodeunt* and *Pange lingua gloriosi, lauream certaminis.* A close friend of St Radegund and her nuns at Holy Cross, he spent most of his life at Poitiers and was eventually elected bishop of that see.
December 14th

VENERABLE BEDE, *see* Bede.

VENERIUS · † 409
He was a deacon of St Ambrose, and succeeded St Simplician as bishop of Milan in 400.
May 4th

VEREMUND · † 1092
Under his rule the Benedictine abbey of Hyrache became the most important in Spain. He wrought many miracles for the relief of the poor.
March 8th

VERENA
Her origin is uncertain, but she is said to have been an Egyptian who settled in Switzerland living in a cave near Solothurn.
September 1st

VERONICA · *First Century*
St Veronica illustrates in a most instructive manner the difficulties of hagiology. There is no mention of the saint in the gospel story, yet there can be little doubt that the majority of devout Christians would have no hesitation in claiming an intimate knowledge of her. The story of the woman who, moved with compassion by the sufferings of Christ on his way to Calvary, pushed her way through the crowd so that she might wipe the blood and sweat from his face is too well known to require reiteration. And the imprint of the divine countenance, the details of which are no longer discernible on the towel preserved in St Peter's in Rome, was felt to be an adequate testimony to the truth of the story. Many, therefore, will be surprised to hear that there is no historical evidence as to the origin of the towel or even as to the existence of such a person as Veronica. In contrast to this lack of factual knowledge, legends

abound. Veronica has been **variously** described as a princess of Edessa, as Martha, the sister of Lazarus, or as the daughter of the Canaanite woman (Matthew 15:22). French tradition has it that she was the wife of Zaccheus, who climbed the tree to see our Lord (Luke 19:2), and that she made an apostolic journey to France, where she died at Bordeaux. Italian tradition, on the other hand, has held that she was the wife of a Roman officer, and was summoned to Rome by the Emperor Tiberius, whom she cured by making him touch the sacred image imprinted upon the towel. The most widely held legend identifies her with the woman who was cured of the issue of blood (Matthew 9:20), but which of these legends is true is unknown. Her story is certainly not included in the early Roman martyrologies, the first written account being in a later Latin edition of a fourth or fifth-century apocryphal work entitled *The Acts of Pilate or the Gospel of Nicodemus.*

There is some evidence that the towel has been preserved in St Peter's since the time of Pope John VII (705–707). It seems probable that the name Veronica was applied to the legendary woman because of the image upon the towel, for Veronica is derived from 'vera icon' or 'true image'. Hence it is more likely that the towel was the primary instrument in the story, and the name Veronica was subsequently applied in an arbitrary fashion to the presumed owner of the towel. Certainly the cult of St Veronica did not appear until the fifteenth century, when the devotion of the stations of the cross was developing.

The person and story of Veronica may therefore be entirely legendary. This, however, need not detract from the value of the story, for the most important function of the accounts of the lives of the saints is to encourage the reader to a greater devotion to God and to the person of Christ. Whether Veronica existed or not, the theme of compassion for the suffering Christ which is enshrined in her story is relevant for all time. And this is especially true of the present time when Christ suffers so grievously in his mystical body, which is the members of the church. If, therefore, as a result of meditation on the story of Veronica we are moved to stretch out the hand of help to those who suffer for Christ today in many countries of the world, her story, whether it be fact or fiction, will have served its ultimate purpose.
July 12th ILLUSTRATION: page 459

VERONICA GIULIANI · 1660–1727
She was born in 1660 at Mercatello in Urbino and became a Capuchiness at Città di Castello when she was only seventeen. Because the bishop who confirmed her had prophesied that she would one day become a saint, she was given a hard novitiate which was further complicated by illness.

In 1694, the crown of thorns was imprinted upon her forehead and in 1697 she received the stigmata; but what is most remarkable is that towards the end of her life she seems to have had an accurate mental picture of the physical constitution of her heart. She even drew a chart on which she indicated the position in the heart of the several emblems of our Lord's passion: a cross, a chalice, a crown of thorns, three nails and seven swords. On her death, the heart was examined by two professors of medicine and surgery before a committee of notable ecclesiastics, and a formal testimony was made that a number of minute objects corresponding to those shown in St Veronica's plan were to be found in the right ventricle.

For a discussion of stigmata *see* St Gemma Galgani.
July 9th

VICELIN   *c.* 1086–1154
In 1126, after his ordination at Magdeburg, he engaged in evangelizing the still pagan tribes of northern Germany. His work suffered badly from pirate raids, and he may never have occupied his see of Staargard (now Oldenburg), of which he was appointed bishop in 1149.
December 12th

VICTOR I   † *c.* 199
An African, he succeeded St Eleutherius as pope in *c.* 189 and strove to establish uniformity in the celebration of Easter.
July 28th

VICTOR MAURUS   *Fourth Century*
A member of the Praetorian guard, he suffered martyrdom in Milan.
May 8th

VICTOR of MARSEILLES   † 290?
He may have been an officer in the Roman Army, who was discovered encouraging the Christians of Marseilles during a persecution. His guards were converted by him and all were executed.
July 21st

VICTOR or VITTRE THE HERMIT
                                        Seventh Century
A priest from Troyes who became a solitary at Arcis, near Plancy-sur-Aube. By his example, more than by his numerous miracles, he won many to God.
February 26th

VICTORIA, *see* Acisclus and Victoria.

VICTORIA and ANATOLIA
Though their passion is fictitious, there are grounds for believing that Victoria was martyred at Tribulano in the Sabine hills, and that Anatolia, her sister, was also a

martyr. Venerated in this part of Italy, nothing else is known for certain about them.
December 23rd

VICTORIAN   † 558
A strong disciplinarian, he lived for many years in France and later ruled a large community at Asan in Aragon.
January 12th

VICTORIAN and his Companions   † 484
All were martyred in Mauretania under Huneric, king of the Vandals, for refusing to conform to Arianism. Victorian, who was a wealthy proconsul from Carthage, is said to have had four companion martyrs.
March 23rd

VICTORICUS, *see* Fuscian, Victoricus and Gentian.

VICTORINUS   † *c.* 303
This bishop of Pettau in Upper Pannonia was a considerable writer. He was probably martyred under Diocletian.
November 2nd

VICTORINUS and his Companions   † 284
Victor, Nicephorus, Claudian, Dioscorus, Serapion and Papias were citizens of Corinth and were martyred at Diospolis in the Thebaïd in Numerian's reign. Some were pounded to death, others were hacked to pieces, but all met their deaths with courage and faith.
February 25th

VICTRICIUS   † *c.* 407
A Christian while still a soldier in the Roman legion, nothing is known of him for certain before his appearance as bishop of Rouen.
August 7th

VIGILIUS   † 405
Born at Trent, and educated in Athens, he returned to his native city of which he was the patron and became bishop in 385. While preaching in the valley of Rendena, he smashed a statue of Saturn and was stoned to death.
June 26th

VIGOR   *Sixth Century*
Born in Artois, he became bishop of Bayeux in 513. Saint-Vigeur-le-Grand, near Bayeux, is named after the monastery founded by him, and he may have been buried there.
November 1st

VINCENT and VALERIUS of SARAGOSSA
                                                   † 304
St Vincent, a deacon, was apprehended with his bishop Valerius during a persecution by the governor of Spain, Dacian. Valerius was banished, but Vincent was sub-

mitted to the fiercest of tortures. His flesh was torn by iron hooks, he was placed on a red hot gridiron and roasted, he was thrown into a dungeon strewn with broken pottery – yet he still survived.

At last his friends were allowed to visit him. They prepared a bed, and as they laid him on it he died.
January 22nd

VINCENT de PAUL   1580–1660

The de Pauls were peasant farmers at Pouy near Dax in Gascony; their third child in a family of six, Vincent, was born about 1580; he spent his childhood watching his father's sheep on the windswept plain of the Landes where, mounted on stilts, he was obliged to pass several hours a day with little to do save observe the countryside or contemplate the heavens. He owed much in later life to this early experience – a practical turn of mind and a genuine humility which are inseparable from the contact with reality that is the countryman's lot.

Vincent was educated by the Franciscans at Dax; to help him in his further studies at the University of Toulouse his father sold livestock, a realization of his scanty capital that on the part of a frugal peasant amounted to an act of faith in his son's future.

After ordination at the early (and uncanonical) age of twenty – no rare event in those days – there follow two years during which we lose sight of Vincent. It was then that occurred his alleged capture by Corsairs as he returned home by sea from Marseille to Narbonne. The evidence for this episode is not entirely satisfactory and it is possible that he was otherwise occupied in the south of France, though it is unlikely that the truth of the matter will ever be discovered at this distance of time. His ecclesiastical career now began. He obtained a benefice, a sinecure in the form of a commendatory priorship, and the appointment as one of the chaplains in the household of Queen Margot of Valois. Coming under the influence of Pierre de Bérulle, founder of the Oratorians and later cardinal, Vincent seems at this time to have begun in earnest to lead a life of self-denial and prayer; on de Bérulle's recommendation he accepted the position of chaplain in the powerful de Gondi family and, while ministering to some of the peasants on their estates, discovered the condition of religious and moral destitution in which these poor people were allowed to remain: the ignorance and laziness of many of the clergy were the main causes of this lamentable state of affairs. Once it was brought home to Vincent he set about remedying it.

He became the friend of the poor, endeavoring with all the means in his power to work for their moral and religious regeneration, concerning himself at the same time with their material needs, making indeed the latter very frequently the means to achieve the former. A short experience as parish priest of Châtillon-les-Dombes showed him more clearly still the extent of the problem, and although he effected a great change in his parish it was increasingly plain to him that he would have to work on a far larger scale. He returned to Paris, and with the support of Madame de Gondi started to relieve distress wherever he found it. He did everything in his power to help the galley slaves left to rot for days in prison in Paris on their way to Marseille, he organized 'charity confraternities' all over France to provide food and clothing for the poor, he began a religious congregation (known as the Lazarists from their principal house in Paris, the disused priory of St Lazare from which the modern railway station takes its name: in English the members of Vincent's congregation are known as Vincentians) whose principal function was to be the preaching of missions to countryfolk and the training of the clergy. From his charity confraternity grew up his Sisters of Charity, whose distinctive costume is known the world over as the emblem of that charity inseparably bound up with the name of Vincent.

The peasant priest from the Landes had become a figure of national importance. From his room at St Lazare he exerted an influence that was felt in France principally but also in Poland, Italy, the Hebrides and far-away Madagascar, for his missionaries were at work in all these places. Anne of Austria, regent until Louis XIV's accession, entrusted him with the appointments to bishoprics; he was in opposition to Mazarin and, having failed to influence that prelate's policy, found himself with more distress and misery on his hands as the result of the ensuing civil war. The wars in Lorraine, to relieve the devastation of which he collected a large sum of money, the redemption of slaves in north Africa, and the needs and government of his now widespread congregation, kept him occupied in his room at St Lazare. There he sat day after day, busy at his interminable correspondence, writing to prelates and poor priests, the great in the land and the unimportant, those long letters in which he stands so clearly revealed. Firmness on occasion, but always gentleness, an all-embracing charity and an overriding concern for the spread of God's kingdom, are mingled with a humanity and a 'man to man' approach that makes the collection of his letters fascinating reading.

His letters and his conferences show him (together with de Bérulle and one or two others) as one of the regenerators of the church in France in the sixteenth century. The retreats that he organized at St Lazare for those about to be ordained, the monthly 'days of recollection' that he instituted for the clergy of Paris (such famous figures as de Retz and Bossuet came to them) were a further potent influence in the work of regeneration.

He remained to the end the peasant, but in the best sense of the term. His humility was outstanding, he was gentle and understanding, dominating with an inflexible will his proneness to swift anger, and though he has left no special mystical teaching and seems to have undergone no striking mystical experience, his work, which was all for God, was impregnated with his constant prayer. There, with his all-embracing charity, is the principal lesson of his life clearly marked by his simplicity in spiritual matters and in his approach to God.

He died in his chair in 1660 when he was about eighty years of age, and was canonized in 1737.

July 19th   ILLUSTRATION: facing page 465

VINCENT FERRER   1350–1419

He was born on January 23rd, 1350, in Valencia, the fourth son of Constantia Miguel and William Ferrer. His father was an Englishman, who had been knighted at the siege of the city. On February 5th, 1367, having completed his studies in philosophy, Vincent became a Dominican. He was moved to Barcelona in the next year, and in 1370 became lecturer in philosophy at the Dominican house in Lerida. In 1373, when he returned to Barcelona to the 'Studium Arabicum et Hebraicum', he was already a famous public preacher.

In 1377 he was sent to Toulouse for further study; there he attracted the attention of the Legate of the future Avignon antipope, Cardinal Pedro de Luna, whose suite he joined, being himself a strong advocate of the claims of the Avignon popes as against those of Rome. From 1385 to 1390 he gave public lectures in theology at the cathedral of Valencia, after which he rejoined the suite of Pedro de Luna. He preached a great deal, particularly to Jews and Moors, and converted a rabbi of Valladolid, who later became Bishop Paul of Burgos, and associated with St Vincent in his strenuous and successful, if not wholly creditable, attempts to convert the Jews of Spain. From 1391 to 1395 he was confessor to Queen Yolanda of Aragon and was at that time cited before the inquisition for preaching the repentance of Judas. Pedro de Luna, who had been elected Pope Benedict XIII in Avignon in October 1394, quashed the process and invited St Vincent to the papal court, making him the papal confessor and penitentiary.

Disillusioned in his attempts to heal the schism between Rome and Avignon, St Vincent saw a vision of our Lord standing between St Dominic and St Francis, commissioning him directly to go about preaching penance. He was released by Benedict XIII in November 1399 to do this, and continued his preaching and wandering throughout western Europe until his death, being followed by a crowd of penitents and flagellants which varied from 300 to 10,000. He was in Aragon when the throne became vacant and with his brother, Boniface,

a Carthusian, was instrumental in choosing as prince Ferdinand of Castille.

In 1416 he withdrew his own allegiance and that of the kingdom of Aragon from Benedict XIII, because the Avignon antipope had made no serious attempt to heal the schism and had refused the request made by the council of Constance that he should resign in order to make possible a new and undisputed election to the papacy. St Vincent's decision had the effect of deposing Benedict and of making possible an end to the schism. St Vincent died on April 5th, 1419, at Vannes in Brittany, where his relics are venerated. He was canonized by Pope Calixtus II in 1455.   ILLUSTRATION: page 460

April 5th

VINCENT MADELGARIUS   c. 615–687

His wife was St Waldetrudis, and all their four children are venerated as saints. When Waldetrudis became a nun, he entered his own foundation of Hautmont and ended his days in another of his foundations, on his estate at Soignies. The writer of his *Life* has, however, pieced it together from the lives of other saints.

September 20th

VINCENT of AGEN   c. 300?

This deacon from Gascony suffered martyrdom when he caused a disturbance at a pagan, probably druidical, ceremony.

June 9th

VINCENT of LÉRINS   † c. 445

A monk of Lérins, he was celebrated for his *Commonitorium* against heresies, a work written after the council of Ephesus, in which for the first time we find asserted that for a dogma to be accepted it must be shown to have been held universally.

May 24th

VINCENT STRAMBI   1745–1824

He joined the Passionists in 1768, and became bishop of Macerata and Tolentino in 1801. He was banished during the reign of Napoleon for refusing to take the oath of allegiance, and returned only when Napoleon had been defeated. When Murat was defeated by the Austrians, it was St Vincent who saved the city of Macerata from destruction.

September 25th

VINCENTIA GEROSA   1784–1847

Closely associated with St Bartholomea Capitanio, and like her a native of Lovere, Catherine (Vincentia) Gerosa undertook educational work in the Austrian part of Italy, combining with it care of the sick. The order of the Sisters of Charity of Lovere was founded to further this work and by 1937 it possessed 7,000 nuns in 500 convents.

June 4th

VINCENTIAN
Seventh Century

He is said to have been brought up by Berald, duke of Aquitaine, and sent to train under St Didier. After suffering brutal treatment from Berald's successor, he became a hermit and was noted for miracles.
January 2nd

VINDICIAN
† 712

A priest from Bullecourt near Bapaume, he succeeded St Aubert as bishop of Cambrai and founded many monasteries, notably that at Arras. By his fearless eloquence he brought King Thierry to do penance for the murder of Bishop St Leger.
March 11th

VIRGIL of ARLES
† 610

Unfortunately very little is known about Virgil beyond his rather attractive name. He was a native of Gascony and educated at Lérins, where he may have joined the community. It is certain that he was a monk, and possibly abbot, of Autun when he became archbishop of Arles. He appears to have been an able administrator and a zealous pastor of souls, perhaps a little too zealous, because his friend, St Gregory the Great, had to reprimand him for trying to convert the Jews of his diocese by force and suggest that he should limit himself to praying for them and preaching. It would seem that he was in some way associated with St Gregory's mission to England and consecrated St Augustine at the request of the pope. He died in the year 610.
March 5th

VIRGIL or FERGAL
† 784

An Irish monk, he became bishop of Salzburg, where he rebuilt the cathedral.
November 27th

VITALIAN
† 672

Vitalian was elected pope in 657, and though troubled by Monothelite tendencies of the emperor and his patriarchs, he achieved much, particularly in the relations between the Holy See and England. St Theodore of Tarsus and St Adrian were both sent by him to assist the English church.
January 27th

VITALIS and AGRICOLA

The existence of these two martyrs was supernaturally revealed to Eusebius, bishop of Bologna, in 393, and St Ambrose of Milan was a witness at their disinterment.
November 4th

VITALIS and VALERIA
Second Century?

Nothing is known for certain of St Vitalis, after whom the great basilica of San Vitale at Ravenna is named. He and his wife Valeria were probably martyred near Milan during the persecution of Marcus Aurelius.
April 28th

VITONUS or VANNE
Sixth Century

He succeeded St Firminus as bishop of Verdun in the reign of King Clovis. The Benedictine congregation which bore his name developed from a college of priests he founded outside the city. They served the basilica in which Vitonus and other early bishops were buried.
November 9th

VITTRE THE HERMIT, *see* Victor.

VITUS, MODESTUS and CRESCENTIA
† *c.* 300?

The story of St Vitus is, briefly, that he was the son of a senator in Sicily, and was converted to Christianity in his boyhood. To escape the persecutions of the local administrator and the displeasure of his father, he fled to southern Italy, taking with him his tutor, Modestus, and an attendant, Crescentia. There they stayed for some time preaching the gospel, and then went on to Rome. Here Vitus wrought a cure on the son of the Emperor Diocletian, but afterwards he and his companions were cruelly tortured because they would not sacrifice to the gods. However, they were set free from their imprisonment by an angel, and they returned to southern Italy, where they died as a result of their sufferings.

This story is legend; the fact that they were martyrs, probably in southern Italy, is vouched for by the very early veneration given to them; but nothing else, not even the date of their martyrdom, is certain. This early devotion has continued down the centuries, and became wide-spread. The reputed relics of St Vitus came to rest in Saxony, thus spreading his fame there; and as well as being the protector of those suffering from what came to be known as St Vitus's Dance and from epilepsy, he was invoked against many varying dangers and disasters: attacks from animals, tempest, even over-sleeping. His connection with Sicily is underlined by the fact that there he is apparently still prayed to for the relief of the insane. He is also the patron of dancers and actors, and is venerated as one of the Fourteen Holy Helpers.
June 15th

VIVIANA, *see* Bibiana.

VLADIMIR of KIEV
c. 957–1015

St Vladimir is remembered above all as the apostle of Russian Christianity. He was the grand-prince of Kiev in the Ukraine, at that time ruled by the barbarous Varangians, who were Scandinavian in origin, and Vladimir was as barbarous as any of them. At about the age of thirty-two he was converted to Christianity. The results were twofold. Vladimir and his people were now in close contact with the riches of Byzantine civilization, and through it with the Christian church, a contact that was made into something very like a political alliance

by his marriage with Anne, daughter of the Emperor Basil II. But this was given heart and life, and a hope of permanence, by the nature of Vladimir's Christianity. Having received baptism he set himself quite simply to be a Christian. He used many of his extensive powers to encourage Christianity among his subjects and to support the work of Greek missionaries. More important, he fundamentally reformed his own way of life. He became generous, humble and devout; he even had scruples as to his right as a Christian ruler to inflict the death penalty, scruples which surprised the Byzantine ecclesiastics whom he consulted, and who were full of good legal assurances which did not entirely satisfy him. This essential simplicity of heart and genuineness of his Christianity showed itself finally on the occasion of his death; he would die a poor man: and he gave away all his personal belongings to his friends and to the poor.
July 15th

VODALUS or VOEL   *Eighth Century*
A Scots missionary preacher, he settled at Soissons outside St Mary's convent where St Adalgard ruled. After a misunderstanding he returned to Scotland, but was divinely guided back to Soissons and died there.
February 5th

VOLUSIAN   † 496
Bishop of Tours, he was driven from his see by the Goths and was said to have been martyred. His wife had such a wicked temper that Ruricius, bishop of Limoges, advised Volusian to fear her more than the Goths.
January 18th

VULFLAGIUS or WULPHY   *Seventh Century*
Although he was married he was ordained to become a pastor of his native town, Rue, near Abbeville; but because he resumed marital relations with his wife his conscience troubled him. He resigned, made an expiatory pilgrimage and lived the rest of his life as a recluse.
June 7th

VULMAR or WULMAR   *Seventh Century*
He left the abbey of Hautmont to live a more secluded life. Near Calais he founded the monastery of Samer and the nunnery of Wierre-aux-Bois.
July 20th

W ALARICUS or VALERY   *Seventh Century*
Educated at the monastery of Autumo, he went from St Germanus near Auxerre to Luxeuil to be under St Columbanus, whose expulsion by King Theodoric caused Walaricus to go on a mission to Neustria; he settled near the mouth of the Somme, where the monastery of Leuconaus grew up around him.
April 1st

WALBURGA   † 779
Sister of SS Willibald and Winebald, she became a nun of Wimborne in Dorset. She accompanied St Lioba on the great mission lead by St Boniface to the Germans and became head of a nunnery of Heidenheim.

We do not know how her name became associated with Walpurgisnacht: the witches' revels in the Hartz mountains on May 1st.
February 25th

WALDEBERT   *Seventh Century*
The third abbot of Luxeuil, this nobleman and ex-soldier changed the rule from that of St Columban to that of St Benedict and secured from the pope freedom from episcopal control.
May 2nd

WALDETRUDIS or WAUDRU   *Seventh Century*
A member of a family of saints; her parents were St Walbert and St Bertilia, her sister St Aldegundis of Maubeuge, her husband St Vincent Madelgar, and their children St Landericus, St Dentelinus, St Aldetrudis and St Madelberta. After the death of her husband she founded the convent of Chateaulieu at Mons.
April 9th

WALFRID   *Eighth Century*
This wealthy citizen of Pisa, with his wife and two friends, founded a monastery and convent at Monte Verde to which they respectively retired. His son, Gimfrid, succeeded him as abbot.
February 15th

WALSTAN   † 1016
He may not have existed, but some sources say that he was born at Baber near Norwich of a wealthy family, that he left home to become a servant, and that he made a vow of celibacy but did not become a monk.
May 30th

WALTER of L'ESTERP   † 1070
Born at the castle of Conflans and educated among the Augustinian canons at Dorat, he became abbot of L'Esterp, and ruled for thirty-eight years.
May 11th

WALTER of PONTOISE   † 1095
A native of Picardy, this man of wide education was forced against his will to become abbot of a new monastery near Pontoise.
April 8th

WALTHEOF or WALTHEN   † c. 1160
The younger son of the Earl of Huntingdon, he left the court of his step-father, St David I of Scotland, and entered an Augustinian monastery. Attracted to the

austerities of the Cistercians, he moved to the abbey of Wardon and was later elected abbot of Melrose.
August 3rd

WANDREGISILUS or WANDRILLE † 668
Although he married at the court of King Dagobert, he and his wife agreed to take up a religious life. He lived as a solitary for some years, and after some wandering, founded the abbey of Fontenelle.
July 22nd

WANDRILLE, *see* Wandregisilus.

WANINGUS or VANENG Seventh Century
Governor of Pays de Caux in Normandy under Clotaire III, he was turned completely to God by a vision of St Eulalia. He assisted St Wandrille in his foundation at Fontenelle. He also founded a convent in the Fécamp valley, where 360 nuns in relays kept up the uninterrupted chanting of the office.
January 9th

WAUDRU, *see* Waldetrudis.

WENCESLAUS of BOHEMIA 907–929
Wenceslaus of Bohemia lived at a time when the country he ruled was only partially Christianized. He himself was well educated and trained in habits of devotion by his grandmother St Ludmila; but his brother, Boleslaus, and his mother, made themselves leaders of an anti-Christian party, and after Wenceslaus's father was killed in battle St Ludmila was murdered by two nobles of the opposing faction. Wenceslaus immediately took strong measures; he made peace with his mother, and set himself to govern the country as a Christian ruler.

His close co-operation with the church, his severity with turbulent nobles, and his policy towards the German king, Henry I, which ensured peace and friendly relations at the expense of what we would now call Bohemian nationalism, created anew a body of bitter opposition. This, when Wenceslaus married and had a son, found its leader in his brother now deprived of hope of the succession. Boleslaus invited Wenceslaus to keep with him the feast of SS Cosmas and Damian. Next day, as Wenceslaus was on the way to mass, he was set on by Boleslaus and his retainers; Wenceslaus died at the door of the chapel, asking God's mercy on his brother. He was speedily proclaimed a martyr by the people; and he became in time patron of Bohemia, and hence of modern Czechoslovakia.

The carol, 'Good King Wenceslaus', is of course famous to English speaking peoples, but only quite recently: the words which were fitted to a medieval tune, were written by the distinguished nineteenth century Anglican hymn-writer, J. M. Neale.
September 28th ILLUSTRATION: page 461

WERBURGA Seventh Century
The beautiful daughter of Wulfhere, King of Mercia, and St Ermenilda, she refused marriage and entered the Ely convent under the great-aunt, St Etheldreda. Later she became superior-general of all Mercian convents. Chester cathedral was built to enshrine her relics.
February 3rd

WIBORADA † 926
After the death of her noble parents, she joined her brother Hatto in a religious life. As a recluse near the church of St Magnus at St Gall, she suffered martyrdom when she refused to flee before the Hungarian invasion.
May 2nd

WIGBERT † c. 738
An English monk, he joined St Boniface in Germany and was made abbot of Fritzlar. From there he moved to Ohrdruf, and made several foundations before retiring to Fritzlar before his death.
August 13th

WILFRID 634–709
St Wilfrid was born in Northumbria in 634, a year after King Oswald had conquered it and sent for a Christian mission from Iona. He was of noble birth, and, as a boy of fourteen with an ardent monastic vocation, he attracted the notice of the Northumbrian queen, Eanfled. Queen Eanfled had been brought up in Kent and she observed Easter after the Roman fashion; since her husband, King Oswy, followed the Celtic custom, this meant that one half of the court was keeping Lent whilst the other half was celebrating Easter. As a boy of fourteen, Wilfrid was sent to St Aidan at Lindisfarne, where he remained for about four years. In 651 Aidan died and another monk of Iona, Finan, succeeded him. Aidan's prestige had prevented much open quarrelling between the Roman and Celtic parties at the Northumbrian court but, after his death, the intolerable situation aroused acute controversy. Wilfrid had never been tonsured, and now Aidan was dead he left Lindisfarne and set out for a pilgrimage to Rome. For a year he stayed in Canterbury and became familiar with many Roman customs hitherto unknown to him. In 653 another traveller reached Canterbury on his way to Rome, Benedict Bishop, the first, but not, fortunately, the last, Englishman to introduce Mediterranean styles of architecture into English building. Wilfrid joined him, but at Lyons they separated, and Wilfrid stayed with the archbishop, St Annemund, who sought with some success to detain him in his city with the offer of a magnificent career. First, however, Wilfrid was permitted to complete his pilgrimage, and then he returned to Lyons. Here he remained three years, receiving the Roman tonsure and looking forward, no doubt, to an

honorable career in the Frankish church. His patron the archbishop was, however, executed by the secular power, but Wilfrid, although eager to suffer with him, was spared and had to return to Northumbria.

Northumbria had now an important convert to the Roman obedience in Alchfrid, King Oswy's son, and under his father, ruler of York. It was to Alchfrid that Wilfrid came, and by Alchfrid that he was commissioned to rule the new monastery of Ripon according to Roman principles. Thus the southern part of Northumbria was now securely attached to Rome, and the northern to Iona when, in 664, matters came to a head and a synod of the Northumbrian church was held at Whitby to settle the issue finally. Wilfrid, although very far from senior, was the spokesman of the Roman party; he pointed to the primacy of Peter and his successor, and to the fact the rest of Christendom agreed with Rome, not Iona. The leader of the Celtic party, Bishop Colman, admitted that our Lord had given the keys of the kingdom of heaven to Peter, and King Oswy replied that in this case he would have no quarrel with Peter and decided the issue in favor of Rome. Colman refused to accept this decision and left for Ireland. His successor died after a few weeks, and Wilfrid was appointed to succeed him. The see then probably moved to York.

Wilfrid refused to accept consecration from a Celtic bishop and left for Gaul, where during a three year absence, never satisfactorily explained, he was consecrated by no less than twelve bishops. In his absence his patron Alchfrid rebelled against his father and disappears from history. King Oswy, moved either by impatience at Wilfrid's absence or distaste for his son's protégé, replaced him by another Northumbrian monk, St Chad. Wilfrid eventually returned to his monastery of Ripon, until his restoration by Archbishop Theodore, in 669. Wilfrid ruled his see in peace until 678, when, having fallen foul of the Northumbrian queen, he was deprived of his see.

From now until the end of his life he was engaged in constant litigation to recover his see and his Northumbrian possessions. He was occasionally successful but never for long, and, although he was undoubtedly hardly used, it is plain that he exasperated everyone, including Archbishop Theodore, by the lack of moderation in his demands. But Wilfrid's litigation, if it failed in its avowed object, achieved far more valuable though unintended consequences than most lawsuits ever have. Wilfrid was the first Englishman to take a lawsuit to Rome, and he began a tradition of appeals to the Pope only interrupted by Henry VIII. In the course of his travels to Rome, he landed in Frisia and spent the winter preaching to the pagan inhabitants; it is thus Wilfrid who has the honor of inaugurating the tremendous Anglo-Saxon mission. Having made Christian

England too hot to hold him, Wilfrid took refuge in Sussex, the last pagan English kingdom; and he had achieved its conversion by the time of his recall to favor. He died, probably in 709, worn out by his exertions and his quarrels.

Although an ardent leader of the Roman party, Wilfrid was in many ways a typical Celtic monk: an all-or-nothing man, an inveterate pilgrim, an indefatigable missionary, who was without tact or discretion. But he never spared himself in good causes or in indifferent ones. He was never wholly in the wrong, and he roused as much love as he caused exasperation; but the good he did altogether eclipses his failings and his absurdities. ILLUSTRATION: page 462
October 12th

WILFRID THE YOUNGER   *Eighth Century*
Educated at Whitby Abbey he was a pupil and disciple of St John of Beverley who nominated him as his successor to the see of York.
April 29th

WILGEFORTIS or LIBERATA
This is a pious fiction to end all pious fictions. It is the story of a girl who was one of nine children born at the same time to the queen of Portugal. She took a vow of virginity, and her prayers for protection against her suitors were answered when she started to grow a beard. Her irate father had her crucified.

In England she was known as St Uncumber because she was thought to deliver women who were encumbered (sic) by an unwanted and troublesome husband. St Thomas More tells us that her image in St Paul's was, therefore, much frequented by the matrons of London.
July 20th

WILLEHAD   † 789
Born in Northumbria and educated at York, he went to the Low Countries as a missionary. In 787 he was appointed bishop to the Saxons, after Charlemagne had subdued them, with Bremen as his episcopal city.
November 8th

WILLIAM   † 1209
Born in Nevers of distinguished parents, he became a monk of Grandmont, seeking that perfect discipline which he eventually found in the Cistercian order. He became abbot of Fontaine-Jean and Châlis, and was appointed archbishop of Bourges. His humility and charity converted many, and he steadfastly refused to invoke the civil power against sinners – a most unusual abstinence on the part of an archbishop at this time.
January 10th

WILLIAM FIRMATUS   *Eleventh Century*
Born at Tours, he lived as a hermit at various places in France. He is said to have had exceptional power over

animals, so that the country people used to apply to him for help against the creatures that raided their crops.
April 24th

WILLIAM of ESKILL † 1203
A Frenchman and canon regular of St Geneviève, he was invited by the bishop of Roskilde in Denmark to come and improve monastic discipline. By founding the monastery of St Thomas on Zealand and reforming other houses, he succeeded in his task.
April 6th

WILLIAM of GELLONE † 812
Son of the count of Toulouse, he served with distinction under Charlemagne, becoming duke of Aquitaine; later he retired to the monastery he had founded at Gellone.
May 28th

WILLIAM of MALEVAL † 1157
He became abbot of a monastery in Tuscany, but finding the discipline lax withdrew to Maleval near Siena. Although he instructed disciples, he lived apart; but at his death they established themselves as the Hermits of St William or Gulielmites.
February 10th

WILLIAM of MONTE VERGINE, *see* William of Vercelli.

WILLIAM of NORWICH, *see* Simon of Trent.

WILLIAM of ROCHESTER † 1201
A native of Perth, he was murdered near Rochester by a foundling boy, whom he had adopted and was taking on a pilgrimage to Jerusalem.
May 23rd

WILLIAM of ROSKILDE † c. 1070
As chaplain to King Canute, this Englishman saw the condition of the people of Denmark. He decided to stay there as a missionary and became bishop of Roskilde.
September 2nd

WILLIAM of SAINT BENIGNUS 962–1031
Born on San Giuglio island near Novara in 962, he was the son of a count. After long training at Cluny, he was appointed abbot of St Benignus at Dijon which became under his strong rule one of the most important centers of monastic reform. He reformed the abbey of Fécamp, where he died.
January 1st

WILLIAM of VERCELLI or WILLIAM of MONTE VERGINE 1085–1142
Born at Vercelli of a Piedmontese family, William lived as a hermit on Monte Virgiliano, between Nola and Benevento. Joined by disciples, he formed them into a community and built a church dedicated to our Lady; hence the present name of the mountain.
June 25th

WILLIAM of YORK † 1154
St William of York, or William Fitzherbert, as he was known during his lifetime, came of noble English-Norman stock. It has been conjectured, but is not completely certain, that he was the son of Emma, the sister of King Stephen, by Count Herbert. In the year 1130 he became a canon of York and appears to have been generous and popular. When Archbishop Thurston died and the chapter chose Waldef of Kirkham, a Cistercian, as his successor, this was vetoed by the king for political reasons, and William was chosen in his place.

The election was bitterly opposed by Osbert, the archdeacon, and by the Cistercians in Yorkshire, on the grounds that it was open to the gravest suspicions of simony and that the candidate's private life was not all that it should have been. Henry de Blois, the bishop of Winchester and papal legate, advised William to take his case to Rome; but no sooner had he set out than the Cistercians sent off a delegation to put their side of the case before the pope. They stopped at Clairvaux on their way and enlisted the support of St Bernard, who threw himself wholeheartedly into the conflict, with characteristic fervor, not hesitating to describe William to the pope as 'a man rotten from the soles of his feet to the crown of his head'. The case was heard in Rome before Pope Innocent II in the year 1142, but, although the evidence was strong against the archbishop-elect, it collapsed for lack of witnesses. The pope packed the litigants back to England and ordered the principals to come to Rome on the third Sunday in Lent during the following year. No settlement was reached the following year, because William insisted on appealing to the testimony of the dean of York, who was not present in Rome.

The pope then transferred the case to England, and made his approval of the election contingent on the dean's swearing that no pressure had been brought to bear on the chapter of York by the king's men. The dean, in the meantime, had become bishop of Durham, and astutely avoided taking the oath by substituting someone else in his place. Later he declared in a letter that nothing would persuade him to take the oath, because he knew the contrary to be true. The substitute had no such scruples, and William was at length consecrated archbishop of York by Henry de Blois, but he had yet to receive the pallium. Innocent II died in 1143 before he could confer it, and was succeeded in rapid succession by Celestine II and Lucius II, who both died before they could take any decisive action in the matter.

Then, in 1145, Eugenius III became pope, and he was a Cistercian as well as a disciple of St Bernard. Determined to settle the York dispute once and for all, he suspended William until the former dean of York should take, in person, the oath required of him by

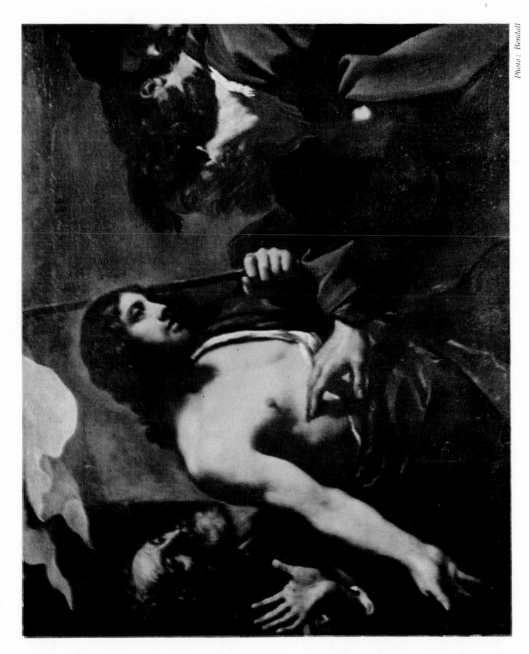

THOMAS THE APOSTLE: painting by Guercino (c.1591 – 1666). (*National Gallery, London*)

PLATE 15

SIXTUS II: engraving.

Photo: Alinari

STANISLAUS of CRACOW: detail of fresco, attributed to Stefano Fiorentino, school of Giotto, early fourteenth century, showing a witness returning from the grave to vindicate Stanislaus.
(Ch. di S. Francesco (lower), Assisi.)

STEPHEN PROTOMARTYR: painting by Vittore Carpaccio (died 1523 – 1526). (*Louvre, Paris.*)

TERESA of AVILA: sculpture by Bernini (1598 – 1680). *(Ch. di S. Maria della Vittoria, Rome.)*

Photo: *Office Centrale de Lisieux*

TERESA of LISIEUX: photograph. Teresa (left) with Sister Geneviève de la
Sainte Face (novice): detail of group at the communal laundry (1895).

Tho: Moor L ͪ Chancelour

THOMAS MORE: drawing by Hans Holbein the younger (1497 - 1543).
(Royal Library, Windsor, reproduced by gracious permission of H.M. the Queen.)

454

THOMAS of CANTERBURY: Harleian MS (early thirteenth century). *(British Museum.)*

URBAN I: limewood bust. Alsatian (c.1500). *(Staatliche Museum, Berlin.)*

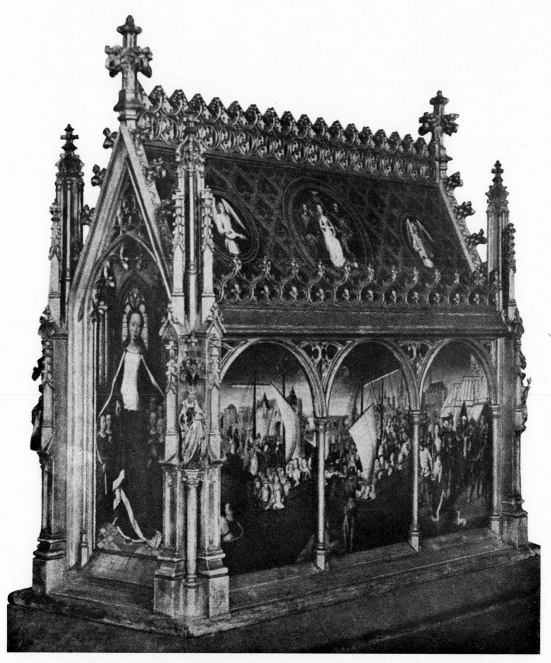

URSULA: casket painted by Hans Memlinc (1430-35–1494). *(Hôpital S. Jean, Bruges.)*

VALENTINE: Valentine curing an epileptic woman, from a German MS.

VERONICA: exterior right hand wing of triptych,
'The Adoration of the Magi', by Hans Memlinc (*c.* 1430–35 – 1494).
(Hôpital S. Jean, Bruges.)

VINCENT FERRER: central panel of altarpiece by Francesco Cossa (1435–1477).
(National Gallery, London.)

WENCESLAUS of BOHEMIA: sculpture by the Brothers Parler (1373).
(Church of St Wenceslaus, Prague.)

WILFRID: fifteenth century figure.
(Ripon Minster, Yorkshire.)

Photo: National Buildings Record

WILLIAM of YORK: mural painting, early fourteenth century.
(St Albans Cathedral, Hertfordshire.)

ZENOBIUS: details from scenes from the life of St Zenobius, painting on wood by Botticelli (1445 – 1510). (National Gallery, London.)

1576. S^t. VINCENT de PAUL. *fondateur et* Ier *Général*. 1660.

VINCENT de PAUL: probably a copy of a portrait by Simon François of Tours, painted 1660.
(*Lazarist Motherhouse, Paris*)

PLATE 16

Innocent II. This he refused to do, and, as a consequence, William was deposed. Thereupon his infuriated supporters raided Fountains Abbey, doing much damage, and William took refuge with Henry de Blois. In the year 1147, within two years of Eugenius's succession, Henry Murdach, a Cistercian, was consecrated archbishop of York. Late in the year 1153, when Murdach and Bernard were both dead and Anastasius IV had succeeded to the see of Peter, William set out for Rome to beg the new pope, who appears to have been his personal friend, to reverse the decision of his predecessor and permit him to succeed Murdach as archbishop of York. Anastasius confirmed his right of succession and conferred on him the pallium with his own hands. William received an enthusiastic ovation from the clergy and people of York and, when the bridge on which they were standing to welcome him back collapsed without injury to anyone, they immediately attributed their safety to his prayers.

In the year 1154, hardly a twelvemonth after he had taken possession of his see, he was seized by violent pains while saying mass on Trinity Sunday and died two days later on June 8th. It was officially denied that he had been poisoned. He was buried in his cathedral and, after many miracles at his tomb, he was canonized by Pope Honorius III in the year 1226.

At this distance of time it is not possible to say how much truth there was in the accusations of his opponents. They were men of the highest integrity, but it is possible for such men, even for such a man as St Bernard, to be carried away by party prejudice. It does not seem improbable that the king did exert undue pressure on the chapter in favor of his kinsman and chaplain, yet the cause of William did not lack the support of devout and serious men. It is difficult to escape the impression that he was used by stronger personalities than himself as a tool to further their own ends, and there is no doubt that his cause suffered from the violence of his supporters. During the short time that he was archbishop he distinguished himself for piety and gentleness, and he showed no resentment at all against such of his old opponents as remained alive. ILLUSTRATION: page 463

June 8th

WILLIAM PINCHON † 1234

Bishop of Saint-Brieuc, his defense of the church led to his banishment by the duke of Brittany, Peter Mauclerc, in 1228, but he was able to return two years later.

July 29th

WILLIAM, STEPHEN, RAYMUND
and their Companions † 1242

When the Dominicans were sent to Toulouse to preach against the Albigensians, a number of priests were lured into a castle at Avignonet and murdered. There were twelve martyrs in all: three Dominicans, two Franscis-cans, two Benedictines, four secular priests and one layman.

May 29th

WILLIBALD † 786

St Willibald was born about 700 of noble West Saxon parents – according to his legend his father was a king called St Richard. He was a relative of St Boniface, and brother of SS Winebald and Walburga. About 720 he made a pilgrimage to Rome, which he extended into a tour of the Holy Land. Many years later his memories were recorded by a nun who knew him well, and the result is the earliest travel book written by an Englishman. He returned to Rome via Constantinople and Naples, and then spent some years as a monk at Monte Cassino. He visited his relative, Boniface, in Germany, was ordained priest and worked in Thuringia. In 741 Boniface made him bishop of Eichstädt. He spent the rest of his life there as a typical Anglo-Saxon monk, mission priest and bishop, dying in 786. He is not to be confused with the Willibald who wrote the first *Life* of St Boniface.

June 7th

WILLIBRORD 658–739

St Willibrord was a Northumbrian born in 658, and was educated in St Wilfrid's monastery of Ripon, the center of the Romanizing party in the Northumbrian church. When Wilfrid was deposed and exiled in 678, Willibrord left Northumbria too, and went to Ireland, where he joined Egbert, that saintly Englishman, who, by his life and example, persuaded the Celtic monks of northern Ireland and Iona to the Roman obedience. Willibrord left Ireland in 690 for Frisia, where the military success of the Christian – and politic – Carolingians had made missionary work possible. Willibrord was given the support and blessing of the Frankish king, but he also chose to go to Rome for the permission and blessing of the pope. Thus Willibrord set the tone of the Anglo-Saxon missions: a political alliance with the Carolingians and a respect for the papacy unusual in western Europe at the time. The political alliance was a *sine qua non* of the missions, but the reverence for Rome was something more deliberate. It was particularly characteristic of Wilfrid's circle; there can be little doubt that it was Willibrord's education at Ripon which was the source of his papalism.

After a second journey to Rome, Willibrord was consecrated archbishop of the Frisians with his see at Utrecht. King Pippin was also consulted and gave his consent. This was the beginning of a momentous collaboration between the Carolingians and the papacy, which led to the founding of the Christian empire in 800. Apart from a dangerous pagan reaction under the anti-Carolingian Duke Radbod from 715-9 (which showed some of the disadvantages of the political affiliations of the mission) Archbishop Clement, as the pope had renamed Willibrord, ruled his see until his death in 739 at the age of eighty-one. His sphere of work was limited, his converts not specially numerous, but his achievement was nevertheless immense. He inaugurated a period of Anglo-Saxon missionary work, attracting young Christians from the different tribal kingdoms to take part in the first common 'English' enterprise, which was the conversion of their continental cousins, the pagan old Saxons of western Germany. The greatest of these missionaries was St Boniface, who very largely completed what Willibrord had begun.

November 7th

WILLIGIS † 1011

Though born of humble parents, he became chancellor of Germany under Otto II, and archbishop of Mainz. During the minority of Otto III, he was joint regent with St Adelaide. An outstanding administrator, he founded many churches and did much to ensure that the power wielded by the heads of the Holy Roman Empire was used to protect the church. It was said of him that 'he spoke little, but his few words carried more weight than many oaths from other people'.

February 23rd

WILTRUDIS *Tenth Century*

St Wiltrudis was the sister of Count Ortulf, and wife of Berthold, duke of Bavaria. When her husband died she founded and became first abbess of the famous Bergen abbey for Benedictine nuns.

January 6th

WINEBALD † 761

A pilgrim from England, he decided to remain in Rome where later, after a visit to England he met St Boniface. He accompanied him to Germany where he joined his brother, St Willibald, and, with his sister, St Walburga, founded a double monastery at Heidenheim in Würtemberg, of which he became abbot.

December 18th

WINIFRID *Seventh Century*

In the first half of the seventh century there lived in Wales a girl who is today famous as St Winifrid. For long after her death her fame was local. It was joined with and subsidiary to that of St Beuno; but by the twelfth century she had a notable cult at Holywell and at Gwytherin and a story which was to become famous. In 1138 her relics were translated from Gwytherin to the abbey of the Black Monks in Shrewsbury, where they were venerated by pilgrims until the dissolution of the monastery and the destruction of the shrine by

Henry VIII and Thomas Cromwell. The government, however, was powerless to put an effective stop to the pilgrimage to her well, which, alone of the British pilgrimages, has continued in full vigor down to the present day.

When the monks set themselves to write her story in the twelfth century, this is what they had to say. St Winifrid was the daughter of patrician parents in Flintshire. Her uncle, St Beuno, obtained from them land on which he built a church. One Sunday, while her parents were at mass, Caradoc, the son of a neighboring prince, hot and thirsty from hunting, came to the house to ask for drink. Finding the girl alone, he set to work to seduce her. Escaping from the house, she fled to the church, pursued by the enraged Caradoc, sword in hand, who caught her on the threshold of the church and hacked her head from her body. St Beuno, coming from the altar, cursed the murderer, and the earth opened and swallowed him. Where her head fell a fountain sprang up. The saint then prayed to God that the girl might be restored to life. His prayer was answered, nor was there any sign of the wound to be seen except a white line encircling her neck. The spring became another pool of Bethesda, in which the maimed, the halt and the blind might hope to be made whole. The saint lived for another fifteen years. When St Beuno went to Clynnog, St Winifrid went, first, to St Deifr at Bodfari, and then to St Sadwrn at Henllan. She was directed by the latter to St Eleri at Gwytherin in a remote valley in the mountains, where she became a nun. The feast of her martyrdom was kept on June 22nd, and of her death on November 3rd. Here, clearly, is a twelfth century reconstruction of earlier and imperfectly understood material.

In spite of the impetus which her cult received from the translation of her relics to Shrewsbury, it was confined to North Wales and the March until 1398. It was then that Roger Waldon, archbishop of Canterbury, ordered her feast to be kept with nine lessons throughout his province. In 1415 his successor Chicheley raised the feast to even higher dignity. The evidence of the manuscript copy of the *Hereford Missal*, now in the library of University College, Oxford, indicates a vigorous cult of the saint in Monmouthshire and in the Welsh part of Herefordshire, where it is significant that St Beuno had a settlement at Llanfeuno. Moreover in medieval Wales the principal road ran from St David's by way of the Cistercian monastery of Strata Florida to Holywell, while at Ludlow a special hospice was built to accommodate the pilgrims who followed the road along the border to Shrewsbury and Holywell.

Today, as one watches the pilgrimage buses roll in from Merseyside, or the Welsh speaking pilgrims of the Cylch Catholig come down the street to the well, with

its late perpendicular chapel, the gift of the mother of Henry VII, one is witnessing, in an entirely contemporary setting, what is, in fact, the oldest thing in modern Wales.
November 3rd

WINNOC † 717?
A Breton monk of the recently-established monastery of St Peter at Sithiu, he so distinguished himself that he was chosen to be one of four monks to make a new foundation near Dunkirk of which he became abbot.
November 6th

WINWALOE or GUÉNOLÉ *Sixth Century*
A widely popular saint, he was probably born in Brittany, and placed by his parents, Fracon and Gwen, in a monastery on Laure island. Following Abbot Budoc's instructions he was joint founder and abbot of the Landevennec monastery at Brest.
March 3rd

WIRO, PLECHELM and OTEGER *Eighth Century*
On a visit to Rome, Wiro and Plechelm were consecrated regionary bishops, and after their return, set out to evangelize in the Netherlands, where Pepin of Herstal gave them St Peter's Hill where they built a church and founded a monastery. Oteger was a deacon who accompanied them.
May 8th

WISDOM, *see* Faith, Hope, Charity and Wisdom.

WISTAN † 849
This grandson of King Wiglaf of Mercia was murdered, possibly because he opposed the marriage of his god-father to his widowed mother.
June 1st

WITHBURGA † *c.* 743
The youngest daughter of Anna, the East Anglian king, she gathered about her a community at Dereham in Norfolk, but died before it was fully established.
July 8th

WIVINA † 1170?
Preferring a religious life to marriage, she settled as a recluse at Grand-Bigard near Brussels. The land nearby was given to her by Count Godfrey of Brabant, and she established a flourishing community there.
December 17th

WOLFGANG *c.* 930–994
Educated at the famous abbey of Reichenau on Lake Constance and at the new school at Würzberg, he became a monk of Einsiedeln in 964. After his ordination he worked as a missionary among the Magyars and was elected bishop of Regensburg (Ratisbon) in 972. Continuing to live as a monk, he reformed many abuses during his rule of twenty-two years.
October 31st

WOLFHARD, *see* Gualfardus.

WULFRAM *Eighth Century*
He succeeded Lambert as archbishop of Sens, but abdicated to become a missionary among the Frisians, taking with him monks from Fontenelle Abbey. He succeeded in stopping the Friesland custom of making human sacrifices, and by his preaching and miracles made many conversions.
March 20th

WULFRIC † 1154
A priest who was more interested in hunting than anything else, he was brought suddenly to repentance. He retired to a cell attached to the parish church at Haselbury Plucknett in Somerset where he lived in great austerity. Instead of the customary hair shirt, he wore chain-mail next to his skin, and he is reputed to have recited the whole psalter while standing immersed in a tub of cold water. He was visited by King Henry I and by King Stephen – whose succession to the throne he prophesied. At his death, his relics were preserved in his church in a small aisle still known as Wulfric's aisle, and his tomb was visited by many pilgrims.
February 20th

WULMAR, *see* Vulmar.

WULPHY, *see* Vulflagius.

WULSIN † 1005
Appointed superior of the revived monastery of Westminster by his close friend St Dunstan, then bishop of London, Wulsin was consecrated abbot in 980 and later became bishop of Sherborne. He was greatly beloved, but it is not certain that he ever received the cultus of a saint.
January 8th

WULSTAN *c.* 1008–1095
Wulstan was born about 1008. His father was probably a thegn of the church of Worcester under St Oswald. As a child Wulstan was sent to the abbey of Evesham for his education and later to Peterborough. His family seem to have lost their property but not their influence in the Viking wars, and Wulstan became a priest and a member of the *familia* of Bishop Britheah of Worcester. Shortly after this Wulstan decided to become a monk, and he entered the cathedral monastery of Worcester, at that time reduced to a mere twelve members. His

rise in the monastery was rapid and he soon became prior, whereupon he undertook a reform of the monastery's affairs both religious and secular, which entitles him to rank with St Oswald as a second founder; during his lifetime the community increased from twelve to fifty. He soon earned a reputation for sanctity, through his care for the poor and his preaching. In 1062 the pope ordered the separation of the see of Worcester from the see of York, and Wulstan was chosen to succeed the archbishop of York as bishop of Worcester – and abbot of the cathedral monastery. In 1066 Wulstan went to Northumbria to persuade the people there to accept Harold Godwinson as king of England, but, after Harold's death at Hastings, Wulstan was one of the first to submit to the Conqueror. After the reform of the English episcopate in 1072, he was the only English-born bishop of an English see, and his loyalty to the new regime was complete – as was that of most sensible Englishmen of the time. He had on occasion to defend Worcester both from revolting barons and perennial Welsh raids.

He succeeded in suppressing the slave trade through Bristol, secured the building of many new parish churches, and he was known for his zeal for the celibacy of the clergy – an ideal more sought after than realized in his day. He also began the rebuilding of the cathedral of Worcester, and his new crypt still survives. During his pontificate the monks of Worcester became involved in a long quarrel with the neighboring monks of Evesham. There is little doubt that right lay with Evesham, and Worcester lost its case. Not long afterwards Abbot Ethelwig of Evesham died, and Wulstan scandalized his monks by praying for Ethelwig's soul, consequently, says his biographer, God struck him with the gout from which Ethelwig had died – a story which nicely shows how much above the monkish pettiness of his time Wulstan stood. In his day there was a close connection between the monks of Worcester and those of the see of Dublin. The second bishop of Dublin, Patrick, was a former monk of Worcester, who wrote a charming poem in Wulstan's honor. Wulstan died in 1095, and he was canonized by Pope Innocent III in 1203.
January 19th

XYSTUS I, *see* Sixtus.

ZACHAEUS, *see* Alphaeus and Zachaeus.

ZACHARY, *see* Elizabeth and Zachary.

ZACHARY † 752
A Greek from Calabria, Zachary succeeded St Gregory III as pope. He negotiated successfully with the Lombards then threatening Rome, allowed his legate, St Boniface, to anoint Pépin the Short as king of France and translated St Gregory's *Dialogues* into Greek.
March 15th

ZENO, *see* Eusebius, Nestabus, Zeno and Nestor.

ZENO of VERONA † 371
Appointed bishop of Verona in 362, he was strong in his opposition to the Arians, and in relieving the sufferings caused by the Gothic invasions.
April 12th

ZENOBIUS *Fourth Century*
The principal patron of Florence, he belonged to the Geronimo family. He was made archdeacon of Florence and then, on his return from a papal mission to Constantinople, bishop. He was associated with St Eugenius and St Crescentius.

He is credited with having brought a number of people back to life, including a child run over by a cart; but the details of his life are unreliable, as no early biography exists. ILLUSTRATION: page 464
May 25th

ZEPHYRINUS † 217
St Zephyrinus succeeded St Victor I as pope round about the year 200. His pontificate lasted eighteen years until 217. Little is really known of him, and one of our main sources is the *Philosophoumena* of his theological opponent, St Hippolytus, who describes him as a man of no personality and little education. He was content to entrust the administration of his see, and even, it would seem, his theology to his archdeacon, St Callistus.

It is said of Zephyrinus that he ordered glass chalices to be used at mass in place of the wooden ones then customary. It is possible that he was martyred during persecutions at the end of his pontificate.
August 26th

ZITA † 1278
A servant from the age of twelve, she led a remarkably humble and pious life in the face of many trials, remaining with the same family for forty-eight years until her death. She is regarded as the patroness of domestic workers, and one of her sayings was, 'A servant is not good if she is not industrious: work-shy piety in people of our position is sham piety'.
April 27th

ZOË, *see* Exsuperius and Zoë.

ZOILUS and his Companions † 304
Zoilus was a martyr who suffered in Cordova during the persecution under Diocletian.
June 27th

ZOSIMUS, *see* Rufus and Zosimus.

ZOSIMUS † 418

A Greek, he succeeded St Innocent I as pope. His short pontificate was continually troubled by problems arising in the African church, particularly by the appeal of Pelagius and Celestius against their condemnation.

December 26th

ZOSIMUS *Seventh Century*

For many years he performed menial tasks in St Lucy's monastery near Syracuse, until the bishop, recognizing his divine grace, appointed him abbot of Santa Lucia. He later held the joint appointment of abbot and bishop of Syracuse, and ruled with exceptional wisdom and charity.

March 30th

THE CALENDAR OF FEAST DAYS

THE CALENDAR OF FEAST DAYS

'SMALL CAPITALS' indicate the chief feast for the day according to the Roman Missal.

'*Italics*' indicate all other feasts mentioned in the Roman Missal.

'Ordinary type' indicates saints whose feasts are not mentioned in the Roman Missal but whose lives are included in this book.

An asterisk '*' indicates those saints who are treated as main entries or form part of such an entry.

Boxed insertions indicate movable feasts.

January 1st

THE CIRCUMCISION OF OUR LORD JESUS CHRIST
Concordius, martyr; Felix of Bourges; Almachius or Telemachus, martyr; Euphrosyne, virgin; Eugendus, abbot; William of Saint Benignus, abbot; Fulgentius, bishop; Clarus, abbot; Peter of Atroa abbot; Odilo, abbot; Fanchea, Virgin.

> On the Sunday between the Circumcision and the Epiphany, or if there is no Sunday on January 2nd occurs:
> THE HOLY NAME OF JESUS

January 2nd

Macarius of Alexandria; Munchin, bishop; Vincentian; Adalhard or Adelard, abbot; Caspar del Bufalo.

January 3rd

Antherus, pope and martyr; Peter Balsam, martyr; Geneviève, virgin*; Bertilia of Mareuil, widow.

January 4th

Gregory of Langres, bishop; Pharaïldis, virgin; Rigobert of Rheims, bishop.

January 5th

TELESPHORUS, POPE AND MARTYR
Apollinaris Syncletica, virgin; Syncletica, virgin; Simeon Stylites*; Convoyon, abbot; Dorotheus the Younger, abbot; Gerlac.

January 6th

THE EPIPHANY OF OUR LORD JESUS CHRIST
Wiltrudis, widow; Erminold, abbot; Guarinus or Guérin, bishop; Charles of Sezze.

> On the first Sunday after the Epiphany occurs:
> THE FEAST OF THE HOLY FAMILY

January 7th

Lucian of Antioch, martyr; Valentine, bishop; Tillo; Aldric, bishop; Reinold; Canute Lavard; Kentigerna, widow.

January 8th

Apollinaris of Hierapolis, bishop; Lucian of Beauvais, martyr; Severinus of Noricum; Severinus of Septempeda, bishop; Erhard, bishop; Gudula, virgin; Pega, virgin; Wulsin, bishop; Thorfinn, bishop.

January 9th

Marciana, virgin and martyr; Julian, Basilissa and Companions, martyrs; Peter of Sebaste, bishop; Waningus or Vaneng; Adrian of Canterbury, abbot; Berhtwald of Canterbury, abbot.

January 10th

Marcian; John the Good, bishop; Agatho, pope; Peter Orseolo; William, bishop.

January 11th

HYGINUS, POPE AND MARTYR
Theodosius the Cenobiarch; Salvius or Sauve, bishop.

January 12th

Arcadius, martyr; Tigrius and Eutropius, martyrs; Caesaria, virgin; Victorian, abbot; Benedict or Benet Biscop, bishop*.

January 13th

COMMEMORATION OF THE BAPTISM OF OUR LORD JESUS CHRIST
Agrecius or Agritius, bishop; Berno, abbot.

January 14th

HILARY OF POITIERS, BISHOP, CONFESSOR AND DOCTOR*
*Felix, Priest and Martyr**
Macrina the Elder, widow; Barbasymas and Companions, martyrs; Datius, bishop; Kentigern or Mungo, bishop*; Sava, bishop.

January 15th

PAUL, THE FIRST HERMIT, CONFESSOR*
Maurus, Abbot
Macarius the Elder; Isidore of Alexandria; John Calybites; Ita, virgin*; Bonet or Bonitus, bishop; Ceowulf.

January 16th

MARCELLUS I, POPE AND MARTYR
Priscilla, matron; Honoratus, bishop; Fursey, abbot*; Henry of Cocket; Berard and Companions, martyrs.

January 17th

ANTONY THE ABBOT*
Speusippus, Eleusippus and Meleusippus, martyrs; Genulf or Genou, bishop; Julian Sabas, hermit; Sabinus of Piacenza, bishop; Richimir, abbot; Sulpicius II or Sulpice.

January 18th

PETER'S CHAIR AT ROME*
Prisca, Virgin and Martyr
Volusian, bishop; Deicolus or Desle, abbot.

January 19th

MARIUS, MARTHA, AUDIFAX AND ABACHUM, MARTYRS
*Canute or Knut, King and Martyr**
Germanicus, martyr; Nathalan, bishop; Albert of Cashel, bishop; Fillan or Foelan, abbot; Wulstan, bishop*; Henry of Uppsala, bishop and martyr.

January 20th

FABIAN, POPE, AND SEBASTIAN*, MARTYRS
Euthymius the Great, abbot; Fechin, abbot.

January 21st

AGNES, VIRGIN AND MARTYR*
Fructuosus of Tarragona, bishop and martyr; Patroclus, martyr; Epiphanius of Pavia, bishop; Meinrad, martyr.

January 22nd

VINCENT OF SARAGOSSA AND
ANASTASIUS THE PERSIAN,
MARTYRS
Blesilla, widow; Dominic of Sora,
abbot; Berhtwald, bishop; Valerius
of Saragossa.

January 23rd

RAYMUND OF PENAFORT,
CONFESSOR
Emerentiana, Virgin and Martyr
Asclas, martyr; Agathangelus and
Clement, martyrs; John the Alms-
giver, patriarch; Ildephonsus,
bishop; Bernard or Barnard, bishop;
Lufthildis, virgin; Maimbod,
martyr.

January 24th

TIMOTHY OF EPHESUS, BISHOP
AND MARTYR*
Babylas, bishop and martyr; Felician, bishop and martyr, and Messalina, martyr; Macedonius.

January 25th

THE CONVERSION OF PAUL
Artemas, martyr; Juventinus and
Maximinus, martyrs; Publius, abbot;
Apollo, abbot; Praejectus or Prix,
bishop and martyr; Poppo, abbot.

January 26th

POLYCARP OF SMYRNA, BISHOP
AND MARTYR*
Paula, widow; Conan, bishop; Al-
beric, abbot*; Eystein, bishop;
Margaret of Hungary, virgin*.

January 27th

JOHN CHRYSOSTOM, BISHOP
AND DOCTOR*
Julian of Le Mans, bishop; Marius
or May, abbot; Vitalian, pope.

January 28th

PETER NOLASCO, CONFESSOR*
Agnes, Virgin and Martyr (Second
Feast)
John of Reomay, abbot; Paulinus of
Aquileia, bishop; Charlemagne;
Amadeus, bishop; Peter Thomas,
bishop.

January 29th

FRANCIS DE SALES, BISHOP,
CONFESSOR AND DOCTOR*
Sabinian, martyr; Gildas the Wise,
abbot; Sulpicius 'Severus', bishop.

January 30th

MARTINA, VIRGIN AND MARTYR*
Barsimaeus, bishop; Bathildis,
widow; Aldegundis, virgin; Adelelmus or Aleaume, abbot; Hyacintha
Mariscotti, virgin.

January 31st

JOHN BOSCO, CONFESSOR*
Cyrus and John, martyrs; Marcella,
widow; Aidan or Maedoc of Ferns,
bishop; Adamnan of Coldingham;
Ulphia, virgin; Eusebius, martyr;
Nicetas of Novgorod, bishop; Francis Xavier Bianchi.

February 1st

IGNATIUS OF ANTIOCH, BISHOP
AND MARTYR*
Pionius, martyr; Brigid or Bride,
virgin*; Sigebert III of Austrasia;
John 'of the Grating', bishop.

February 2nd

THE PURIFICATION OF THE
BLESSED VIRGIN MARY*
Adalbald of Ostrevant, martyr; Joan
of Lestonnac, widow.

February 3rd

BLAISE, BISHOP AND MARTYR
Laurence of Spoleto, bishop; Ia,
virgin; Laurence of Canterbury,
bishop; Werburga, virgin; Anskar,
bishop; Margaret 'of England',
virgin; Aelred of Rievaulx, abbot.*

February 4th

ANDREW CORSINI, BISHOP AND
CONFESSOR*
Theopilus the Penitent; Phileas,
bishop and martyr; Isidore of Pelusium, abbot; Modan, abbot; Nicholas Studites, abbot; Rembert,
bishop; Joan of Valois, matron*;
Joseph of Leonessa; John de Britto,
martyr.

February 5th

AGATHA, VIRGIN AND MARTYR*
Avitus of Vienne, bishop; Bertoul or
Bertulf; Indractus and Dominica,
martyrs; Vodalus or Voel; Adelaide
of Bellich, virgin; The Martyrs of
Japan: Peter Baptist, Martin de
Aguirre, Francis Blanco, Francis-of-
St-Michael, Philip de las Casas,
Gonsalo Garcia, Paul Mike, John
Goto, James Kisai, Caius Francis,
Francis of Miako, Leo Karasuma,
Louis Ibarki, Antony Deynan and
Thomas Kasaki.

February 6th

TITUS, BISHOP
Dorothy, Virgin and Martyr
Mel and Melchu, bishops; Vedast or
Vaast, bishop; Amand, bishop;
Guarinus, bishop; Hildegund,
widow.

February 7th

ROMUALD, ABBOT
Adaucus, martyr; Theodore of
Heraclea, martyr; Moses, bishop;
Richard, 'King'; Luke the Younger.

February 8th

JOHN OF MATHA, CONFESSOR
Nicetius or Nizier of Besançon,
bishop; Elfleda, virgin; Meingold,
martyr; Cuthman; Stephen of Muret,
abbot.

February 9th

CYRIL OF ALEXANDRIA,
BISHOP AND DOCTOR*
Apollonia, Virgin and Martyr
Nicephorus, martyr; Sabinus of
Canosa, bishop; Teilo, bishop*;
Ansbert, bishop; Alto, abbot.

February 10th

SCHOLASTICA, VIRGIN*
Soteris, virgin and martyr; Trum-
win, bishop; Austreberta, virgin;
William of Maleval.

February 11th

APPARITION OF OUR LADY OF
LOURDES
Saturninus, Dativus and Companions, martyrs; Lucius, bishop and
martyr; Lazarus, bishop; Severinus,
abbot; Caedmon; Gregory II, pope;
Benedict of Aniane, abbot; Paschal I,
pope.

February 12th

THE SEVEN FOUNDERS OF THE
SERVITE ORDER, CONFESSORS
Marina, virgin; Julian the Hospi-
taller; Meletius, bishop; Ethelwald,
bishop; Antony Kauleas, bishop;
Ludan.

February 13th

Polyeuctus, martyr; Martinian the
Hermit; Stephen of Rieti, abbot;
Modomnoc; Licinius or Lesin,
bishop; Ermengild or Ermenilda,
widow; Catherine dei Ricci, virgin.

February 14th

VALENTINE, PRIEST AND
MARTYR*
Abraham, bishop; Maro, abbot;
Auxentius; Conran, bishop; Anto-
ninus of Sorrento, abbot; Adolf,
bishop.

February 15th

FAUSTINUS AND JOVITA,
MARTYRS
Agape, virgin and martyr; Walfrid,
abbot; Tanco or Tatto, bishop and
martyr; Sigfrid, bishop.

February 16th

Onesimus, martyr; Juliana, virgin
and martyr; Elias, Jeremy and Companions, martyrs; Gilbert of Sempringham*.

February 17th

Theodulus and Julian, martyrs;
Loman, bishop; Fintan of Cloneenagh, abbot; Finan, bishop; Evermod, bishop; Silvin, bishop.

February 18th

SIMEON, BISHOP AND MARTYR
Leo and Paregorius, martyrs; Flavian, bishop and martyr; Helladius, bishop; Colman of Lindisfarne, bishop*; Angilbert, abbot; Theotonius, abbot.

February 19th

Mesrop, bishop; Barbatus, bishop; Beatus of Liebana; Boniface of Lausanne, bishop; Conrad of Piacenza.

February 20th

Tyrannio, Zenobius and Companions, martyrs; Sadoth, bishop and martyr; Eleutherius of Tournai, bishop; Eucherius of Orleans, bishop; Wulfric.

February 21st

Severian, bishop and martyr; Germanus of Granfel, martyr; George of Amastris, bishop.

February 22nd

PETER'S CHAIR AT ANTIOCH*
Thalassius and Limnaeus; Baradates; Margaret of Cortona*.

February 23rd

PETER DAMIAN, BISHOP, CONFESSOR AND DOCTOR*
Serenus the Gardener or Cerneuf of Billom, martyr; Alexander Akimetes; Dositheus; Boisil or Boswell, abbot; Milburga and Mildgytha, virgins; Willigis, bishop.

February 24th

MATTHIAS, APOSTLE [1]
Montanus, Lucius and Companions, martyrs; Praetextatus or Prix, bishop and martyr.

February 25th

Victorinus and Companions, martyrs; Caesarius Nazianzen; Ethelbert of Kent; Walburga, virgin; Tarasius, bishop; Gerland, bishop.

February 26th

Nestor, bishop and martyr; Alexander of Alexandria, bishop; Porphyry, bishop; Victor or Vittre the Hermit.

February 27th

GABRIEL OF OUR LADY OF SORROWS, CONFESSOR
Besas, Cronion and Julian, martyrs; Thalelaeus the Hermit; Leander, bishop; Baldomerus or Galmier; Alnoth; John of Gorze, abbot.

[1] In Leap Year the feast of Matthias is kept on February 25th, and any feast occurring from February 24th to the end of the month is postponed by one day.

February 28th

Proterius, bishop and martyr; Romanus and Lupicinus, abbots; Hilarus, pope; Oswald of Worcester, bishop*.

March 1st

David or Dewi, bishop*; Felix II (III), pope; Albinus or Aubin of Angers, bishop; Swithbert, bishop; Rudesind or Rosendo, bishop.

March 2nd

Chad or Ceadda, bishop*.

March 3rd

Marinus and Astyrius, martyrs; Chelidonius and Emeterius, martyrs; Arthelais, virgin; Non or Nonnita; Winwaloe or Guénolé, abbot; Anselm of Nonantola, abbot; Cunegund, widow; Gervinus, abbot; Aelred of Rievaulx, abbot*.

March 4th

CASIMIR OF POLAND, CONFESSOR
Lucius I, Pope and Martyr
Adrian and Companions; Peter of Cava, bishop.

March 5th

Adrian and Eubulus, martyrs; Phocas of Antioch, martyr; Eusebius or Cremona; Gerasimus, abbot; Ciaran or Kieran of Saighir, bishop; Piran, abbot; Virgil of Arles, bishop; John Joseph of the Cross.

March 6th

PERPETUA, FELICITY AND COMPANIONS, MARTYRS*
Fridolin, abbot; Cyneburga, Cyneswide and Tibba; Chrodegang, bishop; Balred and Bilfred; Cadroe or Cadroel, abbot; Ollegarius or Oldegar, bishop; Cyril of Constantinople; Colette, virgin.

March 7th

THOMAS AQUINAS, CONFESSOR AND DOCTOR*
Paul the Simple; Drausius or Drausin, bishop; Esterwine, abbot; Ardo; Theophylact, bishop.

March 8th

JOHN OF GOD, CONFESSOR
Pontius; Philemon and Apollonius, martyrs; Senan, bishop*; Felix of Dunwich, bishop; Julian of Toledo, bishop; Humphrey or Hunfrid, bishop; Duthac, bishop; Veremund, abbot; Stephen of Obazine, abbot.

March 9th

FRANCES OF ROME, WIDOW
Pacian, bishop; Gregory of Nyssa, bishop*; Bosa, bishop; Catherine of Bologna, virgin; Dominic Savio.

March 10th

THE FORTY MARTYRS OF SEBASTE
Codratus and Companions, martyrs; Macarius of Jerusalem, bishop; Simplicius, pope; Kessog, bishop and martyr; Anastasia Patricia, virgin; Droctoveus or Drotté, abbot; Attalas, abbot; Himelin.

March 11th

Constantine, martyr; Sophronius, bishop; Vindician, bishop; Benedict Crispus, bishop; Oengus or Aengus, abbot-bishop; Eulogius of Cordova, martyr; Aurea, virgin; Teresa Margaret Redi, virgin.

March 12th

GREGORY THE GREAT, POPE AND DOCTOR*
Maximilian of Theveste, martyr*; Peter, Gorgonius and Dorotheus, martyrs; Paul Aurelian, bishop; Theophanes the Chronicler, abbot; Alphege of Winchester, bishop; Bernard of Capua, bishop; Fina or Seraphina, virgin.

March 13th

Euphrasia or Euphraxia, virgin; Mochoemoc, abbot; Gerald of Mayo, abbot; Nicephorus of Constantinople, bishop; Ansovinus, bishop; Heldrad, abbot; Roderic and Solomon, martyrs.

March 14th

Leobinus or Lubin, bishop; Eutychius or Eustathius, martyr; Matilda, widow.

March 15th

Longinus, martyr; Matrona, virgin and martyr; Zachary, pope; Leocritia or Lucretia, virgin and martyr; Louise de Marillac, widow*; Clement Mary Hofbauer*.

March 16th

Julian of Antioch, martyr; Abraham Kidunia; Finnian Lobhar, abbot; Eusebia, abbess; Gregory Makar, bishop; Heribert, bishop.

March 17th

PATRICK, BISHOP AND CONFESSOR*
Joseph of Arimathea*; Agricola, bishop; Gertrude of Nivelles, virgin; Paul of Cyprus; The Martyrs of the Serapeum.

March 18th

CYRIL, BISHOP OF JERUSALEM, CONFESSOR AND DOCTOR*
Alexander of Jerusalem, bishop and martyr; Frigidian or Frediano, bishop; Edward the Martyr; Anselm of Lucca, bishop; Salvator of Horta.

March 19th

JOSEPH, SPOUSE OF THE BLESSED VIRGIN MARY, CONFESSOR★

John of Panaca; Landoald and Companions; Alcmund, martyr.

March 20th

Photina and Companions, martyrs; Martin of Braga, bishop; Cuthbert, bishop★; Herbert; Wulfram, bishop; The Martyrs of Mar Saba.

March 21st

BENEDICT OF NURSIA, ABBOT★

Serapion, bishop; Enda, abbot.

March 22nd

Paul of Narbonne and Companions; Basil of Ancyra, martyr; Deogratias, bishop; Benvenuto of Osimo, bishop; Nicholas von (of) Flüe★.

March 23rd

Victorian and Companions, martyrs; Benedict the Hermit; Ethelwald or Oidilwald the Hermit; Joseph Oriol.

March 24th

GABRIEL THE ARCHANGEL

Irenaeus of Sirmium, bishop and martyr; Aldemar, abbot; Catherine of Vadstena, virgin; Simon of Trent and William of Norwich.

March 25th

THE ANNUNCIATION OF THE BLESSED VIRGIN MARY★

Dismas★; Barontius; Hermenland, abbot; Alfwold, bishop; Lucy Filippini, virgin.

March 26th

Castulus, martyr; Felix of Trier, bishop; Macartan, bishop; Braulio, bishop; Ludger, bishop; Basil the Younger.

March 27th

JOHN DAMASCENE, CONFESSOR AND DOCTOR

John of Egypt.

March 28th

JOHN OF CAPISTRANO, CONFESSOR

Guntramnus; Tutilo.

March 29th

Barachisius and Jonas, martyrs; Cyril of Heliopolis, martyr, and Mark, bishop; Armogastes, Archinimus and Saturus, martyrs; Gundleus and Gwladys or Gladys; Rupert, bishop; Berthold; Ludolf, bishop.

March 30th

Regulus or Rieul, bishop; John Climacus, abbot; Zosimus, bishop; Osburga, virgin.

March 31st

Balbina, virgin; Acacius or Achatius, bishop; Benjamin, martyr; Guy of Pomposa, abbot.

April 1st

Melito, bishop; Walaricus or Valery, abbot; Macarius the Wonder-Worker; Hugh of Grenoble, bishop; Hugh of Bonnevaux, abbot; Gilbert of Caithness, bishop; Catherine of Palma, virgin.

April 2na

FRANCIS OF PAOLA, CONFESSOR

Apphian and Theodosia, martyrs; Mary of Egypt; Nicetius or Nizier of Lyons, bishop; Ebba the Younger, virgin.

April 3rd

Pancras of Taormina, bishop and martyr; Sixtus or Xystus I, pope and martyr; Agape, Chionia and Irene, virgins and martyrs; Burgundofara or Fare, virgin; Nicetas, abbot; Richard Wyche or Richard of Chichester, bishop.

April 4th

ISIDORE OF SEVILLE, BISHOP AND DOCTOR★

Agathopus and Theodulus, martyrs; Tigernach, bishop; Plato, abbot; Benedict the Black.

April 5th

VINCENT FERRER, CONFESSOR★

Derfel Gadarn; Ethelburga of Lyminge, matron; Gerald of Sauve-Majeure, abbot; Albert of Montecorvino, bishop.

April 6th

The Martyrs in Persia; Marcellinus, martyr; Celestine I, pope; Eutychius, bishop; Prudentius of Troyes, bishop; William of Eskhill, abbot.

April 7th

Hegesippus; Aphraates; George the Younger, bishop; Celsus or Ceallach, bishop; Aybert.

April 8th

Dionysius of Corinth, bishop; Perpetuus, bishop; Walter of Pontoise, abbot.

April 9th

Mary of Cleophas, matron; Waldetrudis or Waudru, widow; Hugh of Rouen, bishop; Gaucherius, abbot.

April 10th

Bademus, abbot; The Martyrs under the Danes; Macarius or Macaire of Ghent; Fulbert, bishop; Paternus of Abdinghof; Michael de Sanctis.

April 11th

LEO THE GREAT, POPE AND DOCTOR★

Barsanuphius; Isaac of Spoleto; Godeberta, virgin; Guthlac★; Gemma Galgani, virgin★.

April 12th

Julius I, pope; Zeno of Verona, bishop; Sabas the Goth, martyr; Alferius, abbot.

April 13th

HERMENEGILD, MARTYR

Agathonica, Papylus and Carpus★, martyrs; Martius or Mars, abbot.

April 14th

JUSTIN, MARTYR

Tiburtius, Valerius and Maximus, Martyrs

Ardalion, martyr; Lambert of Lyons bishop; Bernard of Tiron, abbot; Caradoc; Bénezet; Antony, Eustace and John, martyrs; Lidwina of Schiedam, virgin★.

April 15th

Basilissa and Anastasia, martyrs; Padarn or Patern, bishop; Ruadan of Lothra, abbot; Hunna or Huva, matron.

April 16th

Optatus and Companions and Encratis, virgin, martyrs; Turibius of Astorga, bishop; Paternus or Pair, bishop; Fructuosus of Braga, bishop; Magnus, martyr★; Drogo or Druon; Contardo; Joseph Benedict Labre★; Bernadette Soubirous, virgin★.

April 17th

ANICETUS, POPE AND MARTYR

Mappalicus and Companions, martyrs; Innocent of Tortona, bishop; Donnan and Companions, martyrs★; Robert of Chaise-Dieu, abbot; Stephen Harding, abbot★.

April 18th

Apollonius the Apologist, martyr; Laserian, Laisren or Molaisse, bishop; Idesbald, abbot; Galdinus, bishop.

April 19th

Leo IX, pope; Expeditus★; Ursmar, abbot and bishop; Geroldus; Alphege, bishop and martyr★.

April 20th

Marcellinus of Embrun, bishop; Marcian or Marian; Caedwalla; Hildegund, virgin; Agnes of Montepulciano, virgin.

April 21st

ANSELM, BISHOP, CONFESSOR AND DOCTOR★

Simeon Barsabae, bishop, and Companions, martyrs; Anastasius I of Antioch, bishop; Beuno, abbot★; Malrubius or Maelrubha, abbot; Conrad of Parzham.

April 22nd
SOTER AND CAIUS, POPES AND MARTYRS
Epipodius and Alexander, martyrs; Leonides, martyr; Agapitus I, pope; Theodore of Sykeon, bishop; Opportuna, virgin and abbess.

April 23rd
GEORGE, MARTYR★
Felix, Fortunatus and Achilleus, martyrs; Ibar, bishop; Gerard of Toul, bishop; Adalbert of Prague, bishop and martyr.

April 24th
FIDELIS OF SIGMARINGEN, MARTYR
Mellitus, bishop; Ivo, bishop; Egbert; William Firmatus; Mary Euphrasia Pelletier, virgin.

April 25th
MARK THE EVANGELIST★
Anianus, bishop; Heribald, bishop.

April 26th
CLETUS AND MARCELLINUS, POPES AND MARTYRS
Peter of Braga, bishop; Richarius or Riquier, abbot; Paschasius Radbertus, abbot; Franca of Piacenza, virgin and abbess; Stephen of Perm, bishop.

April 27th
PETER CANISIUS, CONFESSOR AND DOCTOR★
Anthimus, bishop; Asicus or Tassach, bishop; Maughold or Maccul, bishop; Floribert, bishop; Stephen Pechersky, bishop; Zita, virgin; Turibius of Lima, bishop★; Theodore the Sanctified, abbot.

April 28th
PAUL OF THE CROSS, CONFESSOR★
Vitalis, Martyr
Valeria, martyr; Pollio, martyr; Theodora and Didymus, martyrs; Cronan of Roscrea, abbot; Pamphilus of Sulmona, bishop; Cyril of Turov, bishop; Louis Mary of Montfort; Peter Mary Chanel, martyr★.

April 29th
PETER OF VERONA, MARTYR
Wilfrid the Younger, bishop; The Abbots of Cluny★ (Berno, Odo, Mayeul, Odilo, Hugh, Bd Aymard and Peter the Venerable); Robert of Molesme, abbot; Joseph Cottolengo.

April 30th
CATHERINE OF SIENA, VIRGIN★
Maximus, martyr; Eutropius of Saintes, bishop and martyr; James and Marian, martyrs★; Forannan, abbot; Gualfardus or Wolfhard

May 1st
JOSEPH THE WORKMAN, CONFESSOR, SPOUSE OF THE BLESSED VIRGIN MARY★
Amator or Amatre, bishop; Brioc or Brieuc, abbot★; Sigismund of Burgundy; Marculf or Marcoul, abbot; Theodard of Narbonne, bishop; Peregrine Laziosi.

May 2nd
ATHANASIUS, BISHOP, CONFESSOR AND DOCTOR★
Exsuperius or Hesperus and Zoë, martyrs; Waldebert, abbot; Ultan, abbot; Wiborada, virgin and martyr; Mafalda or Matilda.

May 3rd
THE FINDING OF THE HOLY CROSS
Alexander, Eventius and Theodulus, Martyrs; Juvenal, Bishop
Timothy and Maura, martyrs; Philip of Zell.

May 4th
MONICA, WIDOW★
Cyriacus or Judas Quiricus, bishop; Pelagia of Tarsus, virgin and martyr; Venerius, bishop; Godehard or Gothard, bishop; Florian, martyr.

May 5th
PIUS V, POPE AND CONFESSOR★
Hilary of Arles, bishop; Maurantius, abbot; Mauruntius, abbot; Avertinus; Angelo, martyr; Jutta, widow.

May 6th
JOHN, APOSTLE BEFORE THE LATIN GATE
Evodius, bishop; Edbert, bishop; Petronax, abbot.

May 7th
STANISLAUS, BISHOP AND MARTYR★
Domitian, bishop; Liuhard, bishop; Serenicus and Serenus; John of Beverley, bishop★.

May 8th
THE APPARITION OF ST MICHAEL★
Victor Maurus, martyr; Acacius or Agathus, martyr; Gibrian; Desideratus, bishop; Boniface IV, pope; Benedict II, pope; Wiro, Plechlem and Oteger; Peter of Tarentaise, bishop.

May 9th
GREGORY NAZIANZEN, BISHOP, DOCTOR AND CONFESSOR★
Beatus; Pachomius, abbot; Gerontius, bishop.

May 10th
ANTONINUS OF FLORENCE, BISHOP AND CONFESSOR★
Gordian and Epimachus, Martyrs
Calepodius, martyr; Alphius, Cyri-

nus and Philadelphus, martyrs; Catald and Conleth, bishops; Solangia, virgin and martyr.

May 11th
PHILIP AND JAMES THE LESS★, APOSTLES
Mamertus, bishop; Comgall, abbot; Asaph, bishop; Gengulf or Gengoul; Majolus or Mayeule, abbot; Ansfrid, bishop; Walter of L'Esterp, abbot; Francis di Girolamo; Ignatius of Laconi.

May 12th
NEREUS, ACHILLEUS AND DOMITILLA, MARTYRS
Pancras, Martyr
Epiphanius of Salamis, bishop; Modoaldus, bishop; Rictrudis, widow; Germanus of Constantinople, bishop; Dominic of the Causeway.

May 13th
ROBERT BELLARMINE, BISHOP, CONFESSOR AND DOCTOR★
Glyceris, virgin and martyr; Mucius or Mocius, martyr; Servatius or Servais, bishop; John the Silent; Erconwald, bishop★; Euthymius the Illuminator, abbot; Peter Regalatus.

May 14th
BONIFACE OF TARSUS, MARTYR
Pontius, martyr; Carthage, Carthach or Mochuda, abbot; Erembert, bishop; Michael Garicoïts★; Mary Mazzarello, virgin.

May 15th
JOHN BAPTIST DE LA SALLE, CONFESSOR★
Torquatus and Companions, martyrs; Isidore of Chios; Hilary of Galeata, abbot; Dympna and Gerebernus, martyrs★; Bertha and Rupert; Hallvard, martyr; Isaias of Rostov, bishop; Isidore the Husbandman; Peter of Lampsacus and Companions, martyrs.

May 16th
UBALD OF GUBBIO, BISHOP AND CONFESSOR
Peregrine of Auxerre, bishop and martyr; Possidius, bishop; Germerius, bishop; Brendan, abbot★; Domnolus, bishop; Carantoc or Carannog, abbot; Honoratus of Amiens, bishop; Simon Stock★; John Nepomucen, martyr; Andrew Hubert Fournet.★

May 17th
PASCHAL BAYLON, CONFESSOR★
Madron or Madern; Bruno of Würzburg, bishop.

May 18th

VENANTIUS, MARTYR
Theodotus, Thecusa and Companions, martyrs; Potamon, bishop and martyr; Eric of Sweden, martyr; Felix of Cantalice.

May 19th

PETER CELESTINE V, POPE AND CONFESSOR★
Pudentiana and Pudens, martyrs; Calocerus and Parthenius, martyrs; Dunstan, bishop★; Ivo of Kermartin.

May 20th

BERNARDINE OF SIENA, CONFESSOR★
Thalelaeus, martyr; Basilla or Basilissa, virgin and martyr; Baudelius, martyr; Austregisilus or Outril, bishop; Ethelbert, martyr.

May 21st

Godric; Andrew Bobola, martyr; Theophilus of Corte.

May 22nd

Aemilius and Castus, martyrs; Quiteria, virgin and martyr; Romanus; Julia, martyr; Aigulf or Ayoul, bishop; Humility, widow; Rita, widow★.

May 23rd

Desiderius or Didier, bishop and martyr; Guibert; Leonitus of Rostov, bishop and martyr; Ivo of Chartres, bishop★; Euphrosyne of Polotsk, virgin; William of Rochester, martyr; John Baptist Rossi.

May 24th

Donatian and Rogatian, martyrs; Vincent of Lérins; David I, King of Scotland; Nicetas of Pereaslav, martyr.

May 25th

GREGORY VII, POPE AND CONFESSOR★
Urban I, Pope and Martyr
Dionysius of Milan, bishop; Zenobius, bishop; Leo or Lyé, abbot; Aldhelm, bishop★; Gennadius, bishop; Madeleine Sophie Barat, virgin★.

May 26th

PHILIP NERI, CONFESSOR★
Quadratus, bishop; Priscus or Prix and Companions, martyrs; Lambert of Vence, bishop; Marian of Quito, virgin.

May 27th

BEDE THE VENERABLE, DOCTOR AND CONFESSOR★
John I, Pope and Martyr
Restituta of Sora, virgin and martyr; Julius and Companions, martyrs; Eutropius of Orange, bishop; Melangell or Monacella, virgin.

May 28th

AUGUSTINE OF CANTERBURY, BISHOP AND CONFESSOR★
Senator, bishop; Justus of Urgel, bishop; Germanus or Germain, bishop; William of Gellone; Bernard of Menthon or Montjoux★; Ignatius of Rostov, bishop.

May 29th

MARY MAGDALEN DEI PAZZI, VIRGIN
Cyril of Caesarea, martyr; Maximinus, bishop; Sisinnius, Martyrius and Alexander, martyrs; Theodosia, virgin and martyr; William, Stephen, Raymund and Companions, martyrs.

May 30th

FELIX I, POPE AND MARTYR
Isaac of Constantinople, abbot; Exsuperantius, bishop; Madelgisilus or Mauguille; Walstan; Ferdinand III, King of Castile; Joan of Arc, virgin★; Eleutherius, pope.

May 31st

THE QUEENSHIP OF THE BLESSED VIRGIN MARY★
Petronilla, Virgin and Martyr
Cantius, Cantianius and Cantianella, martyrs; Mechtildis of Edelstetten, virgin.

June 1st

ANGELA MERICI, VIRGIN★
Pamphilus and Companions, martyrs; Proculus, 'the soldier' and Proculus of Bologna, bishop, Caprasius or Caprais; Wistan; Simeon of Syracuse; Eneco or Iñigo, abbot; Theobald of Alba.

June 2nd

MARCELLINUS AND PETER, MARTYRS
Erasmus or Elmo, Bishop and Martyr
Pothinus and Companions, martyrs★; Eugenius I, pope; Stephen of Sweden, bishop and martyr; Nicholas the Pilgrim; Blandina, martyr.

June 3rd

Cecilius; Pergentinus and Laurentinus, martyrs; Lucillian and Companions, martyrs; Clotilda, widow; Liphardus and Urbicius, abbots; Kevin or Coegmen, abbot; Genesius of Clermont, bishop; Isaac of Cordova, martyr; Morand.

June 4th

FRANCIS CARACCIOLO, CONFESSOR★
Quirinus, bishop and martyr; Metrophanes, bishop; Optatus of Milevis, bishop; Petroc, abbot★; Vincentia Gerosa, virgin.

June 5th

BONIFACE, BISHOP AND MARTYR★
Dorotheus of Tyre, martyr; Sanctius or Sancho, martyr.

June 6th

NORBERT, BISHOP AND CONFESSOR★
Philip the Deacon★; Ceratius or Cérase, bishop; Eustorgius of Milan, bishop; Jarlath, bishop; Gudwal or Gurval; Claud, bishop.

June 7th

Paul of Constantinople, bishop; Meriadoc, bishop; Colman of Dromore, bishop; Vulflagius or Wulphy; Willibald, bishop★; Gottschalk, martyr; Robert of Newminster, abbot; Antony Gianelli, bishop.

June 8th

Maximinus of Aix; Médard, bishop; Clodulf or Cloud, bishop; William of York, bishop★.

June 9th

PRIMUS AND FELICIAN, MARTYRS
Columba or Columcille, abbot★; Vincent of Agen, martyr; Pelagia of Antioch, virgin and martyr; Richard of Andria, bishop.

June 10th

MARGARET, QUEEN OF SCOTLAND, WIDOW★
Getulius and Companions, martyrs; Ithamar, bishop; Landericus or Landry, bishop; Bogumilus, bishop.

June 11th

BARNABAS, APOSTLE★
Felix and Fortunatus, martyrs; Parisio.

June 12th

JOHN OF SAHAGUN OR OF ST FACUNDO, CONFESSOR
Basilides, Quirinus or Cyrinus, Nabor and Nazarius, Martyrs
Antonina, martyr; Onuphrius; Ternan, bishop; Peter of Mount Athos; Leo III, pope★; Odulf; Eskil, bishop and martyr.

June 13th

ANTONY OF PADUA, DOCTOR AND CONFESSOR★
Felicula, martyr; Aquilina, martyr; Triphyllius, bishop.

June 14th

BASIL THE GREAT, BISHOP, DOCTOR AND CONFESSOR★
Valerius and Rufinus, martyrs; Dogmael; Methodius I of Constantinople, bishop.

June 15th

VITUS, MODESTUS AND CRESCENTIA, MARTYRS*
Hesychius, martyr; Tatian Dulas, martyr; Orsiesius, abbot; Landelinus, abbot; Edburga of Winchester, virgin; Bardo, bishop; Aleydis or Alice, virgin; Germaine of Pibrac, virgin.

June 16th

Ferreolus and Ferrutio, martyrs; Cyricus and Julitta, martyrs; Tychon; bishop; Aurelian, bishop; Benno, bishop; Lutgardis, virgin; John Francis Regis*.

June 17th

Nicander and Marcian, martyrs; Bessarion; Hypatius, abbot; Avitus, abbot; Nectan; Hervé or Harvey, abbot; Botulf or Botolph, abbot; Adulf, bishop; Moling, bishop; Rainerius of Pisa; Teresa and Sanchia of Portugal; Emily de Vialar, virgin.

June 18th

EPHRAEM THE DEACON, CONFESSOR AND DOCTOR*
Mark and Marcellian, Martyrs
Amandus, bishop; Elizabeth of Schönau, virgin.

June 19th

JULIANA FALCONIERI, VIRGIN*
Gervase and Protase, Martyrs
Deodatus or Dié, bishop; Bruno or Boniface of Querfurt, bishop and martyr.

June 20th

SILVERIUS, POPE AND MARTYR
Goban or Gobain, martyr; Bagnus or Bain, bishop; Adalbert of Magdeburg, bishop; John of Matera, abbot.

June 21st

ALOYSIUS GONZAGA, CONFESSOR*
Eusebius of Samosata, bishop; Alban or Albinus of Mainz, martyr; Méen or Mewan, abbot; Engelmund; Leutfridus or Leufroy, abbot; Ralph or Raoul, bishop.

June 22nd

PAULINUS OF NOLA, BISHOP AND CONFESSOR*
Alban, martyr*; Nicetas of Remesiana, bishop; Eberhard, bishop.

June 23rd

Agrippina, virgin and martyr; Etheldreda or Audrey, widow; Lietbertus or Libert, bishop; Joseph Cafasso.

June 24th

THE BIRTHDAY OF JOHN THE BAPTIST*
The Martyrs under Nero; Simplicius, bishop; Bartholomew of Farne.

June 25th

WILLIAM OF VERCELLI, ABBOT
Febronia, virgin and martyr; Gallicanus; Prosper of Aquitaine; Prosper of Reggio, bishop; Maximus of Turin, bishop; Moloc or Luan, bishop; Adalbert of Egmond; Eurosia, virgin and martyr; Gohard, bishop and Companions, martyrs.

June 26th

JOHN AND PAUL, MARTYRS
Vigilius, bishop and martyr; Maxentius, abbot; Salvius or Sauve and Superius; John of the Goths; Pelagius or Pelayo, martyr; Anthelm, bishop.

June 27th

Zoilus and Companions, martyrs; Samson of Constantinople; John of Chinon; George Mtasmindeli of the Black Mountains, abbot; Ladislaus of Hungary; Benvenuto of Gubbio.

June 28th

IRENAEUS, BISHOP AND MARTYR*
Plutarch, Potamiaena and Companions, martyrs; Paul I, pope; Heimrad; Sergius and Germanus of Valaam, abbots.

June 29th

PETER AND PAUL, APOSTLES*
Cassius, bishop; Salome and Judith; Emma, widow.

June 30th

THE COMMEMORATION OF PAUL, APOSTLE*
Martial, bishop; Bertrand of Le Mans, bishop; Erentrude, virgin; Theobald or Thibaud of Provins.

July 1st

THE PRECIOUS BLOOD OF OUR LORD JESUS CHRIST
Shenute, abbot; Theodoric or Thierry, abbot; Carilefus or Calais, abbot; Gall of Clermont, bishop; Eparchius or Cybard; Simeon Salus; Serf or Servanus, bishop.

July 2nd

THE VISITATION OF THE BLESSED VIRGIN MARY*
Processus and Martinian, Martyrs
Monegundis, widow; Otto of Bamberg, bishop.

July 3rd

LEO II, POPE AND CONFESSOR
Anatolius, bishop; Irenaeus and Mustiola, martyrs; Julius and Aaron, martyrs; Heliodorus, bishop; Anatolius of Constantinople, bishop; Rumold or Rombaut, martyr; Bernardino Realino.

July 4th

Bertha, widow; Andrew of Crete, bishop; Odo of Canterbury, bishop; Ulric of Augsburg, bishop.

July 5th

ANTONY MARY ZACCARIA, CONFESSOR
Athanasius the Athonite, abbot.

July 6th

Romulus of Fiesole, bishop and martyr; Dominica, virgin and martyr; Sisoes; Goar; Sexburga, widow; Modwenna, virgin; Godelva, martyr; Mary Goretti, virgin and martyr*.

July 7th

CYRIL AND METHODIUS, BISHOPS AND CONFESSORS
Pantaenus; Palladius, bishop; Felix of Nantes, bishop; Ethelburga, Ercongota and Sethrida, virgins; Hedda, bishop.

July 8th

ELIZABETH, QUEEN OF PORTUGAL, WIDOW*
Aquila and Prisca; Procopius, martyr; Kilian and Companions, martyrs; Withburga, virgin; Adrian III, pope; Grimbald; Sunniva and Companions; Raymund of Toulouse.

July 9th

John Fisher, bishop and martyr*; Thomas More, martyr*; Everild, virgin; The Martyrs of Gorkum: Nicholas Pieck, Jerome Weerden, Leonard Vechel, Nicholas Janssen, Godfrey van Duynen, John van Oosterwyk, John van Hoornaer; Adrian van Hilvarenbeek, James Lacops, Andrew Wouters, Antony van Willehad, and Nicasius van Heeze; Veronica Giuliani, virgin.

July 10th

THE SEVEN HOLY BROTHERS, MARTYRS*
Rufina and Secunda, Virgins and Martyrs
Amalburga, widow; Amalburga, virgin; Antony and Theodosius of Pechersk, abbots.

July 11th

PIUS I, POPE AND MARTYR
Drostan, abbot; John of Bergamo, bishop; Hidulf, bishop; Olga, widow.

July 12th

JOHN GUALBERT, ABBOT
Nabor and Felix, Martyrs
Veronica*; Jason, martyr; Hermagoras and Fortunatus, martyrs; John the Iberian, abbot.

July 13th

ANACLETUS, POPE AND MARTYR
(now identified with Cletus [April 26th])
Silas or Silvanus; Maura and Brigid; Eugenius of Carthage, bishop; Mildred, virgin; James of Voragine, bishop; Francis Solano.

July 14th

BONAVENTURE, BISHOP, DOCTOR AND CONFESSOR★
Deusdedit, bishop; Marchelm; Ulric of Zell, abbot.

July 15th

HENRY THE EMPEROR, CONFESSOR
James of Nisibis, bishop; Barhadbesaba, martyr; Donald; Swithun, bishop★; Athanasius of Naples, bishop; Edith of Polesworth; Vladimir of Kiev★; David of Munktorp, bishop; Pompilio Pirrotti.

July 16th

THE COMMEMORATION OF OUR LADY OF MOUNT CARMEL
Athenogenes, bishop and martyr; Eustathius of Antioch, bishop; Helier, martyr; Reineldis, virgin and martyr; Fulrad, abbot.

July 17th

ALEXIS, CONFESSOR★
Speratus and Companions, the Scillitan Martyrs; Marcellina, virgin; Ennodius, bishop; Kenelm; Leo IV, pope; Clement of Okhrida and Companions, the Seven Apostles of Bulgaria; Nerses Lampronazi, bishop; Mary Magdalen Postel★.

July 18th

CAMILLUS DE LELLIS, CONFESSOR★
Symphorosa and her Seven Sons, Martyrs
Pambo; Philastrius, bishop; Arnulf or Arnoul of Metz, bishop; Frederick of Utrecht, bishop and martyr; Bruno of Segni, bishop.

July 19th

VINCENT DE PAUL, CONFESSOR★
Justa and Rufina, virgins and martyrs; Arsenius; Symmachus, pope; Ambrose Autpert; Macrina the Younger, virgin.

July 20th

JEROME EMILIANI, CONFESSOR
Margaret or Marina, Virgin and Martyr
Wilgefortis or Liberta; Joseph Barsabas; Aurelius, bishop; Flavian and Elias, bishops; Vulmar or Wulmar, abbot; Ansegisus, abbot.

July 21st

PRAXEDES, VIRGIN
Victor of Marseilles, martyr; Arbogast, bishop.

July 22nd

MARY MAGDALENE, PENITENT★
Joseph of Palestine; Wandregisilus or Wandrille, abbot.

July 23rd

APOLLINARIS OF RAVENNA, BISHOP AND MARTYR
Liborius, Bishop
The Three Wise Men; John Cassian, abbot; Romula and her Companions, virgins; Anne or Susanna, virgin; Laurence of Brindisi.

July 24th

CHRISTINA, VIRGIN AND MARTYR
Lewina, virgin and martyr; Declan, bishop; Boris and Gleb, martyrs; Christina the Astonishing, virgin; Christina of Tyre, virgin and martyr.

July 25th

JAMES THE GREATER, APOSTLE★
Christopher, Martyr★
Thea, Valentina and Paul, martyrs; Magnericus, bishop.

July 26th

ANNE★, MOTHER OF THE BLESSED VIRGIN MARY
Simeon the Armenian; Bartholomea Capitanio, virgin.

July 27th

PANTALEON, MARTYR★
The Seven Sleepers of Ephesus; Aurelius, Natalia, Felix and Companions, martyrs; Theobald of Marly, abbot.

July 28th

NAZARIUS AND CELSUS, MARTYRS
Victor I, Pope and Martyr; Innocent I, Pope and Confessor
Samson, bishop★; Botvid.

July 29th

MARTHA, VIRGIN★
Felix 'II', Pope; Simplicius, Faustinus and Beatrice, Martyrs
Lupus or Loup, bishop; Olaf, martyr★; William Pinchon, bishop.

July 30th

ABDON AND SENNEN, MARTYRS
Julitta, widow and martyr.

July 31st

IGNATIUS OF LOYOLA, CONFESSOR★
Neot★; Helen of Skövde, widow; Germanus of Auxerre, bishop★.

August 1st

PETER'S CHAINS★
The Holy Machabees, Martyrs
Faith, Hope, Charity and their mother, Wisdom, martyrs; Aled, Almedha or Eiluned, virgin and martyr; Ethelwold, bishop.

August 2nd

ALPHONSUS OF LIGUORI, BISHOP, DOCTOR AND CONFESSOR★
Stephen I, Pope and Martyr
Theodota, martyr; Thomas of Dover.

August 3rd

THE FINDING OF THE BODY OF STEPHEN, PROTOMARTYR★
Waltheof or Walthen, abbot; Nicodemus.

August 4th

DOMINIC, CONFESSOR★
Ia and Companions, martyrs; Molua or Lughaidh, abbot.

August 5th

THE DEDICATION OF OUR LADY OF THE SNOWS
Addai and Mari, bishops; Afra, martyr; Nonna, matron.

August 6th

THE TRANSFIGURATION OF OUR LORD JESUS CHRIST
Sixtus II, Felicissimus, Agapitus and Companions, Martyrs★
Justus and Pastor, martyrs; Hormisdas, pope.

August 7th

CAJETAN, CONFESSOR★
Donatus of Arezzo, Bishop and Martyr
Claudia, matron; Dometius the Persian, martyr; Victricius, bishop; Albert of Trapani; Donatus of Besançon, bishop.

August 8th

CYRIACUS, LARGUS AND SMARAGDUS, MARTYRS★
The Fourteen Holy Helpers★; Hormisdas, martyr; Altman, bishop.

August 9th

JOHN VIANNEY, CONFESSOR★
Romanus, Martyr
Emygdius, martyr; Nathy and Felim, bishops; Oswald of Northumbria, martyr★.

August 10th

LAURENCE, MARTYR★
Philomena or Philumena★.

August 11th

TIBURTIUS AND SUSANNA, VIRGIN, MARTYRS
Alexander the Charcoal-Burner, bishop and martyr; Equitius, abbot;

Blane, bishop; Attracta or Araght, virgin; Lelia, virgin; Gaugericus or Géry, bishop; Gerard of Gallinaro and Companions.

August 12th
CLARE, VIRGIN★
Euplus, martyr; Murtagh or Muredach, bishop; Porcarius and Companions, martyrs.

August 13th
HIPPOLYTUS★ AND CASSIAN OF IMOLA, MARTYRS
Simplician, bishop; Radegund, matron★; Maximus the Confessor, abbot; Wigbert, abbot; Nerses Klaiëtsi, bishop.

August 14th
Eusebius of Rome, Confessor
Marcellus of Apamea, bishop and martyr; Fachanan, bishop; Athanasia, matron.

August 15th
THE ASSUMPTION OF THE BLESSED VIRGIN MARY★
Tarsicius, martyr; Arnulf or Arnoul of Soissons, bishop.

August 16th
JOACHIM, FATHER OF THE BLESSED VIRGIN MARY, CONFESSOR AND DOCTOR
Arsacius; Armel, abbot; Rock.

August 17th
HYACINTH, CONFESSOR★
Mamas, martyr; Eusebius, pope; Liberatus and Companions, martyrs; Clare of Montefalco, virgin.

August 18th
AGAPITUS, MARTYR
Florus and Laurus, martyrs; Helena, widow★; Alipius, bishop.

August 19th
JOHN EUDES, CONFESSOR★
Andrew the Tribune, martyr; Timothy, Agapius and Thecla, martyrs; Sixtus or Xystus III, pope; Mochta, abbot; Bertulf, abbot; Sebald; Louis of Anjou, bishop.

August 20th
BERNARD, ABBOT, DOCTOR AND CONFESSOR★
Amadour; Oswin, martyr; Philibert, abbot.

August 21st
JOAN FRANCES DE CHANTAL, WIDOW★
Luxorius, Cisellus and Camerinus, martyrs; Bonosus and Maximian, martyrs; Sidonius Apollinaris, bishop; Abraham of Smolensk, abbot.

August 22nd
THE IMMACULATE HEART OF THE BLESSED VIRGIN MARY★
Timothy, Hippolytus and Symphorian, Martyrs
Sigfrid, abbot; Andrew of Fiesole.

August 23rd
PHILIP BENIZI, CONFESSOR★
Claudius, Asterius, Neon, Domnina and Theonilla, martyrs; Eugene or Eoghan, bishop.

August 24th
BARTHOLOMEW, APOSTLE★
The Martyrs of Utica; Audoenus or Ouen, bishop.

August 25th
LOUIS IX, KING OF FRANCE, CONFESSOR★
Genesius the Comedian, martyr; Genesius of Arles; Patricia, virgin; Mennas of Constantinople, bishop; Ebba the Elder, virgin; Gregory of Utrecht, abbot; Joan Antide-Thouret, virgin★; Mary Michaela Desmaisières, virgin.

August 26th
ZEPHYRINUS, POPE AND MARTYR★
Joan Elizabeth Bichier des Ages, virgin★.

August 27th
JOSEPH CALASANCTIUS, CONFESSOR★
Marcellus and Companions, martyrs; Poemen, abbot; Caesarius of Arles, bishop; Syagrius, bishop; Hugh or Little Hugh of Lincoln; Margaret the Barefooted, widow.

August 28th
AUGUSTINE, BISHOP, CONFESSOR AND DOCTOR★
Hermes, Martyr
Julian of Brioude, martyr; Alexander, John III and Paul IV, bishops; Moses the Black; Joachima de Vedruna, widow.

August 29th
THE BEHEADING OF JOHN THE BAPTIST★
Sabina, martyr
Medericus or Merry, abbot.

August 30th
ROSE OF LIMA, VIRGIN★
Felix and Adauctus, Martyrs
Pammachius; Rumon or Ruan; Fantinus, abbot.

August 31st
RAYMUND NONNATUS, CONFESSOR★
Paulinus of Trier, bishop; Aidan of Lindisfarne, bishop★.

September 1st
GILES, ABBOT
The Twelve Brothers, Martyrs
Verena, virgin; Lupus or Leu, bishop; Fiacre★; Sebbe; Drithelm★.

September 2nd
STEPHEN, KING OF HUNGARY, CONFESSOR★
Antoninus of Apamea, martyr; Castor, bishop; Agricolus, bishop; William of Roskilde, bishop; Brocard.

September 3rd
PIUS X, POPE AND CONFESSOR★
Phoebe; Macanisius, bishop; Simeon Stylites the Younger; Remaclus, bishop; Aigulf, martyr; Hildelitha, virgin; Cuthburga, widow.

September 4th
Marcellus and Valerian, martyrs; Marinus; Boniface I, pope; Ultan of Ardbraccan, bishop; Ida of Herzfeld, widow; Rosalia, virgin; Rose of Viterbo, virgin.

September 5th
LAURENCE JUSTINIAN, BISHOP AND CONFESSOR★
Bertinus, abbot.

September 6th
Donatian, Laetus and Companions, bishops and martyrs; Eleutherius, abbot; Chainoaldus or Cagnoald, bishop; Bega or Bee, virgin.

September 7th
Regina or Reine, virgin and martyr; Sozon, martyr; Grimonia, virgin and martyr; John of Nicomedia, martyr; Anastasius the Fuller, martyr; Cloud or Clodoald; Alcmund and Tilbert, bishops.

September 8th
THE BIRTHDAY OF THE BLESSED VIRGIN MARY★
Adrian and Natalia, Martyrs
Eusebius, Nestabus, Zeno and Nestor, martyrs; Disibod; Sergius I, pope; Corbinian, bishop.

September 9th
GORGONIUS, MARTYR
Isaac or Sahak I, bishop; Ciaran or Kieran, abbot★; Audomarus or Omer, bishop; Bettelin; Peter Claver★.

September 10th
NICHOLAS OF TOLENTINO, CONFESSOR★
Nemesian and Companions, martyrs; Menodora, Metrodora and Nymphodora, virgins and martyrs; Pulcheria, virgin; Finnian of Moville, bishop; Salvius of Albi, bishop; Theodard, bishop; Aubert, bishop.

September 11th
PROTUS AND HYACINTH,
MARTYRS★
Theodora of Alexandria; Paphnutius the Great, bishop; Patiens of Lyons, bishop; Deiniol, bishop; Peter of Chavanon; Bodo, bishop.

September 12th
THE MOST HOLY NAME OF MARY★
Ailbhe, bishop; Eanswida; virgin; Guy of Anderlecht.

September 13th
Maurilius, bishop; Eulogius of Alexandria, bishop; Amatus, abbot; Amatus, bishop.

September 14th
THE EXALTATION OF THE HOLY CROSS
Maternus, bishop; Notburga, virgin.

September 15th
THE SEVEN SORROWS OF THE BLESSED VIRGIN MARY★
Nicomedes, Martyr
Nicetas the Goth, martyr; Aichardus or Archard, abbot; Mirin; Catherine of Genoa, widow★.

September 16th
CORNELIUS, POPE AND MARTYR★
Cyprian, Bishop and Martyr★; Euphemia, Lucy and Geminianus, Martyrs
Abundius, Abundantius and Companions, martyrs; Ninian, bishop★; Ludmila, martyr; Edith of Wilton, virgin.

September 17th
THE STIGMATA OF FRANCIS★
Socrates and Stephen, martyrs; Satyrus; Lambert of Maestricht, bishop and martyr; Columba, virgin and martyr; Hildegard, virgin; Peter Arbues, martyr.

September 18th
JOSEPH OF COPERTINO, CONFESSOR★
Ferreolus, martyr; Methodius of Olympus, bishop and martyr; Richardis, widow; Ferreolus of Limoges, bishop.

September 19th
JANUARIUS, BISHOP, AND COMPANIONS, MARTYRS★
Peleus and Companions, martyrs; Sequanus or Seine, abbot; Goericus or Abbo, bishop; Theodore of Tarsus, bishop★; Mary of Cerevellon, virgin; Theodore, David and Constantine; Emily de Rodat, virgin.

September 20th
EUSTACE AND COMPANIONS, MARTYRS
Vincent Madelgarius, abbot.

September 21st
MATTHEW, APOSTLE AND EVANGELIST★
Maura of Troyes, virgin; Michael of Chernigov and Theodore, martyrs.

September 22nd
THOMAS OF VILLANOVA. BISHOP★
Phocas the Gardener, martyr; Maurice, Candidus and Companions, martyrs; Felix III (IV), pope; Salaberga, widow; Emmeramus, bishop.

September 23rd
LINUS, POPE AND MARTYR
Thecla, Virgin and Martyr
Adamnan, abbot; Martha of Persia, virgin and martyr.

September 24th
OUR LADY OF RANSOM
Geremarus or Germer, abbot; Gerard of Csanad, bishop and martyr; Pacifico of San Severino.

September 25th
Firminus, bishop and martyr; Cadoc, abbot; Aunacharius or Aunaire, bishop; Finbar, bishop; Ceolfrid, abbot; Albert of Jerusalem, bishop; Sergius of Radonezh, abbot; Vincent Strambi, bishop.

September 26th
CYPRIAN OF ANTIOCH AND JUSTINA, MARTYRS★
The Martyrs of North America★: René Goupil, John Lalande, Isaac Jogues, Antony Daniel, John de Brébeuf, Gabriel Lalemant, Charles Garnier and Noel Chabanel; Colman of Lann Elo, abbot; John of Meda; Nilus of Rossano, abbot.

September 27th
COSMAS AND DAMIAN, MARTYRS★
Elzear.

September 28th
WENCESLAUS OF BOHEMIA, MARTYR★
Exsuperius, bishop; Eustochium, virgin; Faustus of Riez, bishop; Annemund, bishop; Lioba, virgin.

September 29th
THE DEDICATION OF MICHAEL★, ARCHANGEL
Rhipsime, Gaiana and Companions, virgins and martyrs; Theodota of Philippolis, martyr.

September 30th
JEROME, PRIEST, CONFESSOR AND DOCTOR★
Gregory the Illuminator, bishop; Honorius of Canterbury, bishop; Simon of Crépy.

October 1st
REMIGIUS, BISHOP AND CONFESSOR★
Romanus the Melodist; Melorus Melar or Mylor, martyr; Bavo or Allowin.

October 2nd
THE GUARDIAN ANGELS★
Eleutherius, martyr; Leodegarius or Leger, bishop and martyr.

October 3rd
TERESA OF LISIEUX, VIRGIN★
Hesychius; The Two Ewalds, martyrs; Gerard of Brogne, abbot; Froilan and Attilanus, bishops; Thomas of Hereford, bishop.

October 4th
FRANCIS OF ASSISI, CONFESSOR★
Ammon; Petronius, bishop.

October 5th
PLACID AND OTHERS, MARTYRS
Apollinaris of Valence, bishop; Galla, widow; Magenulf or Meinulf; Flora of Beaulieu, virgin; Bd Aymard of Cluny, abbot.

October 6th
BRUNO, CONFESSOR★
Faith, virgin and martyr; Nicetas of Constantinople; Mary Frances of Naples, virgin.

October 7th
HOLY ROSARY OF THE BLESSED VIRGIN MARY★
Mark, Pope; Sergius and Bacchus, Martyrs
Marcellus and Apuleius, martyrs; Justina, virgin and martyr; Osyth, virgin and martyr; Artaldus or Arthaud, bishop.

October 8th
BRIDGET OF SWEDEN, WIDOW★
Simeon; Pelagia the Penitent; Thaïs; Reparata, virgin and martyr; Demetrius, martyr; Keyne, virgin★.

October 9th
JOHN LEONARDI, CONFESSOR
Dionysius or Denis, Bishop★; Eleutherius and Rusticus, Martyrs
Demetrius of Alexandria, bishop; Publia, widow; Andronicus and Athanasia; Savin; Gislenus or Ghislain, abbot; Gunther; Louis Bertrand.

October 10th

FRANCIS BORGIA, CONFESSOR★
Gereon and Companions, martyrs;
Eulampius and Eulampia, martyrs;
Maharsapor, martyr; Cerbonius,
bishop; Paulinus of York, bishop;
Daniel and Companions, martyrs.

October 11th

THE MOTHERHOOD OF THE
BLESSED VIRGIN MARY★
Andronicus, Tarachus, and Probus,
martyrs; Nectarius, bishop; Canice
or Kenneth, abbot★; Agilbert,
bishop; Gummarus or Gommaire;
Bruno the Great of Cologne,
bishop; Alexander Sauli, bishop.

October 12th

Maximilian, bishop and martyr;
Felix and Cyprian and Companions;
Edwin, martyr; Ethelburga of Bar-
king, virgin; Wilfrid, bishop★.

October 13th

EDWARD THE CONFESSOR★
Faustus, Januarius and Martial,
martyrs; Comgan, abbot; Gerald of
Aurillac; Coloman, martyr; Maurice
of Carnoët, abbot.

October 14th

CALLISTUS OR CALIXTUS, POPE
AND MARTYR★
Justus of Lyons, bishop; Manechildis,
virgin; Angadrisma or Angadrême,
virgin; Burchard, bishop; Dominic
Lauricatus.

October 15th

TERESA OF AVILA, VIRGIN★
Leonard of Vandoeuvre, abbot;
Thecla of Kitzingen, virgin; Euthy-
mius the Younger, abbot.

October 16th

HEDWIG, WIDOW
Martinian and his Companions
and Maxima; Gall★; Mommolinus,
bishop; Bercharius, abbot; Lull,
bishop; Anastasius of Cluny; Bertrand of Comminges, bishop; Gerard
Majella.

October 17th

MARGARET MARY ALACOQUE,
VIRGIN★
John the Dwarf; Anstrudis or
Anstrude, virgin; Nothelm, bishop;
Seraphino.

October 18th

LUKE THE EVANGELIST★
Justus of Beauvais, martyr.

October 19th

PETER OF ALCÁNTARA,
CONFESSOR★
Ptolemaeus and Lucius, martyrs;
Cleopatra, widow and Varus,
martyr; Ethbin; Aquilinus, bishop;
Frideswide, virgin.

October 20th

JOHN OF KANTI OR CANTIUS,
CONFESSOR★
Caprasius, martyr; Artemius, martyr; Acca, bishop; Andrew of Crete,
martyr.

October 21st

HILARION, ABBOT★
Ursula and Companions, Martyrs★
Malchus; Fintan or Munnu of
Taghmon, abbot; Condedus; John
of Bridlington.

October 22nd

Abercius, bishop; Philip of Heraclea,
bishop, and Companions, martyrs;
Mallonius or Mellon, bishop;
Nunilo and Alodia, virgins and
martyrs; Donatus of Fiesole, bishop.

October 23rd

Theodoret, martyr; Severinus or
Seurin, martyr; Severinus Boethius,
martyr; Romanus of Rouen, bishop;
Ignatius of Constantinople, bishop;
Allucio.

October 24th

RAPHAEL, ARCHANGEL★
Felix of Thibiuca, bishop and
martyr; Proclus, bishop; Aretas
and the martyrs of Najran and
Elesbaan; Senoch, abbot; Martin or
Mark; Maglorius or Maelor, bishop;
Martin of Vertou, abbot; Ebregislus
or Evergislus, bishop; Antony Claret,
bishop★.

October 25th

CHRYSANTHUS AND DARIA,
MARTYRS
Crispin and Crispinian, martyrs;
Fronto and George, bishops; Gau-
dentius, bishop.

October 26th

EVARISTUS, POPE AND MARTYR
Lucian and Marcian, martyrs; Rusticus of Narbonne, bishop; Cedd,
bishop★; Eata, bishop; Bean, bishop.

October 27th

Frumentius, bishop; Otteran or
Odhran, abbot.

October 28th

SIMON AND JUDE, APOSTLES★
Anastasia and Cyril, martyrs; Fidelis
of Como, martyr; Salvius or Saire;
Faro, bishop.

October 29th

Narcissus of Jerusalem, bishop;
Theuderius or Chef, abbot; Colman
of Kilmacduagh, bishop; Abraham
of Rostov, abbot.

October 30th

Serapion of Antioch, bishop; Marcellus, martyr★; Asterius, bishop;
Germanus of Capua, bishop; Ethel-
noth, bishop; Alphonsus Rodri-
guez★.

October 31st

Quentin or Quintinius, martyr;
Foillan, abbot; Wolfgang, bishop.

Last Sunday of October:
FEAST OF OUR LORD JESUS
CHRIST THE KING

November 1st

ALL SAINTS
Caesarius and Julian, martyrs; Benignus of Dijon, martyr; Austremonius
or Stremoine, bishop; Mary, virgin
and martyr; Maturinus or Mathurin;
Marcellus of Paris, bishop; Vigor,
bishop; Cadfan, abbot.

November 2nd

COMMEMORATION OF ALL THE
FAITHFUL DEPARTED (ALL SOULS)
Victorinus, bishop and martyr;
Marcian.

November 3rd

Winifrid, virgin and martyr★;
Rumwald; Hubert, bishop; Pirminus, bishop; Amicus; Malachy,
bishop★.

November 4th

CHARLES BORROMEO, BISHOP
AND CONFESSOR★
Vitalis and Agricola, Martyrs
Pierius; John Zedazneli and Com-
panions; Clarus, martyr; Joannicus.

November 5th

Elizabeth and Zachary★; Galation
and Episteme; Bertilla, virgin.

November 6th

Leonard of Noblac; Melaine, bishop;
Illtud or Illtyd, abbot★; Winnoc,
abbot; Demetrian, bishop; Barlaam
of Khutyn, abbot.

November 7th

Herculanus, bishop and martyr;
Florentius of Strasbourg, bishop;
Willibrord, bishop★; Engelbert,
bishop and martyr.

November 8th

THE FOUR CROWNED ONES,
MARTYRS
Cybi or Cuby, abbot; Deusdedit,
pope; Tysilio or Suliau, abbot;
Willehad, bishop; Godfrey of
Amiens, bishop.

November 9th

THE DEDICATION OF THE BASILICA OF ST SAVIOUR OR ST JOHN LATERAN
Theodore Tiro, Martyr
Benignus or Benen, bishop; Vitonus or Vanne, bishop.

November 10th

ANDREW AVELLINO, CONFESSOR★
Trypho, Respicius and Nympha, Martyrs
Theoctista, virgin; Aedh Mac Bricc, bishop; Justus of Canterbury, bishop.

November 11th

MARTIN OF TOURS, BISHOP AND CONFESSOR★
Mennas, Martyr
Theodore the Studite, abbot; Bartholomew of Grottaferrata, abbot.

November 12th

MARTIN I, POPE AND MARTYR★
Nilus the Elder; Emilian Cucullatus, abbot; Machar, bishop; Cunibert, bishop; Cumian, abbot; Livinus, bishop and martyr; Lebuin or Liafwine or Livinius; Benedict of Benevento and Companions, martyrs; Astrik or Anastasius, bishop; Cadwallader★.

November 13th

DIDACUS OR DIEGO, CONFESSOR
Arcadius and Companions, martyrs; Brice or Britius, bishop★; Eugenius of Toledo, bishop; Maxellendis, virgin and martyr; Kilian; Nicholas I, pope; Abbo of Fleury, abbot; Homobonus; Stanislaus Kostka.

November 14th

JOSAPHAT OF POLOTSK, BISHOP AND MARTYR★
Dyfrig, bishop★; Laurence O'Toole, bishop★.

November 15th

ALBERT THE GREAT, BISHOP, CONFESSOR AND DOCTOR★
Abibus, Gurias and Samonas, martyrs; Desiderius or Didier, bishop; Malo, bishop; Fintan of Rheinau; Leopold of Austria.

November 16th

GERTRUDE THE GREAT, VIRGIN★
Mechtilde, virgin★; Eucherius of Lyons, bishop; Afan, bishop; Edmund of Abingdon, bishop★; Agnes of Assisi, virgin.

November 17th

GREGORY THE WONDER-WORKER, BISHOP AND CONFESSOR
Dionysius of Alexandria, bishop; Alphaeus and Zachaeus, martyrs; Acisclus and Victoria, martyrs; Anianus or Aignan of Orleans, bishop; Gregory of Tours, bishop; Hilda, virgin; Hugh of Lincoln, bishop★.

November 18th

THE DEDICATION OF THE BASILICAS OF THE APOSTLES PETER AND PAUL
Romanus of Antioch, martyr; Mawes or Maudez, abbot; Odo of Cluny, abbot★.

November 19th

ELIZABETH OF HUNGARY, WIDOW★
Pontian, Pope and Martyr
Nerses, bishop and martyr; Barlaam, martyr.

November 20th

FELIX OF VALOIS, CONFESSOR
Dasius, martyr; Nerses of Sahgerd, bishop, and Companions, martyrs; Maxentia, virgin and martyr; Edmund the Martyr★; Bernward, bishop.

November 21st

THE PRESENTATION OF THE BLESSED VIRGIN MARY★
Gelasius I, pope; Albert of Louvain, bishop and martyr.

November 22nd

CECILIA OR CECILY, VIRGIN AND MARTYR★
Philemon and Apphia, martyrs.

November 23rd

CLEMENT, POPE AND MARTYR★
Felicity, Martyr★
Amphilochius, bishop; Gregory, bishop; Columbanus, abbot★; Trudo or Trond.

November 24th

JOHN OF THE CROSS, CONFESSOR AND DOCTOR★
Chrysogonus, Martyr
Colman of Cloyne, bishop; Flora and Mary, virgins and martyrs.

November 25th

CATHERINE OF ALEXANDRIA, VIRGIN AND MARTYR
Mercurius, martyr; Moses, martyr.

November 26th

SILVESTER, ABBOT
Peter of Alexandria, Bishop amd Martyr
Siricius, pope; Basolus or Basle; Conrad of Constance, bishop; Nikon 'Metanoeite'; John Berchmans; Leonard of Port Maurice.

November 27th

Barlaam and Josaphat; James Intercisus, martyr; Secundinus or Sechnall, bishop; Maximus of Riez, bishop; Cungar, abbot★; Fergus, bishop; Virgil or Fergal, bishop.

November 28th

Stephen the Younger, martyr; Simeon Metaphrastes; James of the March; Joseph Pignatelli; Catherine Labouré, virgin★.

November 29th

SATURNINUS, MARTYR
Saturninus or Sernin, bishop and martyr; Radbod, bishop.

November 30th

ANDREW, APOSTLE★
Sapor and Isaac, bishops and martyrs.

December 1st

Ansanus, martyr; Agericus or Airy, bishop; Tudwal, bishop; Eligius or Eloi, bishop.

December 2nd

BIBIANA OR VIVIANA, VIRGIN AND MARTYR
Chromatius, bishop.

December 3rd

FRANCIS XAVIER, APOSTLE OF INDIES, CONFESSOR★
Lucius; Claudius, Hilaria and Companions, martyrs; Cassian, martyr★; Sola.

December 4th

PETER CHRYSOLOGUS, BISHOP, CONFESSOR AND DOCTOR★
Barbara, Virgin and Martyr
Maruthas, bishop; Anno, bishop; Osmund, bishop; Bernard of Parma, bishop.

December 5th

SABAS, ABBOT★
Crispina, martyr; Nicetius of Trier, bishop; Birinus, bishop; Sigiramnus or Cyran, abbot.

December 6th

NICHOLAS, BISHOP AND CONFESSOR★
Dionysia, Majoricus and Companions, martyrs; Abraham of Kratia, bishop.

December 7th

AMBROSE, BISHOP, CONFESSOR AND DOCTOR★
Eutychian, pope; Josepha Rosello, virgin.

December 8th

THE IMMACULATE CONCEPTION OF THE BLESSED VIRGIN MARY★
Romaric, abbot.

December 9th

Hipparchus and Companions, martyrs; the Seven Martyrs of Samosata; Leocadia, virgin and martyr; Gorgonia, widow; Budoc or Beuzec, abbot; Peter Fourier.

December 10th

MELCHIADES, POPE AND MARTYR

Mennas, Hermogenes and Eugraphus, martyrs; Eulalia of Merida, virgin and martyr; Gregory III, pope.

December 11th

DAMASUS I, POPE

Barsabas, martyr; Fuscian, Victoricus and Gentian, martyrs; Daniel the Stylite.

December 12th

Epimachus, Alexander and Companions, martyrs; Finnian of Clonard, bishop; Corentin or Cury, bishop; Edburga, virgin; Vicelin, bishop.

December 13th

LUCY, VIRGIN AND MARTYR

Eustratius and Companions, martyrs; Judoc or Josse; Aubert of Cambrai, bishop; Odilia or Ottilia, virgin.

December 14th

Spiridion, bishop; Nicasius, bishop and Companions, martyrs; Venantius Fortunatus, bishop; Dioscorus and others, martyrs.

December 15th

Nino, virgin; Valerian and other martyrs in Africa; Stephen of Surosh, bishop; Paul of Latros; Mary di Rosa, virgin.

December 16th

EUSEBIUS OF VERCELLI, BISHOP AND CONFESSOR

Adelaide, widow*.

December 17th

Lazarus; Olympias, widow; Begga, widow; Sturmi, abbot; Wivina, virgin.

December 18th

Rufus and Zosimus, martyrs; Gatian, bishop; Flannan, bishop; Winebald, abbot.

December 19th

Nemesius, martyr; Anastasius I, pope.

December 20th

Ammon and Companions, martyrs; Philogonius, bishop; Ursicinus, abbot; Dominic of Silos, abbot.

December 21st

THOMAS THE APOSTLE*

Anastasius II of Antioch, bishop and martyr.

December 22nd

Frances Xavier Cabrini, virgin*; Chaeremon Ischyion and other martyrs.

December 23rd

The Ten Martyrs of Crete; Victoria and Anatolia, virgins and martyrs; Servulus; Dagobert II of Austrasia; Thorlac, bishop.

December 24th

THE VIGIL OF CHRISTMAS

Gregory of Spoleto, martyr; Delphinus, bishop; Tharsilla and Emiliana, virgins; Irmina, virgin and Adela, widow.

December 25th

THE BIRTHDAY OF OUR LORD JESUS CHRIST

Anastasia of Sirmium, Martyr

Eugenia, virgin and martyr; The Martyrs of Nicomedia.

December 26th

STEPHEN, THE FIRST MARTYR*

Archelaus, bishop; Dionysius, pope; Zosimus, pope.

December 27th

JOHN THE EVANGELIST*

Fabiola, widow*; Nicarete, virgin; Theodore and Theophanes.

December 28th

THE HOLY INNOCENTS, MARTYRS

Antony of Lérins.

December 29th

THOMAS OF CANTERBURY, BISHOP AND MARTYR*

Trophimus, bishop; Marcellus Akimetes, abbot; Ebrulf or Evroult, abbot; Bd Peter the Venerable, abbot*.

December 30th

Sabinus and Companions, martyrs; Anysia, martyr; Anysius, bishop; Egwin, bishop.

December 31st

SILVESTER I, POPE AND CONFESSOR

Columba of Sens, virgin and martyr; Melania the Younger, widow.

FOR FURTHER READING

ACKNOWLEDGMENTS

ABOUT THE CONTRIBUTORS

For further reading

GENERAL WORKS

A main source of material for the lives of the saints is the *Acta Sanctorum*, which is compiled by an association of Jesuits known as *Bollandists* after their founder, John van Bolland (1596–1665). Their work, which fills nearly seventy volumes, is being continually revised, and they also publish a periodical known as *Analecta Bollandiana*.

One of the greatest Bollandists was Hippolyte Delehaye, their president from 1912 to 1941, and his *The Legends of the Saints*, New York, 1907, is an authoritative introduction to the subject of hagiography. The general reader will, however, find the latest (1956) edition of Butler's *Lives of the Saints* the most useful of all modern works. It was first published by Alban Butler in 1756–9, and has been revised and edited into its present form of four volumes by Herbert Thurston, s.j., and Donald Attwater. It also contains excellent bibliographical references for further reading on particular saints. Other general works of interest are:

Vies des saints et des bienheureux (twelve volumes) edited by the Benedictines of Paris, Paris, 1935–57.

Dictionary of Christian Biography edited by William Smith and Henry Wace, London, 1877–87.

Lives of the Saints by S. Baring-Gould (fifteen volumes), J. Hodges, London, 1872–7.

The Saints and Ourselves (Series I and II) edited by Philip Caraman, s.j., Hollis & Carter, London, 1953; P. J. Kenedy, New York, 1953.

Neglected Saints by E. I. Watkin, Sheed & Ward, London and New York, 1955.

Saints of Our Times edited by Theodore Maynard, Staples Press, London, 1953.

Saints for Now edited by Clare Boothe Luce, Sheed & Ward, London, 1952.

Some Authentic Acts of the Early Martyrs translated by E. C. E. Owen, The Clarendon Press, Oxford, 1927.

The Golden Book of Eastern Saints by D. Attwater, The Bruce Publishing Co., Milwaukee, 1938.

Saga of Saints by Sigrid Undset, Sheed & Ward, London, 1934; Longmans, Green, New York, 1934.

The Shrine of St Peter and the Vatican Excavations by Jocelyn M. C. Toynbee and John Ward Perkins, Longmans, Green, London and New York, 1956.

What are Saints? by C. C. Martindale, s.j., Sheed & Ward, London, 1932.

The Anglo-Saxon Missionaries in Germany edited by C. H. Talbot, Sheed & Ward, New York, 1934.

Stories of the Saints by Norman Painting, edited by Fr Michael Day, Burns & Oates, London, 1956.

WORKS ON INDIVIDUAL SAINTS

AELRED of RIEVAULX: *St Aelred* by J. D. Dalgairns, London, 1903; *The Life of Ailred of Rievaulx* by W. Daniel, Nelson, London, 1950.

ALBERT THE GREAT by S. M. Albert, o.p., Blackfriars, Oxford, 1948; *St Albert, Patron of Scientists* by F. Sherwood Taylor (Aquinas Paper No. 14) Blackfriars, Oxford, 1950.

ALOYSIUS GONZAGA: *St Aloysius Gonzaga* by C. C. Martindale, s.j., The American Press, New York, 1926; *The Vocation of St Aloysius Gonzaga* by C. C. Martindale, s.j., Sheed & Ward, London, 1929.

ALPHONSUS LIGUORI: *The Saints and Ourselves II* edited by Philip Caraman, s.j. (Article by Reginald James Dingle) Hollis & Carter, London, 1953; P. J. Kenedy, New York, 1953.

AMBROSE: *Life and Times of St Ambrose* (two volumes) by Rev. F. H. Dudden, The Clarendon Press, Oxford, 1935.

ANTONY CLARET: *Assignments of Antonio Claret* by D. Sargent, D. X. McMullen, New York, 1948.

ANTONY of PADUA: *St Antony of Padua* by Alice Curtayne, Father Mathew Record Office, Dublin, 1931; *St Anthony; The man who found himself* by Fr Michael Day and Norman Painting, Burns & Oates, London, 1957; Franciscan Herald Press, Chicago, 1957.

ANTONY THE ABBOT: *The Life of St Antony* by St Athanasius, Newman Press, Westminster, Maryland, 1950.

AUGUSTINE: *The Confessions of St Augustine* in a revised translation by Sir Tobie Matthew, edited by Dom Roger

Hudleston, Burns & Oates, London, 1923; also translated by F. J. Sheed, Sheed & Ward, New York, 1942; *A Monument to Saint Augustine* by various Catholic writers, Sheed & Ward, London, 1930; *Saint Augustine of Hippo; Essays dealing with his life and times* by the Very Rev. Hugh Pope, O.P., Sands, London, 1937; *The Young Augustine* by John O'Meara, Longmans, Green, London, 1954.

BEDE (The Venerable Bede): *Ecclesiastical History of the English Nation*, Blackwell, Oxford, 1949.

BENEDICT of NURSIA: *St Benedict* by Abbot J. McCann, Sheed & Ward, New York, 1937, London, 1938; *St Benedict, his Life and Work* by Thomas Fanshawe Lindsay, Burns & Oates, London, 1949.

BERNADETTE SOUBIROUS: *We Saw Her* by B. G. Sandhurst, New York, 1953.

BERNARD of CLAIRVAUX: *Letters of St Bernard of Clairvaux* edited by Rev. Bruno S. James, Burns & Oates, London, 1953; *Life of St Bernard of Clairvaux* by Rev. Bruno S. James, Methuen, London, 1957.

BRIGID or BRIDE: *St Brigid of Ireland* by Alice Curtayne, Browne & Nolan, Dublin, 1934; revised edition, 1955.

BRUNO: *Neglected Saints* by E. I. Watkin, Sheed & Ward, London and New York, 1955.

CAJETAN: *St Cajetan* by M. A. R. de Maulde La Clavière translated by G. H. Ely, Benzinger Brothers, New York, 1902; Duckworth, London, 1902.

CAMILLUS de LELLIS: *St Camillus* by C. C. Martindale, S.J., Sheed & Ward, London, 1940.

CATHERINE of GENOA: *Quartet in Heaven* by Sheila Kaye-Smith, Harper, New York, 1952; *The mystical elements of religion as studied in Saint Catherine of Siena and her Friends* by Baron Friedrich von Hügel, J. M. Dent, second edition, London, 1923.

CATHERINE of SIENA: *St Catherine of Siena* by Alice Curtayne, Sheed & Ward, London, 1929, New York, 1935.

CHARLES BORROMEO: *A Prince of Pastors* by Margaret Yeo, Longmans, Green, New York, 1938.

CUTHBERT: *See* Bede's *Ecclesiastical History of the English Nation*, Blackwell, Oxford, 1949.

DOMINIC: *Life of St Dominic* by Bede Jarrett, O.P., Blackfriars, London, 1955.

ELIZABETH of HUNGARY: Article in *Saints of Our Times* edited by Theodore Maynard, Staples Press, London, 1953.

FRANCIS: *Saint Francis of Assisi* by G. K. Chesterton, Hodder & Stoughton, London and Toronto, 1923; George H. Doran, New York, 1924; *Life of St Francis of Assisi* by Fr Cuthbert, New York, 1948.

FRANCIS of SALES: *Life of St François of Sales* by M. Hamon, translated by H. Burton, London, 1925; *St Francois de Sales* by E. K. Sanders, London, 1938; *Introduction to the Devout Life*, translated by Fr Michael Day, Burns & Oates, London, 1956.

FRANCIS XAVIER: *Saint Francis Xavier* by James Brodrick, S.J., Burns & Oates, London, 1952.

GREGORY THE GREAT: *Gregory the Great: his Place in History and Thought* by F. H. Dudden, Longmans, Green, London and New York, 1905.

HELENA: *The Saints and Ourselves I* edited by Philip Caraman, S.J., (Article by Evelyn Waugh) Hollis & Carter, London, 1953; P. J. Kenedy, New York, 1953; *Helena* by Evelyn Waugh, Chapman & Hall, London, 1950.

HUGH of LINCOLN: *The Life of Saint Hugh of Lincoln*, translated from the French Carthusian Life and edited with large additions by the Rev. Herbert Thurston, S.J., Burns & Oates, London, 1898; *The Saints and Ourselves* I, edited by Philip Caraman, S.J. (Article by Renée Haynes) Hollis & Carter, London, 1953; P. J. Kenedy, New York, 1953; *Neglected Saints* by E. I. Watkin, Sheed & Ward, London and New York, 1955.

IGNATIUS of LOYOLA: *St Ignatius* by Christopher Hollis, Sheed & Ward, London, 1931; Harper Brothers, New York, 1931; *Saint Ignatius Loyola* by James Brodrick, S.J., Burns & Oates, London, 1956; *St Ignatius Loyola* by Leonard von Matt and Walter Hauser, Longmans, Green, London, 1956.

JOAN ANTIDE-THOURET: *Saint Joan Antide Thouret* translated by A. F. Wedd.

JOAN FRANCES de CHANTAL: *Jane de Chantal* by Bishop L. Bourgaud, London, 1895; *The Spirit of St J. F. de Chantal as shown in her letters*, London, 1952.

JOAN of ARC: *Joan of Arc* by Joseph Fabre, Hachette, Paris, 1913; *St Joan, the Woman and the Saint* by Etienne Robo, Burns & Oates, London, 1947; *The Holiness of St Joan of Arc* by Etienne Robo, Catholic Truth Society, London, 1951; *The Retrial of Joan of Arc. The Evidence at the trial for her Rehabilitation* by Régine Perroud, translated by A. M. Cohen, Methuen, London, 1955.

JOHN BAPTISTE de la SALLE: *De la Salle, a Pioneer of Modern Education* by W. J. Battersby, Longmans, Green, London, 1949; *De La Salle, Saint and Spiritual Writer* by W. J. Battersby, Longmans, Green, London, 1950; *The de la Salle Brothers in Great Britain* by W. J. Battersby, Burns & Oates, London, 1954; *St John Baptist de la Salle*, by W. J. Battersby, Burns & Oates, London, 1957.

JOHN BOSCO: *The Secret of St John Bosco* by H. Ghéon, Sheed & Ward, London and New York, 1936; *Don Bosco* by Lancelot Sheppard, Burns & Oates, London, 1957.

JOHN of the CROSS: *John of the Cross* by Fr Bruno de Jésus-Marie, Sheed & Ward, London, 1932; Benziger Brothers, New York, 1932.

JOHN VIANNEY (the Curé d'Ars): *The Curé d'Ars* by Abbé Francis Trochu, Burns & Oates, London, 1927; Westminster, Maryland, 1949; *The Secret of the Curé d'Ars* by H. Ghéon, Longmans, Green, New York, 1929; Sheed & Ward, London, 1929; *Portrait of a Parish Priest* by Lancelot Sheppard, Burns & Oates, London, 1959.

LEO THE GREAT: *Life and Times of Leo the Great* by Rev. T. G. Jalland, Macmillan, New York, 1941; S.P.C.K., London, 1941.

LOUIS IX, KING of FRANCE: *Life of St Louis* by John of Joinville, Sheed & Ward, 1955.

LUKE THE EVANGELIST: *A Portrait of St Luke* by Adrian Green-Armytage, Burns & Oates, London, 1955.

MARGARET MARY ALACOQUE: *The Secret of St Margaret Mary* by H. Ghéon, Sheed & Ward, New York, 1937; *The Nun* by Margaret Trouncer, Hutchinsons, London, 1953.

MARGARET of CORTONA: *A Tuscan Penitent* by Father Cuthbert, Burns & Oates, London, 1907; Benziger Brothers, New York, 1907.

MARGARET of SCOTLAND: *The Saints and Ourselves II* edited by Philip Caraman, s.J. (Article by George Scott-Moncrieff) Hollis & Carter, London, 1953; P. J. Kenedy, New York, 1953.

MARTIN of TOURS: *Neglected Saints* by E. I. Watkin, Sheed & Ward, London and New York, 1955.

MARTYRS of NORTH AMERICA: *The Jesuits in North America* by Francis Parkman, Little, Brown, Boston, 1867.

NICOLAS von (of) FLÜE: *Saints and Ourselves I*, edited by Philip Caraman, s.J. (Article by E. I. Watkin) Hollis & Carter, London, 1953; P. J. Kenedy, New York, 1953.

PATRICK of IRELAND: *The Works of St Patrick* by Ludwig Bieler, Newman Press, Westminster, Maryland, 1953.

PAUL: *St Paul* by C. C. Martindale, s.J., Burns & Oates, London, 1924; *Saint Paul: Apostle of Nations* by Daniel-Rops, Fides Publishers' Association, Chicago, 1953.

PERPETUA: *Perpetua, Saint and Martyr*, Translation by Walter Shewring, Sheed & Ward, London, 1931.

PETER CANISIUS: *St Peter Canisius* by J. Brodrick, Sheed & Ward, London, 1935.

PETER CLAVER: *A Saint in the Slave Trade: Peter Claver* by Sir Arnold Lunn, Sheed & Ward, London, 1935.

PHILIP NERI: *St Philip Neri and the Roman Society and his Times* by Louis Ponnelle and Louis Bordet, translated by the Rev. Francis Kerr, Sheed & Ward, London, 1932; *A Mystic in Motley* by T. Maynard, The Bruce Publishing Co., Milwaukee, 1946.

PIUS X: *St Pius X* by Igino Giordani, Bruce Publishing Co., Milwaukee, 1954; *Pius X* by H. Dal-Gal, Westminster, Maryland, 1954.

ROBERT BELLARMINE: *The Life and Work of Blessed Robert Bellarmine* by J. Brodrick (two volumes), Burns & Oates, London, 1928.

ROSE of LIMA: *Quartet in Heaven* by Sheila Kaye-Smith, Harper, New York, 1952.

STEPHEN HARDING: *Life of St Stephen Harding* by J. D. Dalgairns and H. Thurston, Westminster, Maryland, 1946.

TERESA of AVILA: *The Eagle and the Dove* by V. Sackville West, Michael Joseph, London, 1943; Doubleday, Doran, New York, 1944; *Mother of Carmel* by E. Allison Peers, Morehouse-Goreham, New York, 1946; S. C. M. Press, London, 1946; *Saint Teresa of Avila*, by Marcelle Auclair, translated by Kathleen Pond, Burns & Oates, London, 1953; *St Teresa of Jesus and other Essays* by E. Allison Peers, Faber & Faber, London, 1953.

TERESA of LISIEUX: *Two Portraits of St Teresa* by Etienne Robo, Sand, London & Glasgow, second edition, 1957; *Autobiography of a Saint*, translated by R. A. Knox, Harvill, London, 1958; *The Hidden Face* by Ida Görres, Burns & Oates, London 1959.

THOMAS AQUINAS: *St Thomas Aquinas* by Jacques Maritain, the Dial Press, New York, 1931; Sheed & Ward, London, 1938; *St Thomas Aquinas* by A. Sertillanges, 1933, *St Thomas Aquinas* by Gerald Vann, O.P., Hague & Gill, London, 1940; *St Thomas Aquinas* by A. Walz, Westminster, Maryland, 1951.

THOMAS MORE: *Thomas More* by R. W. Chambers, J. Cape, London and Toronto, 1935; Harcourt, Brace, New York, 1935; *St Thomas More* by E. E. Reynolds, Burns & Oates, London, 1953.

THOMAS of CANTERBURY: *Life of St Thomas Becket* by J. Morris, London, 1885.

THOMAS of VILLANOVA: *Neglected Saints* by E. I. Watkin, Sheed & Ward, London and New York, 1955.

VINCENT de PAUL: *Apostle of Charity* by Theodore Maynard, George Allen & Unwin, London, 1940; *The Life of St Vincent de Paul* by J. Calvet, London, 1952.

VINCENT FERRER: *Saint Vincent Ferrer* by H. Ghéon, translated by F. J. Sheed, Sheed & Ward, London, 1939.

Acknowledgments

We are indebted to the following for lending us photographs and helping us with the selection of illustrations: Her Majesty Queen Elizabeth II; The Rev. V. R. Beddoes; Mrs T. Cox; R. M. M. Dolley, Esq; Mrs A. de Georgi; Dr Rose Graham, C.B.E., M.A.; Miss M. Kay; Mrs G. O'Riordain; David Talbot Rice, Esq, M.B.E.; The Frick Collection, New York; Kunsthistorisches Museum, Vienna; The Louvre, Paris; The Museum of Fine Art, Boston, Mass.; National Buildings Record, London; The National Gallery, London; Schweizerische Landesmuseum, Zurich; The Syndics of the Fitzwilliam Museum, Cambridge; The Trustees of the British Museum; The Wallace Collection, London; Mother Cabrini High School, New York; Convent of the Sacred Heart, Woldingham; The Salesian College, London.

We are also indebted to Philip Caraman S.J. for help in the preparation of the book.

We wish to thank Patrick Kavanagh, Heather McCracken and Irving Yass for their help in the preparation of manuscripts.

About the contributors

Professor HILARY ARMSTRONG, Gladstone Professor of Greek in the University of Liverpool.
Publications include:
Aristotle, Plotinus and St Thomas, Blackfriars, Oxford, 1946.
The Greek Philosophical Background of the Psychology of St Thomas, Blackfriars, Oxford, 1952.
An Introduction to Ancient Philosophy, third edition, Methuen, London, 1957; American edition, 1949.
Plotinus, George Allen & Unwin, London, 1953.

DEBORAH ARMSTRONG.

RACHEL ATTWATER.
Publications include:
The Book Concerning Piers Plowman, (Editor), Everyman's Library, Dent, London, 1957.

The Rev. W. J. BATTERSBY, F.S.C., PH. D. (Lond).
Publications include:
The de la Salle Brothers in Great Britain, Burns & Oates, London, 1954.
St John Baptist de la Salle, Burns & Oates, London, 1957.

DAME ANSELMA BRENNELL, O.S.B., Stanbrook Abbey' Worcester.
Publications include:
British Mediaeval History (Ashley Histories), G. Bell & Sons, London, 1953.
Mediaeval Mystical Tradition and St John of the Cross, Burns & Oates, London, 1954.

The Rev. LAURENCE BRIGHT, O.P., S.T.L., D. PHIL.

MARYVONNE BUTCHER, Literary Editor of *The Tablet*.

The Rt Rev. B. C. BUTLER, Abbot of Downside.
Publications include:
The Originality of St Matthew. A critique of the two-document hypothesis, Cambridge University Press, Cambridge, 1951.
The Church and Infallibility. A reply to the abridged "Salmon", Sheed & Ward, London and New York, 1954.

EDWARD F. CALDIN, D.PHIL. (Oxon), Senior Lecturer in Physical Chemistry in the University of Leeds.
Publications include:
The Power and Limits of Science, Chapman & Hall, London, 1949.
Science and Christian Apologetic, Blackfriars, London, 1951.

The Rev. JOHN CHALLENOR, Priest of the Birmingham Oratory.

T. CHARLES-EDWARDS, Ampleforth College, York.
Publications include:
The Age of the Tudors and Stuarts, (Ashley Histories), G. Bell and Sons, London, 1953.
They saw it Happen, 1689–1897, (with B. Richardson), Basil Blackwell, Oxford, 1957.

JOHN COULSON, Downside School (Editor).

The Rev. FRANCIS COURTNEY, S.J., Heythrop College, Oxon.
Publications include:
Cardinal Robert Pullen. An English Theologian of the twelfth century, Apud Aedes Universitatis Gregorianae, Romae, 1954.

ALICE CURTAYNE.
Publications include:
St Antony of Padua, The Father Mathew Record Office, Dublin, 1931.
St Brigid of Ireland, Browne & Nolan, Dublin, 1934.
St Columcille, the Dove of the Church, Anthonian Press, Dublin, 1934.
St Catherine of Siena, Sheed & Ward, New York, 1935; Catholic Truth Society, London, 1951.

The Rev. WILLIAM DALTON, St Joseph's College, Upholland, Wigan.

The Rev. MICHAEL DAY, Priest of the Birmingham Oratory.
Publications include:
Translation of *The Story of a Soul* (the autobiography of St Teresa of Lisieux), Burns & Oates, London, 1951.
Christian Simplicity in St Thérèse, Burns & Oates, London, 1953.
Introduction to the Devout Life, (Translator), by St Francis of Sales, Burns & Oates, London, 1956.
St Anthony: The Man who found himself, (with Norman Painting), Burns & Oates, London, 1957.

MICHAEL DERRICK, Assistant Editor of *The Tablet*, and Editor of the *Dublin Review*.
Publications include:
The Portugal of Salazar, Paladin Press, London, 1938.

REGINALD JAMES DINGLE.
Publications include:
The Faith and Modern Science, Burns & Oates, London, 1935.

The Very Rev. ILLTUD EVANS, O.P., Prior, St Dominic's Priory, London; Editor of *Blackfriars*.
Publications include:
One and Many, Blackfriars, London, 1957.

H. O. Evennett, Fellow of Trinity College, Cambridge.
Publications include:
The Cardinal of Lorraine and the Council of Trent, Cambridge University Press, Cambridge, 1930.
Martin Luther, Catholic Truth Society, London, 1954.

J. R. Foster, Downside School.
Publications include:
Edition of *Judenbuche* by Droste-Hülshoff, Harrap, London, 1955.
Edition of *Heilige Experiment (The Strong Are Lonely)* by Fritz Hochwälder, Harrap, London, 1957.

Adrian Green-Armytage.
Publications include:
John who saw, Faber & Faber, London, 1952.
A Portrait of St Luke, Burns & Oates, London, 1955.

Dom Bede Griffiths, o.s.b.
Publications include:
The Golden String, (an autobiography), Harvill Press, London, 1954.

Arnold L. Haskell, c.b.e., Director of the Royal Ballet School, London.
Publications include:
Ballet: a complete guide to appreciation, Penguin Books, Harmondsworth, 1938; revised edition, 1955.
In his True Centre, (an interim autobiography), Adam & Charles Black, London, 1951.
Saints Alive: a study of six saints for young people, Allan Wingate, London, 1953.

Renée Haynes.
Publications include:
The Holy Hunger Hutchinsons, London, 1936.
Pan, Caesar and God, William Heinemann, London and Toronto, 1938.
Hilaire Belloc, Longmans, Green, London, 1953.

Christopher Hollis.
Publications include:
St Ignatius, Sheed & Ward, London, 1931; Harper Bro.., New York, 1931.
Erasmus, Eyre & Spottiswoode, London, 1933; The Bruce Publishing Co., Milwaukee, 1933.
Thomas More, Sheed & Ward, London, 1934; The Bruce Publishing Co., Milwaukee, 1934.
Evelyn Waugh, Longmans, Green, London, 1954.

The Rev. Bruno S. James.
Publications include:
Letters of St Bernard of Clairvaux, (Editor), Burns & Oates, London, 1953.
Life of St Bernard of Clairvaux, Methuen, London, 1957.

Julian Jebb.

Eric John, Lecturer in History, Manchester University.

The Rev. Alex Jones, s.t.l., l.s.s., b.c.l., Professor of Studies and Professor of Hebrew and Sacred Scriptures at St Joseph's College, Upholland, Wigan.
Publications include:
The Kingdom of Promise, (with R. Dyson), Burns & Oates, London, 1947.
Unless some Man show me, (on interpreting the Old Testament), Sheed & Ward, London and New York, 1951.
Old Testament Selections for Catholic Schools by the Sisters of St Joseph's Calasanctius, Vorselaar, (Translator) Thomas Nelson, London, 1955.

The Rev. Professor David Knowles, Regius Professor of Modern History in the University of Cambridge.
Publications include:
The Monastic Order in England, Cambridge University Press, Cambridge, 1940; reissued 1950.
The Religious Orders in England, Cambridge University Press, Cambridge, 1948; reissued 1950.
The Episcopal Colleagues of Archbishop Thomas Becket, (Ford Lecture), Cambridge University Press, Cambridge, 1951.
Cistercians and Cluniacs. The Controversy between St Bernard and Peter the Venerable, Oxford University Press, London, 1955.

Thomas Fanshawe Lindsay, Assistant Editor of *The Tablet*, 1936–38.
Publications include:
The Holy Rule for Laymen, Burns & Oates, London, 1947.
St Benedict: His Life and Work, Burns & Oates, London, 1949.

Sir Arnold Lunn, hon. d.phil. (Zurich).
Publications include:
Difficulties, (with Mgr R. Knox), Eyre & Spottiswoode, London; new edition, 1952.
A Saint in the Slave Trade (St Peter Claver), Sheed & Ward, London, 1935.
Science and the Supernatural, (with Professor J. B. S. Haldane), Eyre & Spottiswoode, London, 1935; Sheed & Ward, New York, 1935.

John Marshall, m.d., Reader, Institute of Neurology, University of London.

The Rev. Gervase Mathew, o.p., s.t.l., Lecturer in Greek Patristics, University of Oxford, 1937; Lecturer in Byzantine and Islamic Architecture at Ashmolean Museum, Oxford, 1938; Dean of Blackfriars, Oxford, 1939.
Publications include:
The Reformation and the Contemplative Life, (with

Archbishop Mathew), Sheed & Ward, London, 1934.

Byzantine Painting, Faber & Faber, London, 1950.

The Rev. C. C. MARTINDALE, S.J.

Publications include:

Saint Aloysius Gonzaga, The American Press, New York, 1926.

The Vocation of Aloysius Gonzaga, Sheed & Ward, London, 1929.

What are saints? Sheed & Ward, London, 1932; New York, 1933.

Life of St Camillus, Sheed & Ward, London, 1946.

The Message of Fatima, Burns & Oates, London, 1950.

DOM SEBASTIAN MOORE, O.S.B., D.D., Monk of Downside Abbey and Editor of *The Downside Review*.

NORMAN PAINTING.

Publications include:

Stories of the Saints, (Edited by Fr Michael Day), Burns & Oates, London, 1956; Franciscan Herald Press, Chicago, 1956.

St Anthony: the man who found himself (with Fr Michael Day), Burns & Oates, London, 1957; Franciscan Herald Press, Chicago, 1957.

ALAN PRYCE-JONES, Editor of *The Times Literary Supplement*.

Publications include:

The Spring Journey, Cobden-Sanderson, London, 1931.

Twenty-seven poems, William Heinemann, London and Toronto, 1935.

Prose Literature 1949–50, Published for the British Council by Longmans, Green, London, 1951.

The Rev. GABRIEL REIDY, O.F.M., D.D., St Mary's Friary, East Bergholt, Near Colchester.

E. E. REYNOLDS.

Publications include:

St Thomas More, Burns & Oates, London, 1953.

St John Fisher, Burns & Oates, London, 1955.

The Rev. H. J. RICHARDS, S.T.L., L.S.S., Professor of Sacred Scripture at St Edmund's College, Ware.

The Rev. ETIENNE ROBO.

Publications include:

St Joan, the woman and the saint, Burns & Oates, London, 1947.

Two Portraits of St Teresa of Lisieux, Sands, London and Glasgow, 1955.

DOM RALPH RUSSELL, O.S.B., D.D., Monk of Downside Abbey; Member of the Editorial Board and Associate Editor of the Catholic Commentary on Holy Scripture.

Publications include:

Essays in Reconstruction, (Editor), Sheed & Ward, London, 1946.

JOSEPH RYKWERT.

Publications include:

Ten Books on Architecture, (Editor), by Leone Battista Alberti, Alec Tiranti, London, 1955.

The Very Rev. COLUMBA RYAN, O.P., S.T.L., D.PHIL., (Oxon), Prior, Hawkesyard Priory, Staffs.

Publications include:

Blessed Martin de Porres, Catholic Truth Society, London, 1953.

Professor EDWARD SARMIENTO, PH.D., sometime Professor of Spanish at University College, Cardiff.

Publications include:

The Pleasures of Spanish Literature, University of Wales Press, Cardiff, 1955.

GEORGE IRVING SCOTT-MONCRIEFF.

Publications include:

Tinker's Wind Wishart, London, 1933.

Lowlands of Scotland, Batsford, London, 1939; third edition, 1949.

Death's Bright Shadow, Allan Wingate, London, 1948.

ROGER SHARROCK, B.LITT. (Oxon), Lecturer in English in the University of Southampton.

Publications include:

Songs and Comments, Fortune Press, London, 1945.

John Bunyan, University Library, Hutchinson, London, 1954.

LANCELOT SHEPPARD.

Publications include:

A Guide to the use of the Roman Breviary, Burns & Oates, London, 1927.

The English Carmelites, Burns & Oates, London, 1943.

Don Bosco, Burns & Oates, London, 1957.

WALTER SHEWRING, Ampleforth College, York.

Publications include:

The Golden Epistle of Abbot William, (Translator), Sheed & Ward, London, 1930.

Perpetua, Saint and Martyr, (Translator), Sheed & Ward, London, 1931.

Art in Christian Philosophy, Somer Press, Plainfields, New Jersey, 1946.

Rich and Poor in Christian Tradition, Burns & Oates, London, 1948.

ERIC STRAUSS, D.M., B.CH., F.R.C.P., HON. D.SC. (Frankfurt), Physician for Psychological Medicine, St Bartholomew's Hospital; Lecturer in Psychological Medicine, St Bartholomew's Medical School, London University.

Publications include:

Recent Advances in Neurology, J. & A. Churchill, London, 1929; sixth edition, 1953.

Reason and Unreason in Psychological Medicine, (with Walter R. Brain), H. K. Lewis, London, 1953.

Professor JOCELYN M. C. TOYNBEE, D.PHIL., F.B.A., F.S.A., Laurence Professor of Classical Archaeology in the University of Cambridge.

Publications include:

The Hadrianic School. A chapter in the history of Greek Art, Cambridge University Press, Cambridge, 1934.

Roman Medallions, New York, 1944.

Some notes on Artists in the Roman World, Collection Latomus, (volume 6) Bruxelles, 1951.

The Shrine of St Peter and the Vatican Excavations, (with John Ward Perkins), Longmans, Green, London and New York, 1956.

R. TREVETT.

MARGARET TROUNCER.

Publications include:

The Nun (St Margaret Mary and the Sacred Heart), Hutchinsons, London, 1953.

The Reluctant Abbess, Hutchinsons, London, 1957.

DOM AELRED WATKIN, O.S.B., F.S.A., F.R.HIST.S., Monk of Downside Abbey.

Publications include:

The Great Chartulary of Glastonbury, Somerset Record Society, 1947.

The Heart of the World, Burns & Oates, London, 1954.

E. I. WATKIN.

Publications include:

A Philosophy of Form, Sheed & Ward, third edition, London, 1950.

Poets and Mystics, Sheed & Ward, London, 1953.

Neglected Saints, Sheed & Ward, London, 1955.

Roman Catholicism in England from the Reformation to 1950, Home University Library, Oxford University Press, London, 1957.

EVELYN WAUGH.

Publications include:

Edmund Campion, Hollis & Carter, London, 1947.

Helena, Chapman & Hall, London, 1950.

CHARLES WRONG.

Publications include:

St Francis of Assisi, Sheldon Press, London, 1947